THE MODERN LIBRARY
OF THE WORLD'S BEST BOOKS

THE COMEDIES OF

SHAKESPEARE

The publishers will be pleased to send, upon request, an illustrated folder setting forth the purpose and scope of THE MODERN LIBRARY, *and listing each volume in the series. Every reader of books will find titles he has been looking for, handsomely printed, in definitive editions, and at an unusually low price.*

The Comedies of Shakespeare

VOLUME TWO

THE MODERN LIBRARY

NEW YORK

Random House IS THE PUBLISHER OF

THE MODERN LIBRARY

BENNETT A. CERF · DONALD S. KLOPFER · ROBERT K. HAAS

Manufactured in the United States of America

Printed by Parkway Printing Company   Bound by H. Wolff

CONTENTS

The Merchant of Venice
547

As You Like It
621

The Taming of the Shrew
695

All's Well That Ends Well
769

Twelfth-Night, or What You Will
851

The Winter's Tale
921

Notes
1009

Glossary
1055

THE MERCHANT OF VENICE

CAST OF CHARACTERS

DUKE OF VENICE

PRINCE OF MOROCCO \} *Suitors to Portia*
PRINCE OF ARRAGON

ANTONIO, *a Merchant of Venice*
BASSANIO, *his Friend*

GRATIANO
SALANIO \} *Friends to Antonio and Bassanio*
SALARINO

LORENZO, *in love with Jessica*
SHYLOCK, *a rich Jew*
TUBAL, *a Jew, his Friend*
LAUNCELOT GOBBO, *a Clown, Servant to Shylock*
OLD GOBBO, *Father to Launcelot*
LEONARDO, *Servant to Bassanio*

BALTHAZAR \} *Servants to Portia*
STEPHANO

PORTIA, *a rich Heiress*
NERISSA, *her Waiting-maid*
JESSICA, *Daughter to Shylock*

Magnificoes of Venice, Officers of the Court of Justice, Gaoler, Servants to Portia, and other Attendants

SCENE

Partly at Venice, and partly at Belmont, the seat of Portia, on the Continent

THE MERCHANT OF VENICE

ACT ONE

SCENE ONE

Venice. A Street.

Enter Antonio, Salarino, and Salanio

ANTONIO. In sooth, I know not why I am so sad:
　It wearies me; you say it wearies you;
　But how I caught it, found it, or came by it,
　What stuff 'tis made of, whereof it is born,
　I am to learn;
　And such a want-wit sadness makes of me,
　That I have much ado to know myself.
SALARINO. Your mind is tossing on the ocean;
　There, where your argosies with portly sail,—
　Like signiors and rich burghers on the flood,
　Or, as it were, the pageants of the sea,—
　Do overpeer the petty traffickers,
　That curtsy to them, do them reverence,
　As they fly by them with their woven wings.
SALANIO. Believe me, sir, had I such venture forth,
　The better part of my affections would
　Be with my hopes abroad. I should be still
　Plucking the grass to know where sits the wind;
　Peering in maps for ports, and piers, and roads;
　And every object that might make me fear
　Misfortune to my ventures, out of doubt
　Would make me sad.
SALARINO. 　　　　　　　My wind, cooling my broth
　Would blow me to an ague, when I thought
　What harm a wind too great might do at sea.
　I should not see the sandy hour-glass run
　But I should think of shallows and of flats,

    And see my wealthy Andrew dock'd in sand
Vailing her high-top lower than her ribs
To kiss her burial. Should I go to church
And see the holy edifice of stone,
And not bethink me straight of dangerous rocks,
Which touching but my gentle vessel's side
Would scatter all her spices on the stream,
Enrobe the roaring waters with my silks;
And, in a word, but even now worth this,
And now worth nothing? Shall I have the thought
To think on this, and shall I lack the thought
That such a thing bechanc'd would make me sad?
But tell not me: I know Antonio
Is sad to think upon his merchandise.

ANTONIO. Believe me, no: I thank my fortune for it,
My ventures are not in one bottom trusted,
Nor to one place; nor is my whole estate
Upon the fortune of this present year:
Therefore, my merchandise makes me not sad.

SALARINO. Why, then you are in love.

ANTONIO.   Fie, fie!

SALARINO. Not in love neither? Then let's say you are sad,
Because you are not merry: and 'twere as easy
For you to laugh and leap, and say you are merry,
Because you are not sad. Now, by two-headed Janus,
Nature hath fram'd strange fellows in her time:
Some that will evermore peep through their eyes
And laugh like parrots at a bag-piper,
And other of such vinegar aspect
That they 'll not show their teeth in way of smile,
Though Nestor swear the jest be laughable.

        Enter Bassanio, Lorenzo, and Gratiano

SALANIO. Here comes Bassanio, your most noble kinsman,
Gratiano, and Lorenzo. Fare ye well:
We leave you now with better company.

SALARINO. I would have stay'd till I had made you merry,
If worthier friends had not prevented me.

ANTONIO. Your worth is very dear in my regard.
I take it, your own business calls on you,
And you embrace the occasion to depart.

SALARINO. Good-morrow, my good lords.

BASSANIO. Good signiors both, when shall we laugh? say when?
You grow exceeding strange: must it be so?
SALARINO. We'll make our leisures to attend on yours.
Exeunt Salarino and Salanio
LORENZO. My Lord Bassanio, since you have found Antonio,
We too will leave you; but, at dinner-time,
I pray you, have in mind where we must meet.
BASSANIO. I will not fail you.
GRATIANO. You look not well, Signior Antonio;
You have too much respect upon the world:
They lose it that do buy it with much care:
Believe me, you are marvellously chang'd.
ANTONIO. I hold the world but as the world, Gratiano;
A stage where every man must play a part,
And mine a sad one.
GRATIANO. Let me play the fool:
With mirth and laughter let old wrinkles come,
And let my liver rather heat with wine
Than my heart cool with mortifying groans.
Why should a man, whose blood is warm within,
Sit like his grandsire cut in alabaster?
Sleep when he wakes, and creep into the jaundice
By being peevish? I tell thee what, Antonio—
I love thee, and it is my love that speaks—
There are a sort of men whose visages
Do cream and mantle like a standing pond,
And do a wilful stillness entertain,
With purpose to be dress'd in an opinion
Of wisdom, gravity, profound conceit;
As who should say, 'I am Sir Oracle,
And when I ope my lips let no dog bark!'
O, my Antonio, I do know of these,
That therefore only are reputed wise
For saying nothing; when, I am very sure,
If they should speak, would almost damn those ears
Which, hearing them, would call their brothers fools.
I'll tell thee more of this another time:
But fish not, with this melancholy bait,
For this fool-gudgeon, this opinion.
Come, good Lorenzo. Fare ye well awhile:
I'll end my exhortation after dinner.

LORENZO. Well, we will leave you then till dinner-time.
I must be one of these same dumb wise men,
For Gratiano never lets me speak.

GRATIANO. Well, keep me company but two years moe,
Thou shalt not know the sound of thine own tongue.

ANTONIO. Farewell: I 'll grow a talker for this gear.

GRATIANO. Thanks, i' faith; for silence is only commendable
In a neat's tongue dried and a maid not vendible.

Exeunt Gratiano and Lorenzo

ANTONIO. Is that any thing now?

BASSANIO. Gratiano speaks an infinite deal of nothing, more
than any man in all Venice. His reasons are as two grains
of wheat hid in two bushels of chaff: you shall seek all day
ere you find them, and, when you have them, they are not
worth the search.

ANTONIO. Well, tell me now, what lady is the same
To whom you swore a secret pilgrimage,
That you to-day promis'd to tell me of?

BASSANIO. 'Tis not unknown to you, Antonio,
How much I have disabled mine estate,
By something showing a more swelling port
Than my faint means would grant continuance:
Nor do I now make moan to be abridg'd
From such a noble rate; but my chief care
Is, to come fairly off from the great debts
Wherein my time, something too prodigal,
Hath left me gag'd. To you, Antonio,
I owe the most, in money and in love;
And from your love I have a warranty
To unburthen all my plots and purposes
How to get clear of all the debts I owe.

ANTONIO. I pray you, good Bassanio, let me know it;
And if it stand, as you yourself still do,
Within the eye of honour, be assur'd,
My purse, my person, my extremest means,
Lie all unlock'd to your occasions.

BASSANIO. In my school-days, when I had lost one shaft,
I shot his fellow of the self-same flight
The self-same way with more advised watch,
To find the other forth, and by adventuring both,
I oft found both. I urge this childhood proof,
Because what follows is pure innocence.

I owe you much, and, like a wilful youth,
That which I owe is lost; but if you please
To shoot another arrow that self way
Which you did shoot the first, I do not doubt,
As I will watch the aim, or to find both,
Or bring your latter hazard back again,
And thankfully rest debtor for the first.

ANTONIO. You know me well, and herein spend but time
To wind about my love with circumstance;
And out of doubt you do me now more wrong
In making question of my uttermost
Than if you had made waste of all I have:
Then do but say to me what I should do
That in your knowledge may by me be done,
And I am prest unto it: therefore speak.

BASSANIO. In Belmont is a lady richly left,
And she is fair, and, fairer than that word,
Of wondrous virtues: sometimes from her eyes
I did receive fair speechless messages:
Her name is Portia; nothing undervalu'd
To Cato's daughter, Brutus' Portia:
Nor is the wide world ignorant of her worth,
For the four winds blow in from every coast
Renowned suitors; and her sunny locks
Hang on her temples like a golden fleece;
Which makes her seat of Belmont Colchos' strond,
And many Jasons come in quest of her.
O my Antonio! had I but the means
To hold a rival place with one of them,
I have a mind presages me such thrift,
That I should questionless be fortunate.

ANTONIO. Thou knowest that all my fortunes are at sea;
Neither have I money, nor commodity
To raise a present sum: therefore go forth;
Try what my credit can in Venice do:
That shall be rack'd, even to the uttermost,
To furnish thee to Belmont, to fair Portia.
Go, presently inquire, and so will I,
Where money is, and I no question make
To have it of my trust or for my sake. *Exeunt*

SCENE TWO

Belmont. A Room in Portia's House.

Enter Portia and Nerissa

PORTIA. By my troth, Nerissa, my little body is aweary of this great world.

NERISSA. You would be, sweet madam, if your miseries were in the same abundance as your good fortunes are: and yet, for aught I see, they are as sick that surfeit with too much as they that starve with nothing. It is no mean happiness therefore, to be seated in the mean: superfluity comes sooner by white hairs, but competency lives longer.

PORTIA. Good sentences and well pronounced.

NERISSA. They would be better if well followed.

PORTIA. If to do were as easy as to know what were good to do, chapels had been churches, and poor men's cottages princes' palaces. It is a good divine that follows his own instructions: I can easier teach twenty what were good to be done, than be one of the twenty to follow mine own teaching. The brain may devise laws for the blood, but a hot temper leaps o'er a cold decree: such a hare is madness the youth, to skip o'er the meshes of good counsel the cripple. But this reasoning is not in the fashion to choose me a husband. O me, the word 'choose'! I may neither choose whom I would nor refuse whom I dislike; so is the will of a living daughter curbed by the will of a dead father. Is it not hard, Nerissa, that I cannot choose one nor refuse none?

NERISSA. Your father was ever virtuous, and holy men at their death have good inspirations; therefore, the lottery that he hath devised in these three chests of gold, silver, and lead, whereof who chooses his meaning chooses you, will, no doubt, never be chosen by any rightly but one who you shall rightly love. But what warmth is there in your affection towards any of these princely suitors that are already come?

PORTIA. I pray thee, over-name them, and as thou namest them, I will describe them; and, according to my description, level at my affection.

ACT I · SCENE II

NERISSA. First, there is the Neapolitan prince.

PORTIA. Ay, that's a colt indeed, for he doth nothing but talk of his horse; and he makes it a great appropriation to his own good parts that he can shoe him himself. I am much afeard my lady his mother played false with a smith.

NERISSA. Then is there the County Palatine.

PORTIA. He doth nothing but frown, as who should say, 'An you will not have me, choose.' He hears merry tales, and smiles not: I fear he will prove the weeping philosopher when he grows old, being so full of unmannerly sadness in his youth. I had rather be married to a death's-head with a bone in his mouth than to either of these. God defend me from these two!

NERISSA. How say you by the French lord, Monsieur Le Bon?

PORTIA. God made him, and therefore let him pass for a man. In truth, I know it is a sin to be a mocker; but, he! why, he hath a horse better than the Neapolitan's, a better bad habit of frowning than the Count Palatine; he is every man in no man; if a throstle sing, he falls straight a-capering; he will fence with his own shadow: if I should marry him, I should marry twenty husbands. If he would despise me, I would forgive him, for if he love me to madness, I shall never requite him.

NERISSA. What say you, then, to Falconbridge, the young baron of England?

PORTIA. You know I say nothing to him, for he understands not me, nor I him: he hath neither Latin, French, nor Italian; and you will come into the court and swear that I have a poor pennyworth in the English. He is a proper man's picture, but, alas! who can converse with a dumb-show? How oddly he is suited! I think he bought his doublet in Italy, his round hose in France, his bonnet in Germany, and his behaviour everywhere.

NERISSA. What think you of the Scottish lord, his neighbour?

PORTIA. That he hath a neighbourly charity in him, for he borrowed a box of the ear of the Englishman, and swore he would pay him again when he was able: I think the Frenchman became his surety and sealed under for another.

NERISSA. How like you the young German, the Duke of Saxony's nephew?

PORTIA. Very vilely in the morning, when he is sober, and most vilely in the afternoon, when he is drunk: when he is best, he is a little worse than a man, and when he is worst, he is little better than a beast. An the worst fall that ever fell, I hope I shall make shift to go without him.

NERISSA. If he should offer to choose, and choose the right casket, you should refuse to perform your father's will, if you should refuse to accept him.

PORTIA. Therefore, for fear of the worst, I pray thee, set a deep glass of Rhenish wine on the contrary casket, for, if the devil be within and that temptation without, I know he will choose it. I will do anything, Nerissa, ere I will be married to a sponge.

NERISSA. You need not fear, lady, the having any of these lords: they have acquainted me with their determinations; which is, indeed, to return to their home and to trouble you with no more suit, unless you may be won by some other sort than your father's imposition depending on the caskets.

PORTIA. If I live to be as old as Sibylla, I will die as chaste as Diana, unless I be obtained by the manner of my father's will. I am glad this parcel of wooers are so reasonable, for there is not one among them but I dote on his very absence, and I pray God grant them a fair departure.

NERISSA. Do you not remember, lady, in your father's time, a Venetian, a scholar and a soldier, that came hither in the company of the Marquis of Montferrat?

PORTIA. Yes, yes: it was Bassanio; as I think, he was so called.

NERISSA. True, madam: he, of all the men that ever my foolish eyes looked upon, was the best deserving a fair lady.

PORTIA. I remember him well, and I remember him worthy of thy praise.

Enter a Servant

How now! what news?

SERVANT. The four strangers seek for you, madam, to take their leave; and there is a forerunner come from a fifth, the Prince of Morocco, who brings word the prince his master will be here to-night.

PORTIA. If I could bid the fifth welcome with so good heart as I can bid the other four farewell, I should be glad of his approach: if he have the condition of a saint and the complexion of a devil, I had rather he should shrive me than wive me. Come, Nerissa. Sirrah, go before.

Whiles we shut the gate upon one wooer, another knocks at the door. *Exeunt*

SCENE THREE

Venice. A public Place.

Enter Bassanio and Shylock

SHYLOCK. Three thousand ducats; well?

BASSANIO. Ay, sir, for three months.

SHYLOCK. For three months; well?

BASSANIO. For the which, as I told you, Antonio shall be bound.

SHYLOCK. Antonio shall become bound; well?

BASSANIO. May you stead me? Will you pleasure me? Shall I know your answer?

SHYLOCK. Three thousand ducats, for three months, and Antonio bound.

BASSANIO. Your answer to that.

SHYLOCK. Antonio is a good man.

BASSANIO. Have you heard any imputation to the contrary?

SHYLOCK. Ho, no, no, no, no: my meaning in saying he is a good man is to have you understand me that he is sufficient. Yet his means are in supposition: he hath an argosy bound to Tripolis, another to the Indies; I understand moreover upon the Rialto, he hath a third at Mexico, a fourth for England, and other ventures he hath, squandered abroad. But ships are but boards, sailors but men: there be land-rats and water-rats, land-thieves, and water-thieves,—I mean pirates,—and then there is the peril of waters, winds, and rocks. The man is, notwithstanding, sufficient. Three thousand ducats; I think, I may take his bond.

BASSANIO. Be assured you may.

SHYLOCK. I will be assured I may; and, that I may be assured, I will bethink me. May I speak with Antonio?

BASSANIO. If it please you to dine with us.

SHYLOCK. Yes, to smell pork; to eat of the habitation which your prophet the Nazarite conjured the devil into. I will buy with you, sell with you, talk with you, walk with you, and so following; but I will not eat with you, drink with you, nor pray with you. What news on the Rialto? Who is he comes here?

Enter Antonio

BASSANIO. This is Signior Antonio.

SHYLOCK. (*Aside*) How like a fawning publican he looks!
I hate him for he is a Christian;
But more for that in low simplicity
He lends out money gratis, and brings down
The rate of usance here with us in Venice.
If I can catch him once upon the hip,
I will feed fat the ancient grudge I bear him.
He hates our sacred nation, and he rails,
Even there where merchants most do congregate,
On me, my bargains, and my well-won thrift,
Which he calls interest. Cursed be my tribe,
If I forgive him!

BASSANIO.   Shylock, do you hear?

SHYLOCK. I am debating of my present store,
And, by the near guess of my memory,
I cannot instantly raise up the gross
Of full three thousand ducats. What of that?
Tubal, a wealthy Hebrew of my tribe,
Will furnish me. But soft! how many months
Do you desire? (*To Antonio*) Rest you fair, good signior;
Your worship was the last man in our mouths.

ANTONIO. Shylock, albeit I neither lend nor borrow
By taking nor by giving of excess,
Yet, to supply the ripe wants of my friend,
I'll break a custom. (*To Bassanio*) Is he yet possess'd
How much ye would?

SHYLOCK.   Ay, ay, three thousand ducats.

ANTONIO. And for three months.

SHYLOCK. I had forgot; three months; you told me so.
Well then, your bond; and let me see. But hear you:
Methought you said you neither lend nor borrow
Upon advantage.

ANTONIO.   I do never use it.

SHYLOCK. When Jacob graz'd his uncle Laban's sheep,—
This Jacob from our holy Abram was,
As his wise mother wrought in his behalf,

The third possessor: ay, he was the third,—
ANTONIO. And what of him? Did he take interest?
SHYLOCK. No; not take interest; not, as you would say,
Directly interest: mark what Jacob did.
When Laban and himself were compromis'd,
That all the eanlings that were streak'd and pied
Should fall as Jacob's hire, the ewes, being rank,
In end of autumn turned to the rams;
And, when the work of generation was
Between these woolly breeders in the act,
The skilful shepherd peel'd me certain wands,
And, in the doing of the deed of kind,
He stuck them up before the fulsome ewes,
Who, then conceiving, did in eaning time
Fall parti-colour'd lambs, and those were Jacob's.
This was a way to thrive, and he was blest:
And thrift is blessing, if men steal it not.
ANTONIO. This was a venture, sir, that Jacob serv'd for;
A thing not in his power to bring to pass,
But sway'd and fashion'd by the hand of heaven.
Was this inserted to make interest good?
Or is your gold and silver ewes and rams?
SHYLOCK. I cannot tell; I make it breed as fast:
But note me, signior.
ANTONIO.   Mark you this, Bassanio,
The devil can cite Scripture for his purpose.
An evil soul, producing holy witness,
Is like a villain with a smiling cheek,
A goodly apple rotten at the heart.
O, what a goodly outside falsehood hath!
SHYLOCK. Three thousand ducats; 'tis a good round sum.
Three months from twelve, then let me see the rate.
ANTONIO. Well, Shylock, shall we be beholding to you?
SHYLOCK. Signior Antonio, many a time and oft
In the Rialto you have rated me
About my moneys and my usances:
Still have I borne it with a patient shrug,
For sufferance is the badge of all our tribe.
You call me misbeliever, cut-throat dog,
And spet upon my Jewish gaberdine,
And all for use of that which is mine own.
Well then, it now appears you need my help:

Go to then; you come to me, and you say,
'Shylock, we would have moneys': you say so;
You, that did void your rheum upon my beard,
And foot me as you spurn a stranger cur
Over your threshold: moneys is your suit.
What should I say to you? Should I not say,
'Hath a dog money? Is it possible
A cur can lend three thousand ducats?' or
Shall I bend low, and in a bondman's key,
With bated breath, and whispering humbleness,
Say this:—
'Fair sir, you spet on me on Wednesday last;
You spurn'd me such a day; another time
You call'd me dog; and for these courtesies
I'll lend you thus much moneys'?

ANTONIO. I am as like to call thee so again,
To spet on thee again, to spurn thee too.
If thou wilt lend this money, lend it not
As to thy friends,—for when did friendship take
A breed for barren metal of his friend?—
But lend it rather to thine enemy;
Who if he break, thou mayst with better face
Exact the penalty.

SHYLOCK. Why, look you, how you storm!
I would be friends with you, and have your love,
Forget the shames that you have stain'd me with,
Supply your present wants, and take no doit
Of usance for my moneys, and you'll not hear me:
This is kind I offer.

ANTONIO. This were kindness.

SHYLOCK. This kindness will I show.
Go with me to a notary, seal me there
Your single bond; and, in a merry sport,
If you repay me not on such a day,
In such a place, such sum or sums as are
Express'd in the condition, let the forfeit
Be nominated for an equal pound
Of your fair flesh, to be cut off and taken
In what part of your body pleaseth me.

ANTONIO. Content, i' faith: I'll seal to such a bond,
And say there is much kindness in the Jew.

BASSANIO. You shall not seal to such a bond for me:

I 'll rather dwell in my necessity.

ANTONIO. Why, fear not, man; I will not forfeit it:
Within these two months, that 's a month before
This bond expires, I do expect return
Of thrice three times the value of this bond.

SHYLOCK. O father Abram! what these Christians are,
Whose own hard dealing teaches them suspect
The thoughts of others. Pray you, tell me this;
If he should break his day, what should I gain
By the exaction of the forfeiture?
A pound of man's flesh, taken from a man,
Is not so estimable, profitable neither,
As flesh of muttons, beefs, or goats. I say,
To buy his favour, I extend this friendship:
If he will take it, so; if not, adieu;
And, for my love, I pray you wrong me not.

ANTONIO. Yes, Shylock, I will seal unto this bond.

SHYLOCK. Then meet me forthwith at the notary's;
Give him direction for this merry bond,
And I will go and purse the ducats straight,
See to my house, left in the fearful guard
Of an unthrifty knave, and presently
I will be with you.

ANTONIO.   Hie thee, gentle Jew.   *Exit Shylock*
This Hebrew will turn Christian: he grows kind.

BASSANIO. I like not fair terms and a villain's mind.

ANTONIO. Come on: in this there can be no dismay;
My ships come home a month before the day.   *Exeunt*

ACT TWO

SCENE ONE

Belmont. A Room in Portia's House.

Flourish of Cornets. Enter the Prince of Morocco, and his Followers; Portia, Nerissa, and Others of her Train.

MOROCCO. Mislike me not for my complexion,
The shadow'd livery of the burnish'd sun,
To whom I am a neighbour and near bred.
Bring me the fairest creature northward born,
Where Phœbus' fire scarce thaws the icicles,
And let us make incision for your love,
To prove whose blood is reddest, his or mine.
I tell thee, lady, this aspect of mine
Hath fear'd the valiant: by my love, I swear
The best regarded virgins of our clime
Have lov'd it too: I would not change this hue,
Except to steal your thoughts, my gentle queen.

PORTIA. In terms of choice I am not solely led
By nice direction of a maiden's eyes;
Besides, the lottery of my destiny
Bars me the right of voluntary choosing:
But if my father had not scanted me
And hedg'd me by his wit, to yield myself
His wife who wins me by that means I told you,
Yourself, renowned prince, then stood as fair
As any comer I have look'd on yet
For my affection.

MOROCCO. Even for that I thank you:
Therefore, I pray you, lead me to the caskets
To try my fortune. By this scimitar,—
That slew the Sophy, and a Persian prince
That won three fields of Sultan Solyman,—
I would outstare the sternest eyes that look,

Outbrave the heart most daring on the earth,
Pluck the young sucking cubs from the she-bear,
Yea, mock the lion when he roars for prey,
To win thee, lady. But, alas the while!
If Hercules and Lichas play at dice
Which is the better man, the greater throw
May turn by fortune from the weaker hand:
So is Alcides beaten by his page;
And so may I, blind fortune leading me,
Miss that which one unworthier may attain,
And die with grieving.

PORTIA. You must take your chance;
And either not attempt to choose at all,
Or swear before you choose, if you choose wrong,
Never to speak to lady afterward
In way of marriage: therefore be advis'd.

MOROCCO. Nor will not: come, bring me unto my chance.

PORTIA. First, forward to the temple: after dinner
Your hazard shall be made.

MOROCCO. Good fortune then!
To make me blest or cursed'st among men!

Cornets, and exeunt

SCENE TWO

Venice. A Street.

Enter Launcelot Gobbo

LAUNCELOT. Certainly my conscience will serve me to run from this Jew my master. The fiend is at mine elbow, and tempts me, saying to me, 'Gobbo, Launcelot Gobbo, good Launcelot,' or 'good Gobbo,' or 'good Launcelot Gobbo, use your legs, take the start, run away.' My conscience says, 'No; take heed, honest Launcelot; take heed, honest Gobbo'; or, as aforesaid, 'honest Launcelot Gobbo; do not run; scorn running with thy heels.' Well, the most courageous fiend bids me pack: 'Via!' says the fiend; 'away!' says the fiend; 'for the heavens, rouse up a brave mind,' says the fiend, 'and run.' Well, my conscience, hanging about the neck of my heart, says very wisely to me, 'My honest friend Launcelot, being an honest man's son,'—or rather an honest woman's son;—for, indeed, my father did something smack, something grow to, he had a kind of taste;—well, my conscience says, 'Launcelot, budge not.' 'Budge,' says the fiend. 'Budge not,' says my conscience. 'Conscience,' say I, 'you counsel well'; 'fiend,' say I, 'you counsel well': to be ruled by my conscience, I should stay with the Jew my master, who, God bless the mark! is a kind of devil; and, to run away from the Jew, I should be ruled by the fiend, who, saving your reverence, is the devil himself. Certainly, the Jew is the very devil incarnal; and, in my conscience, my conscience is but a kind of hard conscience, to offer to counsel me to stay with the Jew. The fiend gives the more friendly counsel: I will run, fiend; my heels are at your commandment; I will run.

Enter Old Gobbo, with a basket

GOBBO. Master young man, you; I pray you, which is the way to Master Jew's?

LAUNCELOT. (*Aside*) O heavens! this is my true-begotten father, who, being more than sand-blind, high-gravel blind, knows me not: I will try confusions with him.

GOBBO. Master young gentleman, I pray you, which is the way to Master Jew's?

LAUNCELOT. Turn up on your right hand at the next turning, but, at the next turning of all, on your left; marry, at the very next turning, turn of no hand, but turn down indirectly to the Jew's house.

GOBBO. By God's sonties, 'twill be a hard way to hit. Can you tell me whether one Launcelot, that dwells with him, dwell with him or no?

LAUNCELOT. Talk you of young Master Launcelot? (*Aside*) Mark me now; now will I raise the waters. Talk you of young Master Launcelot?

GOBBO. No master, sir, but a poor man's son: his father, though I say it, is an honest, exceeding poor man, and, God be thanked, well to live.

LAUNCELOT. Well, let his father be what a' will, we talk of young Master Launcelot.

GOBBO. Your worship's friend, and Launcelot, sir.

LAUNCELOT. But I pray you, ergo, old man, ergo, I beseech you, talk you of young Master Launcelot?

GOBBO. Of Launcelot, an 't please your mastership.

LAUNCELOT. Ergo, Master Launcelot. Talk not of Master

Launcelot, father; for the young gentleman,—according to Fates and Destinies and such odd sayings, the Sisters Three and such branches of learning,—is, indeed, deceased; or, as you would say in plain terms, gone to heaven.

GOBBO. Marry, God forbid! the boy was the very staff of my age, my very prop.

LAUNCELOT. (*Aside*) Do I look like a cudgel or a hovel-post, a staff or a prop? Do you know me, father?

GOBBO. Alack the day! I know you not, young gentleman: but I pray you, tell me, is my boy,—God rest his soul!—alive or dead?

LAUNCELOT. Do you not know me, father?

GOBBO. Alack, sir, I am sand-blind; I know you not.

LAUNCELOT. Nay, indeed, if you had your eyes, you might fail of the knowing me: it is a wise father that knows his own child. Well, old man, I will tell you news of your son. Give me your blessing; truth will come to light; murder cannot be hid long; a man's son may, but, in the end, truth will out.

GOBBO. Pray you, sir, stand up. I am sure you are not Launcelot, my boy.

LAUNCELOT. Pray you, let 's have no more fooling about it, but give me your blessing: I am Launcelot, your boy that was, your son that is, your child that shall be.

GOBBO. I cannot think you are my son.

LAUNCELOT. I know not what I shall think of that; but I am Launcelot, the Jew's man, and I am sure Margery your wife is my mother.

GOBBO. Her name is Margery, indeed: I 'll be sworn, if thou be Launcelot, thou art mine own flesh and blood. Lord worshipped might he be! what a beard hast thou got! thou hast got more hair on thy chin than Dobbin my thill-horse has on his tail.

LAUNCELOT. It should seem then that Dobbin's tail grows backward: I am sure he had more hair on his tail than I have on my face, when I last saw him.

GOBBO. Lord! how art thou changed. How dost thou and thy master agree? I have brought him a present. How 'gree you now?

LAUNCELOT. Well, well: but, for mine own part, as I have set up my rest to run away, so I will not rest till I have run some ground. My master 's a very Jew: give him a present! give him a halter: I am famished in his service; you may tell every finger I have with my ribs. Father, I am glad you are come: give me your present to one Master Bassanio, who, indeed, gives rare new liveries. If I serve not him, I will run as far as God has any ground. O rare fortune! here comes the man: to him, father; for I am a Jew, if I serve the Jew any longer.

Enter Bassanio, with Leonardo, and other Followers

BASSANIO. You may do so; but let it be so hasted that supper be ready at the very furthest by five of the clock. See these letters delivered; put the liveries to making; and desire Gratiano to come anon to my lodging. *Exit a Servant*

LAUNCELOT. To him, father.

GOBBO. God bless your worship!

BASSANIO. Gramercy! wouldst thou aught with me?

GOBBO. Here 's my son, sir, a poor boy,—

LAUNCELOT. Not a poor boy, sir, but the rich Jew's man; that would, sir,—as my father shall specify,—

GOBBO. He hath a great infection, sir, as one would say, to serve—

LAUNCELOT. Indeed, the short and the long is, I serve the Jew, and have a desire, as my father shall specify,—

GOBBO. His master and he, saving your worship's reverence, are scarce cater-cousins,—

LAUNCELOT. To be brief, the very truth is that the Jew having done me wrong, doth cause me,—as my father, being, I hope, an old man, shall frutify unto you,—

GOBBO. I have here a dish of doves that I would bestow upon your worship, and my suit is,—

LAUNCELOT. In very brief, the suit is impertinent to myself, as your worship shall know by this honest old man; and, though I say it, though old man, yet poor man, my father.

BASSANIO. One speak for both. What would you?

LAUNCELOT. Serve you, sir.

GOBBO. That is the very defect of the matter, sir.

BASSANIO. I know thee well; thou hast obtain'd thy suit:
Shylock thy master spoke with me this day
And hath preferr'd thee, if it be preferment
To leave a rich Jew's service, to become
The follower of so poor a gentleman.

LAUNCELOT. The old proverb is very well parted between

ACT II : SCENE II

my master Shylock and you, sir: you have the grace of
God, sir, and he hath enough.

BASSANIO. Thou speak'st it well. Go, father, with thy son.
Take leave of thy old master, and inquire
My lodging out. (*To his Followers*) Give him a livery
More guarded than his fellows': see it done.

LAUNCELOT. Father, in. I cannot get a service, no; I have
ne'er a tongue in my head. Well, (*Looking on his palm*)
if any man in Italy have a fairer table which doth offer to
swear upon a book, I shall have good fortune. Go to;
here's a simple line of life: here's a small trifle of wives:
alas! fifteen wives is nothing: a 'leven widows and nine
maids is a simple coming-in for one man; and then to
'scape drowning thrice, and to be in peril of my life with
the edge of a feather-bed; here are simple 'scapes. Well,
if Fortune be a woman, she's a good wench for this gear.
Father, come; I'll take my leave of the Jew in the twinkling of an eye. *Exeunt Launcelot and Old Gobbo*

BASSANIO. I pray thee, good Leonardo, think on this:
These things being bought, and orderly bestow'd,
Return in haste, for I do feast to-night
My best-esteem'd acquaintance: hie thee, go.

LEONARDO. My best endeavours shall be done herein.

Enter Gratiano

GRATIANO. Where is your master?

LEONARDO. Yonder, sir, he walks. *Exit*

GRATIANO. Signior Bassanio!—

BASSANIO. Gratiano!

GRATIANO. I have a suit to you.

BASSANIO. You have obtain'd it.

GRATIANO. You must not deny me: I must go with you to
Belmont.

BASSANIO. Why, then you must. But hear thee, Gratiano;
Thou art too wild, too rude and bold of voice;
Parts that become thee happily enough,
And in such eyes as ours appear not faults;
But where thou art not known, why, there they show
Something too liberal. Pray thee, take pain
To allay with some cold drops of modesty
Thy skipping spirit, lest, through thy wild behaviour,
I be misconstru'd in the place I go to,
And lose my hopes.

GRATIANO. Signior Bassanio, hear me:
If I do not put on a sober habit,
Talk with respect, and swear but now and then,
Wear prayer-books in my pocket, look demurely,
Nay more, while grace is saying, hood mine eyes
Thus with my hat, and sigh, and say 'amen';
Use all the observance of civility,
Like one well studied in a sad ostent
To please his grandam, never trust me more.

BASSANIO. Well, we shall see your bearing.

GRATIANO. Nay, but I bar to-night; you shall not gauge me
By what we do to-night.

BASSANIO. No, that were pity:
I would entreat you rather to put on
Your boldest suit of mirth, for we have friends
That purpose merriment. But fare you well:
I have some business.

GRATIANO. And I must to Lorenzo and the rest;
But we will visit you at supper-time. *Exeunt*

SCENE THREE

The Same. A Room in Shylock's House.

Enter Jessica and Launcelot

JESSICA. I am sorry thou wilt leave my father so:
Our house is hell, and thou, a merry devil,
Didst rob it of some taste of tediousness.
But fare thee well; there is a ducat for thee:
And, Launcelot, soon at supper shalt thou see
Lorenzo, who is thy new master's guest:
Give him this letter; do it secretly;
And so farewell: I would not have my father
See me in talk with thee.

LAUNCELOT. Adieu! tears exhibit my tongue. Most beautiful pagan, most sweet Jew! If a Christian did not play the knave and get thee, I am much deceived. But, adieu! these foolish drops do somewhat drown my manly spirit: adieu!

JESSICA. Farewell, good Launcelot. *Exit Launcelot*
Alack, what heinous sin is it in me

To be asham'd to be my father's child!
But though I am a daughter to his blood,
I am not to his manners. O Lorenzo!
If thou keep promise, I shall end this strife,
Become a Christian, and thy loving wife. *Exit*

SCENE FOUR

The Same. A Street.

Enter Gratiano, Lorenzo, Salarino, and Salanio

LORENZO. Nay, we will slink away in supper-time,
  Disguise us at my lodging, and return
  All in an hour.
GRATIANO. We have not made good preparation.
SALARINO. We have not spoke us yet of torch-bearers.
SALANIO. 'Tis vile, unless it may be quaintly order'd,
  And better, in my mind, not undertook.
LORENZO. 'Tis now but four o'clock: we have two hours
  To furnish us.
      Enter Launcelot, with a letter
          Friend Launcelot, what's the news?
LAUNCELOT. An it shall please you to break up this, it shall seem to signify.
LORENZO. I know the hand: in faith, 'tis a fair hand;
  And whiter than the paper it writ on
  Is the fair hand that writ.
GRATIANO.   Love news, in faith.
LAUNCELOT. By your leave, sir.
LORENZO. Whither goest thou?
LAUNCELOT. Marry, sir, to bid my old master, the Jew, to sup to-night with my new master, the Christian.
LORENZO. Hold there, take this: tell gentle Jessica
  I will not fail her; speak it privately.
  Go, gentlemen,   *Exit Launcelot*
  Will you prepare you for this masque to-night?
  I am provided of a torch-bearer.
SALARINO. Ay, marry, I'll be gone about it straight.
SALANIO. And so will I.
LORENZO.   Meet me and Gratiano
  At Gratiano's lodging some hour hence.

SALARINO. 'Tis good we do so.

Exeunt Salarino and Salanio

GRATIANO. Was not that letter from fair Jessica?
LORENZO. I must needs tell thee all. She hath directed
How I shall take her from her father's house;
What gold and jewels she is furnish'd with;
What page's suit she hath in readiness.
If e'er the Jew her father come to heaven,
It will be for his gentle daughter's sake;
And never dare misfortune cross her foot,
Unless she do it under this excuse,
That she is issue to a faithless Jew.
Come, go with me: peruse this as thou goest.
Fair Jessica shall be my torch-bearer. *Exeunt*

SCENE FIVE

The Same. Before Shylock's House.

Enter Shylock and Launcelot

SHYLOCK. Well, thou shalt see, thy eyes shall be thy judge,
The difference of old Shylock and Bassanio:—
What, Jessica!—thou shalt not gormandize,
As thou hast done with me;—What, Jessica!—
And sleep and snore, and rend apparel out—
Why, Jessica, I say!
LAUNCELOT. Why, Jessica!
SHYLOCK. Who bids thee call? I do not bid thee call.
LAUNCELOT. Your worship was wont to tell me that I could do nothing without bidding.

Enter Jessica

JESSICA. Call you? What is your will?
SHYLOCK. I am bid forth to supper, Jessica:
There are my keys. But wherefore should I go?
I am not bid for love; they flatter me:
But yet I'll go in hate, to feed upon
The prodigal Christian. Jessica, my girl,
Look to my house. I am right loath to go:
There is some ill a-brewing towards my rest,
For I did dream of money-bags to-night.
LAUNCELOT. I beseech you, sir, go: my young master doth expect your reproach.

SHYLOCK. So do I his.

LAUNCELOT. And they have conspired together: I will not say you shall see a masque; but if you do, then it was not for nothing that my nose fell a-bleeding on Black-Monday last, at six o'clock i' the morning, falling out that year on Ash-Wednesday was four year in the afternoon.

SHYLOCK. What! are there masques? Hear you me, Jessica:
Lock up my doors; and when you hear the drum,
And the vile squealing of the wry-neck'd fife,
Clamber not you up to the casements then,
Nor thrust your head into the public street
To gaze on Christian fools with varnish'd faces,
But stop my house's ears, I mean my casements;
Let not the sound of shallow foppery enter
My sober house. By Jacob's staff I swear
I have no mind of feasting forth to-night;
But I will go. Go you before me, sirrah;
Say I will come.

LAUNCELOT. I will go before, sir. Mistress, look out at window, for all this;
       There will come a Christian by,
       Will be worth a Jewess' eye. *Exit Launcelot*

SHYLOCK. What says that fool of Hagar's offspring, ha?

JESSICA. His words were, 'Farewell, mistress'; nothing else.

SHYLOCK. The patch is kind enough, but a huge feeder;
Snail-slow in profit, and he sleeps by day
More than the wild cat: drones hive not with me;
Therefore I part with him, and part with him
To one that I would have him help to waste
His borrow'd purse. Well, Jessica, go in:
Perhaps I will return immediately:
Do as I bid you; shut doors after you:
'Fast bind, fast find,'
A proverb never stale in thrifty mind. *Exit*

JESSICA. Farewell; and if my fortune be not crost,
I have a father, you a daughter, lost. *Exit*

SCENE SIX

The Same.

Enter Gratiano and Salarino, masqued

GRATIANO. This is the penthouse under which Lorenzo
  Desir'd us to make stand.
SALARINO.   His hour is almost past.
GRATIANO. And it is marvel he out-dwells his hour,
  For lovers ever run before the clock.
SALARINO. O! ten times faster Venus' pigeons fly
  To seal love's bonds new-made, than they are wont
  To keep obliged faith unforfeited!
GRATIANO. That ever holds: who riseth from a feast
  With that keen appetite that he sits down?
  Where is the horse that doth untread again
  His tedious measures with the unbated fire
  That he did pace them first? All things that are,
  Are with more spirit chased than enjoy'd.
  How like a younker or a prodigal
  The scarfed bark puts from her native bay,
  Hugg'd and embraced by the strumpet wind!
  How like the prodigal doth she return,
  With over-weather'd ribs and ragged sails,
  Lean, rent, and beggar'd by the strumpet wind!
SALARINO. Here comes Lorenzo: more of this hereafter.

Enter Lorenzo

LORENZO. Sweet friends, your patience for my long abode;
  Not I, but my affairs, have made you wait:
  When you shall please to play the thieves for wives,
  I'll watch as long for you then. Approach;
  Here dwells my father Jew. Ho! who's within?

Enter Jessica above, in boy's clothes

JESSICA. Who are you? Tell me, for more certainty,
  Albeit I'll swear that I do know your tongue.
LORENZO. Lorenzo, and thy love.
JESSICA. Lorenzo, certain; and my love indeed,
  For whom love I so much? And now who knows
  But you, Lorenzo, whether I am yours?
LORENZO. Heaven and thy thoughts are witness that thou
  art.

JESSICA. Here, catch this casket; it is worth the pains.
 I am glad 'tis night, you do not look on me,
 For I am much asham'd of my exchange;
 But love is blind, and lovers cannot see
 The pretty follies that themselves commit;
 For if they could, Cupid himself would blush
 To see me thus transformed to a boy.
LORENZO. Descend, for you must be my torch-bearer.
JESSICA. What! must I hold a candle to my shames?
 They in themselves, good sooth, are too-too light.
 Why, 'tis an office of discovery, love,
 And I should be obscur'd.
LORENZO. So are you, sweet,
 Even in the lovely garnish of a boy.
 But come at once;
 For the close night doth play the runaway,
 And we are stay'd for at Bassanio's feast.
JESSICA. I will make fast the doors, and gild myself
 With some more ducats, and be with you straight.
Exit above
GRATIANO. Now, by my hood, a Gentile, and no Jew.
LORENZO. Beshrew me, but I love her heartily;
 For she is wise, if I can judge of her,
 And fair she is, if that mine eyes be true,
 And true she is, as she hath prov'd herself;
 And therefore, like herself, wise, fair, and true,
 Shall she be placed in my constant soul.
Enter Jessica
What, art thou come? On, gentlemen; away!
Our masquing mates by this time for us stay.
Exit with Jessica and Salarino
Enter Antonio
ANTONIO. Who's there?
GRATIANO. Signior Antonio!
ANTONIO. Fie, fie, Gratiano! where are all the rest?
 'Tis nine o'clock; our friends all stay for you.
 No masque to-night: the wind is come about;
 Bassanio presently will go aboard:
 I have sent twenty out to seek for you.
GRATIANO. I am glad on 't: I desire no more delight
 Than to be under sail and gone to-night. *Exeunt*

SCENE SEVEN

Belmont. A Room in Portia's House.

Flourish of Cornets. Enter Portia, with the Prince of Morocco, and their Trains

PORTIA. Go, draw aside the curtains, and discover
The several caskets to this noble prince.
Now make your choice.

MOROCCO. The first, of gold, which this inscription bears:
'Who chooseth me shall gain what many men desire.'
The second, silver, which this promise carries:
'Who chooseth me shall get as much as he deserves.'
This third, dull lead, with warning all as blunt:
'Who chooseth me must give and hazard all he hath.'
How shall I know if I do choose the right?

PORTIA. The one of them contains my picture, prince:
If you choose that, then I am yours withal.

MOROCCO. Some god direct my judgment! Let me see:
I will survey the inscriptions back again:
What says this leaden casket?
'Who chooseth me must give and hazard all he hath.'
Must give: For what? for lead? hazard for lead?
This casket threatens. Men that hazard all
Do it in hope of fair advantages:
A golden mind stoops not to shows of dross;
I'll then nor give nor hazard aught for lead.
What says the silver with her virgin hue?
'Who chooseth me shall get as much as he deserves.'
As much as he deserves! Pause there, Morocco,
And weigh thy value with an even hand.
If thou be'st rated by thy estimation,
Thou dost deserve enough; and yet enough
May not extend so far as to the lady:
And yet to be afeard of my deserving
Were but a weak disabling of myself.
As much as I deserve! Why, that's the lady:
I do in birth deserve her, and in fortunes,
In graces, and in qualities of breeding;
But more than these, in love I do deserve.

What if I stray'd no further, but chose here?
Let 's see once more this saying grav'd in gold:
'Who chooseth me shall gain what many men desire.'
Why, that 's the lady: all the world desires her:
From the four corners of the earth they come,
To kiss this shrine, this mortal-breathing saint:
The Hyrcanian deserts and the vasty wilds
Of wide Arabia are as throughfares now
For princes to come view fair Portia:
The watery kingdom, whose ambitious head
Spits in the face of heaven, is no bar
To stop the foreign spirits, but they come,
As o'er a brook, to see fair Portia.
One of these three contains her heavenly picture.
Is 't like that lead contains her? 'Twere damnation
To think so base a thought: it were too gross
To rib her cerecloth in the obscure grave.
Or shall I think in silver she 's immur'd,
Being ten times undervalu'd to tried gold?
O sinful thought! Never so rich a gem
Was set in worse than gold. They have in England
A coin that bears the figure of an angel
Stamped in gold, but that 's insculp'd upon;
But here an angel in a golden bed
Lies all within. Deliver me the key:
Here do I choose, and thrive I as I may!

PORTIA. There, take it, prince; and if my form lie there,
Then I am yours. *He unlocks the golden casket*
MOROCCO. O hell! what have we here?
A carrion Death, within whose empty eye
There is a written scroll. I 'll read the writing.
    'All that glisters is not gold;
    Often have you heard that told:
    Many a man his life hath sold
    But my outside to behold:
    Gilded tombs do worms infold.
    Had you been as wise as bold,
    Young in limbs, in judgment old,
    Your answer had not been inscroll'd:
    Fare you well; your suit is cold.'
  Cold, indeed; and labour lost:
  Then, farewell, heat, and welcome, frost!

Portia, adieu. I have too griev'd a heart
To take a tedious leave: thus losers part.
                    Exit with his Train. Flourish of Cornets
PORTIA. A gentle riddance. Draw the curtains: go.
Let all of his complexion choose me so.   *Exeunt*

SCENE EIGHT

Venice. A Street.

Enter Salarino and Salanio

SALARINO. Why, man, I saw Bassanio under sail:
With him is Gratiano gone along;
And in their ship I 'm sure Lorenzo is not.
SALANIO. The villain Jew with outcries rais'd the duke,
Who went with him to search Bassanio's ship.
SALARINO. He came too late, the ship was under sail:
But there the duke was given to understand
That in a gondola were seen together
Lorenzo and his amorous Jessica.
Besides, Antonio certified the duke
They were not with Bassanio in his ship.
SALANIO. I never heard a passion so confus'd,
So strange, outrageous, and so variable,
As the dog Jew did utter in the streets:
'My daughter! O my ducats! O my daughter!
Fled with a Christian! O my Christian ducats!
Justice! the law! my ducats, and my daughter!
A sealed bag, two sealed bags of ducats,
Of double ducats, stol'n from me by my daughter!
And jewels! two stones, two rich and precious stones,
Stol'n by my daughter! Justice! find the girl!
She hath the stones upon her, and the ducats.'
SALARINO. Why, all the boys in Venice follow him,
Crying, his stones, his daughter, and his ducats.
SALANIO. Let good Antonio look he keep his day,
Or he shall pay for this.
SALARINO.   Marry, well remember'd.
I reason'd with a Frenchman yesterday,
Who told me,—in the narrow seas that part

The French and English,—there miscarried
A vessel of our country richly fraught.
I thought upon Antonio when he told me,
And wish'd in silence that it were not his.
SALANIO. You were best to tell Antonio what you hear;
Yet do not suddenly, for it may grieve him.
SALARINO. A kinder gentleman treads not the earth.
I saw Bassanio and Antonio part:
Bassanio told him he would make some speed
Of his return: he answer'd 'Do not so;
Slubber not business for my sake, Bassanio,
But stay the very riping of the time;
And for the Jew's bond which he hath of me,
Let it not enter in your mind of love:
Be merry, and employ your chiefest thoughts
To courtship and such fair ostents of love
As shall conveniently become you there.'
And even there, his eye being big with tears,
Turning his face, he put his hand behind him,
And with affection wondrous sensible
He wrung Bassanio's hand; and so they parted.
SALANIO. I think he only loves the world for him.
I pray thee, let us go and find him out,
And quicken his embraced heaviness
With some delight or other.
SALARINO.   Do we so.   *Exeunt*

SCENE NINE

Belmont. A Room in Portia's House.

Enter Nerissa, with a Servitor

NERISSA. Quick, quick, I pray thee; draw the curtain straight:
The Prince of Arragon hath ta'en his oath
And comes to his election presently.
          *Flourish of Cornets. Enter the
      Prince of Arragon, Portia, and their Trains*
PORTIA. Behold, there stands the caskets, noble prince:
If you choose that wherein I am contain'd,
Straight shall our nuptial rites be solemniz'd;

But if you fail, without more speech, my lord,
You must be gone from hence immediately.

ARRAGON. I am enjoin'd by oath to observe three things:
First, never to unfold to any one
Which casket 'twas I chose; next, if I fail
Of the right casket, never in my life
To woo a maid in way of marriage;
Lastly,
If I do fail in fortune of my choice,
Immediately to leave you and be gone.

PORTIA. To these injunctions every one doth swear
That comes to hazard for my worthless self.

ARRAGON. And so have I address'd me. Fortune now
To my heart's hope! Gold, silver, and base lead.
'Who chooseth me must give and hazard all he hath':
You shall look fairer, ere I give or hazard.
What says the golden chest? ha! let me see:
'Who chooseth me shall gain what many men desire.'
What many men desire! that 'many' may be meant
By the fool multitude, that choose by show,
Not learning more than the fond eye doth teach;
Which pries not to the interior, but, like the martlet,
Builds in the weather on the outward wall,
Even in the force and road of casualty.
I will not choose what many men desire,
Because I will not jump with common spirits
And rank me with the barbarous multitude.
Why, then to thee, thou silver treasure-house;
Tell me once more what title thou dost bear:
'Who chooseth me shall get as much as he deserves.'
And well said too; for who shall go about
To cozen fortune and be honourable
Without the stamp of merit? Let none presume
To wear an undeserved dignity.
O! that estates, degrees, and offices
Were not deriv'd corruptly, and that clear honour
Were purchas'd by the merit of the wearer.
How many then should cover that stand bare;
How many be commanded that command;
How much low peasantry would then be glean'd
From the true seed of honour; and how much honour
Pick'd from the chaff and ruin of the times

To be new varnish'd! Well, but to my choice:
'Who chooseth me shall get as much as he deserves.'
I will assume desert. Give me a key for this,
And instantly unlock my fortunes here.

He opens the silver casket

PORTIA. Too long a pause for that which you find there.
ARRAGON. What's here? the portrait of a blinking idiot,
Presenting me a schedule! I will read it.
How much unlike art thou to Portia!
How much unlike my hopes and my deservings!
'Who chooseth me shall have as much as he deserves.'
Did I deserve no more than a fool's head?
Is that my prize? Are my deserts no better?
PORTIA. To offend, and judge, are distinct offices,
And of opposed natures.
ARRAGON.   What is here?
   'The fire seven times tried this:
   Seven times tried that judgment is
   That did never choose amiss.
   Some there be that shadows kiss;
   Such have but a shadow's bliss:
   There be fools alive, I wis,
   Silver'd o'er; and so was this.
   Take what wife you will to bed,
   I will ever be your head:
   So be gone, sir: you are sped.'
Still more fool I shall appear
By the time I linger here:
With one fool's head I came to woo,
But I go away with two.
Sweet, adieu. I'll keep my oath,
Patiently to bear my wroth. *Exit Arragon with his Train*
PORTIA. Thus hath the candle sing'd the moth.
O, these deliberate fools! When they do choose,
They have the wisdom by their wit to loose.
NERISSA. The ancient saying is no heresy:
'Hanging and wiving goes by destiny.'
PORTIA. Come, draw the curtain, Nerissa.

Enter a Servant

SERVANT. Where is my lady?
PORTIA.   Here; what would my lord?
SERVANT. Madam, there is alighted at your gate

A young Venetian, one that comes before
To signify the approaching of his lord;
From whom he bringeth sensible regreets,
To wit,—besides commends and courteous breath,—
Gifts of rich value. Yet I have not seen
So likely an ambassador of love.
A day in April never came so sweet,
To show how costly summer was at hand,
As this fore-spurrer comes before his lord.

PORTIA. No more, I pray thee: I am half afeard
Thou wilt say anon he is some kin to thee,
Thou spend'st such high-day wit in praising him.
Come, come, Nerissa; for I long to see
Quick Cupid's post that comes so mannerly.

NERISSA. Bassanio, Lord Love, if thy will it be! *Exeunt*

ACT THREE

SCENE ONE

Venice. A Street.

Enter Salanio and Salarino

SALANIO. Now, what news on the Rialto?

SALARINO. Why, yet it lives there unchecked that Antonio hath a ship of rich lading wracked on the narrow seas; the Goodwins, I think they call the place; a very dangerous flat, and fatal, where the carcasses of many a tall ship lie buried, as they say, if my gossip Report be an honest woman of her word.

SALANIO. I would she were as lying a gossip in that as ever knapped ginger, or made her neighbours believe she wept for the death of a third husband. But it is true,—without any slips of prolixity or crossing the plain highway of talk, —that the good Antonio, the honest Antonio,—O, that I had a title good enough to keep his name company!—

SALARINO. Come, the full stop.

SALANIO. Ha! what sayst thou? Why, the end is, he hath lost a ship.

SALARINO. I would it might prove the end of his losses.

SALANIO. Let me say 'amen' betimes, lest the devil cross my prayer, for here he comes in the likeness of a Jew.

Enter Shylock

How now, Shylock! What news among the merchants?

SHYLOCK. You knew, none so well, none so well as you, of my daughter's flight.

SALARINO. That's certain: I, for my part, knew the tailor that made the wings she flew withal.

SALANIO. And Shylock, for his own part, knew the bird was fledged; and then it is the complexion of them all to leave the dam.

SHYLOCK. She is damned for it.

SALARINO. That's certain, if the devil may be her judge.

SHYLOCK. My own flesh and blood to rebel!

SALANIO. Out upon it, old carrion! rebels it at these years?

SHYLOCK. I say my daughter is my flesh and blood.

SALARINO. There is more difference between thy flesh and hers than between jet and ivory; more between your bloods than there is between red wine and Rhenish. But tell us, do you hear whether Antonio have had any loss at sea or no?

SHYLOCK. There I have another bad match: a bankrupt, a prodigal, who dare scarce show his head on the Rialto; a beggar, that used to come so smug upon the mart; let him look to his bond: he was wont to call me usurer; let him look to his bond: he was wont to lend money for a Christian courtesy; let him look to his bond.

SALARINO. Why, I am sure, if he forfeit thou wilt not take his flesh: what's that good for?

SHYLOCK. To bait fish withal: if it will feed nothing else, it will feed my revenge. He hath disgraced me, and hindered me half a million, laughed at my losses, mocked at my gains, scorned my nation, thwarted my bargains, cooled my friends, heated mine enemies; and what's his reason? I am a Jew. Hath not a Jew eyes? hath not a Jew hands, organs, dimensions, senses, affections, passions? fed with the same food, hurt with the same weapons, subject to the same diseases, healed by the same means, warmed and cooled by the same winter and summer, as a Christian is? If you prick us, do we not bleed? if you tickle us, do we not laugh? if you poison us, do we not die? and if you wrong us, shall we not revenge? If we are like you in the rest, we will resemble you in that. If a Jew wrong a Christian, what is his humility? Revenge. If a Christian wrong a Jew, what should his sufferance be by Christian example? Why, revenge. The villany you teach me I will execute, and it shall go hard but I will better the instruction.

Enter a Servant

SERVANT. Gentlemen, my master Antonio is at his house, and desires to speak with you both.

SALARINO. We have been up and down to seek him.

Enter Tubal

SALANIO. Here comes another of the tribe: a third cannot be matched, unless the devil himself turn Jew.

Exeunt Salanio, Salarino and Servant

SHYLOCK. How now, Tubal! What news from Genoa? Hast thou found my daughter?

TUBAL. I often came where I did hear of her, but cannot find her.

SHYLOCK. Why there, there, there! a diamond gone, cost me two thousand ducats in Frankfort! The curse never fell upon our nation till now; I never felt it till now: two thousand ducats in that; and other precious, precious jewels. I would my daughter were dead at my foot, and the jewels in her ear! Would she were hearsed at my foot, and the ducats in her coffin! No news of them? Why, so: and I know not what's spent in the search: Why thou—loss upon loss! the thief gone with so much, and so much to find the thief; and no satisfaction, no revenge: nor no ill luck stirring but what lights on my shoulders; no sighs but of my breathing; no tears but of my shedding.

TUBAL. Yes, other men have ill luck too. Antonio, as I heard in Genoa,—

SHYLOCK. What, what, what? Ill luck, ill luck?

TUBAL. —hath an argosy cast away, coming from Tripolis.

SHYLOCK. I thank God! I thank God! Is it true? Is it true?

TUBAL. I spoke with some of the sailors that escaped the wrack.

SHYLOCK. I thank thee, good Tubal. Good news, good news! ha, ha! Where? in Genoa?

TUBAL. Your daughter spent in Genoa, as I heard, one night, fourscore ducats.

SHYLOCK. Thou stick'st a dagger in me: I shall never see my gold again: fourscore ducats at a sitting! fourscore ducats!

TUBAL. There came divers of Antonio's creditors in my company to Venice, that swear he cannot choose but break.

SHYLOCK. I am very glad of it: I'll plague him; I'll torture him: I am glad of it.

TUBAL. One of them showed me a ring that he had of your daughter for a monkey.

SHYLOCK. Out upon her! Thou torturest me, Tubal: it was my turquoise; I had it of Leah when I was a bachelor: I would not have given it for a wilderness of monkeys.

TUBAL. But Antonio is certainly undone.

SHYLOCK. Nay, that's true, that's very true. Go, Tubal, fee

me an officer; bespeak him a fortnight before. I will have
the heart of him, if he forfeit; for, were he out of Venice, I
can make what merchandise I will. Go, go, Tubal, and
meet me at our synagogue; go, good Tubal; at our synagogue, Tubal. *Exeunt*

SCENE TWO

Belmont. A Room in Portia's House.

*Enter Bassanio, Portia, Gratiano, Nerissa,
and Attendants*

PORTIA. I pray you, tarry: pause a day or two
Before you hazard; for, in choosing wrong,
I lose your company: therefore, forbear awhile.
There's something tells me, but it is not love,
I would not lose you; and you know yourself,
Hate counsels not in such a quality.
But lest you should not understand me well,—
And yet a maiden hath no tongue but thought,—
I would detain you here some month or two
Before you venture for me. I could teach you
How to choose right, but then I am forsworn;
So will I never be: so may you miss me;
But if you do, you'll make me wish a sin,
That I had been forsworn. Beshrew your eyes,
They have o'erlook'd me and divided me:
One half of me is yours, the other half yours,
Mine own, I would say; but if mine, then yours,
And so all yours. O! these naughty times
Put bars between the owners and their rights;
And so, though yours, not yours. Prove it so,
Let fortune go to hell for it, not I.
I speak too long; but 'tis to peise the time,
To eke it and to draw it out in length,
To stay you from election.
BASSANIO.   Let me choose;
For as I am, I live upon the rack.
PORTIA. Upon the rack, Bassanio! Then confess
What treason there is mingled with your love.

BASSANIO. None but that ugly treason of mistrust,
  Which makes me fear th' enjoying of my love:
  There may as well be amity and life
  'Tween snow and fire, as treason and my love.
PORTIA. Ay, but I fear you speak upon the rack,
  Where men enforced do speak anything.
BASSANIO. Promise me life, and I'll confess the truth.
PORTIA. Well then, confess, and live.
BASSANIO.   'Confess' and 'love'
  Had been the very sum of my confession:
  O happy torment, when my torturer
  Doth teach me answers for deliverance!
  But let me to my fortune and the caskets.
PORTIA. Away then! I am lock'd in one of them:
  If you do love me, you will find me out.
  Nerissa and the rest, stand all aloof.
  Let music sound while he doth make his choice;
  Then, if he lose, he makes a swan-like end,
  Fading in music: that the comparison
  May stand more proper, my eye shall be the stream
  And watery death-bed for him. He may win;
  And what is music then? Then music is
  Even as the flourish when true subjects bow
  To a new-crowned monarch: such it is
  As are those dulcet sounds in break of day
  That creep into the dreaming bridegroom's ear,
  And summon him to marriage. Now he goes,
  With no less presence, but with much more love,
  Than young Alcides, when he did redeem
  The virgin tribute paid by howling Troy
  To the sea-monster: I stand for sacrifice;
  The rest aloof are the Dardanian wives,
  With bleared visages, come forth to view
  The issue of the exploit. Go, Hercules!
  Live thou, I live: with much, much more dismay
  I view the fight than thou that mak'st the fray.

*A Song, whilst Bassanio
comments on the caskets to himself*

> Tell me where is fancy bred,
> Or in the heart or in the head?
> How begot, how nourished?
> > Reply, reply.
> It is engender'd in the eyes,
> With gazing fed; and fancy dies
> In the cradle where it lies.
> > Let us all ring fancy's knell:
> > I'll begin it.—Ding, dong, bell.

ALL. Ding, dong, bell.
BASSANIO. So may the outward shows be least themselves:
The world is still deceiv'd with ornament.
In law, what plea so tainted and corrupt
But, being season'd with a gracious voice,
Obscures the show of evil? In religion,
What damned error, but some sober brow
Will bless it and approve it with a text,
Hiding the grossness with fair ornament?
There is no vice so simple but assumes
Some mark of virtue on his outward parts.
How many cowards, whose hearts are all as false
As stairs of sand, wear yet upon their chins
The beards of Hercules and frowning Mars,
Who, inward search'd, have livers white as milk;
And these assume but valour's excrement
To render them redoubted! Look on beauty,
And you shall see 'tis purchas'd by the weight:
Which therein works a miracle in nature,
Making them lightest that wear most of it:
So are those crisped snaky golden locks
Which make such wanton gambols with the wind,
Upon supposed fairness, often known
To be the dowry of a second head,
The skull that bred them, in the sepulchre.
Thus ornament is but the guiled shore
To a most dangerous sea; the beauteous scarf
Veiling an Indian beauty; in a word,
The seeming truth which cunning times put on
To entrap the wisest. Therefore, thou gaudy gold,
Hard food for Midas, I will none of thee;

[103-142] ACT III · SCENE II

    Nor none of thee, thou pale and common drudge
'Tween man and man: but thou, thou meagre lead,
Which rather threat'nest than dost promise aught,
Thy plainness moves me more than eloquence,
And here choose I: joy be the consequence!
PORTIA. (*Aside*) How all the other passions fleet to air,
As doubtful thoughts, and rash-embrac'd despair,
And shuddering fear, and green-ey'd jealousy.
O love! be moderate; allay thy ecstasy;
In measure rain thy joy; scant this excess;
I feel too much thy blessing; make it less,
For fear I surfeit!
BASSANIO.   What find I here?
                              Opening the leaden casket
Fair Portia's counterfeit! What demi-god
Hath come so near creation? Move these eyes?
Or whether, riding on the balls of mine,
Seem they in motion? Here are sever'd lips,
Parted with sugar breath; so sweet a bar
Should sunder such sweet friends. Here, in her hairs
The painter plays the spider, and hath woven
A golden mesh to entrap the hearts of men
Faster than gnats in cobwebs: but her eyes!—
How could he see to do them? Having made one,
Methinks it should have power to steal both his
And leave itself unfurnish'd: yet look, how far
The substance of my praise doth wrong this shadow
In underprizing it, so far this shadow
Doth limp behind the substance. Here's the scroll,
The continent and summary of my fortune.
    'You that choose not by the view,
    Chance as fair and choose as true!
    Since this fortune falls to you,
    Be content and seek no new.
    If you be well pleas'd with this
    And hold your fortune for your bliss,
    Turn you where your lady is
    And claim her with a loving kiss.'
A gentle scroll. Fair lady, by your leave;   *Kissing her*
I come by note, to give and to receive.
Like one of two contending in a prize,
That thinks he hath done well in people's eyes,

Hearing applause and universal shout,
Giddy in spirit, still gazing in a doubt
Whether those peals of praise be his or no;
So, thrice-fair lady, stand I, even so,
As doubtful whether what I see be true,
Until confirm'd, sign'd, ratified by you.

PORTIA. You see me, Lord Bassanio, where I stand,
Such as I am: though for myself alone
I would not be ambitious in my wish,
To wish myself much better; yet, for you
I would be trebled twenty times myself;
A thousand times more fair, ten thousand times
More rich;
That only to stand high in your account,
I might in virtues, beauties, livings, friends,
Exceed account: but the full sum of me
Is sum of nothing; which, to term in gross,
Is an unlesson'd girl, unschool'd, unpractis'd;
Happy in this, she is not yet so old
But she may learn; happier than this,
She is not bred so dull but she can learn;
Happiest of all is that her gentle spirit
Commits itself to yours to be directed,
As from her lord, her governor, her king.
Myself and what is mine to you and yours
Is now converted: but now I was the lord
Of this fair mansion, master of my servants,
Queen o'er myself; and even now, but now,
This house, these servants, and this same myself
Are yours, my lord. I give them with this ring;
Which when you part from, lose, or give away,
Let it presage the ruin of your love,
And be my vantage to exclaim on you.

BASSANIO. Madam, you have bereft me of all words,
Only my blood speaks to you in my veins;
And there is such confusion in my powers,
As, after some oration fairly spoke
By a beloved prince, there doth appear
Among the buzzing pleased multitude;
Where every something, being blent together,
Turns to a wild of nothing, save of joy,
Express'd and not express'd. But when this ring

Parts from this finger, then parts life from hence:
O! then be bold to say Bassanio's dead.
NERISSA. My lord and lady, it is now our time,
That have stood by and seen our wishes prosper,
To cry, good joy. Good joy, my lord and lady!
GRATIANO. My Lord Bassanio and my gentle lady,
I wish you all the joy that you can wish;
For I am sure you can wish none from me:
And when your honours mean to solemnize
The bargain of your faith, I do beseech you,
Even at that time I may be married too.
BASSANIO. With all my heart, so thou canst get a wife.
GRATIANO. I thank your lordship, you have got me one.
My eyes, my lord, can look as swift as yours:
You saw the mistress, I beheld the maid;
You lov'd, I lov'd for intermission.
No more pertains to me, my lord, than you.
Your fortune stood upon the caskets there,
And so did mine too, as the matter falls;
For wooing here until I sweat again,
And swearing till my very roof was dry
With oaths of love, at last, if promise last,
I got a promise of this fair one here
To have her love, provided that your fortune
Achiev'd her mistress.
PORTIA. Is this true, Nerissa?
NERISSA. Madam, it is, so you stand pleas'd withal.
BASSANIO. And do you, Gratiano, mean good faith?
GRATIANO. Yes, faith, my lord.
BASSANIO. Our feast shall be much honour'd in your marriage.
GRATIANO. We'll play with them the first boy for a thousand ducats.
NERISSA. What! and stake down?
GRATIANO. No; we shall ne'er win at that sport, and stake down.
But who comes here? Lorenzo and his infidel?
What! and my old Venetian friend, Salanio?

Enter Lorenzo, Jessica, and Salanio

BASSANIO. Lorenzo, and Salanio, welcome hither,
If that the youth of my new interest here
Have power to bid you welcome. By your leave,

I bid my very friends and countrymen,
Sweet Portia, welcome.

PORTIA. So do I, my lord:
They are entirely welcome.

LORENZO. I thank your honour. For my part, my lord,
My purpose was not to have seen you here;
But meeting with Salanio by the way,
He did entreat me, past all saying nay,
To come with him along.

SALANIO. I did, my lord,
And I have reason for it. Signior Antonio
Commends him to you. *Gives Bassanio a letter*

BASSANIO. Ere I ope his letter,
I pray you, tell me how my good friend doth.

SALANIO. Not sick, my lord, unless it be in mind;
Nor well, unless in mind: his letter there
Will show you his estate.

GRATIANO. Nerissa, cheer yon stranger; bid her welcome.
Your hand, Salanio. What 's the news from Venice?
How doth that royal merchant, good Antonio?
I know he will be glad of our success;
We are the Jasons, we have won the fleece.

SALANIO. I would you had won the fleece that he hath lost.

PORTIA. There are some shrewd contents in yon same paper,
That steal the colour from Bassanio's cheek:
Some dear friend dead, else nothing in the world
Could turn so much the constitution
Of any constant man. What, worse and worse!
With leave, Bassanio; I am half yourself,
And I must freely have the half of anything
That this same paper brings you.

BASSANIO. O sweet Portia!
Here are a few of the unpleasant'st words
That ever blotted paper. Gentle lady,
When I did first impart my love to you,
I freely told you all the wealth I had
Ran in my veins, I was a gentleman:
And then I told you true; and yet, dear lady,
Rating myself at nothing, you shall see
How much I was a braggart. When I told you
My state was nothing, I should then have told you
That I was worse than nothing; for, indeed,

I have engag'd myself to a dear friend,
Engag'd my friend to his mere enemy,
To feed my means. Here is a letter, lady;
The paper as the body of my friend,
And every word in it a gaping wound,
Issuing life-blood. But is it true, Salanio?
Hath all his ventures fail'd? What, not one hit?
From Tripolis, from Mexico, and England,
From Lisbon, Barbary, and India?
And not one vessel 'scape the dreadful touch
Of merchant-marring rocks?

SALANIO. Not one, my lord.
Besides, it should appear, that if he had
The present money to discharge the Jew,
He would not take it. Never did I know
A creature, that did bear the shape of man,
So keen and greedy to confound a man.
He plies the duke at morning and at night,
And doth impeach the freedom of the state,
If they deny him justice: twenty merchants,
The duke himself, and the magnificoes
Of greatest port, have all persuaded with him;
But none can drive him from the envious plea
Of forfeiture, of justice, and his bond.

JESSICA. When I was with him, I have heard him swear
To Tubal and to Chus, his countrymen,
That he would rather have Antonio's flesh
Than twenty times the value of the sum
That he did owe him; and I know, my lord,
If law, authority, and power deny not,
It will go hard with poor Antonio.

PORTIA. Is it your dear friend that is thus in trouble?

BASSANIO. The dearest friend to me, the kindest man,
The best-condition'd and unwearied spirit
In doing courtesies, and one in whom
The ancient Roman honour more appears
Than any that draws breath in Italy.

PORTIA. What sum owes he the Jew?

BASSANIO. For me, three thousand ducats.

PORTIA. What, no more?
Pay him six thousand, and deface the bond;
Double six thousand, and then treble that,

Before a friend of this description
Shall lose a hair thorough Bassanio's fault.
First go with me to church and call me wife,
And then away to Venice to your friend;
For never shall you lie by Portia's side
With an unquiet soul. You shall have gold
To pay the petty debt twenty times over:
When it is paid, bring your true friend along.
My maid Nerissa and myself meantime,
Will live as maids and widows. Come, away!
For you shall hence upon your wedding-day.
Bid your friends welcome, show a merry cheer;
Since you are dear bought, I will love you dear.
But let me hear the letter of your friend.

BASSANIO. 'Sweet Bassanio, my ships have all miscarried, my creditors grow cruel, my estate is very low, my bond to the Jew is forfeit; and since, in paying it, it is impossible I should live, all debts are cleared between you and I, if I might but see you at my death. Notwithstanding, use your pleasure: if your love do not persuade you to come, let not my letter.'

PORTIA. O love, dispatch all business, and be gone!

BASSANIO. Since I have your good leave to go away,
I will make haste; but, till I come again,
No bed shall e'er be guilty of my stay,
Nor rest be interposer 'twixt us twain.   *Exeunt*

SCENE THREE

Venice. A Street.

Enter Shylock, Salarino, Antonio, and Gaoler

SHYLOCK. Gaoler, look to him: tell not me of mercy;
This is the fool that lent out money gratis:
Gaoler, look to him.

ANTONIO.   Hear me yet, good Shylock.

SHYLOCK. I'll have my bond; speak not against my bond:
I have sworn an oath that I will have my bond.
Thou call'dst me dog before thou hadst a cause,
But, since I am a dog, beware my fangs:
The duke shall grant me justice. I do wonder,

[9·36; 1-5]   ACT III · SCENE III   593

    Thou naughty gaoler, that thou art so fond
    To come abroad with him at his request.
ANTONIO. I pray thee, hear me speak.
SHYLOCK. I'll have my bond; I will not hear thee speak:
    I'll have my bond, and therefore speak no more.
    I'll not be made a soft and dull-eyed fool,
    To shake the head, relent, and sigh, and yield
    To Christian intercessors. Follow not;
    I'll have no speaking; I will have my bond.   *Exit*
SALARINO. It is the most impenetrable cur
    That ever kept with men.
ANTONIO.   Let him alone:
    I'll follow him no more with bootless prayers.
    He seeks my life; his reason well I know.
    I oft deliver'd from his forfeitures
    Many that have at times made moan to me;
    Therefore he hates me.
SALARINO.   I am sure the duke
    Will never grant this forfeiture to hold.
ANTONIO. The duke cannot deny the course of law:
    For the commodity that strangers have
    With us in Venice, if it be denied,
    'Twill much impeach the justice of the state;
    Since that the trade and profit of the city
    Consisteth of all nations. Therefore, go:
    These griefs and losses have so bated me,
    That I shall hardly spare a pound of flesh
    To-morrow to my bloody creditor.
    Well, gaoler, on. Pray God, Bassanio come
    To see me pay his debt, and then I care not!   *Exeunt*

SCENE FOUR

Belmont. A Room in Portia's House.

Enter Portia, Nerissa, Lorenzo, Jessica, and Balthazar

LORENZO. Madam, although I speak it in your presence,
    You have a noble and a true conceit
    Of god-like amity; which appears most strongly
    In bearing thus the absence of your lord.
    But if you knew to whom you show this honour,

How true a gentleman you send relief,
How dear a lover of my lord your husband,
I know you would be prouder of the work
Than customary bounty can enforce you.

PORTIA. I never did repent for doing good,
Nor shall not now: for in companions
That do converse and waste the time together,
Whose souls do bear an equal yoke of love,
There must be needs a like proportion
Of lineaments, of manners, and of spirit;
Which makes me think that this Antonio,
Being the bosom lover of my lord,
Must needs be like my lord. If it be so,
How little is the cost I have bestow'd
In purchasing the semblance of my soul
From out the state of hellish cruelty!
This comes too near the praising of myself;
Therefore, no more of it: hear other things.
Lorenzo, I commit into your hands
The husbandry and manage of my house
Until my lord's return: for mine own part,
I have toward heaven breath'd a secret vow
To live in prayer and contemplation,
Only attended by Nerissa here,
Until her husband and my lord's return.
There is a monastery two miles off,
And there will we abide. I do desire you
Not to deny this imposition,
The which my love and some necessity
Now lays upon you.

LORENZO.   Madam, with all my heart:
I shall obey you in all fair commands.

PORTIA. My people do already know my mind,
And will acknowledge you and Jessica
In place of Lord Bassanio and myself.
So fare you well till we shall meet again.

LORENZO. Fair thoughts and happy hours attend on you!

JESSICA. I wish your ladyship all heart's content.

PORTIA. I thank you for your wish, and am well pleas'd
To wish it back on you: fare you well, Jessica.

Exeunt Jessica and Lorenzo

Now, Balthazar,
As I have ever found thee honest-true,
So let me find thee still. Take this same letter,
And use thou all the endeavour of a man
In speed to Padua: see thou render this
Into my cousin's hand, Doctor Bellario;
And, look, what notes and garments he doth give thee,
Bring them, I pray thee, with imagin'd speed
Unto the traject, to the common ferry
Which trades to Venice. Waste no time in words,
But get thee gone: I shall be there before thee.

BALTHAZAR. Madam, I go with all convenient speed. *Exit*

PORTIA. Come on, Nerissa: I have work in hand
 That you yet know not of: we'll see our husbands
 Before they think of us.

NERISSA. Shall they see us?

PORTIA. They shall, Nerissa; but in such a habit
 That they shall think we are accomplished
 With that we lack. I'll hold thee any wager,
 When we are both accoutred like young men,
 I'll prove the prettier fellow of the two,
 And wear my dagger with the braver grace,
 And speak between the change of man and boy
 With a reed voice, and turn two mincing steps
 Into a manly stride, and speak of frays
 Like a fine bragging youth, and tell quaint lies,
 How honourable ladies sought my love,
 Which I denying, they fell sick and died:
 I could not do withal; then I'll repent,
 And wish, for all that, that I had not kill'd them:
 And twenty of these puny lies I'll tell,
 That men shall swear I have discontinu'd school
 Above a twelvemonth. I have within my mind
 A thousand raw tricks of these bragging Jacks,
 Which I will practise.

NERISSA. Why, shall we turn to men?

PORTIA. Fie, what a question's that,
 If thou wert near a lewd interpreter!
 But come: I'll tell thee all my whole device
 When I am in my coach, which stays for us
 At the park gate; and therefore haste away,
 For we must measure twenty miles to-day. *Exeunt*

SCENE FIVE

The Same. A Garden.

Enter Launcelot and Jessica

LAUNCELOT. Yes, truly; for, look you, the sins of the father are to be laid upon the children; therefore, I promise you, I fear you. I was always plain with you, and so now I speak my agitation of the matter: therefore be of good cheer; for, truly, I think you are damned. There is but one hope in it that can do you any good, and that is but a kind of bastard hope neither.

JESSICA. And what hope is that, I pray thee?

LAUNCELOT. Marry, you may partly hope that your father got you not, that you are not the Jew's daughter.

JESSICA. That were a kind of bastard hope, indeed: so the sins of my mother should be visited upon me.

LAUNCELOT. Truly then I fear you are damned both by father and mother: thus when I shun Scylla, your father, I fall into Charybdis, your mother: well, you are gone both ways.

JESSICA. I shall be saved by my husband; he hath made me a Christian.

LAUNCELOT. Truly the more to blame he: we were Christians enow before; e'en as many as could well live one by another. This making of Christians will raise the price of hogs: if we grow all to be pork-eaters, we shall not shortly have a rasher on the coals for money.

JESSICA. I'll tell my husband, Launcelot, what you say: here he comes.

Enter Lorenzo

LORENZO. I shall grow jealous of you shortly, Launcelot, if you thus get my wife into corners.

JESSICA. Nay, you need not fear us, Lorenzo: Launcelot and I are out. He tells me flatly, there is no mercy for me in heaven, because I am a Jew's daughter: and he says you are no good member of the commonwealth, for, in converting Jews to Christians, you raise the price of pork.

LORENZO. I shall answer that better to the commonwealth

ACT III · SCENE V

[34-73]

than you can the getting up of the negro's belly: the Moor is with child by you, Launcelot.

LAUNCELOT. It is much that the Moor should be more than reason; but if she be less than an honest woman, she is indeed more than I took her for.

LORENZO. How every fool can play upon the word! I think the best grace of wit will shortly turn into silence, and discourse grow commendable in none only but parrots. Go in, sirrah: bid them prepare for dinner.

LAUNCELOT. That is done, sir; they have all stomachs.

LORENZO. Goodly Lord, what a wit-snapper are you! Then bid them prepare dinner.

LAUNCELOT. That is done too, sir; only, 'cover' is the word.

LORENZO. Will you cover, then, sir?

LAUNCELOT. Not so, sir, neither; I know my duty.

LORENZO. Yet more quarrelling with occasion! Wilt thou show the whole wealth of thy wit in an instant? I pray thee, understand a plain man in his plain meaning: go to thy fellows; bid them cover the table, serve in the meat, and we will come in to dinner.

LAUNCELOT. For the table, sir, it shall be served in; for the meat, sir, it shall be covered; for your coming in to dinner, sir, why, let it be as humours and conceits shall govern.
Exit

LORENZO. O dear discretion, how his words are suited!
The fool hath planted in his memory
An army of good words: and I do know
A many fools, that stand in better place,
Garnish'd like him, that for a tricksy word
Defy the matter. How cheer'st thou, Jessica?
And now, good sweet, say thy opinion;
How dost thou like the Lord Bassanio's wife?

JESSICA. Past all expressing. It is very meet,
The Lord Bassanio live an upright life,
For, having such a blessing in his lady,
He finds the joys of heaven here on earth;
And if on earth he do not mean it, then
In reason he should never come to heaven.
Why, if two gods should play some heavenly match,
And on the wager lay two earthly women,
And Portia one, there must be something else

Pawn'd with the other, for the poor rude world
Hath not her fellow.
LORENZO.   Even such a husband
Hast thou of me as she is for a wife.
JESSICA. Nay, but ask my opinion too of that.
LORENZO. I will anon; first, let us go to dinner.
JESSICA. Nay, let me praise you while I have a stomach.
LORENZO. No, pray thee, let it serve for table-talk;
Then howsoe'er thou speak'st, 'mong other things
I shall digest it.
JESSICA.   Well, I'll set you forth.   *Exeunt*

ACT FOUR

SCENE ONE

Venice. A Court of Justice.

***Enter the Duke: the Magnificoes; Antonio, Bassanio,
Gratiano, Salarino, Salanio, and Others***

DUKE. What, is Antonio here?
ANTONIO. Ready, so please your Grace.
DUKE. I am sorry for thee: thou art come to answer
 A stony adversary, an inhuman wretch
 Uncapable of pity, void and empty
 From any dram of mercy.
ANTONIO. I have heard
 Your Grace hath ta'en great pains to qualify
 His rigorous course; but since he stands obdurate,
 And that no lawful means can carry me
 Out of his envy's reach, I do oppose
 My patience to his fury, and am arm'd
 To suffer with a quietness of spirit
 The very tyranny and rage of his.
DUKE. Go one, and call the Jew into the court.
SALARINO. He's ready at the door: he comes, my lord.
 Enter Shylock
DUKE. Make room, and let him stand before our face.
 Shylock, the world thinks, and I think so too,
 That thou but lead'st this fashion of thy malice
 To the last hour of act; and then 'tis thought
 Thou 'lt show thy mercy and remorse more strange
 Than is thy strange-apparent cruelty;
 And where thou now exact'st the penalty,—
 Which is a pound of this poor merchant's flesh,—
 Thou wilt not only loose the forfeiture,
 But, touch'd with human gentleness and love,
 Forgive a moiety of the principal;

Glancing an eye of pity on his losses,
That have of late so huddled on his back,
Enow to press a royal merchant down,
And pluck commiseration of his state
From brassy bosoms and rough hearts of flint,
From stubborn Turks and Tartars, never train'd
To offices of tender courtesy.
We all expect a gentle answer, Jew.

SHYLOCK. I have possess'd your Grace of what I purpose;
And by our holy Sabbath have I sworn
To have the due and forfeit of my bond:
If you deny it, let the danger light
Upon your charter and your city's freedom.
You 'll ask me, why I rather choose to have
A weight of carrion flesh than to receive
Three thousand ducats: I 'll not answer that:
But say it is my humour: is it answer'd?
What if my house be troubled with a rat,
And I be pleas'd to give ten thousand ducats
To have it ban'd? What, are you answer'd yet?
Some men there are love not a gaping pig;
Some, that are mad if they behold a cat;
And others, when the bagpipe sings i' the nose,
Cannot contain their urine: for affection,
Mistress of passion, sways it to the mood
Of what it likes, or loathes. Now, for your answer
As there is no firm reason to be render'd,
Why he cannot abide a gaping pig;
Why he, a harmless necessary cat;
Why he, a wauling bagpipe; but of force
Must yield to such inevitable shame
As to offend, himself being offended;
So can I give no reason, nor I will not,
More than a lodg'd hate and a certain loathing
I bear Antonio, that I follow thus
A losing suit against him. Are you answer'd?

BASSANIO. This is no answer, thou unfeeling man,
To excuse the current of thy cruelty.

SHYLOCK. I am not bound to please thee with my answer.

BASSANIO. Do all men kill the things they do not love?

SHYLOCK. Hates any man the thing he would not kill?

BASSANIO. Every offence is not a hate at first.

ACT IV · SCENE I

SHYLOCK. What! wouldst thou have a serpent sting thee
twice?

ANTONIO. I pray you, think you question with the Jew:
You may as well go stand upon the beach,
And bid the main flood bate his usual height;
You may as well use question with the wolf,
Why he hath made the ewe bleat for the lamb;
You may as well forbid the mountain pines
To wag their high tops, and to make no noise
When they are fretted with the gusts of heaven;
You may as well do anything most hard,
As seek to soften that—than which what's harder?—
His Jewish heart: therefore, I do beseech you,
Make no more offers, use no further means;
But with all brief and plain conveniency,
Let me have judgment, and the Jew his will.

BASSANIO. For thy three thousand ducats here is six.

SHYLOCK. If every ducat in six thousand ducats
Were in six parts and every part a ducat,
I would not draw them; I would have my bond.

DUKE. How shalt thou hope for mercy, rendering none?

SHYLOCK. What judgment shall I dread, doing no wrong?
You have among you many a purchas'd slave,
Which, like your asses and your dogs and mules,
You use in abject and in slavish parts,
Because you bought them: shall I say to you,
Let them be free, marry them to your heirs?
Why sweat they under burdens? Let their beds
Be made as soft as yours, and let their palates
Be season'd with such viands? You will answer:
'The slaves are ours': so do I answer you:
The pound of flesh which I demand of him,
Is dearly bought; 'tis mine and I will have it.
If you deny me, fie upon your law!
There is no force in the decrees of Venice.
I stand for judgment: answer; shall I have it?

DUKE. Upon my power I may dismiss this court,
Unless Bellario, a learned doctor,
Whom I have sent for to determine this,
Come here to-day.

SALARINO. My lord, here stays without
A messenger with letters from the doctor,

New come from Padua.

DUKE. Bring us the letters: call the messenger.

BASSANIO. Good cheer, Antonio! What, man, courage yet!
　The Jew shall have my flesh, blood, bones, and all,
　Ere thou shalt lose for me one drop of blood.

ANTONIO. I am a tainted wether of the flock,
　Meetest for death: the weakest kind of fruit
　Drops earliest to the ground; and so let me:
　You cannot better be employ'd, Bassanio,
　Than to live still, and write mine epitaph.

Enter Nerissa, dressed like a lawyer's clerk

DUKE. Came you from Padua, from Bellario?

NERISSA. From both, my lord. Bellario greets your Grace.
　　　　　　　　　　　　　　　　Presents a letter

BASSANIO. Why dost thou whet thy knife so earnestly?

SHYLOCK. To cut the forfeiture from that bankrupt there.

GRATIANO. Not on thy sole, but on thy soul, harsh Jew,
　Thou mak'st thy knife keen; but no metal can,
　No, not the hangman's axe, bear half the keenness
　Of thy sharp envy. Can no prayers pierce thee?

SHYLOCK. No, none that thou hast wit enough to make.

GRATIANO. O, be thou damn'd, inexecrable dog!
　And for thy life let justice be accus'd.
　Thou almost mak'st me waver in my faith
　To hold opinion with Pythagoras,
　That souls of animals infuse themselves
　Into the trunks of men: thy currish spirit
　Govern'd a wolf, who, hang'd for human slaughter,
　Even from the gallows did his fell soul fleet,
　And whilst thou lay'st in thy unhallow'd dam,
　Infus'd itself in thee; for thy desires
　Are wolfish, bloody, starv'd, and ravenous.

SHYLOCK. Till thou canst rail the seal from off my bond,
　Thou but offend'st thy lungs to speak so loud:
　Repair thy wit, good youth, or it will fall
　To cureless ruin. I stand here for law.

DUKE. This letter from Bellario doth commend
　A young and learned doctor to our court.
　Where is he?

NERISSA. 　　　He attendeth here hard by,
　To know your answer, whether you'll admit him.

DUKE. With all my heart: some three or four of you

Go give him courteous conduct to this place.
Meantime, the court shall hear Bellario's letter.

CLERK. (*Reads*) 'Your Grace shall understand that at the receipt of your letter I am very sick; but in the instant that your messenger came, in loving visitation was with me a young doctor of Rome; his name is Balthazar. I acquainted him with the cause in controversy between the Jew and Antonio the merchant: we turned o'er many books together: he is furnished with my opinion; which, bettered with his own learning,—the greatness whereof I cannot enough commend,—comes with him, at my importunity, to fill up your Grace's request in my stead. I beseech you, let his lack of years be no impediment to let him lack a reverend estimation, for I never knew so young a body with so old a head. I leave him to your gracious acceptance, whose trial shall better publish his commendation.'

DUKE. You hear the learn'd Bellario, what he writes:
And here, I take it, is the doctor come.

Enter Portia, dressed like a doctor of laws

Give me your hand. Came you from old Bellario?
PORTIA. I did, my lord.
DUKE. You are welcome: take your place.
Are you acquainted with the difference
That holds this present question in the court?
PORTIA. I am informed throughly of the cause.
Which is the merchant here, and which the Jew?
DUKE. Antonio and old Shylock, both stand forth.
PORTIA. Is your name Shylock?
SHYLOCK. Shylock is my name.
PORTIA. Of a strange nature is the suit you follow;
Yet in such rule that the Venetian law
Cannot impugn you as you do proceed.
(*To Antonio*) You stand within his danger, do you not?
ANTONIO. Ay, so he says.
PORTIA. Do you confess the bond?
ANTONIO. I do.
PORTIA. Then must the Jew be merciful.
SHYLOCK. On what compulsion must I? tell me that.
PORTIA. The quality of mercy is not strain'd,
It droppeth as the gentle rain from heaven
Upon the place beneath: it is twice bless'd;

It blesseth him that gives and him that takes:
'Tis mightiest in the mightiest; it becomes
The thronèd monarch better than his crown;
His sceptre shows the force of temporal power,
The attribute to awe and majesty,
Wherein doth sit the dread and fear of kings;
But mercy is above this sceptred sway,
It is enthronèd in the hearts of kings,
It is an attribute to God himself,
And earthly power doth then show likest God's
When mercy seasons justice. Therefore, Jew,
Though justice be thy plea, consider this,
That in the course of justice none of us
Should see salvation: we do pray for mercy,
And that same prayer doth teach us all to render
The deeds of mercy. I have spoke thus much
To mitigate the justice of thy plea,
Which if thou follow, this strict court of Venice
Must needs give sentence 'gainst the merchant there.

SHYLOCK. My deeds upon my head! I crave the law,
The penalty and forfeit of my bond.

PORTIA. Is he not able to discharge the money?

BASSANIO. Yes, here I tender it for him in the court;
Yea, twice the sum: if that will not suffice,
I will be bound to pay it ten times o'er,
On forfeit of my hands, my head, my heart.
If this will not suffice, it must appear
That malice bears down truth. And, I beseech you,
Wrest once the law to your authority:
To do a great right, do a little wrong,
And curb this cruel devil of his will.

PORTIA. It must not be. There is no power in Venice
Can alter a decree establishèd:
'Twill be recorded for a precedent,
And many an error by the same example
Will rush into the state. It cannot be.

SHYLOCK. A Daniel come to judgment! yea, a Daniel!
O wise young judge, how I do honour thee!

PORTIA. I pray you, let me look upon the bond.

SHYLOCK. Here 'tis, most reverend doctor; here it is.

PORTIA. Shylock, there's thrice thy money offer'd thee.

SHYLOCK. An oath, an oath, I have an oath in heaven:

Shall I lay perjury upon my soul?
No, not for Venice.

PORTIA. Why, this bond is forfeit;
And lawfully by this the Jew may claim
A pound of flesh to be by him cut off
Nearest the merchant's heart. Be merciful:
Take thrice thy money; bid me tear the bond.

SHYLOCK. When it is paid according to the tenour.
It doth appear you are a worthy judge;
You know the law, your exposition
Hath been most sound: I charge you by the law,
Whereof you are a well-deserving pillar,
Proceed to judgment: by my soul I swear
There is no power in the tongue of man
To alter me. I stay here on my bond.

ANTONIO. Most heartily I do beseech the court
To give the judgment.

PORTIA. Why then, thus it is:
You must prepare your bosom for his knife.

SHYLOCK. O noble judge! O excellent young man!

PORTIA. For, the intent and purpose of the law
Hath full relation to the penalty,
Which here appeareth due upon the bond.

SHYLOCK. 'Tis very true! O wise and upright judge!
How much more elder art thou than thy looks!

PORTIA. Therefore lay bare your bosom.

SHYLOCK. Ay, 'his breast':
So says the bond:—doth it not, noble judge?—
'Nearest his heart': those are the very words.

PORTIA. It is so. Are there balance here to weigh
The flesh?

SHYLOCK. I have them ready.

PORTIA. Have by some surgeon, Shylock, on your charge,
To stop his wounds, lest he do bleed to death.

SHYLOCK. Is it so nominated in the bond?

PORTIA. It is not so express'd; but what of that?
'Twere good you do so much for charity.

SHYLOCK. I cannot find it: 'tis not in the bond.

PORTIA. You, merchant, have you any thing to say?

ANTONIO. But little: I am arm'd and well prepar'd.
Give me your hand, Bassanio: fare you well!
Grieve not that I am fallen to this for you;

For herein Fortune shows herself more kind
Than is her custom: it is still her use
To let the wretched man outlive his wealth,
To view with hollow eye and wrinkled brow
An age of poverty; from which lingering penance
Of such a misery doth she cut me off.
Commend me to your honourable wife:
Tell her the process of Antonio's end;
Say how I lov'd you, speak me fair in death;
And, when the tale is told, bid her be judge
Whether Bassanio had not once a love.
Repent not you that you shall lose your friend,
And he repents not that he pays your debt;
For if the Jew do cut but deep enough,
I 'll pay it instantly with all my heart.

BASSANIO. Antonio, I am married to a wife
Which is as dear to me as life itself;
But life itself, my wife, and all the world,
Are not with me esteem'd above thy life:
I would lose all, ay, sacrifice them all,
Here to this devil, to deliver you.

PORTIA. Your wife would give you little thanks for that,
If she were by to hear you make the offer.

GRATIANO. I have a wife, whom, I protest, I love:
I would she were in heaven, so she could
Entreat some power to change this currish Jew.

NERISSA. 'Tis well you offer it behind her back;
The wish would make else an unquiet house.

SHYLOCK. These be the Christian husbands! I have a daughter;
Would any of the stock of Barabbas
Had been her husband rather than a Christian!
We trifle time; I pray thee, pursue sentence.

PORTIA. A pound of that same merchant's flesh is thine.
The court awards it, and the law doth give it.

SHYLOCK. Most rightful judge!

PORTIA. And you must cut this flesh from off his breast:
The law allows it, and the court awards it.

SHYLOCK. Most learned judge! A sentence! come, prepare!

PORTIA. Tarry a little: there is something else.
This bond doth give thee here no jot of blood;
The words expressly are 'a pound of flesh':

    Then take thy bond, take thou thy pound of flesh;
    But, in the cutting it, if thou dost shed
    One drop of Christian blood, thy lands and goods
    Are, by the laws of Venice, confiscate
    Unto the state of Venice.
GRATIANO. O upright judge! Mark, Jew: O learned judge!
SHYLOCK. Is that the law?
PORTIA.   Thyself shalt see the act;
    For, as thou urgest justice, be assur'd
    Thou shalt have justice, more than thou desir'st.
GRATIANO. O learned judge! Mark, Jew: a learned judge!
SHYLOCK. I take this offer then: pay the bond thrice,
    And let the Christian go.
BASSANIO.   Here is the money.
PORTIA. Soft!
    The Jew shall have all justice; soft! no haste:—
    He shall have nothing but the penalty.
GRATIANO. O Jew! an upright judge, a learned judge!
PORTIA. Therefore prepare thee to cut off the flesh.
    Shed thou no blood; nor cut thou less, nor more,
    But just a pound of flesh: if thou tak'st more,
    Or less, than a just pound, be it but so much
    As makes it light or heavy in the substance,
    Or the division of the twentieth part
    Of one poor scruple, nay, if the scale do turn
    But in the estimation of a hair,
    Thou diest and all thy goods are confiscate.
GRATIANO. A second Daniel, a Daniel, Jew!
    Now, infidel, I have thee on the hip.
PORTIA. Why doth the Jew pause? Take thy forfeiture.
SHYLOCK. Give me my principal, and let me go.
BASSANIO. I have it ready for thee; here it is.
PORTIA. He hath refus'd it in the open court:
    He shall have merely justice, and his bond.
GRATIANO. A Daniel, still say I; a second Daniel!
    I thank thee, Jew, for teaching me that word.
SHYLOCK. Shall I not have barely my principal?
PORTIA. Thou shalt have nothing but the forfeiture,
    To be so taken at thy peril, Jew.
SHYLOCK. Why, then the devil give him good of it!
    I'll stay no longer question.
PORTIA.   Tarry, Jew:

The law hath yet another hold on you.
It is enacted in the laws of Venice,
If it be prov'd against an alien
That by direct or indirect attempts
He seek the life of any citizen,
The party 'gainst the which he doth contrive
Shall seize one half his goods; the other half
Comes to the privy coffer of the state;
And the offender's life lies in the mercy
Of the duke only, 'gainst all other voice.
In which predicament, I say, thou stand'st;
For it appears by manifest proceeding,
That indirectly and directly too
Thou hast contrived against the very life
Of the defendant; and thou hast incurr'd
The danger formerly by me rehears'd.
Down therefore and beg mercy of the duke.

GRATIANO. Beg that thou mayst have leave to hang thyself:
And yet, thy wealth being forfeit to the state,
Thou hast not left the value of a cord;
Therefore thou must be hang'd at the state's charge.

DUKE. That thou shalt see the difference of our spirits,
I pardon thee thy life before thou ask it.
For half thy wealth, it is Antonio's;
The other half comes to the general state,
Which humbleness may drive into a fine.

PORTIA. Ay, for the state; not for Antonio.

SHYLOCK. Nay, take my life and all; pardon not that:
You take my house when you do take the prop
That doth sustain my house; you take my life
When you do take the means whereby I live.

PORTIA. What mercy can you render him, Antonio?

GRATIANO. A halter gratis; nothing else, for God's sake!

ANTONIO. So please my lord the duke, and all the court,
To quit the fine for one half of his goods,
I am content; so he will let me have
The other half in use, to render it,
Upon his death, unto the gentleman
That lately stole his daughter:
Two things provided more, that, for this favour,
He presently become a Christian;
The other, that he do record a gift,

Here in the court, of all he dies possess'd,
Unto his son Lorenzo, and his daughter.
DUKE. He shall do this, or else I do recant
The pardon that I late pronounced here.
PORTIA. Art thou contented, Jew? what dost thou say?
SHYLOCK. I am content.
PORTIA.   Clerk, draw a deed of gift.
SHYLOCK. I pray you give me leave to go from hence:
I am not well. Send the deed after me,
And I will sign it.
DUKE.   Get thee gone, but do it.
GRATIANO. In christening thou shalt have two godfathers;
Had I been judge, thou shouldst have had ten more,
To bring thee to the gallows, not the font. *Exit Shylock*
DUKE. Sir, I entreat you home with me to dinner.
PORTIA. I humbly do desire your Grace of pardon:
I must away this night toward Padua,
And it is meet I presently set forth.
DUKE. I am sorry that your leisure serves you not.
Antonio, gratify this gentleman,
For, in my mind, you are much bound to him.
                Exeunt Duke, Magnificoes, and Train
BASSANIO. Most worthy gentleman, I and my friend
Have by your wisdom been this day acquitted
Of grievous penalties; in lieu whereof,
Three thousand ducats, due unto the Jew,
We freely cope your courteous pains withal.
ANTONIO. And stand indebted, over and above,
In love and service to you evermore.
PORTIA. He is well paid that is well satisfied;
And I, delivering you, am satisfied,
And therein do account myself well paid:
My mind was never yet more mercenary.
I pray you, know me when we meet again:
I wish you well, and so I take my leave.
BASSANIO. Dear sir, of force I must attempt you further:
Take some remembrance of us, as a tribute,
Not as a fee. Grant me two things, I pray you,
Not to deny me, and to pardon me.
PORTIA. You press me far, and therefore I will yield.
  (*To Antonio*) Give me your gloves, I 'll wear them for
    your sake;

(*To Bassanio*) And for your love, I'll take this ring from
  you.
Do not draw back your hand; I'll take no more;
And you in love shall not deny me this;
BASSANIO. This ring, good sir? alas! it is a trifle;
I will not shame myself to give you this.
PORTIA. I will have nothing else but only this;
And now methinks I have a mind to it.
BASSANIO. There's more depends on this than on the value.
The dearest ring in Venice will I give you,
And find it out by proclamation:
Only for this, I pray you, pardon me.
PORTIA. I see, sir, you are liberal in offers:
You taught me first to beg, and now methinks
You teach me how a beggar should be answer'd.
BASSANIO. Good sir, this ring was given me by my wife;
And, when she put it on, she made me vow
That I should never sell nor give nor lose it.
PORTIA. That 'scuse serves many men to save their gifts.
An if your wife be not a mad-woman,
And know how well I have deserv'd the ring,
She would not hold out enemy for ever,
For giving it to me. Well, peace be with you.
Exeunt Portia and Nerissa
ANTONIO. My Lord Bassanio, let him have the ring:
Let his deservings and my love withal
Be valu'd 'gainst your wife's commandment.
BASSANIO. Go, Gratiano; run and overtake him;
Give him the ring, and bring him, if thou canst,
Unto Antonio's house. Away! make haste. *Exit Gratiano*
Come, you and I will thither presently,
And in the morning early will we both
Fly toward Belmont. Come, Antonio. *Exeunt*

SCENE TWO

The Same. A Street.

Enter Portia and Nerissa

PORTIA. Inquire the Jew's house out, give him this deed,
And let him sign it. We'll away to-night,
And be a day before our husbands home:
This deed will be well welcome to Lorenzo.

Enter Gratiano

GRATIANO. Fair sir, you are well o'erta'en.
My Lord Bassanio upon more advice
Hath sent you here this ring, and doth entreat
Your company at dinner.
PORTIA. That cannot be:
His ring I do accept most thankfully;
And so, I pray you, tell him: furthermore,
I pray you, show my youth old Shylock's house.
GRATIANO. That will I do.
NERISSA. Sir, I would speak with you.
(*Aside to Portia*) I'll see if I can get my husband's ring
Which I did make him swear to keep for ever.
PORTIA. Thou mayst, I warrant. We shall have old swearing
That they did give the rings away to men;
But we'll outface them, and outswear them too.
Away! make haste: thou know'st where I will tarry.
NERISSA. Come, good sir, will you show me to this house?

Exeunt

ACT FIVE

SCENE ONE

Belmont. The Avenue to Portia's House.

Enter Lorenzo and Jessica

LORENZO. The moon shines bright: in such a night as this,
When the sweet wind did gently kiss the trees
And they did make no noise, in such a night
Troilus methinks mounted the Troyan walls,
And sigh'd his soul toward the Grecian tents,
Where Cressid lay that night.

JESSICA. In such a night
Did Thisbe fearfully o'ertrip the dew,
And saw the lion's shadow ere himself,
And ran dismay'd away.

LORENZO. In such a night
Stood Dido with a willow in her hand
Upon the wild sea-banks, and waft her love
To come again to Carthage.

JESSICA. In such a night
Medea gather'd the enchanted herbs
That did renew old Æson.

LORENZO. In such a night
Did Jessica steal from the wealthy Jew,
And with an unthrift love did run from Venice,
As far as Belmont.

JESSICA. In such a night
Did young Lorenzo swear he lov'd her well,
Stealing her soul with many vows of faith—
And ne'er a true one.

LORENZO. In such a night
Did pretty Jessica, like a little shrew,
Slander her love, and he forgave it her.

JESSICA. I would out-night you, did no body come;

[24-60] ACT V : SCENE I 613

But, hark! I hear the footing of a man.
Enter Stephano
LORENZO. Who comes so fast in silence of the night?
STEPHANO. A friend.
LORENZO. A friend! What friend? your name, I pray you, friend.
STEPHANO. Stephano is my name; and I bring word
My mistress will before the break of day
Be here at Belmont. She doth stray about
By holy crosses, where she kneels and prays
For happy wedlock hours.
LORENZO.   Who comes with her?
STEPHANO. None, but a holy hermit and her maid.
I pray you, is my master yet return'd?
LORENZO. He is not, nor we have not heard from him.
But go we in, I pray thee, Jessica,
And ceremoniously let us prepare
Some welcome for the mistress of the house.
Enter Launcelot
LAUNCELOT. Sola, sola! wo ha, ho! sola, sola!
LORENZO. Who calls?
LAUNCELOT. Sola! did you see Master Lorenzo?
Master Lorenzo! sola, sola!
LORENZO. Leave hollaing, man; here.
LAUNCELOT. Sola! where? where?
LORENZO. Here.
LAUNCELOT. Tell him there's a post come from my master, with his horn full of good news: my master will be here ere morning.   *Exit*
LORENZO. Sweet soul, let's in, and there expect their coming.
And yet no matter; why should we go in?
My friend Stephano, signify, I pray you,
Within the house, your mistress is at hand;
And bring your music forth into the air.   *Exit Stephano*
How sweet the moonlight sleeps upon this bank!
Here will we sit, and let the sounds of music
Creep in our ears: soft stillness and the night
Become the touches of sweet harmony.
Sit, Jessica: look, how the floor of heaven
Is thick inlaid with patines of bright gold:
There's not the smallest orb which thou behold'st

But in his motion like an angel sings,
Still quiring to the young-eyed cherubins;
Such harmony is in immortal souls;
But, whilst this muddy vesture of decay
Doth grossly close it in, we cannot hear it.
Enter Musicians
Come, ho! and wake Diana with a hymn:
With sweetest touches pierce your mistress' ear,
And draw her home with music.   *Music*

JESSICA. I am never merry when I hear sweet music.
LORENZO. The reason is, your spirits are attentive:
For do but note a wild and wanton herd,
Or race of youthful and unhandled colts,
Fetching mad bounds, bellowing and neighing loud,
Which is the hot condition of their blood;
If they but hear perchance a trumpet sound,
Or any air of music touch their ears,
You shall perceive them make a mutual stand,
Their savage eyes turn'd to a modest gaze
By the sweet power of music: therefore the poet
Did feign that Orpheus drew trees, stones, and floods;
Since naught so stockish, hard, and full of rage,
But music for the time doth change his nature,
The man that hath no music in himself,
Nor is not mov'd with concord of sweet sounds,
Is fit for treasons, stratagems, and spoils;
The motions of his spirit are dull as night,
And his affections dark as Erebus:
Let no such man be trusted. Mark the music.
Enter Portia and Nerissa, at a distance
PORTIA. That light we see is burning in my hall.
How far that little candle throws his beams!
So shines a good deed in a naughty world.
NERISSA. When the moon shone, we did not see the candle.
PORTIA. So doth the greater glory dim the less:
A substitute shines brightly as a king
Until a king be by, and then his state
Empties itself, as doth an inland brook
Into the main of waters. Music! hark!
NERISSA. It is your music, madam, of the house.
PORTIA. Nothing is good, I see, without respect:
Methinks it sounds much sweeter than by day.

[101-137] ACT V : SCENE I 615

NERISSA. Silence bestows that virtue on it, madam.
PORTIA. The crow doth sing as sweetly as the lark
When neither is attended, and I think
The nightingale, if she should sing by day,
When every goose is cackling, would be thought
No better a musician than the wren.
How many things by season season'd are
To their right praise and true perfection!
Peace, ho! the moon sleeps with Endymion,
And would not be awak'd! *Music ceases*
LORENZO.   That is the voice,
Or I am much deceiv'd, of Portia.
PORTIA. He knows me, as the blind man knows the cuckoo,
By the bad voice.
LORENZO.   Dear lady, welcome home.
PORTIA. We have been praying for our husbands' welfare,
Which speed, we hope, the better for our words.
Are they return'd?
LORENZO.   Madam, they are not yet;
But there is come a messenger before,
To signify their coming.
PORTIA.   Go in, Nerissa:
Give order to my servants that they take
No note at all of our being absent hence;
Nor you, Lorenzo; Jessica, nor you. *A tucket sounds*
LORENZO. Your husband is at hand; I hear his trumpet:
We are no tell-tales, madam; fear you not.
PORTIA. This night methinks is but the daylight sick;
It looks a little paler: 'tis a day,
Such as the day is when the sun is hid.
Enter Bassanio, Antonio, Gratiano, and their Followers
BASSANIO. We should hold day with the Antipodes,
If you would walk in absence of the sun.
PORTIA. Let me give light, but let me not be light;
For a light wife doth make a heavy husband,
And never be Bassanio so for me:
But God sort all! You are welcome home, my lord.
BASSANIO. I thank you, madam. Give welcome to my friend:
This is the man, this is Antonio,
To whom I am so infinitely bound.
PORTIA. You should in all sense be much bound to him,
For, as I hear, he was much bound for you.

ANTONIO. No more than I am well acquitted of.
PORTIA. Sir, you are very welcome to our house:
 It must appear in other ways than words,
 Therefore I scant this breathing courtesy.
GRATIANO. (*To Nerissa*) By yonder moon I swear you do me wrong;
 In faith, I gave it to the judge's clerk:
 Would he were gelt that had it, for my part,
 Since you do take it, love, so much at heart.
PORTIA. A quarrel, ho, already! what's the matter?
GRATIANO. About a hoop of gold, a paltry ring
 That she did give me, whose posy was
 For all the world like cutlers' poetry
 Upon a knife, 'Love me, and leave me not.'
NERISSA. What talk you of the posy, or the value?
 You swore to me, when I did give it you,
 That you would wear it till your hour of death,
 And that it should lie with you in your grave:
 Though not for me, yet for your vehement oaths,
 You should have been respective and have kept it.
 Gave it a judge's clerk! no, God's my judge,
 The clerk will ne'er wear hair on 's face that had it.
GRATIANO. He will, an if he live to be a man.
NERISSA. Ay, if a woman live to be a man.
GRATIANO. Now, by this hand, I gave it to a youth,
 A kind of boy, a little scrubbed boy,
 No higher than thyself, the judge's clerk.
 A prating boy, that begg'd it as a fee:
 I could not for my heart deny it him.
PORTIA. You were to blame,—I must be plain with you,—
 To part so slightly with your wife's first gift;
 A thing stuck on with oaths upon your finger,
 And riveted so with faith unto your flesh.
 I gave my love a ring and made him swear
 Never to part with it; and here he stands,
 I dare be sworn for him he would not leave it
 Nor pluck it from his finger for the wealth
 That the world masters. Now, in faith, Gratiano,
 You give your wife too unkind a cause of grief:
 An 'twere to me, I should be mad at it.
BASSANIO. (*Aside*) Why, I were best to cut my left hand off,
 And swear I lost the ring defending it.

ACT V : SCENE I

GRATIANO. My Lord Bassanio gave his ring away
  Unto the judge that begg'd it, and indeed
  Deserv'd it too; and then the boy, his clerk,
  That took some pains in writing, he begg'd mine;
  And neither man nor master would take aught
  But the two rings.
PORTIA.   What ring gave you, my lord?
  Not that, I hope, that you receiv'd of me.
BASSANIO. If I could add a lie unto a fault,
  I would deny it; but you see my finger
  Hath not the ring upon it; it is gone.
PORTIA. Even so void is your false heart of truth.
  By heaven, I will ne'er come in your bed
  Until I see the ring.
NERISSA.   Nor I in yours,
  Till I again see mine.
BASSANIO.   Sweet Portia,
  If you did know to whom I gave the ring,
  If you did know for whom I gave the ring,
  And would conceive for what I gave the ring,
  And how unwillingly I left the ring,
  When naught would be accepted but the ring,
  You would abate the strength of your displeasure.
PORTIA. If you had known the virtue of the ring,
  Or half her worthiness that gave the ring,
  Or your own honour to contain the ring,
  You would not then have parted with the ring.
  What man is there so much unreasonable,
  If you had pleas'd to have defended it
  With any terms of zeal, wanted the modesty
  To urge the thing held as a ceremony?
  Nerissa teaches me what to believe:
  I'll die for't but some woman had the ring.
BASSANIO. No, by my honour, madam, by my soul,
  No woman had it; but a civil doctor
  Which did refuse three thousand ducats of me,
  And begg'd the ring, the which I did deny him,
  And suffer'd him to go displeas'd away;
  Even he that did uphold the very life
  Of my dear friend. What should I say, sweet lady?
  I was enforc'd to send it after him;
  I was beset with shame and courtesy;

My honour would not let ingratitude
So much besmear it. Pardon me, good lady,
For, by these blessed candles of the night,
Had you been there, I think you would have begg'd
The ring of me to give the worthy doctor.

PORTIA. Let not that doctor e'er come near my house.
Since he hath got the jewel that I lov'd,
And that which you did swear to keep for me,
I will become as liberal as you;
I'll not deny him any thing I have;
No, not my body, nor my husband's bed.
Know him I shall, I am well sure of it:
Lie not a night from home; watch me like Argus:
If you do not, if I be left alone,
Now by mine honour, which is yet mine own,
I'll have that doctor for my bedfellow.

NERISSA. And I his clerk; therefore be well advis'd
How you do leave me to mine own protection.

GRATIANO. Well, do you so: let me not take him, then;
For if I do, I'll mar the young clerk's pen.

ANTONIO. I am the unhappy subject of these quarrels.

PORTIA. Sir, grieve not you; you are welcome notwithstanding.

BASSANIO. Portia, forgive me this enforced wrong;
And in the hearing of these many friends,
I swear to thee, even by thine own fair eyes,
Wherein I see myself,—

PORTIA.   Mark you but that!
In both my eyes he doubly sees himself;
In each eye, one: swear by your double self,
And there's an oath of credit.

BASSANIO.   Nay, but hear me:
Pardon this fault. and by my soul I swear
I never more will break an oath with thee.

ANTONIO. I once did lend my body for his wealth,
Which, but for him that had your husband's ring,
Had quite miscarried: I dare be bound again,
My soul upon the forfeit, that your lord
Will never more break faith advisedly.

PORTIA. Then you shall be his surety. Give him this,
And bid him keep it better than the other.

ANTONIO. Here, Lord Bassanio; swear to keep this ring.

BASSANIO. By heaven! it is the same I gave the doctor!
PORTIA. I had it of him: pardon me, Bassanio,
   For, by this ring, the doctor lay with me.
NERISSA. And pardon me, my gentle Gratiano;
   For that same scrubbed boy, the doctor's clerk,
   In lieu of this last night did lie with me.
GRATIANO. Why, this is like the mending of high ways
   In summer, where the ways are fair enough.
   What! are we cuckolds ere we have deserv'd it?
PORTIA. Speak not so grossly. You are all amaz'd:
   Here is a letter; read it at your leisure;
   It comes from Padua, from Bellario:
   There you shall find that Portia was the doctor,
   Nerissa, there, her clerk: Lorenzo here
   Shall witness I set forth as soon as you
   And even but now return'd; I have not yet
   Enter'd my house. Antonio, you are welcome;
   And I have better news in store for you
   Than you expect: unseal this letter soon;
   There you shall find three of your argosies
   Are richly come to harbour suddenly.
   You shall not know by what strange accident
   I chanced on this letter.
ANTONIO.   I am dumb.
BASSANIO. Were you the doctor and I knew you not?
GRATIANO. Were you the clerk that is to make me cuckold?
NERISSA. Ay; but the clerk that never means to do it,
   Unless he live until he be a man.
BASSANIO. Sweet doctor, you shall be my bedfellow:
   When I am absent, then, lie with my wife.
ANTONIO. Sweet lady, you have given me life and living;
   For here I read for certain that my ships
   Are safely come to road.
PORTIA.   How now, Lorenzo!
   My clerk hath some good comforts too for you.
NERISSA. Ay, and I'll give them him without a fee.
   There do I give to you and Jessica,
   From the rich Jew, a special deed of gift,
   After his death, of all he dies possess'd of.
LORENZO. Fair ladies, you drop manna in the way
   Of starved people.
PORTIA.   It is almost morning,

    And yet I am sure you are not satisfied
Of these events at full. Let us go in;
And charge us there upon inter'gatories,
And we will answer all things faithfully.
GRATIANO. Let it be so: the first inter'gatory
That my Nerissa shall be sworn on is,
Whe'r till the next night she had rather stay,
Or go to bed now, being two hours to day:
But were the day come, I should wish it dark,
That I were couching with the doctor's clerk.
Well, while I live I'll fear no other thing
So sore as keeping safe Nerissa's ring. *Exeunt*

AS YOU LIKE IT

CAST OF CHARACTERS

DUKE, *living in exile*
FREDERICK, *his Brother, Usurper of his Dominions*

AMIENS }
JAQUES } *Lords attending upon the banished Duke*

LE BEAU, *a Courtier, attending upon Frederick*
CHARLES, *a Wrestler*

OLIVER }
JAQUES } *Sons of Sir Rowland de Boys*
ORLANDO }

ADAM }
DENNIS } *Servants to Oliver*

TOUCHSTONE, *a Clown*
SIR OLIVER MARTEXT, *a Vicar*

CORIN }
SILVIUS } *Shepherds*

WILLIAM, *a Country Fellow, in love with Audrey*
A person representing Hymen

ROSALIND, *Daughter to the banished Duke*
CELIA, *Daughter to Frederick*
PHEBE, *a Shepherdess*
AUDREY, *a Country Wench*

Lords, Pages, Foresters, and Attendants

SCENE

First, Oliver's Orchard near his House; afterwards, in the Usurper's Court, and in the Forest of Arden

AS YOU LIKE IT

ACT ONE

SCENE ONE

An Orchard near Oliver's House.

Enter Orlando and Adam

ORLANDO. As I remember, Adam, it was upon this fashion: he bequeathed me by will but poor a thousand crowns, and, as thou sayest, charged my brother on his blessing, to breed me well: and there begins my sadness. My brother Jaques he keeps at school, and report speaks goldenly of his profit. For my part, he keeps me rustically at home, or, to speak more properly, stays me here at home unkept; for call you that keeping for a gentleman of my birth, that differs not from the stalling of an ox? His horses are bred better; for, besides that they are fair with their feeding, they are taught their manage, and to that end riders dearly hired: but I, his brother, gain nothing under him but growth, for the which his animals on his dunghills are as much bound to him as I. Besides this nothing that he so plentifully gives me, the something that nature gave me, his countenance seems to take from me. He lets me feed with his hinds, bars me the place of a brother, and, as much as in him lies, mines my gentility with my education. This is it, Adam, that grieves me; and the spirit of my father, which I think is within me, begins to mutiny against this servitude. I will no longer endure it, though yet I know no wise remedy how to avoid it.

ADAM. Yonder comes my master, your brother.

ORLANDO. Go apart, Adam, and thou shalt hear how he will shake me up.

Enter Oliver

OLIVER. Now, sir! what make you here?

ORLANDO. Nothing. I am not taught to make anything.

OLIVER. What mar you then, sir.

ORLANDO. Marry, sir, I am helping you to mar that which God made, a poor unworthy brother of yours, with idleness.

OLIVER. Marry, sir, be better employed, and be naught awhile.

ORLANDO. Shall I keep your hogs, and eat husks with them? What prodigal portion have I spent, that I should come to such penury?

OLIVER. Know you where you are, sir?

ORLANDO. O! sir, very well: here in your orchard.

OLIVER. Know you before whom, sir?

ORLANDO. Ay, better than he I am before knows me. I know you are my eldest brother; and, in the gentle condition of blood, you should so know me. The courtesy of nations allows you my better, in that you are the first-born; but the same tradition takes not away my blood, were there twenty brothers betwixt us. I have as much of my father in me as you; albeit, I confess, your coming before me is nearer to his reverence.

OLIVER. What, boy! *Strikes him*

ORLANDO. Come, come, elder brother, you are too young in this. *Seizes him*

OLIVER. Wilt thou lay hands on me, villain?

ORLANDO. I am no villain; I am the youngest son of Sir Rowland de Boys; he was my father, and he is thrice a villain that says such a father begot villains. Wert thou not my brother, I would not take this hand from thy throat till this other had pulled out thy tongue for saying so: thou hast railed on thyself.

ADAM. (*Coming forward*) Sweet masters, be patient: for your father's remembrance, be at accord.

OLIVER. Let me go, I say.

ORLANDO. I will not, till I please: you shall hear me. My father charged you in his will to give me good education: you have trained me like a peasant, obscuring and hiding from me all gentleman-like qualities. The spirit of my father grows strong in me, and I will no longer endure it; therefore allow me such exercises as may become a gentleman, or give me the poor allottery my father left me by testament; with that I will go buy my fortunes.

Releases him

OLIVER. And what wilt thou do? beg, when that is spent? Well, sir, get you in: I will not long be troubled with you; you shall have some part of your will: I pray you, leave me.

ORLANDO. I will no further offend you than becomes me for my good.

OLIVER. Get you with him, you old dog.

ADAM. Is 'old dog' my reward? Most true, I have lost my teeth in your service. God be with my old master! he would not have spoke such a word.

Exeunt Orlando and Adam

OLIVER. Is it even so? begin you to grow upon me? I will physic your rankness, and yet give no thousand crowns neither. Holla, Dennis!

Enter Dennis

DENNIS. Calls your worship?

OLIVER. Was not Charles the duke's wrestler here to speak with me?

DENNIS. So please you, he is here at the door, and importunes access to you.

OLIVER. Call him in. (*Exit Dennis*) 'Twill be a good way; and to-morrow the wrestling is.

Enter Charles

CHARLES. Good-morrow to your worship.

OLIVER. Good Monsieur Charles. What's the new news at the new court?

CHARLES. There's no news at the court, sir, but the old news: that is, the old duke is banished by his younger brother the new duke; and three or four loving lords have put themselves into voluntary exile with him, whose lands and revenues enrich the new duke; therefore he gives them good leave to wander.

OLIVER. Can you tell if Rosalind, the duke's daughter, be banished with her father?

CHARLES. O, no; for the duke's daughter, her cousin, so loves her,—being ever from their cradles bred together,—that she would have followed her exile, or have died to stay behind her. She is at the court, and no less beloved of her uncle than his own daughter; and never two ladies loved as they do.

OLIVER. Where will the old duke live?

CHARLES. They say he is already in the forest of Arden, and a many merry men with him; and there they live like the old Robin Hood of England. They say many young gentlemen flock to him every day, and fleet the time carelessly, as they did in the golden world.

OLIVER. What, you wrestle to-morrow before the new duke?

CHARLES. Marry, do I, sir; and I came to acquaint you with a matter. I am given, sir, secretly to understand that your younger brother Orlando hath a disposition to come in disguised against me to try a fall. To-morrow, sir, I wrestle for my credit, and he that escapes me without some broken limb shall acquit him well. Your brother is but young and tender; and, for your love, I would be loath to foil him as I must, for my own honour, if he come in: therefore, out of my love to you, I came hither to acquaint you withal, that either you might stay him from his intendment, or brook such disgrace well as he shall run into, in that it is a thing of his own search and altogether against my will.

OLIVER. Charles, I thank thee for thy love to me, which thou shalt find I will most kindly requite. I had myself notice of my brother's purpose herein, and have by underhand means laboured to dissuade him from it, but he is resolute. I'll tell thee, Charles, it is the stubbornest young fellow of France; full of ambition, an envious emulator of every man's good parts, a secret and villanous contriver against me his natural brother; therefore use thy discretion. I had as lief thou didst break his neck as his finger. And thou wert best look to 't; for if thou dost him any slight disgrace, or if he do not mightily grace himself on thee, he will practise against thee by poison, entrap thee by some treacherous device, and never leave thee till he hath ta'en thy life by some indirect means or other; for, I assure thee,—and almost with tears I speak it,—there is not one so young and so villanous this day living. I speak but brotherly of him; but should I anatomize him to thee as he is, I must blush and weep, and thou must look pale and wonder.

CHARLES. I am heartily glad I came hither to you. If he come to-morrow, I'll give him his payment: if ever he go alone again, I'll never wrestle for prize more; and so God keep your worship! *Exit*

OLIVER. Farewell, good Charles. Now will I stir this gamester. I hope I shall see an end of him; for my soul, yet I know not why, hates nothing more than he. Yet he 's gentle, never schooled and yet learned, full of noble device, of all sorts enchantingly beloved, and, indeed so much in the heart of the world, and especially of my own people, who best know him, that I am altogether misprised. But it shall not be so long; this wrestler shall clear all: nothing remains but that I kindle the boy thither, which now I 'll go about.

SCENE TWO

A Lawn before the Duke's Palace.

Enter Rosalind and Celia

CELIA. I pray thee, Rosalind, sweet my coz, be merry.

ROSALIND. Dear Celia, I show more mirth than I am mistress of, and would you yet I were merrier? Unless you could teach me to forget a banished father, you must not learn me how to remember any extraordinary pleasure.

CELIA. Herein I see thou lovest me not with the full weight that I love thee. If my uncle, thy banished father, had banished thy uncle, the duke my father, so thou hadst been still with me, I could have taught my love to take thy father for mine: so wouldst thou, if the truth of thy love to me were so righteously tempered as mine is to thee.

ROSALIND. Well, I will forget the condition of my estate, to rejoice in yours.

CELIA. You know my father hath no child but I, nor none is like to have; and, truly, when he dies, thou shalt be his heir: for what he hath taken away from thy father perforce, I will render thee again in affection; by mine honour, I will; and when I break that oath, let me turn monster. Therefore, my sweet Rose, my dear Rose, be merry.

ROSALIND. From henceforth I will, coz, and devise sports. Let me see; what think you of falling in love?

CELIA. Marry, I prithee, do, to make sport withal: but love no man in good earnest; nor no further in sport neither, than with safety of a pure blush thou mayst in honour come off again.

ROSALIND. What shall be our sport then?

CELIA. Let us sit and mock the good housewife Fortune from her wheel, that her gifts may henceforth be bestowed equally.

ROSALIND. I would we could do so, for her benefits are mightily misplaced, and the bountiful blind woman doth most mistake in her gifts to women.

CELIA. 'Tis true; for those that she makes fair she scarce makes honest, and those that she makes honest she makes very ill-favouredly.

ROSALIND. Nay, now thou goest from Fortune's office to Nature's: Fortune reigns in gifts of the world, not in the lineaments of Nature.

Enter Touchstone

CELIA. No? When Nature hath made a fair creature, may she not by Fortune fall into the fire? Though Nature hath given us wit to flout at Fortune, hath not Fortune sent in this fool to cut off the argument?

ROSALIND. Indeed, there is Fortune too hard for Nature, when Fortune makes Nature's natural the cutter-off of Nature's wit.

CELIA. Peradventure this is not Fortune's work neither, but Nature's; who, perceiving our natural wits too dull to reason of such goddesses, hath sent this natural for our whetstone: for always the dullness of the fool is the whetstone of the wits. How now, wit! Whither wander you?

TOUCHSTONE. Mistress, you must come away to your father.

CELIA. Were you made the messenger?

TOUCHSTONE. No, by mine honour; but I was bid to come for you.

ROSALIND. Where learned you that oath, fool?

TOUCHSTONE. Of a certain knight that swore by his honour they were good pancakes, and swore by his honour the mustard was naught. Now, I 'll stand to it, the pancakes were naught and the mustard was good, and yet was not the knight forsworn.

CELIA. How prove you that, in the great heap of your knowledge?

ROSALIND. Ay, marry: now unmuzzle your wisdom.

TOUCHSTONE. Stand you both forth now. Stroke your chins, and swear by your beards that I am a knave.

CELIA. By our beards, if we had them, thou art.

ACT I · SCENE II

TOUCHSTONE. By my knavery, if I had it, then I were; but if you swear by that that is not, you are not forsworn: no more was this knight, swearing by his honour, for he never had any; or if he had, he had sworn it away before ever he saw those pancakes or that mustard.

CELIA. Prithee, who is 't that thou meanest?

TOUCHSTONE. One that old Frederick, your father, loves.

CELIA. My father's love is enough to honour him. Enough! speak no more of him; you 'll be whipped for taxation one of these days.

TOUCHSTONE. The more pity that fools may not speak wisely what wise men do foolishly.

CELIA. By my troth, thou sayest true; for since the little wit that fools have was silenced, the little foolery that wise men have makes a great show. Here comes Monsieur Le Beau.

ROSALIND. With his mouth full of news.

CELIA. Which he will put on us, as pigeons feed their young.

ROSALIND. Then we shall be news-cramm'd.

CELIA. All the better; we shall be more marketable.

Enter Le Beau

Bon jour, Monsieur Le Beau. What 's the news?

LE BEAU. Fair princess, you have lost much good sport.

CELIA. Sport! Of what colour?

LE BEAU. What colour, madam! How shall I answer you?

ROSALIND. As wit and fortune will.

TOUCHSTONE. Or as the Destinies decree.

CELIA. Well said! That was laid on with a trowel.

TOUCHSTONE. Nay, if I keep not my rank,—

ROSALIND. Thou losest thy old smell.

LE BEAU. You amaze me, ladies. I would have told you of good wrestling, which you have lost the sight of.

ROSALIND. Yet tell us the manner of the wrestling.

LE BEAU. I will tell you the beginning; and, if it please your ladyships, you may see the end, for the best is yet to do; and here, where you are, they are coming to perform it.

CELIA. Well, the beginning, that is dead and buried.

LE BEAU. There comes an old man and his three sons,—

CELIA. I could match this beginning with an old tale.

LE BEAU. Three proper young men, of excellent growth and presence;—

ROSALIND. With bills on their necks, 'Be it known unto all men by these presents.'

LE BEAU. The eldest of the three wrestled with Charles, the duke's wrestler; which Charles in a moment threw him and broke three of his ribs, that there is little hope of life in him. So he served the second, and so the third. Yonder they lie; the poor old man, their father, making such pitiful dole over them that all the beholders take his part with weeping.

ROSALIND. Alas!

TOUCHSTONE. But what is the sport, monsieur, that the ladies have lost?

LE BEAU. Why, this that I speak of.

TOUCHSTONE. Thus men may grow wiser every day. It is the first time that ever I heard breaking of ribs was sport for ladies.

CELIA. Or I, I promise thee.

ROSALIND. But is there any else longs to feel this broken music in his sides? Is there yet another dotes upon rib-breaking? Shall we see this wrestling, cousin?

LE BEAU. You must, if you stay here; for here is the place appointed for the wrestling, and they are ready to perform it.

CELIA. Yonder, sure, they are coming. Let us now stay and see it.

*Flourish. Enter Duke Frederick,
Lords, Orlando, Charles, and Attendants*

DUKE FREDERICK. Come on. Since the youth will not be entreated, his own peril on his forwardness.

ROSALIND. Is yonder the man?

LE BEAU. Even he, madam.

CELIA. Alas! he is too young: yet he looks successfully.

DUKE FREDERICK. How now, daughter and cousin! Are you crept hither to see the wrestling?

ROSALIND. Ay, my liege, so please you give us leave.

DUKE FREDERICK. You will take little delight in it, I can tell you, there is such odds in the man. In pity of the challenger's youth I would fain dissuade him, but he will not be entreated. Speak to him, ladies; see if you can move him.

CELIA. Call him hither, good Monsieur Le Beau.

DUKE FREDERICK. Do so. I'll not be by. *Duke goes apart*

LE BEAU. Monsieur the challenger, the princess calls for you.

ORLANDO. I attend them with all respect and duty.

ROSALIND. Young man, have you challenged Charles the wrestler?

ORLANDO. No, fair princess; he is the general challenger: I come but in, as others do, to try with him the strength of my youth.

CELIA. Young gentleman, your spirits are too bold for your years. You have seen cruel proof of this man's strength. If you saw yourself with your eyes or knew yourself with your judgment, the fear of your adventure would counsel you to a more equal enterprise. We pray you, for your own sake, to embrace your own safety and give over this attempt.

ROSALIND. Do, young sir. Your reputation shall not therefore be misprised. We will make it our suit to the duke that the wrestling might not go forward.

ORLANDO. I beseech you, punish me not with your hard thoughts, wherein I confess me much guilty, to deny so fair and excellent ladies anything. But let your fair eyes and gentle wishes go with me to my trial: wherein if I be foiled, there is but one shamed that was never gracious; if killed, but one dead that is willing to be so. I shall do my friends no wrong, for I have none to lament me; the world no injury, for in it I have nothing; only in the world I fill up a place, which may be better supplied when I have made it empty.

ROSALIND. The little strength that I have, I would it were with you.

CELIA. And mine, to eke out hers.

ROSALIND. Fare you well. Pray heaven I be deceived in you!

CELIA. Your heart's desires be with you!

CHARLES. Come, where is this young gallant that is so desirous to lie with his mother earth?

ORLANDO. Ready, sir; but his will hath in it a more modest working.

DUKE FREDERICK. You shall try but one fall.

CHARLES. No, I warrant your Grace, you shall not entreat him to a second, that have so mightily presuaded him from a first.

ORLANDO. You mean to mock me after; you should not have mocked me before: but come your ways.

ROSALIND. Now Hercules be thy speed, young man!

CELIA. I would I were invisible, to catch the strong fellow by the leg. *Charles and Orlando wrestle*

ROSALIND. O excellent young man!

CELIA. If I had a thunderbolt in mine eye, I can tell who should down. *Charles is thrown. Shout*

DUKE FREDERICK. No more, no more.

ORLANDO. Yes, I beseech your Grace. I am not yet well breathed.

DUKE FREDERICK. How dost thou, Charles?

LE BEAU. He cannot speak, my lord.

DUKE FREDERICK. Bear him away. What is thy name, young man? *Charles is borne out*

ORLANDO. Orlando, my liege; the youngest son of Sir Rowland de Boys.

DUKE FREDERICK. I would thou hadst been son to some man else!
The world esteem'd thy father honourable,
But I did find him still mine enemy:
Thou shouldst have better pleas'd me with this deed,
Hadst thou descended from another house.
But fare thee well; thou art a gallant youth:
I would thou hadst told me of another father.
Exeunt Duke Frederick, Train, and Le Beau

CELIA. Were I my father, coz, would I do this?

ORLANDO. I am more proud to be Sir Rowland's son,
His youngest son; and would not change that calling,
To be adopted heir to Frederick.

ROSALIND. My father lov'd Sir Rowland as his soul,
And all the world was of my father's mind:
Had I before known this young man his son,
I should have given him tears unto entreaties,
Ere he should thus have ventur'd.

CELIA. Gentle cousin,
Let us go thank him and encourage him.
My father's rough and envious disposition
Sticks me at heart. Sir, you have well deserv'd.
If you do keep your promises in love
But justly, as you have exceeded all promise,
Your mistress shall be happy.

ROSALIND. Gentleman,
Giving him a chain from her neck
Wear this for me, one out of suits with fortune,
That could give more, but that her hand lacks means.
Shall we go, coz?

CELIA. Ay. Fare you well, fair gentleman.

ORLANDO. Can I not say, I thank you? My better parts
Are all thrown down, and that which here stands up
Is but a quintain, a mere lifeless block.

ROSALIND. He calls us back. My pride fell with my fortunes;
I'll ask him what he would. Did you call, sir?
Sir, you have wrestled well, and overthrown
More than your enemies.

CELIA. Will you go, coz?

ROSALIND. Have with you. Fare you well.
Exeunt Rosalind and Celia

ORLANDO. What passion hangs these weights upon my tongue?
I cannot speak to her, yet she urg'd conference.
O poor Orlando, thou art overthrown!
Or Charles or something weaker masters thee.
Re-enter Le Beau

LE BEAU. Good sir, I do in friendship counsel you
To leave this place. Albeit you have deserv'd
High commendation, true applause and love,
Yet such is now the duke's condition
That he misconstrues all that you have done.
The duke is humorous. What he is indeed,
More suits you to conceive than I to speak of.

ORLANDO. I thank you, sir; and pray you, tell me this;
Which of the two was daughter of the duke,
That here was at the wrestling?

LE BEAU. Neither his daughter, if we judge by manners:
But yet, indeed the smaller is his daughter:
The other is daughter to the banish'd duke,
And here detain'd by her usurping uncle,
To keep his daughter company; whose loves
Are dearer than the natural bond of sisters.
But I can tell you that of late this duke
Hath ta'en displeasure 'gainst his gentle niece,
Grounded upon no other argument
But that the people praise her for her virtues,

And pity her for her good father's sake;
And, on my life, his malice 'gainst the lady
Will suddenly break forth. Sir, fare you well.
Hereafter, in a better world than this,
I shall desire more love and knowledge of you.

ORLANDO. I rest much bounden to you. Fare you well.

Exit Le Beau

Thus must I from the smoke into the smother;
From tyrant duke unto a tyrant brother.
But heavenly Rosalind! *Exit*

SCENE THREE

A Room in the Palace.

Enter Celia and Rosalind

CELIA. Why, cousin! why, Rosalind! Cupid have mercy! Not a word?

ROSALIND. Not one to throw at a dog.

CELIA. No, thy words are too precious to be cast away upon curs; throw some of them at me; come, lame me with reasons.

ROSALIND. Then there were two cousins laid up, when the one should be lamed with reasons and the other mad without any.

CELIA. But is all this for your father?

ROSALIND. No, some of it is for my child's father. O, how full of briers is this working-day world!

CELIA. They are but burrs, cousin, thrown upon thee in holiday foolery. If we walk not in the trodden paths, our very petticoats will catch them.

ROSALIND. I could shake them off my coat. These burrs are in my heart.

CELIA. Hem them away.

ROSALIND. I would try, if I could cry 'hem,' and have him.

CELIA. Come, come; wrestle with thy affections.

ROSALIND. O! they take the part of a better wrestler than myself!

CELIA. O, a good wish upon you! You will try in time, in despite of a fall. But, turning these jests out of service, let us talk in good earnest. Is it possible, on such a sudden,

ACT I · SCENE III

you should fall into so strong a liking with old Sir Rowland's youngest son?

ROSALIND. The duke my father loved his father dearly.

CELIA. Doth it therefore ensue that you should love his son dearly? By this kind of chase, I should hate him, for my father hated his father dearly; yet I hate not Orlando.

ROSALIND. No, faith, hate him not, for my sake.

CELIA. Why should I not? Doth he not deserve well?

ROSALIND. Let me love him for that; and do you love him, because I do. Look, here comes the duke.

CELIA. With his eyes full of anger.

Enter Duke Frederick, with Lords

DUKE FREDERICK. Mistress, dispatch you with your safest haste,
And get you from our court.

ROSALIND. Me, uncle?

DUKE FREDERICK. You, cousin.
Within these ten days if that thou be'st found
So near our public court as twenty miles,
Thou diest for it.

ROSALIND. I do beseech your Grace,
Let me the knowledge of my fault bear with me.
If with myself I hold intelligence,
Or have acquaintance with mine own desires,
If that I do not dream or be not frantic,—
As I do trust I am not,—then, dear uncle,
Never so much as in a thought unborn
Did I offend your Highness.

DUKE FREDERICK. Thus do all traitors.
If their purgation did consist in words,
They are as innocent as grace itself.
Let it suffice thee that I trust thee not.

ROSALIND. Yet your mistrust cannot make me a traitor.
Tell me whereon the likelihood depends.

DUKE FREDERICK. Thou art thy father's daughter; there 's enough.

ROSALIND. So was I when your Highness took his dukedom;
So was I when your Highness banish'd him.
Treason is not inherited, my lord;
Or, if we did derive it from our friends,
What 's that to me? My father was no traitor.
Then, good my liege, mistake me not so much

To think my poverty is treacherous.

CELIA. Dear sovereign, hear me speak.

DUKE FREDERICK. Ay, Celia; we stay'd her for your sake;
Else had she with her father rang'd along.

CELIA. I did not then entreat to have her stay:
It was your pleasure and your own remorse.
I was too young that time to value her;
But now I know her. If she be a traitor,
Why so am I; we still have slept together,
Rose at an instant, learn'd, play'd, eat together;
And wheresoe'er we went, like Juno's swans,
Still we went coupled and inseparable.

DUKE FREDERICK. She is too subtle for thee; and her smoothness,
Her very silence and her patience,
Speak to the people, and they pity her.
Thou art a fool: she robs thee of thy name;
And thou wilt show more bright and seem more virtuous
When she is gone. Then open not thy lips.
Firm and irrevocable is my doom
Which I have pass'd upon her; she is banish'd.

CELIA. Pronounce that sentence then, on me, my liege:
I cannot live out of her company.

DUKE FREDERICK. You are a fool. You, niece, provide yourself.
If you outstay the time, upon mine honour,
And in the greatness of my word, you die.

Exeunt Duke Frederick and Lords

CELIA. O my poor Rosalind! whither wilt thou go?
Wilt thou change fathers? I will give thee mine.
I charge thee, be not thou more griev'd than I am.

ROSALIND. I have more cause.

CELIA.   Thou hast not, cousin.
Prithee, be cheerful; know'st thou not, the duke
Hath banish'd me, his daughter?

ROSALIND.   That he hath not.

CELIA. No, hath not? Rosalind lacks then the love
Which teacheth thee that thou and I am one.
Shall we be sunder'd? Shall we part, sweet girl?
No: let my father seek another heir.
Therefore devise with me how we may fly,
Whither to go, and what to bear with us:

And do not seek to take your change upon you,
To bear your griefs yourself and leave me out;
For, by this heaven, now at our sorrows pale,
Say what thou canst, I 'll go along with thee.

ROSALIND. Why, whither shall we go?

CELIA. To seek my uncle in the forest of Arden.

ROSALIND. Alas, what danger will it be to us,
Maids as we are, to travel forth so far!
Beauty provoketh thieves sooner than gold.

CELIA. I 'll put myself in poor and mean attire,
And with a kind of umber smirch my face;
The like do you. So shall we pass along
And never stir assailants.

ROSALIND. Were it not better,
Because that I am more than common tall,
That I did suit me all points like a man?
A gallant curtle-axe upon my thigh,
A boar-spear in my hand; and,—in my heart
Lie there what hidden woman's fear there will,—
We 'll have a swashing and a martial outside,
As many other mannish cowards have
That do outface it with their semblances.

CELIA. What shall I call thee when thou art a man?

ROSALIND. I 'll have no worse a name than Jove's own page,
And therefore look you call me Ganymede.
But what will you be call'd?

CELIA. Something that hath a reference to my state:
No longer Celia, but Aliena.

ROSALIND. But, cousin, what if we assay'd to steal
The clownish fool out of your father's court?
Would he not be a comfort to our travel?

CELIA. He 'll go along o'er the wide world with me;
Leave me alone to woo him. Let 's away,
And get our jewels and our wealth together,
Devise the fittest time and safest way
To hide us from pursuit that will be made
After my flight. Now go we in content
To liberty and not to banishment. *Exeunt*

ACT TWO

SCENE ONE

The Forest of Arden.

Enter Duke Senior, Amiens, and other Lords, like Foresters

DUKE SENIOR. Now, my co-mates and brothers in exile,
  Hath not old custom made this life more sweet
  Than that of painted pomp? Are not these woods
  More free from peril than the envious court?
  Here feel we but the penalty of Adam,
  The seasons' difference; as, the icy fang
  And churlish chiding of the winter's wind,
  Which, when it bites and blows upon my body,
  Even till I shrink with cold, I smile and say
  'This is no flattery: these are counsellors
  That feelingly persuade me what I am.'
  Sweet are the uses of adversity,
  Which like the toad, ugly and venomous,
  Wears yet a precious jewel in his head;
  And this our life exempt from public haunt,
  Finds tongues in trees, books in the running brook,
  Sermons in stones, and good in every thing.
  I would not change it.
AMIENS.   Happy is your Grace,
  That can translate the stubbornness of fortune
  Into so quiet and so sweet a style.
DUKE SENIOR. Come, shall we go and kill us venison?
  And yet it irks me, the poor dappled fools,
  Being native burghers of this desert city,
  Should in their own confines with forked heads
  Have their round haunches gor'd.
FIRST LORD.   Indeed, my lord,
  The melancholy Jaques grieves at that;
  And, in that kind, swears you do more usurp
  Than doth your brother that hath banish'd you.

To-day my Lord of Amiens and myself
Did steal behind him as he lay along
Under an oak whose antique root peeps out
Upon the brook that brawls along this wood;
To the which place a poor sequester'd stag,
That from the hunters' aim had ta'en a hurt,
Did come to languish; and, indeed, my lord,
The wretched animal heav'd forth such groans
That their discharge did stretch his leathern coat
Almost to bursting, and the big round tears
Cours'd one another down his innocent nose
In piteous chase; and thus the hairy fool,
Much marked of the melancholy Jaques,
Stood on the extremest verge of the swift brook,
Augmenting it with tears.

DUKE SENIOR. But what said Jaques?
Did he not moralize this spectacle?

FIRST LORD. O, yes, into a thousand similes.
First, for his weeping into the needless stream;
'Poor deer,' quoth he, 'thou mak'st a testament
As worldlings do, giving thy sum of more
To that which had too much.' Then, being there alone,
Left and abandon'd of his velvet friends:
' 'Tis right,' quoth he; 'thus misery doth part
The flux of company.' Anon, a careless herd,
Full of the pasture, jumps along by him
And never stays to greet him. 'Ay,' quoth Jaques,
'Sweep on, you fat and greasy citizens;
'Tis just the fashion; wherefore do you look
Upon that poor and broken bankrupt there?'
Thus most invectively he pierceth through
The body of the country, city, court,
Yea, and of this our life, swearing that we
Are mere usurpers, tyrants, and what 's worse,
To fright the animals and to kill them up
In their assign'd and native dwelling-place.

DUKE SENIOR. And did you leave him in this contemplation?

SECOND LORD. We did, my lord, weeping and commenting
Upon the sobbing deer.

DUKE SENIOR. Show me the place.
I love to cope him in these sullen fits,
For then he 's full of matter.

SECOND LORD. I 'll bring you to him straight. *Exeunt*

SCENE TWO

A Room in the Palace.

Enter Duke Frederick, Lords, and Attendants

DUKE FREDERICK. Can it be possible that no man saw them?
  It cannot be. Some villains of my court
  Are of consent and sufferance in this.
FIRST LORD. I cannot hear of any that did see her.
  The ladies, her attendants of her chamber,
  Saw her a-bed; and, in the morning early
  They found the bed untreasur'd of their mistress.
SECOND LORD. My lord, the roynish clown, at whom so oft
  Your Grace was wont to laugh, is also missing.
  Hisperia, the princess' gentlewoman,
  Confesses that she secretly o'erheard
  Your daughter and her cousin much commend
  The parts and graces of the wrestler
  That did but lately foil the sinewy Charles;
  And she believes, wherever they are gone,
  That youth is surely in their company.
DUKE FREDERICK. Send to his brother; fetch that gallant hither;
  If he be absent, bring his brother to me;
  I'll make him find him. Do this suddenly,
  And let not search and inquisition quail
  To bring again these foolish runaways. *Exeunt*

SCENE THREE

Before Oliver's House.

Enter Orlando and Adam, meeting

ORLANDO. Who's there?
ADAM. What! my young master? O my gentle master!
  O my sweet master! O you memory
  Of old Sir Rowland! Why, what make you here?
  Why are you virtuous? Why do people love you?
  And wherefore are you gentle, strong, and valiant?

Why would you be so fond to overcome
The bony priser of the humorous duke?
Your praise is come too swiftly home before you.
Know you not, master, to some kind of men
Their graces serve them but as enemies?
No more do yours. Your virtues, gentle master,
Are sanctified and holy traitors to you.
O, what a world is this, when what is comely
Envenoms him that bears it!

ORLANDO. Why, what's the matter?
ADAM. O unhappy youth!
Come not within these doors; within this roof
The enemy of all your graces lives.
Your brother,—no, no brother; yet the son,—
Yet not the son, I will not call him son
Of him I was about to call his father,—
Hath heard your praises, and this night he means
To burn the lodging where you use to lie,
And you within it. If he fail of that,
He will have other means to cut you off.
I overheard him and his practices.
This is no place; this house is but a butchery.
Abhor it, fear it, do not enter it.

ORLANDO. Why, whither, Adam, wouldst thou have me go?
ADAM. No matter whither, so you come not here.
ORLANDO. What! wouldst thou have me go and beg my food?
Or with a base and boisterous sword enforce
A thievish living on the common road?
This I must do, or know not what to do:
Yet this I will not do, do how I can;
I rather will subject me to the malice
Of a diverted and bloody brother.

ADAM. But do not so. I have five hundred crowns,
The thrifty hire I sav'd under your father,
Which I did store to be my foster-nurse
When service should in my old limbs lie lame,
And unregarded age in corners thrown.
Take that; and He that doth the ravens feed,
Yea, providently caters for the sparrow,
Be comfort to my age! Here is the gold;
All this I give you. Let me be your servant.

Though I look old, yet I am strong and lusty;
For in my youth I never did apply
Hot and rebellious liquors in my blood,
Nor did not with unbashful forehead woo
The means of weakness and debility;
Therefore my age is as a lusty winter,
Frosty, but kindly. Let me go with you;
I 'll do the service of a younger man
In all your business and necessities.
ORLANDO. O good old man! how well in thee appears
The constant service of the antique world,
When service sweat for duty, not for meed!
Thou art not for the fashion of these times,
Where none will sweat but for promotion,
And having that, do choke their service up
Even with the having. It is not so with thee.
But, poor old man, thou prun'st a rotten tree,
That cannot so much as a blossom yield,
In lieu of all thy pains and husbandry.
But come thy ways, we 'll go along together,
And ere we have thy youthful wages spent,
We 'll light upon some settled low content.
ADAM. Master, go on, and I will follow thee
To the last gasp with truth and loyalty.
From seventeen years till now almost fourscore
Here lived I, but now live here no more.
At seventeen years many their fortunes seek;
But at fourscore it is too late a week:
Yet fortune cannot recompense me better
Than to die well and not my master's debtor. *Exeunt*

SCENE FOUR

The Forest of Arden.

Enter Rosalind in boy's clothes, Celia dressed like a shepherdess, and Touchstone

ROSALIND. O Jupiter! how weary are my spirits.

TOUCHSTONE. I care not for my spirits if my legs were not weary.

ROSALIND. I could find it in my heart to disgrace my man's apparel and to cry like a woman; but I must comfort the weaker vessel, as doublet and hose ought to show itself courageous to petticoat. Therefore, courage, good Aliena.

CELIA. I pray you, bear with me. I cannot go no further.

TOUCHSTONE. For my part, I had rather bear with you than bear you; yet I should bear no cross if I did bear you, for I think you have no money in your purse.

ROSALIND. Well, this is the forest of Arden.

TOUCHSTONE. Ay, now am I in Arden; the more fool I; when I was at home, I was in a better place: but travellers must be content.

ROSALIND. Ay, be so, good Touchstone. Look you, who comes here; a young man and an old in solemn talk.

Enter Corin and Silvius

CORIN. That is the way to make her scorn you still.

SILVIUS. O Corin, that thou knew'st how I do love her!

CORIN. I partly guess, for I have lov'd ere now.

SILVIUS. No, Corin; being old, thou canst not guess,
Though in thy youth thou wast as true a lover
As ever sigh'd upon a midnight pillow.
But if thy love were ever like to mine,—
As sure I think did never man love so,—
How many actions most ridiculous
Hast thou been drawn to by thy fantasy?

CORIN. Into a thousand that I have forgotten.

SILVIUS. O! thou didst then ne'er love so heartily.
If thou remember'st not the slightest folly
That ever love did make thee run into,
Thou hast not lov'd.
Or if thou hast not sat as I do now,

Wearing thy hearer with thy mistress' praise,
   Thou hast not lov'd:
   Or if thou hast not broke from company
   Abruptly, as my passion now makes me,
   Thou hast not lov'd. O Phebe, Phebe, Phebe! *Exit*
ROSALIND. Alas, poor shepherd! searching of thy wound,
   I have by hard adventure found mine own.
TOUCHSTONE. And I mine. I remember, when I was in love I broke my sword upon a stone, and bid him take that for coming a-night to Jane Smile; and I remember the kissing of her batler, and the cow's dugs that her pretty chopped hands had milked; and I remember the wooing of a peascod instead of her, from whom I took two cods, and giving her them again, said with weeping tears, 'Wear these for my sake.' We that are true lovers run into strange capers; but as all is mortal in nature, so is all nature in love mortal in folly.
ROSALIND. Thou speakest wiser than thou art ware of.
TOUCHSTONE. Nay, I shall ne'er be ware of mine own wit till I break my shins against it.
ROSALIND. Jove, Jove! this shepherd's passion
      Is much upon my fashion.
TOUCHSTONE. And mine; but it grows something stale with me.
CELIA. I pray you, one of you question yond man,
   If he for gold will give us any food:
   I faint almost to death.
TOUCHSTONE.   Holla, you clown!
ROSALIND. Peace, fool: he's not thy kinsman.
CORIN.   Who calls?
TOUCHSTONE. Your betters, sir.
CORIN.   Else are they very wretched.
ROSALIND. Peace, I say. Good even to you, friend.
CORIN. And to you, gentle sir, and to you all.
ROSALIND. I prithee, shepherd, if that love or gold
   Can in this desert place buy entertainment,
   Bring us where we may rest ourselves and feed.
   Here's a young maid with travel much oppress'd,
   And faints for succour.
CORIN.   Fair sir, I pity her,
   And wish, for her sake more than for mine own,
   My fortunes were more able to relieve her;
   But I am shepherd to another man,

ACT II · SCENE IV

And do not shear the fleeces that I graze:
My master is of churlish disposition
And little recks to find the way to heaven
By doing deeds of hospitality.
Besides, his cote, his flocks, and bounds of feed
Are now on sale; and at our sheepcote now,
By reason of his absence, there is nothing
That you will feed on; but what is, come see,
And in my voice most welcome shall you be.

ROSALIND. What is he that shall buy his flock and pasture?

CORIN. That young swain that you saw here but erewhile,
That little cares for buying any thing.

ROSALIND. I pray thee, if it stand with honesty,
Buy thou the cottage, pasture, and the flock,
And thou shalt have to pay for it of us.

CELIA. And we will mend thy wages. I like this place,
And willingly could waste my time in it.

CORIN. Assuredly the thing is to be sold.
Go with me. If you like upon report
The soil, the profit, and this kind of life,
I will your very faithful feeder be,
And buy it with your gold right suddenly. *Exeunt*

SCENE FIVE

Another part of the Forest.

Enter Amiens, Jaques, and Others

SONG

AMIENS.   Under the greenwood tree
      Who loves to lie with me,
      And turn his merry note
      Unto the sweet bird's throat,
Come hither, come hither, come hither!
      Here shall he see
      No enemy
But winter and rough weather.

JAQUES. More, more, I prithee, more.

AMIENS. It will make you melancholy, Monsieur Jaques.

JAQUES. I thank it. More! I prithee, more. I can suck melancholy out of a song as a weasel sucks eggs. More! I prithee, more.

AMIENS. My voice is ragged; I know I cannot please you.

JAQUES. I do not desire you to please me; I do desire you to sing. Come, more; another stanzo. Call you them stanzos?

AMIENS. What you will, Monsieur Jaques.

JAQUES. Nay, I care not for their names; they owe me nothing. Will you sing?

AMIENS. More at your request than to please myself.

JAQUES. Well then, if ever I thank any man, I'll thank you. But that they call compliment is like the encounter of two dog-apes, and when a man thanks me heartily, methinks I have given him a penny and he renders me the beggarly thanks. Come, sing; and you that will not, hold your tongues.

AMIENS. Well, I'll end the song. Sirs, cover the while; the duke will drink under this tree. He hath been all this day to look you.

JAQUES. And I have been all this day to avoid him. He is too disputable for my company. I think of as many matters as he, but I give heaven thanks, and make no boast of them. Come, warble; come.

SONG

AMIENS.
      Who doth ambition shun *All together here*
      And loves to live i' the sun,
      Seeking the food he eats,
      And pleas'd with what he gets,
Come hither, come hither, come hither:
      Here shall he see
      No enemy
But winter and rough weather.

JAQUES. I'll give you a verse to this note, that I made yesterday in despite of my invention.

AMIENS. And I'll sing it.

JAQUES. Thus it goes:

      If it do come to pass
      That any man turn ass,
      Leaving his wealth and ease,
      A stubborn will to please,
Ducdame, ducdame, ducdame:
      Here shall he see
      Gross fools as he,
And if he will come to me.

AMIENS. What's that 'ducdame'?
JAQUES. 'Tis a Greek invocation to call fools into a circle. I'll go sleep if I can; if I cannot, I'll rail against all the first-born of Egypt.
AMIENS. And I'll go seek the duke. His banquet is prepared. *Exeunt severally*

SCENE SIX

Another Part of the Forest.

Enter Orlando and Adam

ADAM. Dear master, I can go no further. O! I die for food. Here lie I down, and measure out my grave. Farewell, kind master.
ORLANDO. Why, how now, Adam! no greater heart in thee? Live a little; comfort a little; cheer thyself a little. If this uncouth forest yield anything savage, I will either be food for it, or bring it for food to thee. Thy conceit is nearer death than thy powers. For my sake be comfortable, hold death awhile at the arm's end, I will here be with thee presently, and if I bring thee not something to eat, I will give thee leave to die; but if thou diest before I come, thou art a mocker of my labour. Well said! thou lookest cheerly, and I'll be with thee quickly. Yet thou liest in the bleak air: come, I will bear thee to some shelter, and thou shalt not die for lack of a dinner, if there live anything in this desert. Cheerly, good Adam. *Exeunt*

SCENE SEVEN

Another part of the Forest.

A table set out. Enter Duke Senior, Amiens, Lords like Outlaws

DUKE SENIOR. I think he be transform'd into a beast,
For I can nowhere find him like a man.
FIRST LORD. My lord, he is but even now gone hence.
Here was he merry, hearing of a song.
DUKE SENIOR. If he, compact of jars, grow musical,

We shall have shortly discord in the spheres.
Go, seek him: tell him I would speak with him.
FIRST LORD. He saves my labour by his own approach.

Enter Jaques

DUKE SENIOR. Why, how now, monsieur! what a life is this,
That your poor friends must woo your company?
What, you look merrily!
JAQUES. A fool, a fool! I met a fool i' the forest,
A motley fool; a miserable world!
As I do live by food, I met a fool;
Who laid him down and bask'd him in the sun,
And rail'd on Lady Fortune in good terms,
In good set terms, and yet a motley fool.
'Good-morrow, fool,' quoth I. 'No, sir,' quoth he,
'Call me not fool till heaven hath sent me fortune.'
And then he drew a dial from his poke,
And, looking on it with lack-lustre eye,
Says very wisely, 'It is ten o'clock;
Thus may we see,' quoth he, 'how the world wags.
'Tis but an hour ago since it was nine,
And after one hour more 'twill be eleven;
And so, from hour to hour we ripe and ripe,
And then from hour to hour we rot and rot,
And thereby hangs a tale.' When I did hear
The motley fool thus moral on the time,
My lungs began to crow like chanticleer,
That fools should be so deep-contemplative,
And I did laugh sans intermission
An hour by his dial. O noble fool!
A worthy fool! Motley 's the only wear.
DUKE SENIOR. What fool is this?
JAQUES. O worthy fool! One that hath been a courtier,
And says, if ladies be but young and fair,
They have the gift to know it; and in his brain,—
Which is as dry as the remainder biscuit
After a voyage,—he hath strange places cramm'd
With observation, the which he vents
In mangled forms. O that I were a fool!
I am ambitious for a motley coat.
DUKE SENIOR. Thou shalt have one.
JAQUES.   It is my only suit;
Provided that you weed your better judgments

    Of all opinion that grows rank in them
    That I am wise. I must have liberty
    Withal, as large a charter as the wind,
    To blow on whom I please; for so fools have.
    And they that are most galled with my folly,
    They most must laugh. And why, sir, must they so?
    The 'why' is plain as way to parish church:
    He that a fool doth very wisely hit
    Doth very foolishly, although he smart,
    Not to seem senseless of the bob; if not,
    The wise man's folly is anatomiz'd
    Even by the squandering glances of the fool.
    Invest me in my motley; give me leave
    To speak my mind, and I will through and through
    Cleanse the foul body of th' infected world,
    If they will patiently receive my medicine.
DUKE SENIOR. Fie on thee! I can tell what thou wouldst do.
JAQUES. What, for a counter, would I do, but good?
DUKE SENIOR. Most mischievous foul sin, in chiding sin.
    For thou thyself hast been a libertine,
    As sensual as the brutish sting itself;
    And all the embossed sores and headed evils,
    That thou with licence of free foot hast caught,
    Wouldst thou disgorge into the general world.
JAQUES. Why, who cries out on pride,
    That can therein tax any private party?
    Doth it not flow as hugely as the sea,
    Till that the wearer's very means do ebb?
    What woman in the city do I name,
    When that I say the city-woman bears
    The cost of princes on unworthy shoulders?
    Who can come in and say that I mean her,
    When such a one as she such is her neighbour?
    Or what is he of basest function,
    That says his bravery is not on my cost,—
    Thinking that I mean him,—but therein suits
    His folly to the mettle of my speech?
    There then; how then? what then? Let me see wherein
    My tongue hath wrong'd him: if it do him right,
    Then he hath wrong'd himself; if he be free,
    Why then, my taxing like a wild goose flies,
    Unclaim'd of any man. But who comes here?

Enter Orlando, with his sword drawn

ORLANDO. Forbear, and eat no more.
JAQUES. Why, I have eat none yet.
ORLANDO. Nor shalt not, till necessity be serv'd.
JAQUES. Of what kind should this cock come of?
DUKE SENIOR. Art thou thus bolden'd, man, by thy distress,
  Or else a rude despiser of good manners,
  That in civility thou seem'st so empty?
ORLANDO. You touch'd my vein at first: the thorny point
  Of bare distress hath ta'en from me the show
  Of smooth civility; yet I am inland bred
  And know some nurture. But forbear, I say:
  He dies that touches any of this fruit
  Till I and my affairs are answered.
JAQUES. An you will not be answered with reason,
  I must die.
DUKE SENIOR. What would you have? Your gentleness shall force
  More than your force move us to gentleness.
ORLANDO. I almost die for food; and let me have it.
DUKE SENIOR. Sit down and feed, and welcome to our table.
ORLANDO. Speak you so gently? Pardon me, I pray you:
  I thought that all things had been savage here,
  And therefore put I on the countenance
  Of stern commandment. But whate'er you are
  That in this desert inaccessible,
  Under the shade of melancholy boughs,
  Lose and neglect the creeping hours of time;
  If ever you have look'd on better days,
  If ever been where bells have knoll'd to church,
  If ever sat at any good man's feast,
  If ever from your eyelids wip'd a tear,
  And know what 'tis to pity, and be pitied,
  Let gentleness my strong enforcement be:
  In the which hope I blush, and hide my sword.
DUKE SENIOR. True is it that we have seen better days,
  And have with holy bell been knoll'd to church,
  And sat at good men's feasts, and wip'd our eyes
  Of drops that sacred pity hath engender'd;
  And therefore sit you down in gentleness
  And take upon command what help we have
  That to your wanting may be minister'd.

ACT II · SCENE VII

ORLANDO. Then but forbear your food a little while,
  Whiles, like a doe, I go to find my fawn
  And give it food. There is an old poor man,
  Who after me hath many a weary step
  Limp'd in pure love; till he be first suffic'd,
  Oppress'd with two weak evils, age and hunger,
  I will not touch a bit.
DUKE SENIOR.   Go find him out,
  And we will nothing waste till you return.
ORLANDO. I thank ye; and be bless'd for your good comfort!
                                                    Exit

DUKE SENIOR. Thou seest we are not all alone unhappy:
  This wide and universal theatre
  Presents more woful pageants than the scene
  Wherein we play in.
JAQUES.   All the world's a stage,
  And all the men and women merely players.
  They have their exits and their entrances;
  And one man in his time plays many parts,
  His acts being seven ages. At first the infant,
  Mewling and puking in the nurse's arms.
  And then the whining school-boy, with his satchel,
  And shining morning face, creeping like snail
  Unwillingly to school. And then the lover,
  Sighing like furnace, with a woful ballad
  Made to his mistress' eyebrow. Then a soldier,
  Full of strange oaths, and bearded like the pard,
  Jealous in honour, sudden and quick in quarrel,
  Seeking the bubble reputation
  Even in the cannon's mouth. And then the justice,
  In fair round belly with good capon lin'd,
  With eyes severe, and beard of formal cut,
  Full of wise saws and modern instances;
  And so he plays his part. The sixth age shifts
  Into the lean and slipper'd pantaloon,
  With spectacles on nose and pouch on side,
  His youthful hose well sav'd a world too wide
  For his shrunk shank; and his big manly voice,
  Turning again toward childish treble, pipes
  And whistles in his sound. Last scene of all,
  That ends this strange eventful history,
  Is second childishness and mere oblivion,
  Sans teeth, sans eyes, sans taste, sans everything.

Re-enter Orlando, with Adam

DUKE SENIOR. Welcome. Set down your venerable burden,
And let him feed.
ORLANDO.   I thank you most for him.
ADAM. So had you need:
I scarce can speak to thank you for myself.
DUKE SENIOR. Welcome; fall to: I will not trouble you
As yet, to question you about your fortunes.
Give us some music; and, good cousin, sing.

SONG

AMIENS.   Blow, blow, thou winter wind,
                Thou art not so unkind
                    As man's ingratitude;
                Thy tooth is not so keen,
                Because thou art not seen,
                    Although thy breath be rude.
        Heigh-ho! sing, heigh-ho! unto the green holly:
        Most friendship is feigning, most loving mere folly.
                Then heigh-ho! the holly!
                    This life is most jolly.

                Freeze, freeze, thou bitter sky,
                That dost not bite so nigh
                    As benefits forgot:
                Though thou the waters warp,
                Thy sting is not so sharp
                    As friend remember'd not.
        Heigh-ho! sing, heigh-ho! unto the green holly:
        Most friendship is feigning, most loving mere folly.
                Then heigh-ho! the holly!
                    This life is most jolly.

DUKE SENIOR. If that you were the good Sir Rowland's son,
As you have whisper'd faithfully you were,
And as mine eye doth his effigies witness
Most truly limn'd and living in your face,
Be truly welcome hither. I am the duke
That lov'd your father. The residue of your fortune,
Go to my cave and tell me. Good old man,
Thou art right welcome as thy master is.
Support him by the arm. Give me your hand,
And let me all your fortunes understand.   *Exeunt*

ACT THREE

SCENE ONE

A Room in the Palace.

Enter Duke Frederick, Oliver, Lords, and Attendants

DUKE FREDERICK. Not seen him since! Sir, sir, that cannot be:
But were I not the better part made mercy,
I should not seek an absent argument
Of my revenge, thou present. But look to it:
Find out thy brother, wheresoe'er he is;
Seek him with candle; bring him, dead or living,
Within this twelvemonth, or turn thou no more
To seek a living in our territory.
Thy lands and all things that thou dost call thine
Worth seizure, do we seize into our hands,
Till thou canst quit thee by thy brother's mouth
Of what we think against thee.
OLIVER. O that your Highness knew my heart in this!
I never lov'd my brother in my life.
DUKE FREDERICK. More villain thou. Well, push him out of doors;
And let my officers of such a nature
Make an extent upon his house and lands.
Do this expediently and turn him going. *Exeunt*

SCENE TWO

The Forest of Arden.

Enter Orlando, with a paper

ORLANDO. Hang there, my verse, in witness of my love:
    And thou, thrice-crowned queen of night, survey
With thy chaste eye, from thy pale sphere above,
    Thy huntress' name, that my full life doth sway.
O Rosalind! these trees shall be my books,
    And in their barks my thoughts I'll character,
That every eye, which in this forest looks,
    Shall see thy virtue witness'd everywhere.
Run, run, Orlando: carve on every tree
The fair, the chaste, and unexpressive she. *Exit*

Enter Corin and Touchstone

CORIN. And how like you this shepherd's life, Master Touchstone?

TOUCHSTONE. Truly, shepherd, in respect of itself, it is a good life; but in respect that it is a shepherd's life, it is naught. In respect that it is solitary, I like it very well; but in respect that it is private, it is a very vile life. Now, in respect it is in the fields, it pleaseth me well; but in respect it is not in the court, it is tedious. As it is a spare life, look you, it fits my humour well; but as there is no more plenty in it, it goes much against my stomach. Hast any philosophy in thee, shepherd?

CORIN. No more but that I know the more one sickens the worse at ease he is; and that he that wants money, means, and content, is without three good friends; that the property of rain is to wet, and fire to burn; that good pasture makes fat sheep, and that a great cause of the night is lack of the sun; that he that hath learned no wit by nature nor art may complain of good breeding, or comes of a very dull kindred.

TOUCHSTONE. Such a one is a natural philosopher. Wast ever in court, shepherd?

CORIN. No, truly.

TOUCHSTONE. Then thou art damned.

CORIN. Nay, I hope.

TOUCHSTONE. Truly, thou art damned like an ill-roasted egg, all on one side.

CORIN. For not being at court? Your reason.

TOUCHSTONE. Why, if thou never wast at court, thou never sawest good manners; if thou never sawest good manners, then thy manners must be wicked; and wickedness is sin, and sin is damnation. Thou art in a parlous state, shepherd.

CORIN. Not a whit, Touchstone. Those that are good manners at the court are as ridiculous in the country as the behaviour of the country is most mockable at the court. You told me you salute not at the court, but you kiss your hands. That courtesy would be uncleanly if courtiers were shepherds.

TOUCHSTONE. Instance, briefly; come, instance.

CORIN. Why, we are still handling our ewes, and their fells, you know, are greasy.

TOUCHSTONE. Why, do not your courtier's hands sweat? and is not the grease of a mutton as wholesome as the sweat of a man? Shallow, shallow. A better instance, I say; come.

CORIN. Besides, our hands are hard.

TOUCHSTONE. Your lips will feel them the sooner: shallow again. A more sounder instance; come.

CORIN. And they are often tarred over with the surgery of our sheep; and would you have us kiss tar? The courtier's hands are perfumed with civet.

TOUCHSTONE. Most shallow man! Thou worms-meat, in respect of a good piece of flesh, indeed! Learn of the wise, and perpend. Civet is of a baser birth than tar, the very uncleanly flux of a cat. Mend the instance, shepherd.

CORIN. You have too courtly a wit for me. I'll rest.

TOUCHSTONE. Wilt thou rest damned? God help thee, shallow man! God make incision in thee! thou art raw.

CORIN. Sir, I am a true labourer: I earn that I eat, get that I wear, owe no man hate, envy no man's happiness, glad of other men's good, content with my harm; and the greatest of my pride is to see my ewes graze and my lambs suck.

TOUCHSTONE. That is another simple sin in you, to bring the ewes and the rams together, and to offer to get your living by the copulation of cattle; to be bawd to a bell-wether, and to betray a she-lamb of a twelvemonth to a crooked-pated, old, cuckoldy ram, out of all reasonable match. If thou be'st not damned for this, the devil himself will have no shepherds: I cannot see else how thou shouldst 'scape.

CORIN. Here comes young Master Ganymede, my new mistress's brother.

Enter Rosalind, reading a paper

ROSALIND. 'From the east to western Ind,
No jewel is like Rosalind.
Her worth, being mounted on the wind,
Through all the world bears Rosalind.
All the pictures fairest lin'd
Are but black to Rosalind.
Let no face be kept in mind,
But the fair of Rosalind.'

TOUCHSTONE. I'll rime you so, eight years together, dinners and suppers and sleeping hours excepted. It is the right butter-women's rank to market.

ROSALIND. Out, fool!

TOUCHSTONE. For a taste:—
If a hart do lack a hind,
Let him seek out Rosalind.
If the cat will after kind,
So be sure will Rosalind.
Winter-garments must be lin'd,
So must slender Rosalind.
They that reap must sheaf and bind,
Then to cart with Rosalind.
Sweetest nut hath sourest rind,
Such a nut is Rosalind.
He that sweetest rose will find
Must find love's prick and Rosalind.

This is the very false gallop of verses. Why do you infect yourself with them?

ROSALIND. Peace! you dull fool. I found them on a tree.

TOUCHSTONE. Truly the tree yields bad fruit.

ROSALIND. I'll graff it with you, and then I shall graff it with a medlar: then it will be the earliest fruit i' the country; for you'll be rotten ere you be half ripe, and that's the right virtue of the medlar.

TOUCHSTONE. You have said; but whether wisely or no, let the forest judge.

Enter Celia, reading a paper

ROSALIND. Peace!

ACT III : SCENE II

Here comes my sister, reading: stand aside.

CELIA. 'Why should this a desert be?
　　For it is unpeopled? No;
Tongues I'll hang on every tree,
　　That shall civil sayings show.
Some, how brief the life of man
　　Runs his erring pilgrimage,
That the stretching of a span
　　Buckles in his sum of age;
Some, of violated vows
　　'Twixt the souls of friend and friend:
But upon the fairest boughs,
　　Or at every sentence' end,
Will I Rosalinda write;
　　Teaching all that read to know
The quintessence of every sprite
　　Heaven would in little show.
Therefore Heaven Nature charg'd
That one body should be fill'd
With all graces wide enlarg'd.
　　Nature presently distill'd
Helen's cheek, but not her heart,
　　Cleopatra's majesty,
Atalanta's better part,
　　Sad Lucretia's modesty.
Thus Rosalind of many parts
　　By heavenly synod was devis'd,
Of many faces, eyes, and hearts,
　　To have the touches dearest priz'd.
Heaven would that she these gifts should have,
And I to live and die her slave.'

ROSALIND. O most gentle pulpiter! what tedious homily of love have you wearied your parishioners withal, and never cried, 'Have patience, good people!'

CELIA. How now! back, friends! Shepherd, go off a little. Go with him, sirrah.

TOUCHSTONE. Come, shepherd, let us make an honourable retreat; though not with bag and baggage, yet with scrip and scrippage. *Exeunt Corin and Touchstone*

CELIA. Didst thou hear these verses?

ROSALIND. O, yes, I heard them all, and more too; for some of them had in them more feet than the verses would bear.

CELIA. That's no matter. The feet might bear the verses.

ROSALIND. Ay, but the feet were lame, and could not bear themselves without the verse, and therefore stood lamely in the verse.

CELIA. But didst thou hear without wondering, how thy name should be hanged and carved upon these trees?

ROSALIND. I was seven of the nine days out of the wonder before you came; for look here what I found on a palm-tree; I was never so be-rimed since Pythagoras' time, that I was an Irish rat, which I can hardly remember.

CELIA. Trow you who hath done this?

ROSALIND. Is it a man?

CELIA. And a chain, that you once wore, about his neck. Change you colour?

ROSALIND. I prithee, who?

CELIA. O Lord, Lord! it is a hard matter for friends to meet; but mountains may be removed with earthquakes, and so encounter.

ROSALIND. Nay, but who is it?

CELIA. Is it possible?

ROSALIND. Nay, I prithee now, with most petitionary vehemence, tell me who it is.

CELIA. O wonderful, wonderful, and most wonderful wonderful! and yet again wonderful! and after that, out of all whooping!

ROSALIND. Good my complexion! Dost thou think, though I am caparison'd like a man, I have a doublet and hose in my disposition? One inch of delay more is a South-sea of discovery; I prithee, tell me who is it quickly, and speak apace. I would thou couldst stammer, that thou mightst pour this concealed man out of thy mouth, as wine comes out of a narrow-mouth'd bottle; either too much at once, or none at all. I prithee, take the cork out of thy mouth, that I may drink thy tidings.

CELIA. So you may put a man in your belly.

ROSALIND. Is he of God's making? What manner of man? Is his head worth a hat, or his chin worth a beard?

CELIA. Nay, he hath but a little beard.

ROSALIND. Why, God will send more, if the man will be thankful. Let me stay the growth of his beard, if thou delay me not the knowledge of his chin.

CELIA. It is young Orlando, that tripped up the wrestler's

heels and your heart both, in an instant.

ROSALIND. Nay, but the devil take mocking. Speak, sad brow and true maid.

CELIA. I' faith, coz, 'tis he.

ROSALIND. Orlando?

CELIA. Orlando.

ROSALIND. Alas the day! what shall I do with my doublet and hose? What did he when thou sawest him? What said he? How looked he? Wherein went he? What makes he here? Did he ask for me? Where remains he? How parted he with thee, and when shalt thou see him again? Answer me in one word.

CELIA. You must borrow me Gargantua's mouth first: 'tis a word too great for any mouth of this age's size. To say ay and no to these particulars is more than to answer in a catechism.

ROSALIND. But doth he know that I am in this forest and in man's apparel? Looks he as freshly as he did the day he wrestled?

CELIA. It is as easy to count atomies as to resolve the propositions of a lover; but take a taste of my finding him, and relish it with good observance. I found him under a tree, like a dropped acorn.

ROSALIND. It may well be called Jove's tree, when it drops forth such fruit.

CELIA. Give me audience, good madam.

ROSALIND. Proceed.

CELIA. There lay he, stretch'd along like a wounded knight.

ROSALIND. Though it be pity to see such a sight, it well becomes the ground.

CELIA. Cry 'holla!' to thy tongue, I prithee; it curvets unseasonably. He was furnish'd like a hunter.

ROSALIND. O, ominous! he comes to kill my heart.

CELIA. I would sing my song without a burthen. Thou bringest me out of tune.

ROSALIND. Do you not know I am a woman? When I think, I must speak. Sweet, say on.

CELIA. You bring me out. Soft! comes he not here?

ROSALIND. 'Tis he! Slink by, and note him.

Enter Orlando and Jaques

JAQUES. I thank you for your company; but, good faith, I had as lief have been myself alone.

ORLANDO. And so had I; but yet, for fashion' sake, I thank you too for your society.

JAQUES. God be wi' you. Let 's meet as little as we can.

ORLANDO. I do desire we may be better strangers.

JAQUES. I pray you, mar no more trees with writing love-songs in their barks.

ORLANDO. I pray you mar no more of my verses with reading them ill-favouredly.

JAQUES. Rosalind is your love's name?

ORLANDO. Yes, just.

JAQUES. I do not like her name.

ORLANDO. There was no thought of pleasing you when she was christened.

JAQUES. What stature is she of?

ORLANDO. Just as high as my heart.

JAQUES. You are full of pretty answers. Have you not been acquainted with goldsmiths' wives, and conn'd them out of rings?

ORLANDO. Not so; but I answer you right painted cloth, from whence you have studied your questions.

JAQUES. You have a nimble wit. I think 'twas made of Atalanta's heels. Will you sit down with me? and we two will rail against our mistress the world, and all our misery.

ORLANDO. I will chide no breather in the world but myself, against whom I know most faults.

JAQUES. The worst fault you have is to be in love.

ORLANDO. 'Tis a fault I will not change for your best virtue. I am weary of you.

JAQUES. By my troth, I was seeking for a fool when I found you.

ORLANDO. He is drowned in the brook. Look but in, and you shall see him.

JAQUES. There I shall see mine own figure.

ORLANDO. Which I take to be either a fool or a cipher.

JAQUES. I 'll tarry no longer with you. Farewell, good Signior Love.

ORLANDO. I am glad of your departure. Adieu, good Monsieur Melancholy. *Exit Jaques*

ROSALIND. I will speak to him like a saucy lackey, and under that habit play the knave with him. Do you hear, forester?

ORLANDO. Very well. What would you?

ROSALIND. I pray you, what is 't o'clock?

ORLANDO. You should ask me, what time o' day; there 's no clock in the forest.

ROSALIND. Then there is no true lover in the forest; else sighing every minute and groaning every hour would detect the lazy foot of Time as well as a clock.

ORLANDO. And why not the swift foot of Time? Had not that been as proper?

ROSALIND. By no means, sir. Time travels in divers paces with divers persons. I 'll tell you who Time ambles withal, who Time trots withal, who Time gallops withal, and who he stands still withal.

ORLANDO. I prithee, who doth he trot withal?

ROSALIND. Marry, he trots hard with a young maid between the contract of her marriage and the day it is solemnized; if the interim be but a se'nnight, Time's pace is so hard that it seems the length of seven year.

ORLANDO. Who ambles Time withal?

ROSALIND. With a priest that lacks Latin, and a rich man that hath not the gout; for the one sleeps easily because he cannot study, and the other lives merrily because he feels no pain; the one lacking the burden of lean and wasteful learning, the other knowing no burden of heavy tedious penury. These Time ambles withal.

ORLANDO. Who doth he gallop withal?

ROSALIND. With a thief to the gallows; for though he go as softly as foot can fall he thinks himself too soon there.

ORLANDO. Who stays it still withal?

ROSALIND. With lawyers in the vacation; for they sleep between term and term, and then they perceive not how Time moves.

ORLANDO. Where dwell you, pretty youth?

ROSALIND. With this shepherdess, my sister; here in the skirts of the forest, like fringe upon a petticoat.

ORLANDO. Are you native of this place?

ROSALIND. As the cony, that you see dwell where she is kindled.

ORLANDO. Your accent is something finer than you could purchase in so removed a dwelling.

ROSALIND. I have been told so of many: but indeed an old religious uncle of mine taught me to speak, who was in his youth an inland man; one that knew courtship too well, for there he fell in love. I have heard him read many lectures against it; and I thank God, I am not a woman, to be touched with so many giddy offences as he hath generally taxed their whole sex withal.

ORLANDO. Can you remember any of the principal evils that he laid to the charge of women?

ROSALIND. There were none principal; they were all like one another as half-pence are; every one fault seeming monstrous till his fellow fault came to match it.

ORLANDO. I prithee, recount some of them.

ROSALIND. No, I will not cast away my physic, but on those that are sick. There is a man haunts the forest, that abuses our young plants with carving 'Rosalind' on their barks; hangs odes upon hawthorns, and elegies on brambles; all, forsooth, deifying the name of Rosalind: if I could meet that fancy-monger, I would give him some good counsel, for he seems to have the quotidian of love upon him.

ORLANDO. I am he that is so love-shaked. I pray you, tell me your remedy.

ROSALIND. There is none of my uncle's marks upon you: he taught me how to know a man in love; in which cage of rushes I am sure you are not prisoner.

ORLANDO. What were his marks?

ROSALIND. A lean cheek, which you have not; a blue eye and sunken, which you have not; an unquestionable spirit, which you have not; a beard neglected, which you have not: but I pardon you for that, for, simply, your having in beard is a younger brother's revenue. Then, your hose should be ungartered, your bonnet unbanded, your sleeve unbuttoned, your shoe untied, and everything about you demonstrating a careless desolation. But you are no such man: you are rather point-device in your accoutrements; as loving yourself than seeming the lover of any other.

ORLANDO. Fair youth, I would I could make thee believe I love.

ROSALIND. Me believe it! You may as soon make her that you love believe it; which, I warrant, she is apter to do than to confess she does; that is one of the points in the which women still give the lie to their consciences. But, in good sooth, are you he that hangs the verses on the trees, wherein Rosalind is so admired?

ORLANDO. I swear to thee, youth, by the white hand of Rosalind, I am that he, that unfortunate he.

ROSALIND. But are you so much in love as your rimes speak?
ORLANDO. Neither rime nor reason can express how much.
ROSALIND. Love is merely a madness, and, I tell you, deserves as well a dark house and a whip as madmen do; and the reason why they are not so punished and cured is, that the lunacy is so ordinary that the whippers are in love too. Yet I profess curing it by counsel.
ORLANDO. Did you ever cure any so?
ROSALIND. Yes, one; and in this manner. He was to imagine me his love, his mistress; and I set him every day to woo me. At which time would I, being but a moonish youth, grieve, be effeminate, changeable, longing and liking; proud, fantastical, apish, shallow, inconstant, full of tears, full of smiles, for every passion something, and for no passion truly anything, as boys and women are, for the most part, cattle of this colour; would now like him, now loathe him; then entertain him, then forswear him; now weep for him, then spit at him; that I drave my suitor from his mad humour of love to a living humour of madness, which was, to forswear the full stream of the world, and to live in a nook merely monastic. And thus I cured him; and this way will I take upon me to wash your liver as clean as a sound sheep's heart, that there shall not be one spot of love in 't.
ORLANDO. I would not be cured, youth.
ROSALIND. I would cure you, if you would but call me Rosalind, and come every day to my cote and woo me.
ORLANDO. Now, by the faith of my love, I will. Tell me where it is.
ROSALIND. Go with me to it and I'll show it you; and by the way you shall tell me where in the forest you live. Will you go?
ORLANDO. With all my heart, good youth.
ROSALIND. Nay, you must call me Rosalind. Come, sister, will you go? *Exeunt*

SCENE THREE

Another Part of the Forest.

Enter Touchstone and Audrey; Jaques behind

TOUCHSTONE. Come apace, good Audrey. I will fetch up your goats, Audrey. And how, Audrey, am I the man yet? Doth my simple feature content you?

AUDREY. Your features! Lord warrant us! What features?

TOUCHSTONE. I am here with thee and thy goats, as the most capricious poet, honest Ovid, was among the Goths.

JAQUES. (*Aside*) O knowledge ill-inhabited, worse than Jove in a thatch'd house!

TOUCHSTONE. When a man's verses cannot be understood, nor a man's good wit seconded with the forward child Understanding, it strikes a man more dead than a great reckoning in a little room. Truly, I would the gods had made thee poetical.

AUDREY. I do not know what 'poetical' is. Is it honest in deed and word? Is it a true thing?

TOUCHSTONE. No, truly, for the truest poetry is the most feigning; and lovers are given to poetry, and what they swear in poetry may be said as lovers they do feign.

AUDREY. Do you wish then that the gods had made me poetical?

TOUCHSTONE. I do, truly; for thou swearest to me thou art honest: now, if thou wert a poet, I might have some hope thou didst feign.

AUDREY. Would you not have me honest?

TOUCHSTONE. No, truly, unless thou wert hard-favour'd; for honesty coupled to beauty is to have honey a sauce to sugar.

JAQUES. (*Aside*) A material fool.

AUDREY. Well, I am not fair, and therefore I pray the gods make me honest.

TOUCHSTONE. Truly, and to cast away honesty upon a foul slut were to put good meat into an unclean dish.

AUDREY. I am not a slut, though I thank the gods I am foul.

TOUCHSTONE. Well, praised be the gods for thy foulness! Sluttishness may come hereafter. But be it as it may be, I

ACT III · SCENE III

will marry thee; and to that end I have been with Sir Oliver Martext, the vicar of the next village, who hath promised to meet me in this place of the forest, and to couple us.

JAQUES. (*Aside*) I would fain see this meeting.

AUDREY. Well, the gods give us joy!

TOUCHSTONE. Amen. A man may, if he were of a fearful heart, stagger in this attempt; for here we have no temple but the wood, no assembly but horn-beasts. But what though? Courage! As horns are odious, they are necessary. It is said, 'many a man knows no end of his goods.' Right! Many a man has good horns, and knows no end of them. Well, that is the dowry of his wife; 'tis none of his own getting. Horns? Even so. Poor men alone? No, no; the noblest deer hath them as huge as the rascal. Is the single man therefore blessed? No: as a walled town is more worthier than a village, so is the forehead of a married man more honourable than the bare brow of a bachelor; and by how much defence is better than no skill, by so much is a horn more precious than to want. Here comes Sir Oliver.

Enter Sir Oliver Martext

Sir Oliver Martext, you are well met: will you dispatch us here under this tree, or shall we go with you to your chapel?

SIR OLIVER. Is there none here to give the woman?

TOUCHSTONE. I will not take her on gift of any man.

SIR OLIVER. Truly, she must be given, or the marriage is not lawful.

JAQUES. (*Coming forward*) Proceed, proceed! I'll give her.

TOUCHSTONE. Good even, good Master What-ye-call 't: how do you, sir? You are very well met: God 'ild you for your last company. I am very glad to see you. Even a toy in hand here, sir. Nay, pray be covered.

JAQUES. Will you be married, motley?

TOUCHSTONE. As the ox hath his bow, sir, the horse his curb, and the falcon her bells, so man hath his desires; and as pigeons bill, so wedlock would be nibbling.

JAQUES. And will you, being a man of your breeding, be married under a bush, like a beggar? Get you to church, and have a good priest that can tell you what marriage is. This fellow will but join you together as they join wainscot; then one of you will prove a shrunk panel, and like green timber, warp, warp.

TOUCHSTONE. (*Aside*) I am not in the mind but I were better to be married of him than of another: for he is not like to marry me well, and not being well married, it will be a good excuse for me hereafter to leave my wife.

JAQUES. Go thou with me, and let me counsel thee.

TOUCHSTONE. Come, sweet Audrey:
We must be married, or we must live in bawdry.
Farewell, good Master Oliver: not
    O sweet Oliver!
    O brave Oliver!
   Leave me not behind thee:
 but,—
    Wind away,
    Begone, I say,
  I will not to wedding with thee.
   Exeunt Jaques, Touchstone, and Audrey

SIR OLIVER. 'Tis no matter. Ne'er a fantastical knave of them all shall flout me out of my calling. *Exit*

SCENE FOUR

Another Part of the Forest.

Enter Rosalind and Celia

ROSALIND. Never talk to me. I will weep.

CELIA. Do, I prithee; but yet have the grace to consider that tears do not become a man.

ROSALIND. But have I not cause to weep?

CELIA. As good cause as one would desire; therefore weep.

ROSALIND. His very hair is of the dissembling colour.

CELIA. Something browner than Judas's; marry, his kisses are Judas's own children.

ROSALIND. I' faith, his hair is of a good colour.

CELIA. An excellent colour. Your chestnut was ever the only colour.

ROSALIND. And his kissing is as full of sanctity as the touch of holy bread.

CELIA. He hath bought a pair of cast lips of Diana. A nun of winter's sisterhood kisses not more religiously; the very ice of chastity is in them.

ROSALIND. But why did he swear he would come this morning, and comes not?

CELIA. Nay, certainly, there is no truth in him.

ROSALIND. Do you think so?

CELIA. Yes: I think he is not a pick-purse nor a horse-stealer; but for his verity in love, I do think him as concave as a covered goblet or a worm-eaten nut.

ROSALIND. Not true in love?

CELIA. Yes, when he is in; but I think he is not in.

ROSALIND. You have heard him swear downright he was.

CELIA. 'Was' is not 'is.' Besides, the oath of a lover is no stronger than the word of a tapster; they are both the confirmers of false reckonings. He attends here in the forest on the duke your father.

ROSALIND. I met the duke yesterday and had much question with him. He asked me of what parentage I was; I told him, of as good as he; so he laughed, and let me go. But what talk we of fathers, when there is such a man as Orlando?

CELIA. O, that's a brave man! He writes brave verses, speaks brave words, swears brave oaths, and breaks them bravely, quite traverse, athwart the heart of his lover; as a puisny tilter, that spurs his horse but on one side, breaks his staff like a noble goose. But all's brave that youth mounts and folly guides. Who comes here?

Enter Corin

CORIN. Mistress and master, you have oft inquir'd
After the shepherd that complain'd of love,
Who you saw sitting by me on the turf,
Praising the proud disdainful shepherdess
That was his mistress.

CELIA.   Well, and what of him?

CORIN. If you will see a pageant truly play'd,
Between the pale complexion of true love
And the red glow of scorn and proud disdain,
Go hence a little, and I shall conduct you,
If you will mark it.

ROSALIND.   O! come, let us remove:
The sight of lovers feedeth those in love.
Bring us to this sight, and you shall say
I'll prove a busy actor in their play.   *Exeunt*

SCENE FIVE

Another Part of the Forest.

Enter Silvius and Phebe

SILVIUS. Sweet Phebe, do not scorn me; do not, Phebe!
  Say that you love me not, but say not so
  In bitterness. The common executioner,
  Whose heart the accustom'd sight of death makes hard,
  Falls not the axe upon the humbled neck
  But first begs pardon: will you sterner be
  Than he that dies and lives by bloody drops?
    Enter Rosalind, Celia, and Corin, behind
PHEBE. I would not be thy executioner.
  I fly thee, for I would not injure thee.
  Thou tell'st me there is murder in mine eye:
  'Tis pretty, sure, and very probable,
  That eyes, that are the frail'st and softest things,
  Who shut their coward gates on atomies,
  Should be call'd tyrants, butchers, murderers!
  Now I do frown on thee with all my heart;
  And, if mine eyes can wound, now let them kill thee;
  Now counterfeit to swound; why now fall down;
  Or, if thou canst not, O! for shame, for shame,
  Lie not, to say mine eyes are murderers.
  Now show the wound mine eye hath made in thee;
  Scratch thee but with a pin, and there remains
  Some scar of it; lean but upon a rush,
  The cicatrice and capable impressure
  Thy palm some moment keeps; but now mine eyes,
  Which I have darted at thee, hurt thee not,
  Nor, I am sure, there is no force in eyes
  That can do hurt.
SILVIUS.   O dear Phebe,
  If ever,—as that ever may be near,—
  You meet in some fresh cheek the power of fancy,
  Then shall you know the wounds invisible
  That love's keen arrows make.
PHEBE.   But, till that time
  Come not thou near me; and, when that time comes,

Afflict me with thy mocks, pity me not;
As, till that time I shall not pity thee.
ROSALIND. (*Advancing*) And why, I pray you? Who might
be your mother,
That you insult, exult, and all at once,
Over the wretched? What though you have no beauty,—
As by my faith, I see no more in you
Than without candle may go dark to bed,—
Must you be therefore proud and pitiless?
Why, what means this? Why do you look on me?
I see no more in you than in the ordinary
Of nature's sale-work. Od's my little life!
I think she means to tangle my eyes too.
No, faith, proud mistress, hope not after it.
'Tis not your inky brows, your black silk hair,
Your bugle eyeballs, nor your cheek of cream,
That can entame my spirits to your worship.
You foolish shepherd, wherefore do you follow her,
Like foggy south puffing with wind and rain?
You are a thousand times a properer man
Than she a woman. 'Tis such fools as you
That make the world full of ill-favour'd children:
'Tis not her glass, but you, that flatters her;
And out of you she sees herself more proper
Than any of her lineaments can show her.
But, mistress, know yourself. Down on your knees,
And thank heaven, fasting, for a good man's love:
For I must tell you friendly in your ear,
Sell when you can; you are not for all markets.
Cry the man mercy; love him; take his offer:
Foul is most foul, being foul to be a scoffer.
So take her to thee, shepherd. Fare you well.
PHEBE. Sweet youth, I pray you, chide a year together:
I had rather hear you chide than this man woo.
ROSALIND. He's fallen in love with her foulness, and she'll
fall in love with my anger. If it be so, as fast as she answers thee with frowning looks, I'll sauce her with bitter
words. Why look you so upon me?
PHEBE. For no ill will I bear you.
ROSALIND. I pray you, do not fall in love with me,
For I am falser than vows made in wine.
Besides, I like you not. If you will know my house,

'Tis at the tuft of olives here hard by.
Will you go, sister? Shepherd, ply her hard.
Come, sister. Shepherdess, look on him better,
And be not proud: though all the world could see,
None could be so abus'd in sight as he.
Come, to our flock. *Exeunt Rosalind, Celia, and Corin*
PHEBE. Dead shepherd, now I find thy saw of might;
'Who ever lov'd that lov'd not at first sight?'
SILVIUS. Sweet Phebe,—
PHEBE. Ha! what sayst thou, Silvius?
SILVIUS. Sweet Phebe, pity me.
PHEBE. Why, I am sorry for thee, gentle Silvius.
SILVIUS. Wherever sorrow is, relief would be:
If you do sorrow at my grief in love,
By giving love your sorrow and my grief
Were both extermin'd.
PHEBE. Thou hast my love: is not that neighbourly?
SILVIUS. I would have you.
PHEBE. Why, that were covetousness.
Silvius, the time was that I hated thee;
And yet it is not that I bear thee love:
But since that thou canst talk of love so well,
Thy company, which erst was irksome to me,
I will endure, and I 'll employ thee too;
But do not look for further recompense
Than thine own gladness that thou art employ'd.
SILVIUS. So holy and so perfect is my love,
And I in such a poverty of grace,
That I shall think it a most plenteous crop
To glean the broken ears after the man
That the main harvest reaps. Loose now and then
A scatter'd smile, and that I 'll live upon.
PHEBE. Know'st thou the youth that spoke to me erewhile?
SILVIUS. Not very well, but I have met him oft;
And he hath bought the cottage and the bounds
That the old carlot once was master of.
PHEBE. Think not I love him, though I ask for him.
'Tis but a peevish boy; yet he talks well;
But what care I for words? Yet words do well,
When he that speaks them pleases those that hear.
It is a pretty youth: not very pretty:
But sure, he 's proud; and yet his pride becomes him.

He 'll make a proper man. The best thing in him
Is his complexion; and faster than his tongue
Did make offence his eye did heal it up.
He is not very tall; yet for his years he 's tall.
His leg is but so so; and yet 'tis well.
There was a pretty redness in his lip,
A little riper and more lusty red
Than that mix'd in his cheek; 'twas just the difference
Betwixt the constant red and mingled damask.
There be some women, Silvius, had they mark'd him
In parcels as I did, would have gone near
To fall in love with him; but, for my part,
I love him not nor hate him not; and yet
Have more cause to hate him than to love him:
For what had he to do to chide at me?
He said mine eyes were black and my hair black;
And, now I am remember'd, scorn'd at me.
I marvel why I answer'd not again.
But that 's all one; omittance is no quittance.
I 'll write to him a very taunting letter,
And thou shalt bear it. Wilt thou, Silvius?
SILVIUS. Phebe, with all my heart.
PHEBE.   I 'll write it straight;
The matter 's in my head and in my heart:
I will be bitter with him and passing short.
Go with me, Silvius.   *Exeunt*

ACT FOUR

SCENE ONE

The Forest of Arden.

Enter Rosalind, Celia, and Jaques

JAQUES. I prithee, pretty youth, let me be better acquainted with thee.

ROSALIND. They say you are a melancholy fellow.

JAQUES. I am so; I do love it better than laughing.

ROSALIND. Those that are in extremity of either are abominable fellows, and betray themselves to every modern censure worse than drunkards.

JAQUES. Why, 'tis good to be sad and say nothing.

ROSALIND. Why, then, 'tis good to be a post.

JAQUES. I have neither the scholar's melancholy, which is emulation; nor the musician's, which is fantastical; nor the courtier's, which is proud; nor the soldier's, which is ambitious; nor the lawyer's, which is politic; nor the lady's, which is nice; nor the lover's, which is all these: but it is a melancholy of mine own, compounded of many simples, extracted from many objects, and indeed the sundry contemplation of my travels, which, by often rumination, wraps me in a most humorous sadness.

ROSALIND. A traveller! By my faith, you have great reason to be sad. I fear you have sold your own lands to see other men's; then, to have seen much and to have nothing, is to have rich eyes and poor hands.

JAQUES. Yes, I have gained my experience.

ROSALIND. And your experience makes you sad. I had rather have a fool to make me merry than experience to make me sad: and to travel for it too!

Enter Orlando

ORLANDO. Good day, and happiness, dear Rosalind!

JAQUES. Nay then, God be wi' you, an you talk in blank verse. *Exit*

ROSALIND. Farewell, Monsieur Traveller. Look you lisp, and wear strange suits, disable all the benefits of your own country, be out of love with your nativity, and almost chide God for making you that countenance you are; or I will scarce think you have swam in a gondola. Why, how now, Orlando! Where have you been all this while? You a lover! An you serve me such another trick, never come in my sight more.

ORLANDO. My fair Rosalind, I come within an hour of my promise.

ROSALIND. Break an hour's promise in love! He that will divide a minute into a thousand parts, and break but a part of the thousandth part of a minute in the affairs of love, it may be said of him that Cupid hath clapped him o' the shoulder, but I 'll warrant him heart-whole.

ORLANDO. Pardon me, dear Rosalind.

ROSALIND. Nay, an you be so tardy, come no more in my sight. I had as lief be wooed of a snail.

ORLANDO. Of a snail!

ROSALIND. Ay, of a snail; for though he comes slowly, he carries his house on his head; a better jointure, I think, than you make a woman. Besides, he brings his destiny with him.

ORLANDO. What 's that?

ROSALIND. Why, horns; that such as you are fain to be beholding to your wives for: but he comes armed in his fortune and prevents the slander of his wife.

ORLANDO. Virtue is no horn-maker; and my Rosalind is virtuous.

ROSALIND. And I am your Rosalind?

CELIA. It pleases him to call you so; but he hath a Rosalind of a better leer than you.

ROSALIND. Come, woo me, woo me; for now I am in a holiday humour, and like enough to consent. What would you say to me now, an I were your very very Rosalind?

ORLANDO. I would kiss before I spoke.

ROSALIND. Nay, you were better speak first, and when you were gravelled for lack of matter, you might take occasion to kiss. Very good orators, when they are out, they will spit; and for lovers lacking,—God warn us!—matter, the cleanliest shift is to kiss.

ORLANDO. How if the kiss be denied?

ROSALIND. Then she puts you to entreaty, and there begins new matter.

ORLANDO. Who could be out, being before his beloved mistress?

ROSALIND. Marry, that should you, if I were your mistress; or I should think my honesty ranker than my wit.

ORLANDO. What, of my suit?

ROSALIND. Not out of your apparel, and yet out of your suit. Am not I your Rosalind?

ORLANDO. I take some joy to say you are, because I would be talking of her.

ROSALIND. Well, in her person I say I will not have you.

ORLANDO. Then in mine own person I die.

ROSALIND. No, faith, die by attorney. The poor world is almost six thousand years old, and in all this time there was not any man died in his own person, videlicet, in a lovecause. Troilus had his brains dashed out with a Grecian club; yet he did what he could to die before, and he is one of the patterns of love. Leander, he would have lived many a fair year, though Hero had turned nun, if it had not been for a hot midsummer night; for, good youth, he went but forth to wash him in the Hellespont, and being taken with the cramp was drowned; and the foolish coroners of that age found it was 'Hero of Sestos.' But these are all lies; men have died from time to time, and worms have eaten them, but not for love.

ORLANDO. I would not have my right Rosalind of this mind; for, I protest, her frown might kill me.

ROSALIND. By this hand, it will not kill a fly. But come, now I will be your Rosalind in a more coming-on disposition; and ask me what you will, I will grant it.

ORLANDO. Then love me, Rosalind.

ROSALIND. Yes, faith will I, Fridays and Saturdays and all.

ORLANDO. And wilt thou have me?

ROSALIND. Ay, and twenty such.

ORLANDO. What sayest thou?

ROSALIND. Are you not good?

ORLANDO. I hope so.

ROSALIND. Why then, can one desire too much of a good

thing?—Come, sister, you shall be the priest and marry us.—Give me your hand, Orlando. What do you say, sister?

ORLANDO. Pray thee, marry us.

CELIA. I cannot say the words.

ROSALIND. You must begin,—'Will you, Orlando,'—

CELIA. Go to.—Will you, Orlando, have to wife this Rosalind?

ORLANDO. I will.

ROSALIND. Ay, but when?

ORLANDO. Why now; as fast as she can marry us.

ROSALIND. Then you must say, 'I take thee, Rosalind, for wife.'

ORLANDO. I take thee, Rosalind, for wife.

ROSALIND. I might ask you for your commission; but, I do take thee, Orlando, for my husband. There's a girl goes before the priest; and, certainly, a woman's thought runs before her actions.

ORLANDO. So do all thoughts; they are winged.

ROSALIND. Now tell me how long you would have her after you have possessed her?

ORLANDO. For ever and a day.

ROSALIND. Say 'a day,' without the 'ever.' No, no, Orlando; men are April when they woo, December when they wed: maids are May when they are maids, but the sky changes when they are wives. I will be more jealous of thee than a Barbary cock-pigeon over his hen; more clamorous than a parrot against rain; more new-fangled than an ape; more giddy in my desires than a monkey: I will weep for nothing, like Diana in the fountain, and I will do that when you are disposed to be merry; I will laugh like a hyen, and that when thou art inclined to sleep.

ORLANDO. But will my Rosalind do so?

ROSALIND. By my life, she will do as I do.

ORLANDO. O! but she is wise.

ROSALIND. Or else she could not have the wit to do this: the wiser, the waywarder: make the doors upon a woman's wit, and it will out at the casement; shut that, and 'twill out at the key-hole; stop that, 'twill fly with the smoke out at the chimney.

ORLANDO. A man that hath a wife with such a wit, he might say, 'Wit, whither wilt?'

ROSALIND. Nay, you might keep that check for it till you met your wife's wit going to your neighbour's bed.

ORLANDO. And what wit could wit have to excuse that?

ROSALIND. Marry, to say she came to seek you there. You shall never take her without her answer, unless you take her without her tongue. O! that woman that cannot make her fault her husband's occasion, let her never nurse her child herself, for she will breed it like a fool.

ORLANDO. For these two hours, Rosalind, I will leave thee.

ROSALIND. Alas! dear love, I cannot lack thee two hours.

ORLANDO. I must attend the duke at dinner. By two o'clock I will be with thee again.

ROSALIND. Ay, go your ways, go your ways; I knew what you would prove, my friends told me as much, and I thought no less. That flattering tongue of yours won me. 'Tis but one cast away, and so, come, death! Two o'clock is your hour?

ORLANDO. Ay, sweet Rosalind.

ROSALIND. By my troth, and in good earnest, and so God mend me, and by all pretty oaths that are not dangerous, if you break one jot of your promise or come one minute behind your hour, I will think you the most pathetical break-promise, and the most hollow lover, and the most unworthy of her you call Rosalind, that may be chosen out of the gross band of the unfaithful. Therefore, beware my censure, and keep your promise.

ORLANDO. With no less religion than if thou wert indeed my Rosalind: so, adieu.

ROSALIND. Well, Time is the old justice that examines all such offenders, and let Time try. Adieu.   *Exit Orlando*

CELIA. You have simply misused our sex in your love-prate. We must have your doublet and hose plucked over your head, and show the world what the bird hath done to her own nest.

ROSALIND. O coz, coz, coz, my pretty little coz, that thou didst know how many fathom deep I am in love! But it cannot be sounded. My affection hath an unknown bottom, like the bay of Portugal.

CELIA. Or rather, bottomless; that as fast as you pour affection in, it runs out.

ROSALIND. No; that same wicked bastard of Venus, that was begot of thought, conceived of spleen, and born of madness, that blind rascally boy that abuses every one's eyes because his own are out, let him be judge how deep I am in love. I'll tell thee, Aliena, I cannot be out of the sight of Orlando. I'll go find a shadow and sigh till he come.

CELIA. And I'll sleep. *Exeunt*

SCENE TWO

Another Part of the Forest.

Enter Jaques, Lords, and Foresters

JAQUES. Which is he that killed the deer?

FIRST LORD. Sir, it was I.

JAQUES. Let's present him to the duke, like a Roman conqueror; and it would do well to set the deer's horns upon his head for a branch of victory. Have you no song, forester, for this purpose?

SECOND LORD. Yes, sir.

JAQUES. Sing it: 'tis no matter how it be in tune so it make noise enough.

SONG

What shall he have that kill'd the deer?
His leather skin and horns to wear.
    Then sing him home.   *The rest shall bear this burden*

Take thou no scorn to wear the horn;
It was a crest ere thou wast born:
    Thy father's father wore it,
    And thy father bore it.
The horn, the horn, the lusty horn
Is not a thing to laugh to scorn.   *Exeunt*

SCENE THREE

Another Part of the Forest.

Enter Rosalind and Celia

ROSALIND. How say you now? Is it not past two o'clock?
And here much Orlando!
CELIA. I warrant you, with pure love and a troubled brain,
he hath ta'en his bow and arrows, and is gone forth to
sleep. Look, who comes here.

Enter Silvius

SILVIUS. My errand is to you, fair youth.
My gentle Phebe did bid me give you this. *Giving a letter*
I know not the contents; but, as I guess
By the stern brow and waspish action
Which she did use as she was writing of it,
It bears an angry tenour. Pardon me;
I am but as a guiltless messenger.
ROSALIND. Patience herself would startle at this letter,
And play the swaggerer. Bear this, bear all:
She says I am not fair; that I lack manners;
She calls me proud, and that she could not love me
Were man as rare as phœnix. 'Od 's my will!
Her love is not the hare that I do hunt.
Why writes she so to me? Well, shepherd, well,
This is a letter of your own device.
SILVIUS. No, I protest, I know not the contents.
Phebe did write it.
ROSALIND. Come, come, you are a fool,
And turn'd into the extremity of love.
I saw her hand: she has a leathern hand,
A freestone-colour'd hand; I verily did think
That her old gloves were on, but 'twas her hands.
She has a housewife's hand; but that 's no matter.
I say she never did invent this letter;
This is a man's invention, and his hand.
SILVIUS. Sure, it is hers.
ROSALIND. Why, 'tis a boisterous and a cruel style,
A style for challengers; why, she defies me,
Like Turk to Christian! Woman's gentle brain

Could not drop forth such giant-rude invention,
Such Ethiop words, blacker in their effect
Than in their countenance. Will you hear the letter?
SILVIUS. So please you, for I never heard it yet;
Yet heard too much of Phebe's cruelty.
ROSALIND. She Phebes me. Mark how the tyrant writes.
(*Reads*)
> 'Art thou god to shepherd turn'd,
> That a maiden's heart hath burn'd?'
Can a woman rail thus?
SILVIUS. Call you this railing?
ROSALIND. (*Reads*)
> 'Why, thy godhead laid apart,
> Warr'st thou with a woman's heart?'
Did you ever hear such railing?
> 'Whiles the eye of man did woo me,
> That could do no vengeance to me.'
Meaning me a beast.
> 'If the scorn of your bright eyne
> Have power to raise such love in mine,
> Alack! in me what strange effect
> Would they work in mild aspect.
> Whiles you chid me, I did love;
> How then might your prayers move!
> He that brings this love to thee
> Little knows this love in me;
> And by him seal up thy mind;
> Whether that thy youth and kind
> Will the faithful offer take
> Of me and all that I can make;
> Or else by him my love deny,
> And then I'll study how to die.'
SILVIUS. Call you this chiding?
CELIA. Alas, poor shepherd!
ROSALIND. Do you pity him? No, he deserves no pity. Wilt thou love such a woman? What, to make thee an instrument and play false strains upon thee! not to be endured! Well, go your way to her, for I see love hath made thee a tame snake, and say this to her: that if she love me, I charge her to love thee: if she will not, I will never have her, unless thou entreat for her. If you be a true lover, hence, and not a word, for here comes more company.
Exit Silvius

Enter Oliver

OLIVER. Good-morrow, fair ones. Pray you if you know,
  Where in the purlieus of this forest stands
  A sheepcote fenc'd about with olive-trees?
CELIA. West of this place, down in the neighbour bottom.
  The rank of osiers by the murmuring stream
  Left on your right hand brings you to the place.
  But at this hour the house doth keep itself;
  There's none within.
OLIVER. If that an eye may profit by a tongue,
  Then should I know you by description;
  Such garments, and such years: 'The boy is fair,
  Of female favour, and bestows himself
  Like a ripe sister: but the woman low,
  And browner than her brother.' Are not you
  The owner of the house I did inquire for?
CELIA. It is no boast, being ask'd, to say, we are.
OLIVER. Orlando doth commend him to you both,
  And to that youth he calls his Rosalind
  He sends this bloody napkin. Are you he?
ROSALIND. I am. What must we understand by this?
OLIVER. Some of my shame; if you will know of me
  What man I am, and how, and why, and where
  This handkercher was stain'd.
CELIA.   I pray you, tell it.
OLIVER. When last the young Orlando parted from you
  He left a promise to return again
  Within an hour; and, pacing through the forest,
  Chewing the food of sweet and bitter fancy,
  Lo, what befell! he threw his eye aside,
  And mark what object did present itself:
  Under an oak, whose boughs were moss'd with age,
  And high top bald with dry antiquity,
  A wretched ragged man, o'ergrown with hair,
  Lay sleeping on his back: about his neck
  A green and gilded snake had wreath'd itself,
  Who with her head nimble in threats approach'd
  The opening of his mouth; but suddenly,
  Seeing Orlando, it unlink'd itself,
  And with indented glides did slip away
  Into a bush; under which bush's shade
  A lioness, with udders all drawn dry,

ACT IV : SCENE III

Lay couching, head on ground, with catlike watch,
When that the sleeping man should stir; for 'tis
The royal disposition of that beast
To prey on nothing that doth seem as dead:
This seen, Orlando did approach the man,
And found it was his brother, his elder brother.

CELIA. O! I have heard him speak of that same brother;
And he did render him the most unnatural
That liv'd 'mongst men.

OLIVER. And well he might so do,
For well I know he was unnatural.

ROSALIND. But, to Orlando: did he leave him there,
Food to the suck'd and hungry lioness?

OLIVER. Twice did he turn his back and purpos'd so;
But kindness, nobler ever than revenge,
And nature, stronger than his just occasion,
Made him give battle to the lioness,
Who quickly fell before him: in which hurtling
From miserable slumber I awak'd.

CELIA. Are you his brother?

ROSALIND. Was it you he rescu'd?

CELIA. Was 't you that did so oft contrive to kill him?

OLIVER. 'Twas I; but 'tis not I. I do not shame
To tell you what I was, since my conversion
So sweetly tastes, being the thing I am.

ROSALIND. But, for the bloody napkin?

OLIVER. By and by.
When from the first to last, betwixt us two,
Tears our recountments had most kindly bath'd,
As how I came into that desert place:—
In brief, he led me to the gentle duke,
Who gave me fresh array and entertainment,
Committing me unto my brother's love;
Who led me instantly unto his cave,
There stripp'd himself; and here, upon his arm
The lioness had torn some flesh away,
Which all this while had bled; and now he fainted,
And cried, in fainting, upon Rosalind.
Brief, I recover'd him, bound up his wound;
And, after some small space, being strong at heart,
He sent me hither, stranger as I am,
To tell this story, that you might excuse

His broken promise; and to give this napkin,
Dy'd in his blood, unto the shepherd youth
That he in sport doth call his Rosalind.

CELIA. (*Rosalind swoons*) Why, how now, Ganymede! sweet Ganymede!

OLIVER. Many will swoon when they do look on blood.

CELIA. There is more in it. Cousin! Ganymede!

OLIVER. Look, he recovers.

ROSALIND. I would I were at home.

CELIA. We'll lead you thither. I pray you, will you take him by the arm?

OLIVER. Be of good cheer, youth. You a man! You lack a man's heart.

ROSALIND. I do so, I confess it. Ah, sirrah! a body would think this was well counterfeited. I pray you, tell your brother how well I counterfeited. Heigh-ho!

OLIVER. This was not counterfeit. There is too great testimony in your complexion that it was a passion of earnest.

ROSALIND. Counterfeit, I assure you.

OLIVER. Well then, take a good heart and counterfeit to be a man.

ROSALIND. So I do; but, i' faith, I should have been a woman by right.

CELIA. Come; you look paler and paler. Pray you, draw homewards. Good sir, go with us.

OLIVER. That will I, for I must bear answer back
How you excuse my brother, Rosalind.

ROSALIND. I shall devise something. But, I pray you, commend my counterfeiting to him. Will you go? *Exeunt*

ACT FIVE

SCENE ONE

The Forest of Arden.

Enter Touchstone and Audrey

TOUCHSTONE. We shall find a time, Audrey. Patience, gentle Audrey.
AUDREY. Faith, the priest was good enough, for all the old gentleman's saying.
TOUCHSTONE. A most wicked Sir Oliver, Audrey; a most vile Martext. But, Audrey, there is a youth here in the forest lays claim to you.
AUDREY. Ay, I know who 'tis. He hath no interest in me in the world. Here comes the man you mean.

Enter William

TOUCHSTONE. It is meat and drink to me to see a clown. By my troth, we that have good wits have much to answer for. We shall be flouting; we cannot hold.
WILLIAM. Good even, Audrey.
AUDREY. God ye good even, William.
WILLIAM. And good even to you, sir.
TOUCHSTONE. Good even, gentle friend. Cover thy head, cover thy head; nay, prithee, be covered. How old are you, friend?
WILLIAM. Five-and-twenty, sir.
TOUCHSTONE. A ripe age. Is thy name William?
WILLIAM. William, sir.
TOUCHSTONE. A fair name. Wast born i' the forest here?
WILLIAM. Ay, sir, I thank God.
TOUCHSTONE. 'Thank God'; a good answer. Art rich?
WILLIAM. Faith, sir, so so.
TOUCHSTONE. 'So so,' is good, very good, very excellent good: and yet it is not; it is but so so. Art thou wise?
WILLIAM. Ay, sir, I have a pretty wit.

TOUCHSTONE. Why, thou sayest well. I do now remember a saying, 'The fool doth think he is wise, but the wise man knows himself to be a fool.' The heathen philosopher, when he had a desire to eat a grape, would open his lips when he put it into his mouth; meaning thereby that grapes were made to eat and lips to open. You do love this maid?

WILLIAM. I do, sir.

TOUCHSTONE. Give me your hand. Art thou learned?

WILLIAM. No, sir.

TOUCHSTONE. Then learn this of me: to have, is to have; for it is a figure in rhetoric, that drink, being poured out of a cup into a glass, by filling the one doth empty the other; for all your writers do consent that ipse is he: now, you are not ipse, for I am he.

WILLIAM. Which he, sir?

TOUCHSTONE. He, sir, that must marry this woman. Therefore, you clown, abandon,—which is in the vulgar, leave, —the society,—which in the boorish is, company,—of this female,—which in the common is, woman; which together is, abandon the society of this female, or, clown, thou perishest; or, to thy better understanding, diest; or, to wit, I kill thee, make thee away, translate thy life into death, thy liberty into bondage. I will deal in poison with thee, or in bastinado, or in steel; I will bandy with thee in faction; I will o'errun thee with policy; I will kill thee a hundred and fifty ways: therefore tremble, and depart.

AUDREY. Do, good William.

WILLIAM. God rest you merry, sir. *Exit*

Enter Corin

CORIN. Our master and mistress seek you. Come, away, away!

TOUCHSTONE. Trip, Audrey! trip, Audrey! I attend, I attend.
Exeunt

ACT V : SCENE II

SCENE TWO

Another Part of the Forest.

Enter Orlando and Oliver

ORLANDO. Is 't possible that on so little acquaintance you should like her? that, but seeing, you should love her? and, loving, woo? and, wooing, she should grant? and will you persever to enjoy her?

OLIVER. Neither call the giddiness of it in question, the poverty of her, the small acquaintance, my sudden wooing, nor her sudden consenting; but say with me, I love Aliena; say with her that she loves me; consent with both that we may enjoy each other: it shall be to your good; for my father's house and all the revenue that was old Sir Rowland's will I estate upon you, and here live and die a shepherd.

ORLANDO. You have my consent. Let your wedding be tomorrow. Thither will I invite the duke and all 's contented followers. Go you and prepare Aliena; for, look you, here comes my Rosalind.

Enter Rosalind

ROSALIND. God save you, brother.

OLIVER. And you, fair sister. *Exit*

ROSALIND. O! my dear Orlando, how it grieves me to see thee wear thy heart in a scarf.

ORLANDO. It is my arm.

ROSALIND. I thought thy heart had been wounded with the claws of a lion.

ORLANDO. Wounded it is, but with the eyes of a lady.

ROSALIND. Did your brother tell you how I counterfeited to swound when he showed me your handkercher?

ORLANDO. Ay, and greater wonders than that.

ROSALIND. O! I know where you are. Nay, 'tis true. There was never anything so sudden but the fight of two rams, and Cæsar's thrasonical brag of 'I came, saw, and overcame': for your brother and my sister no sooner met, but they looked; no sooner looked but they loved; no sooner loved but they sighed; no sooner sighed but they asked one another the reason; no sooner knew the reason but they sought the remedy: and in these degrees have they made a pair of stairs to marriage which they will climb incontinent, or else be incontinent before marriage. They are in the very wrath of love, and they will together. Clubs cannot part them.

ORLANDO. They shall be married to-morrow, and I will bid the duke to the nuptial. But, O! how bitter a thing it is to look into happiness through another man's eyes. By so much the more shall I to-morrow be at the height of heart-heaviness, by how much I shall think my brother happy in having what he wishes for.

ROSALIND. Why then, to-morrow I cannot serve your turn for Rosalind?

ORLANDO. I can live no longer by thinking.

ROSALIND. I will weary you then no longer with idle talking. Know of me then,—for now I speak to some purpose,—that I know you are a gentleman of good conceit. I speak not this that you should bear a good opinion of my knowledge, insomuch I say I know you are; neither do I labour for a greater esteem than may in some little measure draw a belief from you, to do yourself good, and not to grace me. Believe then, if you please, that I can do strange things. I have, since I was three years old, conversed with a magician, most profound in his art and yet not damnable. If you do love Rosalind so near the heart as your gesture cries it out, when your brother marries Aliena, shall you marry her. I know into what straits of fortune she is driven; and it is not impossible to me, if it appear not inconvenient to you, to set her before your eyes to-morrow, human as she is, and without any danger.

ORLANDO. Speakest thou in sober meanings?

ROSALIND. By my life, I do; which I tender dearly, though I say I am a magician. Therefore, put you in your best array; bid your friends; for if you will be married to-morrow, you shall; and to Rosalind, if you will. Look, here comes a lover of mine, and a lover of hers.

Enter Silvius and Phebe

PHEBE. Youth, you have done me much ungentleness,
To show the letter that I writ to you.

ROSALIND. I care not if I have: it is my study
To seem despiteful and ungentle to you.
You are there follow'd by a faithful shepherd.
Look upon him, love him; he worships you.

PHEBE. Good shepherd, tell this youth what 'tis to love.
SILVIUS. It is to be all made of sighs and tears;
And so am I for Phebe.
PHEBE. And I for Ganymede.
ORLANDO. And I for Rosalind.
ROSALIND. And I for no woman.
SILVIUS. It is to be all made of faith and service;
And so am I for Phebe.
PHEBE. And I for Ganymede.
ORLANDO. And I for Rosalind.
ROSALIND. And I for no woman.
SILVIUS. It is to be all made of fantasy,
All made of passion, and all made of wishes;
All adoration, duty, and observance;
All humbleness, all patience, and impatience;
All purity, all trial, all obeisance;
And so am I for Phebe.
PHEBE. And so am I for Ganymede.
ORLANDO. And so am I for Rosalind.
ROSALIND. And so am I for no woman.
PHEBE. (*To Rosalind*) If this be so, why blame you me to love you?
SILVIUS. (*To Phebe*) If this be so, why blame you me to love you?
ORLANDO. If this be so, why blame you me to love you?
ROSALIND. Who do you speak to, 'Why blame you me to love you'?
ORLANDO. To her that is not here, nor doth not hear.
ROSALIND. Pray you, no more of this: 'tis like the howling of Irish wolves against the moon. (*To Silvius*) I will help you, if I can. (*To Phebe*) I would love you, if I could. To-morrow meet me all together. (*To Phebe*) I will marry you, if ever I marry woman, and I'll be married to-morrow. (*To Orlando*) I will satisfy you, if ever I satisfied man, and you shall be married to-morrow. (*To Silvius*) I will content you, if what pleases you contents you, and you shall be married to-morrow. (*To Orlando*) As you love Rosalind, meet. (*To Silvius*) As you love Phebe, meet: and as I love no woman, I'll meet. So, fare you well. I have left you commands.
SILVIUS. I'll not fail, if I live.
PHEBE. Nor I.
ORLANDO. Nor I. *Exeunt*

SCENE THREE

Another Part of the Forest.

Enter Touchstone and Audrey

TOUCHSTONE. To-morrow is the joyful day, Audrey; to-morrow will we be married.

AUDREY. I do desire it with all my heart, and I hope it is no dishonest desire to desire to be a woman of the world. Here come two of the banished duke's pages.

Enter two Pages

FIRST PAGE. Well met, honest gentleman.

TOUCHSTONE. By my troth, well met. Come, sit, sit, and a song.

SECOND PAGE. We are for you: sit i' the middle.

FIRST PAGE. Shall we clap into 't roundly, without hawking or spitting, or saying we are hoarse, which are the only prologues to a bad voice?

SECOND PAGE. I' faith, i' faith; and both in a tune, like two gipsies on a horse.

SONG

    It was a lover and his lass,
        With a hey, and a ho, and a hey nonino,
    That o'er the green corn-field did pass,
        In the spring time, the only pretty ring time,
    When birds do sing, hey ding a ding, ding;
    Sweet lovers love the spring.
    Between the acres of the rye,
        With a hey, and a ho, and a hey nonino,
    These pretty country folks would lie,
        In the spring time, &c.
    This carol they began that hour,
        With a hey, and a ho, and a hey nonino,
    How that a life was but a flower
        In the spring time, &c.
    And therefore take the present time,
        With a hey, and a ho, and a hey nonino;
    For love is crowned with the prime
        In the spring time, &c.

ACT V : SCENE III

TOUCHSTONE. Truly, young gentlemen, though there was no great matter in the ditty, yet the note was very untuneable.

FIRST PAGE. You are deceived, sir. We kept time; we lost not our time.

TOUCHSTONE. By my troth, yes; I count it but time lost to hear such a foolish song. God be wi' you; and God mend your voices! Come, Audrey. *Exeunt*

SCENE FOUR

Another Part of the Forest.

Enter Duke Senior, Amiens, Jaques, Orlando, Oliver, and Celia

DUKE SENIOR. Dost thou believe, Orlando, that the boy
Can do all this that he hath promised?

ORLANDO. I sometimes do believe, and sometimes do not;
As those that fear they hope, and know they fear.

Enter Rosalind, Silvius, and Phebe

ROSALIND. Patience once more, whiles our compact is urg'd.
(*To the Duke*) You say, if I bring in your Rosalind,
You will bestow her on Orlando here?

DUKE SENIOR. That would I, had I kingdoms to give with her.

ROSALIND. (*To Orlando*) And you say, you will have her when I bring her?

ORLANDO. That would I, were I of all kingdoms king.

ROSALIND. (*To Phebe*) You say, that you'll marry me, if I be willing?

PHEBE. That will I, should I die the hour after.

ROSALIND. But if you do refuse to marry me,
You'll give yourself to this most faithful shepherd?

PHEBE. So is the bargain.

ROSALIND. (*To Silvius*) You say, that you'll have Phebe, if she will?

SILVIUS. Though to have her and death were both one thing.

ROSALIND. I have promis'd to make all this matter even.
Keep you your word, O duke, to give your daughter;
You yours, Orlando, to receive his daughter;
Keep your word, Phebe, that you'll marry me,

Or else, refusing me, to wed this shepherd;
Keep your word, Silvius, that you 'll marry her,
If she refuse me: and from hence I go,
To make these doubts all even. *Exeunt Rosalind and Celia*

DUKE SENIOR. I do remember in this shepherd boy
Some lively touches of my daughter's favour.

ORLANDO. My lord, the first time that I ever saw him,
Methought he was a brother to your daughter;
But, my good lord, this boy is forest-born,
And hath been tutor'd in the rudiments
Of many desperate studies by his uncle,
Whom he reports to be a great magician,
Obscured in the circle of this forest.

Enter Touchstone and Audrey

JAQUES. There is, sure, another flood toward, and these couples are coming to the ark. Here comes a pair of very strange beasts, which in all tongues are called fools.

TOUCHSTONE. Salutation and greeting to you all!

JAQUES. Good my lord, bid him welcome. This is the motley-minded gentleman that I have so often met in the forest. He hath been a courtier, he swears.

TOUCHSTONE. If any man doubt that, let him put me to my purgation. I have trod a measure; I have flattered a lady; I have been politic with my friend, smooth with mine enemy; I have undone three tailors; I have had four quarrels, and like to have fought one.

JAQUES. And how was that ta'en up?

TOUCHSTONE. Faith, we met, and found the quarrel was upon the seventh cause.

JAQUES. How seventh cause? Good my lord, like this fellow.

DUKE SENIOR. I like him very well.

TOUCHSTONE. God 'ild you, sir; I desire you of the like. I press in here, sir, amongst the rest of the country copulatives, to swear, and to forswear, according as marriage binds and blood breaks. A poor virgin, sir, an ill-favoured thing, sir, but mine own: a poor humour of mine, sir, to take that that no man else will. Rich honesty dwells like a miser, sir, in a poor house, as your pearl in your foul oyster.

DUKE SENIOR. By my faith, he is very swift and sententious.

TOUCHSTONE. According to the fool's bolt, sir, and such dulcet diseases.

ACT V : SCENE IV

JAQUES. But, for the seventh cause; how did you find the quarrel on the seventh cause?

TOUCHSTONE. Upon a lie seven times removed:—bear your body more seeming, Audrey:—as thus, sir. I did dislike the cut of a certain courtier's beard: he sent me word, if I said his beard was not cut well, he was in the mind it was: this is called 'the retort courteous.' If I sent him word again, it was not well cut, he would send me word, he cut it to please himself: this is called the 'quip modest.' If again, it was not well cut, he disabled my judgment: this is called the 'reply churlish.' If again, it was not well cut, he would answer, I spake not true: this is called the 'reproof valiant': if again, it was not well cut, he would say, I lie: this is called the 'countercheck quarrelsome': and so to the 'lie circumstantial,' and the 'lie direct.'

JAQUES. And how oft did you say his beard was not well cut?

TOUCHSTONE. I durst go no further than the 'lie circumstantial,' nor he durst not give me the 'lie direct': and so we measured swords and parted.

JAQUES. Can you nominate in order now the degrees of the lie?

TOUCHSTONE. O sir, we quarrel in print; by the book, as you have books for good manners: I will name you the degrees. The first, the 'retort courteous'; the second, the 'quip modest'; the third, the 'reply churlish'; the fourth, the 'reproof valiant'; the fifth, the 'countercheck quarrelsome'; the sixth, the 'lie with circumstance'; the seventh, the 'lie direct.' All these you may avoid but the lie direct; and you may avoid that too, with an 'if.' I knew when seven justices could not take up a quarrel; but when the parties were met themselves, one of them thought but of an 'if,' as 'If you said so, then I said so'; and they shook hands and swore brothers. Your 'if' is the only peacemaker; much virtue in 'if.'

JAQUES. Is not this a rare fellow, my lord? He 's as good at any thing, and yet a fool.

DUKE SENIOR. He uses his folly like a stalking-horse, and under the presentation of that he shoots his wit.

Enter Hymen, leading Rosalind in woman's clothes, and Celia
Still Music

HYMEN.   Then is there mirth in heaven,
                When earthly things made even
                    Atone together.
              Good duke, receive thy daughter;
                Hymen from heaven brought her;
                    Yea, brought her hither,
              That thou mightst join her hand with his,
                Whose heart within her bosom is.

ROSALIND. *(To Duke Senior)* To you I give myself, for I am yours.

(To Orlando) To you I give myself, for I am yours.

DUKE SENIOR. If there be truth in sight, you are my daughter.

ORLANDO. If there be truth in sight, you are my Rosalind.

PHEBE. If sight and shape be true,
Why then, my love adieu!

ROSALIND. *(To Duke Senior)* I 'll have no father, if you be not he.

(To Orlando) I 'll have no husband, if you be not he.

(To Phebe) Nor ne'er wed woman, if you be not she.

HYMEN.   Peace, ho, ho! I bar confusion:
                'Tis I must make conclusion
                    Of these most strange events:
              Here 's eight that must take hands
                To join in Hymen's bands,
                    If truth holds true contents.

(To Orlando and Rosalind) You and you no cross shall part.

(To Oliver and Celia) You and you are heart in heart.

(To Phebe) You to his love must accord,
Or have a woman to your lord:

(To Touchstone and Audrey) You and you are sure together,
As the winter to foul weather.
Whiles a wedlock hymn we sing,
Feed yourselves with questioning,
That reason wonder may diminish,
How thus we met, and these things finish.

SONG

Wedding is great Juno's crown:
    O blessed bond of board and bed!
'Tis Hymen peoples every town;
    High wedlock then be honoured.

Honour, high honour, and renown,
To Hymen, god of every town!
DUKE SENIOR. O my dear niece! welcome thou art to me.
Even daughter, welcome in no less degree.
PHEBE. (*To Silvius*) I will not eat my word, now thou art mine;
Thy faith my fancy to thee doth combine.

Enter Jaques de Boys

JAQUES DE BOYS. Let me have audience for a word or two:
I am the second son of old Sir Rowland,
That bring these tidings to this fair assembly.
Duke Frederick, hearing how that every day
Men of great worth resorted to this forest,
Address'd a mighty power, which were on foot
In his own conduct, purposely to take
His brother here and put him to the sword:
And to the skirts of this wild wood he came,
Where, meeting with an old religious man,
After some question with him, was converted
Both from his enterprise and from the world;
His crown bequeathing to his banish'd brother,
And all their lands restor'd to them again
That were with him exil'd. This to be true,
I do engage my life.
DUKE SENIOR.   Welcome, young man;
Thou offer'st fairly to thy brothers' wedding:
To one, his lands withheld; and to the other
A land itself at large, a potent dukedom.
First, in this forest, let us do those ends
That here were well begun and well begot;
And after, every of this happy number
That have endur'd shrewd days and nights with us,
Shall share the good of our returned fortune,
According to the measure of their states.
Meantime, forget this new-fall'n dignity,
And fall into our rustic revelry.
Play, music! and you, brides and bridegrooms all,
With measure heap'd in joy, to the measures fall.
JAQUES. Sir, by your patience. If I heard you rightly,
The duke hath put on a religious life,
And thrown into neglect the pompous court?
JAQUES DE BOYS. He hath.

JAQUES. To him will I. Out of these convertites
   There is much matter to be heard and learn'd.
   (*To Duke Senior*) You to your former honour I bequeath;
   Your patience and your virtue well deserve it.
   (*To Orlando*) You to a love that your true faith doth merit:
   (*To Oliver*) You to your land, and love, and great allies:
   (*To Silvius*) You to a long and well-deserved bed:
   (*To Touchstone*) And you to wrangling; for thy loving voyage
   Is but for two months victual'd. So, to your pleasures!
   I am for other than for dancing measures.
DUKE SENIOR. Stay, Jaques, stay.
JAQUES. To see no pastime, I! What you would have
   I'll stay to know at your abandon'd cave.   *Exit*
DUKE SENIOR. Proceed, proceed. We will begin these rites,
   As we do trust they'll end, in true delights.
                              A dance. Exeunt

EPILOGUE

Spoken by Rosalind

It is not the fashion to see the lady the epilogue; but it is no more unhandsome than to see the lord the prologue. If it be true that good wine needs no bush, 'tis true that a good play needs no epilogue; yet to good wine they do use good bushes, and good plays prove the better by the help of good epilogues. What a case am I in then, that am neither a good epilogue, nor cannot insinuate with you in the behalf of a good play! I am not furnished like a beggar, therefore to beg will not become me. My way is, to conjure you; and I'll begin with the women. I charge you, O women! for the love you bear to men, to like as much of this play as please you: and I charge you, O men! for the love you bear to women,—as I perceive by your simpering none of you hate them,—that between you and the women, the play may please. If I were a woman I would kiss as many of you as had beards that pleased me, complexions that liked me, and breaths that I defied not; and, I am sure, as many as have good beards, or good faces, or sweet breaths, will, for my kind offer, when I make curtsy, bid me farewell.   *Exeunt*

THE TAMING OF THE SHREW

CAST OF CHARACTERS

A Lord

CHRISTOPHER SLY, *a Tinker*
Hostess, Page, Players, Huntsmen, and Servants
} *Persons in the Induction*

BAPTISTA, *a rich Gentleman of Padua*
VINCENTIO, *an old Gentleman of Pisa*
LUCENTIO, *son to Vincentio; in love with Bianca*
PETRÚCHIO, *a Gentleman of Verona; Suitor to Katharina*

GREMIO
HORTENSIO
} *Suitors to Bianca*

TRANIO
BIONDELLO
} *Servants to Lucentio*

GRUMIO
CURTIS
} *Servants to Petruchio*

Pedant, set up to personate Vincentio

KATHARINA, *the Shrew*
BIANCA
} *Daughters to Baptista*

Widow

Tailor, Haberdasher, and Servants attending on Baptista and Petruchio

SCENE

Padua; and in Petruchio's House in the Country

THE TAMING OF THE SHREW

INDUCTION

SCENE ONE

Before an Alehouse on a Heath.

Enter Hostess and Sly

SLY. I'll pheeze you, in faith.

HOSTESS. A pair of stocks, you rogue!

SLY. Y' are a baggage: the Slys are no rogues; look in the chronicles; we came in with Richard Conqueror. Therefore, paucas pallabris; let the world slide. Sessa!

HOSTESS. You will not pay for the glasses you have burst?

SLY. No, not a denier. Go by, Jeronimy, go to thy cold bed, and warm thee.

HOSTESS. I know my remedy: I must go fetch the thirdborough. *Exit*

SLY. Third, or fourth, or fifth borough, I'll answer him by law. I'll not budge an inch, boy: let him come, and kindly.
     Lies down on the ground, and falls asleep
     Horns winded. Enter a
 Lord from hunting, with Huntsmen and Servants

LORD. Huntsman, I charge thee, tender well my hounds:
Brach Merriman, the poor cur is emboss'd,
And couple Clowder with the deep-mouth'd brach.
Saw'st thou not, boy, how Silver made it good
At the hedge-corner, in the coldest fault?
I would not lose the dog for twenty pound.

FIRST HUNTSMAN. Why, Bellman is as good as he, my lord;
He cried upon it at the merest loss,
And twice to-day pick'd out the dullest scent:
Trust me, I take him for the better dog.

LORD. Thou art a fool: if Echo were as fleet,

I would esteem him worth a dozen such.
But sup them well, and look unto them all:
To-morrow I intend to hunt again.

FIRST HUNTSMAN. I will, my lord.

LORD. (*Sees Sly*) What's here? one dead, or drunk? See,
doth he breathe?

SECOND HUNTSMAN. He breathes, my lord. Were he not
warm'd with ale,
This were a bed but cold to sleep so soundly.

LORD. O monstrous beast! how like a swine he lies!
Grim death, how foul and loathsome is thine image!
Sirs, I will practise on this drunken man.
What think you, if he were convey'd to bed,
Wrapp'd in sweet clothes, rings put upon his fingers,
A most delicious banquet by his bed,
And brave attendants near him when he wakes,
Would not the beggar then forget himself?

FIRST HUNTSMAN. Believe me, lord, I think he cannot choose.

SECOND HUNTSMAN. It would seem strange unto him when
he wak'd.

LORD. Even as a flattering dream or worthless fancy.
Then take him up and manage well the jest.
Carry him gently to my fairest chamber,
And hang it round with all my wanton pictures;
Balm his foul head in warm distilled waters,
And burn sweet wood to make the lodging sweet.
Procure me music ready when he wakes,
To make a dulcet and a heavenly sound;
And if he chance to speak, be ready straight,
And with a low submissive reverence
Say, 'What is it your honour will command?'
Let one attend him with a silver basin
Full of rose-water, and bestrew'd with flowers;
Another bear the ewer, the third a diaper,
And say, 'Will't please your lordship cool your hands?'
Some one be ready with a costly suit,
And ask him what apparel he will wear;
Another tell him of his hounds and horse,
And that his lady mourns at his disease.
Persuade him that he hath been lunatic;
And, when he says he is——say that he dreams,
For he is nothing but a mighty lord.

This do, and do it kindly, gentle sirs:
It will be pastime passing excellent,
If it be husbanded with modesty.

FIRST HUNTSMAN. My lord, I warrant you we will play our part,
As he shall think, by our true diligence,
He is no less than what we say he is.

LORD. Take him up gently, and to bed with him,
And each one to his office when he wakes.

Sly is borne out. A trumpet sounds

Sirrah, go see what trumpet 'tis that sounds: *Exit Servant*
Belike, some noble gentleman that means,
Travelling some journey, to repose him here.

Re-enter Servant

How now! who is it?

SERVANT. An it please your honour,
Players that offer service to your lordship.

LORD. Bid them come near.

Enter Players

Now, fellows, you are welcome.

PLAYERS. We thank your honour.

LORD. Do you intend to stay with me to-night?

A PLAYER. So please your lordship to accept our duty.

LORD. With all my heart. This fellow I remember,
Since once he play'd a farmer's eldest son:
'Twas where you woo'd the gentlewoman so well.
I have forgot your name; but, sure, that part
Was aptly fitted and naturally perform'd.

A PLAYER. I think 'twas Soto that your honour means.

LORD. 'Tis very true: thou didst it excellent.
Well, you are come to me in happy time,
The rather for I have some sport in hand
Wherein your cunning can assist me much.
There is a lord will hear you play to-night;
But I am doubtful of your modesties,
Lest, over-eyeing of his odd behaviour,—
For yet his honour never heard a play,—
You break into some merry passion
And so offend him; for I tell you, sirs,
If you should smile he grows impatient.

A PLAYER. Fear not, my lord: we can contain ourselves
Were he the veriest antick in the world.

LORD. Go, sirrah, take them to the buttery,
And give them friendly welcome every one:
Let them want nothing that my house affords.

Exeunt one with the Players

Sirrah, go you to Barthol'mew my page,
And see him dress'd in all suits like a lady:
That done, conduct him to the drunkard's chamber;
And call him 'madam,' do him obeisance.
Tell him from me,—as he will win my love,—
He bear himself with honourable action,
Such as he hath observ'd in noble ladies
Unto their lords, by them accomplished:
Such duty to the drunkard let him do
With soft low tongue and lowly courtesy;
And say, 'What is 't your honour will command,
Wherein your lady and your humble wife
May show her duty, and make known her love?'
And then, with kind embracements, tempting kisses,
And with declining head into his bosom,
Bid him shed tears, as being overjoy'd
To see her noble lord restor'd to health,
Who for this seven years hath esteemed him
No better than a poor and loathsome beggar.
And if the boy have not a woman's gift
To rain a shower of commanded tears,
An onion will do well for such a shift,
Which in a napkin being close convey'd,
Shall in despite enforce a watery eye.
See this dispatch'd with all the haste thou canst:
Anon I'll give thee more instructions. *Exit Servant*
I know the boy will well usurp the grace,
Voice, gait, and action of a gentlewoman:
I long to hear him call the drunkard husband,
And how my men will stay themselves from laughter
When they do homage to this simple peasant.
I'll in to counsel them: haply, my presence
May well abate the over merry spleen
Which otherwise would grow into extremes. *Exeunt*

SCENE TWO

A Bedchamber in the Lord's House.

Sly is discovered in a rich nightgown, with Attendants: some with apparel, others with basin, ewer, and other appurtenances; and Lord, dressed like a servant

SLY. For God's sake! a pot of small ale.

FIRST SERVANT. Will 't please your lordship drink a cup of sack?

SECOND SERVANT. Will 't please your honour taste of these conserves?

THIRD SERVANT. What raiment will your honour wear to-day?

SLY. I am Christophero Sly; call not me honour, nor lordship: I ne'er drank sack in my life; and if you give me any conserves, give me conserves of beef. Ne'er ask me what raiment I 'll wear, for I have no more doublets than backs, no more stockings than legs, nor no more shoes than feet: nay, sometime more feet than shoes, or such shoes as my toes look through the over-leather.

LORD. Heaven cease this idle humour in your honour!
O, that a mighty man, of such descent,
Of such possessions, and so high esteem,
Should be infused with so foul a spirit!

SLY. What! would you make me mad? Am not I Christopher Sly, old Sly's son, of Burton-heath; by birth a pedlar, by education a card-maker, by transmutation a bear-herd, and now by present profession a tinker? Ask Marian Hacket, the fat ale-wife of Wincot, if she know me not: if she say I am not fourteen pence on the score for sheer ale, score me up for the lyingest knave in Christendom. What! I am not bestraught: here 's—

FIRST SERVANT. O! this it is that makes your lady mourn.

SECOND SERVANT. O! this it is that makes your servants droop.

LORD. Hence comes it that your kindred shuns your house,
As beaten hence by your strange lunacy.
O noble lord, bethink thee of thy birth,
Call home thy ancient thoughts from banishment,
And banish hence these abject lowly dreams.

Look how thy servants do attend on thee,
Each in his office ready at thy beck:
Wilt thou have music? hark! Apollo plays, *Music*
And twenty caged nightingales do sing:
Or wilt thou sleep? We 'll have thee to a couch
Softer and sweeter than the lustful bed
On purpose trimm'd up for Semiramis.
Say thou wilt walk, we will bestrew the ground:
Or wilt thou ride? Thy horses shall be trapp'd,
Their harness studded all with gold and pearl.
Dost thou love hawking? Thou hast hawks will soar
Above the morning lark: or wilt thou hunt?
Thy hounds shall make the welkin answer them,
And fetch shrill echoes from the hollow earth.

FIRST SERVANT. Say thou wilt course; thy greyhounds are as swift
As breathed stags, ay, fleeter than the roe.

SECOND SERVANT. Dost thou love pictures? we will fetch thee straight
Adonis painted by a running brook,
And Cytherea all in sedges hid,
Which seem to move and wanton with her breath,
Even as the waving sedges play with wind.

LORD. We 'll show thee Io as she was a maid,
And how she was beguiled and surpris'd,
As lively painted as the deed was done.

THIRD SERVANT. Or Daphne roaming through a thorny wood,
Scratching her legs that one shall swear she bleeds;
And at that sight shall sad Apollo weep,
So workmanly the blood and tears are drawn.

LORD. Thou art a lord and nothing but a lord:
Thou hast a lady far more beautiful
Than any woman in this waning age.

FIRST SERVANT. And till the tears that she hath shed for thee
Like envious floods o'er-run her lovely face,
She was the fairest creature in the world;
And yet she is inferior to none.

SLY. Am I a lord? and have I such a lady?
Or do I dream? or have I dream'd till now?
I do not sleep; I see, I hear, I speak;
I smell sweet savours, and I feel soft things:
Upon my life, I am a lord indeed;

And not a tinker, nor Christophero Sly.
Well, bring our lady hither to our sight;
And once again, a pot o' the smallest ale.
SECOND SERVANT. Will 't please your mightiness to wash
your hands? *Servants present a ewer, basin, and napkin*
O, how we joy to see your wit restor'd!
O, that once more you knew but what you are!
These fifteen years you have been in a dream,
Or, when you wak'd, so wak'd as if you slept.
SLY. These fifteen years! by my fay, a goodly nap.
But did I never speak of all that time?
FIRST SERVANT. O! yes, my lord, but very idle words;
For though you lay here in this goodly chamber,
Yet would you say ye were beaten out of door,
And rail upon the hostess of the house,
And say you would present her at the leet,
Because she brought stone jugs and no seal'd quarts.
Sometimes you would call out for Cicely Hacket.
SLY. Ay, the woman's maid of the house.
THIRD SERVANT. Why, sir, you know no house, nor no such maid,
Nor no such men as you have reckon'd up,
As Stephen Sly, and old John Naps of Greece,
And Peter Turf, and Henry Pimpernell,
And twenty more such names and men as these,
Which never were nor no man ever saw.
SLY. Now, Lord be thanked for my good amends!
ALL. Amen.
SLY. I thank thee; thou shalt not lose by it.
Enter the Page, as a lady, with Attendants
PAGE. How fares my noble lord?
SLY. Marry, I fare well, for here is cheer enough.
Where is my wife?
PAGE. Here, noble lord: what is thy will with her?
SLY. Are you my wife, and will not call me husband?
My men should call me lord: I am your goodman.
PAGE. My husband and my lord, my lord and husband;
I am your wife in all obedience.
SLY. I know it well. What must I call her?
LORD. Madam.
SLY. Al'ce madam, or Joan madam?
LORD. Madam, and nothing else: so lords call ladies.

SLY. Madam wife, they say that I have dream'd
And slept above some fifteen year or more.
PAGE. Ay, and the time seems thirty unto me,
Being all this time abandon'd from your bed.
SLY. 'Tis much. Servants, leave me and her alone.
Madam, undress you, and come now to bed.
PAGE. Thrice noble lord, let me entreat of you
To pardon me yet for a night or two,
Or, if not so, until the sun be set:
For your physicians have expressly charg'd,
In peril to incur your former malady,
That I should yet absent me from your bed:
I hope this reason stands for my excuse.
SLY. Ay, it stands so, that I may hardly tarry so long; but I would be loath to fall into my dreams again: I will therefore tarry, in spite of the flesh and the blood.

Enter a Servant

SERVANT. Your honour's players, hearing your amendment,
Are come to play a pleasant comedy;
For so your doctors hold it very meet,
Seeing too much sadness hath congeal'd your blood,
And melancholy is the nurse of frenzy:
Therefore they thought it good you hear a play,
And frame your mind to mirth and merriment,
Which bars a thousand harms and lengthens life.
SLY. Marry, I will; let them play it. Is not a commonty a Christmas gambold or a tumbling-trick?
PAGE. No, my good lord; it is more pleasing stuff.
SLY. What! household stuff?
PAGE. It is a kind of history.
SLY. Well, we'll see 't. Come, madam wife, sit by my side,
And let the world slip: we shall ne'er be younger.

Flourish

ACT ONE

SCENE ONE

Padua. A public Place.

Enter Lucentio and Tranio

LUCENTIO. Tranio, since for the great desire I had
To see fair Padua, nursery of arts,
I am arriv'd for fruitful Lombardy,
The pleasant garden of great Italy;
And by my father's love and leave am arm'd
With his good will and thy good company,
My trusty servant well approv'd in all,
Here let us breathe, and haply institute
A course of learning and ingenious studies.
Pisa, renowned for grave citizens,
Gave me my being and my father first,
A merchant of great traffic through the world,
Vincentio, come of the Bentivolii.
Vincentio's son, brought up in Florence,
It shall become to serve all hopes conceiv'd,
To deck his fortune with his virtuous deeds:
And therefore, Tranio, for the time I study,
Virtue and that part of philosophy
Will I apply that treats of happiness
By virtue specially to be achiev'd.
Tell me thy mind; for I have Pisa left
And am to Padua come, as he that leaves
A shallow plash to plunge him in the deep,
And with satiety seeks to quench his thirst.
TRANIO. Mi perdonate, gentle master mine,
I am in all affected as yourself,
Glad that you thus continue your resolve
To suck the sweets of sweet philosophy.
Only, good master, while we do admire

This virtue and this moral discipline,
Let 's be no stoics nor no stocks, I pray;
Or so devote to Aristotle's checks
As Ovid be an outcast quite abjur'd.
Balk logic with acquaintance that you have,
And practise rhetoric in your common talk;
Music and poesy use to quicken you;
The mathematics and the metaphysics,
Fall to them as you find your stomach serves you:
No profit grows where is no pleasure ta'en;
In brief, sir, study what you most affect.

LUCENTIO. Gramercies, Tranio, well dost thou advise.
If, Biondello, thou wert come ashore,
We could at once put us in readiness,
And take a lodging fit to entertain
Such friends as time in Padua shall beget.
But stay awhile: what company is this?

TRANIO. Master, some show to welcome us to town.

*Enter Baptista, Katharina, Bianca,
Gremio, and Hortensio. Lucentio and Tranio stand aside*

BAPTISTA. Gentlemen, importune me no further,
For how I firmly am resolv'd you know;
That is, not to bestow my youngest daughter
Before I have a husband for the elder.
If either of you both love Katharina,
Because I know you well and love you well,
Leave shall you have to court her at your pleasure.

GREMIO. To cart her rather: she 's too rough for me.
There, there, Hortensio, will you any wife?

KATHARINA. (*To Baptista*) I pray you, sir, is it your will
To make a stale of me amongst these mates?

HORTENSIO. Mates, maid! how mean you that? no mates for you,
Unless you were of gentler, milder mould.

KATHARINA. I' faith, sir, you shall never need to fear:
I wis it is not half way to her heart;
But if it were, doubt not her care should be
To comb your noddle with a three-legg'd stool,
And paint your face, and use you like a fool.

HORTENSIO. From all such devils, good Lord deliver us!

GREMIO. And me too, good Lord!

TRANIO. Hush, master! here is some good pastime toward:

That wench is stark mad or wonderful froward.
LUCENTIO. But in the other's silence do I see
Maid's mild behaviour and sobriety.
Peace, Tranio!
TRANIO. Well said, master; mum! and gaze your fill.
BAPTISTA. Gentlemen, that I may soon make good
What I have said,—Bianca, get you in:
And let it not displease thee, good Bianca,
For I will love thee ne'er the less, my girl.
KATHARINA. A pretty peat! it is best
Put finger in the eye, an she knew why.
BIANCA. Sister, content you in my discontent.
Sir, to your pleasure humbly I subscribe:
My books and instruments shall be my company,
On them to look and practise by myself.
LUCENTIO. Hark, Tranio! thou mayst hear Minerva speak.
HORTENSIO. Signior Baptista, will you be so strange?
Sorry am I that our good will effects
Bianca's grief.
GREMIO.   Why will you mew her up,
Signior Baptista, for this fiend of hell,
And make her bear the penance of her tongue?
BAPTISTA. Gentlemen, content ye; I am resolv'd.
Go in, Bianca.   *Exit Bianca*
And for I know she taketh most delight
In music, instruments, and poetry,
Schoolmasters will I keep within my house,
Fit to instruct her youth. If you, Hortensio,
Or Signior Gremio, you, know any such,
Prefer them hither; for to cunning men
I will be very kind, and liberal
To mine own children in good bringing up.
And so, farewell. Katharina, you may stay;
For I have more to commune with Bianca.   *Exit*
KATHARINA. Why, and I trust I may go too; may I not?
What! shall I be appointed hours, as though, belike,
I knew not what to take, and what to leave? Ha!   *Exit*
GREMIO. You may go to the devil's dam: your gifts are so
good, here's none will hold you. Their love is not so great,
Hortensio, but we may blow our nails together, and fast it
fairly out: our cake's dough on both sides. Farewell: yet,
for the love I bear my sweet Bianca, if I can by any means

light on a fit man to teach her that wherein she delights, I will wish him to her father.

HORTENSIO. So will I, Signior Gremio: but a word, I pray. Though the nature of our quarrel yet never brooked parle, know now, upon advice, it toucheth us both,—that we may yet again have access to our fair mistress and be happy rivals in Bianca's love,—to labour and effect one thing specially.

GREMIO. What's that, I pray?

HORTENSIO. Marry, sir, to get a husband for her sister.

GREMIO. A husband! a devil.

HORTENSIO. I say, a husband.

GREMIO. I say, a devil. Thinkest thou, Hortensio, though her father be very rich, any man is so very a fool to be married to hell?

HORTENSIO. Tush, Gremio! though it pass your patience and mine to endure her loud alarums, why, man, there be good fellows in the world, an a man could light on them, would take her with all faults, and money enough.

GREMIO. I cannot tell; but I had as lief take her dowry with this condition, to be whipped at the high-cross every morning.

HORTENSIO. Faith, as you say, there's small choice in rotten apples. But, come; since this bar in law makes us friends, it shall be so far forth friendly maintained, till by helping Baptista's eldest daughter to a husband, we set his youngest free for a husband, and then have to 't afresh. Sweet Bianca! Happy man be his dole! He that runs fastest gets the ring. How say you, Signior Gremio?

GREMIO. I am agreed: and would I had given him the best horse in Padua to begin his wooing, that would thoroughly woo her, wed her, and bed her, and rid the house of her. Come on. *Exeunt Gremio and Hortensio*

TRANIO. I pray, sir, tell me, is it possible
That love should of a sudden take such hold?

LUCENTIO. O Tranio! till I found it to be true,
I never thought it possible or likely;
But see, while idly I stood looking on,
I found the effect of love in idleness;
And now in plainness do confess to thee,
That art to me as secret and as dear
As Anna to the Queen of Carthage was,

Tranio, I burn, I pine, I perish, Tranio,
If I achieve not this young modest girl.
Counsel me, Tranio, for I know thou canst:
Assist me, Tranio, for I know thou wilt.
TRANIO. Master, it is no time to chide you now;
Affection is not rated from the heart:
If love have touch'd you, nought remains but so,
Redime te captum, quam queas minimo.
LUCENTIO. Gramercies, lad; go forward: this contents:
The rest will comfort, for thy counsel's sound.
TRANIO. Master, you look'd so longly on the maid,
Perhaps you mark'd not what's the pith of all.
LUCENTIO. O yes, I saw sweet beauty in her face,
Such as the daughter of Agenor had,
That made great Jove to humble him to her hand,
When with his knees he kiss'd the Cretan strand.
TRANIO. Saw you no more? Mark'd you not how her sister
Began to scold and raise up such a storm
That mortal ears might hardly endure the din?
LUCENTIO. Tranio, I saw her coral lips to move,
And with her breath she did perfume the air;
Sacred and sweet was all I saw in her.
TRANIO. Nay, then, 'tis time to stir him from his trance.
I pray, awake, sir: if you love the maid,
Bend thoughts and wits to achieve her. Thus it stands:
Her elder sister is so curst and shrewd,
That till the father rid his hands of her,
Master, your love must live a maid at home;
And therefore has he closely mew'd her up,
Because she will not be annoy'd with suitors.
LUCENTIO. Ah, Tranio, what a cruel father's he!
But art thou not advis'd he took some care
To get her cunning schoolmasters to instruct her?
TRANIO. Ay, marry, am I, sir; and now 'tis plotted.
LUCENTIO. I have it, Tranio.
TRANIO. Master, for my hand,
Both our inventions meet and jump in one.
LUCENTIO. Tell me thine first.
TRANIO. You will be schoolmaster,
And undertake the teaching of the maid:
That's your device.
LUCENTIO. It is: may it be done?

TRANIO. Not possible; for who shall bear your part,
And be in Padua here Vincentio's son?
Keep house and ply his book, welcome his friends;
Visit his countrymen, and banquet them?
LUCENTIO. Basta; content thee; for I have it full.
We have not yet been seen in any house,
Nor can we be distinguish'd by our faces
For man, or master: then, it follows thus:
Thou shalt be master, Tranio, in my stead,
Keep house, and port, and servants, as I should:
I will some other be; some Florentine,
Some Neapolitan, or meaner man of Pisa.
'Tis hatch'd and shall be so: Tranio, at once
Uncase thee, take my colour'd hat and cloak:
When Biondello comes, he waits on thee;
But I will charm him first to keep his tongue.

They exchange habits

TRANIO. So had you need.
In brief then, sir, sith it your pleasure is,
And I am tied to be obedient;
For so your father charg'd me at our parting,
'Be serviceable to my son,' quoth he,
Although I think 'twas in another sense:
I am content to be Lucentio,
Because so well I love Lucentio.
LUCENTIO. Tranio, be so, because Lucentio loves;
And let me be a slave, to achieve that maid
Whose sudden sight hath thrall'd my wounded eye.
Here comes the rogue.

Enter Biondello

Sirrah, where have you been?
BIONDELLO. Where have I been! Nay, how now! where are you?
Master, has my fellow Tranio stol'n your clothes,
Or you stol'n his? or both? pray, what's the news?
LUCENTIO. Sirrah, come hither: 'tis no time to jest,
And therefore frame your manners to the time.
Your fellow Tranio, here, to save my life,
Puts my apparel and my countenance on,
And I for my escape have put on his;
For in a quarrel since I came ashore
I kill'd a man, and fear I was descried.

Wait you on him, I charge you, as becomes,
While I make way from hence to save my life:
You understand me?
BIONDELLO.   I, sir! Ne'er a whit.
LUCENTIO. And not a jot of Tranio in your mouth:
Tranio is changed to Lucentio.
BIONDELLO. The better for him: would I were so too!
TRANIO. So would I, faith, boy, to have the next wish after,
That Lucentio indeed had Baptista's youngest daughter.
But, sirrah, not for my sake, but your master's, I advise
You use your manners discreetly in all kind of companies:
When I am alone, why, then I am Tranio;
But in all places else your master, Lucentio.
LUCENTIO. Tranio, let's go. One thing more rests, that thyself execute, to make one among these wooers: if thou ask me why, sufficeth my reasons are both good and weighty.
Exeunt

The Presenters above speak

FIRST SERVANT. My lord, you nod; you do not mind the play.
SLY. Yes, by Saint Anne, I do. A good matter, surely: comes there any more of it?
PAGE. My lord, 'tis but begun.
SLY. 'Tis a very excellent piece of work, madam lady: would 'twere done!   *They sit and mark*

SCENE TWO

The Same. Before Hortensio's House.

Enter Petruchio and Grumio

PETRUCHIO. Verona, for awhile I take my leave,
To see my friends in Padua; but, of all
My best beloved and approved friend,
Hortensio; and I trow this is his house.
Here, sirrah Grumio; knock, I say.
GRUMIO. Knock, sir! Whom should I knock? Is there any man has rebused your worship?
PETRUCHIO. Villain, I say, knock me here soundly.
GRUMIO. Knock you here, sir! Why, sir, what am I, sir, that I should knock you here, sir?

PETRUCHIO. Villain, I say, knock me at this gate;
And rap me well, or I'll knock your knave's pate.
GRUMIO. My master is grown quarrelsome. I should knock you first,
And then I know after who comes by the worst.
PETRUCHIO. Will it not be?
Faith, sirrah, and you'll not knock, I'll ring it;
I'll try how you can sol, fa, and sing it.
He wrings Grumio by the ears
GRUMIO. Help, masters, help! My master is mad.
PETRUCHIO. Now, knock when I bid you, sirrah villain!
Enter Hortensio
HORTENSIO. How now! what's the matter? My old friend Grumio! and my good friend Petruchio! How do you all at Verona?
PETRUCHIO. Signior Hortensio, come you to part the fray?
Con tutto il cuore ben trovato, may I say.
HORTENSIO. Alla nostra casa ben venuto; molto honorato signior mio Petruchio.
Rise, Grumio, rise: we will compound this quarrel.
GRUMIO. Nay, 'tis no matter, sir, what he 'leges in Latin. If this be not a lawful cause for me to leave his service, look you, sir, he bid me knock him and rap him soundly, sir: well, was it fit for a servant to use his master so; being, perhaps, for aught I see, two-and-thirty, a pip out?
Whom would to God, I had well knock'd at first,
Then had not Grumio come by the worst.
PETRUCHIO. A senseless villain! Good Hortensio,
I bade the rascal knock upon your gate,
And could not get him for my heart to do it.
GRUMIO. Knock at the gate! O heavens! Spake you not these words plain, 'Sirrah, knock me here, rap me here, knock me well, and knock me soundly'? And come you now with 'knocking at the gate'?
PETRUCHIO. Sirrah, be gone, or talk not, I advise you.
HORTENSIO. Petruchio, patience; I am Grumio's pledge.
Why, this's a heavy chance 'twixt him and you,
Your ancient, trusty, pleasant servant Grumio.
And tell me now, sweet friend, what happy gale
Blows you to Padua here from old Verona?
PETRUCHIO. Such wind as scatters young men through the world

    To seek their fortunes further than at home,
    Where small experience grows. But in a few,
    Signior Hortensio, thus it stands with me:
    Antonio, my father, is deceas'd,
    And I have thrust myself into this maze,
    Haply to wive and thrive as best I may.
    Crowns in my purse I have and goods at home,
    And so am come abroad to see the world.
HORTENSIO. Petruchio, shall I then come roundly to thee,
    And wish thee to a shrewd ill-favour'd wife?
    Thou 'dst thank me but a little for my counsel;
    And yet I 'll promise thee she shall be rich,
    And very rich: but thou 'rt too much my friend,
    And I 'll not wish thee to her.
PETRUCHIO. Signior Hortensio, 'twixt such friends as we,
    Few words suffice; and therefore, if thou know
    One rich enough to be Petruchio's wife,
    As wealth is burden of my wooing dance,
    Be she as foul as was Florentius' love,
    As old as Sibyl, and as curst and shrewd
    As Socrates' Xanthippe, or a worse,
    She moves me not, or not removes, at least,
    Affection's edge in me, were she as rough
    As are the swelling Adriatic seas:
    I come to wive it wealthily in Padua;
    If wealthily, then happily in Padua.
GRUMIO. Nay, look you, sir, he tells you flatly what his mind is: why, give him gold enough and marry him to a puppet or an aglet-baby; or an old trot with ne'er a tooth in her head, though she have as many diseases as two-and-fifty horses: why, nothing comes amiss, so money comes withal.
HORTENSIO. Petruchio, since we are stepp'd thus far in,
    I will continue that I broach'd in jest.
    I can, Petruchio, help thee to a wife
    With wealth enough, and young and beauteous,
    Brought up as best becomes a gentlewoman:
    Her only fault,—and that is faults enough,—
    Is, that she is intolerable curst
    And shrewd and froward, so beyond all measure,
    That, were my state far worser than it is,
    I would not wed her for a mine of gold.

PETRUCHIO. Hortensio, peace! thou know'st not gold's
  effect:
  Tell me her father's name, and 'tis enough;
  For I will board her, though she chide as loud
  As thunder when the clouds in autumn crack.
HORTENSIO. Her father is Baptista Minola,
  An affable and courteous gentleman;
  Her name is Katharina Minola,
  Renown'd in Padua for her scolding tongue.
PETRUCHIO. I know her father, though I know not her;
  And he knew my deceased father well.
  I will not sleep, Hortensio, till I see her;
  And therefore let me be thus bold with you,
  To give you over at this first encounter,
  Unless you will accompany me thither.
GRUMIO. I pray you, sir, let him go while the humour lasts.
  O' my word, an she knew him as well as I do, she would
  think scolding would do little good upon him. She may,
  perhaps, call him half a score knaves or so: why, that's
  nothing: an he begin once, he'll rail in his rope-tricks. I'll
  tell you what, sir, an she stand him but a little, he will
  throw a figure in her face, and so disfigure her with it that
  she shall have no more eyes to see withal than a cat. You
  know him not, sir.
HORTENSIO. Tarry, Petruchio, I must go with thee,
  For in Baptista's keep my treasure is:
  He hath the jewel of my life in hold,
  His youngest daughter, beautiful Bianca,
  And her withholds from me and other more,
  Suitors to her and rivals in my love;
  Supposing it a thing impossible,
  For those defects I have before rehears'd,
  That ever Katharina will be woo'd:
  Therefore this order hath Baptista ta'en,
  That none shall have access unto Bianca,
  Till Katharine the curst have got a husband.
GRUMIO. Katharine the curst!
  A title for a maid of all titles the worst.
HORTENSIO. Now shall my friend Petruchio do me grace,
  And offer me, disguis'd in sober robes,
  To old Baptista as a schoolmaster
  Well seen in music, to instruct Bianca;

That so I may, by this device at least
Have leave and leisure to make love to her,
And unsuspected court her by herself.

GRUMIO. Here's no knavery! See, to beguile the old folks,
how the young folks lay their heads together!

*Enter Gremio, and
Lucentio disguised, with books under his arm*

Master, master, look about you: who goes there, ha?

HORTENSIO. Peace, Grumio! 'tis the rival of my love.
Petruchio, stand by awhile.

GRUMIO. A proper stripling, and an amorous!

GREMIO. O! very well; I have perus'd the note.
Hark you, sir; I'll have them very fairly bound:
All books of love, see that at any hand,
And see you read no other lectures to her.
You understand me. Over and beside
Signior Baptista's liberality,
I'll mend it with a largess. Take your papers too,
And let me have them very well perfum'd;
For she is sweeter than perfume itself
To whom they go to. What will you read to her?

LUCENTIO. Whate'er I read to her, I'll plead for you,
As for my patron, stand you so assur'd,
As firmly as yourself were still in place;
Yea, and perhaps with more successful words
Than you, unless you were a scholar, sir.

GREMIO. O! this learning, what a thing it is.

GRUMIO. O! this woodcock, what an ass it is.

PETRUCHIO. Peace, sirrah!

HORTENSIO. Grumio, mum! God save you, Signior Gremio!

GREMIO. And you're well met, Signior Hortensio.
Trow you whither I am going? To Baptista Minola.
I promis'd to inquire carefully
About a schoolmaster for the fair Bianca;
And, by good fortune, I have lighted well
On this young man; for learning and behaviour
Fit for her turn; well read in poetry
And other books, good ones, I warrant ye.

HORTENSIO. 'Tis well: and I have met a gentleman
Hath promis'd me to help me to another,
A fine musician to instruct our mistress:
So shall I no whit be behind in duty

To fair Bianca, so belov'd of me.
GREMIO. Belov'd of me, and that my deeds shall prove.
GRUMIO. (*Aside*) And that his bags shall prove.
HORTENSIO. Gremio, 'tis now no time to vent our love:
Listen to me, and if you speak me fair,
I'll tell you news indifferent good for either.
Here is a gentleman whom by chance I met,
Upon agreement from us to his liking,
Will undertake to woo curst Katharine;
Yea, and to marry her, if her dowry please.
GREMIO. So said, so done, is well.
Hortensio, have you told him all her faults?
PETRUCHIO. I know she is an irksome, brawling scold:
If that be all, masters, I hear no harm.
GREMIO. No, sayst me so, friend? What countryman?
PETRUCHIO. Born in Verona, old Antonio's son:
My father dead, my fortune lives for me;
And I do hope good days and long to see.
GREMIO. O, sir, such a life, with such a wife, were strange!
But if you have a stomach, to 't i' God's name:
You shall have me assisting you in all.
But will you woo this wild-cat?
PETRUCHIO.   Will I live?
GRUMIO. Will he woo her? ay, or I'll hang her.
PETRUCHIO. Why came I hither but to that intent?
Think you a little din can daunt mine ears?
Have I not in my time heard lions roar?
Have I not heard the sea, puff'd up with winds,
Rage like an angry boar chafed with sweat?
Have I not heard great ordnance in the field,
And heaven's artillery thunder in the skies?
Have I not in a pitched battle heard
Loud 'larums, neighing steeds, and trumpets' clang?
And do you tell me of a woman's tongue,
That gives not half so great a blow to hear
As will a chestnut in a farmer's fire?
Tush, tush! fear boys with bugs.
GRUMIO.   (*Aside*) For he fears none.
GREMIO. Hortensio, hark:
This gentleman is happily arriv'd,
My mind presumes, for his own good and ours.
HORTENSIO. I promis'd we would be contributors,

And bear his charge of wooing, whatsoe'er.
GREMIO. And so we will, provided that he win her.
GRUMIO. (*Aside*) I would I were as sure of a good dinner.
Enter Tranio, bravely apparelled; and Biondello
TRANIO. Gentlemen, God save you! If I may be bold,
Tell me, I beseech you, which is the readiest way
To the house of Signior Baptista Minola?
BIONDELLO. He that has the two fair daughters: is 't he you mean?
TRANIO. Even he, Biondello!
GREMIO. Hark you, sir; you mean not her to—
TRANIO. Perhaps, him and her, sir: what have you to do?
PETRUCHIO. Not her that chides, sir, at any hand, I pray.
TRANIO. I love no chiders, sir. Biondello, let 's away.
LUCENTIO. (*Aside*) Well begun, Tranio.
HORTENSIO.   Sir, a word ere you go.
Are you a suitor to the maid you talk of, yea or no?
TRANIO. And if I be, sir, is it any offence?
GREMIO. No; if without more words you will get you hence.
TRANIO. Why, sir, I pray, are not the streets as free
For me as for you?
GREMIO.   But so is not she.
TRANIO. For what reason, I beseech you?
GREMIO. For this reason, if you 'll know,
That she 's the choice love of Signior Gremio.
HORTENSIO. That she 's the chosen of Signior Hortensio.
TRANIO. Softly, my masters! if you be gentlemen,
Do me this right; hear me with patience.
Baptista is a noble gentleman,
To whom my father is not all unknown;
And were his daughter fairer than she is,
She may more suitors have, and me for one.
Fair Leda's daughter had a thousand wooers;
Then well one more may fair Bianca have,
And so she shall; Lucentio shall make one,
Though Paris came in hope to speed alone.
GREMIO. What! this gentleman will out-talk us all.
LUCENTIO. Sir, give him head: I know he 'll prove a jade.
PETRUCHIO. Hortensio, to what end are all these words?
HORTENSIO. Sir, let me be so bold as ask you,
Did you yet ever see Baptista's daughter?
TRANIO. No, sir; but hear I do that he hath two,

The one as famous for a scolding tongue
　　　As is the other for beauteous modesty.
PETRUCHIO. Sir, sir, the first 's for me; let her go by.
GREMIO. Yea, leave that labour to great Hercules,
　　　And let it be more than Alcides' twelve.
PETRUCHIO. Sir, understand you this of me in sooth:
　　　The youngest daughter, whom you hearken for,
　　　Her father keeps from all access of suitors,
　　　And will not promise her to any man
　　　Until the elder sister first be wed;
　　　The younger then is free, and not before.
TRANIO. If it be so, sir, that you are the man
　　　Must stead us all, and me among the rest;
　　　And if you break the ice, and do this feat,
　　　Achieve the elder, set the younger free
　　　For our access, whose hap shall be to have her
　　　Will not so graceless be to be ingrate.
HORTENSIO. Sir, you say well, and well you do conceive;
　　　And since you do profess to be a suitor,
　　　You must, as we do, gratify this gentleman,
　　　To whom we all rest generally beholding.
TRANIO. Sir, I shall not be slack: in sign whereof,
　　　Please ye we may contrive this afternoon,
　　　And quaff carouses to our mistress' health,
　　　And do as adversaries do in law,
　　　Strive mightily, but eat and drink as friends.
GRUMIO.　　　} O excellent motion! Fellows, let 's be gone.
BIONDELLO.　}
HORTENSIO. The motion 's good indeed, and be it so:—
　　　Petruchio, I shall be your ben venuto.　　　　　*Exeunt*

ACT TWO

SCENE ONE

Padua. A Room in Baptista's House.

Enter Katharina and Bianca

BIANCA. Good sister, wrong me not, nor wrong yourself,
To make a bondmaid and a slave of me;
That I disdain: but for these other gawds,
Unbind my hands, I'll pull them off myself,
Yea, all my raiment, to my petticoat;
Or what you will command me will I do,
So well I know my duty to my elders.

KATHARINA. Of all thy suitors, here I charge thee, tell
Whom thou lov'st best: see thou dissemble not.

BIANCA. Believe me, sister, of all the men alive
I never yet beheld that special face
Which I could fancy more than any other.

KATHARINA. Minion, thou liest. Is 't not Hortensio?

BIANCA. If you affect him, sister, here I swear
I'll plead for you myself, but you shall have him.

KATHARINA. O! then, belike, you fancy riches more:
You will have Gremio to keep you fair.

BIANCA. Is it for him you do envy me so?
Nay, then you jest; and now I well perceive
You have but jested with me all this while:
I prithee, sister Kate, untie my hands.

KATHARINA. If that be jest, then all the rest was so.
Strikes her

Enter Baptista

BAPTISTA. Why, how now, dame! whence grows this insolence?
Bianca, stand aside. Poor girl! she weeps.
Go ply thy needle; meddle not with her.
For shame, thou hilding of a devilish spirit,

Why dost thou wrong her that did ne'er wrong thee?
When did she cross thee with a bitter word?
KATHARINA. Her silence flouts me, and I'll be reveng'd.
Flies after Bianca
BAPTISTA. What! in my sight? Bianca, get thee in.
Exit Bianca
KATHARINA. What! will you not suffer me? Nay, now I see
She is your treasure, she must have a husband;
I must dance bare-foot on her wedding-day,
And, for your love to her, lead apes in hell.
Talk not to me: I will go sit and weep
Till I can find occasion of revenge. *Exit*
BAPTISTA. Was ever gentleman thus griev'd as I?
But who comes here?
*Enter Gremio, with Lucentio in the habit
of a mean man; Petruchio, with Hortensio as a Musician; and
Tranio, with Biondello bearing a lute and books*
GREMIO. Good-morrow, neighbour Baptista.
BAPTISTA. Good-morrow, neighbour Gremio. God save you, gentlemen!
PETRUCHIO. And you, good sir. Pray, have you not a daughter
Call'd Katharina, fair and virtuous?
BAPTISTA. I have a daughter, sir, call'd Katharina.
GREMIO. You are too blunt: go to it orderly.
PETRUCHIO. You wrong me, Signior Gremio: give me leave.
I am a gentleman of Verona, sir,
That, hearing of her beauty and her wit,
Her affability and bashful modesty,
Her wondrous qualities and mild behaviour,
Am bold to show myself a forward guest
Within your house, to make mine eye the witness
Of that report which I so oft have heard.
And, for an entrance to my entertainment,
I do present you with a man of mine, *Presenting Hortensio*
Cunning in music and the mathematics,
To instruct her fully in those sciences,
Whereof I know she is not ignorant.
Accept of him, or else you do me wrong:
His name is Licio, born in Mantua.
BAPTISTA. You're welcome, sir; and he, for your good sake.
But for my daughter Katharine, this I know,

She is not for your turn, the more my grief.
PETRUCHIO. I see you do not mean to part with her,
Or else you like not of my company.
BAPTISTA. Mistake me not; I speak but as I find.
Whence are you, sir? What may I call your name?
PETRUCHIO. Petruchio is my name; Antonio's son;
A man well known throughout all Italy.
BAPTISTA. I know him well: you are welcome for his sake.
GREMIO. Saving your tale, Petruchio, I pray,
Let us, that are poor petitioners, speak too.
Backare! you are marvellous forward.
PETRUCHIO. O, pardon me, Signior Gremio; I would fain be doing.
GREMIO. I doubt it not, sir; but you will curse your wooing. Neighbour, this is a gift very grateful, I am sure of it. To express the like kindness, myself, that have been more kindly beholding to you than any, freely give unto you this young scholar, (*Presenting Lucentio*) that has been long studying at Rheims; as cunning in Greek, Latin, and other languages, as the other in music and mathematics. His name is Cambio; pray accept his service.
BAPTISTA. A thousand thanks, Signior Gremio; welcome, good Cambio.— (*To Tranio*) But, gentle sir, methinks you walk like a stranger: may I be so bold to know the cause of your coming?
TRANIO. Pardon me, sir, the boldness is mine own,
That, being a stranger in this city here,
Do make myself a suitor to your daughter,
Unto Bianca, fair and virtuous.
Nor is your firm resolve unknown to me,
In the preferment of the eldest sister.
This liberty is all that I request,
That, upon knowledge of my parentage,
I may have welcome 'mongst the rest that woo,
And free access and favour as the rest:
And, toward the education of your daughters,
I here bestow a simple instrument,
And this small packet of Greek and Latin books:
If you accept them, then their worth is great.
BAPTISTA. Lucentio is your name, of whence, I pray?
TRANIO. Of Pisa, sir; son to Vincentio.
BAPTISTA. A mighty man of Pisa; by report

I know him well: you are very welcome, sir.
(*To Hortensio*) Take you the lute, (*To Lucentio*) and you the set of books;
You shall go see your pupils presently.
Holla, within!

Enter a Servant

Sirrah, lead these gentlemen
To my two daughters, and then tell them both
These are their tutors: bid them use them well.

Exit Servant, with Hortensio, Lucentio, and Biondello

We will go walk a little in the orchard,
And then to dinner. You are passing welcome,
And so I pray you all to think yourselves.

PETRUCHIO. Signior Baptista, my business asketh haste,
And every day I cannot come to woo.
You knew my father well, and in him me,
Left solely heir to all his lands and goods,
Which I have better'd rather than decreas'd:
Then tell me, if I get your daughter's love,
What dowry shall I have with her to wife?

BAPTISTA. After my death the one half of my lands,
And in possession twenty thousand crowns.

PETRUCHIO. And, for that dowry, I'll assure her of
Her widowhood, be it that she survive me,
In all my lands and leases whatsoever.
Let specialties be therefore drawn between us,
That covenants may be kept on either hand.

BAPTISTA. Ay, when the special thing is well obtain'd,
That is, her love; for that is all in all.

PETRUCHIO. Why, that is nothing; for I tell you, father,
I am as peremptory as she proud-minded;
And where two raging fires meet together
They do consume the thing that feeds their fury:
Though little fire grows great with little wind,
Yet extreme gusts will blow out fire and all;
So I to her, and so she yields to me;
For I am rough and woo not like a babe.

BAPTISTA. Well mayst thou woo, and happy be thy speed!
But be thou arm'd for some unhappy words.

PETRUCHIO. Ay, to the proof; as mountains are for winds,
That shake not, though they blow perpetually.

Re-enter Hortensio, with his head broke

ACT II · SCENE I

BAPTISTA. How now, my friend! Why dost thou look so pale?
HORTENSIO. For fear, I promise you, if I look pale.
BAPTISTA. What, will my daughter prove a good musician?
HORTENSIO. I think she'll sooner prove a soldier:
   Iron may hold with her, but never lutes.
BAPTISTA. Why, then thou canst not break her to the lute?
HORTENSIO. Why, no; for she hath broke the lute to me.
   I did but tell her she mistook her frets,
   And bow'd her hand to teach her fingering;
   When, with a most impatient devilish spirit,
   'Frets, call you these?' quoth she; 'I'll fume with them';
   And, with that word, she struck me on the head,
   And through the instrument my pate made way;
   And there I stood amazed for a while,
   As on a pillory, looking through the lute;
   While she did call me rascal fiddler,
   And twangling Jack; with twenty such vile terms
   As she had studied to misuse me so.
PETRUCHIO. Now, by the world, it is a lusty wench!
   I love her ten times more than e'er I did:
   O! how I long to have some chat with her!
BAPTISTA. (*To Hortensio*) Well, go with me, and be not so discomfited:
   Proceed in practice with my younger daughter;
   She's apt to learn, and thankful for good turns.
   Signior Petruchio, will you go with us,
   Or shall I send my daughter Kate to you?
PETRUCHIO. I pray you do; I will attend her here,
         Exeunt Baptista, Gremio, Tranio, and Hortensio
   And woo her with some spirit when she comes.
   Say that she rail; why then I'll tell her plain
   She sings as sweetly as a nightingale:
   Say that she frown; I'll say she looks as clear
   As morning roses newly wash'd with dew:
   Say she be mute and will not speak a word;
   Then I'll commend her volubility,
   And say she uttereth piercing eloquence:
   If she do bid me pack, I'll give her thanks,
   As though she bid me stay by her a week:
   If she deny to wed, I'll crave the day
   When I shall ask the banns, and when be married.
   But here she comes; and now, Petruchio, speak.

Enter Katharina

Good-morrow, Kate; for that's your name, I hear.

KATHARINA. Well have you heard, but something hard of hearing:
They call me Katharine that do talk of me.

PETRUCHIO. You lie, in faith; for you are call'd plain Kate,
And bonny Kate, and sometimes Kate the curst;
But, Kate, the prettiest Kate in Christendom;
Kate of Kate-Hall, my super-dainty Kate,
For dainties are all cates: and therefore, Kate,
Take this of me, Kate of my consolation;
Hearing thy mildness prais'd in every town,
Thy virtues spoke of, and thy beauty sounded,—
Yet not so deeply as to thee belongs,—
Myself am mov'd to woo thee for my wife.

KATHARINA. Mov'd! in good time: let him that mov'd you hither
Remove you hence. I knew you at the first,
You were a moveable.

PETRUCHIO. Why, what's a moveable?

KATHARINA. A joint-stool.

PETRUCHIO. Thou hast hit it: come, sit on me.

KATHARINA. Asses are made to bear, and so are you.

PETRUCHIO. Women are made to bear, and so are you.

KATHARINA. No such jade as bear you, if me you mean.

PETRUCHIO. Alas! good Kate, I will not burden thee;
For, knowing thee to be but young and light,—

KATHARINA. Too light for such a swain as you to catch,
And yet as heavy as my weight should be.

PETRUCHIO. Should be! should buzz!

KATHARINA. Well ta'en, and like a buzzard.

PETRUCHIO. O slow-wing'd turtle! shall a buzzard take thee?

KATHARINA. Ay, for a turtle, as he takes a buzzard.

PETRUCHIO. Come, come, you wasp; i' faith you are too angry.

KATHARINA. If I be waspish, best beware my sting.

PETRUCHIO. My remedy is, then, to pluck it out.

KATHARINA. Ay, if the fool could find it where it lies.

PETRUCHIO. Who knows not where a wasp does wear his sting?
In his tail.

KATHARINA. In his tongue.

PETRUCHIO. Whose tongue?
KATHARINA. Yours, if you talk of tails; and so farewell.
PETRUCHIO. What! with my tongue in your tail? nay, come again.
Good Kate, I am a gentleman.
KATHARINA. That I'll try. *Striking him*
PETRUCHIO. I swear I'll cuff you if you strike again.
KATHARINA. So may you lose your arms:
If you strike me, you are no gentleman;
And if no gentleman, why then no arms.
PETRUCHIO. A herald, Kate? O! put me in thy books.
KATHARINA. What is your crest? a coxcomb?
PETRUCHIO. A combless cock, so Kate will be my hen.
KATHARINA. No cock of mine; you crow too like a craven.
PETRUCHIO. Nay, come, Kate, come; you must not look so sour.
KATHARINA. It is my fashion when I see a crab.
PETRUCHIO. Why, here's no crab, and therefore look not sour.
KATHARINA. There is, there is.
PETRUCHIO. Then show it me.
KATHARINA. Had I a glass, I would.
PETRUCHIO. What, you mean my face?
KATHARINA. Well aim'd of such a young one.
PETRUCHIO. Now, by Saint George, I am too young for you.
KATHARINA. Yet you are wither'd.
PETRUCHIO. 'Tis with cares.
KATHARINA. I care not.
PETRUCHIO. Nay, hear you, Kate: in sooth, you 'scape not so.
KATHARINA. I chafe you, if I tarry: let me go.
PETRUCHIO. No, not a whit: I find you passing gentle.
'Twas told me you were rough and coy and sullen,
And now I find report a very liar;
For thou art pleasant, gamesome, passing courteous,
But slow in speech, yet sweet as spring-time flowers:
Thou canst not frown, thou canst not look askance,
Nor bite the lip, as angry wenches will;
Nor hast thou pleasure to be cross in talk;
But thou with mildness entertain'st thy wooers,
With gentle conference, soft and affable.
Why does the world report that Kate doth limp?
O slanderous world! Kate, like the hazel-twig,

Is straight and slender, and as brown in hue
As hazel-nuts, and sweeter than the kernels.
O! let me see thee walk: thou dost not halt.

KATHARINA. Go, fool, and whom thou keep'st command.

PETRUCHIO. Did ever Dian so become a grove
As Kate this chamber with her princely gait?
O! be thou Dian, and let her be Kate,
And then let Kate be chaste, and Dian sportful!

KATHARINA. Where did you study all this goodly speech?

PETRUCHIO. It is extempore, from my mother-wit.

KATHARINA. A witty mother! witless else her son.

PETRUCHIO. Am I not wise?

KATHARINA. Yes; keep you warm.

PETRUCHIO. Marry, so I mean, sweet Katharine, in thy bed:
And therefore, setting all this chat aside,
Thus in plain terms: your father hath consented
That you shall be my wife; your dowry 'greed on;
And will you, nill you, I will marry you.
Now, Kate, I am a husband for your turn;
For, by this light, whereby I see thy beauty,—
Thy beauty that doth make me like thee well,—
Thou must be married to no man but me:
For I am he am born to tame you, Kate;
And bring you from a wild Kate to a Kate
Conformable as other household Kates.
Here comes your father: never make denial;
I must and will have Katharine to my wife.

Re-enter Baptista, Gremio, and Tranio

BAPTISTA. Now, Signior Petruchio, how speed you with my daughter?

PETRUCHIO. How but well, sir? how but well?
It were impossible I should speed amiss.

BAPTISTA. Why, how now, daughter Katharine! in your dumps?

KATHARINA. Call you me daughter? Now, I promise you
You have show'd a tender fatherly regard,
To wish me wed to one half lunatic;
A mad-cap ruffian and a swearing Jack,
That thinks with oaths to face the matter out.

PETRUCHIO. Father, 'tis thus: yourself and all the world,
That talk'd of her, have talk'd amiss of her:
If she be curst, it is for policy,

> For she 's not froward, but modest as the dove;
> She is not hot, but temperate as the morn;
> For patience she will prove a second Grissel,
> And Roman Lucrece for her chastity;
> And to conclude, we have 'greed so well together,
> That upon Sunday is the wedding-day.

KATHARINA. I 'll see thee hang'd on Sunday first.

GREMIO. Hark, Petruchio: she says she 'll see thee hang'd first.

TRANIO. Is this your speeding? Nay then, good-night our part!

PETRUCHIO. Be patient, gentlemen; I choose her for myself:
> If she and I be pleas'd, what 's that to you?
> 'Tis bargain'd 'twixt us twain, being alone,
> That she shall still be curst in company.
> I tell you, 'tis incredible to believe
> How much she loves me: O! the kindest Kate!
> She hung about my neck, and kiss on kiss
> She vied so fast, protesting oath on oath,
> That in a twink she won me to her love.
> O! you are novices: 'tis a world to see,
> How tame, when men and women are alone,
> A meacock wretch can make the curstest shrew.
> Give me thy hand, Kate: I will unto Venice
> To buy apparel 'gainst the wedding-day.
> Provide the feast, father, and bid the guests;
> I will be sure my Katharine shall be fine.

BAPTISTA. I know not what to say; but give me your hands.
> God send you joy, Petruchio! 'tis a match.

GREMIO. } Amen, say we: we will be witnesses.
TRANIO.

PETRUCHIO. Father, and wife, and gentlemen, adieu.
> I will to Venice; Sunday comes apace:
> We will have rings, and things, and fine array;
> And, kiss me, Kate, we will be married o' Sunday.

Exeunt Petruchio and Katharina, severally

GREMIO. Was ever match clapp'd up so suddenly?

BAPTISTA. Faith, gentlemen, now I play a merchant's part,
> And venture madly on a desperate mart.

TRANIO. 'Twas a commodity lay fretting by you:
> 'Twill bring you gain, or perish on the seas.

BAPTISTA. The gain I seek is, quiet in the match.

GREMIO. No doubt but he hath got a quiet catch.
  But now, Baptista, to your younger daughter:
  Now is the day we long have looked for:
  I am your neighbour, and was suitor first.
TRANIO. And I am one that love Bianca more
  Than words can witness, or your thoughts can guess.
GREMIO. Youngling, thou canst not love so dear as I.
TRANIO. Greybeard, thy love doth freeze.
GREMIO.   But thine doth fry.
  Skipper, stand back: 'tis age that nourisheth.
TRANIO. But youth in ladies' eyes that flourisheth.
BAPTISTA. Content you, gentlemen; I'll compound this strife:
  'Tis deeds must win the prize; and he, of both
  That can assure my daughter greatest dower
  Shall have my Bianca's love.
  Say, Signior Gremio, what can you assure her?
GREMIO. First, as you know, my house within the city
  Is richly furnished with plate and gold:
  Basins and ewers to lave her dainty hands;
  My hangings all of Tyrian tapestry;
  In ivory coffers I have stuff'd my crowns;
  In cypress chests my arras counterpoints,
  Costly apparel, tents, and canopies,
  Fine linen, Turkey cushions boss'd with pearl,
  Valance of Venice gold in needle-work,
  Pewter and brass, and all things that belong
  To house or housekeeping: then, at my farm
  I have a hundred milch-kine to the pail,
  Six score fat oxen standing in my stalls,
  And all things answerable to this portion.
  Myself am struck in years, I must confess;
  And if I die to-morrow, this is hers,
  If whilst I live she will be only mine.
TRANIO. That 'only' came well in. Sir, list to me:
  I am my father's heir and only son:
  If I may have your daughter to my wife,
  I'll leave her houses three or four as good,
  Within rich Pisa walls, as any one
  Old Signior Gremio has in Padua;
  Besides two thousand ducats by the year
  Of fruitful land, all of which shall be her jointure.

What, have I pinch'd you, Signior Gremio?
GREMIO. Two thousand ducats by the year of land!
My land amounts not to so much in all:
That she shall have; besides an argosy
That now is lying in Marseilles' road.
What, have I chok'd you with an argosy?
TRANIO. Gremio, 'tis known my father hath no less
Than three great argosies, besides two galliasses,
And twelve tight galleys; these I will assure her,
And twice as much, whate'er thou offer'st next.
GREMIO. Nay, I have offer'd all, I have no more;
And she can have no more than all I have:
If you like me, she shall have me and mine.
TRANIO. Why, then the maid is mine from all the world,
By your firm promise. Gremio is out-vied.
BAPTISTA. I must confess your offer is the best;
And, let your father make her the assurance,
She is your own; else, you must pardon me:
If you should die before him, where 's her dower?
TRANIO. That 's but a cavil: he is old, I young.
GREMIO. And may not young men die as well as old?
BAPTISTA. Well, gentlemen,
I am thus resolv'd. On Sunday next, you know,
My daughter Katharine is to be married:
Now, on the Sunday following, shall Bianca
Be bride to you, if you make this assurance;
If not, to Signior Gremio:
And so, I take my leave, and thank you both.
GREMIO. Adieu, good neighbour. (*Exit Baptista*) Now I
fear thee not:
Sirrah young gamester, your father were a fool
To give thee all, and in his waning age
Set foot under thy table. Tut! a toy!
An old Italian fox is not so kind, my boy. *Exit*
TRANIO. A vengeance on your crafty wither'd hide!
Yet I have fac'd it with a card of ten.
'Tis in my head to do my master good:
I see no reason, but suppos'd Lucentio
Must get a father, called 'suppos'd Vincentio';
And that 's a wonder: fathers, commonly,
Do get their children; but in this case of wooing,
A child shall get a sire, if I fail not of my cunning. *Exit*

ACT THREE

SCENE ONE

Padua. A Room in Baptista's House.

Enter Lucentio, Hortensio, and Bianca

LUCENTIO. Fiddler, forbear; you grow too forward, sir:
  Have you so soon forgot the entertainment
  Her sister Katharine welcom'd you withal?
HORTENSIO. But, wrangling pedant, this is
  The patroness of heavenly harmony:
  Then give me leave to have prerogative;
  And when in music we have spent an hour,
  Your lecture shall have leisure for as much.
LUCENTIO. Preposterous ass, that never read so far
  To know the cause why music was ordain'd!
  Was it not to refresh the mind of man
  After his studies or his usual pain?
  Then give me leave to read philosophy,
  And while I pause, serve in your harmony.
HORTENSIO. Sirrah, I will not bear these braves of thine.
BIANCA. Why, gentlemen, you do me double wrong,
  To strive for that which resteth in my choice.
  I am no breeching scholar in the schools;
  I'll not be tied to hours nor 'pointed times,
  But learn my lessons as I please myself.
  And, to cut off all strife, here sit we down:
  Take you your instrument, play you the whiles;
  His lecture will be done ere you have tun'd.
HORTENSIO. You'll leave his lecture when I am in tune?
                                            Retires
LUCENTIO. That will be never: tune your instrument.
BIANCA. Where left we last?
LUCENTIO. Here, madam:—

[28-66]

> Hic ibat Simois; hic est Sigeia tellus;
> Hic steterat Priami regia celsa senis.

BIANCA. Construe them.

LUCENTIO. 'Hic ibat,' as I told you before, 'Simois,' I am Lucentio, 'hic est,' son unto Vincentio of Pisa, 'Sigeia tellus,' disguised thus to get your love; 'Hic steterat,' and that Lucentio that comes a-wooing, 'Priami,' is my man Tranio, 'regia,' bearing my port, 'celsa senis,' that we might beguile the old pantaloon.

HORTENSIO. (*Returning*) Madam, my instrument's in tune.

BIANCA. Let's hear.— *Hortensio plays*
O fie! the treble jars.

LUCENTIO. Spit in the hole, man, and tune again.

BIANCA. Now let me see if I can construe it: 'Hic ibat Simois,' I know you not, 'hic est Sigeia tellus,' I trust you not; 'Hic steterat Priami,' take heed he hear us not, 'regia,' presume not; 'celsa senis,' despair not.

HORTENSIO. Madam, 'tis now in tune.

LUCENTIO. All but the base.

HORTENSIO. The base is right; 'tis the base knave that jars.
How fiery and forward our pedant is!
(*Aside*) Now, for my life, the knave doth court my love;
Pedascule, I'll watch you better yet.

BIANCA. In time I may believe, yet I mistrust.

LUCENTIO. Mistrust it not; for, sure, Æacides
Was Ajax, call'd so from his grandfather.

BIANCA. I must believe my master; else, I promise you,
I should be arguing still upon that doubt:
But let it rest. Now, Licio, to you.
Good masters, take it not unkindly, pray,
That I have been thus pleasant with you both.

HORTENSIO. (*To Lucentio*) You may go walk, and give me leave a while:
My lessons make no music in three parts.

LUCENTIO. Are you so formal, sir? (*Aside*) Well, I must wait,
And watch withal; for, but I be deceiv'd,
Our fine musician groweth amorous.

HORTENSIO. Madam, before you touch the instrument,
To learn the order of my fingering,
I must begin with rudiments of art;
To teach you gamut in a briefer sort,

More pleasant, pithy, and effectual,
Than hath been taught by any of my trade:
And there it is in writing, fairly drawn.
BIANCA. Why, I am past my gamut long ago.
HORTENSIO. Yet read the gamut of Hortensio.
BIANCA.
' "Gamut" I am, the ground of all accord,
   "A re," to plead Hortensio's passion;
"B mi," Bianca, take him for thy lord,
   "C fa ut," that loves with all affection:
"D sol re," one clef, two notes have I;
"E la mi," show pity, or I die.'
Call you this gamut? Tut, I like it not:
Old fashions please me best; I am not so nice,
To change true rules for odd inventions.

Enter a Servant

SERVANT. Mistress, your father prays you leave your books,
And help to dress your sister's chamber up:
You know to-morrow is the wedding-day.
BIANCA. Farewell, sweet masters both: I must be gone.

Exeunt Bianca and Servant

LUCENTIO. Faith, mistress, then I have no cause to stay. *Exit*
HORTENSIO. But I have cause to pry into this pedant:
Methinks he looks as though he were in love.
Yet if thy thoughts, Bianca, be so humble
To cast thy wandering eyes on every stale,
Seize thee that list: if once I find thee ranging,
Hortensio will be quit with thee by changing.   *Exit*

SCENE TWO

The Same. Before Baptista's House.

*Enter Baptista, Gremio, Tranio, Katharina, Bianca,
Lucentio, and Attendants*

BAPTISTA. (*To Tranio*) Signior Lucentio, this is the 'pointed day
That Katharine and Petruchio should be married,
And yet we hear not of our son-in-law.
What will be said? What mockery will it be
To want the bridegroom when the priest attends

To speak the ceremonial rites of marriage!
What says Lucentio to this shame of ours?

KATHARINA. No shame but mine: I must, forsooth, be forc'd
To give my hand oppos'd against my heart
Unto a mad-brain rudesby, full of spleen;
Who woo'd in haste and means to wed at leisure.
I told you, I, he was a frantic fool,
Hiding his bitter jests in blunt behaviour;
And to be noted for a merry man,
He'll woo a thousand, 'point the day of marriage,
Make friends invite, and proclaim the banns;
Yet never means to wed where he hath woo'd.
Now must the world point at poor Katharine,
And say, 'Lo! there is mad Petruchio's wife,
If it would please him come and marry her.'

TRANIO. Patience, good Katharine, and Baptista too.
Upon my life, Petruchio means but well,
Whatever fortune stays him from his word:
Though he be blunt, I know him passing wise;
Though he be merry, yet withal he's honest.

KATHARINA. Would Katharine had never seen him though!
Exit weeping, followed by Bianca and others

BAPTISTA. Go, girl: I cannot blame thee now to weep,
For such an injury would vex a very saint,
Much more a shrew of thy impatient humour.
Enter Biondello

BIONDELLO. Master, master! news! old news, and such news as you never heard of!

BAPTISTA. Is it new and old too? How may that be?

BIONDELLO. Why, is it not news to hear of Petruchio's coming?

BAPTISTA. Is he come?

BIONDELLO. Why, no, sir.

BAPTISTA. What then?

BIONDELLO. He is coming.

BAPTISTA. When will he be here?

BIONDELLO. When he stands where I am and sees you there.

TRANIO. But, say, what to thine old news?

BIONDELLO. Why, Petruchio is coming, in a new hat and an old jerkin; a pair of old breeches thrice turned; a pair of boots that have been candle-cases, one buckled, another laced; an old rusty sword ta'en out of the town-armoury, with a broken hilt, and chapeless; with two broken points: his horse hipped with an old mothy saddle and stirrups of no kindred; besides, possessed with the glanders and like to mose in the chine; troubled with the lampass, infected with the fashions, full of windgalls, sped with spavins, rayed with the yellows, past cure of the fives, stark spoiled with the staggers, begnawn with the bots, swayed in the back, and shoulder-shotten; near-legged before, and with a half-checked bit, and a head-stall of sheep's leather, which, being restrained to keep him from stumbling, hath been often burst and now repaired with knots; one girth six times pieced, and a woman's crupper of velure, which hath two letters for her name fairly set down in studs, and here and there pieced with packthread.

BAPTISTA. Who comes with him?

BIONDELLO. O, sir! his lackey, for all the world caparisoned like the horse; with a linen stock on one leg and a kersey boot-hose on the other, gartered with a red and blue list; an old hat, and the 'humour of forty fancies' pricked in 't for a feather: a monster, a very monster in apparel, and not like a Christian footboy or a gentleman's lackey.

TRANIO. 'Tis some odd humour pricks him to this fashion;
Yet oftentimes he goes but mean-apparell'd.

BAPTISTA. I am glad he is come, howsoe'er he comes.

BIONDELLO. Why, sir, he comes not.

BAPTISTA. Didst thou not say he comes?

BIONDELLO. Who? that Petruchio came?

BAPTISTA. Ay, that Petruchio came.

BIONDELLO. No, sir; I say his horse comes, with him on his back.

BAPTISTA. Why, that's all one.

BIONDELLO.   Nay, by Saint Jamy,
           I hold you a penny,
           A horse and a man
           Is more than one,
           And yet not many.

Enter Petruchio and Grumio

PETRUCHIO. Come, where be these gallants? Who is at home?

BAPTISTA. You are welcome, sir.

PETRUCHIO.   And yet I come not well.

BAPTISTA. And yet you halt not.

ACT III : SCENE II

TRANIO. Not so well apparell'd
  As I wish you were.
PETRUCHIO. Were it better, I should rush in thus.
  But where is Kate? where is my lovely bride?
  How does my father? Gentles, methinks you frown:
  And wherefore gaze this goodly company,
  As if they saw some wondrous monument,
  Some comet, or unusual prodigy?
BAPTISTA. Why, sir, you know this is your wedding-day:
  First were we sad, fearing you would not come;
  Now sadder, that you come so unprovided.
  Fie! doff this habit, shame to your estate,
  An eye-sore to our solemn festival.
TRANIO. And tell us what occasion of import
  Hath all so long detain'd you from your wife,
  And sent you hither so unlike yourself?
PETRUCHIO. Tedious it were to tell, and harsh to hear:
  Sufficeth, I am come to keep my word,
  Though in some part enforced to digress;
  Which, at more leisure, I will so excuse
  As you shall well be satisfied withal.
  But where is Kate? I stay too long from her:
  The morning wears, 'tis time we were at church.
TRANIO. See not your bride in these unreverent robes:
  Go to my chamber; put on clothes of mine.
PETRUCHIO. Not I, believe me: thus I 'll visit her.
BAPTISTA. But thus, I trust, you will not marry her.
PETRUCHIO. Good sooth, even thus; therefore ha' done with words:
  To me she 's married, not unto my clothes.
  Could I repair what she will wear in me
  As I can change these poor accoutrements,
  'Twere well for Kate and better for myself.
  But what a fool am I to chat with you
  When I should bid good-morrow to my bride,
  And seal the title with a lovely kiss!
          Exeunt Petruchio, Grumio, and Biondello
TRANIO. He hath some meaning in his mad attire.
  We will persuade him, be it possible,
  To put on better ere he go to church.
BAPTISTA. I 'll after him, and see the event of this.
          Exeunt Baptista, Gremio, and Attendants

TRANIO. But to her love concerneth us to add
  Her father's liking: which to bring to pass,
  As I before imparted to your worship,
  I am to get a man,—whate'er he be
  It skills not much, we'll fit him to our turn,—
  And he shall be Vincentio of Pisa,
  And make assurance here in Padua,
  Of greater sums than I have promised.
  So shall you quietly enjoy your hope,
  And marry sweet Bianca with consent.
LUCENTIO. Were it not that my fellow schoolmaster
  Doth watch Bianca's steps so narrowly,
  'Twere good, methinks, to steal our marriage;
  Which once perform'd, let all the world say no,
  I'll keep mine own, despite of all the world.
TRANIO. That by degrees we mean to look into,
  And watch our vantage in this business.
  We'll over-reach the greybeard, Gremio,
  The narrow-prying father, Minola,
  The quaint musician, amorous Licio;
  All for my master's sake, Lucentio.
      Re-enter Gremio
  Signior Gremio, came you from the church?
GREMIO. As willingly as e'er I came from school.
TRANIO. And is the bride and bridegroom coming home?
GREMIO. A bridegroom say you? 'Tis a groom indeed,
  A grumbling groom, and that the girl shall find.
TRANIO. Curster than she? Why, 'tis impossible.
GREMIO. Why, he's a devil, a devil, a very fiend.
TRANIO. Why, she's a devil, a devil, the devil's dam.
GREMIO. Tut! she's a lamb, a dove, a fool to him.
  I'll tell you, Sir Lucentio: when the priest
  Should ask, if Katharine should be his wife,
  'Ay, by gogs-wouns!' quoth he; and swore so loud,
  That, all amaz'd, the priest let fall the book;
  And, as he stoop'd again to take it up,
  The mad-brain'd bridegroom took him such a cuff
  That down fell priest and book and book and priest:
  'Now take them up,' quoth he, 'if any list.'
TRANIO. What said the wench when he arose again?
GREMIO. Trembled and shook; for why, he stampt and
    swore,

As if the vicar meant to cozen him.
But after many ceremonies done,
He calls for wine: 'A health!' quoth he; as if
He had been aboard, carousing to his mates
After a storm; quaff'd off the muscadel,
And threw the sops all in the sexton's face;
Having no other reason
But that his beard grew thin and hungerly,
And seem'd to ask him sops as he was drinking.
This done, he took the bride about the neck,
And kiss'd her lips with such a clamorous smack
That at the parting all the church did echo:
And I, seeing this, came thence for very shame;
And after me, I know, the rout is coming.
Such a mad marriage never was before.
Hark, hark! I hear the minstrels play. *Music*

*Re-enter Petruchio, Katharina,
Bianca, Baptista, Hortensio, Grumio, and Train*

PETRUCHIO. Gentlemen and friends, I thank you for your pains:
I know you think to dine with me to-day,
And have prepar'd great store of wedding cheer;
But so it is, my haste doth call me hence,
And therefore here I mean to take my leave.
BAPTISTA. Is 't possible you will away to-night?
PETRUCHIO. I must away to-day, before night come.
Make it no wonder: if you knew my business,
You would entreat me rather go than stay.
And, honest company, I thank you all,
That have beheld me give away myself
To this most patient, sweet, and virtuous wife.
Dine with my father, drink a health to me,
For I must hence; and farewell to you all.
TRANIO. Let us entreat you stay till after dinner.
PETRUCHIO. It may not be.
GREMIO.   Let me entreat you.
PETRUCHIO. It cannot be.
KATHARINA.   Let me entreat you.
PETRUCHIO. I am content.
KATHARINA.   Are you content to stay?
PETRUCHIO. I am content you shall entreat me stay,
But yet not stay, entreat me how you can.

KATHARINA. Now, if you love me, stay.
PETRUCHIO. Grumio, my horse!
GRUMIO. Ay, sir, they be ready: the oats have eaten the horses.
KATHARINA. Nay, then,
Do what thou canst, I will not go to-day;
No, nor to-morrow, nor till I please myself.
The door is open, sir, there lies your way;
You may be jogging whiles your boots are green;
For me, I 'll not be gone till I please myself.
'Tis like you 'll prove a jolly surly groom,
That take it on you at the first so roundly.
PETRUCHIO. O Kate! content thee: prithee, be not angry.
KATHARINA. I will be angry: what hast thou to do?
Father, be quiet; he shall stay my leisure.
GREMIO. Ay, marry, sir, now it begins to work.
KATHARINA. Gentlemen, forward to the bridal dinner:
I see a woman may be made a fool,
If she had not a spirit to resist.
PETRUCHIO. They shall go forward, Kate, at thy command.
Obey the bride, you that attend on her;
Go to the feast, revel and domineer,
Carouse full measure to her maidenhead,
Be mad and merry, or go hang yourselves:
But for my bonny Kate, she must with me.
Nay, look not big, nor stamp, nor stare, nor fret;
I will be master of what is mine own.
She is my goods, my chattels; she is my house,
My household stuff, my field, my barn,
My horse, my ox, my ass, my any thing;
And here she stands, touch her whoever dare;
I 'll bring mine action on the proudest he
That stops my way in Padua. Grumio,
Draw forth thy weapon, we 're beset with thieves;
Rescue thy mistress, if thou be a man.
Fear not, sweet wench; they shall not touch thee, Kate:
I 'll buckler thee against a million.
Exeunt Petruchio, Katharina, and Grumio
BAPTISTA. Nay, let them go, a couple of quiet ones.
GREMIO. Went they not quickly I should die with laughing.
TRANIO. Of all mad matches never was the like.
LUCENTIO. Mistress, what 's your opinion of your sister?

BIANCA. That, being mad herself, she's madly mated.
GREMIO. I warrant him, Petruchio is Kated.
BAPTISTA. Neighbours and friends, though bride and bride-
  groom wants
  For to supply the places at the table,
  You know there wants no junkets at the feast.
  Lucentio, you shall supply the bridegroom's place,
  And let Bianca take her sister's room.
TRANIO. Shall sweet Bianca practise how to bride it?
BAPTISTA. She shall, Lucentio. Come, gentlemen, let's go.
Exeunt

ACT FOUR

SCENE ONE

A Hall in Petruchio's Country House.

Enter Grumio

GRUMIO. Fie, fie, on all tired jades, on all mad masters, and all foul ways! Was ever man so beaten? Was ever man so rayed? Was ever man so weary? I am sent before to make a fire, and they are coming after to warm them. Now, were not I a little pot and soon hot, my very lips might freeze to my teeth, my tongue to the roof of my mouth, my heart in my belly, ere I should come by a fire to thaw me; but I, with blowing the fire, shall warm myself; for, considering the weather, a taller man than I will take cold. Holla, ho! Curtis.

Enter Curtis

CURTIS. Who is that calls so coldly?

GRUMIO. A piece of ice: if thou doubt it, thou mayst slide from my shoulder to my heel with no greater a run but my head and my neck. A fire, good Curtis.

CURTIS. Is my master and his wife coming, Grumio?

GRUMIO. O, ay! Curtis, ay; and therefore fire, fire; cast on no water.

CURTIS. Is she so hot a shrew as she's reported?

GRUMIO. She was, good Curtis, before this frost; but, thou knowest, winter tames man, woman, and beast; for it hath tamed my old master, and my new mistress, and myself, fellow Curtis.

CURTIS. Away, you three-inch fool! I am no beast.

GRUMIO. Am I but three inches? Why, thy horn is a foot; and so long am I at the least. But wilt thou make a fire, or shall I complain on thee to our mistress, whose hand,—she being now at hand,—thou shalt soon feel, to thy cold comfort, for being slow in thy hot office?

CURTIS. I prithee, good Grumio, tell me, how goes the world?

GRUMIO. A cold world, Curtis, in every office but thine; and therefore, fire. Do thy duty, and have thy duty, for my master and mistress are almost frozen to death.

CURTIS. There's fire ready; and therefore, good Grumio, the news?

GRUMIO. Why, 'Jack, boy! ho, boy!' and as much news as thou wilt.

CURTIS. Come, you are so full of cony-catching.

GRUMIO. Why, therefore fire: for I have caught extreme cold. Where's the cook? Is supper ready, the house trimmed, rushes strewed, cobwebs swept; the serving-men in their new fustian, their white stockings, and every officer his wedding-garment on? Be the Jacks fair within, the Jills fair without, and carpets laid, and everything in order?

CURTIS. All ready; and therefore, I pray thee, news?

GRUMIO. First, know, my horse is tired; my master and mistress fallen out.

CURTIS. How?

GRUMIO. Out of their saddles into the dirt; and thereby hangs a tale.

CURTIS. Let's ha't, good Grumio.

GRUMIO. Lend thine ear.

CURTIS. Here.

GRUMIO. (*Striking him*) There.

CURTIS. This is to feel a tale, not to hear a tale.

GRUMIO. And therefore it is called a sensible tale; and this cuff was but to knock at your ear and beseech listening. Now I begin: Imprimis, we came down a foul hill, my master riding behind my mistress,—

CURTIS. Both of one horse?

GRUMIO. What's that to thee?

CURTIS. Why, a horse.

GRUMIO. Tell thou the tale: but hadst thou not crossed me thou shouldst have heard how her horse fell, and she under her horse; thou shouldst have heard in how miry a place, how she was bemoiled; how he left her with the horse upon her; how he beat me because her horse stumbled; how she waded through the dirt to pluck him off me: how he swore; how she prayed, that never prayed before;

how I cried; how the horses ran away; how her bridle was burst; how I lost my crupper; with many things of worthy memory, which now shall die in oblivion, and thou return unexperienced to thy grave.

CURTIS. By this reckoning he is more shrew than she.

GRUMIO. Ay; and that, thou and the proudest of you all shall find when he comes home. But what talk I of this? Call forth Nathaniel, Joseph, Nicholas, Philip, Walter, Sugarsop, and the rest: let their heads be sleekly combed, their blue coats brushed, and their garters of an indifferent knit: let them curtsy with their left legs, and not presume to touch a hair of my master's horsetail till they kiss their hands. Are they all ready?

CURTIS. They are.

GRUMIO. Call them forth.

CURTIS. Do you hear? ho! you must meet my master to countenance my mistress.

GRUMIO. Why, she hath a face of her own.

CURTIS. Who knows not that?

GRUMIO. Thou, it seems, that callest for company to countenance her.

CURTIS. I call them forth to credit her.

GRUMIO. Why, she comes to borrow nothing of them.

Enter several Servants

NATHANIEL. Welcome home, Grumio!

PHILIP. How now, Grumio?

JOSEPH. What, Grumio!

NICHOLAS. Fellow Grumio!

NATHANIEL. How now, old lad!

GRUMIO. Welcome, you; how now, you; what, you; fellow, you; and thus much for greeting. Now, my spruce companions, is all ready, and all things neat?

NATHANIEL. All things is ready. How near is our master?

GRUMIO. E'en at hand, alighted by this; and therefore be not,—Cock's passion, silence! I hear my master.

Enter Petruchio and Katharina

PETRUCHIO. Where be these knaves? What! no man at door
To hold my stirrup nor to take my horse?
Where is Nathaniel, Gregory, Philip?—

ALL SERVANTS. Here, here, sir; here, sir.

PETRUCHIO. Here, sir! here, sir! here, sir! here, sir!
You logger-headed and unpolish'd grooms!

What, no attendance? no regard? no duty?
Where is the foolish knave I sent before?

GRUMIO. Here, sir; as foolish as I was before.

PETRUCHIO. You peasant swain! you whoreson malt-horse drudge!
Did I not bid thee meet me in the park,
And bring along these rascal knaves with thee?

GRUMIO. Nathaniel's coat, sir, was not fully made,
And Gabriel's pumps were all unpink'd i' the heel,
There was no link to colour Peter's hat,
And Walter's dagger was not come from sheathing,
There was none fine but Adam, Ralph, and Gregory;
The rest were ragged, old, and beggarly;
Yet, as they are, here are they come to meet you.

PETRUCHIO. Go, rascals, go, and fetch my supper in.
Exeunt some of the Servants
'Where is the life that late I led?'
Where are those—? Sit down, Kate, and welcome.
Soud, soud, soud, soud!
Re-enter Servants with supper
Why, when, I say?—Nay, good sweet Kate, be merry.—
Off with my boots, you rogues! you villains! When?
  It was the friar of orders grey,
  As he forth walked on his way:
Out, you rogue! you pluck my foot awry: *Strikes him*
Take that, and mend the plucking off the other.
Be merry, Kate. Some water, here; what, ho!
Where's my spaniel Troilus? Sirrah, get you hence
And bid my cousin Ferdinand come hither: *Exit Servant*
One, Kate, that you must kiss, and be acquainted with.
Where are my slippers? Shall I have some water?
Come, Kate, and wash, and welcome heartily.—
Servant lets the ewer fall. Petruchio strikes him
You whoreson villain! will you let it fall?

KATHARINA. Patience, I pray you; 'twas a fault unwilling.

PETRUCHIO. A whoreson, beetle-headed, flap-ear'd knave!
Come, Kate, sit down; I know you have a stomach.
Will you give thanks, sweet Kate, or else shall I?—
What's this? mutton?

FIRST SERVANT.   Ay.

PETRUCHIO.   Who brought it?

FIRST SERVANT.   I.

PETRUCHIO. 'Tis burnt; and so is all the meat.
What dogs are these! Where is the rascal cook?
How durst you, villains, bring it from the dresser,
And serve it thus to me that love it not?
Throws the meat, &c., at them
There, take it to you, trenchers, cups, and all.
You heedless joltheads and unmanner'd slaves!
What! do you grumble? I 'll be with you straight.
KATHARINA. I pray you, husband, be not so disquiet:
The meat was well if you were so contented.
PETRUCHIO. I tell thee, Kate, 'twas burnt and dried away;
And I expressly am forbid to touch it,
For it engenders choler, planteth anger;
And better 'twere that both of us did fast,
Since, of ourselves, ourselves are choleric,
Than feed it with such over-roasted flesh.
Be patient; to-morrow 't shall be mended,
And for this night we 'll fast for company:
Come, I will bring thee to thy bridal chamber.
Exeunt Petruchio, Katharina, and Curtis
NATHANIEL. Peter, didst ever see the like?
PETER. He kills her in her own humour.
Re-enter Curtis
GRUMIO. Where is he?
CURTIS. In her chamber, making a sermon of continency to her;
And rails, and swears, and rates, that she, poor soul,
Knows not which way to stand, to look, to speak,
And sits as one new-risen from a dream.
Away, away! for he is coming hither. *Exeunt*
Re-enter Petruchio
PETRUCHIO. Thus have I politicly begun my reign,
And 'tis my hope to end successfully.
My falcon now is sharp and passing empty,
And till she stoop she must not be full-gorg'd,
For then she never looks upon her lure.
Another way I have to man my haggard,
To make her come and know her keeper's call;
That is, to watch her, as we watch these kites
That bate and beat and will not be obedient.
She eat no meat to-day, nor none shall eat;
Last night she slept not, nor to-night she shall not:

As with the meat, some undeserved fault
I'll find about the making of the bed;
And here I'll fling the pillow, there the bolster,
This way the coverlet, another way the sheets:
Ay, and amid this hurly I intend
That all is done in reverend care of her;
And in conclusion she shall watch all night:
And if she chance to nod I'll rail and brawl,
And with the clamour keep her still awake.
This is a way to kill a wife with kindness;
And thus I'll curb her mad and headstrong humour.
He that knows better how to tame a shrew,
Now let him speak: 'tis charity to show. *Exit*

SCENE TWO

Padua. Before Baptista's House.

Enter Tranio and Hortensio

TRANIO. Is't possible, friend Licio, that Mistress Bianca
Doth fancy any other but Lucentio?
I tell you, sir, she bears me fair in hand.
HORTENSIO. Sir, to satisfy you in what I have said,
Stand by, and mark the manner of his teaching.
They stand aside
Enter Bianca and Lucentio
LUCENTIO. Now, mistress, profit you in what you read?
BIANCA. What, master, read you? First resolve me that.
LUCENTIO. I read that I profess, the Art to Love.
BIANCA. And may you prove, sir, master of your art!
LUCENTIO. While you, sweet dear, prove mistress of my
heart. *They retire*
HORTENSIO. Quick proceeders, marry! Now, tell me, I pray,
You that durst swear that your mistress Bianca
Lov'd none in the world so well as Lucentio.
TRANIO. O despiteful love! unconstant womankind!
I tell thee, Licio, this is wonderful.
HORTENSIO. Mistake no more: I am not Licio,
Nor a musician, as I seem to be;
But one that scorns to live in this disguise,
For such a one as leaves a gentleman,

And makes a god of such a cullion:
Know, sir, that I am call'd Hortensio.

TRANIO. Signior Hortensio, I have often heard
Of your entire affection to Bianca;
And since mine eyes are witness of her lightness,
I will with you, if you be so contented,
Forswear Bianca and her love for ever.

HORTENSIO. See, how they kiss and court! Signior Lucentio,
Here is my hand, and here I firmly vow
Never to woo her more; but do forswear her,
As one unworthy all the former favours
That I have fondly flatter'd her withal.

TRANIO. And here I take the like unfeigned oath,
Never to marry with her though she would entreat.
Fie on her! See how beastly she doth court him.

HORTENSIO. Would all the world, but he had quite forsworn!
For me, that I may surely keep mine oath,
I will be married to a wealthy widow
Ere three days pass, which hath as long lov'd me
As I have lov'd this proud disdainful haggard.
And so farewell, Signior Lucentio.
Kindness in women, not their beauteous looks,
Shall win my love: and so I take my leave,
In resolution as I swore before.

Exit Hortensio. Lucentio and Bianca advance

TRANIO. Mistress Bianca, bless you with such grace
As 'longeth to a lover's blessed case!
Nay, I have ta'en you napping, gentle love,
And have forsworn you with Hortensio.

BIANCA. Tranio, you jest. But have you both forsworn me?

TRANIO. Mistress, we have.

LUCENTIO. Then we are rid of Licio.

TRANIO. I' faith, he'll have a lusty widow now,
That shall be woo'd and wedded in a day.

BIANCA. God give him joy!

TRANIO. Ay, and he'll tame her.

BIANCA. He says so, Tranio.

TRANIO. Faith, he is gone unto the taming-school.

BIANCA. The taming-school! what, is there such a place?

TRANIO. Ay, mistress, and Petruchio is the master;
That teacheth tricks eleven and twenty long,
To tame a shrew, and charm her chattering tongue.

ACT IV · SCENE II

Enter Biondello, running

BIONDELLO. O master, master! I have watch'd so long
That I 'm dog-weary; but at last I spied
An ancient angel coming down the hill
Will serve the turn.

TRANIO. What is he, Biondello?

BIONDELLO. Master, a mercatante, or a pedant,
I know not what; but formal in apparel,
In gait and countenance surely like a father.

LUCENTIO. And what of him, Tranio?

TRANIO. If he be credulous and trust my tale,
I 'll make him glad to seem Vincentio,
And give assurance to Baptista Minola,
As if he were the right Vincentio.
Take in your love, and then let me alone.

Exeunt Lucentio and Bianca
Enter a Pedant

PEDANT. God save you, sir!

TRANIO. And you, sir! you are welcome.
Travel you far on, or are you at the farthest?

PEDANT. Sir, at the farthest for a week or two;
But then up farther, and as far as Rome;
And so to Tripoli, if God lend me life.

TRANIO. What countryman, I pray?

PEDANT. Of Mantua.

TRANIO. Of Mantua, sir! marry, God forbid!
And come to Padua, careless of your life?

PEDANT. My life, sir! How, I pray? For that goes hard.

TRANIO. 'Tis death for any one in Mantua
To come to Padua. Know you not the cause?
Your ships are stay'd at Venice; and the duke,—
For private quarrel 'twixt your duke and him,—
Hath publish'd and proclaim'd it openly.
'Tis marvel, but that you are but newly come,
You might have heard it else proclaim'd about.

PEDANT. Alas, sir! it is worse for me than so;
For I have bills for money by exchange
From Florence, and must here deliver them.

TRANIO. Well, sir, to do you courtesy,
This will I do, and this I will advise you:
First, tell me, have you ever been at Pisa?

PEDANT. Ay, sir, in Pisa have I often been;

Pisa, renowned for grave citizens.
TRANIO. Among them, know you one Vincentio?
PEDANT. I know him not, but I have heard of him;
 A merchant of incomparable wealth.
TRANIO. He is my father, sir; and, sooth to say,
 In countenance somewhat doth resemble you.
BIONDELLO. (*Aside*) As much as an apple doth an oyster,
 and all one.
TRANIO. To save your life in this extremity,
 This favour will I do you for his sake;
 And think it not the worst of all your fortunes
 That you are like to Sir Vincentio.
 His name and credit shall you undertake,
 And in my house you shall be friendly lodg'd,
 Look that you take upon you as you should!
 You understand me, sir; so shall you stay
 Till you have done your business in the city.
 If this be courtesy, sir, accept of it.
PEDANT. O sir, I do; and will repute you ever
 The patron of my life and liberty.
TRANIO. Then go with me to make the matter good.
 This, by the way, I let you understand:
 My father is here look'd for every day,
 To pass assurance of a dower in marriage
 'Twixt me and one Baptista's daughter here:
 In all these circumstances I'll instruct you.
 Go with me to clothe you as becomes you.   *Exeunt*

SCENE THREE

A Room in Petruchio's House.

Enter Katharina and Grumio

GRUMIO. No, no, forsooth; I dare not, for my life.
KATHARINA. The more my wrong the more his spite appears.
 What, did he marry me to famish me?
 Beggars, that come unto my father's door,
 Upon entreaty have a present alms;
 If not, elsewhere they meet with charity:
 But I, who never knew how to entreat,
 Nor never needed that I should entreat,

ACT IV : SCENE III

Am starv'd for meat, giddy for lack of sleep;
With oaths kept waking, and with brawling fed.
And that which spites me more than all these wants,
He does it under name of perfect love;
As who should say, if I should sleep or eat
'Twere deadly sickness, or else present death.
I prithee go and get me some repast;
I care not what, so it be wholesome food.

GRUMIO. What say you to a neat's foot?

KATHARINA. 'Tis passing good: I prithee let me have it.

GRUMIO. I fear it is too choleric a meat.
How say you to a fat tripe finely broil'd?

KATHARINA. I like it well: good Grumio, fetch it me.

GRUMIO. I cannot tell; I fear 'tis choleric.
What say you to a piece of beef and mustard?

KATHARINA. A dish that I do love to feed upon.

GRUMIO. Ay, but the mustard is too hot a little.

KATHARINA. Why, then the beef, and let the mustard rest.

GRUMIO. Nay, then I will not: you shall have the mustard,
Or else you get no beef of Grumio.

KATHARINA. Then both, or one, or anything thou wilt.

GRUMIO. Why then, the mustard without the beef.

KATHARINA. Go, get thee gone, thou false deluding slave,
Beats him
That feed'st me with the very name of meat.
Sorrow on thee and all the pack of you,
That triumph thus upon my misery!
Go, get thee gone, I say.

Enter Petruchio with a dish of meat; and Hortensio

PETRUCHIO. How fares my Kate? What, sweeting, all amort?

HORTENSIO. Mistress, what cheer?

KATHARINA. Faith, as cold as can be.

PETRUCHIO. Pluck up thy spirits; look cheerfully upon me.
Here, love; thou seest how diligent I am,
To dress thy meat myself and bring it thee:
Sets the dish on a table
I am sure, sweet Kate, this kindness merits thanks.
What! not a word? Nay then, thou lov'st it not,
And all my pains is sorted to no proof.
Here, take away this dish.

KATHARINA. I pray you, let it stand.

PETRUCHIO. The poorest service is repaid with thanks,

And so shall mine, before you touch the meat.

KATHARINA. I thank you, sir.

HORTENSIO. Signior Petruchio, fie! you are to blame.
Come, Mistress Kate, I'll bear you company.

PETRUCHIO. (*Aside*) Eat it up all, Hortensio, if thou lov'st me.
Much good do it unto thy gentle heart!
Kate, eat apace: and now, my honey love,
Will we return unto thy father's house,
And revel it as bravely as the best,
With silken coats and caps and golden rings,
With ruffs and cuffs and farthingales and things;
With scarfs and fans and double change of bravery,
With amber bracelets, beads and all this knavery.
What! hast thou din'd? The tailor stays thy leisure,
To deck thy body with his ruffling treasure.

Enter Tailor

Come, tailor, let us see these ornaments;
Lay forth the gown.—

Enter Haberdasher

What news with you, sir?

HABERDASHER. Here is the cap your worship did bespeak.

PETRUCHIO. Why, this was moulded on a porringer;
A velvet dish: fie, fie! 'tis lewd and filthy:
Why, 'tis a cockle or a walnut-shell,
A knack, a toy, a trick, a baby's cap:
Away with it! Come, let me have a bigger.

KATHARINA. I'll have no bigger: this doth fit the time,
And gentlewomen wear such caps as these.

PETRUCHIO. When you are gentle, you shall have one too;
And not till then.

HORTENSIO. (*Aside*) That will not be in haste.

KATHARINA. Why, sir, I trust I may have leave to speak,
And speak I will; I am no child, no babe:
Your betters have endur'd me say my mind,
And if you cannot, best you stop your ears.
My tongue will tell the anger of my heart,
Or else my heart, concealing it, will break:
And rather than it shall, I will be free
Even to the uttermost, as I please, in words.

PETRUCHIO. Why, thou sayst true; it is a paltry cap,
A custard-coffin, a bauble, a silken pie.

I love thee well in that thou lik'st it not.

KATHARINA. Love me or love me not, I like the cap,
And it I will have, or I will have none. *Exit Haberdasher*

PETRUCHIO. Thy gown? why, ay: come, tailor, let us see 't.
O mercy, God! what masquing stuff is here?
What 's this? a sleeve? 'Tis like a demi-cannon:
What! up and down, carv'd like an apple-tart?
Here 's snip and nip and cut and slish and slash,
Like to a censer in a barber's shop.
Why, what, i' devil's name, tailor, call'st thou this?

HORTENSIO. (*Aside*) I see, she's like to have neither cap nor gown.

TAILOR. You bid me make it orderly and well,
According to the fashion and the time.

PETRUCHIO. Marry, and did: but if you be remember'd,
I did not bid you mar it to the time.
Go, hop me over every kennel home,
For you shall hop without my custom, sir.
I 'll none of it: hence! make your best of it.

KATHARINA. I never saw a better-fashion'd gown,
More quaint, more pleasing, nor more commendable.
Belike you mean to make a puppet of me.

PETRUCHIO. Why, true; he means to make a puppet of thee

TAILOR. She says your worship means to make a puppet of her.

PETRUCHIO. O monstrous arrogance! Thou liest, thou thread,
Thou thimble,
Thou yard, three-quarters, half-yard, quarter, nail!
Thou flea, thou nit, thou winter-cricket thou!
Brav'd in mine own house with a skein of thread!
Away! thou rag, thou quantity, thou remnant,
Or I shall so be-mete thee with thy yard
As thou shalt think on prating whilst thou liv'st!
I tell thee, I, that thou hast marr'd her gown.

TAILOR. Your worship is deceiv'd: the gown is made
Just as my master had direction.
Grumio gave order how it should be done.

GRUMIO. I gave him no order; I gave him the stuff.

TAILOR. But how did you desire it should be made?

GRUMIO. Marry, sir, with needle and thread.

TAILOR. But did you not request to have it cut?

GRUMIO. Thou hast faced many things.

TAILOR. I have.

GRUMIO. Face not me: thou hast braved many men; brave not me: I will neither be faced nor braved. I say unto thee, I bid thy master cut out the gown; but I did not bid him cut it to pieces: ergo, thou liest.

TAILOR. Why, here is the note of the fashion to testify.

PETRUCHIO. Read it.

GRUMIO. The note lies in 's throat if he say I said so.

TAILOR. 'Imprimis. A loose-bodied gown.'

GRUMIO. Master, if ever I said loose-bodied gown, sew me in the skirts of it, and beat me to death with a bottom of brown thread. I said, a gown.

PETRUCHIO. Proceed.

TAILOR. 'With a small compassed cape.'

GRUMIO. I confess the cape.

TAILOR. 'With a trunk sleeve.'

GRUMIO. I confess two sleeves.

TAILOR. 'The sleeves curiously cut.'

PETRUCHIO. Ay, there 's the villany.

GRUMIO. Error i' the bill, sir; error i' the bill. I commanded the sleeves should be cut out and sewed up again; and that I 'll prove upon thee, though thy little finger be armed in a thimble.

TAILOR. This is true that I say: an I had thee in place where thou shouldst know it.

GRUMIO. I am for thee straight: take thou the bill, give me thy mete-yard, and spare not me.

HORTENSIO. God-a-mercy, Grumio! then he shall have no odds.

PETRUCHIO. Well, sir, in brief, the gown is not for me.

GRUMIO. You are i' the right, sir; tis for my mistress.

PETRUCHIO. Go, take it up unto thy master's use.

GRUMIO. Villain, not for thy life! take up my mistress' gown for thy master's use!

PETRUCHIO. Why, sir, what 's your conceit in that?

GRUMIO. O, sir, the conceit is deeper than you think for. Take up my mistress' gown to his master's use! O, fie, fie, fie!

PETRUCHIO. (*Aside*) Hortensio, say thou wilt see the tailor paid.

(*To Tailor*) Go take it hence; be gone, and say no more.

ACT IV : SCENE III

HORTENSIO. (*Aside to Tailor*) Tailor, I'll pay thee for thy
  gown to-morrow:
  Take no unkindness of his hasty words.
  Away! I say; commend me to thy master. *Exit Tailor*
PETRUCHIO. Well, come, my Kate; we will unto your father's,
  Even in these honest mean habiliments.
  Our purses shall be proud, our garments poor;
  For 'tis the mind that makes the body rich;
  And as the sun breaks through the darkest clouds,
  So honour peereth in the meanest habit.
  What is the jay more precious than the lark
  Because his feathers are more beautiful?
  Or is the adder better than the eel
  Because his painted skin contents the eye?
  O, no, good Kate; neither art thou the worse
  For this poor furniture and mean array.
  If thou account'st it shame, lay it on me;
  And therefore frolic: we will hence forthwith,
  To feast and sport us at thy father's house.
  Go, call my men, and let us straight to him;
  And bring our horses unto Long-lane end;
  There will we mount, and thither walk on foot.
  Let's see; I think 'tis now some seven o'clock,
  And well we may come there by dinner-time.
KATHARINA. I dare assure you, sir, 'tis almost two;
  And 'twill be supper-time ere you come there.
PETRUCHIO. It shall be seven ere I go to horse.
  Look, what I speak, or do, or think to do,
  You are still crossing it. Sirs, let 't alone:
  I will not go to-day; and ere I do,
  It shall be what o'clock I say it is.
HORTENSIO. Why, so this gallant will command the sun.
  Exeunt

SCENE FOUR

Padua. Before Baptista's House.

Enter Tranio, and the Pedant dressed like Vincentio

TRANIO. Sir, this is the house: please it you that I call?
PEDANT. Ay, what else? and, but I be deceived,
  Signior Baptista may remember me,
  Near twenty years ago, in Genoa,
  Where we were lodgers at the Pegasus.
TRANIO. 'Tis well; and hold your own, in any case,
  With such austerity as 'longeth to a father.
PEDANT. I warrant you. But, sir, here comes your boy;
  'Twere good he were school'd.
      Enter Biondello
TRANIO. Fear you not him. Sirrah Biondello,
  Now do your duty throughly, I advise you:
  Imagine 'twere the right Vincentio.
BIONDELLO. Tut! fear not me.
TRANIO. But hast thou done thy errand to Baptista?
BIONDELLO. I told him that your father was at Venice,
  And that you look'd for him this day in Padua.
TRANIO. Thou 'rt a tall fellow: hold thee that to drink.
  Here comes Baptista. Set your countenance, sir.
      Enter Baptista and Lucentio
  Signior Baptista, you are happily met.
  (*To the Pedant*) Sir, this is the gentleman I told you of:
  I pray you, stand good father to me now,
  Give me Bianca for my patrimony.
PEDANT. Soft, son!
  Sir, by your leave: having come to Padua
  To gather in some debts, my son Lucentio
  Made me acquainted with a weighty cause
  Of love between your daughter and himself:
  And,—for the good report I hear of you,
  And for the love he beareth to your daughter,
  And she to him,—to stay him not too long,
  I am content, in a good father's care,
  To have him match'd; and, if you please to like
  No worse than I, upon some agreement

Me shall you find ready and willing
With one consent to have her so bestow'd;
For curious I cannot be with you,
Signior Baptista, of whom I hear so well.

BAPTISTA. Sir, pardon me in what I have to say:
Your plainness and your shortness please me well.
Right true it is, your son Lucentio here
Doth love my daughter and she loveth him,
Or both dissemble deeply their affections:
And therefore, if you say no more than this,
That like a father you will deal with him
And pass my daughter a sufficient dower,
The match is made, and all is done:
Your son shall have my daughter with consent.

TRANIO. I thank you, sir. Where, then, do you know best
We be affied and such assurance ta'en
As shall with either part's agreement stand?

BAPTISTA. Not in my house, Lucentio; for, you know,
Pitchers have ears, and I have many servants.
Besides, old Gremio is hearkening still,
And happily we might be interrupted.

TRANIO. Then at my lodging, an it like you:
There doth my father lie, and there this night
We'll pass the business privately and well.
Send for your daughter by your servant here;
My boy shall fetch the scrivener presently.
The worst is this, that, at so slender warning,
You're like to have a thin and slender pittance.

BAPTISTA. It likes me well. Cambio, hie you home,
And bid Bianca make her ready straight;
And, if you will, tell what hath happened:
Lucentio's father is arriv'd in Padua,
And how she's like to be Lucentio's wife.

LUCENTIO. I pray the gods she may with all my heart!

TRANIO. Dally not with the gods, but get thee gone.
Signior Baptista, shall I lead the way?
Welcome! one mess is like to be your cheer.
Come, sir; we will better it in Pisa.

BAPTISTA. I follow you.

Exeunt Tranio, Pedant, and Baptista

BIONDELLO. Cambio!

LUCENTIO. What sayst thou, Biondello?

BIONDELLO. You saw my master wink and laugh upon you?
LUCENTIO. Biondello, what of that?
BIONDELLO. Faith, nothing; but he has left me here behind to expound the meaning or moral of his signs and tokens.
LUCENTIO. I pray thee, moralize them.
BIONDELLO. Then thus. Baptista is safe, talking with the deceiving father of a deceitful son.
LUCENTIO. And what of him?
BIONDELLO. His daughter is to be brought by you to the supper.
LUCENTIO. And then?
BIONDELLO. The old priest at Saint Luke's church is at your command at all hours.
LUCENTIO. And what of all this?
BIONDELLO. I cannot tell, expect they are busied about a counterfeit assurance: take you assurance of her, cum privilegio ad imprimendum solum. To the church! Take the priest, clerk, and some sufficient honest witnesses.
If this be not that you look for, I have no more to say,
But bid Bianca farewell for ever and a day. *Going*
LUCENTIO. Hearest thou, Biondello?
BIONDELLO. I cannot tarry: I knew a wench married in an afternoon as she went to the garden for parsley to stuff a rabbit; and so may you, sir; and so, adieu, sir. My master hath appointed me to go to Saint Luke's, to bid the priest be ready to come against you come with your appendix.

Exit

LUCENTIO. I may, and will, if she be so contented:
She will be pleas'd; then wherefore should I doubt?
Hap what hap may, I'll roundly go about her:
It shall go hard if Cambio go without her. *Exit*

SCENE FIVE

A public Road.

Enter Petruchio, Katharina, Hortensio, and Servants

PETRUCHIO. Come on, i' God's name; once more toward our father's.
Good Lord, how bright and goodly shines the moon!
KATHARINA. The moon! the sun: it is not moonlight now.

[4-41] ACT IV : SCENE V 757

PETRUCHIO. I say it is the moon that shines so bright.
KATHARINA. I know it is the sun that shines so bright.
PETRUCHIO. Now, by my mother's son, and that's myself,
  It shall be moon, or star, or what I list,
  Or ere I journey to your father's house.
  Go one and fetch our horses back again.
  Evermore cross'd and cross'd; nothing but cross'd!
HORTENSIO. Say as he says, or we shall never go.
KATHARINA. Forward, I pray, since we have come so far,
  And be it moon, or sun, or what you please.
  An if you please to call it a rush-candle,
  Henceforth I vow it shall be so for me.
PETRUCHIO. I say it is the moon.
KATHARINA.   I know it is the moon.
PETRUCHIO. Nay, then you lie; it is the blessed sun.
KATHARINA. Then God be bless'd, it is the blessed sun:
  But sun it is not when you say it is not,
  And the moon changes even as your mind.
  What you will have it nam'd, even that it is;
  And so, it shall be so for Katharine.
HORTENSIO. Petruchio, go thy ways; the field is won.
PETRUCHIO. Well, forward, forward! thus the bowl should run,
  And not unluckily against the bias.
  But soft! what company is coming here?
      Enter Vincentio, in a travelling dress
  (*To Vincentio*) Good-morrow, gentle mistress: where away?
  Tell me, sweet Kate, and tell me truly too,
  Hast thou beheld a fresher gentlewoman?
  Such war of white and red within her cheeks!
  What stars do spangle heaven with such beauty,
  As those two eyes become that heavenly face?
  Fair lovely maid, once more good day to thee.
  Sweet Kate, embrace her for her beauty's sake.
HORTENSIO. A' will make the man mad, to make a woman of him.
KATHARINA. Young budding virgin, fair and fresh and sweet,
  Whither away, or where is thy abode?
  Happy the parents of so fair a child;
  Happier the man, whom favourable stars
  Allot thee for his lovely bed-fellow!

PETRUCHIO. Why, how now, Kate! I hope thou art not mad:
    This is a man, old, wrinkled, faded, wither'd,
    And not a maiden, as thou sayst he is.
KATHARINA. Pardon, old father, my mistaking eyes,
    That have been so bedazzled with the sun
    That everything I look on seemeth green:
    Now I perceive thou art a reverend father;
    Pardon, I pray thee, for my mad mistaking.
PETRUCHIO. Do, good old grandsire; and withal make known
    Which way thou travellest: if along with us,
    We shall be joyful of thy company.
VINCENTIO. Fair sir, and you my merry mistress,
    That with your strange encounter much amaz'd me,
    My name is called Vincentio; my dwelling, Pisa;
    And bound I am to Padua, there to visit
    A son of mine, which long I have not seen.
PETRUCHIO. What is his name?
VINCENTIO. Lucentio, gentle sir.
PETRUCHIO. Happily met; the happier for thy son.
    And now by law, as well as reverend age,
    I may entitle thee my loving father:
    The sister to my wife, this gentlewoman,
    Thy son by this hath married. Wonder not,
    Nor be not griev'd: she is of good esteem,
    Her dowry wealthy, and of worthy birth;
    Beside, so qualified as may beseem
    The spouse of any noble gentleman.
    Let me embrace with old Vincentio;
    And wander we to see thy honest son,
    Who will of thy arrival be full joyous.
VINCENTIO. But is this true? or is it else your pleasure,
    Like pleasant travellers, to break a jest
    Upon the company you overtake?
HORTENSIO. I do assure thee, father, so it is.
PETRUCHIO. Come, go along, and see the truth hereof;
    For our first merriment hath made thee jealous.
                              Exeunt all but Hortensio
HORTENSIO. Well, Petruchio, this has put me in heart.
    Have to my widow! and if she be froward,
    Then hast thou taught Hortensio to be untoward.   *Exit*

ACT FIVE

SCENE ONE

Padua. Before Lucentio's House.

*Enter on one side Biondello, Lucentio, and Bianca;
Gremio walking on the other side*

BIONDELLO. Softly and swiftly, sir, for the priest is ready.
LUCENTIO. I fly, Biondello: but they may chance to need thee at home; therefore leave us.
BIONDELLO. Nay, faith, I'll see the church o' your back; and then come back to my master as soon as I can.
  Exeunt Lucentio, Bianca, and Biondello
GREMIO. I marvel Cambio comes not all this while.
  Enter Petruchio, Katharina, Vincentio, and Attendants
PETRUCHIO. Sir, here's the door, this is Lucentio's house:
  My father's bears more toward the market-place;
  Thither must I, and here I leave you, sir.
VINCENTIO. You shall not choose but drink before you go.
  I think I shall command your welcome here,
  And, by all likelihood, some cheer is toward. *Knocks*
GREMIO. They're busy within; you were best knock louder.
  Enter Pedant above, at a window
PEDANT. What's he that knocks as he would beat down the gate?
VINCENTIO. Is Signior Lucentio within, sir?
PEDANT. He's within, sir, but not to be spoken withal.
VINCENTIO. What if a man bring him a hundred pound or two, to make merry withal?
PEDANT. Keep your hundred pounds to yourself: he shall need none so long as I live.
PETRUCHIO. Nay, I told you your son was well beloved in Padua. Do you hear, sir? To leave frivolous circumstances, I pray you, tell Signior Lucentio that his father is come from Pisa, and is here at the door to speak with him.

PEDANT. Thou liest: his father is come from Padua, and here looking out at the window.

VINCENTIO. Art thou his father?

PEDANT. Ay, sir; so his mother says, if I may believe her.

PETRUCHIO. (*To Vincentio*) Why, how now, gentleman! why, this is flat knavery, to take upon you another man's name.

PEDANT. Lay hands on the villain: I believe, a' means to cozen somebody in this city under my countenance.

Re-enter Biondello

BIONDELLO. I have seen them in the church together: God send 'em good shipping! But who is here? Mine old master, Vincentio! Now we are undone and brought to nothing.

VINCENTIO. (*Seeing Biondello*) Come hither, crack-hemp.

BIONDELLO. I hope I may choose, sir.

VINCENTIO. Come hither, you rogue. What, have you forgot me?

BIONDELLO. Forgot you! no, sir: I could not forget you, for I never saw you before in all my life.

VINCENTIO. What, you notorious villain! Didst thou never see thy master's father, Vincentio?

BIONDELLO. What, my old, worshipful old master? Yes, marry, sir. See where he looks out of the window.

VINCENTIO. Is 't so, indeed? *Beats Biondello*

BIONDELLO. Help, help, help! Here 's a madman will murder me. *Exit*

PEDANT. Help, son! Help, Signior Baptista!
Exit from the window

PETRUCHIO. Prithee, Kate, let 's stand aside, and see the end of this controversy. *They retire*

Re-enter Pedant below; Baptista, Tranio, and Servants

TRANIO. Sir, what are you that offer to beat my servant?

VINCENTIO. What am I, sir! nay, what are you, sir? O immortal gods! O fine villain! A silken doublet! a velvet hose! a scarlet cloak! and a copatain hat! O, I am undone! I am undone! while I play the good husband at home, my son and my servant spend all at the university.

TRANIO. How now! What 's the matter?

BAPTISTA. What, is the man lunatic?

TRANIO. Sir, you seem a sober ancient gentleman by your habit, but your words show you a madman. Why, sir, what

ACT V : SCENE I

VINCENTIO. Thy father! O villain! He is a sailmaker in Bergamo.
BAPTISTA. You mistake, sir, you mistake, sir. Pray, what do you think is his name?
VINCENTIO. His name! As if I knew not his name: I have brought him up ever since he was three years old, and his name is Tranio.
PEDANT. Away, away, mad ass! His name is Lucentio; and he is mine only son, and heir to the lands of me, Signior Vincentio.
VINCENTIO. Lucentio! O! he hath murdered his master. Lay hold on him, I charge you in the duke's name. O my son, my son! tell me, thou villain, where is my son Lucentio?
TRANIO. Call forth an officer.
Enter one with an Officer
Carry this mad knave to the gaol. Father Baptista,
I charge you see that he be forthcoming.
VINCENTIO. Carry me to the gaol!
GREMIO. Stay, officer: he shall not go to prison.
BAPTISTA. Talk not, Signior Gremio: I say he shall go to prison.
GREMIO. Take heed, Signior Baptista, lest you be cony-catched in this business: I dare swear this is the right Vincentio.
PEDANT. Swear, if thou darest.
GREMIO. Nay, I dare not swear it.
TRANIO. Then thou wert best say that I am not Lucentio.
GREMIO. Yes, I know thee to be Signior Lucentio.
BAPTISTA. Away with the dotard! To the gaol with him!
VINCENTIO. Thus strangers may be haled and abused:
O monstrous villain!
Re-enter Biondello, with Lucentio and Bianca
BIONDELLO. O! we are spoiled; and yonder he is: deny him, forswear him, or else we are all undone.
LUCENTIO. (*Kneeling*) Pardon, sweet father.
VINCENTIO.   Lives my sweetest son?
Biondello, Tranio, and Pedant run out
BIANCA. (*Kneeling*) Pardon, dear father.
BAPTISTA.   How hast thou offended?
Where is Lucentio?

LUCENTIO. Here's Lucentio,
Right son to the right Vincentio;
That have by marriage made thy daughter mine,
While counterfeit supposes blear'd thine eyne.

GREMIO. Here's packing, with a witness, to deceive us all!

VINCENTIO. Where is that damned villain Tranio,
That fac'd and brav'd me in this matter so?

BAPTISTA. Why, tell me, is not this my Cambio?

BIANCA. Cambio is chang'd into Lucentio.

LUCENTIO. Love wrought these miracles. Bianca's love
Made me exchange my state with Tranio,
While he did bear my countenance in the town;
And happily I have arriv'd at last
Unto the wished haven of my bliss.
What Tranio did, myself enforc'd him to;
Then pardon him, sweet father, for my sake.

VINCENTIO. I'll slit the villain's nose, that would have sent me to the gaol.

BAPTISTA. (*To Lucentio*) But do you hear, sir?
Have you married my daughter without asking my good will?

VINCENTIO. Fear not, Baptista; we will content you, go to:
but I will in, to be revenged for this villany. *Exit*

BAPTISTA. And I, to sound the depth of this knavery. *Exit*

LUCENTIO. Look not pale, Bianca; thy father will not frown.
Exeunt Lucentio and Bianca

GREMIO. My cake is dough; but I'll in among the rest,
Out of hope of all, but my share of the feast. *Exit*

Petruchio and Katharina advance

KATHARINA. Husband, let's follow, to see the end of this ado.

PETRUCHIO. First kiss me, Kate, and we will.

KATHARINA. What! in the midst of the street?

PETRUCHIO. What! art thou ashamed of me?

KATHARINA. No, sir, God forbid; but ashamed to kiss.

PETRUCHIO. Why, then let's home again. Come, sirrah, let's away.

KATHARINA. Nay, I will give thee a kiss: now pray thee, love, stay.

PETRUCHIO. Is not this well? Come, my sweet Kate:
Better once than never, for never too late. *Exeunt*

SCENE TWO

A Room in Lucentio's House.

A Banquet set out. Enter Baptista, Vincentio, Gremio, the Pedant, Lucentio, Bianca, Petruchio, Katharina, Hortensio, and Widow. Tranio, Biondello, Grumio. and Others, attending

LUCENTIO. At last, though long, our jarring notes agree:
And time it is, when raging war is done,
To smile at 'scapes and perils overblown.
My fair Bianca, bid my father welcome,
While I with self-same kindness welcome thine.
Brother Petruchio, sister Katharina,
And thou, Hortensio, with thy loving widow,
Feast with the best, and welcome to my house:
My banquet is to close our stomachs up,
After our great good cheer. Pray you, sit down;
For now we sit to chat as well as eat.   *They sit at table*

PETRUCHIO. Nothing but sit and sit, and eat and eat!

BAPTISTA. Padua affords this kindness, son Petruchio.

PETRUCHIO. Padua affords nothing but what is kind.

HORTENSIO. For both our sakes I would that word were true.

PETRUCHIO. Now, for my life, Hortensio fears his widow.

WIDOW. Then never trust me, if I be afeard.

PETRUCHIO. You are very sensible, and yet you miss my sense:
I mean, Hortensio is afeard of you.

WIDOW. He that is giddy thinks the world turns round.

PETRUCHIO. Roundly replied.

KATHARINA.   Mistress, how mean you that?

WIDOW. Thus I conceive by him.

PETRUCHIO. Conceives by me! How likes Hortensio that?

HORTENSIO. My widow says, thus she conceives her tale.

PETRUCHIO. Very well mended. Kiss him for that, good widow.

KATHARINA. 'He that is giddy thinks the world turns round':
I pray you, tell me what you meant by that.

WIDOW. Your husband, being troubled with a shrew,
Measures my husband's sorrow by his woe:

And now you know my meaning.
KATHARINA. A very mean meaning.
WIDOW.   Right, I mean you.
KATHARINA. And I am mean, indeed, respecting you.
PETRUCHIO. To her, Kate!
HORTENSIO. To her, widow!
PETRUCHIO. A hundred marks, my Kate does put her down.
HORTENSIO. That's my office.
PETRUCHIO. Spoke like an officer: ha' to thee, lad.
Drinks to Hortensio
BAPTISTA. How likes Gremio these quick-witted folks?
GREMIO. Believe me, sir, they butt together well.
BIANCA. Head and butt! a hasty-witted body
Would say your head and butt were head and horn.
VINCENTIO. Ay, mistress bride, hath that awaken'd you?
BIANCA. Ay, but not frighted me; therefore I'll sleep again.
PETRUCHIO. Nay, that you shall not; since you have begun,
Have at you for a bitter jest or two.
BIANCA. Am I your bird? I mean to shift my bush;
And then pursue me as you draw your bow.
You are welcome all.
Exeunt Bianca, Katharina, and Widow
PETRUCHIO. She hath prevented me. Here, Signior Tranio;
This bird you aim'd at, though you hit her not:
Therefore a health to all that shot and miss'd.
TRANIO. O sir! Lucentio slipp'd me, like his greyhound,
Which runs himself, and catches for his master.
PETRUCHIO. A good swift simile, but something currish.
TRANIO. 'Tis well, sir, that you hunted for yourself:
'Tis thought your deer does hold you at a bay.
BAPTISTA. O ho, Petruchio! Tranio hits you now.
LUCENTIO. I thank thee for that gird, good Tranio.
HORTENSIO. Confess, confess, hath he not hit you here?
PETRUCHIO. A' has a little gall'd me, I confess;
And, as the jest did glance away from me,
'Tis ten to one it maim'd you two outright.
BAPTISTA. Now, in good sadness, son Petruchio,
I think thou hast the veriest shrew of all.
PETRUCHIO. Well, I say no: and therefore, for assurance,
Let's each one send unto his wife;
And he whose wife is most obedient
To come at first when he doth send for her,

ACT V : SCENE II

Shall win the wager which we will propose.
HORTENSIO. Content. What is the wager?
LUCENTIO.   Twenty crowns.
PETRUCHIO. Twenty crowns!
  I'll venture so much of my hawk or hound,
  But twenty times so much upon my wife.
LUCENTIO. A hundred then.
HORTENSIO.   Content.
PETRUCHIO.   A match! 'tis done.
HORTENSIO. Who shall begin?
LUCENTIO.   That will I.
  Go, Biondello, bid your mistress come to me.
BIONDELLO. I go.   *Exit*
BAPTISTA. Son, I will be your half, Bianca comes.
LUCENTIO. I'll have no halves; I'll bear it all myself.
          Re-enter Biondello
  How now! what news?
BIONDELLO.   Sir, my mistress sends you word
  That she is busy and she cannot come.
PETRUCHIO. How! she is busy, and she cannot come!
  Is that an answer?
GREMIO.   Ay, and a kind one too:
  Pray God, sir, your wife send you not a worse.
PETRUCHIO. I hope, better.
HORTENSIO. Sirrah Biondello, go and entreat my wife
  To come to me forthwith.   *Exit Biondello*
PETRUCHIO.   O ho! entreat her!
  Nay, then she must needs come.
HORTENSIO.   I am afraid, sir,
  Do what you can, yours will not be entreated.
          Re-enter Biondello
  Now, where's my wife?
BIONDELLO. She says you have some goodly jest in hand:
  She will not come: she bids you come to her.
PETRUCHIO. Worse and worse; she will not come! O vile,
  Intolerable, not to be endur'd!
  Sirrah Grumio, go to your mistress; say,
  I command her come to me.   *Exit Grumio*
HORTENSIO.   I know her answer.
PETRUCHIO. What?
HORTENSIO. She will not.
PETRUCHIO. The fouler fortune mine, and there an end.

Re-enter Katharina

BAPTISTA. Now, by my holidame, here comes Katharina!
KATHARINA. What is your will, sir, that you send for me?
PETRUCHIO. Where is your sister, and Hortensio's wife?
KATHARINA. They sit conferring by the parlour fire.
PETRUCHIO. Go, fetch them hither: if they deny to come,
  Swinge me them soundly forth unto their husbands.
  Away, I say, and bring them hither straight.
                                    Exit Katharina
LUCENTIO. Here is a wonder, if you talk of a wonder.
HORTENSIO. And so it is. I wonder what it bodes.
PETRUCHIO. Marry, peace it bodes, and love, and quiet life,
  An awful rule and right supremacy;
  And, to be short, what not that's sweet and happy.
BAPTISTA. Now fair befall thee, good Petruchio!
  The wager thou hast won; and I will add
  Unto their losses twenty thousand crowns;
  Another dowry to another daughter,
  For she is chang'd, as she had never been.
PETRUCHIO. Nay, I will win my wager better yet,
  And show more sign of her obedience,
  Her new-built virtue and obedience.
  See where she comes, and brings your froward wives
  As prisoners to her womanly persuasion.
      Re-enter Katharina, with Bianca and Widow
  Katharine, that cap of yours becomes you not:
  Off with that bauble, throw it under foot.
        Katharina pulls off her cap and throws it down
WIDOW. Lord! let me never have a cause to sigh,
  Till I be brought to such a silly pass!
BIANCA. Fie! what a foolish duty call you this?
LUCENTIO. I would your duty were as foolish too:
  The wisdom of your duty, fair Bianca,
  Hath cost me an hundred crowns since supper-time.
BIANCA. The more fool you for laying on my duty.
PETRUCHIO. Katharine, I charge thee, tell these headstrong women
  What duty they do owe their lords and husbands.
WIDOW. Come, come, you're mocking: we will have no telling.
PETRUCHIO. Come on, I say; and first begin with her.
WIDOW. She shall not.

PETRUCHIO. I say she shall: and first begin with her.
KATHARINA. Fie, fie! unknit that threatening unkind brow,
And dart not scornful glances from those eyes,
To wound thy lord, thy king, thy governor:
It blots thy beauty as frosts do bite the meads,
Confounds thy fame as whirlwinds shake fair buds,
And in no sense is meet or amiable.
A woman mov'd is like a fountain troubled,
Muddy, ill-seeming, thick, bereft of beauty;
And while it is so, none so dry or thirsty
Will deign to sip or touch one drop of it.
Thy husband is thy lord, thy life, thy keeper,
Thy head, thy sovereign; one that cares for thee,
And for thy maintenance commits his body
To painful labour both by sea and land,
To watch the night in storms, the day in cold,
Whilst thou liest warm at home, secure and safe;
And craves no other tribute at thy hands
But love, fair looks, and true obedience;
Too little payment for so great a debt.
Such duty as the subject owes the prince,
Even such a woman oweth to her husband;
And when she 's froward, peevish, sullen, sour,
And not obedient to his honest will,
What is she but a foul contending rebel,
And graceless traitor to her loving lord?—
I am asham'd that women are so simple
To offer war where they should kneel for peace,
Or seek for rule, supremacy, and sway,
When they are bound to serve, love, and obey.
Why are our bodies soft, and weak, and smooth,
Unapt to toil and trouble in the world,
But that our soft conditions and our hearts
Should well agree with our external parts?
Come, come, you froward and unable worms!
My mind hath been as big as one of yours,
My heart as great, my reason haply more,
To bandy word for word and frown for frown;
But now I see our lances are but straws,
Our strength as weak, our weakness past compare,
That seeming to be most which we indeed least are.
Then vail your stomachs, for it is no boot,

And place your hands below your husband's foot:
In token of which duty, if he please,
My hand is ready; may it do him ease.

PETRUCHIO. Why, there's a wench! Come on, and kiss me, Kate.

LUCENTIO. Well, go thy ways, old lad, for thou shalt ha 't.

VINCENTIO. 'Tis a good hearing when children are toward.

LUCENTIO. But a harsh hearing when women are froward.

PETRUCHIO. Come, Kate, we'll to bed.
We three are married, but you two are sped.
'Twas I won the wager, (*To Lucentio*) though you hit the white;
And, being a winner, God give you good night!

Exeunt Petruchio and Katharina

HORTENSIO. Now, go thy ways; thou hast tam'd a curst shrew.

LUCENTIO. 'Tis a wonder, by your leave, she will be tam'd so. *Exeunt*

ALL'S WELL THAT ENDS WELL

CAST OF CHARACTERS

KING OF FRANCE
DUKE OF FLORENCE
BERTRAM, *Count of Rousillon*
LAFEU, *an old Lord*
PAROLLES, *a follower of Bertram*
Steward to the Countess of Rousillon
LAVACHE, *a Clown in her household*
A Page

COUNTESS OF ROUSILLON, *Mother to Bertram*
HELENA, *a Gentlewoman protected by the Countess*
An Old Widow of Florence
DIANA, *Daughter to the Widow*
VIOLENTA }
MARIANA } *Neighbours and Friends to the Widow*
Lords, Officers, Soldiers, &c., French and Florentine

SCENE
Rousillon, Paris, Florence, Marseilles

ALL'S WELL THAT ENDS WELL

ACT ONE

SCENE ONE

Rousillon. A Room in the Countess's Palace.

Enter Bertram, the Countess of Rousillon, Helena, and Lafeu, all in black

COUNTESS. In delivering my son from me, I bury a second husband.

BERTRAM. And I, in going, madam, weep o'er my father's death anew; but I must attend his Majesty's command, to whom I am now in ward, evermore in subjection.

LAFEU. You shall find of the king a husband, madam; you, sir, a father. He that so generally is at all times good, must of necessity hold his virtue to you, whose worthiness would stir it up where it wanted rather than lack it where there is such abundance.

COUNTESS. What hope is there of his Majesty's amendment?

LAFEU. He hath abandoned his physicians, madam; under whose practices he hath persecuted time with hope, and finds no other advantage in the process but only the losing of hope by time.

COUNTESS. This young gentlewoman had a father,—O, that 'had'! how sad a passage 'tis!—whose skill was almost as great as his honesty; had it stretched so far, would have made nature immortal, and death should have play for lack of work. Would, for the king's sake, he were living! I think it would be the death of the king's disease.

LAFEU. How called you the man you speak of, madam?

COUNTESS. He was famous, sir, in his profession, and it was his great right to be so: Gerard de Narbon.

LAFEU. He was excellent indeed, madam: the king very lately spoke of him admiringly and mourningly. He was skilful enough to have lived still, if knowledge could be set up against mortality.

BERTRAM. What is it, my good lord, the king languishes of?

LAFEU. A fistula, my lord.

BERTRAM. I heard not of it before.

LAFEU. I would it were not notorious. Was this gentlewoman the daughter of Gerard de Narbon?

COUNTESS. His sole child, my lord; and bequeathed to my overlooking. I have those hopes of her good that her education promises: her dispositions she inherits, which makes fair gifts fairer; for where an unclean mind carries virtuous qualities, there commendations go with pity; they are virtues and traitors too: in her they are the better for their simpleness; she derives her honesty and achieves her goodness.

LAFEU. Your commendations, madam, get from her tears.

COUNTESS. 'Tis the best brine a maiden can season her praise in. The remembrance of her father never approaches her heart but the tyranny of her sorrows takes all livelihood from her cheek. No more of this, Helena, go to, no more; lest it be rather thought you affect a sorrow, than have it.

HELENA. I do affect a sorrow indeed, but I have it too.

LAFEU. Moderate lamentation is the right of the dead, excessive grief the enemy to the living.

HELENA. If the living be enemy to the grief, the excess makes it soon mortal.

BERTRAM. Madam, I desire your holy wishes.

LAFEU. How understand we that?

COUNTESS. Be thou blest, Bertram; and succeed thy father
In manners, as in shape! Thy blood and virtue
Contend for empire in thee; and thy goodness
Share with thy birthright! Love all, trust a few,
Do wrong to none: be able for thine enemy
Rather in power than use, and keep thy friend
Under thy own life's key: be check'd for silence,
But never tax'd for speech. What heaven more will
That thee may furnish, and my prayers pluck down,
Fall on thy head! Farewell, my lord;
'Tis an unseason'd courtier; good my lord,
Advise him.

ACT I · SCENE I

LAFEU. He cannot want the best
 That shall attend his love.
COUNTESS. Heaven bless him! Farewell, Bertram. *Exit*
BERTRAM. (*To Helena*) The best wishes that can be forged
 in your thoughts be servants to you! Be comfortable to my
 mother, your mistress, and make much of her.
LAFEU. Farewell, pretty lady: you must hold the credit of
 your father. *Exeunt Bertram and Lafeu*
HELENA. O! were that all. I think not on my father;
 And these great tears grace his remembrance more
 Than those I shed for him. What was he like?
 I have forgot him: my imagination
 Carries no favour in 't but Bertram's.
 I am undone: there is no living, none,
 If Bertram be away. It were all one
 That I should love a bright particular star
 And think to wed it, he is so above me:
 In his bright radiance and collateral light
 Must I be comforted, not in his sphere.
 The ambition in my love thus plagues itself:
 The hind that would be mated by the lion
 Must die for love. 'Twas pretty, though a plague,
 To see him every hour; to sit and draw
 His arched brows, his hawking eye, his curls,
 In our heart's table; heart too capable
 Of every line and trick of his sweet favour:
 But now he's gone, and my idolatrous fancy
 Must sanctify his reliques. Who comes here?
 One that goes with him; I love him for his sake;
 And yet I know him a notorious liar,
 Think him a great way fool, solely a coward;
 Yet these fix'd evils sit so fit in him,
 That they take place, when virtue's steely bones
 Look bleak in the cold wind: withal, full oft we see
 Cold wisdom waiting on superfluous folly.
  Enter Parolles
PAROLLES. Save you, fair queen!
HELENA. And you, monarch!
PAROLLES. No.
HELENA. And no.
PAROLLES. Are you meditating on virginity?
HELENA. Ay. You have some stain of soldier in you; let me

ask you a question. Man is enemy to virginity; how may we barricade it against him?

PAROLLES. Keep him out.

HELENA. But he assails; and our virginity, though valiant in the defence, yet is weak. Unfold to us some warlike resistance.

PAROLLES. There is none: man, sitting down before you, will undermine you and blow you up.

HELENA. Bless our poor virginity from underminers and blowers up! Is there no military policy, how virgins might blow up men?

PAROLLES. Virginity being blown down, man will quicklier be blown up: marry, in blowing him down again, with the breach yourselves made, you lose your city. It is not politic in the commonwealth of nature to preserve virginity. Loss of virginity is rational increase, and there was never virgin got till virginity was first lost. That you were made of is metal to make virgins. Virginity, by being once lost, may be ten times found: by being ever kept, it is ever lost. 'Tis too cold a companion: away with 't!

HELENA. I will stand for 't a little, though therefore I die a virgin.

PAROLLES. There's little can be said in 't; 'tis against the rule of nature. To speak on the part of virginity is to accuse your mothers, which is most infallible disobedience. He that hangs himself is a virgin: virginity murders itself, and should be buried in highways, out of all sanctified limit, as a desperate offendress against nature. Virginity breeds mites, much like a cheese, consumes itself to the very paring, and so dies with feeding his own stomach. Besides, virginity is peevish, proud, idle, made of self-love, which is the most inhibited sin in the canon. Keep it not; you cannot choose but lose by 't! Out with 't! within the year it will make itself two, which is a goodly increase, and the principal itself not much the worse. Away with 't!

HELENA. How might one do, sir, to lose it to her own liking?

PAROLLES. Let me see: marry, ill, to like him that ne'er it likes. 'Tis a commodity that will lose the gloss with lying; the longer kept, the less worth: off with 't, while 'tis vendible; answer the time of request. Virginity, like an old courtier, wears her cap out of fashion; richly suited, but unsuitable: just like the brooch and the tooth-pick, which wear not now. Your date is better in your pie and your porridge than in your cheek: and your virginity, your old virginity, is like one of our French withered pears; it looks ill, it eats drily; marry, 'tis a withered pear; it was formerly better; marry, yet 'tis a withered pear. Will you anything with it?

HELENA. Not my virginity yet.
There shall your master have a thousand loves,
A mother, and a mistress, and a friend,
A phœnix, captain, and an enemy,
A guide, a goddess, and a sovereign,
A counsellor, a traitress, and a dear;
His humble ambition, proud humility,
His jarring concord, and his discord dulcet,
His faith, his sweet disaster; with a world
Of pretty, fond, adoptious christendoms,
That blinking Cupid gossips. Now shall he—
I know not what he shall. God send him well!
The court's a learning-place, and he is one—

PAROLLES. What one, i' faith?

HELENA. That I wish well. 'Tis pity—

PAROLLES. What's pity?

HELENA. That wishing well had not a body in 't,
Which might be felt; that we, the poorer born,
Whose baser stars do shut us up in wishes,
Might with effects of them follow our friends,
And show what we alone must think, which never
Returns us thanks.

Enter a Page

PAGE. Monsieur Parolles, my lord calls for you.

PAROLLES. Little Helen, farewell: if I can remember thee, I will think of thee at court.

HELENA. Monsieur Parolles, you were born under a charitable star.

PAROLLES. Under Mars, I.

HELENA. I especially think, under Mars.

PAROLLES. Why under Mars?

HELENA. The wars have so kept you under that you must needs be born under Mars.

PAROLLES. When he was predominant.

HELENA. When he was retrograde, I think rather.

PAROLLES. Why think you so?

HELENA. You go so much backward when you fight.
PAROLLES. That's for advantage.
HELENA. So is running away, when fear proposes the safety: but the composition that your valour and fear makes in you is a virtue of a good wing, and I like the wear well.
PAROLLES. I am so full of businesses I cannot answer thee acutely. I will return perfect courtier; in the which, my instruction shall serve to naturalize thee, so thou wilt be capable of a courtier's counsel, and understand what advice shall thrust upon thee; else thou diest in thine unthankfulness, and thine ignorance makes thee away: farewell. When thou hast leisure, say thy prayers; when thou hast none, remember thy friends. Get thee a good husband, and use him as he uses thee: so, farewell. *Exit*
HELENA. Our remedies oft in ourselves do lie
Which we ascribe to heaven: the fated sky
Gives us free scope; only doth backward pull
Our slow designs when we ourselves are dull.
What power is it which mounts my love so high;
That makes me see, and cannot feed mine eye?
The mightiest space in fortune nature brings
To join like likes, and kiss like native things.
Impossible be strange attempts to those
That weigh their pains in sense, and do suppose
What hath been cannot be: who ever strove
To show her merit, that did miss her love?
The king's disease,—my project may deceive me,
But my intents are fix'd and will not leave me. *Exit*

SCENE TWO

Paris. A Room in the King's Palace.

Flourish of Cornets. Enter the King of France, with letters; Lords and Others Attending.

KING. The Florentines and Senoys are by the ears;
Have fought with equal fortune, and continue
A braving war.
FIRST LORD. So 'tis reported, sir.
KING. Nay, 'tis most credible: we here receive it
A certainty, vouch'd from our cousin Austria,

    With caution that the Florentine will move us
For speedy aid; wherein our dearest friend
Prejudicates the business, and would seem
To have us make denial.
FIRST LORD.   His love and wisdom,
    Approv'd so to your Majesty, may plead
For amplest credence.
KING.   He hath arm'd our answer,
    And Florence is denied before he comes:
Yet, for our gentlemen that mean to see
The Tuscan service, freely have they leave
To stand on either part.
SECOND LORD.   It well may serve
    A nursery to our gentry, who are sick
For breathing and exploit.
KING.   What's he comes here?
    Enter Bertram, Lafeu, and Parolles
FIRST LORD. It is the Count Rousillon, my good lord,
    Young Bertram.
KING.   Youth, thou bear'st thy father's face;
    Frank nature, rather curious than in haste,
Hath well compos'd thee. Thy father's moral parts
Mayst thou inherit too! Welcome to Paris.
BERTRAM. My thanks and duty are your Majesty's.
KING. I would I had that corporal soundness now,
    As when thy father and myself in friendship
First tried our soldiership! He did look far
Into the service of the time and was
Discipled of the bravest: he lasted long;
But on us both did haggish age steal on,
And wore us out of act. It much repairs me
To talk of your good father. In his youth
He had the wit which I can well observe
To-day in our young lords; but they may jest
Till their own scorn return to them unnoted
Ere they can hide their levity in honour.
So like a courtier, contempt nor bitterness
Were in his pride or sharpness; if they were,
His equal had awak'd them; and his honour,
Clock to itself, knew the true minute when
Exception bid him speak, and at this time
His tongue obey'd his hand: who were below him

He us'd as creatures of another place,
And bow'd his eminent top to their low ranks,
Making them proud of his humility,
In their poor praise he humbled. Such a man
Might be a copy to these younger times,
Which, follow'd well, would demonstrate them now
But goers backward.

BERTRAM. His good remembrance, sir,
Lies richer in your thoughts than on his tomb;
So in approof lives not his epitaph
As in your royal speech.

KING. Would I were with him! He would always say,—
Methinks I hear him now: his plausive words
He scatter'd not in ears, but grafted them,
To grow there and to bear. 'Let me not live,'—
Thus his good melancholy oft began,
On the catastrophe and heel of pastime,
When it was out,—'Let me not live,' quoth he,
'After my flame lacks oil, to be the snuff
Of younger spirits, whose apprehensive senses
All but new things disdain; whose judgments are
Mere fathers of their garments; whose constancies
Expire before their fashions.' This he wish'd:
I, after him, do after him wish too,
Since I nor wax nor honey can bring home,
I quickly were dissolved from my hive,
To give some labourers room.

SECOND LORD. You are lov'd, sir;
They that least lend it you shall lack you first.

KING. I fill a place, I know 't. How long is 't, count,
Since the physician at your father's died?
He was much fam'd.

BERTRAM. Some six months since, my lord.

KING. If he were living, I would try him yet:
Lend me an arm: the rest have worn me out
With several applications: nature and sickness
Debate it at their leisure. Welcome, count;
My son 's no dearer.

BERTRAM. Thank your Majesty. *Exeunt. Flourish*

SCENE THREE

Rousillon. A Room in the Countess's Palace.

Enter Countess, Steward, and Clown

COUNTESS. I will now hear: what say you of this gentlewoman?

STEWARD. Madam, the care I have had to even your content, I wish might be found in the calendar of my past endeavours; for then we wound our modesty and make foul the clearness of our deservings, when of ourselves we publish them.

COUNTESS. What does this knave here? Get you gone, sirrah: the complaints I have heard of you I do not all believe: 'tis my slowness that I do not; for I know you lack not folly to commit them, and have ability enough to make such knaveries yours.

CLOWN. 'Tis not unknown to you, madam, I am a poor fellow.

COUNTESS. Well, sir.

CLOWN. No, madam, 'tis not so well that I am poor, though many of the rich are damned. But, if I may have your ladyship's good will to go to the world, Isbel the woman and I will do as we may.

COUNTESS. Wilt thou needs be a beggar?

CLOWN. I do beg your good will in this case.

COUNTESS. In what case?

CLOWN. In Isbel's case and mine own. Service is no heritage; and I think I shall never have the blessing of God till I have issue o' my body, for they say barnes are blessings.

COUNTESS. Tell me thy reason why thou wilt marry.

CLOWN. My poor body, madam, requires it: I am driven on by the flesh; and he must needs go that the devil drives.

COUNTESS. Is this all your worship's reason?

CLOWN. Faith, madam, I have other holy reasons, such as they are.

COUNTESS. May the world know them?

CLOWN. I have been, madam, a wicked creature, as you and all flesh and blood are; and, indeed, I do marry that I may repent.

COUNTESS. Thy marriage, sooner than thy wickedness.

CLOWN. I am out o' friends, madam; and I hope to have friends for my wife's sake.

COUNTESS. Such friends are thine enemies, knave.

CLOWN. You 're shallow, madam, in great friends; for the knaves come to do that for me which I am aweary of. He that ears my land spares my team, and gives me leave to in the crop: if I be his cuckold, he 's my drudge. He that comforts my wife is the cherisher of my flesh and blood; he that cherishes my flesh and blood loves my flesh and blood; he that loves my flesh and blood is my friend: ergo, he that kisses my wife is my friend. If men could be contented to be what they are, there were no fear in marriage; for young Charbon the puritan, and old Poysam the papist, howsome'er their hearts are severed in religion, their heads are both one; they may joul horns together like any deer i' the herd.

COUNTESS. Wilt thou ever be a foul-mouthed and calumnious knave?

CLOWN. A prophet I, madam; and I speak the truth the next way:

> For I the ballad will repeat,
>   Which men full true shall find;
>   Your marriage comes by destiny,
>   Your cuckoo sings by kind.

COUNTESS. Get you gone, sir: I 'll talk with you more anon.

STEWARD. May it please you, madam, that he bid Helen come to you: of her I am to speak.

COUNTESS. Sirrah, tell my gentlewoman I would speak with her; Helen I mean.

CLOWN.
> Was this fair face the cause, quoth she,
>   Why the Grecians sacked Troy?
> Fond done, done fond,
>   Was this King Priam's joy?
> With that she sighed as she stood,
> With that she sighed as she stood
>   And gave this sentence then;
> Among nine bad if one be good,
> Among nine bad if one be good,
>   There 's yet one good in ten.

COUNTESS. What! one good in ten? You corrupt the song, sirrah.

ACT I · SCENE III

CLOWN. One good woman in ten, madam; which is a purifying o' the song. Would God would serve the world so all the year! We 'd find no fault with the tithe-woman if I were the parson. One in ten, quoth a'! An we might have a good woman born but for every blazing star, or at an earthquake, 'twould mend the lottery well: a man may draw his heart out ere a' pluck one.

COUNTESS. You 'll be gone, sir knave, and do as I command you!

CLOWN. That man should be at woman's command, and yet no hurt done! Though honesty be no puritan, yet it will do no hurt; it will wear the surplice of humility over the black gown of a big heart. I am going, forsooth: the business is for Helen to come hither. *Exit*

COUNTESS. Well, now.

STEWARD. I know, madam, you love your gentlewoman entirely.

COUNTESS. Faith, I do: her father bequeathed her to me: and she herself, without other advantage, may lawfully make title to as much love as she finds: there is more owing her than is paid, and more shall be paid her than she 'll demand.

STEWARD. Madam, I was very late more near her than I think she wished me: alone she was, and did communicate to herself her own words to her own ears; she thought, I dare vow for her, they touched not any stranger sense. Her matter was, she loved your son: Fortune, she said, was no goddess, that had put such difference betwixt their two estates: Love no god, that would not extend his might, only where qualities were level; Dian no queen of virgins, that would suffer her poor knight surprised, without rescue in the first assault or ransom afterward. This she delivered in the most bitter touch of sorrow that e'er I heard virgin exclaim in; which I held my duty speedily to acquaint you withal, sithence in the loss that may happen, it concerns you something to know it.

COUNTESS. You have discharged this honestly: keep it to yourself. Many likelihoods informed me of this before, which hung so tottering in the balance that I could neither believe nor misdoubt. Pray you, leave me: stall this in your bosom; and I thank you for your honest care. I will speak with you further anon. *Exit Steward*

Enter Helena

Even so it was with me when I was young:
    If ever we are nature's, these are ours; this thorn
Doth to our rose of youth rightly belong;
    Our blood to us, this to our blood is born:
It is the show and seal of nature's truth,
Where love's strong passion is impress'd in youth:
By our remembrances of days foregone,
Such were our faults; or then we thought them none.
Her eye is sick on 't: I observe her now.

HELENA. What is your pleasure, madam?

COUNTESS.   You know, Helen,
I am a mother to you.

HELENA. Mine honourable mistress.

COUNTESS.   Nay, a mother:
Why not a mother? When I said, 'a mother,'
Methought you saw a serpent: what's in 'mother'
That you start at it? I say, I am your mother;
And put you in the catalogue of those
That were enwombed mine: 'tis often seen
Adoption strives with nature, and choice breeds
A native slip to us from foreign seeds;
You ne'er oppress'd me with a mother's groan,
Yet I express to you a mother's care.
God's mercy, maiden! does it curd thy blood
To say I am thy mother? What's the matter,
That this distemper'd messenger of wet,
The many-colour'd Iris, rounds thine eye?
Why? that you are my daughter?

HELENA.   That I am not.

COUNTESS. I say, I am your mother.

HELENA.   Pardon, madam;
The Count Rousillon cannot be my brother:
I am from humble, he from honour'd name;
No note upon my parents, his all noble:
My master, my dear lord he is; and I
His servant live, and will his vassal die.
He must not be my brother.

COUNTESS.   Nor I your mother?

HELENA. You are my mother, madam: would you were,—
So that my lord your son were not my brother,—
Indeed my mother! or were you both our mothers,

    I care no more for than I do for heaven,
    So I were not his sister. Can 't no other,
    But, I your daughter, he must be my brother?
COUNTESS. Yes, Helen, you might be my daughter-in-law:
    God shield you mean it not! daughter and mother
    So strive upon your pulse. What, pale again?
    My fear hath catch'd your fondness: now I see
    The mystery of your loneliness, and find
    Your salt tears' head: now to all sense 'tis gross
    You love my son: invention is asham'd
    Against the proclamation of thy passion,
    To say thou dost not: therefore tell me true;
    But tell me then, 'tis so; for, look, thy cheeks
    Confess it, th' one to th' other; and thine eyes
    See it so grossly shown in thy behaviours
    That in their kind they speak it: only sin
    And hellish obstinacy tie thy tongue,
    That truth should be suspected. Speak, is 't so?
    If it be so, you have wound a goodly clew;
    If it be not, forswear 't: howe'er, I charge thee,
    As heaven shall work in me for thine avail,
    To tell me truly.
HELENA.   Good madam, pardon me!
COUNTESS. Do you love my son?
HELENA.   Your pardon, noble mistress!
COUNTESS. Love you my son?
HELENA.   Do not you love him, madam?
COUNTESS. Go not about; my love hath in 't a bond
    Whereof the world takes note: come, come, disclose
    The state of your affection, for your passions
    Have to the full appeach'd.
HELENA.   Then, I confess,
    Here on my knee, before high heaven and you,
    That before you, and next unto high heaven,
    I love your son.
    My friends were poor, but honest; so 's my love:
    Be not offended, for it hurts not him
    That he is lov'd of me: I follow him not
    By any token of presumptuous suit;
    Nor would I have him till I do deserve him;
    Yet never know how that desert should be.
    I know I love in vain, strive against hope;

Yet, in this captious and intenible sieve
I still pour in the waters of my love,
And lack not to lose still. Thus, Indian-like,
Religious in mine error, I adore
The sun, that looks upon his worshipper,
But knows of him no more. My dearest madam,
Let not your hate encounter with my love
For loving where you do: but, if yourself,
Whose aged honour cites a virtuous youth,
Did ever in so true a flame of liking
Wish chastely and love dearly, that your Dian
Was both herself and Love; O! then, give pity
To her, whose state is such that cannot choose
But lend and give where she is sure to lose;
That seeks not to find that her search implies,
But, riddle-like, lives sweetly where she dies.

COUNTESS. Had you not lately an intent, speak truly,
To go to Paris?

HELENA. Madam, I had.

COUNTESS. Wherefore? tell true.

HELENA. I will tell truth; by grace itself I swear.
You know my father left me some prescriptions
Of rare and prov'd effects, such as his reading
And manifest experience had collected
For general sovereignty; and that he will'd me
In heedfull'st reservation to bestow them,
As notes whose faculties inclusive were
More than they were in note. Amongst the rest,
There is a remedy, approv'd, set down
To cure the desperate languishings whereof
The king is render'd lost.

COUNTESS. This was your motive
For Paris, was it? Speak.

HELENA. My lord your son made me to think of this;
Else Paris, and the medicine, and the king,
Had from the conversation of my thoughts
Haply been absent then.

COUNTESS. But think you, Helen,
If you should tender your supposed aid,
He would receive it? He and his physicians
Are of a mind; he, that they cannot help him,
They, that they cannot help. How shall they credit

A poor unlearned virgin, when the schools,
Embowell'd of their doctrine, have left off
The danger to itself?
HELENA. There's something in 't,
More than my father's skill, which was the great'st
Of his profession, that his good receipt
Shall for my legacy be sanctified
By the luckiest stars in heaven: and, would your honour
But give me leave to try success, I 'd venture
The well-lost life of mine on his Grace's cure,
By such a day, and hour.
COUNTESS. Dost thou believe 't?
HELENA. Ay, madam, knowingly.
COUNTESS. Why, Helen, thou shalt have my leave and love,
Means, and attendants, and my loving greetings
To those of mine in court. I 'll stay at home
And pray God's blessing into thy attempt.
Be gone to-morrow; and be sure of this,
What I can help thee to thou shalt not miss. *Exeunt*

ACT TWO

SCENE ONE

Paris. A Room in the King's Palace.

Flourish. Enter the King, with divers young Lords taking leave for the Florentine War; Bertram, Parolles, and Attendants

KING. Farewell, young lords: these warlike principles
  Do not throw from you: and you, my lords, farewell:
  Share the advice betwixt you; if both gain, all
  The gift doth stretch itself as 'tis receiv'd,
  And is enough for both.
FIRST LORD.   'Tis our hope, sir,
  After well enter'd soldiers, to return
  And find your Grace in health.
KING. No, no, it cannot be; and yet my heart
  Will not confess he owes the malady
  That doth my life besiege. Farewell, young lords;
  Whether I live or die, be you the sons
  Of worthy Frenchmen: let higher Italy—
  Those bated that inherit but the fall
  Of the last monarchy—see that you come
  Not to woo honour, but to wed it; when
  The bravest questant shrinks, find what you seek,
  That fame may cry you loud: I say, farewell.
SECOND LORD. Health, at your bidding, serve your Majesty!
KING. Those girls of Italy, take heed of them:
  They say, our French lack language to deny
  If they demand: beware of being captives,
  Before your serve.
BOTH LORDS.   Our hearts receive your warnings.
KING. Farewell. Come hither to me.   *Exit, attended*
FIRST LORD. O my sweet lord, that you will stay behind us!
PAROLLES. 'Tis not his fault, the spark.

SECOND LORD. O! 'tis brave wars.
PAROLLES. Most admirable: I have seen those wars.
BERTRAM. I am commanded here, and kept a coil with
'Too young,' and 'the next year,' and ' 'tis too early.'
PAROLLES. An thy mind stand to 't, boy, steal away bravely.
BERTRAM. I shall stay here the forehorse to a smock,
Creaking my shoes on the plain masonry,
Till honour be bought up and no sword worn
But one to dance with! By heaven! I 'll steal away.
FIRST LORD. There 's honour in the theft.
PAROLLES. Commit it, count.
SECOND COUNT. I am your accessory; and so farewell.
BERTRAM. I grow to you, and our parting is a tortured body
FIRST LORD. Farewell, captain.
SECOND LORD. Sweet Monsieur Parolles!
PAROLLES. Noble heroes, my sword and yours are kin. Good sparks and lustrous, a word, good metals: you shall find in the regiment of the Spinii, one Captain Spurio, with his cicatrice, an emblem of war, here on his sinister cheek: it was this very sword entrenched it: say to him, I live, and observe his reports for me.
SECOND LORD. We shall, noble captain. *Exeunt Lords*
PAROLLES. Mars dote on you for his novices! What will ye do?
BERTRAM. Stay; the king.
Re-enter King; Parolles and Bertram retire
PAROLLES. Use a more spacious ceremony to the noble lords; you have restrained yourself within the list of too cold an adieu: be more expressive to them; for they wear themselves in the cap of the time, there do muster true gait, eat, speak, and move under the influence of the most received star; and though the devil lead the measure, such are to be followed. After them, and take a more dilated farewell.
BERTRAM. And I will do so.
PAROLLES. Worthy fellows; and like to prove most sinewy swordmen. *Exeunt Bertram and Parolles*
Enter Lafeu
LAFEU. (*Kneeling*) Pardon, my lord, for me and for my tidings.
KING. I 'll fee thee to stand up.

LAFEU. Then here's a man stands that has brought his pardon.
 I would you had kneel'd, my lord, to ask me mercy,
 And that at my bidding you could so stand up.

KING. I would I had; so I had broke thy pate,
 And ask'd thee mercy for 't.

LAFEU. Good faith, across: but, my good lord, 'tis thus;
 Will you be cur'd of your infirmity?

KING. No.

LAFEU. O! will you eat no grapes, my royal fox?
 Yes, but you will my noble grapes an if
 My royal fox could reach them. I have seen a medicine
 That 's able to breathe life into a stone,
 Quicken a rock, and make you dance canary
 With spritely fire and motion; whose simple touch
 Is powerful to araise King Pepin, nay,
 To give great Charlemain a pen in 's hand
 And write to her a love-line.

KING. What 'her' is this?

LAFEU. Why, Doctor She. My lord, there 's one arriv'd
 If you will see her: now, by my faith and honour,
 If seriously I may convey my thoughts
 In this my light deliverance, I have spoke
 With one, that in her sex, her years, profession,
 Wisdom, and constancy, hath amaz'd me more
 Than I dare blame my weakness. Will you see her,
 For that is her demand, and know her business?
 That done, laugh well at me.

KING. Now, good Lafeu,
 Bring in the admiration, that we with thee
 May spend our wonder too, or take off thine
 By wondering how thou took'st it.

LAFEU. Nay, I 'll fit you,
 And not be all day neither. *Exit*

KING. Thus he his special nothing ever prologues.

Re-enter Lafeu, with Helena

LAFEU. Nay, come your ways.

KING. This haste hath wings indeed.

LAFEU. Nay, come your ways;
 This is his Majesty, say your mind to him:
 A traitor you do look like; but such traitors
 His Majesty seldom fears: I am Cressid's uncle,

That dare leave two together. Fare you well. *Exit*
KING. Now, fair one, does your business follow us?
HELENA. Ay, my good lord.
Gerard de Narbon was my father;
In what he did profess well found.
KING.   I knew him.
HELENA. The rather will I spare my praises towards him;
Knowing him is enough. On 's bed of death
Many receipts he gave me; chiefly one,
Which, as the dearest issue of his practice,
And of his old experience the only darling,
He bade me store up as a triple eye,
Safer than mine own two, more dear. I have so;
And, hearing your high Majesty is touch'd
With that malignant cause wherein the honour
Of my dear father's gift stands chief in power,
I come to tender it and my appliance,
With all bound humbleness.
KING.   We thank you, maiden;
But may not be so credulous of cure,
When our most learned doctors leave us, and
The congregated college have concluded
That labouring art can never ransom nature
From her inaidable estate; I say we must not
So stain our judgment, or corrupt our hope,
To prostitute our past-cure malady
To empirics, or to dissever so
Our great self and our credit, to esteem
A senseless help when help past sense we deem.
HELENA. My duty then, shall pay me for my pains:
I will no more enforce mine office on you;
Humbly entreating from your royal thoughts
A modest one, to bear me back again.
KING. I cannot give thee less, to be call'd grateful.
Thou thought'st to help me, and such thanks I give
As one near death to those that wish him live;
But what at full I know, thou know'st no part,
I knowing all my peril, thou no art.
HELENA. What I can do can do no hurt to try,
Since you set up your rest 'gainst remedy.
He that of greatest works is finisher
Oft does them by the weakest minister:

So holy writ in babes hath judgment shown,
When judges have been babes; great floods have flown
From simple sources; and great seas have dried
When miracles have by the greatest been denied.
Oft expectation fails, and most oft there
Where most it promises; and oft it hits
Where hope is coldest and despair most fits.

KING. I must not hear thee: fare thee well, kind maid.
Thy pains, not us'd, must by thyself be paid:
Proffers not took reap thanks for their reward.

HELENA. Inspired merit so by breath is barr'd.
It is not so with Him that all things knows,
As 'tis with us that square our guess by shows;
But most it is presumption in us when
The help of heaven we count the act of men.
Dear sir, to my endeavours give consent;
Of heaven, not me, make an experiment.
I am not an impostor that proclaim
Myself against the level of mine aim;
But know I think, and think I know most sure,
My art is not past power nor you past cure.

KING. Art thou so confident? Within what space
Hop'st thou my cure?

HELENA.   The great'st grace lending grace,
Ere twice the horses of the sun shall bring
Their fiery torcher his diurnal ring,
Ere twice in murk and occidental damp
Moist Hesperus hath quench'd his sleepy lamp,
Or four and twenty times the pilot's glass
Hath told the thievish minutes how they pass,
What is infirm from your sound parts shall fly,
Health shall live free, and sickness freely die.

KING. Upon thy certainty and confidence
What dar'st thou venture?

HELENA.   Tax of impudence,
A strumpet's boldness, a divulged shame,
Traduc'd by odious ballads: my maiden's name
Sear'd otherwise; nay worse—if worse—extended
With vilest torture let my life be ended.

KING. Methinks in thee some blessed spirit doth speak,
His powerful sound within an organ weak;
And what impossibility would slay

ACT II · SCENE I

In common sense, sense saves another way.
Thy life is dear; for all that life can rate
Worth name of life in thee hath estimate;
Youth, beauty, wisdom, courage, virtue, all
That happiness and prime can happy call:
Thou this to hazard needs must intimate
Skill infinite or monstrous desperate.
Sweet practiser, thy physic I will try,
That ministers thine own death if I die.

HELENA. If I break time, or flinch in property
Of what I spoke, unpitied let me die,
And well deserv'd. Not helping, death 's my fee;
But, if I help, what do you promise me?

KING. Make thy demand.

HELENA. But will you make it even?

KING. Ay, be my sceptre, and my hopes of heaven.

HELENA. Then shalt thou give me with thy kingly hand
What husband in thy power I will command.
Exempted be from me the arrogance
To choose from forth the royal blood of France,
My low and humble name to propagate
With any branch or image of thy state;
But such a one, thy vassal, whom I know
Is free for me to ask, thee to bestow.

KING. Here is my hand; the premises observ'd,
Thy will be my performance shall be serv'd:
So make the choice of thy own time, for I,
Thy resolv'd patient, on thee still rely.
More should I question thee, and more I must,
Though more to know could not be more to trust,
From whence thou cam'st, how tended on; but rest
Unquestion'd welcome and undoubted blest.
Give me some help here, ho! If thou proceed
As high as word, my deed shall match thy deed.

Flourish. Exeunt

SCENE TWO

Rousillon. A Room in the Countess's Palace.

Enter Countess and Clown

COUNTESS. Come on, sir; I shall now put you to the height of your breeding.

CLOWN. I will show myself highly fed and lowly taught. I know my business is but to the court.

COUNTESS. To the court! Why, what place make you special, when you put off that with such contempt? 'But to the court'!

CLOWN. Truly, madam, if God have lent a man any manners, he may easily put it off at court: he that cannot make a leg, put off 's cap, kiss his hand, and say nothing, has neither leg, hands, lip, nor cap; and indeed such a fellow, to say precisely, were not for the court. But, for me, I have an answer will serve all men.

COUNTESS. Marry, that 's a bountiful answer that fits all questions.

CLOWN. It is like a barber's chair that fits all buttocks; the pin-buttock, the quatch-buttock, the brawn-buttock, or any buttock.

COUNTESS. Will your answer serve fit to all questions?

CLOWN. As fit as ten groats is for the hand of an attorney, as your French crown for your taffeta punk, as Tib's rush for Tom's forefinger, as a pancake for Shrove-Tuesday, a morris for May-day, as the nail to his hole, the cuckold to his horn, as a scolding quean to a wrangling knave, as the nun's lip to the friar's mouth; nay, as the pudding to his skin.

COUNTESS. Have you, I say, an answer of such fitness for all questions?

CLOWN. From below your duke to beneath your constable, it will fit any question.

COUNTESS. It must be an answer of most monstrous size that must fit all demands.

CLOWN. But a trifle neither, in good faith, if the learned should speak truth of it. Here it is, and all that belongs to 't: ask me if I am a courtier; it shall do you no harm to learn.

COUNTESS. To be young again, if we could. I will be a fool in question, hoping to be the wiser by your answer. I pray you, sir, are you a courtier?

CLOWN. O Lord, sir! There's a simple putting off. More, more, a hundred of them.

COUNTESS. Sir, I am a poor friend of yours, that loves you.

CLOWN. O Lord, sir! Thick, thick, spare not me.

COUNTESS. I think, sir, you can eat none of this homely meat

CLOWN. O Lord, sir! Nay, put me to 't, I warrant you.

COUNTESS. You were lately whipped, sir, as I think.

CLOWN. O Lord, sir! Spare not me.

COUNTESS. Do you cry, 'O Lord, sir!' at your whipping, and 'Spare not me'? Indeed your 'O Lord, sir!' is very sequent to your whipping: you would answer very well to a whipping, if you were but bound to 't.

CLOWN. I ne'er had worse luck in my life in my 'O Lord, sir!' I see things may serve long, but not serve ever.

COUNTESS. I play the noble housewife with the time,
To entertain 't so merrily with a fool.

CLOWN. O Lord, sir! why, there 't serves well again.

COUNTESS. An end, sir: to your business. Give Helen this,
And urge her to a present answer back:
Commend me to my kinsmen and my son.
This is not much.

CLOWN. Not much commendation to them.

COUNTESS. Not much employment for you: you understand me?

CLOWN. Most fruitfully: I am there before my legs.

COUNTESS. Haste you again. *Exeunt severally*

SCENE THREE

Paris. A Room in the King's Palace.

Enter Bertram, Lafeu, and Parolles

LAFEU. They say miracles are past; and we have our philosophical persons, to make modern and familiar, things supernatural and causeless. Hence is it that we make trifles of terrors, ensconcing ourselves into seeming knowledge, when we should submit ourselves to an unknown fear.

PAROLLES. Why, 'tis the rarest argument of wonder that hath shot out in our latter times.

BERTRAM. And so 'tis.

LAFEU. To be relinquished of the artists,—

PAROLLES. So I say.

LAFEU. Both of Galen and Paracelsus.

PAROLLES. So I say.

LAFEU. Of all the learned and authentic fellows,—

PAROLLES. Right; so I say.

LAFEU. That gave him out incurable,—

PAROLLES. Why, there 'tis; so say I too.

LAFEU. Not to be helped,—

PAROLLES. Right; as 'twere, a man assured of a—

LAFEU. Uncertain life, and sure death.

PAROLLES. Just, you say well: so would I have said.

LAFEU. I may truly say it is a novelty to the world.

PAROLLES. It is, indeed: if you will have it in showing, you shall read it in—what do you call there—

LAFEU. A showing of a heavenly effect in an earthly actor.

PAROLLES. That's it I would have said; the very same.

LAFEU. Why, your dolphin is not lustier: 'fore me, I speak in respect—

PAROLLES. Nay, 'tis strange, tis very strange, that is the brief and the tedious of it; and he is of a most facinorous spirit, that will not acknowledge it to be the—

LAFEU. Very hand of heaven—

PAROLLES. Ay, so I say.

LAFEU. In a most weak and debile minister, great power, great transcendence: which should, indeed, give us a further use to be made than alone the recovery of the king, as to be generally thankful.

PAROLLES. I would have said it; you say well. Here comes the king.

Enter King, Helena, and Attendants

LAFEU. Lustig, as the Dutchman says: I'll like a maid the better, whilst I have a tooth in my head. Why, he's able to lead her a coranto.

PAROLLES. Mort du vinaigre! Is not this Helen?

LAFEU. 'Fore God, I think so.

KING. Go, call before me all the lords in court.

Exit an Attendant

Sit, my preserver, by thy patient's side:
And with this healthful hand, whose banish'd sense
Thou hast repeal'd, a second time receive
The confirmation of my promis'd gift,
Which but attends thy naming.
               Enter several Lords
Fair maid, send forth thine eye: this youthful parcel
Of noble bachelors stand at my bestowing,
O'er whom both sovereign power and father's voice
I have to use: thy frank election make;
Thou hast power to choose, and they none to forsake.
HELENA. To each of you one fair and virtuous mistress
Fall, when Love please! marry, to each, but one.
LAFEU. I'd give bay Curtal, and his furniture,
My mouth no more were broken than these boys'
And writ as little beard.
KING.   Peruse them well:
Not one of those but had a noble father.
HELENA. Gentlemen,
Heaven hath through me restor'd the king to health.
ALL. We understand it, and thank heaven for you.
HELENA. I am a simple maid; and therein wealthiest
That I protest I simply am a maid.
Please it your Majesty, I have done already:
The blushes in my cheeks thus whisper me,
'We blush, that thou shouldst choose; but, be refus'd,
Let the white death sit on thy cheek for ever;
We'll ne'er come there again.'
KING.   Make choice; and see,
Who shuns thy love, shuns all his love in me.
HELENA. Now, Dian, from thy altar do I fly,
And to imperial Love, that god most high,
Do my sighs stream. Sir, will you hear my suit?
FIRST LORD. And grant it.
HELENA.   Thanks, sir; all the rest is mute.
LAFEU. I had rather be in this choice than throw ames-ace
for my life.
HELENA. The honour, sir, that flames in your fair eyes,
Before I speak, too threateningly replies:
Love make your fortunes twenty times above
Her that so wishes, and her humble love!
SECOND LORD. No better, if you please.

HELENA.   My wish receive,
    Which great Love grant! and so I take my leave.
LAFEU. Do all they deny her? An they were sons of mine,
    I'd have them whipp'd or I would send them to the Turk
    to make eunuchs of.
HELENA. *(To third Lord)* Be not afraid that I your hand
        should take;
    I'll never do you wrong for your own sake:
    Blessing upon your vows! and in your bed
    Find fairer fortune, if you ever wed!
LAFEU. These boys are boys of ice, they'll none have her:
    sure, they are bastards to the English; the French ne'er
    got 'em.
HELENA. You are too young, too happy, and too good,
    To make yourself a son out of my blood.
FOURTH LORD. Fair one, I think not so.
LAFEU. There's one grape yet. I am sure thy father drunk
    wine. But if thou be'st not an ass, I am a youth of fourteen:
    I have known thee already.
HELENA. *(To Bertram)* I dare not say I take you; but I give
    Me and my service, ever whilst I live,
    Into your guiding power. This is the man.
KING. Why then, young Bertram, take her; she's thy wife.
BERTRAM. My wife, my liege! I shall beseech your Highness
    In such a business give me leave to use
    The help of mine own eyes.
KING.   Know'st thou not, Bertram,
    What she has done for me?
BERTRAM.   Yes, my good lord;
    But never hope to know why I should marry her.
KING. Thou know'st she has rais'd me from my sickly bed.
BERTRAM. But follows it, my lord, to bring me down
    Must answer for your raising? I know her well:
    She had her breeding at my father's charge.
    A poor physician's daughter my wife! Disdain
    Rather corrupt me ever!
KING. 'Tis only title thou disdain'st in her, the which
    I can build up. Strange is it that our bloods,
    Of colour, weight, and heat, pour'd all together,
    Would quite confound distinction, yet stand off
    In differences so mighty. If she be
    All that is virtuous, save what thou dislik'st,

ACT II · SCENE III

A poor physician's daughter, thou dislik'st
Of virtue for the name; but do not so:
From lowest place when virtuous things proceed,
The place is dignified by the doer's deed:
Where great additions swell 's, and virtue none,
It is a dropsied honour. Good alone
Is good without a name: vileness is so:
The property by what it is should go,
Not by the title. She is young, wise, fair;
In these to nature she's immediate heir,
And these breed honour: that is honour's scorn
Which challenges itself as honour's born,
And is not like the sire: honours thrive
When rather from our acts we them derive
Than our foregoers. The mere word's a slave,
Debosh'd on every tomb, on every grave
A lying trophy, and as oft is dumb
Where dust and damn'd oblivion is the tomb
Of honour'd bones indeed. What should be said?
If thou canst like this creature as a maid,
I can create the rest: virtue and she
Is her own dower; honour and wealth from me.

BERTRAM. I cannot love her, nor will strive to do 't.

KING. Thou wrong'st thyself if thou shouldst strive to choose.

HELENA. That you are well restor'd, my lord, I'm glad:
Let the rest go.

KING. My honour's at the stake, which to defeat
I must produce my power. Here, take her hand,
Proud scornful boy, unworthy this good gift,
That dost in vile misprision shackle up
My love and her desert; thou canst not dream
We, poising us in her defective scale,
Shall weigh thee to the beam; that wilt not know,
It is in us to plant thine honour where
We please to have it grow. Check thy contempt:
Obey our will, which travails in thy good:
Believe not thy disdain, but presently
Do thine own fortunes that obedient right
Which both thy duty owes and our power claims;
Or I will throw thee from my care for ever
Into the staggers and the careless lapse
Of youth and ignorance; both my revenge and hate

Loosing upon thee, in the name of justice,
Without all terms of pity. Speak; thine answer.

BERTRAM. Pardon, my gracious lord; for I submit
My fancy to your eyes. When I consider
What great creation and what dole of honour
Flies where you bid it, I find that she, which late
Was in my nobler thoughts most base, is now
The praised of the king; who, so ennobled,
Is, as 'twere, born so.

KING.   Take her by the hand,
And tell her she is thine: to whom I promise
A counterpoise, if not to thy estate
A balance more replete.

BERTRAM.   I take her hand.

KING. Good fortune and the favour of the king
Smile upon this contract; whose ceremony
Shall seem expedient on the now-born brief,
And be perform'd to-night: the solemn feast
Shall more attend upon the coming space,
Expecting absent friends. As thou lov'st her,
Thy love's to me religious; else, does err.

Exeunt King, Bertram, Helena, Lords and Attendants

LAFEU. Do you hear, monsieur? A word with you.

PAROLLES. Your pleasure, sir?

LAFEU. Your lord and master did well to make his recantation.

PAROLLES. Recantation! My lord! My master!

LAFEU. Ay; is it not a language I speak?

PAROLLES. A most harsh one, and not to be understood without bloody succeeding. My master!

LAFEU. Are you companion to the Count Rousillon?

PAROLLES. To any count; to all counts; to what is man.

LAFEU. To what is count's man: count's master is of another style.

PAROLLES. You are too old, sir; let it satisfy you, you are too old.

LAFEU. I must tell thee, sirrah, I write man; to which title age cannot bring thee.

PAROLLES. What I dare too well do, I dare not do.

LAFEU. I did think thee, for two ordinaries, to be a pretty wise fellow: thou didst make tolerable vent of thy travel; it might pass: yet the scarfs and the bannerets about thee did manifoldly dissuade me from believing thee a vessel of too great a burden. I have now found thee; when I lose thee again, I care not; yet art thou good for nothing but taking up, and that thou'rt scarce worth.

PAROLLES. Hadst thou not the privilege of antiquity upon thee,—

LAFEU. Do not plunge thyself too far in anger, lest thou hasten thy trial; which if—Lord have mercy on thee for a hen! So, my good window of lattice, fare thee well: thy casement I need not open, for I look through thee. Give me thy hand.

PAROLLES. My lord, you give me most egregious indignity.

LAFEU. Ay, with all my heart; and thou art worthy of it.

PAROLLES. I have not, my lord, deserved it.

LAFEU. Yes, good faith, every dram of it; and I will not bate thee a scruple.

PAROLLES. Well, I shall be wiser.

LAFEU. E'en as soon as thou canst, for thou hast to pull at a smack o' the contrary. If ever thou be'st bound in thy scarf and beaten, thou shalt find what it is to be proud of thy bondage. I have a desire to hold my acquaintance with thee, or rather my knowledge, that I may say in the default, he is a man I know.

PAROLLES. My lord, you do me most insupportable vexation.

LAFEU. I would it were hell-pains for thy sake, and my poor doing eternal: for doing I am past; as I will by thee, in what motion age will give me leave. *Exit*

PAROLLES. Well, thou hast a son shall take this disgrace off me; scurvy, old, filthy, scurvy lord! Well, I must be patient; there is no fettering of authority. I'll beat him, by my life, if I can meet him with any convenience, an he were double and double a lord. I'll have no more pity of his age than I would have of—I'll beat him, an if I could but meet him again!

Re-enter Lafeu

LAFEU. Sirrah, your lord and master's married; there's news for you: you have a new mistress.

PAROLLES. I most unfeignedly beseech your lordship to make some reservation of your wrongs: he is my good lord: whom I serve above is my master.

LAFEU. Who? God?

PAROLLES. Ay, sir.

800 ALL'S WELL THAT ENDS WELL [242-280]

LAFEU. The devil it is that 's thy master. Why dost thou garter up thy arms o' this fashion? dost make hose of thy sleeves? do other servants so? Thou wert best set thy lower part where thy nose stands. By mine honour, if I were but two hours younger, I 'd beat thee: methinks thou art a general offence, and every man should beat thee: I think thou wast created for men to breathe themselves upon thee.

PAROLLES. This is hard and undeserved measure, my lord.

LAFEU. Go to, sir; you were beaten in Italy for picking a kernel out of a pomegranate; you are a vagabond and no true traveller: you are more saucy with lords and honourable personages than the heraldry of your birth and virtue gives you commission. You are not worth another word, else I 'd call you knave. I leave you. *Exit*

PAROLLES. Good, very good; it is so then: good, very good. Let it be concealed awhile.

Re-enter Bertram

BERTRAM. Undone, and forfeited to cares for ever!

PAROLLES. What is the matter, sweet heart?

BERTRAM. Although before the solemn priest I have sworn, I will not bed her.

PAROLLES. What, what, sweet heart?

BERTRAM. O my Parolles, they have married me!
I 'll to the Tuscan wars, and never bed her.

PAROLLES. France is a dog-hole, and it no more merits
The tread of a man's foot. To the wars!

BERTRAM. There's letters from my mother: what the import is
I know not yet.

PAROLLES. Ay, that would be known. To the wars, my boy!
to the wars!
He wears his honour in a box, unseen,
That hugs his kicky-wicky here at home,
Spending his manly marrow in her arms,
Which should sustain the bound and high curvet
Of Mars's fiery steed. To other regions!
France is a stable; we that dwell in 't jades;
Therefore, to the war!

BERTRAM. It shall be so: I 'll send her to my house,
Acquaint my mother with my hate to her,
And wherefore I am fled; write to the king
That which I durst not speak: his present gift

Shall furnish me to those Italian fields,
Where noble fellows strike. War is no strife
To the dark house and the detested wife.

PAROLLES. Will this capriccio hold in thee? art sure?

BERTRAM. Go with me to my chamber, and advise me.
I'll send her straight away: to-morrow
I'll to the wars, she to her single sorrow.

PAROLLES. Why, these balls bound; there's noise in it. 'Tis hard:
A young man married is a man that's marr'd:
Therefore away, and leave her bravely; go:
The king has done you wrong: but, hush! 'tis so. *Exeunt*

SCENE FOUR

The Same. Another Room in the Palace.

Enter Helena and Clown

HELENA. My mother greets me kindly: is she well?

CLOWN. She is not well; but yet she has her health; she's very merry; but yet she is not well: but thanks be given, she's very well, and wants nothing i' the world; but yet she is not well.

HELENA. If she be very well, what does she ail that she's not very well?

CLOWN. Truly, she's very well indeed, but for two things.

HELENA. What two things?

CLOWN. One, that she's not in heaven, whither God send her quickly! the other, that she's in earth, from whence God send her quickly!

Enter Parolles

PAROLLES. Bless you, my fortunate lady!

HELENA. I hope, sir, I have your good will to have mine own good fortunes.

PAROLLES. You had my prayers to lead them on; and to keep them on, have them still. O! my knave, how does my old lady?

CLOWN. So that you had her wrinkles, and I her money, I would she did as you say.

PAROLLES. Why, I say nothing.

CLOWN. Marry, you are the wiser man; for many a man's

tongue shakes out his master's undoing. To say nothing, to do nothing, to know nothing, and to have nothing, is to be a great part of your title; which is within a very little of nothing.

PAROLLES. Away! thou 'rt a knave.

CLOWN. You should have said, sir, before a knave thou 'rt a knave; that is before me thou 'rt a knave: this had been truth, sir.

PAROLLES. Go to, thou art a witty fool; I have found thee.

CLOWN. Did you find me in yourself, sir? or were you taught to find me? The search, sir, was profitable; and much fool may you find in you, even to the world's pleasure and the increase of laughter.

PAROLLES. A good knave, i' faith, and well fed.
Madam, my lord will go away to-night;
A very serious business calls on him.
The great prerogative and rite of love,
Which, as your due, time claims, he does acknowledge,
But puts it off to a compell'd restraint;
Whose want, and whose delay, is strew'd with sweets,
Which they distil now in the curbed time,
To make the coming hour o'erflow with joy,
And pleasure drown the brim.

HELENA.   What 's his will else?

PAROLLES. That you will take your instant leave o' the king,
And make this haste as your own good proceeding,
Strengthen'd with what apology you think
May make it probable need.

HELENA.   What more commands he?

PAROLLES. That, having this obtain'd, you presently
Attend his further pleasure.

HELENA. In everything I wait upon his will.

PAROLLES. I shall report it so.

HELENA.   I pray you. Come, sirrah.

Exeunt

SCENE FIVE

Another Room in the Same.

Enter Lafeu and Bertram

LAFEU. But I hope your lordship thinks not him a soldier.
BERTRAM. Yes, my lord, and of very valiant approof.
LAFEU. You have it from his own deliverance.
BERTRAM. And by other warranted testimony.
LAFEU. Then my dial goes not true: I took this lark for a bunting.
BERTRAM. I do assure you, my lord, he is very great in knowledge, and accordingly valiant.
LAFEU. I have then sinned against his experience and transgressed against his valour; and my state that way is dangerous, since I cannot yet find in my heart to repent. Here he comes; I pray you, make us friends; I will pursue the amity.

Enter Parolles

PAROLLES. (*To Bertram*) These things shall be done, sir.
LAFEU. Pray you, sir, who's his tailor?
PAROLLES. Sir?
LAFEU. O! I know him well. Ay, sir; he, sir, is a good workman, a very good tailor.
BERTRAM. (*Aside to Parolles*) Is she gone to the king?
PAROLLES. She is.
BERTRAM. Will she away to-night?
PAROLLES. As you'll have her.
BERTRAM. I have writ my letters, casketed my treasure,
Given orders for our horses; and to-night,
When I should take possession of the bride,
End ere I do begin.
LAFEU. A good traveller is something at the latter end of a dinner; but one that lies three thirds, and uses a known truth to pass a thousand nothings with, should be once heard and thrice beaten. God save you, captain.
BERTRAM. Is there any unkindness between my lord and you, monsieur?
PAROLLES. I know not how I have deserved to run into my lord's displeasure.

LAFEU. You have made shift to run into 't, boots and spurs and all, like him that leaped into the custard; and out of it you 'll run again, rather than suffer question for your residence.

BERTRAM. It may be you have mistaken him, my lord.

LAFEU. And shall do so ever, though I took him at his prayers. Fare you well, my lord; and believe this of me, there can be no kernel in this light nut; the soul of this man is his clothes. Trust him not in matter of heavy consequence; I have kept of them tame, and know their natures. Farewell, monsieur: I have spoken better of you than you have or will to deserve at my hand; but we must do good against evil. *Exit*

PAROLLES. An idle lord, I swear.

BERTRAM. I think not so.

PAROLLES. Why, do you not know him?

BERTRAM. Yes, I do know him well; and common speech
Gives him a worthy pass. Here comes my clog.

Enter Helena

HELENA. I have, sir, as I was commanded from you,
Spoke with the king, and have procur'd his leave
For present parting; only, he desires
Some private speech with you.

BERTRAM.   I shall obey his will.
You must not marvel, Helen, at my course,
Which holds not colour with the time, nor does
The ministration and required office
On my particular: prepar'd I was not
For such a business; therefore am I found
So much unsettled. This drives me to entreat you
That presently you take your way for home;
And rather muse than ask why I entreat you;
For my respects are better than they seem,
And my appointments have in them a need
Greater than shows itself at the first view
To you that know them not. This to my mother.

Giving a letter

'Twill be two days ere I shall see you, so
I leave you to your wisdom.

HELENA.   Sir, I can nothing say,
But that I am your most obedient servant.

BERTRAM. Come, come, no more of that.

ACT II : SCENE V

HELENA. And ever shall
With true observance seek to eke out that
Wherein toward me my homely stars have fail'd
To equal my great fortune.
BERTRAM. Let that go:
My haste is very great. Farewell: hie home.
HELENA. Pray sir, your pardon.
BERTRAM. Well, what would you say?
HELENA. I am not worthy of the wealth I owe,
Nor dare I say 'tis mine, and yet it is;
But, like a timorous thief, most fain would steal
What law does vouch mine own.
BERTRAM. What would you have?
HELENA. Something, and scarce so much: nothing indeed.
I would not tell you what I would, my lord:—
Faith, yes;
Strangers and foes do sunder, and not kiss.
BERTRAM. I pray you, stay not, but in haste to horse.
HELENA. I shall not break your bidding, good my lord.
BERTRAM. (*To Parolles*) Where are my other men, monsieur? (*To Helena*) Farewell. *Exit Helena*
Go thou toward home; where I will never come
Whilst I can shake my sword or hear the drum.
Away! and for our flight.
PAROLLES. Bravely, coragio! *Exeunt*

ACT THREE

SCENE ONE

Florence. A Room in the Duke's Palace.

Flourish. Enter the Duke, attended; two French Lords, and Soldiers

DUKE. So that from point to point now have you heard
  The fundamental reasons of this war,
  Whose great decision hath much blood let forth,
  And more thirsts after.
FIRST LORD.   Holy seems the quarrel
  Upon your Grace's part; black and fearful
  On the opposer.
DUKE. Therefore we marvel much our cousin France
  Would in so just a business shut his bosom
  Against our borrowing prayers.
FIRST LORD.   Good my lord,
  The reasons of our state I cannot yield,
  But like a common and an outward man,
  That the great figure of a council frames
  By self-unable motion: therefore dare not
  Say what I think of it, since I have found
  Myself in my incertain grounds to fail
  As often as I guess'd.
DUKE.   Be it his pleasure.
SECOND LORD. But I am sure the younger of our nature,
  That surfeit on their ease, will day by day
  Come here for physic.
DUKE.   Welcome shall they be,
  And all the honours that can fly from us
  Shall on them settle. You know your places well;
  When better fall, for your avails they fell.
  To-morrow to the field.   *Flourish. Exeunt*

SCENE TWO

Rousillon. A Room in the Countess's Palace.

Enter Countess and Clown

COUNTESS. It hath happened all as I would have had it, save that he comes not along with her.
CLOWN. By my troth, I take my young lord to be a very melancholy man.
COUNTESS. By what observance, I pray you?
CLOWN. Why, he will look upon his boot and sing; mend the ruff and sing; ask questions and sing; pick his teeth and sing. I know a man that had this trick of melancholy sold a goodly manor for a song.
COUNTESS. (*Opening a letter*) Let me see what he writes, and when he means to come.
CLOWN. I have no mind to Isbel since I was at court. Our old ling and our Isbels o' the country are nothing like your old ling and your Isbels o' the court: the brains of my Cupid's knocked out, and I begin to love, as an old man loves money, with no stomach.
COUNTESS. What have we here?
CLOWN. E'n that you have there. *Exit*
COUNTESS. 'I have sent you a daughter-in-law: she hath recovered the king, and undone me. I have wedded her, not bedded her; and sworn to make the "not" eternal. You shall hear I am run away: know it before the report come. If there be breadth enough in the world, I will hold a long distance. My duty to you.

Your unfortunate son,
'Bertram.'

This is not well: rash and unbridled boy,
To fly the favours of so good a king!
To pluck his indignation on thy head
By the misprising of a maid too virtuous
For the contempt of empire!

Re-enter Clown

CLOWN. O madam! yonder is heavy news within between two soldiers and my young lady.
COUNTESS. What is the matter?

CLOWN. Nay, there is some comfort in the news, some comfort; your son will not be killed so soon as I thought he would.

COUNTESS. Why should he be killed?

CLOWN. So say I, madam, if he run away, as I hear he does: the danger is in standing to 't; that 's the loss of men, though it be the getting of children. Here they come will tell you more; for my part, I only hear your son was run away. *Exit*

Enter Helena and two Gentlemen

FIRST GENTLEMAN. Save you, good madam.

HELENA. Madam, my lord is gone, for ever gone.

SECOND GENTLEMAN. Do not say so.

COUNTESS. Think upon patience. Pray you, gentlemen,
I have felt so many quirks of joy and grief,
That the first face of neither, on the start,
Can woman me unto 't. Where is my son, I pray you?

SECOND GENTLEMAN. Madam, he 's gone to serve the Duke of Florence:
We met him thitherward; for thence we came,
And, after some dispatch in hand at court,
Thither we bend again.

HELENA. Look on his letter, madam; here 's my passport.
'When thou canst get the ring upon my finger, which never shall come off, and show me a child begotten of thy body that I am father to, then call me husband: but in such a "then" I write a "never."'
This is a dreadful sentence.

COUNTESS. Brought you this letter, gentlemen?

FIRST GENTLEMAN. Ay, madam;
And for the contents' sake are sorry for our pains.

COUNTESS. I prithee, lady, have a better cheer;
If thou engrossest all the griefs are thine,
Thou robb'st me of a moiety: he was my son,
But I do wash his name out of my blood,
And thou art all my child. Towards Florence is he?

SECOND GENTLEMAN. Ay, madam.

COUNTESS. And to be a soldier?

SECOND GENTLEMAN. Such is his noble purpose; and, believe 't,
The duke will lay upon him all the honour
That good convenience claims.

COUNTESS. Return you thither?

FIRST GENTLEMAN. Ay, madam, with the swiftest wing of
    speed.
HELENA. 'Till I have no wife, I have nothing in France.'
    'Tis bitter.
COUNTESS. Find you that there?
HELENA.   Ay, madam.
FIRST GENTLEMAN. 'Tis but the boldness of his hand, haply,
    which his heart was not consenting to.
COUNTESS. Nothing in France until he have no wife!
    There's nothing here that is too good for him
    But only she; and she deserves a lord
    That twenty such rude boys might tend upon,
    And call her hourly mistress. Who was with him?
FIRST GENTLEMAN. A servant only, and a gentleman
    Which I have sometime known.
COUNTESS.   Parolles, was it not?
FIRST GENTLEMAN. Ay, my good lady, he.
COUNTESS. A very tainted fellow, and full of wickedness.
    My son corrupts a well-derived nature
    With his inducement.
FIRST GENTLEMAN.   Indeed, good lady,
    The fellow has a deal of that too much,
    Which holds him much to have.
COUNTESS. Y' are welcome, gentlemen.
    I will entreat you, when you see my son,
    To tell him that his sword can never win
    The honour that he loses: more I 'll entreat you
    Written to bear along.
SECOND GENTLEMAN.   We serve you, madam,
    In that and all your worthiest affairs.
COUNTESS. Not so, but as we change our courtesies.
    Will you draw near?   *Exeunt Countess and Gentlemen*
HELENA. 'Till I have no wife, I have nothing in France.'
    Nothing in France until he has no wife!
    Thou shalt have none, Rousillon, none in France;
    Then hast thou all again. Poor lord! is 't I
    That chase thee from thy country, and expose
    Those tender limbs of thine to the event
    Of the none-sparing war? and is it I
    That drive thee from the sportive court, where thou
    Wast shot at with fair eyes, to be the mark
    Of smoky muskets? O you leaden messengers,
    That ride upon the violent speed of fire,

Fly with false aim; move the still-piecing air,
That sings with piercing; do not touch my lord!
Whoever shoots at him, I set him there;
Whoever charges on his forward breast,
I am the caitiff that do hold him to 't;
And, though I kill him not, I am the cause
His death was so effected: better 'twere
I met the ravin lion when he roar'd
With sharp constraint of hunger; better 'twere
That all the miseries which nature owes
Were mine at once. No, come thou home, Rousillon,
Whence honour but of danger wins a scar,
As oft it loses all: I will be gone;
My being here it is that holds thee hence:
Shall I stay here to do 't? No, no, although
The air of paradise did fan the house,
And angels offic'd all: I will be gone,
That pitiful rumour may report my flight,
To consolate thine ear. Come, night; end, day!
For with the dark, poor thief, I 'll steal away. *Exit*

SCENE THREE

Florence. Before the Duke's Palace.

*Flourish. Enter Duke, Bertram, Parolles, Soldiers.
Drum and Trumpets.*

DUKE. The general of our horse thou art; and we,
Great in our hope, lay our best love and credence
Upon thy promising fortune.
BERTRAM.   Sir, it is
A charge too heavy for my strength, but yet
We 'll strive to bear it for your worthy sake
To the extreme edge of hazard.
DUKE.   Then go thou forth,
And fortune play upon thy prosperous helm
As thy auspicious mistress!
BERTRAM.   This very day,
Great Mars, I put myself into thy file:
Make me but like my thoughts, and I shall prove
A lover of thy drum, hater of love. *Exeunt*

SCENE FOUR

Rousillon. A Room in the Countess's Palace.

Enter Countess and Steward

COUNTESS. Alas! and would you take the letter of her?
Might you not know she would do as she has done,
By sending me a letter? Read it again.
STEWARD. 'I am Saint Jaques' pilgrim, thither gone:
　　Ambitious love hath so in me offended
　That bare-foot plod I the cold ground upon
　　With sainted vow my faults to have amended.
　Write, write, that from the bloody course of war,
　　My dearest master, your dear son, may hie:
　Bless him at home in peace, whilst I from far
　　His name with zealous fervour sanctify:
　His taken labours bid him me forgive;
　　I, his despiteful Juno, sent him forth
　From courtly friends, with camping foes to live,
　　Where death and danger dog the heels of worth:
　He is too good and fair for Death and me;
　Whom I myself embrace, to set him free.'
COUNTESS. Ah, what sharp stings are in her mildest words!
Rinaldo, you did never lack advice so much,
As letting her pass so: had I spoke with her,
I could have well diverted her intents,
Which thus she hath prevented.
STEWARD. 　　　　　　　　Pardon me, madam:
If I had given you this at over-night
She might have been o'erta'en; and yet she writes,
Pursuit would be but vain.
COUNTESS. 　　　　　　　What angel shall
Bless this unworthy husband? He cannot thrive,
Unless her prayers, whom heaven delights to hear
And loves to grant, reprieve him from the wrath
Of greatest justice. Write, write, Rinaldo,
To this unworthy husband of his wife;
Let every word weigh heavy of her worth
That he does weigh too light: my greatest grief,
Though little he do feel it, set down sharply.

Dispatch the most convenient messenger:
When haply he shall hear that she is gone,
He will return; and hope I may that she,
Hearing so much, will speed her foot again,
Led hither by pure love. Which of them both
Is dearest to me I have no skill in sense
To make distinction. Provide this messenger.
My heart is heavy and mine age is weak;
Grief would have tears, and sorrow bids me speak. *Exeunt*

SCENE FIVE

Without the Walls of Florence.

A tucket afar off. Enter a Widow of Florence, Diana, Violenta, Mariana, and other Citizens

WIDOW. Nay, come; for if they do approach the city we shall lose all the sight.

DIANA. They say the French Count has done most honourable service.

WIDOW. It is reported that he has taken their greatest commander, and that with his own hand he slew the duke's brother. We have lost our labour; they are gone a contrary way. Hark! you may know by their trumpets.

MARIANA. Come; let's return again, and suffice ourselves with the report of it. Well, Diana, take heed of this French earl: the honour of a maid is her name, and no legacy is so rich as honesty.

WIDOW. I have told my neighbour how you have been solicited by a gentleman his companion.

MARIANA. I know that knave; hang him! one Parolles: a filthy officer he is in those suggestions for the young earl. Beware of them, Diana; their promises, enticements, oaths, tokens, and all these engines of lust, are not the things they go under: many a maid hath been seduced by them; and the misery is, example, that so terrible shows in the wrack of maidenhood, cannot for all that dissuade succession, but that they are limed with the twigs that threaten them. I hope I need not to advise you further; but I hope your own grace will keep you where you are,

ACT III · SCENE V

though there were no further danger known but the modesty which is so lost.

DIANA. You shall not need to fear me.

WIDOW. I hope so. Look, here comes a pilgrim: I know she will lie at my house; thither they send one another. I'll question her.

Enter Helena in the dress of a Pilgrim

God save you, pilgrim! Whither are you bound?

HELENA. To Saint Jaques le Grand.
Where do the palmers lodge, I do beseech you?

WIDOW. At the Saint Francis, here beside the port.

HELENA. Is this the way?

WIDOW. Ay, marry, is 't. Hark you!

A march afar off

They come this way. If you will tarry, holy pilgrim,
But till the troops come by,
I will conduct you where you shall be lodg'd:
The rather, for I think I know your hostess
As ample as myself.

HELENA. Is it yourself?

WIDOW. If you shall please so, pilgrim.

HELENA. I thank you, and will stay upon your leisure

WIDOW. You came, I think, from France?

HELENA. I did so.

WIDOW. Here you shall see a countryman of yours
That has done worthy service.

HELENA. His name, I pray you.

DIANA. The Count Rousillon: know you such a one?

HELENA. But by the ear, that hears most nobly of him;
His face I know not.

DIANA. Whatsoe'er he is,
He's bravely taken here. He stole from France,
As 'tis reported, for the king had married him
Against his liking. Think you it is so?

HELENA. Ay, surely, mere the truth: I know his lady.

DIANA. There is a gentleman that serves the count
Reports but coarsely of her.

HELENA. What's his name?

DIANA. Monsieur Parolles.

HELENA. O! I believe with him,
In argument of praise, or to the worth
Of the great count himself, she is too mean

To have her name repeated: all her deserving
Is a reserved honesty, and that
I have not heard examin'd.

DIANA. Alas, poor lady!
'Tis a hard bondage to become the wife
Of a detesting lord.

WIDOW. Ay, right; good creature, wheresoe'er she is,
Her heart weighs sadly. This young maid might do her
A shrewd turn if she pleas'd.

HELENA. How do you mean?
May be the amorous count solicits her
In the unlawful purpose.

WIDOW. He does, indeed;
And brokes with all that can in such a suit
Corrupt the tender honour of a maid:
But she is arm'd for him and keeps her guard
In honestest defence.

MARIANA. The gods forbid else!

Enter, with drum and colours,
a party of the Florentine army, Bertram and Parolles

WIDOW. So, now they come.
That is Antonio, the duke's eldest son;
That, Escalus.

HELENA. Which is the Frenchman?

DIANA. He;
That with the plume: 'tis a most gallant fellow;
I would he lov'd his wife. If he were honester,
He were much goodlier; is 't not a handsome gentleman?

HELENA. I like him well.

DIANA. 'Tis pity he is not honest. Yond 's that same knave
That leads him to these places: were I his lady
I would poison that vile rascal.

HELENA. Which is he?

DIANA. That jack-an-apes with scarfs. Why is he melancholy?

HELENA. Perchance he 's hurt i' the battle.

PAROLLES. Lose our drum! well.

MARIANA. He 's shrewdly vexed at something. Look, he has spied us.

WIDOW. Marry, hang you!

MARIANA. And your courtesy, for a ring-carrier!

Exeunt Bertram, Parolles, Officers, and Soldiers

WIDOW. The troop is past. Come, pilgrim, I will bring you
  Where you shall host: of enjoin'd penitents
  There's four or five, to great Saint Jaques bound,
  Already at my house.
HELENA.   I humbly thank you.
  Please it this matron and this gentle maid
  To eat with us to-night, the charge and thanking
  Shall be for me; and, to requite you further,
  I will bestow some precepts of this virgin
  Worthy the note.
BOTH.   We'll take your offer kindly. *Exeunt*

SCENE SIX

Camp before Florence.

Enter Bertram and the two French Lords

FIRST LORD. Nay, good my lord, put him to 't: let him have his way.
SECOND LORD. If your lordship find him not a hilding, hold me no more in your respect.
FIRST LORD. On my life, my lord, a bubble.
BERTRAM. Do you think I am so far deceived in him?
FIRST LORD. Believe it, my lord, in mine own direct knowledge, without any malice, but to speak of him as my kinsman, he's a most notable coward, an infinite and endless liar, an hourly promise-breaker, the owner of no one good quality worthy your lordship's entertainment.
SECOND LORD. It were fit you knew him; lest, reposing too far in his virtue, which he hath not, he might at some great and trusty business in a main danger fail you.
BERTRAM. I would I knew in what particular action to try him.
SECOND LORD. None better than to let him fetch off his drum, which you hear him so confidently undertake to do.
FIRST LORD. I, with a troop of Florentines, will suddenly surprise him: such I will have whom I am sure he knows not from the enemy. We will bind and hoodwink him so, that he shall suppose no other but that he is carried into the leaguer of the adversaries, when we bring him to our own tents. Be but your lordship present at his examination: if

he do not, for the promise of his life and in the highest compulsion of base fear, offer to betray you and deliver all the intelligence in his power against you, and that with the divine forfeit of his soul upon oath, never trust my judgment in anything.

SECOND LORD. O! for the love of laughter, let him fetch his drum: he says he has a stratagem for 't. When your lordship sees the bottom of his success in 't, and to what metal this counterfeit lump of ore will be melted, if you give him not John Drum's entertainment, your inclining cannot be removed. Here he comes.

FIRST LORD. O! for the love of laughter, hinder not the honour of his design: let him fetch off his drum in any hand.

Enter Parolles

BERTRAM. How now, monsieur! This drum sticks sorely in your disposition.

SECOND LORD. A pox on 't! let it go: 'tis but a drum.

PAROLLES. 'But a drum'! Is 't 'but a drum'? A drum so lost! There was excellent command, to charge in with our horse upon our own wings, and to rend our own soldiers!

SECOND LORD. That was not to be blamed in the command of the service: it was a disaster of war that Cæsar himself could not have prevented if he had been there to command.

BERTRAM. Well, we cannot greatly condemn our success: some dishonour we had in the loss of that drum; but it is not to be recovered.

PAROLLES. It might have been recovered.

BERTRAM. It might; but it is not now.

PAROLLES. It is to be recovered. But that the merit of service is seldom attributed to the true and exact performer, I would have that drum or another, or *hic jacet*.

BERTRAM. Why, if you have a stomach to 't, monsieur, if you think your mystery in stratagem can bring this instrument of honour again into its native quarter, be magnanimous in the enterprise and go on; I will grace the attempt for a worthy exploit: if you speed well in it, the duke shall both speak of it, and extend to you what further becomes his greatness, even to the utmost syllable of your worthiness.

PAROLLES. By the hand of a soldier, I will undertake it.

BERTRAM. But you must not now slumber in it.

PAROLLES. I'll about it this evening: and I will presently pen down my dilemmas, encourage myself in my certainty, put myself into my mortal preparation, and by midnight look to hear further from me.

BERTRAM. May I be bold to acquaint his Grace you are gone about it?

PAROLLES. I know not what the success will be, my lord; but the attempt I vow.

BERTRAM. I know thou 'rt valiant; and, to the possibility of thy soldiership will subscribe for thee. Farewell.

PAROLLES. I love not many words. *Exit*

FIRST LORD. No more than a fish loves water. Is not this a strange fellow, my lord, that so confidently seems to undertake this business, which he knows is not to be done; damns himself to do, and dares better be damned than to do 't?

SECOND LORD. You do not know him, my lord, as we do: certain it is, that he will steal himself into a man's favour, and for a week escape a great deal of discoveries; but when you find him out you have him ever after.

BERTRAM. Why, do you think he will make no deed at all of this that so seriously he does address himself unto?

FIRST LORD. None in the world; but return with an invention and clap upon you two or three probable lies. But we have almost embossed him, you shall see his fall to-night; for, indeed, he is not for your lordship's respect.

SECOND LORD. We 'll make you some sport with the fox ere we case him. He was first smoked by the old Lord Lafeu: when his disguise and he is parted, tell me what a sprat you shall find him; which you shall see this very night.

FIRST LORD. I must go look my twigs: he shall be caught.

BERTRAM. Your brother, he shall go along with me.

FIRST LORD. As 't please your lordship: I 'll leave you. *Exit*

BERTRAM. Now will I lead you to the house, and show you
The lass I spoke of.

SECOND LORD. But you say she 's honest.

BERTRAM. That 's all the fault. I spoke with her but once,
And found her wondrous cold; but I sent to her,
By this same coxcomb that we have i' the wind,
Tokens and letters which she did re-send;
And this is all I have done. She 's a fair creature;
Will you go see her?

SECOND LORD. With all my heart, my lord. *Exeunt*

SCENE SEVEN

Florence. A Room in the Widow's House.

Enter Helena and Widow

HELENA. If you misdoubt me that I am not she,
I know not how I shall assure you further,
But I shall lose the grounds I work upon.
WIDOW. Though my estate be fall'n, I was well born,
Nothing acquainted with these businesses;
And would not put my reputation now
In any staining act.
HELENA. Nor would I wish you.
First, give me trust, the county is my husband,
And what to your sworn counsel I have spoken
Is so from word to word; and then you cannot,
By the good aid that I of you shall borrow,
Err in bestowing it.
WIDOW. I should believe you:
For you have show'd me that which well approves
You're great in fortune.
HELENA. Take this purse of gold,
And let me buy your friendly help thus far,
Which I will over-pay and pay again
When I have found it. The county woos your daughter,
Lays down his wanton siege before her beauty
Resolv'd to carry her: let her in fine consent,
As we'll direct her how 'tis best to bear it.
Now, his important blood will naught deny
That she'll demand: a ring the county wears,
That downward hath succeeded in his house
From son to son, some four or five descents
Since the first father wore it: this ring he holds
In most rich choice; yet, in his idle fire,
To buy his will, it would not seem too dear,
Howe'er repented after.
WIDOW. Now I see
The bottom of your purpose.
HELENA. You see it lawful then. It is no more,
But that your daughter, ere she seems as won,

Desires this ring, appoints him an encounter,
In fine, delivers me to fill the time,
Herself most chastely absent. After this,
To marry her, I'll add three thousand crowns
To what is past already.

WIDOW. I have yielded.
Instruct my daughter how she shall persever,
That time and place with this deceit so lawful
May prove coherent. Every night he comes
With musics of all sorts and songs compos'd
To her unworthiness: it nothing steads us
To chide him from our eaves, for he persists
As if his life lay on 't.

HELENA. Why then to-night
Let us assay our plot; which, if it speed,
Is wicked meaning in a lawful deed,
And lawful meaning in a lawful act,
Where both not sin, and yet a sinful fact.
But let's about it. *Exeunt*

ACT FOUR

SCENE ONE

Without the Florentine Camp.

Enter First French Lord, with five or six Soldiers in ambush

FIRST LORD. He can come no other way but by this hedge-corner. When you sally upon him, speak what terrible language you will: though you understand it not yourselves, no matter; for we must not seem to understand him, unless some one among us, whom we must produce for an interpreter.

FIRST SOLDIER. Good captain, let me be the interpreter.

FIRST LORD. Art not acquainted with him? Knows he not thy voice?

FIRST SOLDIER. No, sir, I warrant you.

FIRST LORD. But what linsey-woolsey hast thou to speak to us again?

FIRST SOLDIER. Even such as you speak to me.

FIRST LORD. He must think us some band of strangers i' the adversary's entertainment. Now, he hath a smack of all neighbouring languages; therefore we must every one be a man of his own fancy, not to know what we speak one to another; so we seem to know, is to know straight our purpose: chough's language, gabble enough, and good enough. As for you, interpreter, you must seem very politic. But couch, ho! here he comes, to beguile two hours in a sleep, and then to return and swear the lies he forges.

Enter Parolles

PAROLLES. Ten o'clock: within these three hours 'twill be time enough to go home. What shall I say I have done? It must be a very plausive invention that carries it. They begin to smoke me, and disgraces have of late knocked too often at my door. I find my tongue is too foolhardy; but my heart hath the fear of Mars before it and of his creatures, not daring the reports of my tongue.

FIRST LORD. This is the first truth that e'er thine own tongue was guilty of.

PAROLLES. What the devil should move me to undertake the recovery of this drum, being not ignorant of the impossibility, and knowing I had no such purpose? I must give myself some hurts and say I got them in exploit. Yet slight ones will not carry it: they will say, 'Came you off with so little?' and great ones I dare not give. Wherefore, what's the instance. Tongue, I must put you into a butter-woman's mouth, and buy myself another Bajazet's mule, if you prattle me into these perils.

FIRST LORD. Is it possible he should know what he is, and be that he is?

PAROLLES. I would the cutting of my garments would serve the turn or the breaking of my Spanish sword.

FIRST LORD. We cannot afford you so.

PAROLLES. Or the baring of my beard, and to say it was in stratagem.

FIRST LORD. 'Twould not do.

PAROLLES. Or to drown my clothes, and say I was stripped.

FIRST LORD. Hardly serve.

PAROLLES. Though I swore I leaped from the window of the citadel—

FIRST LORD. How deep?

PAROLLES. Thirty fathom.

FIRST LORD. Three great oaths would scarce make that be believed.

PAROLLES. I would I had any drum of the enemy's: I would swear I recovered it.

FIRST LORD. Thou shalt hear one anon.

PAROLLES. A drum now of the enemy's! *Alarum within*

FIRST LORD. Throca movousus, cargo, cargo, cargo.

ALL. Cargo, cargo, villianda par corbo, cargo.

They seize and blindfold him

PAROLLES. O! ransom, ransom! Do not hide mine eyes.

FIRST SOLDIER. Boskos thromuldo boskos.

PAROLLES. I know you are the Muskos' regiment;
And I shall lose my life for want of language.
If there be here German, or Dane, low Dutch,

Italian, or French, let him speak to me:
I will discover that which shall undo
The Florentine.

FIRST SOLDIER. Boskos vauvado:
I understand thee, and can speak thy tongue:
Kerelybonto: Sir,
Betake thee to thy faith, for seventeen poniards
Are at thy bosom.

PAROLLES. O!

FIRST SOLDIER. O! pray, pray, pray.
Manka revania dulche.

FIRST LORD. Oscorbidulchos volivorco.

FIRST SOLDIER. The general is content to spare thee yet;
And, hoodwink'd as thou art, will lead thee on
To gather from thee: haply thou may'st inform
Something to save thy life.

PAROLLES. O! let me live,
And all the secrets of our camp I'll show,
Their force, their purposes; nay, I'll speak that
Which you will wonder at.

FIRST SOLDIER. But wilt thou faithfully?

PAROLLES. If I do not, damn me.

FIRST SOLDIER. Acordo linta.
Come on; thou art granted space.

Exit, with Parolles guarded. A short alarum within

FIRST LORD. Go, tell the Count Rousillon, and my brother,
We have caught the woodcock, and will keep him muffled
Till we do hear from them.

SECOND SOLDIER. Captain, I will.

FIRST LORD. A' will betray us all unto ourselves:
Inform on that.

SECOND SOLDIER. So I will, sir.

FIRST LORD. Till then, I'll keep him dark and safely lock'd.

Exeunt

SCENE TWO

Florence. A Room in the Widow's House.

Enter Bertram and Diana

BERTRAM. They told me that your name was Fontibell.
DIANA. No, my good lord, Diana.
BERTRAM.   Titled goddess;
And worth it, with addition! But, fair soul,
In your fine frame hath love no quality?
If the quick fire of youth light not your mind,
You are no maiden, but a monument:
When you are dead, you should be such a one
As you are now, for you are cold and stern;
And now you should be as your mother was
When your sweet self was got.
DIANA. She then was honest.
BERTRAM.   So should you be.
DIANA.   No:
My mother did but duty; such, my lord,
As you owe to your wife.
BERTRAM.   No more o' that!
I prithee do not strive against my vows.
I was compell'd to her; but I love thee
By love's own sweet constraint, and will for ever
Do thee all rights of service.
DIANA.   Ay, so you serve us
Till we serve you; but when you have our roses,
You barely leave our thorns to prick ourselves
And mock us with our bareness.
BERTRAM.   How have I sworn!
DIANA. 'Tis not the many oaths that make the truth,
But the plain single vow that is vow'd true.
What is not holy, that we swear not by,
But take the Highest to witness: then, pray you, tell me,
If I should swear by God's great attributes
I lov'd you dearly, would you believe my oaths,
When I did love you ill? This has no holding,
To swear by him whom I protest to love,
That I will work against him: therefore your oaths

Are words and poor conditions, but unseal'd;
At least in my opinion.

BERTRAM. Change it, change it.
Be not so holy-cruel: love is holy;
And my integrity ne'er knew the crafts
That you do charge men with. Stand no more off,
But give thyself unto my sick desires,
Who then recover: say thou art mine, and ever
My love as it begins shall so persever.

DIANA. I see that men make ropes in such a scarr
That we 'll forsake ourselves. Give me that ring.

BERTRAM. I 'll lend it thee, my dear; but have no power
To give it from me.

DIANA. Will you not, my lord?

BERTRAM. It is an honour 'longing to our house,
Bequeathed down from many ancestors,
Which were the greatest obloquy i' the world
In me to lose.

DIANA. Mine honour 's such a ring
My chastity 's the jewel of our house,
Bequeathed down from many ancestors,
Which were the greatest obloquy i' the world
In me to lose. Thus your own proper wisdom
Brings in the champion honour on my part
Against your vain assault.

BERTRAM. Here, take my ring:
My house, mine honour, yea, my life, be thine,
And I 'll be bid by thee.

DIANA. When midnight comes, knock at my chamber-window:
I 'll order take my mother shall not hear.
Now will I charge you in the band of truth,
When you have conquer'd my yet maiden bed,
Remain there but an hour, nor speak to me.
My reasons are most strong; and you shall know them
When back again this ring shall be deliver'd:
And on your finger in the night I 'll put
Another ring, that what in time proceeds
May token to the future our past deeds.
Adieu, till then; then, fail not. You have won
A wife of me, though there my hope be done.

BERTRAM. A heaven on earth I have won by wooing thee.

Exit

DIANA. For which live long to thank both heaven and me!
You may so in the end.
My mother told me just how he would woo
As if she sat in 's heart; she says all men
Have the like oaths: he had sworn to marry me
When his wife 's dead; therefore I 'll lie with him
When I am buried. Since Frenchmen are so braid,
Marry that will, I live and die a maid:
Only in this disguise I think 't no sin
To cozen him that would unjustly win. *Exit*

SCENE THREE

The Florentine Camp.

Enter the two French Lords, and two or three Soldiers

FIRST LORD. You have not given him his mother's letter?

SECOND LORD. I have delivered it an hour since: there is something in 't that stings his nature, for on the reading it he changed almost into another man.

FIRST LORD. He has much worthy blame laid upon him for shaking off so good a wife and so sweet a lady.

SECOND LORD. Especially he hath incurred the everlasting displeasure of the king, who had even tuned his bounty to sing happiness to him. I will tell you a thing, but you shall let it dwell darkly with you.

FIRST LORD. When you have spoken it, 'tis dead, and I am the grave of it.

SECOND LORD. He hath perverted a young gentle-woman here in Florence, of a most chaste renown; and this night he fleshes his will in the spoil of her honour: he hath given her his monumental ring, and thinks himself made in the unchaste composition.

FIRST LORD. Now, God delay our rebellion! As we are ourselves, what things are we!

SECOND LORD. Merely our own traitors: and as in the common course of all treasons, we still see them reveal themselves, till they attain to their abhorred ends, so he that in this action contrives against his own nobility, in his proper stream o'erflows himself.

FIRST LORD. Is it not most damnable in us, to be trumpeters of our unlawful intents? We shall not then have his company to-night?

SECOND LORD. Not till after midnight, for he is dieted to his hour.

FIRST LORD. That approaches apace: I would gladly have him see his company anatomized, that he might take a measure of his own judgments, wherein so curiously he had set this counterfeit.

SECOND LORD. We will not meddle with him till he come, for his presence must be the whip of the other.

FIRST LORD. In the meantime what hear you of these wars?

SECOND LORD. I hear there is an overture of peace.

FIRST LORD. Nay, I assure you, a peace concluded.

SECOND LORD. What will Count Rousillon do then? Will he travel higher, or return again into France?

FIRST LORD. I perceive by this demand, you are not altogether of his council.

SECOND LORD. Let it be forbid, sir; so should I be a great deal of his act.

FIRST LORD. Sir, his wife some two months since fled from his house: her pretence is a pilgrimage to Saint Jaques le Grand; which holy undertaking with most austere sanctimony she accomplished; and, there residing, the tenderness of her nature became as a prey to her grief; in fine, made a groan of her last breath, and now she sings in heaven.

SECOND LORD. How is this justified?

FIRST LORD. The stronger part of it by her own letters, which make her story true, even to the point of her death: her death itself, which could not be her office to say is come, was faithfully confirmed by the rector of the place.

SECOND LORD. Hath the count all this intelligence?

FIRST LORD. Ay, and the particular confirmations, point from point, to the full arming of the verity.

SECOND LORD. I am heartily sorry that he'll be glad of this.

FIRST LORD. How mightily sometimes we make us comforts of our losses!

SECOND LORD. And how mightily some other times we drown our gain in tears! The great dignity that his valour hath here acquired for him shall at home be encountered with a shame as ample.

FIRST LORD. The web of our life is of a mingled yarn, good and ill together: our virtues would be proud if our faults whipped them not; and our crimes would despair if they were not cherished by our virtues.

Enter a Servant

How now! where's your master?

SERVANT. He met the duke in the street, sir, of whom he hath taken a solemn leave: his lordship will next morning for France. The duke hath offered him letters of commendations to the king.

SECOND LORD. They shall be no more than needful there, if they were more than they can commend.

FIRST LORD. They cannot be too sweet for the king's tartness. Here's his lordship now.

Enter Bertram

How now, my lord: is't not after midnight?

BERTRAM. I have to-night dispatched sixteen businesses, a month's length a-piece, by an abstract of success: I have conge'd with the duke, done my adieu with his nearest, buried a wife, mourned for her, writ to my lady mother I am returning, entertained my convoy; and between these main parcels of dispatch effected many nicer needs: the last was the greatest, but that I have not ended yet.

SECOND LORD. If the business be of any difficulty, and this morning your departure hence, it requires haste of your lordship.

BERTRAM. I mean, the business is not ended, as fearing to hear of it hereafter. But shall we have this dialogue between the fool and the soldier? Come, bring forth this counterfeit model: he has deceived me, like a double-meaning prophesier.

SECOND LORD. Bring him forth. (*Exeunt Soldiers*) Has sat i' the stocks all night, poor gallant knave.

BERTRAM. No matter; his heels have deserved it, in usurping his spurs so long. How does he carry himself?

FIRST LORD. I have told your lordship already, the stocks carry him. But to answer you as you would be understood; he weeps like a wench that had shed her milk: he hath confessed himself to Morgan,—whom he supposes to be a friar,—from the time of his remembrance to this very instant disaster of his setting i' the stocks: and what think you he hath confessed?

BERTRAM. Nothing of me, has a'?

SECOND LORD. His confession is taken, and it shall be read to his face: if your lordship be in 't, as I believe you are, you must have the patience to hear it.

Re-enter Soldiers with Parolles

BERTRAM. A plague upon him! muffled! he can say nothing of me: hush! hush!

FIRST LORD. Hoodman comes! Porto tartarossa.

FIRST SOLDIER. He calls for the tortures: what will you say without 'em?

PAROLLES. I will confess what I know without constraint: if ye pinch me like a pasty, I can say no more.

FIRST SOLDIER. Bosko chimurcho.

FIRST LORD. Boblibindo chicurmurco.

FIRST SOLDIER. You are a merciful general. Our general bids you answer to what I shall ask you out of a note.

PAROLLES. And truly, as I hope to live.

FIRST SOLDIER. 'First, demand of him how many horse the duke is strong.' What say you to that?

PAROLLES. Five or six thousand; but very weak and unserviceable: the troops are all scattered, and the commanders very poor rogues, upon my reputation and credit, and as I hope to live.

FIRST SOLDIER. Shall I set down your answer so?

PAROLLES. Do: I'll take the sacrament on 't, how and which way you will.

BERTRAM. All 's one to him. What a past-saving slave is this!

FIRST LORD. You are deceived, my lord: this is Monsieur Parolles, the gallant militarist,—that was his own phrase,—that had the whole theorick of war in the knot of his scarf, and the practice in the chape of his dagger.

SECOND LORD. I will never trust a man again for keeping his sword clean; nor believe he can have everything in him by wearing his apparel neatly.

FIRST SOLDIER. Well, that 's set down.

PAROLLES. Five or six thousand horse, I said,—I will say true, —or thereabouts, set down, for I'll speak truth.

FIRST LORD. He 's very near the truth in this.

BERTRAM. But I con him no thanks for 't, in the nature he delivers it.

PAROLLES. Poor rogues, I pray you, say.

FIRST SOLDIER. Well, that's set down.

PAROLLES. I humbly thank you, sir. A truth's a truth; the rogues are marvellous poor.

FIRST SOLDIER. 'Demand of him, of what strength they are afoot.' What say you to that?

PAROLLES. By my troth, sir, if I were to live this present hour, I will tell true. Let me see: Spurio, a hundred and fifty; Sebastian, so many; Corambus, so many; Jaques, so many; Guiltian, Cosmo, Lodowick, and Gratii, two hundred fifty each; mine own company, Chitopher, Vaumond, Bentii, two hundred fifty each: so that the muster-file, rotten and sound, upon my life, amounts not to fifteen thousand poll; half of the which dare not shake the snow from off their cassocks, lest they shake themselves to pieces.

BERTRAM. What shall be done to him?

FIRST LORD. Nothing, but let him have thanks. Demand of him my condition, and what credit I have with the duke.

FIRST SOLDIER. Well, that's set down. 'You shall demand of him, whether one Captain Dumain be i' the camp, a Frenchman; what his reputation is with the duke; what his valour, honesty, and expertness in wars; or whether he thinks it were not possible, with well-weighing sums of gold, to corrupt him to a revolt.' What say you to this? What do you know of it?

PAROLLES. I beseech you, let me answer to the particular of the inter'gatories: demand them singly.

FIRST SOLDIER. Do you know this Captain Dumain?

PAROLLES. I know him: a' was a botcher's 'prentice in Paris, from whence he was whipped for getting the shrieve's fool with child; a dumb innocent, that could not say him nay.

Dumain lifts up his hand in anger

BERTRAM. Nay, by your leave, hold your hands; though I know his brains are forfeit to the next tile that falls.

FIRST SOLDIER. Well, is this captain in the Duke of Florence's camp?

PAROLLES. Upon my knowledge he is, and lousy.

FIRST LORD. Nay, look not so upon me; we shall hear of your lordship anon.

FIRST SOLDIER. What is his reputation with the duke?

PAROLLES. The duke knows him for no other but a poor officer of mine, and writ to me this other day to turn him out o' the band: I think I have his letter in my pocket.

FIRST SOLDIER. Marry, we'll search.

PAROLLES. In good sadness, I do not know: either it is there, or it is upon a file with the duke's other letters in my tent.

FIRST SOLDIER. Here 'tis; here's a paper; shall I read it to you?

PAROLLES. I do not know if it be it or no.

BERTRAM. Our interpreter does it well.

FIRST LORD. Excellently.

FIRST SOLDIER. 'Dian, the count's a fool, and full of gold'—

PAROLLES. That is not the duke's letter, sir; that is an advertisement to a proper maid in Florence, one Diana, to take heed of the allurement of one Count Rousillon, a foolish idle boy, but for all that very ruttish. I pray you, sir, put it up again.

FIRST SOLDIER. Nay, I'll read it first, by your favour.

PAROLLES. My meaning in 't, I protest, was very honest in the behalf of the maid; for I knew the young count to be a dangerous and lascivious boy, who is a whale to virginity, and devours up all the fry it finds.

BERTRAM. Damnable both-sides rogue!

FIRST SOLDIER. 'When he swears oaths, bid him drop gold
    and take it;
After he scores, he never pays the score:
Half won is match well made; match, and well make it;
    He ne'er pays after-debts; take it before,
And say a soldier, Dian, told thee this,
Men are to mell with, boys are not to kiss;
For count of this, the count's a fool, I know it,
Who pays before, but not when he does owe it.
    Thine, as he vow'd to thee in thine ear,   Parolles.'

BERTRAM. He shall be whipped through the army with this rime in 's forehead.

FIRST LORD. This is your devoted friend, sir; the manifold linguist and the armipotent soldier.

BERTRAM. I could endure anything before but a cat, and now he's a cat to me.

FIRST SOLDIER. I perceive, sir, by our general's looks, we shall be fain to hang you.

PAROLLES. My life, sir, in any case! Not that I am afraid to die; but that, my offences being many, I would repent out

ACT IV : SCENE III

the remainder of nature. Let me live, sir, in a dungeon, i' the stocks, or anywhere, so I may live.

FIRST SOLDIER. We'll see what may be done, so you confess freely: therefore, once more to this Captain Dumain. You have answered to his reputation with the duke and to his valour: what is his honesty?

PAROLLES. He will steal, sir, an egg out of a cloister; for rapes and ravishments he parallels Nessus; he professes not keeping of oaths; in breaking 'em he is stronger than Hercules; he will lie, sir, with such volubility, that you would think truth were a fool; drunkenness is his best virtue, for he will be swine-drunk, and in his sleep he does little harm, save to his bed-clothes about him; but they know his conditions, and lay him in straw. I have but little more to say, sir, of his honesty: he has everything that an honest man should not have; what an honest man should have, he has nothing.

FIRST LORD. I begin to love him for this.

BERTRAM. For this description of thine honesty? A pox upon him for me! He is more and more a cat.

FIRST SOLDIER. What say you to his expertness in war?

PAROLLES. Faith, sir, he has led the drum before the English tragedians,—to belie him I will not,—and more of his soldiership I know not; except, in that country, he had the honour to be the officer at a place there called Mile-end, to instruct for the doubling of files: I would do the man what honour I can, but of this I am not certain.

FIRST LORD. He hath out-villained villany so far, that the rarity redeems him.

BERTRAM. A pox on him! He's a cat still.

FIRST SOLDIER. His qualities being at this poor price, I need not ask you, if gold will corrupt him to revolt.

PAROLLES. Sir, for a cardecu he will sell the fee-simple of his salvation, the inheritance of it; and cut the entail from all remainders, and a perpetual succession for it perpetually.

FIRST SOLDIER. What's his brother, the other Captain Dumain?

SECOND LORD. Why does he ask him of me?

FIRST SOLDIER. What's he?

PAROLLES. E'en a crow o' the same nest; not altogether so great as the first in goodness, but greater a great deal in evil. He excels his brother for a coward, yet his brother is reputed one of the best that is. In a retreat he outruns any lackey; marry, in coming on he has the cramp.

FIRST SOLDIER. If your life be saved, will you undertake to betray the Florentine?

PAROLLES. Ay, and the captain of his horse, Count Rousillon.

FIRST SOLDIER. I'll whisper with the general, and know his pleasure.

PAROLLES. (*Aside*) I'll no more drumming; a plague of all drums! Only to seem to deserve well, and to beguile the supposition of that lascivious young boy the count, have I run into this danger. Yet who would have suspected an ambush where I was taken?

FIRST SOLDIER. There is no remedy, sir, but you must die. The general says, you, that have so traitorously discovered the secrets of your army, and made such pestiferous reports of men very nobly held, can serve the world for no honest use; therefore you must die. Come, headsman, off with his head.

PAROLLES. O Lord, sir, let me live, or let me see my death!

FIRST SOLDIER. That shall you, and take your leave of all your friends. *Unmuffling him*
So, look about you: know you any here?

BERTRAM. Good-morrow, noble captain.

SECOND LORD. God bless you, Captain Parolles.

FIRST LORD. God save you, noble captain.

SECOND LORD. Captain, what greeting will you to my Lord Lafeu? I am for France.

FIRST LORD. Good captain, will you give me a copy of the sonnet you writ to Diana in behalf of the Count Rousillon? An I were not a very coward I'd compel it of you; but fare you well. *Exeunt Bertram and Lords*

FIRST SOLDIER. You are undone, captain; all but your scarf; that has a knot on 't yet.

PAROLLES. Who cannot be crushed with a plot?

FIRST SOLDIER. If you could find out a country where but women were that had received so much shame, you might begin an impudent nation. Fare ye well, sir; I am for France too: we shall speak of you there. *Exit*

PAROLLES. Yet am I thankful: if my heart were great
'Twould burst at this. Captain I'll be no more;
But I will eat and drink, and sleep as soft
As captain shall: simply the thing I am

Shall make me live. Who knows himself a braggart,
Let him fear this; for it will come to pass
That every braggart shall be found an ass.
Rust, sword! cool, blushes! and Parolles, live
Safest in shame! being fool'd, by foolery thrive!
There 's place and means for every man alive.
I 'll after them. *Exit*

SCENE FOUR

Florence. A Room in the Widow's House.

Enter Helena, Widow, and Diana

HELENA. That you may well perceive I have not wrong'd you,
One of the greatest in the Christian world
Shall be my surety; 'fore whose throne 'tis needful,
Ere I can perfect mine intents, to kneel.
Time was I did him a desired office,
Dear almost as his life; which gratitude
Through flinty Tartar's bosom would peep forth,
And answer, thanks. I duly am inform'd
His Grace is at Marseilles; to which place
We have convenient convoy. You must know,
I am supposed dead: the army breaking,
My husband hies him home; where, heaven aiding,
And by the leave of my good lord the king,
We 'll be before our welcome.
WIDOW. Gentle madam,
You never had a servant to whose trust
Your business was more welcome.
HELENA. Nor you, mistress,
Ever a friend whose thoughts more truly labour
To recompense your love. Doubt not but heaven
Hath brought me up to be your daughter's dower,
As it hath fated her to be my motive
And helper to a husband. But, O strange men!
That can such sweet use make of what they hate,
When saucy trusting of the cozen'd thoughts
Defiles the pitchy night: so lust doth play
With what it loathes for that which is away.

But more of this hereafter. You, Diana,
Under my poor instructions yet must suffer
Something in my behalf.

DIANA. Let death and honesty
Go with your impositions, I am yours
Upon your will to suffer.

HELENA. Yet, I pray you:
But with the word the time will bring on summer,
When briers shall have leaves as well as thorns,
And be as sweet as sharp. We must away;
Our waggon is prepar'd, and time revives us:
All 's well that ends well: still the fine 's the crown;
Whate'er the course, the end is the renown. *Exeunt*

SCENE FIVE

Rousillon. A Room in the Countess's Palace.

Enter Countess, Lafeu, and Clown

LAFEU. No, no, no; your son was misled with a snipt-taffeta fellow there, whose villanous saffron would have made all the unbaked and doughy youth of a nation in his colour. your daughter-in-law had been alive at this hour, and your son here at home, more advanced by the king than by that red-tailed humble-bee I speak of.

COUNTESS. I would I had not known him; it was the death of the most virtuous gentlewoman that ever nature had praise for creating. If she had partaken of my flesh, and cost me the dearest groans of a mother, I could not have owed her a more rooted love.

LAFEU. 'Twas a good lady, 'twas a good lady: we may pick a thousand salads ere we light on such another herb.

CLOWN. Indeed, sir, she was the sweet-marjoram of the salad, or, rather the herb of grace.

LAFEU. They are not salad-herbs, you knave; they are nose-herbs.

CLOWN. I am no great Nebuchadnezzar, sir; I have not much skill in grass.

LAFEU. Whether dost thou profess thyself, a knave, or a fool?

CLOWN. A fool, sir, at a woman's service, and a knave at a man's.
LAFEU. Your distinction?
CLOWN. I would cozen the man of his wife, and do his service.
LAFEU. So you were a knave at his service, indeed.
CLOWN. And I would give his wife my bauble, sir, to do her service.
LAFEU. I will subscribe for thee, thou art both knave and fool.
CLOWN. At your service.
LAFEU. No, no, no.
CLOWN. Why, sir, if I cannot serve you, I can serve as great a prince as you are.
LAFEU. Who's that? a Frenchman?
CLOWN. Faith, sir, a' has an English name; but his phisnomy is more hotter in France than there.
LAFEU. What prince is that?
CLOWN. The black prince, sir; alias, the prince of darkness; alias, the devil.
LAFEU. Hold thee, there's my purse. I give thee not this to suggest thee from thy master thou talkest of: serve him still.
CLOWN. I am a woodland fellow, sir, that always loved a great fire; and the master I speak of, ever keeps a good fire. But, sure, he is the prince of the world; let his nobility remain in 's court. I am for the house with the narrow gate, which I take to be too little for pomp to enter: some that humble themselves may; but the many will be too chill and tender, and they 'll be for the flowery way that leads to the broad gate and the great fire.
LAFEU. Go thy ways, I begin to be aweary of thee; and I tell thee so before, because I would not fall out with thee. Go thy ways: let my horses be well looked to, without any tricks.
CLOWN. If I put any tricks upon 'em, sir, they shall be jades' tricks, which are their own right by the law of nature.

Exit

LAFEU. A shrewd knave and an unhappy.
COUNTESS. So he is. My lord that's gone made himself much sport out of him: by his authority he remains here, which

he thinks is a patent for his sauciness; and, indeed, he has no pace, but runs where he will.

LAFEU. I like him well; 'tis not amiss. And I was about to tell you, since I heard of the good lady's death, and that my lord your son was upon his return home, I moved the king my master to speak in the behalf of my daughter; which, in the minority of them both, his Majesty, out of a self-gracious remembrance, did first propose. His Highness hath promised me to do it; and to stop up the displeasure he hath conceived against your son, there is no fitter matter. How does your ladyship like it?

COUNTESS. With very much content, my lord; and I wish it happily effected.

LAFEU. His Highness comes post from Marseilles, of as able body as when he numbered thirty: he will be here to-morrow, or I am deceived by him that in such intelligence hath seldom failed.

COUNTESS. It rejoices me that I hope I shall see him ere I die. I have letters that my son will be here to-night: I shall beseech your lordship to remain with me till they meet together.

LAFEU. Madam, I was thinking with what manners I might safely be admitted.

COUNTESS. You need but plead your honourable privilege.

LAFEU. Lady, of that I have made a bold charter; but I thank my God it holds yet.

Re-enter Clown

CLOWN. O madam! yonder's my lord your son with a patch of velvet on 's face: whether there be a scar under it or no, the velvet knows; but 'tis a goodly patch of velvet. His left cheek is a cheek of two pile and a half, but his right cheek is worn bare.

LAFEU. A scar nobly got, or a noble scar, is a good livery of honour; so belike is that.

CLOWN. But it is your carbonadoed face.

LAFEU. Let us go see your son, I pray you: I long to talk with the young noble soldier.

CLOWN. Faith, there's a dozen of 'em, with delicate fine hats and most courteous feathers, which bow the head and nod at every man. *Exeunt*

ACT FIVE

SCENE ONE

Marseilles. A Street.

Enter Helena, Widow, and Diana, with two Attendants

HELENA. But this exceeding posting, day and night,
Must wear your spirits low; we cannot help it:
But since you have made the days and nights as one,
To wear your gentle limbs in my affairs,
Be bold you do so grow in my requital
As nothing can unroot you. In happy time;
Enter a gentle Astringer
This man may help me to his Majesty's ear,
If he would spend his power. God save you, sir.

ASTRINGER. And you.

HELENA. Sir, I have seen you in the court of France.

ASTRINGER. I have been sometimes there.

HELENA. I do presume, sir, that you are not fallen
From the report that goes upon your goodness;
And therefore, goaded with most sharp occasions,
Which lay nice manners by, I put you to
The use of your own virtues, for the which
I shall continue thankful.

ASTRINGER. What's your will?

HELENA. That it will please you
To give this poor petition to the king,
And aid me with that store of power you have
To come into his presence.

ASTRINGER. The king's not here.

HELENA. Not here, sir!

ASTRINGER. Not, indeed:
He hence remov'd last night, and with more haste
Than is his use.

WIDOW. Lord, how we lose our pains!

HELENA. All's well that ends well yet,
    Though time seems so adverse and means unfit.
    I do beseech you, whither is he gone?
ASTRINGER. Marry, as I take it, to Rousillon;
    Whither I am going.
HELENA.   I do beseech you, sir,
    Since you are like to see the king before me,
    Commend the paper to his gracious hand;
    Which I presume shall render you no blame
    But rather make you thank your pains for it.
    I will come after you with what good speed
    Our means will make us means.
ASTRINGER.   This I'll do for you.
HELENA. And you shall find yourself to be well thank'd,
    Whate'er falls more. We must to horse again:
    Go, go, provide.   *Exeunt*

SCENE TWO

Rousillon. The inner Court of the Countess's Palace.

Enter Clown and Parolles

PAROLLES. Good Monsieur Lavache, give my Lord Lafeu this letter. I have ere now, sir, been better known to you, when I have held familiarity with fresher clothes; but I am now, sir, muddied in Fortune's mood, and smell somewhat strong of her strong displeasure.

CLOWN. Truly, Fortune's displeasure is but sluttish if it smell so strongly as thou speakest of: I will henceforth eat no fish of Fortune's buttering. Prithee, allow the wind.

PAROLLES. Nay, you need not to stop your nose, sir: I spake but by a metaphor.

CLOWN. Indeed, sir, if your metaphor stink, I will stop my nose; or against any man's metaphor. Prithee, get thee further.

PAROLLES. Pray you, sir, deliver me this paper.

CLOWN. Foh! prithee, stand away: a paper from Fortune's close-stool to give to a nobleman! Look, here he comes himself.

Enter Lafeu

Here is a purr of Fortune's, sir, or of Fortune's cat—but not a musk-cat—that has fallen into the unclean fishpond of her displeasure, and, as he says, is muddied withal. Pray you, sir, use the carp as you may, for he looks like a poor, decayed, ingenious, foolish, rascally knave. I do pity his distress in my similes of comfort, and leave him to your lordship. *Exit*

PAROLLES. My lord, I am a man whom Fortune hath cruelly scratched.

LAFEU. And what would you have me to do? 'Tis too late to pare her nails now. Wherein have you played the knave with Fortune that she should scratch you, who of herself is a good lady, and would not have knaves thrive long under her? There's a cardecu for you. Let the justices make you and Fortune friends; I am for other business.

PAROLLES. I beseech your honour to hear me one single word.

LAFEU. You beg a single penny more: come, you shall ha 't; save your word.

PAROLLES. My name, my good lord, is Parolles.

LAFEU. You beg more than one word then. Cox my passion! Give me your hand. How does your drum?

PAROLLES. O, my good lord! You were the first that found me.

LAFEU. Was I, in sooth? And I was the first that lost thee.

PAROLLES. It lies in you, my lord, to bring me in some grace, for you did bring me out.

LAFEU. Out upon thee, knave! Dost thou put upon me at once both the office of God and the devil? One brings thee in grace and the other brings thee out. (*Trumpets sound*) The king's coming; I know by his trumpets. Sirrah, inquire further after me; I had talk of you last night: though you are a fool and a knave, you shall eat: go to, follow.

PAROLLES. I praise God for you. *Exeunt*

SCENE THREE

The Same. A Room in the Countess's Palace.

Flourish. Enter King, Countess, Lafeu, Lords, Gentlemen, Guards, &c.

KING. We lost a jewel of her, and our esteem
Was made much poorer by it: but your son,
As mad in folly, lack'd the sense to know
Her estimation home.
COUNTESS.   'Tis past, my liege;
And I beseech your Majesty to make it
Natural rebellion, done i' the blaze of youth;
When oil and fire, too strong for reason's force,
O'erbears it and burns on.
KING.   My honour'd lady,
I have forgiven and forgotten all,
Though my revenges were high bent upon him,
And watch'd the time to shoot.
LAFEU.   This I must say,—
But first I beg my pardon,—the young lord
Did to his Majesty, his mother, and his lady,
Offence of mighty note, but to himself
The greatest wrong of all: he lost a wife
Whose beauty did astonish the survey
Of richest eyes, whose words all ears took captive,
Whose dear perfection hearts that scorn'd to serve
Humbly call'd mistress.
KING.   Praising what is lost
Makes the remembrance dear. Well, call him hither;
We are reconcil'd, and the first view shall kill
All repetition. Let him not ask our pardon:
The nature of his great offence is dead,
And deeper than oblivion we do bury
The incensing relics of it: let him approach,
A stranger, no offender; and inform him
So 'tis our will he should.
GENTLEMAN.   I shall, my liege.   *Exit*
KING. What says he to your daughter? have you spoke?
LAFEU. All that he is hath reference to your Highness.

KING. Then shall we have a match. I have letters sent me,
That set him high in fame.

Enter Bertram

LAFEU. He looks well on 't.
KING. I am not a day of season,
For thou mayst see a sunshine and a hail
In me at once; but to the brightest beams
Distracted clouds give way: so stand thou forth;
The time is fair again.
BERTRAM. My high-repented blames,
Dear sovereign, pardon to me.
KING. All is whole;
Not one word more of the consumed time.
Let's take the instant by the forward top,
For we are old, and on our quick'st decrees
The inaudible and noiseless foot of time
Steals ere we can effect them. You remember
The daughter of this lord?
BERTRAM. Admiringly, my liege:
At first I stuck my choice upon her, ere my heart
Durst make too bold a herald of my tongue,
Where the impression of mine eye infixing,
Contempt his scornful perspective did lend me,
Which warp'd the line of every other favour;
Scorn'd a fair colour, or express'd it stolen;
Extended or contracted all proportions
To a most hideous object: thence it came
That she, whom all men prais'd, and whom myself,
Since I have lost, have lov'd, was in mine eye
The dust that did offend it.
KING. Well excus'd:
That thou didst love her, strikes some scores away
From the great compt. But love that comes too late,
Like a remorseful pardon slowly carried,
To the great sender turns a sour offence,
Crying, 'That's good that's gone.' Our rasher faults
Make trivial price of serious things we have,
Not knowing them until we know their grave:
Oft our displeasures, to ourselves unjust,
Destroy our friends and after weep their dust:
Our own love waking cries to see what's done,
While shameful hate sleeps out the afternoon.

Be this sweet Helen's knell, and now forget her.
Send forth your amorous token for fair Maudlin:
The main consents are had; and here we 'll stay
To see our widower's second marriage-day.

COUNTESS. Which better than the first, O dear heaven, bless!
Or, ere they meet, in me, O nature, cesse!

LAFEU. Come on, my son, in whom my house's name
Must be digested, give a favour from you
To sparkle in the spirits of my daughter,
That she may quickly come. *Bertram gives a ring*
                                By my old beard,
And every hair that's on 't, Helen, that's dead,
Was a sweet creature; such a ring as this,
The last that e'er I took her leave at court,
I saw upon her finger.

BERTRAM. Hers it was not.

KING. Now, pray you, let me see it; for mine eye,
While I was speaking, oft was fasten'd to 't.—
This ring was mine; and, when I gave it Helen,
I bade her, if her fortunes ever stood
Necessitied to help, that by this token
I would relieve her. Had you that craft to reave her
Of what should stead her most?

BERTRAM.   My gracious sovereign,
Howe'er it pleases you to take it so,
The ring was never hers.

COUNTESS.   Son, on my life,
I have seen her wear it; and she reckon'd it
At her life's rate.

LAFEU.   I am sure I saw her wear it.

BERTRAM. You are deceiv'd, my lord, she never saw it:
In Florence was it from a casement thrown me,
Wrapp'd in a paper, which contain'd the name
Of her that threw it. Noble she was, and thought
I stood engag'd: but when I had subscrib'd
To mine own fortune, and inform'd her fully
I could not answer in that course of honour
As she had made the overture, she ceas'd,
In heavy satisfaction, and would never
Receive the ring again.

KING.   Plutus himself,
That knows the tinct and multiplying medicine,

[103-139] ACT V : SCENE III

Hath not in nature's mystery more science
Than I have in this ring: 'twas mine, 'twas Helen's,
Whoever gave it you. Then, if you know
That you are well acquainted with yourself,
Confess 'twas hers, and by what rough enforcement
You got it from her. She call'd the saints to surety,
That she would never put it from her finger
Unless she gave it to yourself in bed,
Where you have never come, or sent it us
Upon her great disaster.

BERTRAM. She never saw it.

KING. Thou speak'st it falsely, as I love mine honour;
And mak'st conjectural fears to come into me
Which I would fain shut out. If it should prove
That thou art so inhuman,—'twill not prove so;—
And yet I know not: thou didst hate her deadly,
And she is dead; which nothing, but to close
Her eyes myself, could win me to believe,
More than to see this ring. Take him away.

Guards seize Bertram

My fore-past proofs, howe'er the matter fall,
Shall tax my fears of little vanity,
Having vainly fear'd too little. Away with him!
We'll sift this matter further.

BERTRAM. If you shall prove
This ring was ever hers, you shall as easy
Prove that I husbanded her bed in Florence,
Where yet she never was. *Exit guarded*

KING. I am wrapp'd in dismal thinkings.

Enter the gentle Astringer

ASTRINGER. Gracious sovereign,
Whether I have been to blame or no, I know not:
Here's a petition from a Florentine,
Who hath, for four or five removes, come short
To tender it herself. I undertook it,
Vanquish'd thereto by the fair grace and speech
Of the poor suppliant, who by this I know
Is here attending: her business looks in her
With an importing visage, and she told me,
In a sweet verbal brief, it did concern
Your Highness with herself.

KING. 'Upon his many protestations to marry me when his

wife was dead, I blush to say it, he won me. Now is the
Count Rousillon a widower: his vows are forfeited to me,
and my honour 's paid to him. He stole from Florence, tak-
ing no leave, and I follow him to his country for justice.
Grant it me, O king! In you it best lies; otherwise a seducer
flourishes, and a poor maid is undone.
                                              'Diana Capilet.'
LAFEU. I will buy me a son-in-law in a fair, and toll for this:
  I 'll none of him.
KING. The heavens have thought well on thee, Lafeu,
  To bring forth this discovery. Seek these suitors:
  Go speedily and bring again the count.
        Exeunt the gentle Astringer, and some Attendants
  I am afeard the life of Helen, lady,
  Was foully snatch'd.
COUNTESS.   Now, justice on the doers!
              Re-enter Bertram, guarded
KING. I wonder, sir, sith wives are monsters to you,
  And that you fly them as you swear them lordship,
  Yet you desire to marry.
      Re-enter the gentle Astringer, with Widow and Diana
                                  What woman 's that?
DIANA. I am, my lord, a wretched Florentine,
  Derived from the ancient Capilet:
  My suit, as I do understand, you know,
  And therefore know how far I may be pitied.
WIDOW. I am her mother, sir, whose age and honour
  Both suffer under this complaint we bring,
  And both shall cease, without your remedy.
KING. Come hither, county; do you know these women?
BERTRAM. My lord, I neither can nor will deny
  But that I know them: do they charge me further?
DIANA. Why do you look so strange upon your wife?
BERTRAM. She 's none of mine, my lord.
DIANA.   If you shall marry,
  You give away this hand, and that is mine;
  You give away heaven's vows, and those are mine;
  You give away myself, which is known mine;
  For I by vow am so embodied yours
  That she which marries you must marry me;
  Either both or none.
LAFEU. (*To Bertram*) Your reputation comes too short for

ACT V : SCENE III

my daughter: you are no husband for her.

BERTRAM. My lord, this is a fond and desperate creature,
Whom sometime I have laugh'd with: let your Highness
Lay a more noble thought upon mine honour
Than for to think that I would sink it here.

KING. Sir, for my thoughts, you have them ill to friend,
Till your deeds gain them: fairer prove your honour,
Than in my thought it lies.

DIANA. Good my lord,
Ask him upon his oath, if he does think
He had not my virginity.

KING. What sayst thou to her?

BERTRAM. She's impudent, my lord;
And was a common gamester to the camp.

DIANA. He does me wrong, my lord; if I were so,
He might have bought me at a common price:
Do not believe him. O! behold this ring,
Whose high respect and rich validity
Did lack a parallel; yet for all that
He gave it to a commoner o' the camp,
If I be one.

COUNTESS. He blushes, and 'tis it:
Of six preceding ancestors, that gem
Conferr'd by testament to the sequent issue,
Hath it been ow'd and worn. This is his wife:
That ring's a thousand proofs.

KING. Methought you said
You saw one here in court could witness it.

DIANA. I did, my lord, but loath am to produce
So bad an instrument: his name's Parolles.

LAFEU. I saw the man to-day, if man he be.

KING. Find him, and bring him hither. *Exit an Attendant.*

BERTRAM. What of him?
He's quoted for a most perfidious slave,
With all the spots of the world tax'd and debosh'd,
Whose nature sickens but to speak a truth.
Am I or that or this for what he'll utter,
That will speak anything?

KING. She hath that ring of yours.

BERTRAM. I think she has: certain it is I lik'd her,
And boarded her i' the wanton way of youth.
She knew her distance and did angle for me,

Madding my eagerness with her restraint,
As all impediments in fancy's course
Are motives of more fancy; and, in fine,
Her infinite cunning, with her modern grace,
Subdued me to her rate: she got the ring,
And I had that which any inferior might
At market-price have bought.

DIANA. I must be patient;
You, that have turn'd off a first so noble wife,
May justly diet me. I pray you yet,—
Since you lack virtue I will lose a husband,—
Send for your ring; I will return it home,
And give me mine again.

BERTRAM. I have it not.

KING. What ring was yours, I pray you?

DIANA. Sir, much like
The same upon your finger.

KING. Know you this ring? This ring was his of late.

DIANA. And this was it I gave him, being a-bed.

KING. The story then goes false you threw it him
Out of a casement.

DIANA. I have spoke the truth.

Re-enter Attendant with Parolles

BERTRAM. My lord, I do confess the ring was hers.

KING. You boggle shrewdly, every feather starts you.
Is this the man you speak of?

DIANA. Ay, my lord.

KING. Tell me, sirrah, but tell me true, I charge you,
Not fearing the displeasure of your master,—
Which, on your just proceeding I'll keep off,—
By him and by this woman here what know you?

PAROLLES. So please your Majesty, my master hath been an honourable gentleman: tricks he hath had in him, which gentlemen have.

KING. Come, come, to the purpose: did he love this woman?

PAROLLES. Faith, sir, he did love her; but how?

KING. How, I pray you?

PAROLLES. He did love her, sir, as a gentleman loves a woman.

KING. How is that?

PAROLLES. He loved her, sir, and loved her not.

KING. As thou art a knave, and no knave.

What an equivocal companion is this!

PAROLLES. I am a poor man, and at your Majesty's command.

LAFEU. He is a good drum, my lord, but a naughty orator.

DIANA. Do you know he promised me marriage?

PAROLLES. Faith, I know more than I 'll speak.

KING. But wilt thou not speak all thou knowest?

PAROLLES. Yes, so please your Majesty. I did go between them, as I said; but more than that, he loved her, for, indeed, he was mad for her, and talked of Satan, and of limbo, and of Furies, nd I know not what: yet I was in that credit with them at that time, that I knew of their going to bed, and of other motions, as promising her marriage, and things which would derive me ill will to speak of: therefore I will not speak what I know.

KING. Thou hast spoken all already, unless thou canst say they are married: but thou art too fine in thy evidence, therefore stand aside. This ring, you say, was yours?

DIANA. Ay, my good lord.

KING. Where did you buy it? or who gave it you?

DIANA. It was not given me, nor I did not buy it.

KING. Who lent it you?

DIANA. It was not lent me neither.

KING. Where did you find it, then?

DIANA. I found it not.

KING. If it were yours by none of all these ways,
How could you give it him?

DIANA. I never gave it him.

LAFEU. This woman 's an easy glove, my lord: she goes off and on at pleasure.

KING. This ring was mine: I gave it his first wife.

DIANA. It might be yours or hers, for aught I know.

KING. Take her away; I do not like her now.
To prison with her; and away with him.
Unless thou tell'st me where thou hadst this ring
Thou diest within this hour.

DIANA. I 'll never tell you.

KING. Take her away.

DIANA. I 'll put in bail, my liege.

KING. I think thee now some common customer.

DIANA. By Jove, if ever I knew man, 'twas you.

KING. Wherefore hast thou accus'd him all this while?

DIANA. Because he's guilty, and he is not guilty.
He knows I am no maid, and he'll swear to 't;
I'll swear I am a maid, and he knows not.
Great king, I am no strumpet, by my life;
I am either maid, or else this old man's wife.

Pointing to Lafeu

KING. She does abuse our ears: to prison with her!
DIANA. Good mother, fetch my bail. (*Exit Widow*) Stay,
royal sir;
The jeweller that owes the ring is sent for,
And he shall surety me. But for this lord,
Who hath abus'd me, as he knows himself,
Though yet he never harm'd me, here I quit him:
He knows himself my bed he hath defil'd,
And at that time he got his wife with child:
Dead though she be, she feels her young one kick:
So there's my riddle: one that's dead is quick;
And now behold the meaning.

Re-enter Widow, with Helena

KING.   Is there no exorcist
Beguiles the truer office of mine eyes?
Is 't real that I see?
HELENA.   No, my good lord;
'Tis but the shadow of a wife you see;
The name and not the thing.
BERTRAM.   Both, both. O! pardon.
HELENA. O my good lord! when I was like this maid,
I found you wondrous kind. There is your ring;
And, look you, here's your letter; this it says:
'When from my finger you can get this ring,
And are by me with child,' &c. This is done:
Will you be mine, now you are doubly won?
BERTRAM. If she, my liege, can make me know this clearly,
I'll love her dearly, ever, ever dearly.
HELENA. If it appear not plain, and prove untrue,
Deadly divorce step between me and you!
O! my dear mother; do I see you living?
LAFEU. Mine eyes smell onions; I shall weep anon. (*To Parolles*) Good Tom Drum, lend me a handkercher: so, I thank thee. Wait on me home, I'll make sport with thee: let thy curtsies alone, they are scurvy ones.

KING. Let us from point to point this story know,
  To make the even truth in pleasure flow.
  (*To Diana*) If thou be'st yet a fresh uncropped flower,
  Choose thou thy husband, and I'll pay thy dower;
  For I can guess that by thy honest aid
  Thou keptst a wife herself, thyself a maid.
  Of that, and all the progress, more and less,
  Resolvedly more leisure shall express:
  All yet seems well; and if it end so meet,
  The bitter past, more welcome is the sweet.
                              Flourish. Exeunt

EPILOGUE

Spoken by the King

The king's a beggar, now the play is done:
All is well ended if this suit be won,
That you express content; which we will pay,
With strife to please you, day exceeding day:
Ours be your patience then, and yours our parts;
Your gentle hands lend us, and take our hearts.   *Exeunt*

TWELFTH-NIGHT; OR, WHAT YOU WILL

CAST OF CHARACTERS

ORSINO, *Duke of Illyria*
SEBASTIAN, *Brother to Viola*
ANTONIO, *a Sea Captain, Friend to Sebastian*
A Sea Captain, *Friend to Viola*

VALENTINE } *Gentlemen attending on the Duke*
CURIO

SIR TOBY BELCH, *Uncle to Olivia*
SIR ANDREW AGUECHEEK
MALVOLIO, *Steward to Olivia*

FABIAN } *Servants to Olivia*
FESTE, *a Clown*

OLIVIA, *a rich Countess*
VIOLA, *in love with the Duke*
MARIA, *Olivia's Woman*

Lords, Priests, Sailors, Officers, Musicians, and other Attendants

SCENE
A City in Illyria; and the Sea-coast near it

TWELFTH-NIGHT;
OR, WHAT YOU WILL

ACT ONE

SCENE ONE

A Room in the Duke's Palace.

Enter Duke, Curio, Lords; Musicians attending

DUKE. If music be the food of love, play on;
 Give me excess of it, that, surfeiting,
 The appetite may sicken, and so die.
 That strain again! It had a dying fall:
 O! it came o'er my ear like the sweet sound
 That breathes upon a bank of violets,
 Stealing and giving odour. Enough! no more:
 'Tis not so sweet now as it was before.
 O spirit of love! how quick and fresh art thou,
 That, notwithstanding thy capacity
 Receiveth as the sea, naught enters there,
 Of what validity and pitch soe'er,
 But falls into abatement and low price,
 Even in a minute: so full of shapes is fancy,
 That it alone is high fantastical.
CURIO. Will you go hunt, my lord?
DUKE.   What, Curio?
CURIO. The hart.
DUKE. Why, so I do, the noblest that I have.
 O! when mine eyes did see Olivia first,
 Methought she purg'd the air of pestilence.
 That instant was I turn'd into a hart,
 And my desires, like fell and cruel hounds,
 E'er since pursue me.
     Enter Valentine

How now! what news from her?

VALENTINE. So please my lord, I might not be admitted;
But from her handmaid to return this answer:
The element itself, till seven years' heat,
Shall not behold her face at ample view;
But, like a cloistress, she will veiled walk,
And water once a day her chamber round
With eye-offending brine: all this, to season
A brother's dead love, which she would keep fresh
And lasting in her sad remembrance.

DUKE. O! she that hath a heart of that fine frame
To pay this debt of love but to a brother,
How will she love, when the rich golden shaft
Hath kill'd the flock of all affections else
That live in her; when liver, brain, and heart,
These sovereign thrones, are all supplied, and fill'd
Her sweet perfections with one self king.
Away before me to sweet beds of flowers;
Love-thoughts lie rich when canopied with bowers.

Exeunt

SCENE TWO

The Sea-coast.

Enter Viola, Captain, and Sailors

VIOLA. What country, friends, is this?
CAPTAIN.   This is Illyria, lady.
VIOLA. And what should I do in Illyria?
My brother he is in Elysium.
Perchance he is not drown'd. What think you sailors?
CAPTAIN. It is perchance that you yourself were sav'd.
VIOLA. O my poor brother! and so perchance may he be.
CAPTAIN. True, madam: and, to comfort you with chance,
Assure yourself, after our ship did split,
When you and those poor number sav'd with you
Hung on our driving boat, I saw your brother,
Most provident in peril, bind himself,—
Courage and hope both teaching him the practice,—
To a strong mast that liv'd upon the sea;
Where, like Arion on the dolphin's back,

ACT I · SCENE II

I saw him hold acquaintance with the waves
So long as I could see.
VIOLA. For saying so there's gold.
Mine own escape unfoldeth to my hope,
Whereto thy speech serves for authority,
The like of him. Know'st thou this country?
CAPTAIN. Ay, madam, well; for I was bred and born
Not three hours' travel from this very place.
VIOLA. Who governs here?
CAPTAIN. A noble duke, in nature as in name.
VIOLA. What is his name?
CAPTAIN. Orsino.
VIOLA. Orsino! I have heard my father name him:
He was a bachelor then.
CAPTAIN. And so is now, or was so very late;
For but a month ago I went from hence,
And then 'twas fresh in murmur,—as, you know,
What great ones do the less will prattle of,—
That he did seek the love of fair Olivia.
VIOLA. What's she?
CAPTAIN. A virtuous maid, the daughter of a count
That died some twelvemonth since; then leaving her
In the protection of his son, her brother,
Who shortly also died: for whose dear love,
They say she hath abjur'd the company
And sight of men.
VIOLA. O! that I serv'd that lady,
And might not be deliver'd to the world,
Till I had made mine own occasion mellow,
What my estate is.
CAPTAIN. That were hard to compass,
Because she will admit no kind of suit,
No, not the duke's.
VIOLA. There is a fair behaviour in thee, captain;
And though that nature with a beauteous wall
Doth oft close in pollution, yet of thee
I will believe thou hast a mind that suits
With this thy fair and outward character.
I prithee,—and I'll pay thee bounteously,—
Conceal me what I am, and be my aid
For such disguise as haply shall become
The form of my intent. I'll serve this duke:

Thou shall present me as a eunuch to him:
It may be worth thy pains; for I can sing
And speak to him in many sorts of music
That will allow me very worth his service.
What else may hap to time I will commit;
Only shape thou thy silence to my wit.

CAPTAIN. Be you his eunuch, and your mute I'll be:
When my tongue blabs, then let mine eyes not see.

VIOLA. I thank thee: lead me on. *Exeunt*

SCENE THREE

A Room in Olivia's House.

Enter Sir Toby Belch and Maria

SIR TOBY. What a plague means my niece, to take the death of her brother thus? I am sure care's an enemy to life.

MARIA. By my troth, Sir Toby, you must come in earlier o' nights: your cousin, my lady, takes great exceptions to your ill hours.

SIR TOBY. Why, let her except before excepted.

MARIA. Ay, but you must confine yourself within the modest limits of order.

SIR TOBY. Confine! I'll confine myself no finer than I am. These clothes are good enough to drink in, and so be these boots too: an they be not, let them hang themselves in their own straps.

MARIA. That quaffing and drinking will undo you: I heard my lady talk of it yesterday; and of a foolish knight that you brought in one night here to be her wooer.

SIR TOBY. Who? Sir Andrew Aguecheek?

MARIA. Ay, he.

SIR TOBY. He's as tall a man as any's in Illyria.

MARIA. What's that to the purpose?

SIR TOBY. Why, he has three thousand ducats a year.

MARIA. Ay, but he'll have but a year in all these ducats: he's a very fool and a prodigal.

SIR TOBY. Fie, that you'll say so! He plays o' the viol-de-gamboys, and speaks three or four languages word for word without book, and hath all the good gifts of nature.

MARIA. He hath indeed, almost natural; for, besides that he's a fool, he's a great quarreller; and but that he hath the gift of a coward to allay the gust he hath in quarrelling, 'tis thought among the prudent he would quickly have the gift of a grave.

SIR TOBY. By this hand, they are scoundrels and substractors that say so of him. Who are they?

MARIA. They that add, moreover, he's drunk nightly in your company.

SIR TOBY. With drinking healths to my niece. I'll drink to her as long as there is a passage in my throat and drink in Illyria. He's a coward and a coystril, that will not drink to my niece till his brains turn o' the toe like a parish-top. What, wench! Castiliano vulgo! for here comes Sir Andrew Agueface.

Enter Sir Andrew Aguecheek

SIR ANDREW. Sir Toby Belch! How now, Sir Toby Belch!

SIR TOBY. Sweet Sir Andrew!

SIR ANDREW. Bless you, fair shrew.

MARIA. And you too, sir.

SIR TOBY. Accost, Sir Andrew, accost.

SIR ANDREW. What's that?

SIR TOBY. My niece's chambermaid.

SIR ANDREW. Good Mistress Accost, I desire better acquaintance.

MARIA. My name is Mary, sir.

SIR ANDREW. Good Mistress Mary Accost,—

SIR TOBY. You mistake, knight: 'accost' is, front her, board her, woo her, assail her.

SIR ANDREW. By my troth, I would not undertake her in this company. Is that the meaning of 'accost'?

MARIA. Fare you well, gentlemen.

SIR TOBY. An thou let her part so, Sir Andrew, would thou mightst never draw sword again!

SIR ANDREW. An you part so, mistress, I would I might never draw sword again. Fair lady, do you think you have fools in hand?

MARIA. Sir, I have not you by the hand.

SIR ANDREW. Marry, but you shall have; and here's my hand.

MARIA. Now, sir, 'thought is free': I pray you, bring your hand to the buttery-bar and let it drink.

SIR ANDREW. Wherefore, sweetheart? What's your metaphor?

MARIA. It's dry, sir.

SIR ANDREW. Why, I think so: I am not such an ass but I can keep my hand dry. But what's your jest?

MARIA. A dry jest, sir.

SIR ANDREW. Are you full of them?

MARIA. Ay, sir, I have them at my fingers' ends: marry, now I let go your hand, I am barren. *Exit*

SIR TOBY. O knight! thou lackest a cup of canary: when did I see thee so put down?

SIR ANDREW. Never in your life, I think; unless you see canary put me down. Methinks sometimes I have no more wit than a Christian or an ordinary man has; but I am a great eater of beef, and I believe that does harm to my wit.

SIR TOBY. No question.

SIR ANDREW. An I thought that, I'd forswear it. I'll ride home to-morrow, Sir Toby.

SIR TOBY. Pourquoi, my dear knight?

SIR ANDREW. What is 'pourquoi'? Do or not do? I would I had bestowed that time in the tongues that I have in fencing, dancing, and bear-baiting. O! had I but followed the arts!

SIR TOBY. Then hadst thou had an excellent head of hair.

SIR ANDREW. Why, would that have mended my hair?

SIR TOBY. Past question; for thou seest it will not curl by nature.

SIR ANDREW. But it becomes me well enough, does't not?

SIR TOBY. Excellent; it hangs like flax on a distaff, and I hope to see a housewife take thee between her legs, and spin it off.

SIR ANDREW. Faith, I'll home to-morrow, Sir Toby: your niece will not be seen; or if she be, it's four to one she'll none of me. The count himself here hard by woos her.

SIR TOBY. She'll none o' the count; she'll not match above her degree, neither in estate, years, nor wit; I have heard her swear it. Tut, there's life in't, man.

SIR ANDREW. I'll stay a month longer. I am a fellow o' the strangest mind i' the world; I delight in masques and revels sometimes altogether.

SIR TOBY. Art thou good at these kickchawses, knight?

SIR ANDREW. As any man in Illyria, whatsoever he be, under

[106-127; 1-12] ACT I : SCENE III   859

the degree of my betters: and yet I will not compare with an old man.

SIR TOBY. What is thy excellence in a galliard, knight?

SIR ANDREW. Faith, I can cut a caper.

SIR TOBY. And I can cut the mutton to 't.

SIR ANDREW. And I think I have the back-trick simply as strong as any man in Illyria.

SIR TOBY. Wherefore are these things hid? Wherefore have these gifts a curtain before 'em? Are they like to take dust, like Mistress Mall's picture? Why dost thou not go to church in a galliard, and come home in a coranto? My very walk should be a jig: I would not so much as make water but in a sink-a-pace. What dost thou mean? Is it a world to hide virtues in? I did think, by the excellent constitution of thy leg, it was formed under the star of a galliard.

SIR ANDREW. Ay, 'tis strong, and it does indifferent well in a flame-coloured stock. Shall we set about some revels?

SIR TOBY. What shall we do else? Were we not born under Taurus?

SIR ANDREW. Taurus! that's sides and heart.

SIR TOBY. No, sir, it is legs and thighs. Let me see thee caper. Ha! higher: ha, ha! excellent!   *Exeunt*

SCENE FOUR

A Room in the Duke's Palace.

Enter Valentine, and Viola in man's attire

VALENTINE. If the duke continue these favours towards you, Cesario, you are like to be much advanced: he hath known you but three days, and already you are no stranger.

VIOLA. You either fear his humour or my negligence, that you call in question the continuance of his love. Is he inconstant, sir, in his favours?

VALENTINE. No, believe me.

VIOLA. I thank you. Here comes the count.

Enter Duke, Curio, and Attendants

DUKE. Who saw Cesario? ho!

VIOLA. On your attendance, my lord; here.

DUKE. Stand you awhile aloof. Cesario,
  Thou know'st no less but all; I have unclasp'd

    To thee the book even of my secret soul:
    Therefore, good youth, address thy gait unto her,
    Be not denied access, stand at her doors,
    And tell them, there thy fixed foot shall grow
    Till thou have audience.
VIOLA.   Sure, my noble lord,
    If she be so abandon'd to her sorrow
    As it is spoke, she never will admit me.
DUKE. Be clamorous and leap all civil bounds
    Rather than make unprofited return.
VIOLA. Say I do speak with her, my lord, what then?
DUKE. O! then unfold the passion of my love;
    Surprise her with discourse of my dear faith:
    It shall become thee well to act my woes;
    She will attend it better in thy youth
    Than in a nuncio of more grave aspect.
VIOLA. I think not so, my lord.
DUKE.   Dear lad, believe it;
    For they shall yet belie thy happy years
    That say thou art a man: Diana's lip
    Is not more smooth and rubious; thy small pipe
    Is as the maiden's organ, shrill and sound;
    And all is semblative a woman's part.
    I know thy constellation is right apt
    For this affair. Some four or five attend him;
    All, if you will; for I myself am best
    When least in company. Prosper well in this,
    And thou shalt live as freely as thy lord,
    To call his fortunes thine.
VIOLA.   I'll do my best
    To woo your lady: (*Aside*) yet, a barful strife!
    Whoe'er I woo, myself would be his wife.   *Exeunt*

SCENE FIVE

A Room in Olivia's House.

Enter Maria and Clown

MARIA. Nay, either tell me where thou hast been, or I will not open my lips so wide as a bristle may enter in way of thy excuse. My lady will hang thee for thy absence.

CLOWN. Let her hang me: he that is well hanged in this world needs to fear no colours.

MARIA. Make that good.

CLOWN. He shall see none to fear.

MARIA. A good lenten answer: I can tell thee where that saying was born, of 'I fear no colours.'

CLOWN. Where, good Mistress Mary?

MARIA. In the wars; and that may you be bold to say in your foolery.

CLOWN. Well, God give them wisdom that have it; and those that are fools, let them use their talents.

MARIA. Yet you will be hanged for being so long absent; or, to be turned away, is not that as good as a hanging to you?

CLOWN. Many a good hanging prevents a bad marriage; and, for turning away, let summer bear it out.

MARIA. You are resolute then?

CLOWN. Not so, neither; but I am resolved on two points.

MARIA. That if one break, the other will hold; or, if both break, your gaskins fall.

CLOWN. Apt, in good faith; very apt. Well, go thy way: if Sir Toby would leave drinking, thou wert as witty a piece of Eve's flesh as any in Illyria.

MARIA. Peace, you rogue, no more o' that. Here comes my lady: make your excuse wisely, you were best. *Exit*

CLOWN. Wit, an 't be thy will, put me into good fooling! Those wits that think they have thee, do very oft prove fools; and I, that am sure I lack thee, may pass for a wise man: for what says Quinapalus? 'Better a witty fool than a foolish wit.'

Enter Olivia with Malvolio

God bless thee, lady!

OLIVIA. Take the fool away.

CLOWN. Do you not hear, fellows? Take away the lady.

OLIVIA. Go to, you're a dry fool; I'll no more of you: besides, you grow dishonest.

CLOWN. Two faults, madonna, that drink and good counsel will amend: for give the dry fool drink, then is the fool not dry; bid the dishonest man mend himself: if he mend, he is no longer dishonest; if he cannot, let the botcher mend him. Anything that's mended is but patched: virtue that transgresses is but patched with sin; and sin that amends is but patched with virtue. If that this simple syllogism will serve, so; if it will not, what remedy? As there is no true cuckold but calamity, so beauty's a flower. The lady bade take away the fool; therefore, I say again, take her away.

OLIVIA. Sir, I bade them take away you.

CLOWN. Misprision in the highest degree! Lady, cucullus non facit monachum; that's as much to say as I wear not motley in my brain. Good madonna, give me leave to prove you a fool.

OLIVIA. Can you do it?

CLOWN. Dexteriously, good madonna.

OLIVIA. Make your proof.

CLOWN. I must catechise you for it, madonna: good my mouse of virtue, answer me.

OLIVIA. Well, sir, for want of other idleness, I'll bide your proof.

CLOWN. Good madonna, why mournest thou?

OLIVIA. Good fool, for my brother's death.

CLOWN. I think his soul is in hell, madonna.

OLIVIA. I know his soul is in heaven, fool.

CLOWN. The more fool, madonna, to mourn for your brother's soul being in heaven. Take away the fool, gentlemen.

OLIVIA. What think you of this fool, Malvolio? Doth he not mend?

MALVOLIO. Yes, and shall do, till the pangs of death shake him: infirmity, that decays the wise, doth ever make the better fool.

CLOWN. God send you, sir, a speedy infirmity, for the better increasing your folly! Sir Toby will be sworn that I am no fox, but he will not pass his word for two pence that you are no fool.

OLIVIA. How say you to that, Malvolio?

MALVOLIO. I marvel your ladyship takes delight in such a barren rascal: I saw him put down the other day with an ordinary fool that has no more brain than a stone. Look you now, he 's out of his guard already; unless you laugh and minister occasion to him, he is gagged. I protest, I take these wise men, that crow so at these set kind of fools, no better than the fools' zanies.

OLIVIA. O! you are sick of self-love, Malvolio, and taste with a distempered appetite. To be generous, guiltless, and of free disposition, is to take those things for bird-bolts that you deem cannon-bullets. There is no slander in an allowed fool, though he do nothing but rail; nor no railing in a known discreet man, though he do nothing but reprove.

CLOWN. Now, Mercury endue thee with leasing, for thou speakest well of fools!

Re-enter Maria

MARIA. Madam, there is at the gate a young gentleman much desires to speak with you.

OLIVIA. From the Count Orsino, is it?

MARIA. I know not, madam: 'tis a fair young man, and well attended.

OLIVIA. Who of my people hold him in delay?

MARIA. Sir Toby, madam, your kinsman.

OLIVIA. Fetch him off, I pray you: he speaks nothing but madman. Fie on him! (*Exit Maria*) Go you, Malvolio: if it be a suit from the count, I am sick, or not at home; what you will, to dismiss it. (*Exit Malvolio*) Now you see, sir, how your fooling grows old, and people dislike it.

CLOWN. Thou hast spoken for us, madonna, as if thy eldest son should be a fool; whose skull Jove cram with brains! for here comes one of thy kin has a most weak pia mater.

Enter Sir Toby Belch

OLIVIA. By mine honour, half drunk. What is he at the gate, cousin?

SIR TOBY. A gentleman.

OLIVIA. A gentleman! What gentleman?

SIR TOBY. 'Tis a gentleman here,—a plague o' these pickle herring! How now, sot!

CLOWN. Good Sir Toby.

OLIVIA. Cousin, cousin, how have you come so early by this lethargy?

864   TWELFTH-NIGHT   [116-155]

SIR TOBY. Lechery! I defy lechery! There's one at the gate.

CLOWN. Ay, marry, what is he?

SIR TOBY. Let him be the devil, an he will, I care not: give
   me faith, say I. Well, it's all one.   *Exit*

OLIVIA. What's a drunken man like, fool?

CLOWN. Like a drowned man, a fool, and a madman: one
   draught above heat makes him a fool, the second mads
   him, and a third drowns him.

OLIVIA. Go thou and seek the crowner, and let him sit o' my
   coz; for he's in the third degree of drink, he's drowned:
   go, look after him.

CLOWN. He is but mad yet, madonna; and the fool shall look
   to the madman.   *Exit*

Re-enter Malvolio

MALVOLIO. Madam, yond young fellow swears he will speak
   with you. I told him you were sick: he takes on him to understand so much, and therefore comes to speak with you.
   I told him you were asleep: he seems to have a foreknowl-
   edge of that too, and therefore comes to speak with you.
   What is to be said to him, lady? He's fortified against any
   denial.

OLIVIA. Tell him he shall not speak with me.

MALVOLIO. Has been told so; and he says, he'll stand at your
   door like a sheriff's post, and be the supporter to a bench,
   but he'll speak with you.

OLIVIA. What kind o' man is he?

MALVOLIO. Why, of mankind.

OLIVIA. What manner of man?

MALVOLIO. Of very ill manner. He'll speak with you, will
   you or no.

OLIVIA. Of what personage and years is he?

MALVOLIO. Not yet old enough for a man, nor young enough
   for a boy; as a squash is before 'tis a peascod, or a codling
   when 'tis almost an apple: 'tis with him in standing water,
   between boy and man. He is very well-favoured, and he
   speaks very shrewishly: one would think his mother's milk
   were scarce out of him.

OLIVIA. Let him approach. Call in my gentlewoman.

MALVOLIO. Gentlewoman, my lady calls.   *Exit*

Re-enter Maria

OLIVIA. Give me my veil: come, throw it o'er my face.
   We'll once more hear Orsino's embassy.

Enter Viola and Attendants

VIOLA. The honourable lady of the house, which is she?

OLIVIA. Speak to me; I shall answer for her. Your will?

VIOLA. Most radiant, exquisite, and unmatchable beauty,— I pray you tell me if this be the lady of the house, for I never saw her: I would be loath to cast away my speech; for, besides that it is excellently well penned, I have taken great pains to con it. Good beauties, let me sustain no scorn; I am very comptible, even to the least sinister usage.

OLIVIA. Whence came you, sir?

VIOLA. I can say little more than I have studied, and that question's out of my part. Good gentle one, give me modest assurance if you be the lady of the house, that I may proceed in my speech.

OLIVIA. Are you a comedian?

VIOLA. No, my profound heart; and yet, by the very fangs of malice I swear I am not that I play. Are you the lady of the house?

OLIVIA. If I do not usurp myself, I am.

VIOLA. Most certain, if you are she, you do usurp yourself; for, what is yours to bestow is not yours to reserve. But this is from my commission: I will on with my speech in your praise, and then show you the heart of my message.

OLIVIA. Come to what is important in 't: I forgive you the praise.

VIOLA. Alas! I took great pains to study it, and 'tis poetical.

OLIVIA. It is the more like to be feigned: I pray you keep it in. I heard you were saucy at my gates, and allowed your approach rather to wonder at you than to hear you. If you be not mad, be gone; if you have reason, be brief: 'tis not that time of moon with me to make one in so skipping a dialogue.

MARIA. Will you hoist sail, sir? Here lies your way.

VIOLA. No, good swabber; I am to hull here a little longer. Some mollification for your giant, sweet lady.

OLIVIA. Tell me your mind.

VIOLA. I am a messenger.

OLIVIA. Sure, you have some hideous matter to deliver, when the courtesy of it is so fearful. Speak your office.

VIOLA. It alone concerns your ear. I bring no overture of

war, no taxation of homage: I hold the olive in my hand; my words are as full of peace as matter.

OLIVIA. Yet you began rudely. What are you? What would you?

VIOLA. The rudeness that hath appear'd in me have I learn'd from my entertainment. What I am, and what I would, are as secret as maidenhead; to your ears, divinity; to any other's, profanation.

OLIVIA. Give us the place alone: we will hear this divinity. (*Exit Maria and attendants*) Now, sir; what is your text?

VIOLA. Most sweet lady,—

OLIVIA. A comfortable doctrine, and much may be said of it. Where lies your text?

VIOLA. In Orsino's bosom.

OLIVIA. In his bosom! In what chapter of his bosom?

VIOLA. To answer by the method, in the first of his heart.

OLIVIA. O! I have read it: it is heresy. Have you no more to say?

VIOLA. Good madam, let me see your face.

OLIVIA. Have you any commission from your lord to negotiate with my face? You are now out of your text: but we will draw the curtain and show you the picture. (*Unveiling*) Look you, sir, such a one I was as this present: is 't not well done?

VIOLA. Excellently done, if God did all.

OLIVIA. 'Tis in grain, sir; 'twill endure wind and weather.

VIOLA. 'Tis beauty truly blent, whose red and white
Nature's own sweet and cunning hand laid on:
Lady, you are the cruell'st she alive,
If you will lead these graces to the grave
And leave the world no copy.

OLIVIA. O! sir, I will not be so hard-hearted; I will give out divers schedules of my beauty: it shall be inventoried, and every particle and utensil labelled to my will: as Item, Two lips, indifferent red; Item, Two grey eyes, with lids to them; Item, One neck, one chin, and so forth. Were you sent hither to praise me?

VIOLA. I see you what you are: you are too proud;
But, if you were the devil, you are fair.
My lord and master loves you: O! such love
Could be but recompens'd, though you were crown'd
The nonpareil of beauty.

OLIVIA. How does he love me?
VIOLA. With adorations, with fertile tears,
With groans that thunder love, with sighs of fire.
OLIVIA. Your lord does know my mind; I cannot love him;
Yet I suppose him virtuous, know him noble,
Of great estate, of fresh and stainless youth;
In voices well divulg'd, free, learn'd, and valiant;
And, in dimension and the shape of nature
A gracious person; but yet I cannot love him:
He might have took his answer long ago.
VIOLA. If I did love you in my master's flame,
With such a suffering, such a deadly life,
In your denial I would find no sense;
I would not understand it.
OLIVIA. Why, what would you?
VIOLA. Make me a willow cabin at your gate,
And call upon my soul within the house;
Write loyal cantons of contemned love,
And sing them loud even in the dead of night;
Holla your name to the reverberate hills,
And make the babbling gossip of the air
Cry out, 'Olivia!' O! you should not rest
Between the elements of air and earth,
But you should pity me!
OLIVIA. You might do much. What is your parentage?
VIOLA. Above my fortunes, yet my state is well:
I am a gentleman.
OLIVIA. Get you to your lord:
I cannot love him. Let him send no more,
Unless, perchance, you come to me again,
To tell me how he takes it. Fare you well:
I thank you for your pains: spend this for me.
VIOLA. I am no fee'd post, lady; keep your purse:
My master, not myself, lacks recompense.
Love make his heart of flint that you shall love,
And let your fervour, like my master's, be
Plac'd in contempt! Farewell, fair cruelty. *Exit*
OLIVIA. 'What is your parentage?'
'Above my fortunes, yet my state is well:
I am a gentleman.' I'll be sworn thou art:
Thy tongue, thy face, thy limbs, actions, and spirit,
Do give thee five-fold blazon. Not too fast: soft! soft!

Unless the master were the man. How now?
Even so quickly may one catch the plague?
Methinks I feel this youth's perfections
With an invisible and subtle stealth
To creep in at mine eyes. Well, let it be.
What, ho! Malvolio!

Re-enter Malvolio

MALVOLIO. Here, madam, at your service.
OLIVIA. Run after that same peevish messenger,
The county's man: he left this ring behind him,
Would I, or not: tell him I'll none of it.
Desire him not to flatter with his lord,
Nor hold him up with hopes: I'm not for him.
If that the youth will come this way to-morrow,
I'll give him reasons for 't. Hie thee, Malvolio.
MALVOLIO. Madam, I will. *Exit*
OLIVIA. I do I know not what, and fear to find
Mine eye too great a flatterer for my mind.
Fate, show thy force: ourselves we do not owe;
What is decreed must be, and be this so! *Exit*

ACT TWO

SCENE ONE

The Sea-coast.

Enter Antonio and Sebastian

ANTONIO. Will you stay no longer? nor will you not that I go with you?

SEBASTIAN. By your patience, no. My stars shine darkly over me; the malignancy of my fate might, perhaps, distemper yours; therefore I shall crave of you your leave that I may bear my evils alone. It were a bad recompense for your love to lay any of them on you.

ANTONIO. Let me yet know of you whither you are bound.

SEBASTIAN. No, sooth, sir: my determinate voyage is mere extravagancy. But I perceive in you so excellent a touch of modesty that you will not extort from me what I am willing to keep in; therefore, it charges me in manners the rather to express myself. You must know of me then, Antonio, my name is Sebastian, which I called Roderigo. My father was that Sebastian of Messaline, whom I know you have heard of. He left behind him myself and a sister, both born in an hour: if the heavens had been pleased, would we had so ended! but you, sir, altered that; for some hour before you took me from the breach of the sea was my sister drowned.

ANTONIO. Alas the day!

SEBASTIAN. A lady, sir, though it was said she much resembled me, was yet of many accounted beautiful: but, though I could not with such estimable wonder overfar believe that, yet thus far I will boldly publish her: she bore a mind that envy could not but call fair. She is drowned already, sir, with salt water, though I seem to drown her remembrance again with more.

ANTONIO. Pardon me, sir, your bad entertainment.

SEBASTIAN. O good Antonio! forgive me your trouble!

ANTONIO. If you will not murder me for my love, let me be your servant.

SEBASTIAN. If you will not undo what you have done, that is, kill him whom you have recovered, desire it not. Fare ye well at once: my bosom is full of kindness; and I am yet so near the manners of my mother, that upon the least occasion more mine eyes will tell tales of me. I am bound to the Count Orsino's court: farewell. *Exit*

ANTONIO. The gentleness of all the gods go with thee!
I have many enemies in Orsino's court,
Else would I very shortly see thee there;
But, come what may, I do adore thee so,
That danger shall seem sport, and I will go. *Exit*

SCENE TWO

A Street.

Enter Viola; Malvolio following

MALVOLIO. Were not you even now with the Countess Olivia?

VIOLA. Even now, sir: on a moderate pace I have since arrived but hither.

MALVOLIO. She returns this ring to you, sir: you might have saved me my pains, to have taken it away yourself. She adds, moreover, that you should put your lord into a desperate assurance she will none of him. And one thing more; that you be never so hardy to come again in his affairs, unless it be to report your lord's taking of this. Receive it so.

VIOLA. She took the ring of me; I'll none of it.

MALVOLIO. Come, sir, you peevishly threw it to her; and her will is it should be so returned: if it be worth stooping for, there it lies in your eye; if not, be it his that finds it. *Exit*

VIOLA. I left no ring with her: what means this lady?
Fortune forbid my outside have not charm'd her!
She made good view of me; indeed, so much,
That sure methought her eyes had lost her tongue,
For she did speak in starts distractedly.
She loves me, sure; the cunning of her passion

Invites me in this churlish messenger.
None of my lord's ring! why, he sent her none.
I am the man: if it be so, as 'tis,
Poor lady, she were better love a dream.
Disguise, I see, thou art a wickedness,
Wherein the pregnant enemy does much.
How easy is it for the proper-false
In women's waxen hearts to set their forms!
Alas! our frailty is the cause, not we!
For such as we are made of, such we be.
How will this fadge? My master loves her dearly;
And I, poor monster, fond as much on him;
And she, mistaken, seems to dote on me.
What will become of this? As I am man,
My state is desperate for my master's love;
As I am woman,—now alas the day!—
What thriftless sighs shall poor Olivia breathe!
O time! thou must untangle this, not I;
It is too hard a knot for me to untie. *Exit*

SCENE THREE

A Room in Olivia's House.

Enter Sir Toby Belch and Sir Andrew Aguecheek

SIR TOBY. Approach, Sir Andrew: not to be a-bed after midnight is to be up betimes; and *diluculo surgere,* thou knowest,—

SIR ANDREW. Nay, by my troth, I know not; but I know, to be up late is to be up late.

SIR TOBY. A false conclusion: I hate it as an unfilled can. To be up after midnight and to go to bed then, is early; so that to go to bed after midnight is to go to bed betimes. Does not our life consist of the four elements?

SIR ANDREW. Faith, so they say; but, I think, it rather consists of eating and drinking.

SIR TOBY. Thou art a scholar; let us therefore eat and drink. Marian, I say! a stoup of wine!

Enter Clown

SIR ANDREW. Here comes the fool, i' faith.

CLOWN. How now, my hearts! Did you never see the picture of 'we three'?

SIR TOBY. Welcome, ass. Now let's have a catch.

SIR ANDREW. By my troth, the fool has an excellent breast. I had rather than forty shillings I had such a leg, and so sweet a breath to sing, as the fool has. In sooth, thou wast in very gracious fooling last night, when thou spokest of Pigrogromitus, of the Vapians passing the equinoctial of Queubus: 'twas very good, i' faith. I sent thee sixpence for thy leman: hadst it?

CLOWN. I did impeticos thy gratillity; for Malvolio's nose is no whipstock: my lady has a white hand, and the Myrmidons are not bottle-ale houses.

SIR ANDREW. Excellent! Why, this is the best fooling, when all is done. Now, a song.

SIR TOBY. Come on; there is sixpence for you: let's have a song.

SIR ANDREW. There's a testril of me too: if one knight give a—

CLOWN. Would you have a love-song, or a song of good life?

SIR TOBY. A love-song, a love-song.

SIR ANDREW. Ay, ay; I care not for good life.

CLOWN.   O mistress mine! where are you roaming?
        O! stay and hear; your true love's coming,
          That can sing both high and low.
    Trip no further, pretty sweeting;
    Journeys end in lovers meeting,
        Every wise man's son doth know.

SIR ANDREW. Excellent good, i' faith.

SIR TOBY. Good, good.

CLOWN.   What is love? 'Tis not hereafter;
    Present mirth hath present laughter;
        What's to come is still unsure:
    In delay there lies no plenty;
    Then come kiss me, sweet and twenty,
        Youth's a stuff will not endure.

SIR ANDREW. A mellifluous voice, as I am true knight.

SIR TOBY. A contagious breath.

SIR ANDREW. Very sweet and contagious, i' faith.

SIR TOBY. To hear by the nose, it is dulcet in contagion. But shall we make the welkin dance indeed? Shall we rouse the night-owl in a catch that will draw three souls out of one weaver? Shall we do that?

SIR ANDREW. An you love me, let's do't: I am dog at a catch.

CLOWN. By 'r lady, sir, and some dogs will catch well.

SIR ANDREW. Most certain. Let our catch be, 'Thou knave.'

CLOWN. 'Hold thy peace, thou knave,' knight? I shall be constrain'd in 't to call thee knave, knight.

SIR ANDREW. 'Tis not the first time I have constrained one to call me knave. Begin, fool: it begins, 'Hold thy peace.'

CLOWN. I shall never begin if I hold my peace.

SIR ANDREW. Good, i' faith. Come, begin. *They sing a catch*
Enter Maria

MARIA. What a caterwauling do you keep here! If my lady have not called up her steward Malvolio and bid him turn you out of doors, never trust me.

SIR TOBY. My lady 's a Cataian; we are politicians; Malvolio 's a Peg-a-Ramsey, and 'Three merry men be we.' Am not I consanguineous? Am I not of her blood? Tilly-vally, lady!
'There dwelt a man in Babylon, lady, lady!'

CLOWN. Beshrew me, the knight 's in admirable fooling.

SIR ANDREW. Ay, he does well enough if he be disposed, and so do I too: he does it with a better grace, but I do it more natural.

SIR TOBY. 'O! the twelfth day of December,'—

MARIA. For the love o' God, peace!
Enter Malvolio

MALVOLIO. My masters, are you mad? or what are you? Have you no wit, manners, nor honesty, but to gabble like tinkers at this time of night? Do ye make an alehouse of my lady's house, that ye squeak out your coziers' catches without any mitigation or remorse of voice? Is there no respect of place, persons, nor time, in you?

SIR TOBY. We did keep time, sir, in our catches. Sneck up!

MALVOLIO. Sir Toby, I must be round with you. My lady bade me tell you, that, though she harbours you as her kinsman, she 's nothing allied to your disorders. If you can separate yourself and your misdemeanours, you are welcome to the house; if not, an it would please you to take leave of her, she is very willing to bid you farewell.

SIR TOBY. 'Farewell, dear heart, since I must needs be gone.'

MARIA. Nay, good Sir Toby.

CLOWN. 'His eyes do show his days are almost done.'
MALVOLIO. Is 't even so?
SIR TOBY. 'But I will never die.'
CLOWN. Sir Toby, there you lie.
MALVOLIO. This is much credit to you.
SIR TOBY. 'Shall I bid him go?'
CLOWN. 'What an if you do?'
SIR TOBY. 'Shall I bid him go, and spare not?'
CLOWN. 'O! no, no, no, no, you dare not.'
SIR TOBY. 'Out o' time!' Sir, ye lie. Art any more than a steward? Dost thou think, because thou art virtuous, there shall be no more cakes and ale?
CLOWN. Yes, by Saint Anne; and ginger shall be hot i' the mouth too.
SIR TOBY. Thou 'rt i' the right. Go, sir, rub your chain with crumbs. A stoup of wine, Maria!
MALVOLIO. Mistress Mary, if you prized my lady's favour at anything more than contempt, you would not give means for this uncivil rule: she shall know of it, by this hand. *Exit*
MARIA. Go shake your ears.
SIR ANDREW. 'Twere as good a deed as to drink when a man 's a-hungry, to challenge him the field, and then to break promise with him and make a fool of him.
SIR TOBY. Do 't, knight: I 'll write thee a challenge; or I 'll deliver thy indignation to him by word of mouth.
MARIA. Sweet Sir Toby, be patient for to-night: since the youth of the count's was to-day with my lady, she is much out of quiet. For Monsieur Malvolio, let me alone with him: if I do not gull him into a nayword, and make him a common recreation, do not think I have wit enough to lie straight in my bed. I know I can do it.
SIR TOBY. Possess us, possess us; tell us something of him.
MARIA. Marry, sir, sometimes he is a kind of puritan.
SIR ANDREW. O! if I thought that, I 'd beat him like a dog.
SIR TOBY. What, for being a puritan? Thy exquisite reason, dear knight?
SIR ANDREW. I have no exquisite reason for 't, but I have reason good enough.
MARIA. The devil a puritan that he is, or anything constantly but a time-pleaser; an affectioned ass, that cons state without book, and utters it by great swarths: the best persuaded of himself; so crammed, as he thinks, with excel-

lences, that it is his ground of faith that all that look on him love him; and on that vice in him will my revenge find notable cause to work.

SIR TOBY. What wilt thou do?

MARIA. I will drop in his way some obscure epistles of love; wherein, by the colour of his beard, the shape of his leg, the manner of his gait, the expressure of his eye, forehead, and complexion, he shall find himself most feelingly personated. I can write very like my lady your niece; on a forgotten matter we can hardly make distinction of our hands.

SIR TOBY. Excellent! I smell a device.

SIR ANDREW. I have 't in my nose too.

SIR TOBY. He shall think, by the letters that thou wilt drop, that they come from my niece, and that she is in love with him.

MARIA. My purpose is, indeed, a horse of that colour.

SIR ANDREW. And your horse now would make him an ass.

MARIA. Ass, I doubt not.

SIR ANDREW. O! 'twill be admirable.

MARIA. Sport royal, I warrant you: I know my physic will work with him. I will plant you two, and let the fool make a third, where he shall find the letter: observe his construction of it. For this night, to bed, and dream on the event. Farewell. *Exit*

SIR TOBY. Good night, Penthesilea.

SIR ANDREW. Before me, she's a good wench.

SIR TOBY. She's a beagle, true-bred, and one that adores me: what o' that?

SIR ANDREW. I was adored once too.

SIR TOBY. Let 's to bed, knight. Thou hadst need send for more money.

SIR ANDREW. If I cannot recover your niece, I am a foul way out.

SIR TOBY. Send for money, knight: if thou hast her not i' the end, call me cut.

SIR ANDREW. If I do not, never trust me, take it how you will.

SIR TOBY. Come, come: I'll go burn some sack; 'tis too late to go to bed now. Come, knight; come, knight. *Exeunt*

SCENE FOUR

A Room in the Duke's Palace.

Enter Duke, Viola, Curio, and Others

DUKE. Give me some music. Now, good-morrow, friends:
Now, good Cesario, but that piece of song,
That old and antique song we heard last night;
Methought it did relieve my passion much,
More than light airs and recollected terms
Of these most brisk and giddy-paced times:
Come; but one verse.

CURIO. He is not here, so please your lordship, that should sing it.

DUKE. Who was it?

CURIO. Feste, the jester, my lord; a fool that the Lady Olivia's father took much delight in. He is about the house.

DUKE. Seek him out, and play the tune the while.

Exit Curio. Music

Come hither, boy: if ever thou shalt love,
In the sweet pangs of it remember me;
For such as I am all true lovers are:
Unstaid and skittish in all motions else
Save in the constant image of the creature
That is belov'd. How dost thou like this tune?

VIOLA. It gives a very echo to the seat
Where love is thron'd.

DUKE. Thou dost speak masterly.
My life upon 't, young though thou art, thine eye
Hath stay'd upon some favour that it loves;
Hath it not, boy?

VIOLA. A little, by your favour.

DUKE. What kind of woman is 't?

VIOLA. Of your complexion.

DUKE. She is not worth thee, then. What years, i' faith?

VIOLA. About your years, my lord.

DUKE. Too old, by heaven. Let still the woman take
An elder than herself, so wears she to him,
So sways she level in her husband's heart:
For, boy, however we do praise ourselves,

ACT II : SCENE IV

Our fancies are more giddy and unfirm,
More longing, wavering, sooner lost and worn,
Than women's are.
VIOLA. I think it well, my lord.
DUKE. Then, let thy love be younger than thyself,
Or thy affection cannot hold the bent;
For women are as roses, whose fair flower
Being once display'd, doth fall that very hour.
VIOLA. And so they are: alas, that they are so;
To die, even when they to perfection grow!
Re-enter Curio with Clown
DUKE. O, fellow! come, the song we had last night.
Mark it, Cesario; it is old and plain;
The spinsters and the knitters in the sun,
And the free maids that weave their thread with bones,
Do use to chant it: it is silly sooth,
And dallies with the innocence of love,
Like the old age.
CLOWN. Are you ready, sir?
DUKE. Ay; prithee, sing. *Music*
CLOWN. Come away, come away, death,
  And in sad cypress let me be laid;
 Fly away, fly away, breath;
  I am slain by a fair cruel maid.
My shroud of white, stuck all with yew,
  O! prepare it.
My part of death, no one so true
  Did share it.
Not a flower, not a flower sweet,
 On my black coffin let there be strown;
Not a friend, not a friend greet
 My poor corse, where my bones shall be thrown.
 A thousand thousand sighs to save,
  Lay me, O! where
 Sad true lover never find my grave,
  To weep there.
DUKE. There's for thy pains.
CLOWN. No pains, sir; I take pleasure in singing, sir.
DUKE. I'll pay thy pleasure then.
CLOWN. Truly, sir, and pleasure will be paid, one time or another.
DUKE. Give me now leave to leave thee.

CLOWN. Now, the melancholy god protect thee, and the
tailor make thy doublet of changeable taffeta, for thy mind
is a very opal! I would have men of such constancy put to
sea, that their business might be every thing and their intent everywhere; for that's it that always makes a good
voyage of nothing. Farewell. *Exit*

DUKE. Let all the rest give place.
Exeunt Curio and attendants
Once more, Cesario,
Get thee to yond same sovereign cruelty:
Tell her, my love, more noble than the world,
Prizes not quantity of dirty lands;
The parts that fortune hath bestow'd upon her,
Tell her, I hold as giddily as fortune;
But 'tis that miracle and queen of gems
That nature pranks her in attracts my soul.

VIOLA. But if she cannot love you, sir?

DUKE. I cannot be so answer'd.

VIOLA. Sooth, but you must.
Say that some lady, as perhaps there is,
Hath for your love as great a pang of heart
As you have for Olivia: you cannot love her;
You tell her so; must she not then be answer'd?

DUKE. There is no woman's sides
Can bide the beating of so strong a passion
As love doth give my heart; no woman's heart
So big, to hold so much; they lack retention.
Alas! their love may be call'd appetite,
No motion of the liver, but the palate,
That suffer surfeit, cloyment, and revolt;
But mine is all as hungry as the sea,
And can digest as much. Make no compare
Between that love a woman can bear me
And that I owe Olivia.

VIOLA. Ay, but I know,—

DUKE. What dost thou know?

VIOLA. Too well what love women to men may owe:
In faith, they are as true of heart as we.
My father had a daughter lov'd a man,
As it might be, perhaps, were I a woman,
I should your lordship.

DUKE. And what's her history?

VIOLA. A blank, my lord. She never told her love,
But let concealment, like a worm i' the bud,
Feed on her damask cheek: she pin'd in thought,
And with a green and yellow melancholy,
She sat like Patience on a monument,
Smiling at grief. Was not this love indeed?
We men may say more, swear more; but indeed
Our shows are more than will, for still we prove
Much in our vows, but little in our love.
DUKE. But died thy sister of her love, my boy?
VIOLA. I am all the daughters of my father's house,
And all the brothers too; and yet I know not.
Sir, shall I to this lady?
DUKE. Ay, that's the theme.
To her in haste; give her this jewel; say
My love can give no place, bide no denay. *Exeunt*

SCENE FIVE

Olivia's Garden.

Enter Sir Toby Belch, Sir Andrew Aguecheek, and Fabian

SIR TOBY. Come thy ways, Signior Fabian.
FABIAN. Nay, I'll come: if I lose a scruple of this sport, let me be boiled to death with melancholy.
SIR TOBY. Wouldst thou not be glad to have the niggardly rascally sheep-biter come by some notable shame?
FABIAN. I would exult, man: you know he brought me out o' favour with my lady about a bear-baiting here.
SIR TOBY. To anger him we'll have the bear again; and we will fool him black and blue. Shall we not, Sir Andrew?
SIR ANDREW. An we do not, it is pity of our lives.
SIR TOBY. Here comes the little villain.

Enter Maria

How now, my metal of India!
MARIA. Get ye all three into the box-tree. Malvolio's coming down this walk: he has been yonder i' the sun practising behaviour to his own shadow this half-hour. Observe him, for the love of mockery; for I know this letter will make a contemplative idiot of him. Close, in the name of jesting!

Lie thou there: (*Throws down a letter*) for here comes the trout that must be caught with tickling. *Exit*

Enter Malvolio

MALVOLIO. 'Tis but fortune; all is fortune. Maria once told me she did affect me; and I have heard herself come thus near, that should she fancy, it should be one of my complexion. Besides, she uses me with a more exalted respect than anyone else that follows her. What should I think on 't?

SIR TOBY. Here 's an over-weening rogue!

FABIAN. O, peace! Contemplation makes a rare turkey-cock of him: how he jets under his advanced plumes!

SIR ANDREW. 'Slight, I could so beat the rogue!

SIR TOBY. Peace! I say.

MALVOLIO. To be Count Malvolio!

SIR TOBY. Ah, rogue!

SIR ANDREW. Pistol him, pistol him.

SIR TOBY. Peace! peace!

MALVOLIO. There is example for 't: the lady of the Strachy married the yeoman of the wardrobe.

SIR ANDREW. Fie on him, Jezebel!

FABIAN. O, peace! now he 's deeply in; look how imagination blows him.

MALVOLIO. Having been three months married to her, sitting in my state,—

SIR TOBY. O! for a stone-bow, to hit him in the eye!

MALVOLIO. Calling my officers about me, in my branched velvet gown; having come from a day-bed, where I have left Olivia sleeping,—

SIR TOBY. Fire and brimstone!

FABIAN. O, peace! peace!

MALVOLIO. And then to have the humour of state: and after a demure travel of regard, telling them I know my place, as I would they should do theirs, to ask for my kinsman Toby,—

SIR TOBY. Bolts and shackles!

FABIAN. O, peace, peace, peace! now, now.

MALVOLIO. Seven of my people, with an obedient start, make out for him. I frown the while; and perchance wind up my watch, or play with my—some rich jewel. Toby approaches; curtsies there to me,—

SIR TOBY. Shall this fellow live?
FABIAN. Though our silence be drawn from us with ears, yet peace!
MALVOLIO. I extend my hand to him thus, quenching my familiar smile with an austere regard of control,—
SIR TOBY. And does not Toby take you a blow o' the lips then?
MALVOLIO. Saying, 'Cousin Toby, my fortunes having cast me on your niece give me this prerogative of speech,'—
SIR TOBY. What, what?
MALVOLIO. 'You must amend your drunkenness.'
SIR TOBY. Out, scab!
FABIAN. Nay, patience, or we break the sinews of our plot.
MALVOLIO. 'Besides, you waste the treasure of your time with a foolish knight,'—
SIR ANDREW. That's me, I warrant you.
MALVOLIO. 'One Sir Andrew,'—
SIR ANDREW. I knew 'twas I; for many do call me fool.
MALVOLIO. (*Seeing the letter*) What employment have we here?
FABIAN. Now is the woodcock near the gin.
SIR TOBY. O, peace! and the spirit of humours intimate reading aloud to him!
MALVOLIO. (*Taking up the letter*) By my life, this is my lady's hand! These be her very C's, her U's, and her T's; and thus makes she her great P's. It is, in contempt of question, her hand.
SIR ANDREW. Her C's, her U's, and her T's: why that—
MALVOLIO. (*Reads*) 'To the unknown beloved, this and my good wishes.' Her very phrases! By your leave, wax. Soft! and the impressure her Lucrece, with which she uses to seal: 'tis my lady. To whom should this be?
FABIAN. This wins him, liver and all.
MALVOLIO.   'Jove knows I love;
                    But who?
              Lips, do not move:
              No man must know.'
'No man must know.' What follows? the numbers altered.
'No man must know': if this should be thee, Malvolio!
SIR TOBY. Marry, hang thee, brock!

MALVOLIO. (*Reads*)
> 'I may command where I adore;
>   But silence, like a Lucrece knife,
> With bloodless stroke my heart doth gore:
>   M, O, A, I, doth sway my life.'

FABIAN. A fustian riddle!

SIR TOBY. Excellent wench, say I.

MALVOLIO. 'M, O, A, I, doth sway my life.' Nay, but first, let me see, let me see, let me see.

FABIAN. What dish o' poison has she dressed him!

SIR TOBY. And with what wing the staniel checks at it!

MALVOLIO. 'I may command where I adore.' Why, she may command me: I serve her; she is my lady. Why, this is evident to any formal capacity; there is no obstruction in this. And the end, what should that alphabetical position portend? if I could make that resemble something in me,—Softly!—M, O, A, I,—

SIR TOBY. O! ay, make up that: he is now at a cold scent.

FABIAN. Sowter will cry upon 't, for all this, though it be as rank as a fox.

MALVOLIO. M, Malvolio; M, why, that begins my name.

FABIAN. Did not I say he would work it out? The cur is excellent at faults.

MALVOLIO. M,—But then there is no consonancy in the sequel; that suffers under probation: A should follow, but O does.

FABIAN. And O shall end, I hope.

SIR TOBY. Ay, or I'll cudgel him, and make him cry, O!

MALVOLIO. And then I comes behind.

FABIAN. Ay, an you had any eye behind you, you might see more detraction at your heels than fortunes before you.

MALVOLIO. M, O, A, I; this simulation is not as the former; and yet, to crush this a little, it would bow to me, for every one of these letters are in my name. Soft! here follows prose.

(*Reads*) 'If this fall into thy hand, revolve. In my stars I am above thee; but be not afraid of greatness: some are born great, some achieve greatness, and some have greatness thrust upon them. Thy Fates open their hands; let thy blood and spirit embrace them; and to inure thyself to what thou art like to be, cast thy humble slough, and appear fresh. Be opposite with a kinsman, surly with servants; let thy tongue tang arguments of state; put thyself into the trick of singularity. She thus advises thee that sighs for thee. Remember who commended thy yellow stockings, and wished to see thee ever cross-gartered: I say, remember. Go to, thou art made, if thou desirest to be so; if not, let me see thee a steward still, the fellow of servants, and not worthy to touch Fortune's fingers. Farewell. She that would alter services with thee,

'The Fortunate-Unhappy.'

Daylight and champian discovers not more: this is open. I will be proud, I will read politic authors, I will baffle Sir Toby, I will wash off gross acquaintance, I will be point-devise the very man. I do not now fool myself, to let imagination jade me, for every reason excites to this, that my lady loves me. She did commend my yellow stockings of late, she did praise my leg being cross-gartered; and in this she manifests herself to my love, and, with a kind of injunction drives me to these habits of her liking. I thank my stars I am happy. I will be strange, stout, in yellow stockings, and cross-gartered, even with the swiftness of putting on. Jove and my stars be praised! Here is yet a postscript.

'Thou canst not choose but know who I am. If thou entertainest my love, let it appear in thy smiling; thy smiles become thee well; therefore in my presence still smile, dear my sweet, I prithee.'

Jove, I thank thee. I will smile: I will do everything that thou wilt have me. *Exit*

FABIAN. I will not give my part of this sport for a pension of thousands to be paid from the Sophy.

SIR TOBY. I could marry this wench for this device.

SIR ANDREW. So could I too.

SIR TOBY. And ask no other dowry with her but such another jest.

SIR ANDREW. Nor I neither.

FABIAN. Here comes my noble gull-catcher.

Re-enter Maria

SIR TOBY. Wilt thou set thy foot 'o my neck?

SIR ANDREW. Or o' mine either?

SIR TOBY. Shall I play my freedom at tray-trip, and become thy bond-slave?

SIR ANDREW. I' faith, or I either?

SIR TOBY. Why, thou hast put him in such a dream, that when the image of it leaves him he must run mad.

MARIA. Nay, but say true; does it work upon him?

SIR TOBY. Like aqua-vitæ with a midwife.

MARIA. If you will, then, see the fruits of the sport, mark his first approach before my lady; he will come to her in yellow stockings, and 'tis a colour she abhors; and cross-gartered, a fashion she detests; and he will smile upon her, which will now be so unsuitable to her disposition, being addicted to a melancholy as she is, that it cannot but turn him into a notable contempt. If you will see it, follow me.

SIR TOBY. To the gates of Tartar, thou most excellent devil of wit!

SIR ANDREW. I'll make one too. *Exeunt*

ACT THREE

SCENE ONE

Olivia's Garden.

Enter Viola, and Clown with a tabor

VIOLA. Save thee, friend, and thy music. Dost thou live by thy tabor?
CLOWN. No, sir, I live by the church.
VIOLA. Art thou a churchman?
CLOWN. No such matter, sir: I do live by the church; for I do live at my house, and my house doth stand by the church.
VIOLA. So thou mayst say, the king lies by a beggar, if a beggar dwell near him; or, the church stands by thy tabor, if thy tabor stand by the church.
CLOWN. You have said, sir. To see this age! A sentence is but a cheveril glove to a good wit: how quickly the wrong side may be turned outward!
VIOLA. Nay, that's certain: they that dally nicely with words may quickly make them wanton.
CLOWN. I would therefore my sister had had no name, sir.
VIOLA. Why, man?
CLOWN. Why, sir, her name's a word; and to dally with that word might make my sister wanton. But indeed, words are very rascals since bonds disgraced them.
VIOLA. Thy reason, man?
CLOWN. Troth, sir, I can yield you none without words; and words are grown so false, I am loath to prove reason with them.
VIOLA. I warrant thou art a merry fellow, and carest for nothing.
CLOWN. Not so, sir, I do care for something; but in my conscience, sir, I do not care for you: if that be to care for nothing, sir, I would it would make you invisible.
VIOLA. Art not thou the Lady Olivia's fool?

CLOWN. No, indeed, sir; the Lady Olivia has no folly: she will keep no fool, sir, till she be married; and fools are as like husbands as pilchards are to herrings—the husband's the bigger. I am indeed not her fool, but her corrupter of words.

VIOLA. I saw thee late at the Count Orsino's.

CLOWN. Foolery, sir, does walk about the orb like the sun; it shines everywhere. I would be sorry, sir, but the fool should be as oft with your master as with my mistress. I think I saw your wisdom there.

VIOLA. Nay, an thou pass upon me, I'll no more with thee. Hold, there's sixpence for thee. *Gives a piece of money*

CLOWN. Now Jove, in his next commodity of hair, send thee a beard!

VIOLA. By my troth, I'll tell thee, I am almost sick for one, though I would not have it grow on my chin. Is thy lady within?

CLOWN. (*Pointing to the coin*) Would not a pair of these have bred, sir?

VIOLA. Yes, being kept together and put to use.

CLOWN. I would play Lord Pandarus of Phrygia, sir, to bring a Cressida to this Troilus.

VIOLA. I understand you, sir; 'tis well begg'd.

CLOWN. The matter, I hope, is not great, sir, begging but a beggar: Cressida was a beggar. My lady is within, sir. I will conster to them whence you come; who you are and what you would are out of my welkin; I might say 'element,' but the word is overworn. *Exit*

VIOLA. This fellow's wise enough to play the fool,
And to do that well craves a kind of wit:
He must observe their mood on whom he jests,
The quality of persons, and the time,
And, like the haggard, check at every feather
That comes before his eye. This is a practice
As full of labour as a wise man's art;
For folly that he wisely shows is fit;
But wise men folly-fall'n, quite taint their wit.

Enter Sir Toby Belch and Sir Andrew Aguecheek

SIR TOBY. Save you, gentleman.

VIOLA. And you, sir.

SIR ANDREW. Dieu vous garde, monsieur.

VIOLA. Et vous aussi; votre serviteur.

SIR ANDREW. I hope, sir, you are; and I am yours.

SIR TOBY. Will you encounter the house? My niece is desirous you should enter, if your trade be to her.

VIOLA. I am bound to your niece, sir: I mean, she is the list of my voyage.

SIR TOBY. Taste your legs, sir: put them to motion.

VIOLA. My legs do better understand me, sir, than I understand what you mean by bidding me taste my legs.

SIR TOBY. I mean, to go, sir, to enter.

VIOLA. I will answer you with gait and entrance. But we are prevented.

Enter Olivia and Maria

Most excellent accomplished lady, the heavens rain odours on you!

SIR ANDREW. That youth 's a rare courtier. 'Rain odours'! well.

VIOLA. My matter hath no voice, lady, but to your own most pregnant and vouchsafed ear.

SIR ANDREW. 'Odours,' 'pregnant,' and 'vouchsafed.' I 'll get 'em all three all ready.

OLIVIA. Let the garden door be shut, and leave me to my hearing. *Exeunt Sir Toby, Sir Andrew, and Maria*
Give me your hand, sir.

VIOLA. My duty, madam, and most humble service.

OLIVIA. What is your name?

VIOLA. Cesario is your servant's name, fair princess.

OLIVIA. My servant, sir! 'Twas never merry world
Since lowly feigning was call'd compliment.
You 're servant to the Count Orsino, youth.

VIOLA. And he is yours, and his must needs be yours:
Your servant's servant is your servant, madam.

OLIVIA. For him, I think not on him: for his thoughts,
Would they were blanks rather than fill'd with me!

VIOLA. Madam, I come to whet your gentle thoughts
On his behalf.

OLIVIA. O! by your leave, I pray you,
I bade you never speak again of him:
But, would you undertake another suit,
I had rather hear you to solicit that
Than music from the spheres.

VIOLA. Dear lady,—

OLIVIA. Give me leave, beseech you. I did send,

    After the last enchantment you did here,
    A ring in chase of you: so did I abuse
    Myself, my servant, and, I fear me, you:
    Under your hard construction must I sit,
    To force that on you, in a shameful cunning,
    Which you knew none of yours: what might you think?
    Have you not set mine honour at the stake,
    And baited it with all th' unmuzzled thoughts
    That tyrannous heart can think? To one of your receiving
    Enough is shown; a cypress, not a bosom,
    Hideth my heart. So, let me hear you speak.
VIOLA. I pity you.
OLIVIA. That's a degree to love.
VIOLA. No, not a grize; for 'tis a vulgar proof
    That very oft we pity enemies.
OLIVIA. Why, then methinks 'tis time to smile again.
    O world! how apt the poor are to be proud.
    If one should be a prey, how much the better
    To fall before the lion than the wolf!   *Clock strikes*
    The clock upbraids me with the waste of time.
    Be not afraid, good youth, I will not have you:
    And yet, when wit and youth is come to harvest,
    Your wife is like to reap a proper man:
    There lies your way, due west.
VIOLA.   Then westward-ho!
    Grace and good disposition attend your ladyship!
    You'll nothing, madam, to my lord by me?
OLIVIA. Stay:
    I prithee, tell me what thou think'st of me.
VIOLA. That you do think you are not what you are.
OLIVIA. If I think so, I think the same of you.
VIOLA. Then think you right: I am not what I am.
OLIVIA. I would you were as I would have you be!
VIOLA. Would it be better, madam, than I am?
    I wish it might, for now I am your fool.
OLIVIA. O! what a deal of scorn looks beautiful
    In the contempt and anger of his lip.
    A murderous guilt shows not itself more soon
    Than love that would seem hid; love's night is noon.
    Cesario, by the roses of the spring,
    By maidhood, honour, truth, and every thing.
    I love thee so, that, maugre all thy pride,

Nor wit nor reason can my passion hide.
Do not extort thy reasons from this clause,
For that I woo, thou therefore hast no cause;
But rather reason thus with reason fetter,
Love sought is good, but giv'n unsought is better.

VIOLA. By innocence I swear, and by my youth,
I have one heart, one bosom, and one truth,
And that no woman has; nor never none
Shall mistress be of it, save I alone.
And so adieu, good madam: never more
Will I my master's tears to you deplore.

OLIVIA. Yet come again, for thou perhaps mayst move
That heart, which now abhors, to like his love. *Exeunt*

SCENE TWO

A Room in Olivia's House.

*Enter Sir Toby Belch, Sir Andrew Aguecheek,
and Fabian*

SIR ANDREW. No, faith, I'll not stay a jot longer.
SIR TOBY. Thy reason, dear venom; give thy reason.
FABIAN. You must needs yield your reason, Sir Andrew.
SIR ANDREW. Marry, I saw your niece do more favours to the count's serving-man than ever she bestowed upon me; I saw't i' the orchard.
SIR TOBY. Did she see thee the while, old boy? Tell me that.
SIR ANDREW. As plain as I see you now.
FABIAN. This was a great argument of love in her toward you.
SIR ANDREW. 'Slight! will you make an ass o' me?
FABIAN. I will prove it legitimate, sir, upon the oaths of judgment and reason.
SIR TOBY. And they have been grand-jurymen since before Noah was a sailor.
FABIAN. She did show favour to the youth in your sight only to exasperate you, to awake your dormouse valour, to put fire in your heart, and brimstone in your liver. You should then have accosted her, and with some excellent jests, fire-new from the mint, you should have banged the youth into dumbness. This was looked for at your hand, and this was

balked: the double gilt of this opportunity you let time wash off, and you are now sailed into the north of my lady's opinion; where you will hang like an icicle on a Dutchman's beard, unless you do redeem it by some laudable attempt, either of valour or policy.

SIR ANDREW. An 't be any way, it must be with valour, for policy I hate: I had as lief be a Brownist as a politician.

SIR TOBY. Why, then, build me thy fortunes upon the basis of valour: challenge me the count's youth to fight with him; hurt him in eleven places: my niece shall take note of it; and assure thyself, there is no love-broker in the world can more prevail in man's commendation with woman than report of valour.

FABIAN. There is no way but this, Sir Andrew.

SIR ANDREW. Will either of you bear me a challenge to him?

SIR TOBY. Go, write it in a martial hand; be curst and brief; it is no matter how witty, so it be eloquent, and full of invention: taunt him with the licence of ink: if thou thou'st him some thrice, it shall not be amiss; and as many lies as will lie in thy sheet of paper, although the sheet were big enough for the bed of Ware in England, set 'em down: go, about it. Let there be gall enough in thy ink, though thou write with a goose-pen, no matter: about it.

SIR ANDREW. Where shall I find you?

SIR TOBY. We 'll call thee at the cubiculo: go.

Exit Sir Andrew

FABIAN. This is a dear manikin to you, Sir Toby.

SIR TOBY. I have been dear to him, lad, some two thousand strong, or so.

FABIAN. We shall have a rare letter from him; but you 'll not deliver it.

SIR TOBY. Never trust me, then; and by all means stir on the youth to an answer. I think oxen and wain-ropes cannot hale them together. For Andrew, if he were opened, and you find so much blood in his liver as will clog the foot of a flea, I 'll eat the rest of the anatomy.

FABIAN. And his opposite, the youth, bears in his visage no great presage of cruelty.

SIR TOBY. Look, where the youngest wren of nine comes.

Enter Maria

MARIA. If you desire the spleen, and will laugh yourselves into stitches, follow me. Yond gull Malvolio is turned heathen, a very renegado; for there is no Christian, that means to be saved by believing rightly, can ever believe such impossible passages of grossness. He 's in yellow stockings.

SIR TOBY. And cross-gartered?

MARIA. Most villanously; like a pedant that keeps a school i' the church. I have dogged him like his murderer. He does obey every point of the letter that I dropped to betray him: he does smile his face into more lines than are in the new map with the augmentation of the Indies. You have not seen such a thing as 'tis; I can hardly forbear hurling things at him. I know my lady will strike him: if she do, he 'll smile and take 't for a great favour.

SIR TOBY. Come, bring us, bring us where he is. *Exeunt*

SCENE THREE

A Street.

Enter Sebastian and Antonio

SEBASTIAN. I would not by my will have troubled you;
But since you make your pleasure of your pains,
I will no further chide you.

ANTONIO. I could not stay behind you: my desire,
More sharp than filed steel, did spur me forth;
And not all love to see you,—though so much
As might have drawn one to a longer voyage,—
But jealousy what might befall your travel,
Being skilless in these parts; which to a stranger,
Unguided and unfriended, often prove
Rough and unhospitable: my willing love,
The rather by these arguments of fear,
Set forth in your pursuit.

SEBASTIAN.   My kind Antonio,
I can no other answer make but thanks,
And thanks, and ever thanks; for oft good turns
Are shuffled off with such uncurrent pay:
But, were my worth, as is my conscience, firm,
You should find better dealing. What 's to do?
Shall we go see the reliques of this town?

ANTONIO. To-morrow, sir: best first go see your lodging.

SEBASTIAN. I am not weary, and 'tis long to night:
    I pray you, let us satisfy our eyes
    With the memorials and the things of fame
    That do renown this city.
ANTONIO.   Would you 'd pardon me;
    I do not without danger walk these streets:
    Once, in a sea-fight 'gainst the Count his galleys,
    I did some service; of such note indeed,
    That were I ta'en here it would scarce be answer'd.
SEBASTIAN. Belike you slew great number of his people?
ANTONIO. The offence is not of such a bloody nature,
    Albeit the quality of the time and quarrel
    Might well have given us bloody argument.
    It might have since been answer'd in repaying
    What we took from them; which, for traffic's sake,
    Most of our city did: only myself stood out;
    For which, if I be lapsed in this place,
    I shall pay dear.
SEBASTIAN.   Do not then walk too open.
ANTONIO. It doth not fit me. Hold, sir; here 's my purse.
    In the south suburbs, at the Elephant,
    Is best to lodge: I will bespeak our diet,
    Whiles you beguile the time and feed your knowledge
    With viewing of the town: there shall you have me.
SEBASTIAN. Why I your purse?
ANTONIO. Haply your eye shall light upon some toy
    You have desire to purchase; and your store,
    I think, is not for idle markets, sir.
SEBASTIAN. I 'll be your purse-bearer and leave you for an hour.
ANTONIO. To the Elephant.
SEBASTIAN. I do remember.   *Exeunt*

SCENE FOUR

Olivia's Garden.

Enter Olivia and Maria

OLIVIA. I have sent after him: he says he 'll come;
How shall I feast him? what bestow of him?
For youth is bought more oft than begg'd or borrow'd.
I speak too loud.
Where is Malvolio? He is sad, and civil,
And suits well for a servant with my fortunes:
Where is Malvolio?

MARIA. He 's coming, madam; but in very strange manner.
He is sure possess'd, madam.

OLIVIA. Why, what 's the matter? Does he rave?

MARIA. No, madam; he does nothing but smile: your ladyship were best to have some guard about you if he come, for sure the man is tainted in 's wits.

OLIVIA. Go call him hither. *Exit Maria*
I am as mad as he,
If sad and merry madness equal me.

Re-enter Maria, with Malvolio

How now, Malvolio!

MALVOLIO. Sweet lady, ho, ho.

OLIVIA. Smil'st thou?
I sent for thee upon a sad occasion.

MALVOLIO. Sad, lady! I could be sad: this does make some obstruction in the blood, this cross-gartering; but what of that? If it please the eye of one, it is with me as the very true sonnet is, 'Please one and please all.'

OLIVIA. Why, how dost thou, man? What is the matter with thee?

MALVOLIO. Not black in my mind, though yellow in my legs. It did come to his hands, and commands shall be executed: I think we do know the sweet Roman hand.

OLIVIA. Wilt thou go to bed, Malvolio?

MALVOLIO. To bed! ay, sweetheart; and I 'll come to thee.

OLIVIA. God comfort thee! Why dost thou smile so and kiss thy hand so oft?

MARIA. How do you, Malvolio?

MALVOLIO. At your request! Yes; nightingales answer daws.
MARIA. Why appear you with this ridiculous boldness before my lady?
MALVOLIO. 'Be not afraid of greatness': 'Twas well writ.
OLIVIA. What meanest thou by that, Malvolio?
MALVOLIO. 'Some are born great,'—
OLIVIA. Ha!
MALVOLIO. 'Some achieve greatness,'—
OLIVIA. What sayst thou?
MALVOLIO. 'And some have greatness thrust upon them.'
OLIVIA. Heaven restore thee!
MALVOLIO. 'Remember who commended thy yellow stockings,'—
OLIVIA. Thy yellow stockings!
MALVOLIO. 'And wished to see thee cross-gartered.'
OLIVIA. Cross-gartered!
MALVOLIO. 'Go to, thou art made, if thou desirest to be so,'—
OLIVIA. Am I made?
MALVOLIO. 'If not, let me see thee a servant still.'
OLIVIA. Why, this is very midsummer madness.

Enter Servant

SERVANT. Madam, the young gentleman of the Count Orsino's is returned. I could hardly entreat him back: he attends your ladyship's pleasure.
OLIVIA. I'll come to him. (*Exit Servant*) Good Maria, let this fellow be looked to. Where's my cousin Toby? Let some of my people have a special care of him: I would not have him miscarry for the half of my dowry.

Exeunt Olivia and Maria

MALVOLIO. Oh, ho! do you come near me now? No worse man than Sir Toby to look to me! This concurs directly with the letter: she sends him on purpose, that I may appear stubborn to him; for she incites me to that in the letter. 'Cast thy humble slough,' says she; 'be opposite with a kinsman, surly with servants; let thy tongue tang with arguments of state; put thyself into the trick of singularity'; and consequently sets down the manner how; as, a sad face, a reverend carriage, a slow tongue, in the habit of some sir of note, and so forth. I have limed her; but it is Jove's doing, and Jove make me thankful! And when she went away now, 'Let this fellow be looked to'; fellow! not Malvolio, nor after my degree, but 'fellow.' Why, every-

ACT III · SCENE IV

thing adheres together, that no dram of a scruple, no scruple of a scruple, no obstacle, no incredulous or unsafe circumstance—What can be said? Nothing that can be can come between me and the full prospect of my hopes. Well, Jove, not I, is the doer of this, and he is to be thanked.

Re-enter Maria, with Sir Toby Belch and Fabian

SIR TOBY. Which way is he, in the name of sanctity? If all the devils in hell be drawn in little, and Legion himself possess'd him, yet I 'll speak to him.

FABIAN. Here he is, here he is. How is 't with you, sir? How is 't with you, man?

MALVOLIO. Go off; I discard you. Let me enjoy my private; go off.

MARIA. Lo, how hollow the fiend speaks within him! Did not I tell you? Sir Toby, my lady prays you to have a care of him.

MALVOLIO. Ah, ha! does she so?

SIR TOBY. Go to, go to: peace! peace! we must deal gently with him; let me alone. How do you, Malvolio? How is 't with you? What, man! defy the devil: consider, he 's an enemy to mankind.

MALVOLIO. Do you know what you say?

MARIA. La you! an you speak ill of the devil, how he takes it at heart. Pray God, he be not bewitched!

FABIAN. Carry his water to the wise-woman.

MARIA. Marry, and it shall be done to-morrow morning, if I live. My lady would not lose him for more than I 'll say.

MALVOLIO. How now, mistress!

MARIA. O Lord!

SIR TOBY. Prithee, hold thy peace; this is not the way: do you not see you move him? Let me alone with him.

FABIAN. No way but gentleness; gently, gently: the fiend is rough, and will not be roughly used.

SIR TOBY. Why, how now, my bawcock! How dost thou, chuck?

MALVOLIO. Sir!

SIR TOBY. Ay, Biddy, come with me. What, man! 'tis not for gravity to play at cherry-pit with Satan. Hang him, foul collier!

MARIA. Get him to say his prayers, good Sir Toby, get him to pray.

MALVOLIO. My prayers, minx!

MARIA. No, I warrant you, he will not hear of godliness.

MALVOLIO. Go, hang yourselves all! You are idle shallow things: I am not of your element. You shall know more hereafter. *Exit*

SIR TOBY. Is 't possible?

FABIAN. If this were played upon a stage now, I could condemn it as an improbable fiction.

SIR TOBY. His very genius hath taken the infection of the device, man.

MARIA. Nay, pursue him now, lest the device take air, and taint.

FABIAN. Why, we shall make him mad indeed.

MARIA. The house will be the quieter.

SIR TOBY. Come, we 'll have him in a dark room, and bound. My niece is already in the belief that he 's mad: we may carry it thus, for our pleasure and his penance, till our very pastime, tired out of breath, prompt us to have mercy on him; at which time we will bring the device to the bar, and crown thee for a finder of madmen. But see, but see.

Enter Sir Andrew Aguecheek

FABIAN. More matter for a May morning.

SIR ANDREW. Here 's the challenge; read it: I warrant there 's vinegar and pepper in 't.

FABIAN. Is 't so saucy?

SIR ANDREW. Ay, is 't, I warrant him. Do but read.

SIR TOBY. Give me. 'Youth, whatsoever thou art, thou art but a scurvy fellow.'

FABIAN. Good, and valiant.

SIR TOBY. 'Wonder not, nor admire not in thy mind, why I do call thee so, for I will show thee no reason for 't.'

FABIAN. A good note, that keeps you from the blow of the law.

SIR TOBY. 'Thou comest to the Lady Olivia, and in my sight she uses thee kindly: but thou liest in thy throat; that is not the matter I challenge thee for.'

FABIAN. Very brief, and to exceeding good sense—less.

SIR TOBY. 'I will waylay thee going home; where, if it be thy chance to kill me,'—

FABIAN. Good.

SIR TOBY. 'Thou killest me like a rogue and a villain.'

FABIAN. Still you keep o' the windy side of the law: good.

SIR TOBY. 'Fare thee well; and God have mercy upon one of

our souls! He may have mercy upon mine, but my hope is better; and so look to thyself. Thy friend, as thou usest him, and thy sworn enemy,

'Andrew Aguecheek.'

If this letter move him not, his legs cannot. I'll give't him.

MARIA. You may have very fit occasion for 't: he is now in some commerce with my lady, and will by and by depart.

SIR TOBY. Go, Sir Andrew; scout me for him at the corner of the orchard like a bum-baily: so soon as ever thou seest him, draw; and, as thou drawest, swear horrible; for it comes to pass oft that a terrible oath, with a swaggering accent sharply twanged off, gives manhood more approbation than ever proof itself would have earned him. Away!

SIR ANDREW. Nay, let me alone for swearing. *Exit*

SIR TOBY. Now will not I deliver his letter: for the behaviour of the young gentleman gives him out to be of good capacity and breeding; his employment between his lord and my niece confirms no less: therefore this letter, being so excellently ignorant, will breed no terror in the youth: he will find it comes from a clodpole. But, sir, I will deliver his challenge by word of mouth; set upon Aguecheek a notable report of valour; and drive the gentleman,—as I know his youth will aptly receive it,—into a most hideous opinion of his rage, skill, fury, and impetuosity. This will so fright them both that they will kill one another by the look, like cockatrices.

FABIAN. Here he comes with your niece: give them way till he take leave, and presently after him.

SIR TOBY. I will meditate the while upon some horrid message for a challenge.

Exeunt Sir Toby, Fabian, and Maria
Re-enter Olivia, with Viola

OLIVIA. I have said too much unto a heart of stone,
And laid mine honour too unchary out:
There's something in me that reproves my fault,
But such a headstrong potent fault it is
That it but mocks reproof.

VIOLA. With the same haviour that your passion bears
Goes on my master's griefs.

OLIVIA. Here; wear this jewel for me, 'tis my picture;
Refuse it not; it hath no tongue to vex you;
And I beseech you come again to-morrow.

What shall you ask of me that I 'll deny,
That honour sav'd may upon asking give?
VIOLA. Nothing but this; your true love for my master.
OLIVIA. How with mine honour may I give him that
Which I have given to you?
VIOLA. I will acquit you.
OLIVIA. Well, come again to-morrow: fare thee well:
A fiend like thee might bear my soul to hell. *Exit*
Re-enter Sir Toby Belch and Fabian
SIR TOBY. Gentleman, God save thee.
VIOLA. And you, sir.
SIR TOBY. That defence thou hast, betake thee to 't: of what nature the wrongs are thou hast done him, I know not; but thy intercepter, full of despite, bloody as the hunter, attends thee at the orchard-end. Dismount thy tuck, be yare in thy preparation, for thy assailant is quick, skilful, and deadly.
VIOLA. You mistake, sir: I am sure no man hath any quarrel to me: my remembrance is very free and clear from any image of offence done to any man.
SIR TOBY. You 'll find it otherwise, I assure you: therefore, if you hold your life at any price, betake you to your guard; for your opposite hath in him what youth, strength, skill, and wrath, can furnish man withal.
VIOLA. I pray you, sir, what is he?
SIR TOBY. He is knight dubbed with unhatched rapier, and on carpet consideration; but he is a devil in private brawl: souls and bodies hath he divorced three, and his incensement at this moment is so implacable that satisfaction can be none but by pangs of death and sepulchre. Hob, nob, is his word: give 't or take 't.
VIOLA. I will return again into the house and desire some conduct of the lady: I am no fighter. I have heard of some kind of men that put quarrels purposely on others to taste their valour; belike this is a man of that quirk.
SIR TOBY. Sir, no; his indignation derives itself out of a very competent injury: therefore get you on and give him his desire. Back you shall not to the house, unless you undertake that with me which with as much safety you might answer him: therefore, on, or strip your sword stark naked; for meddle you must, that 's certain, or forswear to wear iron about you.

VIOLA. This is as uncivil as strange. I beseech you, do me this courteous office, as to know of the knight what my offence to him is: it is something of my negligence, nothing of my purpose.

SIR TOBY. I will do so. Signior Fabian, stay you by this gentleman till my return. *Exit*

VIOLA. Pray you, sir, do you know of this matter?

FABIAN. I know the knight is incensed against you, even to a mortal arbitrement, but nothing of the circumstance more.

VIOLA. I beseech you, what manner of man is he?

FABIAN. Nothing of that wonderful promise, to read him by his form, as you are like to find him in the proof of his valour. He is, indeed, sir, the most skilful, bloody, and fatal opposite that you could possibly have found in any part of Illyria. Will you walk towards him? I will make your peace with him if I can.

VIOLA. I shall be much bound to you for 't: I am one that had rather go with sir priest than sir knight: I care not who knows so much of my mettle. *Exeunt*

Re-enter Sir Toby, with Sir Andrew

SIR TOBY. Why, man, he 's a very devil: I have not seen such a firago. I had a pass with him, rapier, scabbard and all, and he gives me the stuck in with such a mortal motion that it is inevitable; and on the answer, he pays you as surely as your feet hit the ground they step on. They say he has been fencer to the Sophy.

SIR ANDREW. Pox on 't, I 'll not meddle with him.

SIR TOBY. Ay, but he will not now be pacified: Fabian can scarce hold him yonder.

SIR ANDREW. Plague on 't; an I thought he had been valiant and so cunning in fence I 'd have seen him damned ere I 'd have challenged him. Let him let the matter slip, and I 'll give him my horse, grey Capilet.

SIR TOBY. I 'll make the motion. Stand here; make a good show on 't: this shall end without the perdition of souls.— (*Aside*) Marry, I 'll ride your horse as well as I ride you.

Re-enter Fabian and Viola

(*To Fabian*) I have his horse to take up the quarrel. I have persuaded him the youth 's a devil.

FABIAN. He is as horribly conceited of him; and pants and looks pale, as if a bear were at his heels.

SIR TOBY. There 's no remedy, sir: he will fight with you for his oath's sake. Marry, he hath better bethought him of his quarrel, and he finds that now scarce to be worth talking of: therefore draw for the supportance of his vow: he protests he will not hurt you.

VIOLA. *(Aside)* Pray God defend me! A little thing would make me tell them how much I lack of a man.

FABIAN. Give ground, if you see him furious.

SIR TOBY. Come, Sir Andrew, there 's no remedy: the gentleman will, for his honour's sake, have one bout with you; he cannot by the duello avoid it: but he has promised me, as he is a gentleman and a soldier, he will not hurt you. Come on; to 't.

SIR ANDREW. Pray God, he keep his oath! *Draws*

VIOLA. I do assure you, 'tis against my will. *Draws*

Enter Antonio

ANTONIO. Put up your sword. If this young gentleman
Have done offence, I take the fault on me:
If you offend him, I for him defy you. *Drawing*

SIR TOBY. You, sir! Why, what are you?

ANTONIO. One, sir, that for his love dares yet do more
Than you have heard him brag to you he will.

SIR TOBY. Nay, if you be an undertaker, I am for you. *Draws*

FABIAN. O, good sir Toby, hold! Here come the officers.

SIR TOBY. I 'll be with you anon.

VIOLA. *(To Sir Andrew)* Pray, sir, put your sword up, if you please.

SIR ANDREW. Marry, will I, sir; and, for that I promised you, I 'll be as good as my word. He will bear you easily and reins well.

Enter two Officers

FIRST OFFICER. This is the man; do thy office.

SECOND OFFICER. Antonio, I arrest thee at the suit
Of Count Orsino.

ANTONIO. You do mistake me, sir.

FIRST OFFICER. No, sir, no jot: I know your favour well,
Though now you have no sea-cap on your head.
Take him away: he knows I know him well.

ANTONIO. I must obey.—*(To Viola)* This comes with seeking you:
But there 's no remedy: I shall answer it.
What will you do, now my necessity
Makes me to ask you for my purse? It grieves me

Much more for what I cannot do for you
Than what befalls myself. You stand amaz'd:
But be of comfort.
SECOND OFFICER. Come, sir, away.
ANTONIO. I must entreat of you some of that money.
VIOLA. What money, sir?
For the fair kindness you have show'd me here,
And part, being prompted by your present trouble,
Out of my lean and low ability
I'll lend you something: my having is not much:
I'll make division of my present with you.
Hold, there is half my coffer.
ANTONIO. Will you deny me now?
Is 't possible that my deserts to you
Can lack persuasion? Do not tempt my misery,
Lest that it make me so unsound a man
As to upbraid you with those kindnesses
That I have done for you.
VIOLA. I know of none;
Nor know I you by voice or any feature.
I hate ingratitude more in a man
Than lying, vainness, babbling drunkenness,
Or any taint of vice whose strong corruption
Inhabits our frail blood.
ANTONIO. O heavens themselves!
SECOND OFFICER. Come, sir: I pray you, go.
ANTONIO. Let me speak a little. This youth that you see here
I snatch'd one-half out of the jaws of death,
Reliev'd him with such sanctity of love,
And to his image, which methought did promise
Most venerable worth, did I devotion.
FIRST OFFICER. What's that to us? The time goes by: away!
ANTONIO. But O! how vile an idol proves this god.
Thou hast, Sebastian, done good feature shame.
In nature there's no blemish but the mind;
None can be call'd deform'd but the unkind:
Virtue is beauty, but the beauteous evil
Are empty trunks o'erflourish'd by the devil.
FIRST OFFICER. The man grows mad: away with him! Come, come, sir.
ANTONIO. Lead me on. *Exeunt Officers with Antonio*
VIOLA. Methinks his words do from such passion fly,

> That he believes himself; so do not I.
> Prove true, imagination, O, prove true,
> That I, dear brother, be now ta'en for you!

SIR TOBY. Come hither, knight; come hither, Fabian: we'll whisper o'er a couplet or two of most sage saws.

VIOLA. He nam'd Sebastian: I my brother know
> Yet living in my glass; even such and so
> In favour was my brother; and he went
> Still in this fashion, colour, ornament,
> For him I imitate. O! if it prove,
> Tempests are kind, and salt waves fresh in love! *Exit*

SIR TOBY. A very dishonest paltry boy, and more a coward than a hare. His dishonesty appears in leaving his friend here in necessity, and denying him; and for his cowardship, ask Fabian.

FABIAN. A coward, a most devout coward, religious in it.

SIR ANDREW. 'Slid, I'll after him again and beat him.

SIR TOBY. Do; cuff him soundly, but never draw thy sword.

SIR ANDREW. An I do not,— *Exit*

FABIAN. Come, let's see the event.

SIR TOBY. I dare lay any money 'twill be nothing yet. *Exeunt*

ACT FOUR

SCENE ONE

The Street adjoining Olivia's House.

Enter Sebastian and Clown

CLOWN. Will you make me believe that I am not sent for you?
SEBASTIAN. Go to, go to; thou art a foolish fellow:
Let me be clear of thee.
CLOWN. Well held out, i' faith! No, I do not know you; nor I am not sent to you by my lady to bid you come speak with her; nor your name is not Master Cesario; nor this is not my nose neither. Nothing that is so is so.
SEBASTIAN. I prithee, vent thy folly somewhere else. Thou know'st not me.
CLOWN. Vent my folly! He has heard that word of some great man, and now applies it to a fool. Vent my folly! I am afraid this great lubber, the world, will prove a cockney. I prithee now, ungird thy strangeness and tell me what I shall vent to my lady. Shall I vent to her that thou art coming?
SEBASTIAN. I prithee, foolish Greek, depart from me:
There 's money for thee: if you tarry longer
I shall give worse payment.
CLOWN. By my troth, thou hast an open hand. These wise men that give fools money get themselves a good report after fourteen years' purchase.

Enter Sir Andrew

SIR ANDREW. Now, sir, have I met you again? There 's for you.   *Striking Sebastian*
SEBASTIAN. Why, there 's for thee, and there, and there, and there!   *Beating Sir Andrew*
Are all the people mad?

Enter Sir Toby and Fabian

SIR TOBY. Hold, sir, or I'll throw your dagger o'er the house.
CLOWN. This will I tell my lady straight. I would not be in some of your coats for twopence. *Exit*
SIR TOBY. (*Holding Sebastian*) Come on, sir: hold.
SIR ANDREW. Nay, let him alone; I'll go another way to work with him: I'll have an action of battery against him if there be any law in Illyria. Though I struck him first, yet it's no matter for that.
SEBASTIAN. Let go thy hand.
SIR TOBY. Come, sir, I will not let you go. Come, my young soldier, put up your iron: you are well fleshed; come on.
SEBASTIAN. I will be free from thee. (*Disengaging himself*) What wouldst thou now?
If thou dar'st tempt me further, draw thy sword.
SIR TOBY. What, what! Nay then, I must have an ounce or two of this malapert blood from you. *Draws*

Enter Olivia

OLIVIA. Hold, Toby! On thy life I charge thee, hold!
SIR TOBY. Madam!
OLIVIA. Will it be ever thus? Ungracious wretch!
Fit for the mountains and the barbarous caves,
Where manners ne'er were preach'd. Out of my sight!
Be not offended, dear Cesario.
Rudesby, be gone!

Exeunt Sir Toby, Sir Andrew, and Fabian

I prithee, gentle friend,
Let thy fair wisdom, not thy passion, sway
In this uncivil and unjust extent
Against thy peace. Go with me to my house,
And hear thou there how many fruitless pranks
This ruffian hath botch'd up, that thou thereby
Mayst smile at this. Thou shalt not choose but go:
Do not deny. Beshrew his soul for me,
He started one poor heart of mine in thee.
SEBASTIAN. What relish is in this? How runs the stream?
Or I am mad, or else this is a dream:
Let fancy still my sense in Lethe steep;
If it be thus to dream, still let me sleep!
OLIVIA. Nay; come, I prithee. Would thou'dst be rul'd by me!
SEBASTIAN. Madam, I will.
OLIVIA. O! say so, and so be! *Exeunt*

SCENE TWO

A Room in Olivia's House.

Enter Maria and Clown; Malvolio in a dark chamber adjoining

MARIA. Nay, I prithee, put on this gown and this beard; make him believe thou art Sir Topas the curate: do it quickly; I'll call Sir Toby the whilst. *Exit*

CLOWN. Well, I'll put it on and I will dissemble myself in 't: and I would I were the first that ever dissembled in such a gown. I am not tall enough to become the function well, nor lean enough to be thought a good student; but to be said an honest man and a good housekeeper goes as fairly as to say a careful man and a great scholar. The competitors enter.

Enter Sir Toby Belch and Maria

SIR TOBY. God bless thee, Master parson.

CLOWN. Bonos dies, Sir Toby: for, as the old hermit of Prague, that never saw pen and ink, very wittily said to a niece of King Gorboduc, 'That, that is, is'; so I, being Master parson, am Master parson; for, what is 'that,' but 'that,' and 'is,' but 'is'?

SIR TOBY. To him, Sir Topas.

CLOWN. What ho! I say. Peace in this prison!

SIR TOBY. The knave counterfeits well; a good knave.

MALVOLIO. (*Within*) Who calls there?

CLOWN. Sir Topas, the curate, who comes to visit Malvolio the lunatic.

MALVOLIO. Sir Topas, Sir Topas, good Sir Topas, go to my lady.

CLOWN. Out, hyperbolical fiend! How vexest thou this man! Talkest thou nothing but of ladies?

SIR TOBY. Well said, Master Parson.

MALVOLIO. (*Within*) Sir Topas, never was man thus wronged. Good Sir Topas, do not think I am mad. They have laid me here in hideous darkness.

CLOWN. Fie, thou dishonest Satan! I call thee by the most modest terms; for I am one of those gentle ones that will use the devil himself with courtesy. Sayst thou that house is dark?

MALVOLIO. As hell, Sir Topas.

CLOWN. Why, it hath bay-windows transparent as barricadoes, and the clerestories toward the south-north are as lustrous as ebony; and yet complainest thou of obstruction?

MALVOLIO. I am not mad, Sir Topas. I say to you, this house is dark.

CLOWN. Madman, thou errest. I say, there is no darkness but ignorance, in which thou art more puzzled than the Egyptians in their fog.

MALVOLIO. I say this house is as dark as ignorance, though ignorance were as dark as hell; and I say, there was never man thus abused. I am no more mad than you are. Make the trial of it in any constant question.

CLOWN. What is the opinion of Pythagoras concerning wild fowl?

MALVOLIO. That the soul of our grandam might haply inhabit a bird.

CLOWN. What thinkest thou of his opinion?

MALVOLIO. I think nobly of the soul, and no way approve his opinion.

CLOWN. Fare thee well. Remain thou still in darkness. Thou shalt hold the opinion of Pythagoras ere I will allow of thy wits, and fear to kill a woodcock, lest thou dispossess the soul of thy grandam. Fare thee well.

MALVOLIO. Sir Topas! Sir Topas!

SIR TOBY. My most exquisite Sir Topas!

CLOWN. Nay, I am for all waters.

MARIA. Thou mightst have done this without thy beard and gown. He sees thee not.

SIR TOBY. To him in thine own voice, and bring me word how thou findest him: I would we were well rid of this knavery. If he may be conveniently delivered, I would he were; for I am now so far in offence with my niece that I cannot pursue with any safety this sport to the upshot. Come by and by to my chamber.

Exeunt Sir Toby and Maria

CLOWN. Hey Robin, jolly Robin,
 Tell me how thy lady does.

MALVOLIO. Fool!

CLOWN. 'My lady is unkind, perdy!'
MALVOLIO. Fool!
CLOWN. 'Alas, why is she so?'
MALVOLIO. Fool, I say!
CLOWN. 'She loves another.'
  Who calls, ha?
MALVOLIO. Good fool, as ever thou wilt deserve well at my hand, help me to a candle, and pen, ink, and paper. As I am a gentleman, I will live to be thankful to thee for 't.
CLOWN. Master Malvolio!
MALVOLIO. Ay, good fool.
CLOWN. Alas, sir, how fell you beside your five wits?
MALVOLIO. Fool, there was never man so notoriously abused. I am as well in my wits, fool, as thou art.
CLOWN. But as well? Then you are mad indeed, if you be no better in your wits than a fool.
MALVOLIO. They have here propertied me; keep me in darkness, send ministers to me, asses! and do all they can to face me out of my wits.
CLOWN. Advise you what you say. The minister is here. Malvolio, Malvolio, thy wits the heavens restore! Endeavour thyself to sleep, and leave thy vain bibble-babble.
MALVOLIO. Sir Topas!
CLOWN. Maintain no words with him, good fellow.—Who, I, sir? not I, sir. God be wi' you, good Sir Topas. Marry, amen. I will, sir, I will.
MALVOLIO. Fool, fool, fool, I say!
CLOWN. Alas, sir, be patient. What say you, sir? I am shent for speaking to you.
MALVOLIO. Good fool, help me to some light and some paper: I tell thee I am as well in my wits as any man in Illyria.
CLOWN. Well-a-day, that you were, sir!
MALVOLIO. By this hand, I am. Good fool, some ink, paper, and light; and convey what I will set down to my lady: it shall advantage thee more than ever the bearing of letter did.
CLOWN. I will help you to 't. But tell me true, are you not mad indeed? or do you but counterfeit?
MALVOLIO. Believe me, I am not: I tell thee true.
CLOWN. Nay, I'll ne'er believe a madman till I see his brains. I will fetch you light and paper and ink.

MALVOLIO. Fool, I'll requite it in the highest degree: I
prithee, be gone.
CLOWN. (*Sings*) I am gone, sir,
   And anon, sir,
  I'll be with you again
   In a trice,
   Like to the old Vice,
  Your need to sustain;
 Who with dagger of lath,
 In his rage and his wrath,
  Cries, Ah, ah! to the devil:
 Like a mad lad,
 Pare thy nails, dad;
  Adieu, goodman drivel. *Exit*

SCENE THREE

Olivia's Garden.

Enter Sebastian

SEBASTIAN. This is the air; that is the glorious sun;
This pearl she gave me, I do feel 't and see 't;
And though 'tis wonder that enwraps me thus,
Yet 'tis not madness. Where 's Antonio then?
I could not find him at the Elephant;
Yet there he was, and there I found this credit,
That he did range the town to seek me out.
His counsel now might do me golden service;
For though my soul disputes well with my sense
That this may be some error, but no madness,
Yet doth this accident and flood of fortune
So far exceed all instance, all discourse,
That I am ready to distrust mine eyes,
And wrangle with my reason that persuades me
To any other trust but that I am mad
Or else the lady's mad: yet, if 'twere so,
She could not sway her house, command her followers,
Take and give back affairs and their dispatch
With such a smooth, discreet, and stable bearing
As I perceive she does. There's something in 't
That is deceivable. But here the lady comes.

ACT IV · SCENE III

Enter Olivia and a Priest

OLIVIA. Blame not this haste of mine. If you mean well,
Now go with me and with this holy man
Into the chantry by; there, before him,
And underneath that consecrated roof,
Plight me the full assurance of your faith;
That my most jealous and too doubtful soul
May live at peace. He shall conceal it
Whiles you are willing it shall come to note,
What time we will our celebration keep
According to my birth. What do you say?

SEBASTIAN. I 'll follow this good man, and go with you;
And, having sworn truth, ever will be true.

OLIVIA. Then lead the way, good father; and heavens so shine
That they may fairly note this act of mine! *Exeunt*

ACT FIVE

SCENE ONE

The Street before Olivia's House.

Enter Clown and Fabian

FABIAN. Now, as thou lovest me, let me see his letter.
CLOWN. Good Master Fabian, grant me another request.
FABIAN. Anything.
CLOWN. Do not desire to see this letter.
FABIAN. This is, to give a dog, and, in recompense desire my dog again.

Enter Duke, Viola, Curio, and Attendants

DUKE. Belong you to the Lady Olivia, friends?
CLOWN. Ay, sir; we are some of her trappings.
DUKE. I know thee well. How dost thou, my good fellow?
CLOWN. Truly, sir, the better for my foes and the worse for my friends.
DUKE. Just the contrary; the better for thy friends.
CLOWN. No, sir, the worse.
DUKE. How can that be?
CLOWN. Marry, sir, they praise me and make an ass of me; now my foes tell me plainly I am an ass: so that by my foes, sir, I profit in the knowledge of myself, and by my friends I am abused: so that, conclusions to be as kisses, if your four negatives make your two affirmatives, why then, the worse for my friends and the better for my foes.
DUKE. Why, this is excellent.
CLOWN. By my troth, sir, no; though it please you to be one of my friends.
DUKE. Thou shalt not be the worse for me. There's gold.
CLOWN. But that it would be double-dealing, sir, I would you could make it another.
DUKE. O, you give me ill counsel.

ACT V · SCENE I

CLOWN. Put your grace in your pocket, sir, for this once, and let your flesh and blood obey it.

DUKE. Well, I will be so much a sinner to be a double-dealer: there's another.

CLOWN. Primo, secundo, tertio, is a good play; and the old saying is, 'the third pays for all': the triplex, sir, is a good tripping measure; or the bells of Saint Bennet, sir, may put you in mind; one, two, three.

DUKE. You can fool no more money out of me at this throw. If you will let your lady know I am here to speak with her, and bring her along with you, it may awake my bounty further.

CLOWN. Marry, sir, lullaby to your bounty till I come again. I go, sir; but I would not have you to think that my desire of having is the sin of covetousness; but as you say, sir, let your bounty take a nap, I will awake it anon. *Exit*

VIOLA. Here comes the man, sir, that did rescue me.

Enter Antonio and Officers

DUKE. That face of his I do remember well;
Yet when I saw it last, it was besmear'd
As black as Vulcan in the smoke of war.
A bawbling vessel was he captain of,
For shallow draught and hulk unprizable;
With which such scathful grapple did he make
With the most noble bottom of our fleet,
That very envy and the tongue of loss
Cried fame and honour on him. What's the matter?

FIRST OFFICER. Orsino, this is that Antonio
That took the Phœnix and her fraught from Candy;
And this is he that did the Tiger board,
When your young nephew Titus lost his leg.
Here in the streets, desperate of shame and state,
In private brabble did we apprehend him.

VIOLA. He did me kindness, sir, drew on my side;
But in conclusion put strange speech upon me:
I know not what 'twas but distraction.

DUKE. Notable pirate! thou salt-water thief!
What foolish boldness brought thee to their mercies
Whom thou, in terms so bloody and so dear,
Hast made thine enemies?

ANTONIO.   Orsino, noble sir,
Be pleas'd that I shake off these names you give me:

Antonio never yet was thief or pirate,
Though I confess, on base and ground enough,
Orsino's enemy. A witchcraft drew me hither:
That most ingrateful boy there by your side,
From the rude sea's enrag'd and foamy mouth
Did I redeem; a wrack past hope he was:
His life I gave him, and did thereto add
My love, without retention or restraint,
All his in dedication; for his sake
Did I expose myself, pure for his love,
Into the danger of this adverse town;
Drew to defend him when he was beset:
Where being apprehended, his false cunning,
Not meaning to partake with me in danger,
Taught him to face me out of his acquaintance,
And grew a twenty years removed thing
While one would wink, denied me mine own purse,
Which I had recommended to his use
Not half an hour before.

VIOLA. How can this be?

DUKE. When came he to this town?

ANTONIO. To-day, my lord; and for three months before,—
No interim, not a minute's vacancy,—
Both day and night did we keep company.

Enter Olivia and Attendants

DUKE. Here comes the countess: now heaven walks on earth!
But for thee, fellow; fellow, thy words are madness:
Three months this youth hath tended upon me;
But more of that anon. Take him aside.

OLIVIA. What would my lord, but that he may not have,
Wherein Olivia may seem serviceable?
Cesario, you do not keep promise with me.

VIOLA. Madam!

DUKE. Gracious Olivia.—

OLIVIA. What do you say, Cesario? Good my lord,—

VIOLA. My lord would speak; my duty hushes me.

OLIVIA. If it be aught to the old tune, my lord,
It is as fat and fulsome to mine ear
As howling after music.

DUKE. Still so cruel?

OLIVIA. Still so constant, lord.

DUKE. What, to perverseness? You uncivil lady,

ACT V : SCENE I

To whose ingrate and unauspicious altars
My soul the faithfull'st offerings hath breath'd out
That e'er devotion tender'd! What shall I do?

OLIVIA. Even what it please my lord, that shall become him.

DUKE. Why should I not, had I the heart to do it,
Like to the Egyptian thief at point of death,
Kill what I love?—a savage jealousy
That sometimes savours nobly. But hear me this:
Since you to non-regardance cast my faith,
And that I partly know the instrument
That screws me from my true place in your favour,
Live you, the marble-breasted tyrant still;
But this your minion, whom I know you love,
And whom, by heaven I swear, I tender dearly,
Him will I tear out of that cruel eye,
Where he sits crowned in his master's spite.
Come, boy, with me; my thoughts are ripe in mischief;
I 'll sacrifice the lamb that I do love,
To spite a raven's heart within a dove. *Going*

VIOLA. And I, most jocund, apt, and willingly,
To do you rest, a thousand deaths would die. *Following*

OLIVIA. Where goes Cesario?

VIOLA. After him I love
More than I love these eyes, more than my life,
More, by all mores, than e'er I shall love wife.
If I do feign, you witnesses above
Punish my life for tainting of my love!

OLIVIA. Ah me, detested! How am I beguil'd!

VIOLA. Who does beguile you? Who does do you wrong?

OLIVIA. Hast thou forgot thyself? Is it so long?
Call forth the holy father. *Exit an Attendant*

DUKE. (*To Viola*) Come away.

OLIVIA. Whither, my lord? Cesario, husband, stay.

DUKE. Husband?

OLIVIA. Ay, husband: can he that deny?

DUKE. Her husband, sirrah?

VIOLA. No, my lord, not I.

OLIVIA. Alas! it is the baseness of thy fear
That makes thee strangle thy propriety.
Fear not, Cesario; take thy fortunes up;
Be that thou know'st thou art, and then thou art
As great as that thou fear'st.

Enter Priest

O, welcome, father!
Father, I charge thee, by thy reverence,
Here to unfold,—though lately we intended
To keep in darkness what occasion now
Reveals before 'tis ripe,—what thou dost know
Hath newly pass'd between this youth and me.

PRIEST. A contract of eternal bond of love,
Confirm'd by mutual joinder of your hands,
Attested by the holy close of lips,
Strengthen'd by interchangement of your rings;
And all the ceremony of this compact
Seal'd in my function, by my testimony:
Since when, my watch hath told me, toward my grave
I have travell'd but two hours.

DUKE. O, thou dissembling cub! What wilt thou be
When time hath sow'd a grizzle on thy case?
Or will not else thy craft so quickly grow
That thine own trip shall be thine overthrow?
Farewell, and take her; but direct thy feet
Where thou and I henceforth may never meet.

VIOLA. My lord, I do protest,—

OLIVIA. O! do not swear:
Hold little faith, though thou hast too much fear.

Enter Sir Andrew Aguecheek, with his head broken

SIR ANDREW. For the love of God, a surgeon! Send one presently to Sir Toby.

OLIVIA. What's the matter?

SIR ANDREW. He has broke my head across, and has given Sir Toby a bloody coxcomb too. For the love of God, your help! I had rather than forty pound I were at home.

OLIVIA. Who has done this, Sir Andrew?

SIR ANDREW. The count's gentleman, one Cesario: we took him for a coward, but he's the very devil incarnate.

DUKE. My gentleman, Cesario?

SIR ANDREW. Od's lifelings! here he is. You broke my head for nothing! and that that I did, I was set on to do 't by Sir Toby.

VIOLA. Why do you speak to me? I never hurt you:
You drew your sword upon me without cause;
But I bespake you fair, and hurt you not.

SIR ANDREW. If a bloody coxcomb be a hurt, you have hurt

me: I think you set nothing by a bloody coxcomb. Here comes Sir Toby halting;

Enter Sir Toby Belch, drunk, led by the Clown

you shall hear more: but if he had not been in drink he would have tickled you othergates than he did.

DUKE. How now, gentleman! How is 't with you?

SIR TOBY. That 's all one: he has hurt me, and there 's the end on 't. Sot, didst see Dick Surgeon, sot?

CLOWN. O! he 's drunk, Sir Toby, an hour agone: his eyes were set at eight i' the morning.

SIR TOBY. Then he 's a rogue, and a passy-measures pavin. I hate a drunken rogue.

OLIVIA. Away with him! Who hath made this havoc with them?

SIR ANDREW. I 'll help you, Sir Toby, because we 'll be dressed together.

SIR TOBY. Will you help? An ass-head and a coxcomb and a knave, a thin-faced knave, a gull!

OLIVIA. Get him to bed, and let his hurt be look'd to.

Exeunt Clown, Fabian, Sir Toby, and Sir Andrew
Enter Sebastian

SEBASTIAN. I am sorry, madam, I have hurt your kinsman;
But, had it been the brother of my blood,
I must have done no less with wit and safety.
You throw a strange regard upon me, and by that
I do perceive it hath offended you:
Pardon me, sweet one, even for the vows
We made each other but so late ago.

DUKE. One face, one voice, one habit, and two persons;
A natural perspective, that is, and is not!

SEBASTIAN. Antonio! O my dear Antonio!
How have the hours rack'd and tortur'd me
Since I have lost thee!

ANTONIO. Sebastian are you?

SEBASTIAN. Fear'st thou that, Antonio?

ANTONIO. How have you made division of yourself?
An apple cleft in two is not more twin
Than these two creatures. Which is Sebastian?

OLIVIA. Most wonderful!

SEBASTIAN. Do I stand there? I never had a brother;
Nor can there be that deity in my nature,
Of here and every where. I had a sister,

Whom the blind waves and surges have devour'd.
Of charity, what kin are you to me?
What countryman? what name? what parentage?

VIOLA. Of Messaline: Sebastian was my father;
Such a Sebastian was my brother too,
So went he suited to his watery tomb.
If spirits can assume both form and suit
You come to fright us.

SEBASTIAN.   A spirit I am indeed;
But am in that dimension grossly clad
Which from the womb I did participate.
Were you a woman, as the rest goes even,
I should my tears let fall upon your cheek,
And say, 'Thrice welcome, drowned Viola!'

VIOLA. My father had a mole upon his brow.

SEBASTIAN. And so had mine.

VIOLA. And died that day when Viola from her birth
Had number'd thirteen years.

SEBASTIAN. O! that record is lively in my soul.
He finished indeed his mortal act
That day that made my sister thirteen years.

VIOLA. If nothing lets to make us happy both
But this my masculine usurp'd attire,
Do not embrace me till each circumstance
Of place, time, fortune, do cohere and jump
That I am Viola: which to confirm,
I'll bring you to a captain in this town,
Where lie my maiden weeds: by whose gentle help
I was preserv'd to serve this noble count.
All the occurrence of my fortune since
Hath been between this lady and this lord.

SEBASTIAN. (*To Olivia*) So comes it, lady, you have been mistook:
But nature to her bias drew in that.
You would have been contracted to a maid;
Nor are you therein, by my life, deceiv'd;
You are betroth'd both to a maid and man.

DUKE. Be not amaz'd; right noble is his blood.
If this be so, as yet the glass seems true,
I shall have share in this most happy wrack.
(*To Viola*) Boy, thou hast said to me a thousand times
Thou never shouldst love woman like to me.

ACT V : SCENE I

VIOLA. And all those sayings will I over-swear,
And all those swearings keep as true in soul
As doth that orbed continent the fire
That severs day from night.
DUKE. Give me thy hand;
And let me see thee in thy woman's weeds.
VIOLA. The captain that did bring me first on shore
Hath my maid's garments: he upon some action
Is now in durance at Malvolio's suit,
A gentleman and follower of my lady's.
OLIVIA. He shall enlarge him. Fetch Malvolio hither.
And yet, alas, now I remember me,
They say, poor gentleman, he 's much distract.
A most extracting frenzy of mine own
From my remembrance clearly banish'd his.
Re-enter Clown with a letter, and Fabian
How does he, sirrah?
CLOWN. Truly, madam, he holds Belzebub at the stave's end as well as a man in his case may do. He has here writ a letter to you: I should have given it to you to-day morning; but as a madman's epistles are no gospels, so it skills not much when they are delivered.
OLIVIA. Open it, and read it.
CLOWN. Look then to be well edified, when the fool delivers the madman.
'By the Lord, madam,'—
OLIVIA. How now! Art thou mad?
CLOWN. No, madam, I do but read madness: an your ladyship will have it as it ought to be, you must allow vox.
OLIVIA. Prithee, read i' thy right wits.
CLOWN. So I do, madonna; but to read his right wits is to read thus: therefore perpend, my princess, and give ear.
OLIVIA. (*To Fabian*) Read it you, sirrah.
FABIAN. (*Reads*) 'By the Lord, madam, you wrong me, and the world shall know it: though you have put me into darkness, and given your drunken cousin rule over me, yet have I the benefit of my senses as well as your ladyship. I have your own letter that induced me to the semblance I put on; with the which I doubt not but to do myself much right, or you much shame. Think of me as you please. I leave my duty a little unthought of, and speak out of my injury.
'The madly-used Malvolio.'

OLIVIA. Did he write this?
CLOWN. Ay, madam.
DUKE. This savours not much of distraction.
OLIVIA. See him deliver'd, Fabian; bring him hither.
Exit Fabian
  My lord, so please you, these things further thought on,
  To think me as well a sister as a wife,
  One day shall crown the alliance on 't, so please you,
  Here at my house and at my proper cost.
DUKE. Madam, I am most apt to embrace your offer.
  (*To Viola*) Your master quits you; and, for your service done him,
  So much against the mettle of your sex,
  So far beneath your soft and tender breeding;
  And since you call'd me master for so long,
  Here is my hand: you shall from this time be
  Your master's mistress.
OLIVIA.   A sister! you are she.
      Re-enter Fabian, with Malvolio
DUKE. Is this the madman?
OLIVIA.   Ay, my lord, this same.
  How now, Malvolio!
MALVOLIO.   Madam, you have done me wrong,
  Notorious wrong.
OLIVIA.   Have I, Malvolio? No.
MALVOLIO. Lady, you have. Pray you peruse that letter.
  You must not now deny it is your hand:
  Write from it, if you can, in hand or phrase,
  Or say 'tis not your seal nor your invention:
  You can say none of this. Well, grant it then,
  And tell me, in the modesty of honour,
  Why you have given me such clear lights of favour,
  Bade me come smiling and cross-garter'd to you,
  To put on yellow stockings, and to frown
  Upon Sir Toby and the lighter people;
  And, acting this in an obedient hope,
  Why have you suffer'd me to be imprison'd,
  Kept in a dark house, visited by the priest,
  And made the most notorious geck and gull
  That e'er invention play'd on? Tell me why.
OLIVIA. Alas! Malvolio, this is not my writing,
  Though, I confess, much like the character;

But, out of question, 'tis Maria's hand:
And now I do bethink me, it was she
First told me thou wast mad; then cam'st in smiling,
And in such forms which here were presuppos'd
Upon thee in the letter. Prithee, be content:
This practice hath most shrewdly pass'd upon thee;
But when we know the grounds and authors of it,
Thou shalt be both the plaintiff and the judge
Of thine own cause.
FABIAN.   Good madam, hear me speak,
And let no quarrel nor no brawl to come
Taint the condition of this present hour,
Which I have wonder'd at. In hope it shall not,
Most freely I confess, myself and Toby
Set this device against Malvolio here,
Upon some stubborn and uncourteous parts
We had conceiv'd against him. Maria writ
The letter at Sir Toby's great importance;
In recompense whereof he hath married her.
How with a sportful malice it was follow'd,
May rather pluck on laughter than revenge,
If that the injuries be justly weigh'd
That have on both sides past.
OLIVIA. Alas, poor fool, how have they baffled thee!
CLOWN. Why, 'some are born great, some achieve greatness, and some have greatness thrown upon them.' I was one, sir, in this interlude; one Sir Topas, sir; but that's all one. 'By the Lord, fool, I am not mad': But do you remember? 'Madam, why laugh you at such a barren rascal? An you smile not, he's gagged': and thus the whirligig of time brings in his revenges.
MALVOLIO. I'll be reveng'd on the whole pack of you. *Exit*
OLIVIA. He hath been most notoriously abus'd.
DUKE. Pursue him, and entreat him to a peace;—
He hath not told us of the captain yet:
When that is known and golden time convents,
A solemn combination shall be made
Of our dear souls. Meantime, sweet sister,
We will not part from hence. Cesario, come;
For so you shall be, while you are a man;
But when in other habits you are seen,
Orsino's mistress, and his fancy's queen.
Exeunt all except Clown

SONG

CLOWN. When that I was and a little tiny boy,
    With hey, ho, the wind and the rain;
A foolish thing was but a toy,
    For the rain it raineth every day.

But when I came to man's estate,
    With hey, ho, the wind and the rain;
'Gainst knaves and thieves men shut their gates,
    For the rain it raineth every day.

But when I came, alas! to wive,
    With hey, ho, the wind and the rain;
By swaggering could I never thrive,
    For the rain it raineth every day.

But when I came unto my beds,
    With hey, ho, the wind and the rain;
With toss-pots still had drunken heads,
    For the rain it raineth every day.

A great while ago the world begun,
    With hey, ho, the wind and the rain;
But that's all one, our play is done,
    And we'll strive to please you every day. *Exit*

THE WINTER'S TALE

CAST OF CHARACTERS

LEONTES, *King of Sicilia*
MAMILLIUS, *young Prince of Sicilia*

CAMILLO
ANTIGONUS } *Lords of Sicilia*
CLEOMENES
DION

POLIXENES, *King of Bohemia*
FLORIZEL, *his Son*
ARCHIDAMUS, *a Lord of Bohemia*

A Mariner
A Gaoler
An old Shepherd, reputed Father of Perdita
Clown, his Son
Servant to the old Shepherd

AUTOLYCUS, *a Rogue*

HERMIONE, *Queen to Leontes*
PERDITA, *Daughter to Leontes and Hermione*
PAULINA, *Wife to Antigonus*

EMILIA, *a Lady* } *attending the Queen*
Other Ladies

MOPSA } *Shepherdesses*
DORCAS

Sicilian Lords and Ladies, Attendants, Guards, Satyrs, Shepherds, Shepherdesses, &c.

Time, as Chorus

SCENE

Sometimes in Sicilia, sometimes in Bohemia

THE WINTER'S TALE

ACT ONE

SCENE ONE

Sicilia. An Antechamber in Leontes' Palace.

Enter Camillo and Archidamus

ARCHIDAMUS. If you shall chance, Camillo, to visit Bohemia, on the like occasion whereon my services are now on foot, you shall see, as I have said, great difference betwixt our Bohemia and your Sicilia.

CAMILLO. I think, this coming summer, the King of Sicilia means to pay Bohemia the visitation which he justly owes him.

ARCHIDAMUS. Wherein our entertainment shall shame us we will be justified in our loves: for, indeed,—

CAMILLO. Beseech you,—

ARCHIDAMUS. Verily, I speak it in the freedom of my knowledge: we cannot with such magnificence—in so rare—I know not what to say. We will give you sleepy drinks, that your senses, unintelligent of our insufficiency, may, though they cannot praise us. as little accuse us.

CAMILLO. You pay a great deal too dear for what's given freely.

ARCHIDAMUS. Believe me, I speak as my understanding instructs me, and as mine honesty puts it to utterance.

CAMILLO. Sicilia cannot show himself over-kind to Bohemia. They were trained together in their childhoods; and there rooted betwixt them then such an affection which cannot choose but branch now. Since their more mature dignities and royal necessities made separation of their society, their encounters, though not personal, have been royally attorneyed with interchange of gifts, letters, loving embassies; that they have seemed to be together, though absent, shook hands, as over a vast, and embraced, as it were, from the ends of opposed winds. The heavens continue their loves!

ARCHIDAMUS. I think there is not in the world either malice or matter to alter it. You have an unspeakable comfort of your young Prince Mamillius: it is a gentleman of the greatest promise that ever came into my note.

CAMILLO. I very well agree with you in the hopes of him. It is a gallant child; one that indeed physics the subject, makes old hearts fresh; they that went on crutches ere he was born desire yet their life to see him a man.

ARCHIDAMUS. Would they else be content to die?

CAMILLO. Yes; if there were no other excuse why they should desire to live.

ARCHIDAMUS. If the king had no son, they would desire to live on crutches till he had one. *Exeunt*

SCENE TWO

The Same. A Room of State in the Palace.

Enter Leontes, Polixenes, Hermione, Mamillius, Camillo, and Attendants

POLIXENES. Nine changes of the watery star have been
The shepherd's note since we have left our throne
Without a burden. Time as long again
Would be fill'd up, my brother, with our thanks;
And yet we should for perpetuity
Go hence in debt: and therefore, like a cipher,
Yet standing in rich place, I multiply
With one 'We thank you' many thousands moe
That go before it.

LEONTES. 	Stay your thanks awhile,
And pay them when you part.

POLIXENES. 	Sir, that's to-morrow.
I am question'd by my fears, of what may chance
Or breed upon our absence; that may blow
No sneaping winds at home, to make us say,
'This is put forth too truly!' Besides, I have stay'd
To tire your royalty.

ACT I · SCENE II

LEONTES.   We are tougher, brother,
  Than you can put us to 't.
POLIXENES.   No longer stay.
LEONTES. One seven-night longer.
POLIXENES.   Very sooth, to-morrow.
LEONTES. We 'll part the time between 's then; and in that
  I 'll no gainsaying.
POLIXENES.   Press me not, beseech you, so.
  There is no tongue that moves, none, none i' the world,
  So soon as yours could win me: so it should now,
  Were there necessity in your request, although
  'Twere needful I denied it. My affairs
  Do even drag me homeward; which to hinder
  Were in your love a whip to me; my stay
  To you a charge and trouble: to save both,
  Farewell, our brother.
LEONTES.   Tongue-tied, our queen? Speak you.
HERMIONE. I had thought, sir, to have held my peace until
  You had drawn oaths from him not to stay. You, sir,
  Charge him too coldly: tell him, you are sure
  All in Bohemia 's well: this satisfaction
  The by-gone day proclaim'd: say this to him,
  He 's beat from his best ward.
LEONTES.   Well said, Hermione.
HERMIONE. To tell he longs to see his son were strong:
  But let him say so then, and let him go;
  But let him swear so, and he shall not stay,
  We 'll thwack him hence with distaffs.
  (*To Polixenes*) Yet of your royal presence I 'll adventure
  The borrow of a week. When at Bohemia
  You take my lord, I 'll give him my commission
  To let him there a month behind the gest
  Prefix'd for 's parting: yet, good deed, Leontes,
  I love thee not a jar o' the clock behind
  What lady she her lord. You 'll stay?
POLIXENES.   No, madam.
HERMIONE. Nay, but you will?
POLIXENES.   I may not, verily.
HERMIONE. Verily!
  You put me off with limber vows; but I,
  Though you would seek to unsphere the stars with oaths,
  Should yet say, 'Sir, no going.' Verily,

You shall not go: a lady's 'verily' 's
As potent as a lord's. Will you go yet?
Force me to keep you as a prisoner,
Not like a guest; so you shall pay your fees
When you depart, and save your thanks. How say you?
My prisoner, or my guest? By your dread 'verily,'
One of them you shall be.

POLIXENES. Your guest, then, madam:
To be your prisoner should import offending;
Which is for me less easy to commit
Than you to punish.

HERMIONE. Not your gaoler then,
But your kind hostess. Come, I'll question you
Of my lord's tricks and yours when you were boys.
You were pretty lordings then?

POLIXENES. We were, fair queen,
Two lads that thought there was no more behind
But such a day to-morrow as to-day,
And to be boy eternal.

HERMIONE. Was not my lord the verier wag o' the two?

POLIXENES. We were as twinn'd lambs that did frisk i' the sun,
And bleat the one at the other: what we chang'd
Was innocence for innocence; we knew not
The doctrine of ill-doing, nor dream'd
That any did. Had we pursu'd that life,
And our weak spirits ne'er been higher rear'd
With stronger blood, we should have answer'd heaven
Boldly, 'not guilty'; the imposition clear'd
Hereditary ours.

HERMIONE. By this we gather
You have tripp'd since.

POLIXENES. O! my most sacred lady,
Temptations have since then been born to 's; for
In those unfledg'd days was my wife a girl;
Your precious self had then not cross'd the eyes
Of my young playfellow.

HERMIONE. Grace to boot!
Of this make no conclusion, lest you say
Your queen and I are devils; yet go on:
The offences we have made you do we'll answer;
If you first sinn'd with us, and that with us

ACT I · SCENE II

You did continue fault, and that you slipp'd not
With any but with us.
LEONTES.   Is he won yet?
HERMIONE. He 'll stay, my lord.
LEONTES.   At my request he would **not**
Hermione, my dearest, thou never spok'st
To better purpose.
HERMIONE.   Never?
LEONTES.   Never, but once.
HERMIONE. What! have I twice said well? When was 't
  before?
I prithee tell me; cram 's with praise, and make 's
As fat as tame things: one good deed, dying tongueless,
Slaughters a thousand waiting upon that.
Our praises are our wages: you may ride 's
With one soft kiss a thousand furlongs ere
With spur we heat an acre. But to the goal:
My last good deed was to entreat his stay:
What was my first? It has an elder sister,
Or I mistake you: O! would her name were Grace.
But once before I spoke to the purpose. When?
Nay, let me have 't; I long.
LEONTES.   Why, that was when
Three crabbed months had sour'd themselves to death,
Ere I could make thee open thy white hand
And clap thyself my love: then didst thou utter,
'I am yours for ever.'
HERMIONE.   'Tis grace indeed.
Why, lo you now, I have spoke to the purpose twice.
The one for ever earn'd a royal husband,
The other for some while a friend.
                              Giving her hand to Polixenes
LEONTES. (*Aside*) Too hot, too hot!
To mingle friendship far is mingling bloods.
I have tremor cordis on me: my heart dances;
But not for joy; not joy. This entertainment
May a free face put on, derive a liberty
From heartiness, from bounty, fertile bosom,
And well become the agent: 't may I grant:
But to be paddling palms and pinching fingers,
As now they are, and making practis'd smiles,
As in a looking-glass; and then to sigh, as 'twere

The mort o' the deer; O! that is entertainment
My bosom likes not, nor my brows. Mamillius,
Art thou my boy?
MAMILLIUS. Ay, my good lord.
LEONTES. I' fecks?
Why, that's my bawcock. What! hast smutch'd thy nose?
They say it is a copy out of mine. Come, captain,
We must be neat; not neat, but cleanly, captain:
And yet the steer, the heifer, and the calf,
Are all call'd neat. Still virginalling
Upon his palm! How now, you wanton calf!
Art thou my calf?
MAMILLIUS. Yes, if you will, my lord.
LEONTES. Thou want'st a rough pash and the shoots that I have,
To be full like me: yet they say we are
Almost as like as eggs; women say so,
That will say anything: but were they false
As o'er-dy'd blacks, as wind, as waters, false
As dice are to be wish'd by one that fixes
No bourn 'twixt his and mine, yet were it true
To say this boy were like me. Come, sir page,
Look on me with your welkin eye: sweet villain!
Most dear'st! my collop! Can thy dam?—may 't be?—
Affection! thy intention stabs the centre:
Thou dost make possible things not so held,
Communicat'st with dreams;—how can this be?—
With what's unreal thou co-active art,
And fellow'st nothing: then, 'tis very credent
Thou mayst co-join with something; and thou dost,
And that beyond commission, and I find it,
And that to the infection of my brains
And hardening of my brows.
POLIXENES. What means Sicilia?
HERMIONE. He something seems unsettled.
POLIXENES. How, my lord!
What cheer? how is 't with you, best brother?
HERMIONE. You look
As if you held a brow of much distraction:
Are you mov'd, my lord?
LEONTES. No, in good earnest.
How sometimes nature will betray its folly,

Its tenderness, and make itself a pastime
To harder bosoms! Looking on the lines
Of my boy's face, methoughts I did recoil
Twenty-three years, and saw myself unbreech'd,
In my green velvet coat, my dagger muzzled,
Lest it should bite its master, and so prove,
As ornaments oft do, too dangerous:
How like, methought, I then was to this kernel,
This squash, this gentleman. Mine honest friend,
Will you take eggs for money?
MAMILLIUS. No, my lord, I'll fight.
LEONTES. You will? Why, happy man be his dole! My brother,
Are you so fond of your young prince as we
Do seem to be of ours?
POLIXENES. If at home, sir,
He's all my exercise, my mirth, my matter,
Now my sworn friend and then mine enemy;
My parasite, my soldier, statesman, all:
He makes a July's day short as December,
And with his varying childness cures in me
Thoughts that would thick my blood.
LEONTES. So stands this squire
Offic'd with me. We two will walk, my lord,
And leave you to your graver steps. Hermione,
How thou lov'st us, show in our brother's welcome:
Let what is dear in Sicily be cheap:
Next to thyself and my young rover, he's
Apparent to my heart.
HERMIONE. If you would seek us,
We are yours i' the garden: shall's attend you there?
LEONTES. To your own bents dispose you: you'll be found,
Be you beneath the sky.—(*Aside*) I am angling now,
Though you perceive me not how I give line.
Go to, go to!
How she holds up the neb, the bill to him!
And arms her with the boldness of a wife
To her allowing husband!
Exeunt Polixenes, Hermione, and Attendants
Gone already!
Inch-thick, knee-deep, o'er head and ears a fork'd one!
Go play, boy, play; thy mother plays, and I

Play too, but so disgrac'd a part, whose issue
Will hiss me to my grave: contempt and clamour
Will be my knell. Go play, boy, play. There have been,
Or I am much deceiv'd, cuckolds ere now;
And many a man there is even at this present,
Now, while I speak this, holds his wife by the arm,
That little thinks she has been sluic'd in 's absence,
And his pond fish'd by his next neighbour, by
Sir Smile, his neighbour: nay, there's comfort in 't,
Whiles other men have gates, and those gates open'd,
As mine, against their will. Should all despair
That have revolted wives, the tenth of mankind
Would hang themselves. Physic for 't there is none;
It is a bawdy planet, that will strike
Where 'tis predominant; and 'tis powerful, think it,
From east, west, north, and south: be it concluded,
No barricado for a belly: know 't;
It will let in and out the enemy
With bag and baggage. Many a thousand on 's
Have the disease, and feel 't not. How now, boy!

MAMILLIUS. I am like you, they say.
LEONTES.   Why, that's some comfort.
What! Camillo there?
CAMILLO. Ay, my good lord.
LEONTES. Go play, Mamillius; thou 'rt an honest man.

Exit Mamillius

Camillo, this great sir will yet stay longer.
CAMILLO. You had much ado to make his anchor hold:
When you cast out, it still came home.
LEONTES.   Didst note it?
CAMILLO. He would not stay at your petitions; made
His business more material.
LEONTES.   Didst perceive it?
(*Aside*) They 're here with me already, whispering, rounding
'Sicilia is a so-forth.' 'Tis far gone,
When I shall gust it last. How came 't, Camillo,
That he did stay?
CAMILLO.   At the good queen's entreaty.
LEONTES. At the queen's, be 't: 'good' should be pertinent;
But so it is, it is not. Was this taken
By any understanding pate but thine?

For thy conceit is soaking; will draw in
More than the common blocks. Not noted, is 't,
But of the finer natures? by some severals
Of head-piece extraordinary? Lower messes
Perchance are to this business purblind? Say.

CAMILLO. Business, my lord! I think most understand
Bohemia stays here longer.

LEONTES. Ha!

CAMILLO. Stays here longer.

LEONTES. Ay, but why?

CAMILLO. To satisfy your Highness and the entreaties
Of our most gracious mistress.

LEONTES. Satisfy!
The entreaties of your mistress! satisfy!
Let that suffice. I have trusted thee, Camillo,
With all the nearest things to my heart, as well
My chamber-councils, wherein, priest-like, thou
Hast cleans'd my bosom: I from thee departed
Thy penitent reform'd; but we have been
Deceiv'd in thy integrity, deceiv'd
In that which seems so.

CAMILLO. Be it forbid, my lord!

LEONTES. To bide upon 't, thou art not honest; or,
If thou inclin'st that way, thou art a coward,
Which hoxes honesty behind, restraining
From course requir'd; or else thou must be counted
A servant grafted in my serious trust,
And therein negligent; or else a fool
That seest a game play'd home, the rich stake drawn,
And tak'st it all for jest.

CAMILLO. My gracious lord,
I may be negligent, foolish, and fearful;
In every one of these no man is free,
But that his negligence, his folly, fear,
Among the infinite doings of the world,
Sometime puts forth. In your affairs, my lord,
If ever I were wilful-negligent,
It was my folly; if industriously
I play'd the fool, it was my negligence,
Not weighing well the end; if ever fearful
To do a thing, where I the issue doubted,
Whereof the execution did cry out

Against the non-performance, 'twas a fear
Which oft infects the wisest: these, my lord,
Are such allow'd infirmities that honesty
Is never free of: but, beseech your Grace,
Be plainer with me; let me know my trespass
By its own visage; if I then deny it,
'Tis none of mine.
LEONTES. Ha' not you seen, Camillo,—
But that's past doubt; you have, or your eye-glass
Is thicker than a cuckold's horn,—or heard,—
For to a vision so apparent rumour
Cannot be mute,—or thought,—for cogitation
Resides not in that man that does not think,—
My wife is slippery? If thou wilt confess,—
Or else be impudently negative,
To have nor eyes, nor ears, nor thought,—then say
My wife's a hobby-horse; deserves a name
As rank as any flax-wench that puts to
Before her troth-plight: say 't and justify 't.
CAMILLO. I would not be a stander-by, to hear
My sovereign mistress clouded so, without
My present vengeance taken: 'shrew my heart,
You never spoke what did become you less
Than this; which to reiterate were sin
As deep as that, though true.
LEONTES. Is whispering nothing?
Is leaning cheek to cheek? Is meeting noses?
Kissing with inside lip? stopping the career
Of laughter with a sigh?—a note infallible
Of breaking honesty,—horsing foot on foot?
Skulking in corners? wishing clocks more swift?
Hours, minutes? noon, midnight? and all eyes
Blind with the pin and web but theirs, theirs only,
That would unseen be wicked? Is this nothing?
Why, then the world and all that's in 't is nothing;
The covering sky is nothing; Bohemia nothing;
My wife is nothing; nor nothing have these nothings,
If this be nothing.
CAMILLO. Good my lord, be cur'd
Of this diseas'd opinion, and betimes;
For 'tis most dangerous.
LEONTES. Say it be, 'tis true.

CAMILLO. No, no, my lord.
LEONTES. It is; you lie, you lie:
  I say thou liest, Camillo, and I hate thee;
  Pronounce thee a gross lout, a mindless slave,
  Or else a hovering temporizer, that
  Canst with thine eyes at once see good and evil,
  Inclining to them both: were my wife's liver
  Infected as her life, she would not live
  The running of one glass.
CAMILLO.   Who does infect her?
LEONTES. Why, he that wears her like her medal, hanging
  About his neck, Bohemia: who, if I
  Had servants true about me, that bare eyes
  To see alike mine honour as their profits,
  Their own particular thrifts, they would do that
  Which should undo more doing: ay, and thou,
  His cup-bearer,—whom I from meaner form
  Have bench'd and rear'd to worship, who mayst see
  Plainly, as heaven sees earth, and earth sees heaven,
  How I am galled,—mightst bespice a cup,
  To give mine enemy a lasting wink;
  Which draught to me were cordial.
CAMILLO.   Sir, my lord,
  I could do this, and that with no rash potion,
  But with a lingering dram that should not work
  Maliciously like poison: but I cannot
  Believe this crack to be in my dread mistress,
  So sovereignly being honourable.
  I have lov'd thee,—
LEONTES.   Make that thy question, and go rot!
  Dost think I am so muddy, so unsettled,
  To appoint myself in this vexation; sully
  The purity and whiteness of my sheets,
  Which to preserve is sleep; which being spotted
  Is goads, thorns, nettles, tails of wasps?
  Give scandal to the blood o' the prince my son,
  Who I do think is mine, and love as mine,
  Without ripe moving to 't? Would I do this?
  Could man so blench?
CAMILLO.   I must believe you, sir:
  I do; and will fetch off Bohemia for 't;
  Provided that when he's remov'd, your Highness

Will take again your queen as yours at first,
Even for your son's sake; and thereby for sealing
The injury of tongues in courts and kingdoms
Known and allied to yours.

LEONTES.   Thou dost advise me
Even so as I mine own course have set down:
I'll give no blemish to her honour, none.

CAMILLO. My lord,
Go then; and with a countenance as clear
As friendship wears at feasts, keep with Bohemia,
And with your queen. I am his cup-bearer;
If from me he have wholesome beverage,
Account me not your servant.

LEONTES.   This is all:
Do 't, and thou hast the one half of my heart;
Do 't not, thou split'st thine own.

CAMILLO.   I'll do 't, my lord.

LEONTES. I will seem friendly, as thou hast advis'd me. *Exit*

CAMILLO. O miserable lady! But, for me,
What case stand I in? I must be the poisoner
Of good Polixenes; and my ground to do 't
Is the obedience to a master; one
Who, in rebellion with himself will have
All that are his so too. To do this deed
Promotion follows. If I could find example
Of thousands that had struck anointed kings,
And flourish'd after, I'd not do 't; but since
Nor brass nor stone nor parchment bears not one,
Let villany itself forswear 't. I must
Forsake the court: to do 't, or no, is certain
To me a break-neck. Happy star reign now!
Here comes Bohemia.

Re-enter Polixenes

POLIXENES.   This is strange: methinks
My favour here begins to warp. Not speak?—
Good day, Camillo.

CAMILLO.   Hail, most royal sir!

POLIXENES. What is the news i' the court?

CAMILLO.   None rare, my lord.

POLIXENES. The king hath on him such a countenance
As he had lost some province and a region
Lov'd as he loves himself: even now I met him

With customary compliment, when he,
Wafting his eyes to the contrary, and falling
A lip of much contempt, speeds from me and
So leaves me to consider what is breeding
That changes thus his manners.

CAMILLO. I dare not know, my lord.

POLIXENES. How! dare not! do not! Do you know, and dare not
Be intelligent to me? 'Tis thereabouts;
For, to yourself, what you do know, you must,
And cannot say you dare not. Good Camillo,
Your chang'd complexions are to me a mirror
Which shows me mine chang'd too; for I must be
A party in this alteration, finding
Myself thus alter'd with 't.

CAMILLO. There is a sickness
Which puts some of us in distemper; but
I cannot name the disease, and it is caught
Of you that yet are well.

POLIXENES. How! caught of me?
Make me not sighted like the basilisk:
I have look'd on thousands, who have sped the better
By my regard, but kill'd none so. Camillo,—
As you are certainly a gentleman, thereto
Clerk-like experienc'd, which no less adorns
Our gentry than our parents' noble names,
In whose success we are gentle,—I beseech you,
If you know aught which does behove my knowledge
Thereof to be inform'd, imprison it not
In ignorant concealment.

CAMILLO. I may not answer.

POLIXENES. A sickness caught of me, and yet I well!
I must be answer'd. Dost thou hear, Camillo;
I conjure thee, by all the parts of man
Which honour does acknowledge,—whereof the least
Is not this suit of mine,—that thou declare
What incidency thou dost guess of harm
Is creeping toward me; how far off, how near;
Which way to be prevented if to be;
If not, how best to bear it.

CAMILLO. Sir, I will tell you;
Since I am charg'd in honour and by him

That I think honourable. Therefore mark my counsel,
Which must be even as swiftly follow'd as
I mean to utter it, or both yourself and me
Cry 'lost,' and so good-night!

POLIXENES. On, good Camillo.
CAMILLO. I am appointed him to murder you.
POLIXENES. By whom, Camillo?
CAMILLO. By the king.
POLIXENES. For what?
CAMILLO. He thinks, nay, with all confidence he swears,
As he had seen 't or been an instrument
To vice you to 't, that you have touch'd his queen
Forbiddenly.
POLIXENES. O, then my best blood turn
To an infected jelly, and my name
Be yok'd with his that did betray the Best!
Turn then my freshest reputation to
A savour, that may strike the dullest nostril
Where I arrive; and my approach be shunn'd,
Nay, hated too, worse than the great'st infection
That e'er was heard or read!
CAMILLO. Swear his thought over
By each particular star in heaven and
By all their influences, you may as well
Forbid the sea for to obey the moon
As or by oath remove or counsel shake
The fabric of his folly, whose foundation
Is pil'd upon his faith, and will continue
The standing of his body.
POLIXENES. How should this grow?
CAMILLO. I know not: but I am sure 'tis safer to
Avoid what 's grown than question how 'tis born.
If therefore you dare trust my honesty,
That lies enclosed in this trunk, which you
Shall bear along impawn'd, away to-night!
Your followers I will whisper to the business,
And will by twos and threes at several posterns
Clear them o' the city. For myself, I'll put
My fortunes to your service, which are here
By this discovery lost. Be not uncertain;
For, by the honour of my parents, I
Have utter'd truth, which, if you seek to prove,

I dare not stand by; nor shall you be safer
Than one condemn'd by the king's own mouth, thereon
His execution sworn.
POLIXENES. I do believe thee:
I saw his heart in 's face. Give me thy hand:
Be pilot to me and thy places shall
Still neighbour mine. My ships are ready and
My people did expect my hence departure
Two days ago. This jealousy
Is for a precious creature: as she 's rare
Must it be great, and, as his person 's mighty
Must it be violent, and, as he does conceive
He is dishonour'd by a man which ever
Profess'd to him, why, his revenges must
In that be made more bitter. Fear o'ershades me:
Good expedition be my friend, and comfort
The gracious queen, part of his theme, but nothing
Of his ill-ta'en suspicion! Come, Camillo;
I will respect thee as a father if
Thou bear'st my life off hence: let us avoid.
CAMILLO. It is in mine authority to command
The keys of all the posterns: please your Highness
To take the urgent hour. Come, sir, away! *Exeunt*

ACT TWO

SCENE ONE

Sicilia. A Room in the Palace.

Enter Hermione, Mamillius, and Ladies

HERMIONE. Take the boy to you: he so troubles me,
'Tis past enduring.
FIRST LADY. Come, my gracious lord,
Shall I be your playfellow?
MAMILLIUS. No, I'll none of you.
FIRST LADY. Why, my sweet lord?
MAMILLIUS. You'll kiss me hard and speak to me as if
I were a baby still. I love you better.
SECOND LADY. And why so, my lord?
MAMILLIUS. Not for because
Your brows are blacker; yet black brows, they say,
Become some women best, so that there be not
Too much hair there, but in a semicircle,
Or a half-moon made with a pen.
SECOND LADY. Who taught you this?
MAMILLIUS. I learn'd it out of women's faces. Pray now,
What colour are your eyebrows?
FIRST LADY. Blue, my lord.
MAMILLIUS. Nay, that's a mock: I have seen a lady's nose
That has been blue, but not her eyebrows.
SECOND LADY. Hark ye;
The queen your mother rounds apace: we shall
Present our services to a fine new prince
One of these days; and then you'd wanton with us,
If we would have you.
FIRST LADY. She is spread of late
Into a goodly bulk: good time encounter her!
HERMIONE. What wisdom stirs amongst you? Come sir, now
I am for you again: pray you, sit by us,

And tell 's a tale.
MAMILLIUS. Merry or sad shall 't be?
HERMIONE. As merry as you will.
MAMILLIUS. A sad tale 's best for winter.
I have one of sprites and goblins.
HERMIONE. Let 's have that, good sir.
Come on, sit down: come on, and do your best
To fright me with your sprites; you 're powerful at it.
MAMILLIUS. There was a man,—
HERMIONE. Nay, come, sit down; then on.
MAMILLIUS. Dwelt by a churchyard. I will tell it softly;
Yond crickets shall not hear it.
HERMIONE. Come on then,
And give 't me in mine ear.

Enter Leontes, Antigonus, Lords, and Others

LEONTES. Was he met there? his train? Camillo with him?
FIRST LORD. Behind the tuft of pines I met them: never
Saw I men scour so on their way: I ey'd them
Even to their ships.
LEONTES. How blest am I
In my just censure, in my true opinion!
Alack, for lesser knowledge! How accurs'd
In being so blest! There may be in the cup
A spider steep'd, and one may drink, depart,
And yet partake no venom, for his knowledge
Is not infected; but if one present
The abhorr'd ingredient to his eye, make known
How he hath drunk, he cracks his gorge, his sides,
With violent hefts. I have drunk, and seen the spider.
Camillo was his help in this, his pandar:
There is a plot against my life, my crown;
All 's true that is mistrusted: that false villain
Whom I employ'd was pre-employ'd by him:
He has discover'd my design, and I
Remain a pinch'd thing; yea, a very trick
For them to play at will. How came the posterns
So easily open?
FIRST LORD. By his great authority;
Which often hath no less prevail'd than so
On your command.
LEONTES. I know 't too well.

(*To Hermione*) Give me the boy: I am glad you did not
  nurse him:
Though he does bear some signs of me, yet you
Have too much blood in him.

HERMIONE. What is this? sport?

LEONTES. Bear the boy hence; he shall not come about her;
  Away with him!—(*Exit Mamillius, attended*) and let her
    sport herself
  With that she's big with; for 'tis Polixenes
  Has made thee swell thus.

HERMIONE. But I'd say he had not,
  And I'll be sworn you would believe my saying,
  Howe'er you lean to the nayward.

LEONTES. You, my lords,
  Look on her, mark her well; be but about
  To say, 'she is a goodly lady,' and
  The justice of your hearts will thereto add
  ''Tis pity she's not honest, honourable':
  Praise her but for this her without-door form,—
  Which on my faith deserves high speech,—and straight
  The shrug, the hum or ha, these petty brands
  That calumny doth use,—O, I am out!—
  That mercy does, for calumny will sear
  Virtue itself: these shrugs, these hums and ha's,
  When you have said 'she's goodly,' come between
  Ere you can say 'she's honest.' But be 't known,
  From him that has most cause to grieve it should be,
  She's an adulteress.

HERMIONE. Should a villain say so,
  The most replenish'd villain in the world,
  He were as much more villain: you, my lord,
  Do but mistake.

LEONTES. You have mistook, my lady,
  Polixenes for Leontes. O thou thing!
  Which I'll not call a creature of thy place,
  Lest barbarism, making me the precedent,
  Should a like language use to all degrees,
  And mannerly distinguishment leave out
  Betwixt the prince and beggar: I have said
  She's an adulteress; I have said with whom:
  More, she's a traitor, and Camillo is
  A federary with her, and one that knows

> What she should shame to know herself
> But with her most vile principal, that she's
> A bed-swerver, even as bad as those
> That vulgars give bold'st titles; ay, and privy
> To this their late escape.
>
> HERMIONE. No, by my life,
> Privy to none of this. How will this grieve you
> When you shall come to clearer knowledge that
> You thus have publish'd me! Gentle my lord,
> You scarce can right me throughly then to say
> You did mistake.
>
> LEONTES. No; if I mistake
> In those foundations which I build upon,
> The centre is not big enough to bear
> A schoolboy's top. Away with her to prison!
> He who shall speak for her is afar off guilty
> But that he speaks.
>
> HERMIONE. There 's some ill planet reigns:
> I must be patient till the heavens look
> With an aspect more favourable. Good my lords,
> I am not prone to weeping, as our sex
> Commonly are; the want of which vain dew
> Perchance shall dry your pities; but I have
> That honourable grief lodg'd here which burns
> Worse than tears drown. Beseech you all, my lords,
> With thoughts so qualified as your charities
> Shall best instruct you, measure me; and so
> The king's will be perform'd!
>
> LEONTES. *(To the Guards)* Shall I be heard?
>
> HERMIONE. Who is 't that goes with me? Beseech your Highness,
> My women may be with me; for you see
> My plight requires it. Do not weep, good fools;
> There is no cause: when you shall know your mistress
> Has deserv'd prison, then abound in tears
> As I come out: this action I now go on
> Is for my better grace. Adieu, my lord:
> I never wish'd to see you sorry; now
> I trust I shall. My women, come; you have leave.
>
> LEONTES. Go, do our bidding: hence!
>
> *Exeunt Queen guarded, and Ladies*
>
> FIRST LORD. Beseech your Highness call the queen again.

ANTIGONUS. Be certain what you do, sir, lest your justice
  Prove violence: in the which three great ones suffer,
  Yourself, your queen, your son.
FIRST LORD.   For her, my lord,
  I dare my life lay down, and will do 't, sir,
  Please you to accept it,—that the queen is spotless
  I' the eyes of heaven and to you: I mean,
  In this which you accuse her.
ANTIGONUS.   If it prove
  She 's otherwise, I 'll keep my stables where
  I lodge my wife; I 'll go in couples with her;
  Than when I feel and see her no further trust her;
  For every inch of woman in the world,
  Ay, every dram of woman's flesh is false,
  If she be.
LEONTES.   Hold your peaces!
FIRST LORD.   Good my lord,—
ANTIGONUS. It is for you we speak, not for ourselves.
  You are abus'd, and by some putter-on
  That will be damn'd for 't; would I knew the villain,
  I would land-damn him. Be she honour-flaw'd,—
  I have three daughters; the eldest is eleven,
  The second and the third, nine and some five;
  If this prove true, they 'll pay for 't: by mine honour,
  I 'll geld thee all; fourteen they shall not see,
  To bring false generations: they are co-heirs;
  And I had rather glib myself than they
  Should not produce fair issue.
LEONTES.   Cease! no more.
  You smell this business with a sense as cold
  As is a dead man's nose; but I do see 't and feel 't,
  As you feel doing thus, and see withal
  The instruments that feel.
ANTIGONUS.   If it be so,
  We need no grave to bury honesty:
  There 's not a grain of it the face to sweeten
  Of the whole dungy earth.
LEONTES.   What! lack I credit?
FIRST LORD. I had rather you did lack than I, my lord,
  Upon this ground; and more it would content me
  To have her honour true than your suspicion,
  Be blam'd for 't how you might.

LEONTES. Why, what need we
Commune with you of this, but rather follow
Our forceful instigation? Our prerogative
Calls not your counsels, but our natural goodness
Imparts this; which, if you,—or stupefied
Or seeming so in skill,—cannot or will not
Relish a truth like us, inform yourselves
We need no more of your advice: the matter,
The loss, the gain, the ordering on 't, is all
Properly ours.

ANTIGONUS. And I wish, my liege,
You had only in your silent judgment tried it,
Without more overture.

LEONTES. How could that be?
Either thou art most ignorant by age,
Or thou wert born a fool. Camillo's flight,
Added to their familiarity,
Which was as gross as ever touch'd conjecture,
That lack'd sight only, naught for approbation
But only seeing, all other circumstances
Made up to the deed, doth push on this proceeding:
Yet, for a greater confirmation,—
For in an act of this importance 'twere
Most piteous to be wild,—I have dispatch'd in post
To sacred Delphos, to Apollo's temple,
Cleomenes and Dion, whom you know
Of stuff'd sufficiency. Now, from the oracle
They will bring all; whose spiritual counsel had,
Shall stop or spur me. Have I done well?

FIRST LORD. Well done, my lord.

LEONTES. Though I am satisfied and need no more
Than what I know, yet shall the oracle
Give rest to the minds of others, such as he
Whose ignorant credulity will not
Come up to the truth. So have we thought it good
From our free person she should be confin'd,
Lest that the treachery of the two fled hence
Be left her to perform. Come, follow us:
We are to speak in public; for this business
Will raise us all.

ANTIGONUS. (*Aside*) To laughter, as I take it,
If the good truth were known. *Exeunt*

SCENE TWO

The Same. The outer Room of a Prison.

Enter Paulina and Attendants

PAULINA. The keeper of the prison, call to him;
Let him have knowledge who I am.—*Exit an Attendant*
Good lady,
No court in Europe is too good for thee;
What dost thou then in prison?
    Re-enter Attendant, with the Gaoler
        Now, good sir,
You know me, do you not?
GAOLER.   For a worthy lady
And one whom much I honour.
PAULINA.   Pray you then,
Conduct me to the queen.
GAOLER. I may not, madam: to the contrary
I have express commandment.
PAULINA.   Here's ado,
To lock up honesty and honour from
The access of gentle visitors! Is 't lawful, pray you,
To see her women? any of them? Emilia?
GAOLER. So please you, madam,
To put apart these your attendants, I
Shall bring Emilia forth.
PAULINA.   I pray now, call her.
Withdraw yourselves.   *Exeunt Attendants*
GAOLER.   And, madam,
I must be present at your conference.
PAULINA. Well, be 't so, prithee.   *Exit Gaoler*
Here's such ado to make no stain a stain,
As passes colouring.
    Re-enter Gaoler, with Emilia
      Dear gentlewoman,
How fares our gracious lady?
EMILIA. As well as one so great and so forlorn
May hold together. On her frights and griefs,—
Which never tender lady hath borne greater,—
She is something before her time deliver'd.

PAULINA. A boy?
EMILIA. A daughter; and a goodly babe,
Lusty and like to live: the queen receives
Much comfort in 't; says, 'My poor prisoner,
I am innocent as you.'
PAULINA. I dare be sworn:
These dangerous unsafe lunes i' the king, beshrew them!
He must be told on 't, and he shall: the office
Becomes a woman best; I 'll take 't upon me.
If I prove honey-mouth'd, let my tongue blister,
And never to my red-look'd anger be
The trumpet any more. Pray you, Emilia,
Commend my best obedience to the queen.
If she dares trust me with her little babe,
I 'll show it to the king and undertake to be
Her advocate to the loud'st. We do not know
How he may soften at the sight of the child.
The silence often of pure innocence
Persuades when speaking fails.
EMILIA. Most worthy madam,
Your honour and your goodness is so evident
That your free undertaking cannot miss
A thriving issue: there is no lady living
So meet for this great errand. Please your ladyship
To visit the next room, I 'll presently
Acquaint the queen of your most noble offer,
Who but to-day hammer'd of this design,
But durst not tempt a minister of honour,
Lest she should be denied.
PAULINA. Tell her, Emilia,
I 'll use that tongue I have: if wit flow from 't
As boldness from my bosom, let it not be doubted
I shall do good.
EMILIA. Now be you blest for it!
I 'll to the queen. Please you, come something nearer.
GAOLER. Madam, if 't please the queen to send the babe,
I know not what I shall incur to pass it,
Having no warrant.
PAULINA. You need not fear it, sir:
The child was prisoner to the womb, and is
By law and process of great nature thence
Freed and enfranchis'd; not a party to

The anger of the king, nor guilty of,
If any be, the trespass of the queen.
GAOLER. I do believe it.
PAULINA. Do not you fear: upon mine honour, I
Will stand betwixt you and danger.   *Exeunt*

SCENE THREE

The Same. A Room in the Palace.

Enter Leontes, Antigonus, Lords, and other Attendants

LEONTES. Nor night, nor day, no rest; it is but weakness
To bear the matter thus; mere weakness. If
The cause were not in being,—part o' the cause,
She the adultress; for the harlot king
Is quite beyond mine arm, out of the blank
And level of my brain, plot-proof; but she
I can hook to me: say, that she were gone,
Given to the fire, a moiety of my rest
Might come to me again. Who 's there?
FIRST ATTENDANT.   (*Advancing*) My lord?
LEONTES. How does the boy?
FIRST ATTENDANT. He took good rest to-night;
'Tis hop'd his sickness is discharg'd.
LEONTES.   To see his nobleness!
Conceiving the dishonour of his mother,
He straight declin'd, droop'd, took it deeply,
Fasten'd and fix'd the shame on 't in himself,
Threw off his spirit, his appetite, his sleep,
And downright languish'd. Leave me solely: go,
See how he fares. (*Exit Attendant*)—Fie, fie! no thought
  of him;
The very thought of my revenges that way
Recoil upon me: in himself too mighty,
And in his parties, his alliance; let him be
Until a time may serve: for present vengeance,
Take it on her. Camillo and Polixenes
Laugh at me; make their pastime at my sorrow:
They should not laugh, if I could reach them, **nor**
Shall she within my power.
          Enter Paulina, with a Child

ACT II · SCENE III

FIRST LORD. You must not enter.
PAULINA. Nay, rather, good my lords, be second to me:
Fear you his tyrannous passion more, alas,
Than the queen's life? a gracious innocent soul,
More free than he is jealous.
ANTIGONUS. That's enough.
SECOND ATTENDANT. Madam, he hath not slept to-night; commanded
None should come at him.
PAULINA. Not so hot, good sir;
I come to bring him sleep. 'Tis such as you,
That creep like shadows by him and do sigh
At each his needless heavings, such as you
Nourish the cause of his awaking. I
Do come with words as med'cinal as true,
Honest as either, to purge him of that humour
That presses him from sleep.
LEONTES. What noise there, ho?
PAULINA. No noise, my lord; but needful conference
About some gossips for your Highness.
LEONTES. How!
Away with that audacious lady! Antigonus,
I charg'd thee that she should not come about me.
I knew she would.
ANTIGONUS. I told her so, my lord,
On your displeasure's peril, and on mine,
She should not visit you.
LEONTES. What! canst not rule her?
PAULINA. From all dishonesty he can: in this,
Unless he take the course that you have done,
Commit me for committing honour, trust it,
He shall not rule me.
ANTIGONUS. La you now! you hear;
When she will take the rein I let her run;
But she'll not stumble.
PAULINA. Good my liege, I come,
And I beseech you, hear me, who professes
Myself your loyal servant, your physician,
Your most obedient counsellor, yet that dares
Less appear so in comforting your evils
Than such as most seem yours. I say, I come
From your good queen.

LEONTES. Good queen!
PAULINA. Good queen, my lord, good queen; I say, good
    queen;
  And would by combat make her good, so were I
  A man, the worst about you.
LEONTES. Force her hence.
PAULINA. Let him that makes but trifles of his eyes
  First hand me: on mine own accord I'll off;
  But first I'll do my errand. The good queen,
  For she is good, hath brought you forth a daughter:
  Here 'tis; commends it to your blessing.
            Laying down the Child
LEONTES. Out!
  A mankind witch! Hence with her, out o' door:
  A most intelligencing bawd!
PAULINA. Not so;
  I am as ignorant in that as you
  In so entitling me, and no less honest
  Than you are mad; which is enough, I'll warrant,
  As this world goes, to pass for honest.
LEONTES. Traitors!
  Will you not push her out? Give her the bastard.
  (*To Antigonus*) Thou dotard! thou art woman-tir'd, un-
    roosted
  By thy dame Partlet here. Take up the bastard;
  Take 't up, I say; give 't to thy crone.
PAULINA. For ever
  Unvenerable be thy hands, if thou
  Tak'st up the princess by that forced baseness
  Which he has put upon 't!
LEONTES. He dreads his wife.
PAULINA. So I would you did; then, 'twere past all doubt,
  You'd call your children yours.
LEONTES. A nest of traitors!
ANTIGONUS. I am none, by this good light.
PAULINA. Nor I; nor any
  But one that's here, and that's himself; for he
  The sacred honour of himself, his queen's,
  His hopeful son's, his babe's, betrays to slander,
  Whose sting is sharper than the sword's; and will not,—
  For, as the case now stands, it is a curse
  He cannot be compell'd to 't,—once remove

The root of his opinion, which is rotten
As ever oak or stone was sound.
LEONTES. A callat
Of boundless tongue, who late hath beat her husband
And now baits me! This brat is none of mine;
It is the issue of Polixenes:
Hence with it; and, together with the dam
Commit them to the fire!
PAULINA. It is yours;
And, might we lay the old proverb to your charge,
'So like you, 'tis the worse.' Behold, my lords,
Although the print be little, the whole matter
And copy of the father; eye, nose, lip,
The trick of 's frown, his forehead, nay, the valley,
The pretty dimples of his chin and cheek, his smiles,
The very mould and frame of hand, nail, finger:
And thou, good goddess Nature, which hast made it
So like to him that got it, if thou hast
The ordering of the mind too, 'mongst all colours
No yellow in 't; lest she suspect, as he does,
Her children not her husband's.
LEONTES. A gross hag!
And, lozel, thou art worthy to be hang'd,
That wilt not stay her tongue.
ANTIGONUS. Hang all the husbands
That cannot do that feat, you 'll leave yourself
Hardly one subject.
LEONTES. Once more, take her hence.
PAULINA. A most unworthy and unnatural lord
Can do no more.
LEONTES. I 'll ha' thee burn'd.
PAULINA. I care not:
It is a heretic that makes the fire,
Not she which burns in 't. I 'll not call you tyrant;
But this most cruel usage of your queen,—
Not able to produce more accusation
Than your own weak-hing'd fancy,—something savours
Of tyranny, and will ignoble make you,
Yea, scandalous to the world.
LEONTES. On your allegiance,
Out of the chamber with her! Were I a tyrant,
Where were her life? She durst not call me so

If she did know me one. Away with her!
PAULINA. I pray you do not push me; I'll be gone.
Look to your babe, my lord; 'tis yours. Jove send her
A better guiding spirit! What need these hands?
You, that are thus so tender o'er his follies,
Will never do him good, not one of you.
So, so: farewell; we are gone. *Exit*
LEONTES. Thou, traitor, hast set on thy wife to this.
My child! away with 't!—even thou, that hast
A heart so tender o'er it, take it hence
And see it instantly consum'd with fire.
Even thou and none but thou. Take it up straight!
Within this hour bring me word 'tis done,—
And by good testimony,—or I'll seize thy life,
With what thou else call'st thine. If thou refuse
And wilt encounter with my wrath, say so;
The bastard brains with these my proper hands
Shall I dash out. Go, take it to the fire:
For thou sett'st on thy wife.
ANTIGONUS. I did not, sir:
These lords, my noble fellows, if they please,
Can clear me in 't.
FIRST LORD. We can, my royal liege,
He is not guilty of her coming hither.
LEONTES. You are liars all.
FIRST LORD. Beseech your Highness, give us better credit:
We have always truly serv'd you, and beseech you
So to esteem of us; and on our knees we beg,
As recompense of our dear services
Past and to come, that you do change this purpose,
Which being so horrible, so bloody, must
Lead on to some foul issue. We all kneel.
LEONTES. I am a feather for each wind that blows.
Shall I live on to see this bastard kneel
And call me father? Better burn it now
Than curse it then. But, be it; let it live:
It shall not neither.—(*To Antigonus*) You, sir, come you hither;
You that have been so tenderly officious
With Lady Margery, your midwife there,
To save this bastard's life,—for 'tis a bastard,
So sure as thy beard's grey,—what will you adventure

To save this brat's life?
ANTIGONUS. Any thing, my lord,
That my ability may undergo,
And nobleness impose: at least, thus much:
I 'll pawn the little blood which I have left,
To save the innocent: any thing possible.
LEONTES. It shall be possible. Swear by this sword
Thou wilt perform my bidding.
ANTIGONUS. I will, my lord.
LEONTES. Mark and perform it,—seest thou!—for the fail
Of any point in 't shall not only be
Death to thyself, but to thy lewd-tongu'd wife,
Whom for this time we pardon. We enjoin thee,
As thou art liegeman to us, that thou carry
This female bastard hence; and that thou bear it
To some remote and desert place quite out
Of our dominions; and that there thou leave it,
Without more mercy, to its own protection,
And favour of the climate. As by strange fortune
It came to us, I do in justice charge thee,
On thy soul's peril and thy body's torture,
That thou commend it strangely to some place,
Where chance may nurse or end it. Take it up.
ANTIGONUS. I swear to do this, though a present death
Had been more merciful. Come on, poor babe:
Some powerful spirit instruct the kites and ravens
To be thy nurses! Wolves and bears, they say,
Casting their savageness aside have done
Like offices of pity. Sir, be prosperous
In more than this deed doth require! And blessing
Against this cruelty fight on thy side,
Poor thing, condemn'd to loss! *Exit with the Child*
LEONTES. No; I 'll not rear
Another's issue.

Enter a Servant

SERVANT. Please your Highness, posts
From those you sent to the oracle are come
An hour since: Cleomenes and Dion,
Being well arriv'd from Delphos, are both landed,
Hasting to the court.
FIRST LORD. So please you, sir, their speed
Hath been beyond account.

LEONTES. Twenty-three days
They have been absent: 'tis good speed; foretells
The great Apollo suddenly will have
The truth of this appear. Prepare you, lords;
Summon a session, that we may arraign
Our most disloyal lady; for, as she hath
Been publicly accus'd, so shall she have
A just and open trial. While she lives
My heart will be a burden to me. Leave me,
And think upon my bidding. *Exeunt*

ACT THREE

SCENE ONE

A Sea-port in Sicilia.

Enter Cleomenes and Dion

CLEOMENES. The climate's delicate, the air most sweet,
  Fertile the isle, the temple much surpassing
  The common praise it bears.
DION.   I shall report,
  For most it caught me, the celestial habits,—
  Methinks I so should term them,—and the reverence
  Of the grave wearers. O, the sacrifice!
  How ceremonious, solemn, and unearthly
  It was i' the offering!
CLEOMENES.   But of all, the burst
  And the ear-deafening voice o' the oracle,
  Kin to Jove's thunder, so compris'd my sense,
  That I was nothing.
DION.   If the event o' the journey
  Prove as successful to the queen,—O, be 't so!—
  As it hath been to us rare, pleasant, speedy,
  The time is worth the use on 't.
CLEOMENES.   Great Apollo
  Turn all to the best! These proclamations,
  So forcing faults upon Hermione,
  I little like.
DION.   The violent carriage of it
  Will clear or end the business: when the oracle,
  Thus by Apollo's great divine seal'd up,
  Shall the contents discover, something rare
  Even then will rush to knowledge.—Go:—fresh horses!
  And gracious be the issue!   *Exeunt*

SCENE TWO

Sicilia. A Court of Justice.

Leontes, Lords, and Officers

LEONTES. This sessions, to our great grief we pronounce,
  Even pushes 'gainst our heart: the party tried
  The daughter of a king, our wife, and one
  Of us too much belov'd. Let us be clear'd
  Of being tyrannous, since we so openly
  Proceed in justice, which shall have due course,
  Even to the guilt or the purgation.
  Produce the prisoner.

OFFICER. It is his Highness' pleasure that the queen
  Appear in person here in court. Silence!

Enter Hermione guarded; Paulina and Ladies attending

LEONTES. Read the indictment.

OFFICER. (*Reads*) 'Hermione, queen to the worthy Leontes, King of Sicilia, thou art here accused and arraigned of high treason, in committing adultery with Polixenes, King of Bohemia, and conspiring with Camillo to take away the life of our sovereign lord the king, thy royal husband: the pretence whereof being by circumstances partly laid open, thou, Hermione, contrary to the faith and allegiance of a true subject, didst counsel and aid them, for their better safety, to fly away by night.'

HERMIONE. Since what I am to say must be but that
  Which contradicts my accusation, and
  The testimony on my part no other
  But what comes from myself, it shall scarce boot me
  To say 'Not guilty': mine integrity
  Being counted falsehood, shall, as I express it,
  Be so receiv'd. But thus: if powers divine
  Behold our human actions, as they do,
  I doubt not then but innocence shall make
  False accusation blush, and tyranny
  Tremble at patience. You, my lord, best know,—
  Who least will seem to do so,—my past life
  Hath been as continent, as chaste, as true,
  As I am now unhappy; which is more

[35-73]

Than history can pattern, though devis'd
And play'd to take spectators. For behold me,
A fellow of the royal bed, which owe
A moiety of the throne, a great king's daughter,
The mother to a hopeful prince, here standing
To prate and talk for life and honour 'fore
Who please to come and hear. For life, I prize it
As I weigh grief, which I would spare: for honour,
'Tis a derivative from me to mine,
And only that I stand for. I appeal
To your own conscience, sir, before Polixenes
Came to your court, how I was in your grace,
How merited to be so; since he came,
With what encounter so uncurrent I
Have strain'd, to appear thus: if one jot beyond
The bound of honour, or in act or will
That way inclining, harden'd be the hearts
Of all that hear me, and my near'st of kin
Cry fie upon my grave!

LEONTES.   I ne'er heard yet
That any of these bolder vices wanted
Less impudence to gainsay what they did
Than to perform it first.

HERMIONE.   That's true enough;
Though 'tis a saying, sir, not due to me.

LEONTES. You will not own it.

HERMIONE.   More than mistress of
Which comes to me in name of fault, I must not
At all acknowledge. For Polixenes,—
With whom I am accus'd,—I do confess
I lov'd him as in honour he requir'd,
With such a kind of love as might become
A lady like me; with a love even such,
So and no other, as yourself commanded:
Which not to have done I think had been in me
Both disobedience and ingratitude
To you and toward your friend, whose love had spoke
Even since it could speak, from an infant, freely
That it was yours. Now, for conspiracy,
I know not how it tastes, though it be dish'd
For me to try how: all I know of it
Is that Camillo was an honest man;

And why he left your court, the gods themselves,
Wotting no more than I, are ignorant.

LEONTES. You knew of his departure, as you know
What you have underta'en to do in 's absence.

HERMIONE. Sir,
You speak a language that I understand not:
My life stands in the level of your dreams,
Which I'll lay down.

LEONTES.   Your actions are my dreams:
You had a bastard by Polixenes,
And I but dream'd it. As you were past all shame,—
Those of your fact are so,—so past all truth:
Which to deny concerns more than avails; for as
Thy brat hath been cast out, like to itself,
No father owning it,—which is, indeed,
More criminal in thee than it,—so thou
Shalt feel our justice, in whose easiest passage
Look for no less than death.

HERMIONE.   Sir, spare your threats:
The bug which you would fright me with I seek.
To me can life be no commodity:
The crown and comfort of my life, your favour,
I do give lost; for I do feel it gone,
But know not how it went. My second joy,
And first-fruits of my body, from his presence
I am barr'd, like one infectious. My third comfort,
Starr'd most unluckily, is from my breast,
The innocent milk in its most innocent mouth,
Hal'd out to murder: myself on every post
Proclaim'd a strumpet: with immodest hatred
The child-bed privilege denied, which 'longs
To women of all fashion: lastly, hurried
Here to this place, i' the open air, before
I have got strength of limit. Now, my liege,
Tell me what blessings I have here alive,
That I should fear to die? Therefore proceed.
But yet hear this; mistake me not; no life,
I prize it not a straw:—but for mine honour,
Which I would free, if I shall be condemn'd
Upon surmises, all proofs sleeping else
But what your jealousies awake, I tell you
'Tis rigour and not law. Your honours all,

ACT III : SCENE II

I do refer me to the oracle:
Apollo be my judge!
FIRST LORD. This your request
Is altogether just: therefore, bring forth,
And in Apollo's name, his oracle. *Exeunt certain Officers*
HERMIONE. The Emperor of Russia was my father.
O! that he were alive, and here beholding
His daughter's trial; that he did but see
The flatness of my misery; yet with eyes
Of pity, not revenge!

Re-enter Officers, with Cleomenes and Dion

OFFICER. You here shall swear upon this sword of justice,
That you, Cleomenes and Dion, have
Been both at Delphos, and from thence have brought
This seal'd-up oracle, by the hand deliver'd
Of great Apollo's priest, and that since then
You have not dar'd to break the holy seal,
Nor read the secrets in 't.
CLEOMENES.
DION. All this we swear.
LEONTES. Break up the seals, and read.
OFFICER. 'Hermione is chaste; Polixenes blameless; Camillo
a true subject; Leontes a jealous tyrant; his innocent babe
truly begotten; and the king shall live without an heir if
that which is lost be not found!'
LORDS. Now blessed be the great Apollo!
HERMIONE. Praised!
LEONTES. Hast thou read truth?
OFFICER. Ay, my lord; even so
As it is here set down.
LEONTES. There is no truth at all i' the oracle:
The sessions shall proceed. This is mere falsehood!

Enter a Servant

SERVANT. My lord the king, the king!
LEONTES. What is the business?
SERVANT. O sir! I shall be hated to report it:
The prince your son, with mere conceit and fear
Of the queen's speed, is gone.
LEONTES. How! gone!
SERVANT. Is dead.
LEONTES. Apollo's angry; and the heavens themselves
Do strike at my injustice. *Hermione swoons*

How now, there!

PAULINA. This news is mortal to the queen:—look down,
And see what death is doing.

LEONTES. Take her hence:
Her heart is but o'ercharg'd; she will recover:
I have too much believ'd mine own suspicion:
Beseech you, tenderly apply to her
Some remedies for life.—

Exeunt Paulina and Ladies, with Hermione

Apollo, pardon
My great profaneness 'gainst thine oracle!
I'll reconcile me to Polixenes,
New woo my queen, recall the good Camillo,
Whom I proclaim a man of truth, of mercy;
For, being transported by my jealousies
To bloody thoughts and to revenge, I chose
Camillo for the minister to poison
My friend Polixenes: which had been done,
But that the good mind of Camillo tardied
My swift command; though I with death and with
Reward did threaten and encourage him,
Not doing it, and being done: he, most humane
And fill'd with honour, to my kingly guest
Unclasp'd my practice, quit his fortunes here,
Which you knew great, and to the certain hazard
Of all incertainties himself commended,
No richer than his honour: how he glisters
Thorough my rust! and how his piety
Does my deeds make the blacker!

Re-enter Paulina

PAULINA. Woe the while!
O, cut my lace, lest my heart, cracking it,
Break too!

FIRST LORD. What fit is this, good lady?

PAULINA. What studied torments, tyrant, hast for me?
What wheels? racks? fires? What flaying? or what boiling
In leads, or oils? What old or newer torture
Must I receive, whose every word deserves
To taste of thy most worst? Thy tyranny,
Together working with thy jealousies,
Fancies too weak for boys, too green and idle
For girls of nine, O! think what they have done,

ACT III · SCENE II

And then run mad indeed, stark mad; for all
Thy by-gone fooleries were but spices of it.
That thou betray'dst Polixenes, 'twas nothing;
That did but show thee of a fool, inconstant
And damnable ingrateful; nor was 't much
Thou wouldst have poison'd good Camillo's honour
To have him kill a king; poor trespasses,
More monstrous standing by: whereof I reckon
The casting forth to crows thy baby daughter
To be or none or little; though a devil
Would have shed water out of fire ere done 't:
Nor is 't directly laid to thee, the death
Of the young prince, whose honourable thoughts,—
Thoughts high for one so tender,—cleft the heart
That could conceive a gross and foolish sire
Blemish'd his gracious dam: this is not, no,
Laid to thy answer: but the last,—O lords!
When I have said, cry, 'woe!'—the queen, the queen,
The sweetest, dearest creature 's dead, and vengeance for 't
Not dropp'd down yet.

FIRST LORD. The higher powers forbid!

PAULINA. I say she 's dead; I 'll swear it: if word nor oath
Prevail not, go and see: if you can bring
Tincture or lustre in her lip, her eye,
Heat outwardly, or breath within, I 'll serve you
As I would do the gods. But, O thou tyrant!
Do not repent these things, for they are heavier
Than all thy woes can stir; therefore betake thee
To nothing but despair. A thousand knees
Ten thousand years together, naked, fasting,
Upon a barren mountain, and still winter
In storm perpetual, could not move the gods
To look that way thou wert.

LEONTES. Go on, go on;
Thou canst not speak too much: I have deserv'd
All tongues to talk their bitterest.

FIRST LORD. Say no more:
Howe'er the business goes, you have made fault
I' the boldness of your speech.

PAULINA. I am sorry for 't:
All faults I make, when I shall come to know them,

I do repent. Alas! I have show'd too much
The rashness of a woman: he is touch'd
To the noble heart. What's gone and what's past help
Should be past grief: do not receive affliction
At my petition; I beseech you, rather
Let me be punish'd, that have minded you
Of what you should forget. Now, good my liege,
Sir, royal sir, forgive a foolish woman:
The love I bore your queen,—lo, fool again!—
I'll speak of her no more, nor of your children;
I'll not remember you of my own lord,
Who is lost too: take your patience to you,
And I'll say nothing.

LEONTES. Thou didst speak but well,
When most the truth, which I receive much better
Than to be pitied of thee. Prithee, bring me
To the dead bodies of my queen and son:
One grave shall be for both: upon them shall
The causes of their death appear, unto
Our shame perpetual. Once a day I'll visit
The chapel where they lie, and tears shed there
Shall be my recreation: so long as nature
Will bear up with this exercise, so long
I daily vow to use it. Come and lead me
Unto these sorrows.

Exeunt

SCENE THREE

Bohemia. A desert Country near the Sea.

Enter Antigonus, with the Child; and a Mariner

ANTIGONUS. Thou art perfect, then, our ship hath touch'd upon
The deserts of Bohemia?

MARINER. Ay, my lord; and fear
We have landed in ill time: the skies look grimly
And threaten present blusters. In my conscience,
The heavens with that we have in hand are angry,
And frown upon's.

ANTIGONUS. Their sacred wills be done! Go, get aboard;
Look to thy bark: I'll not be long before

[9-45] ACT III · SCENE III

 I call upon thee.
MARINER.   Make your best haste, and go not
 Too far i' the land: 'tis like to be loud weather;
 Besides, this place is famous for the creatures
 Of prey that keep upon 't.
ANTIGONUS.   Go thou away:
 I'll follow instantly.
MARINER.   I am glad at heart
 To be so rid of the business.   *Exit*
ANTIGONUS.   Come, poor babe:
 I have heard, but not believ'd, the spirits o' the dead
 May walk again: if such thing be, thy mother
 Appear'd to me last night, for ne'er was dream
 So like a waking. To me comes a creature,
 Sometimes her head on one side, some another;
 I never saw a vessel of like sorrow,
 So fill'd, and so becoming: in pure white robes,
 Like very sanctity, she did approach
 My cabin where I lay; thrice bow'd before me,
 And, gasping to begin some speech, her eyes
 Became two spouts: the fury spent, anon
 Did this break from her: 'Good Antigonus,
 Since fate, against thy better disposition,
 Hath made thy person for the thrower-out
 Of my poor babe, according to thine oath,
 Places remote enough are in Bohemia,
 There weep and leave it crying; and, for the babe
 Is counted lost for ever, Perdita,
 I prithee, call 't: for this ungentle business,
 Put on thee by my lord, thou ne'er shalt see
 Thy wife Paulina more': and so, with shrieks,
 She melted into air. Affrighted much,
 I did in time collect myself, and thought
 This was so and no slumber. Dreams are toys;
 Yet for this once, yea, superstitiously,
 I will be squar'd by this. I do believe
 Hermione hath suffer'd death; and that
 Apollo would, this being indeed the issue
 Of King Polixenes, it should here be laid,
 Either for life or death, upon the earth
 Of its right father. Blossom, speed thee well!
         Laying down the Child

There lie; and there thy character: there these;
Laying down a bundle
Which may, if fortune please, both breed thee, pretty,
And still rest thine. The storm begins: poor wretch!
That for thy mother's fault art thus expos'd
To loss and what may follow. Weep I cannot,
But my heart bleeds, and most accurs'd am I
To be by oath enjoin'd to this. Farewell!
The day frowns more and more: thou art like to have
A lullaby too rough. I never saw
The heavens so dim by day. A savage clamour!
Well may I get aboard! This is the chase.
I am gone for ever. *Exit, pursued by a bear*
Enter a Shepherd

SHEPHERD. I would there were no age between sixteen and three-and-twenty, or that youth would sleep out the rest; for there is nothing in the between but getting wenches with child, wronging the ancientry, stealing, fighting. Hark you now! Would any but these boiled brains of nineteen and two-and-twenty hunt this weather? They have scared away two of my best sheep; which I fear the wolf will sooner find than the master: if anywhere I have them, 'tis by the sea-side, browsing of ivy. Good luck, an 't be thy will! what have we here? (*Taking up the Child*) Mercy on 's, a barne; a very pretty barne! A boy or a child, I wonder? A pretty one; a very pretty one; sure some scape: though I am not bookish, yet I can read waiting-gentlewoman in the scape. This has been some stair-work, some trunk-work, some behind-door-work; they were warmer that got this than the poor thing is here. I 'll take it up for pity; yet I 'll tarry till my son come; he hollaed but even now. Whoa, ho, hoa!

Enter Clown

CLOWN. Hilloa, loa!

SHEPHERD. What! art so near? If thou 'lt see a thing to talk on when thou art dead and rotten, come hither. What ailest thou, man?

CLOWN. I have seen two such sights by sea and by land! But I am not to say it is a sea, for it is now the sky: betwixt the firmament and it you cannot thrust a bodkin's point.

SHEPHERD. Why, boy, how is it?

CLOWN. I would you did but see how it chafes, how it rages,

how it takes up the shore! But that's not to the point. O! the most piteous cry of the poor souls; sometimes to see 'em, and not to see 'em; now the ship boring the moon with her mainmast, and anon swallowed with yeast and froth, as you'd thrust a cork into a hogshead. And then for the land-service: to see how the bear tore out his shoulder-bone; how he cried to me for help and said his name was Antigonus, a nobleman. But to make an end of the ship: to see how the sea flapdragoned it: but, first, how the poor souls roared, and the sea mocked them; and how the poor gentleman roared, and the bear mocked him, both roaring louder than the sea or weather.

SHEPHERD. Name of mercy! when was this, boy?

CLOWN. Now, now; I have not winked since I saw these sights: the men are not yet cold under water, nor the bear half dined on the gentleman: he's at it now.

SHEPHERD. Would I had been by, to have helped the old man!

CLOWN. I would you had been by the ship's side, to have helped her: there your charity would have lacked footing.

SHEPHERD. Heavy matters! heavy matters! But look thee here, boy. Now bless thyself: thou mettest with things dying, I with things new born. Here's a sight for thee; look thee, a bearing-cloth for a squire's child! Look thee here: take up, take up, boy; open 't. So, let's see: it was told me, I should be rich by the fairies: this is some changeling.—Open 't. What's within, boy?

CLOWN. You're a made old man: if the sins of your youth are forgiven you, you're well to live. Gold! all gold!

SHEPHERD. This is fairy gold, boy, and 'twill prove so: up with 't, keep it close: home, home, the next way. We are lucky, boy; and to be so still requires nothing but secrecy. Let my sheep go. Come, good boy, the next way home.

CLOWN. Go you the next way with your findings. I'll go see if the bear be gone from the gentleman, and how much he hath eaten: they are never curst but when they are hungry. If there be any of him left, I'll bury it.

SHEPHERD. That's a good deed. If thou mayst discern by that which is left of him what he is, fetch me to the sight of him.

CLOWN. Marry, will I; and you shall help to put him i' the ground.

SHEPHERD. 'Tis a lucky day, boy, and we'll do good deeds
Exeunt

ACT FOUR

Enter Time, the Chorus

TIME. I, that please some, try all, both joy and terror
   Of good and bad, that make and unfold error,
   Now take upon me, in the name of Time,
   To use my wings. Impute it not a crime
   To me or my swift passage, that I slide
   O'er sixteen years, and leave the growth untried
   Of that wide gap; since it is in my power
   To o'erthrow law, and in one self-born hour
   To plant and o'erwhelm custom. Let me pass
   The same I am, ere ancient'st order was
   Or what is now receiv'd: I witness to
   The times that brought them in; so shall I do
   To the freshest things now reigning, and make stale
   The glistering of this present, as my tale
   Now seems to it. Your patience this allowing,
   I turn my glass and give my scene such growing
   As you had slept between. Leontes leaving,—
   The effects of his fond jealousies so grieving,
   That he shuts up himself,—imagine me,
   Gentle spectators, that I now may be
   In fair Bohemia; and remember well,
   I mention'd a son o' the king's, which Florizel
   I now name to you; and with speed so pace
   To speak of Perdita, now grown in grace
   Equal with wondering. What of her ensues
   I list not prophesy; but let Time's news
   Be known when 'tis brought forth. A shepherd's daughter,
   And what to her adheres, which follows after,
   Is th' argument of Time. Of this allow,
   If ever you have spent time worse ere now:
   If never, yet that Time himself doth say
   He wishes earnestly you never may. *Exit*

SCENE ONE

Bohemia. A Room in the Palace of Polixenes.

Enter Polixenes and Camillo

POLIXENES. I pray thee, good Camillo, be no more importunate; 'tis a sickness denying thee any thing; a death to grant this.

CAMILLO. It is fifteen years since I saw my country: though I have for the most part been aired abroad, I desire to lay my bones there. Besides, the penitent king, my master, hath sent for me; to whose feeling sorrows I might be some allay, or I o'erween to think so, which is another spur to my departure.

POLIXENES. As thou lovest me, Camillo, wipe not out the rest of thy services by leaving me now. The need I have of thee thine own goodness hath made. Better not to have had thee than thus to want thee. Thou, having made me businesses which none without thee can sufficiently manage, must either stay to execute them thyself or take away with thee the very services thou hast done; which if I have not enough considered,—as too much I cannot,—to be more thankful to thee shall be my study, and my profit therein, the heaping friendships. Of that fatal country, Sicilia, prithee speak no more, whose very naming punishes me with the remembrance of that penitent, as thou callest him, and reconciled king, my brother; whose loss of his most precious queen and children are even now to be afresh lamented. Say to me, when sawest thou the Prince Florizel, my son? Kings are no less unhappy, their issue not being gracious, than they are in losing them when they have approved their virtues.

CAMILLO. Sir, it is three days since I saw the prince. What his happier affairs may be, are to me unknown; but I have missingly noted he is of late much retired from court, and is less frequent to his princely exercises than formerly he hath appeared.

POLIXENES. I have considered so much, Camillo, and with some care; so far, that I have eyes under my service which look upon his removedness; from whom I have this intelligence, that he is seldom from the house of a most homely shepherd; a man, they say, that from very nothing, and beyond the imagination of his neighbours, is grown into an unspeakable estate.

CAMILLO. I have heard, sir, of such a man, who hath a daughter of most rare note. The report of her is extended more than can be thought to begin from such a cottage.

POLIXENES. That's likewise part of my intelligence; but, I fear, the angle that plucks our son thither. Thou shalt accompany us to the place; where we will, not appearing what we are, have some question with the shepherd; from whose simplicity I think it not uneasy to get the cause of my son's resort thither. Prithee, be my present partner in this business, and lay aside the thoughts of Sicilia.

CAMILLO. I willingly obey your command.

POLIXENES. My best Camillo!—We must disguise ourselves.

Exeunt

SCENE TWO

The Same. A Road near the Shepherd's Cottage.

Enter Autolycus, singing

When daffodils begin to peer,
   With heigh! the doxy, over the dale,
Why, then comes in the sweet o' the year;
   For the red blood reigns in the winter's pale.
The white sheet bleaching on the hedge,
   With heigh! the sweet birds, O, how they sing!
Doth set my pugging tooth on edge;
   For a quart of ale is a dish for a king.
The lark, that tirra-lirra chants,
   With heigh! with heigh! the thrush and the jay,
Are summer songs for me and my aunts,
   While we lie tumbling in the hay.

I have served Prince Florizel, and in my time wore three pile; but now I am out of service:
   But shall I go mourn for that, my dear?
   The pale moon shines by night;
   And when I wander here and there,
   I then do most go right.

If tinkers may have leave to live,
    And bear the sow-skin budget,
Then my account I well may give,
    And in the stocks avouch it.

My traffic is sheets; when the kite builds, look to lesser linen. My father named me Autolycus; who being, as I am, littered under Mercury, was likewise a snapper-up of unconsidered trifles. With die and drab I purchased this caparison, and my revenue is the silly cheat. Gallows and knock are too powerful on the highway: beating and hanging are terrors to me: for the life to come, I sleep out the thought of it. A prize! a prize!

Enter Clown

CLOWN. Let me see: every 'leven wether tods; every tod yields pound and odd shilling: fifteen hundred shorn, what comes the wool to?

AUTOLYCUS. (*Aside*) If the springe hold, the cock's mine.

CLOWN. I cannot do 't without compters. Let me see; what am I to buy for our sheep-shearing feast? 'Three pound of sugar; five pound of currants; rice,' what will this sister of mine do with rice? But my father hath made her mistress of the feast, and she lays it on. She hath made me four-and-twenty nosegays for the shearers, three-man songmen all, and very good ones; but they are most of them means and bases: but one puritan amongst them, and he sings psalms to hornpipes. I must have saffron, to colour the warden pies; mace, dates,—none; that 's out of my note:—nutmegs seven; a race or two of ginger,—but that I may beg;—four pound of prunes, and as many of raisins o' the sun.

AUTOLYCUS. O! that ever I was born!

Grovelling on the ground

CLOWN. I' the name of me!—

AUTOLYCUS. O! help me, help me! Pluck but off these rags, and then death, death!

CLOWN. Alack, poor soul! thou hast need of more rags to lay on thee, rather than have these off.

AUTOLYCUS. O, sir! the loathsomeness of them offends me more than the stripes I have received, which are mighty ones and millions.

CLOWN. Alas, poor man! A million of beating may come to a great matter.

AUTOLYCUS. I am robbed, sir, and beaten; my money and apparel ta'en from me, and these detestable things put upon me.

CLOWN. What, by a horseman or a footman?

AUTOLYCUS. A footman, sweet sir, a footman.

CLOWN. Indeed, he should be a footman, by the garments he hath left with thee: if this be a horseman's coat, it hath seen very hot service. Lend me thy hand, I'll help thee: come, lend me thy hand. *Helping him up*

AUTOLYCUS. O! good sir, tenderly, O!

CLOWN. Alas, poor soul!

AUTOLYCUS. O! good sir; softly, good sir! I fear, sir, my shoulder-blade is out.

CLOWN. How now! Canst stand?

AUTOLYCUS. Softly, dear sir; (*Picks his pocket*) good sir, softly. You ha' done me a charitable office.

CLOWN. Dost lack any money? I have a little money for thee.

AUTOLYCUS. No, good sweet sir: no, I beseech you, sir. I have a kinsman not past three-quarters of a mile hence, unto whom I was going: I shall there have money, or any thing I want. Offer me no money, I pray you! that kills my heart.

CLOWN. What manner of fellow was he that robbed you?

AUTOLYCUS. A fellow, sir, that I have known to go about with trol-my-dames: I knew him once a servant of the prince. I cannot tell, good sir, for which of his virtues it was, but he was certainly whipped out of the court.

CLOWN. His vices, you would say. There's no virtue whipped out of the court. They cherish it, to make it stay there, and yet it will no more but abide.

AUTOLYCUS. Vices, I would say, sir. I know this man well. He hath been since an ape-bearer; then a process-server, a bailiff; then he compassed a motion of the Prodigal Son, and married a tinker's wife within a mile where my land and living lies; and having flown over many knavish professions, he settled only in rogue. Some call him Autolycus.

CLOWN. Out upon him! Prig, for my life, prig! He haunts wakes, fairs, and bear-baitings.

AUTOLYCUS. Very true, sir; he, sir, he. That's the rogue that put me into this apparel.

CLOWN. Not a more cowardly rogue in all Bohemia. If you had but looked big and spit at him, he'd have run.

ACT IV · SCENE II

AUTOLYCUS. I must confess to you, sir, I am no fighter. I am false of heart that way, and that he knew, I warrant him.
CLOWN. How do you now?
AUTOLYCUS. Sweet sir, much better than I was. I can stand and walk. I will even take my leave of you, and pace softly towards my kinsman's.
CLOWN. Shall I bring thee on the way?
AUTOLYCUS. No, good-faced sir; no, sweet sir.
CLOWN. Then fare thee well. I must go buy spices for our sheep-shearing.
AUTOLYCUS. Prosper you, sweet sir!—(*Exit Clown*) Your purse is not hot enough to purchase your spice. I'll be with you at your sheep-shearing too. If I make not this cheat bring out another, and the shearers prove sheep, let me be unrolled, and my name put in the book of virtue.

> Jog on, jog on, the footpath way,
>   And merrily hent the stile-a:
> A merry heart goes all the day,
>   Your sad tires in a mile-a. *Exit*

SCENE THREE

The Same. A Lawn before the Shepherd's Cottage.

Enter Florizel and Perdita

FLORIZEL. These your unusual weeds to each part of you
Do give a life: no shepherdess, but Flora
Peering in April's front. This your sheep-shearing
Is as a meeting of the petty gods,
And you the queen on't.
PERDITA.   Sir, my gracious lord,
To chide at your extremes it not becomes me:
O! pardon, that I name them. Your high self,
The gracious mark o' the land, you have obscur'd
With a swain's wearing, and me, poor lowly maid,
Most goddess-like prank'd up. But that our feasts
In every mess have folly, and the feeders
Digest it with a custom, I should blush
To see you so attired,—swoon, I think,
To show myself a glass.
FLORIZEL.   I bless the time

When my good falcon made her flight across
Thy father's ground.

PERDITA. Now, Jove afford you cause!
To me the difference forges dread; your greatness
Hath not been us'd to fear. Even now I tremble
To think, your father, by some accident,
Should pass this way as you did. O, the Fates!
How would he look, to see his work, so noble,
Vilely bound up? What would he say? Or how
Should I, in these my borrow'd flaunts, behold
The sternness of his presence?

FLORIZEL. Apprehend
Nothing but jollity. The gods themselves,
Humbling their deities to love, have taken
The shapes of beasts upon them: Jupiter
Became a bull, and bellow'd; the green Neptune
A ram, and bleated; and the fire-rob'd god,
Golden Apollo, a poor humble swain,
As I seem now. Their transformations
Were never for a piece of beauty rarer,
Nor in a way so chaste, since my desires
Run not before mine honour, nor my lusts
Burn hotter than my faith.

PERDITA. O! but, sir,
Your resolution cannot hold, when 'tis
Oppos'd, as it must be, by the power of the king.
One of these two must be necessities,
Which then will speak, that you must change this **purpose**,
Or I my life.

FLORIZEL. Thou dearest Perdita,
With these forc'd thoughts, I prithee, darken not
The mirth o' the feast: or I'll be thine, my fair,
Or not my father's; for I cannot be
Mine own, nor any thing to any, if
I be not thine: to this I am most constant,
Though destiny say no. Be merry, gentle;
Strangle such thoughts as these with any thing
That you behold the while. Your guests are coming:
Lift up your countenance, as it were the day
Of celebration of that nuptial which
We two have sworn shall come.

PERDITA. O lady Fortune,

ACT IV · SCENE III

Stand you auspicious!

FLORIZEL. See, your guests approach:
Address yourself to entertain them sprightly.
And let 's be red with mirth.

*Enter Shepherd, with Polixenes and
Camillo disguised; Clown, Mopsa, Dorcas, and Others*

SHEPHERD. Fie, daughter! When my old wife liv'd, upon
This day she was both pantler, butler, cook;
Both dame and servant; welcom'd all, serv'd all,
Would sing her song and dance her turn; now here,
At upper end o' the table, now i' the middle;
On his shoulder, and his; her face o' fire
With labour and the thing she took to quench it,
She would to each one sip. You are retir'd,
As if you were a feasted one and not
The hostess of the meeting. Pray you, bid
These unknown friends to 's welcome; for it is
A way to make us better friends, more known.
Come, quench your blushes and present yourself
That which you are, mistress o' the feast: come on,
And bid us welcome to your sheep-shearing,
As your good flock shall prosper.

PERDITA. *(To Polixenes)* Sir, welcome:
It is my father's will I should take on me
The hostess-ship o' the day. *(To Camillo)* You 're welcome, sir.
Give me those flowers there, Dorcas. Reverend sirs,
For you there 's rosemary and rue; these keep
Seeming and savour all the winter long.
Grace and remembrance be to you both,
And welcome to our shearing!

POLIXENES. Shepherdess,—
A fair one are you,—well you fit our ages
With flowers of winter.

PERDITA. Sir, the year growing ancient,
Not yet on summer's death, nor on the birth
Of trembling winter, the fairest flowers o' the season
Are our carnations, and streak'd gillyvors,
Which some call nature's bastards: of that kind
Our rustic garden 's barren, and I care not
To get slips of them.

POLIXENES. Wherefore, gentle maiden,

Do you neglect them?
PERDITA. For I have heard it said
There is an art which in their piedness shares
With great creating nature.
POLIXENES. Say there be;
Yet nature is made better by no mean
But nature makes that mean: so, over that art,
Which you say adds to nature, is an art
That nature makes. You see, sweet maid, we marry
A gentler scion to the wildest stock,
And make conceive a bark of baser kind
By bud of nobler race. This is an art
Which does mend nature, change it rather, but
The art itself is nature.
PERDITA. So it is.
POLIXENES. Then make your garden rich in gillyvors,
And do not call them bastards.
PERDITA. I'll not put
The dibble in earth to set one slip of them;
No more than, were I painted, I would wish
This youth should say, 'twere well, and only therefore
Desire to breed by me. Here's flowers for you;
Hot lavender, mints, savory, marjoram;
The marigold, that goes to bed wi' the sun,
And with him rises weeping: these are flowers
Of middle summer, and I think they are given
To men of middle age. You're very welcome.
CAMILLO. I should leave grazing, were I of your flock,
And only live by gazing.
PERDITA. Out, alas!
You'd be so lean, that blasts of January
Would blow you through and through. Now, my fair'st friend,
I would I had some flower's o' the spring that might
Become your time of day; and yours, and yours,
That wear upon your virgin branches yet
Your maidenheads growing: O Proserpina!
For the flowers now that frighted thou let'st fall
From Dis's waggon! daffodils,
That come before the swallow dares, and take
The winds of March with beauty; violets dim,
But sweeter than the lids of Juno's eyes

Or Cytherea's breath; pale prime-roses,
That die unmarried, ere they can behold
Bright Phœbus in his strength, a malady
Most incident to maids; bold oxlips and
The crown imperial; lilies of all kinds,
The flower-de-luce being one. O! these I lack
To make you garlands of, and my sweet friend,
To strew him o'er and o'er!

FLORIZEL. What! like a corse?

PERDITA. No, like a bank for love to lie and play on;
Not like a corse; or if,—not to be buried,
But quick and in mine arms. Come, take your flowers:
Methinks I play as I have seen them do
In Whitsun pastorals: sure this robe of mine
Does change my disposition.

FLORIZEL. What you do
Still betters what is done. When you speak, sweet,
I'd have you do it ever: when you sing,
I'd have you buy and sell so; so give alms;
Pray so; and, for the ordering your affairs,
To sing them too: when you do dance, I wish you
A wave o' the sea, that you might ever do
Nothing but that; move still, still so,
And own no other function: each your doing,
So singular in each particular,
Crowns what you are doing in the present deed,
That all your acts are queens.

PERDITA. O Doricles!
Your praises are too large: but that your youth,
And the true blood which fairly peeps through it,
Do plainly give you out an unstain'd shepherd,
With wisdom I might fear, my Doricles,
You woo'd me the false way.

FLORIZEL. I think you have
As little skill to fear as I have purpose
To put you to 't. But, come; our dance, I pray.
Your hand, my Perdita. So turtles pair
That never mean to part.

PERDITA. I'll swear for 'em.

POLIXENES. This is the prettiest low-born lass that ever
Ran on the greensward: nothing she does or seems
But smacks of something greater than herself;

Too noble for this place.
CAMILLO.   He tells her something
That makes her blood look out. Good sooth, she is
The queen of curds and cream.
CLOWN.   Come on, strike up.
DORCAS. Mopsa must be your mistress: marry, garlic,
To mend her kissing with.
MOPSA.   Now, in good time!
CLOWN. Not a word, a word: we stand upon our manners.
Come, strike up.   *Music. Here a dance
                          of Shepherds and Shepherdesses*
POLIXENES. Pray, good shepherd, what fair swain is this
Which dances with your daughter?
SHEPHERD. They call him Doricles, and boasts himself
To have a worthy feeding; but I have it
Upon his own report and I believe it:
He looks like sooth. He says he loves my daughter:
I think so too; for never gaz'd the moon
Upon the water as he'll stand and read
As 'twere my daughter's eyes; and, to be plain,
I think there is not half a kiss to choose
Who loves another best.
POLIXENES.   She dances featly.
SHEPHERD. So she does any thing, though I report it
That should be silent. If young Doricles
Do light upon her, she shall bring him that
Which he not dreams of.
                    Enter a Servant
SERVANT. O master! if you did but hear the pedlar at the
door, you would never dance again after a tabor and pipe;
no, the bagpipe could not move you. He sings several
tunes faster than you'll tell money; he utters them as he
had eaten ballads and all men's ears grew to his tunes.
CLOWN. He could never come better. He shall come in. I
love a ballad but even too well, if it be doleful matter merrily set down, or a very pleasant thing indeed and sung
lamentably.
SERVANT. He hath songs for man or woman, of all sizes; no
milliner can so fit his customers with gloves: he has the
prettiest love-songs for maids; so without bawdry, which
is strange; with such delicate burthens of dildos and fadings, 'jump her and thump her'; and where some stretch-

mouthed rascal would, as it were, mean mischief and break a foul gap into the matter, he makes the maid to answer, 'Whoop, do me no harm, good man'; puts him off, slights him with 'Whoop, do me no harm, good man.'

POLIXENES. This is a brave fellow.

CLOWN. Believe me, thou talkest of an admirable conceited fellow. Has he any unbraided wares?

SERVANT. He hath ribands of all the colours i' the rainbow; points more than all the lawyers in Bohemia can learnedly handle, though they come to him by the gross; inkles, caddisses, cambrics, lawns. Why, he sings 'em over, as they were gods or goddesses. You would think a smock were a she-angel, he so chants to the sleevehand and the work about the square on 't.

CLOWN. Prithee, bring him in, and let him approach singing.

PERDITA. Forewarn him that he use no scurrilous words in 's tunes. *Exit Servant*

CLOWN. You have of these pedlars that have more in them than you 'd think, sister.

PERDITA. Ay, good brother, or go about to think.

Enter Autolycus, singing

> Lawn as white as driven snow;
> Cyprus black as e'er was crow;
> Gloves as sweet as damask roses;
> Masks for faces and for noses;
> Bugle-bracelet, necklace-amber,
> Perfume for a lady's chamber;
> Golden quoifs and stomachers,
> For my lads to give their dears;
> Pins and poking-sticks of steel;
> What maids lack from head to heel:
> Come buy of me, come; come buy, come buy;
> Buy, lads, or else your lasses cry:
> Come buy.

CLOWN. If I were not in love with Mopsa, thou shouldst take no money of me; but being enthralled as I am, it will also be the bondage of certain ribands and gloves.

MOPSA. I was promised them against the feast; but they come not too late now.

DORCAS. He hath promised you more than that, or there be liars.

MOPSA. He hath paid you all he promised you. May be he

has paid you more, which will shame you to give him again.

CLOWN. Is there no manners left among maids? Will they wear their plackets where they should bear their faces? Is there not milking-time, when you are going to bed, or kiln-hole, to whistle off these secrets, but you must be tittle-tattling before all our guests? 'Tis well they are whispering. Clamour your tongues, and not a word more.

MOPSA. I have done. Come, you promised me a tawdry lace and a pair of sweet gloves.

CLOWN. Have I not told thee how I was cozened by the way, and lost all my money?

AUTOLYCUS. And indeed, sir, there are cozeners abroad; therefore it behoves men to be wary.

CLOWN. Fear not thou, man, thou shalt lose nothing here.

AUTOLYCUS. I hope so, sir; for I have about me many parcels of charge.

CLOWN. What hast here? ballads?

MOPSA. Pray now, buy some. I love a ballad in print, a-life, for then we are sure they are true.

AUTOLYCUS. Here's one to a very doleful tune, how a usurer's wife was brought to bed of twenty money-bags at a burden; and how she longed to eat adders' heads and toads carbonadoed.

MOPSA. Is it true too, think you?

AUTOLYCUS. Very true, and but a month old.

DORCAS. Bless me from marrying a usurer!

AUTOLYCUS. Here's the midwife's name to 't, one Mistress Taleporter, and five or six honest wives' that were present. Why should I carry lies abroad?

MOPSA. Pray you now, buy it.

CLOWN. Come on, lay it by: and let's first see moe ballads; we'll buy the other things anon.

AUTOLYCUS. Here's another ballad of a fish that appeared upon the coast on Wednesday the fourscore of April, forty thousand fathom above water, and sung this ballad against the hard hearts of maids. It was thought she was a woman and was turned into a cold fish for she would not exchange flesh with one that loved her. The ballad is very pitiful and as true.

DORCAS. Is it true too, think you?

AUTOLYCUS. Five justices' hands at it, and witnesses more than my pack will hold.

CLOWN. Lay it by too. Another.
AUTOLYCUS. This is a merry ballad, but a very pretty one.
MOPSA. Let's have some merry ones.
AUTOLYCUS. Why, this is a passing merry one, and goes to the tune of 'Two maids wooing a man.' There's scarce a maid westward but she sings it. 'Tis in request, I can tell you.
MOPSA. We can both sing it. If thou 'lt bear a part thou shalt hear; 'tis in three parts.
DORCAS. We had the tune on't a month ago.
AUTOLYCUS. I can bear my part; you must know 'tis my occupation. Have at it with you!

AUTOLYCUS. Get you hence, for I must go,
            Where it fits not you to know.
DORCAS.   Whither?
MOPSA.   O! whither?
DORCAS.   Whither?
MOPSA.   It becomes thy oath full well,
            Thou to me thy secrets tell.
DORCAS.   Me too: let me go thither.
MOPSA.   Or thou go'st to the grange or mill.
DORCAS.   If to either, thou dost ill.
AUTOLYCUS.   Neither.
DORCAS.   What, neither?
AUTOLYCUS.   Neither.
DORCAS.   Thou hast sworn my love to be.
MOPSA.   Thou hast sworn it more to me:
            Then whither go'st? Say, whither?

CLOWN. We'll have this song out anon by ourselves. My father and the gentlemen are in sad talk, and we'll not trouble them. Come, bring away thy pack after me. Wenches, I'll buy for you both. Pedlar, let's have the first choice. Follow me, girls. *Exit with Dorcas and Mopsa*
AUTOLYCUS. And you shall pay well for 'em.
            Will you buy any tape,
              Or lace for your cape,
           My dainty duck, my dear-a?
              Any silk, any thread,
              Any toys for your head,
           Of the new'st and fin'st, fin'st wear-a?
              Come to the pedlar;
              Money's a meddler,
           That doth utter all men's ware-a.   *Exit*

Re-enter Servant

SERVANT. Master, there is three carters, three shepherds, three neat-herds, three swine-herds, that have made themselves all men of hair; they call themselves Saltiers; and they have a dance which the wenches say is a gallimaufry of gambols, because they are not in 't; but they themselves are o' the mind,—if it be not too rough for some that know little but bowling,—it will please plentifully.

SHEPHERD. Away! we 'll none on 't. Here has been too much homely foolery already. I know, sir, we weary you.

POLIXENES. You weary those that refresh us. Pray let 's see these four threes of herdsmen.

SERVANT. One three of them, by their own report, sir, hath danced before the king; and not the worst of the three but jumps twelve foot and a half by the squire.

SHEPHERD. Leave your prating. Since these good men are pleased, let them come in: but quickly now.

SERVANT. Why, they stay at door, sir. *Exit*

Re-enter Servant, with twelve Rustics habited like Satyrs. They dance, and then exeunt

POLIXENES. (*To Shepherd*) O, father! you 'll know more of that hereafter.

(*To Camillo*) Is it not too far gone? 'Tis time to part them. He 's simple and tells much. (*To Florizel*) How now, fair shepherd!
Your heart is full of something that does take
Your mind from feasting. Sooth, when I was young,
And handed love as you do, I was wont
To load my she with knacks. I would have ransack'd
The pedlar's silken treasury and have pour'd it
To her acceptance. You have let him go
And nothing marted with him. If your lass
Interpretation should abuse and call this
Your lack of love or bounty, you were straited
For a reply, at least if you make a care
Of happy holding her.

FLORIZEL. Old sir, I know
She prizes not such trifles as these are.
The gifts she looks from me are pack'd and lock'd
Up in my heart, which I have given already,
But not deliver'd. O! hear me breathe my life
Before this ancient sir, who, it should seem,

Hath sometime lov'd. I take thy hand; this hand,
As soft as dove's down, and as white as it,
Or Ethiopian's tooth, or the fann'd snow
That's bolted by the northern blasts twice o'er.
POLIXENES. What follows this?
How prettily the young swain seems to wash
The hand was fair before! I have put you out:
But to your protestation: let me hear
What you profess.
FLORIZEL. Do, and be witness to 't.
POLIXENES. And this my neighbour too?
FLORIZEL. And he, and more
Than he, and men, the earth, the heavens, and all;
That, were I crown'd the most imperial monarch,
Thereof most worthy, were I the fairest youth
That ever made eye swerve, had force and knowledge
More than was ever man's I would not prize them
Without her love: for her employ them all;
Commend them and condemn them to her service
Or to their own perdition.
POLIXENES. Fairly offer'd.
CAMILLO. This shows a sound affection.
SHEPHERD. But, my daughter,
Say you the like to him?
PERDITA. I cannot speak
So well, nothing so well; no, nor mean better.
By the pattern of mine own thoughts I cut out
The purity of his.
SHEPHERD. Take hands; a bargain;
And, friends unknown, you shall bear witness to 't:
I give my daughter to him, and will make
Her portion equal his.
FLORIZEL. O! that must be
I' the virtue of your daughter: one being dead,
I shall have more than you can dream of yet;
Enough then for your wonder. But, come on;
Contract us 'fore these witnesses.
SHEPHERD. Come, your hand;
And, daughter, yours.
POLIXENES. Soft, swain, awhile, beseech you.
Have you a father?
FLORIZEL. I have; but what of him?

POLIXENES. Knows he of this?
FLORIZEL.   He neither does nor shall.
POLIXENES. Methinks a father
  Is, at the nuptial of his son, a guest
  That best becomes the table. Pray you, once more,
  Is not your father grown incapable
  Of reasonable affairs? Is he not stupid
  With age and altering rheums? can he speak? hear?
  Know man from man? dispute his own estate?
  Lies he not bed-rid? And again does nothing
  But what he did being childish?
FLORIZEL.   No, good sir:
  He has his health and ampler strength indeed
  Than most have of his age.
POLIXENES.   By my white beard,
  You offer him, if this be so, a wrong
  Something unfilial. Reason my son
  Should choose himself a wife, but as good reason
  The father,—all whose joy is nothing else
  But fair posterity,—should hold some counsel
  In such a business.
FLORIZEL.   I yield all this;
  But for some other reasons, my grave sir,
  Which 'tis not fit you know, I not acquaint
  My father of this business.
POLIXENES.   Let him know 't.
FLORIZEL. He shall not.
POLIXENES.   Prithee, let him.
FLORIZEL.   No, he must not.
SHEPHERD. Let him, my son: he shall not need to grieve
  At knowing of thy choice.
FLORIZEL.   Come, come, he must not.
  Mark our contract.
POLIXENES.   Mark your divorce, young sir,
                               Discovering himself
  Whom son I dare not call: thou art too base
  To be acknowledged: thou a sceptre's heir,
  That thus affect'st a sheep-hook! Thou old traitor,
  I am sorry that by hanging thee I can
  But shorten thy life one week. And thou, fresh piece
  Of excellent witchcraft, who of force must know

The royal fool thou cop'st with,—
SHEPHERD. O, my heart!
POLIXENES. I'll have thy beauty scratch'd with briers, and made
  More homely than thy state. For thee, fond boy,
  If I may ever know thou dost but sigh
  That thou no more shalt see this knack,—as never
  I mean thou shalt,—we'll bar thee from succession;
  Not hold thee of our blood, no, not our kin,
  Far than Deucalion off: mark thou my words:
  Follow us to the court. Thou, churl, for this time,
  Though full of our displeasure, yet we free thee
  From the dead blow of it. And you, enchantment,—
  Worthy enough a herdsman; yea, him too,
  That makes himself, but for our honour therein,
  Unworthy thee,—if ever henceforth thou
  These rural latches to his entrance open,
  Or hoop his body more with thy embraces,
  I will devise a death as cruel for thee
  As thou art tender to't. *Exit*
PERDITA. Even here undone!
  I was not much afeard; for once or twice
  I was about to speak and tell him plainly,
  The self-same sun that shines upon his court
  Hides not his visage from our cottage, but
  Looks on alike. Will't please you, sir, be gone?
  I told you what would come of this: beseech you,
  Of your own state take care: this dream of mine—
  Being now awake, I'll queen it no inch farther,
  But milk my ewes and weep.
CAMILLO. Why, how now, father!
  Speak, ere thou diest.
SHEPHERD. I cannot speak, nor think,
  Nor dare to know that which I know. O sir!
  You have undone a man of fourscore three,
  That thought to fill his grave in quiet, yea,
  To die upon the bed my father died,
  To lie close by his honest bones: but now
  Some hangman must put on my shroud and lay me
  Where no priest shovels in dust. O cursed wretch!
  That knew'st this was the prince, and wouldst adventure

> To mingle faith with him. Undone! undone!
> If I might die within this hour, I have liv'd
> To die when I desire. *Exit*

FLORIZEL. Why look you so upon me?
> I am but sorry, not afeard; delay'd,
> But nothing alter'd. What I was, I am:
> More straining on for plucking back; not following
> My leash unwillingly.

CAMILLO. Gracious my lord,
> You know your father's temper: at this time
> He will allow no speech, which I do guess
> You do not purpose to him; and as hardly
> Will he endure your sight as yet, I fear:
> Then, till the fury of his Highness settle,
> Come not before him.

FLORIZEL. I not purpose it.
> I think, Camillo?

CAMILLO. Even he, my lord.

PERDITA. How often have I told you 'twould be thus!
> How often said my dignity would last
> But till 'twere known!

FLORIZEL. It cannot fail but by
> The violation of my faith; and then
> Let nature crush the sides o' the earth together
> And mar the seeds within! Lift up thy looks:
> From my succession wipe me, father; I
> Am heir to my affection.

CAMILLO. Be advis'd.

FLORIZEL. I am; and by my fancy: if my reason
> Will thereto be obedient, I have reason;
> If not, my senses, better pleas'd with madness,
> Do bid it welcome.

CAMILLO. This is desperate, sir.

FLORIZEL. So call it; but it does fulfil my vow,
> I needs must think it honesty. Camillo,
> Not for Bohemia, nor the pomp that may
> Be thereat glean'd, for all the sun sees or
> The close earth wombs or the profound sea hides
> In unknown fathoms, will I break my oath
> To this my fair belov'd. Therefore, I pray you,
> As you have ever been my father's honour'd friend,

When he shall miss me,—as, in faith, I mean not
To see him any more,—cast your good counsels
Upon his passion: let myself and fortune
Tug for the time to come. This you may know
And so deliver, I am put to sea
With her whom here I cannot hold on shore;
And most opportune to our need, I have
A vessel rides fast by, but not prepar'd
For this design. What course I mean to hold
Shall nothing benefit your knowledge, nor
Concern me the reporting.

CAMILLO. O my lord!
I would your spirit were easier for advice,
Or stronger for your need.

FLORIZEL. Hark, Perdita. *Takes her aside*
(*To Camillo*) I 'll hear you by and by.

CAMILLO. He 's irremovable,
Resolv'd for flight. Now were I happy if
His going I could frame to serve my turn,
Save him from danger, do him love and honour,
Purchase the sight again of dear Sicilia
And that unhappy king, my master, whom
I so much thirst to see.

FLORIZEL. Now, good Camillo,
I am so fraught with curious business that
I leave out ceremony.

CAMILLO. Sir, I think
You have heard of my poor services, i' the love
That I have borne your father?

FLORIZEL. Very nobly
Have you deserv'd: it is my father's music
To speak your deeds, not little of his care
To have them recompens'd as thought on.

CAMILLO. Well, my lord,
If you may please to think I love the king
And through him what 's nearest to him, which is
Your gracious self, embrace but my direction.
If your more ponderous and settled project
May suffer alteration, on mine honour
I 'll point you where you shall have such receiving
As shall become your Highness; where you may
Enjoy your mistress,—from the whom, I see,

There 's no disjunction to be made, but by,
As, heavens forfend! your ruin,—marry her;
And with my best endeavours in your absence
Your discontenting father strive to qualify,
And bring him up to liking.

FLORIZEL. How, Camillo,
May this, almost a miracle, be done?
That I may call thee something more than man,
And after that trust to thee.

CAMILLO. Have you thought on
A place whereto you 'll go?

FLORIZEL. Not any yet;
But as the unthought-on accident is guilty
To what we wildly do, so we profess
Ourselves to be the slaves of chance and flies
Of every wind that blows.

CAMILLO. Then list to me:
This follows; if you will not change your purpose
But undergo this flight, make for Sicilia,
And there present yourself and your fair princess,—
For so, I see, she must be,—'fore Leontes;
She shall be habited as it becomes
The partner of your bed. Methinks I see
Leontes opening his free arms and weeping
His welcomes forth; asks thee, the son, forgiveness
As 'twere i' the father's person; kisses the hands
Of your fresh princess; o'er and o'er divides him
'Twixt his unkindness and his kindness: the one
He chides to hell, and bids the other grow
Faster than thought or time.

FLORIZEL. Worthy Camillo,
What colour for my visitation shall I
Hold up before him?

CAMILLO. Sent by the king your father
To greet him and to give him comforts. Sir,
The manner of your bearing towards him, with
What you as from your father shall deliver,
Things known betwixt us three, I 'll write you down.
The which shall point you forth at every sitting
What you must say; that he shall not perceive
But that you have your father's bosom there
And speak his very heart.

FLORIZEL. I am bound to you.
There is some sap in this.

CAMILLO. A course more promising
Than a wild dedication of yourselves
To unpath'd waters, undream'd shores, most certain
To miseries enough: no hope to help you,
But as you shake off one to take another;
Nothing so certain as your anchors, who
Do their best office, if they can but stay you
Where you'll be loath to be. Besides, you know
Prosperity's the very bond of love,
Whose fresh complexion and whose heart together
Affliction alters.

PERDITA. One of these is true:
I think affliction may subdue the cheek,
But not take in the mind.

CAMILLO. Yea, say you so?
There shall not at your father's house these seven years
Be born another such.

FLORIZEL. My good Camillo,
She is as forward of her breeding as
She is i' the rear o' her birth.

CAMILLO. I cannot say 'tis pity
She lacks instructions, for she seems a mistress
To most that teach.

PERDITA. Your pardon, sir; for this
I'll blush you thanks.

FORIZEL. My prettiest Perdita!
But O! the thorns we stand upon. Camillo,
Preserver of my father, now of me,
The medicine of our house, how shall we do?
We are not furnish'd like Bohemia's son,
Nor shall appear in Sicilia.

CAMILLO. My lord,
Fear none of this: I think you know my fortunes
Do all lie there. It shall be so my care
To have you royally appointed as if
The scene you play were mine. For instance, sir,
That you may know you shall not want, one word.

They talk aside

Enter Autolycus

AUTOLYCUS. Ha, ha! what a fool Honesty is! and Trust, his sworn brother, a very simple gentleman! I have sold all my trumpery: not a counterfeit stone, not a riband, glass, pomander, brooch, table-book, ballad, knife, tape, glove, shoe-tie, bracelet, horn-ring, to keep my pack from fasting; they throng who should buy first, as if my trinkets had been hallowed and brought a benediction to the buyer: by which means I saw whose purse was best in picture; and what I saw, to my good use I remembered. My clown,—who wants but something to be a reasonable man,—grew so in love with the wenches' song that he would not stir his pettitoes till he had both tune and words; which so drew the rest of the herd to me that all their other senses stuck in ears: you might have pinched a placket, it was senseless; 'twas nothing to geld a codpiece of a purse; I would have filed keys off that hung in chains: no hearing, no feeling, but my sir's song, and admiring the nothing of it; so that, in this time of lethargy I picked and cut most of their festival purses; and had not the old man come in with a whoo-bub against his daughter and the king's son, and scared my choughs from the chaff, I had not left a purse alive in the whole army.

Camillo, Florizel, and Perdita come forward

CAMILLO. Nay, but my letters, by this means being there
So soon as you arrive, shall clear that doubt.

FLORIZEL. And those that you 'll procure from King Leontes—

CAMILLO. Shall satisfy your father.

PERDITA. Happy be you!
All that you speak shows fair.

CAMILLO. (*Seeing Autolycus*) Whom have we here?
We 'll make an instrument of this: omit
Nothing may give us aid.

AUTOLYCUS. (*Aside*) If they have overheard me now, why, hanging.

CAMILLO. How now, good fellow! Why shakest thou so? Fear not, man; here 's no harm intended to thee.

AUTOLYCUS. I am a poor fellow, sir.

CAMILLO. Why, be so still. Here 's nobody will steal that from thee; yet, for the outside of thy poverty we must make an exchange; therefore, discase thee instantly,—thou must think, there 's a necessity in 't,—and change garments with this gentleman: though the pennyworth on his side

be the worst, yet hold thee, there's some boot.
AUTOLYCUS. I am a poor fellow, sir.—(*Aside*) I know ye well enough.
CAMILLO. Nay, prithee, dispatch: the gentleman is half flayed already.
AUTOLYCUS. Are you in earnest, sir? (*Aside*) I smell the trick on 't.
FLORIZEL. Dispatch, I prithee.
AUTOLYCUS. Indeed, I have had earnest; but I cannot with conscience take it.
CAMILLO. Unbuckle, unbuckle.—
Florizel and Autolycus exchange garments
Fortunate mistress,—let my prophecy
Come home to ye!—you must retire yourself
Into some covert: take your sweetheart's hat
And pluck it o'er your brows; muffle your face;
Dismantle you, and, as you can, disliken
The truth of your own seeming; that you may,—
For I do fear eyes over you,—to shipboard
Get undescried.
PERDITA.   I see the play so lies
That I must bear a part.
CAMILLO.   No remedy.
Have you done there?
FLORIZEL.   Should I now meet my father
He would not call me son.
CAMILLO.   Nay, you shall have no hat.
Giving it to Perdita
Come, lady, come. Farewell, my friend.
AUTOLYCUS.   Adieu, sir.
FLORIZEL. O Perdita, what have we twain forgot!
Pray you, a word.   *They converse apart*
CAMILLO. (*Aside*) What I do next shall be to tell the king
Of this escape, and whither they are bound;
Wherein my hope is I shall so prevail
To force him after: in whose company
I shall review Sicilia, for whose sight
I have a woman's longing.
FLORIZEL.   Fortune speed us!
Thus we set on, Camillo, to the sea-side.
CAMILLO. The swifter speed the better.
Exeunt Florizel, Perdita, and Camillo

AUTOLYCUS. I understand the business; I hear it. To have an open ear, a quick eye, and a nimble hand, is necessary for a cut-purse: a good nose is requisite also, to smell out work for the other senses. I see this is the time that the unjust man doth thrive. What an exchange had this been without boot! What a boot is here with this exchange! Sure, the gods do this year connive at us, and we may do anything extempore. The prince himself is about a piece of iniquity; stealing away from his father with his clog at his heels. If I thought it were a piece of honesty to acquaint the king withal, I would not do 't. I hold it the more knavery to conceal it, and therein am I constant to my profession. Aside, aside! Here is more matter for a hot brain. Every lane's end, every shop, church, session, hanging, yields a careful man work.

Re-enter Clown and Shepherd

CLOWN. See, see, what a man you are now! There is no other way but to tell the king she 's a changeling and none of your flesh and blood.

SHEPHERD. Nay, but hear me.

CLOWN. Nay, but hear me.

SHEPHERD. Go to, then.

CLOWN. She being none of your flesh and blood, your flesh and blood has not offended the king; and so your flesh and blood is not to be punished by him. Show those things you found about her; those secret things, all but what she has with her. This being done, let the law go whistle: I warrant you.

SHEPHERD. I will tell the king all, every word, yea, and his son's pranks too; who, I may say, is no honest man neither to his father nor to me, to go about to make me the king's brother-in-law.

CLOWN. Indeed, brother-in-law was the furthest off you could have been to him, and then your blood had been the dearer by I know not how much an ounce.

AUTOLYCUS. (*Aside*) Very wisely, puppies!

SHEPHERD. Well, let us to the king. There is that in this fardel will make him scratch his beard.

AUTOLYCUS. (*Aside*) I know not what impediment this complaint may be to the flight of my master.

CLOWN. Pray heartily he be at palace.

AUTOLYCUS. (*Aside*) Though I am not naturally honest, I am

so sometimes by chance. Let me pocket up my pedlar's excrement. (*Takes off his false beard*) How now, rustics! Whither are you bound?

SHEPHERD. To the palace, an it like your worship.

AUTOLYCUS. Your affairs there, what, with whom, the condition of that fardel, the place of your dwelling, your names, your ages, of what having, breeding, and anything that is fitting to be known, discover.

CLOWN. We are but plain fellows, sir.

AUTOLYCUS. A lie! You are rough and hairy. Let me have no lying; it becomes none but tradesmen, and they often give us soldiers the lie; but we pay them for it with stamped coin, not stabbing steel; therefore they do not give us the lie.

CLOWN. Your worship had like to have given us one, if you had not taken yourself with the manner.

SHEPHERD. Are you a courtier, an 't like you, sir?

AUTOLYCUS. Whether it like me or no, I am a courtier. Seest thou not the air of the court in these enfoldings? Hath not my gait in it the measure of the court? Receives not thy nose court-odour from me? Reflect I not on thy baseness court-contempt? Think'st thou, for that I insinuate, or toaze from thee thy business, I am therefore no courtier? I am courtier, cap-a-pe, and one that will either push on or pluck back thy business there. Whereupon I command thee to open thy affair.

SHEPHERD. My business, sir, is to the king.

AUTOLYCUS. What advocate hast thou to him?

SHEPHERD. I know not, an 't like you.

CLOWN. Advocate 's the court-word for a pheasant. Say you have none.

SHEPHERD. None, sir; I have no pheasant, cock nor hen.

AUTOLYCUS. How bless'd are we that are not simple men!
Yet nature might have made me as these are,
Therefore I 'll not disdain.

CLOWN. This cannot be but a great courtier.

SHEPHERD. His garments are rich, but he wears them not handsomely.

CLOWN. He seems to be the more noble in being fantastical: a great man, I 'll warrant; I know by the picking on 's teeth.

AUTOLYCUS. The fardel there? What 's i' the fardel? Wherefore that box?

SHEPHERD. Sir, there lies such secrets in this fardel and box which none must know but the king; and which he shall know within this hour if I may come to the speech of him.

AUTOLYCUS. Age, thou hast lost thy labour.

SHEPHERD. Why, sir?

AUTOLYCUS. The king is not at the palace; he is gone aboard a new ship to purge melancholy and air himself: for, if thou be'st capable of things serious, thou must know the king is full of grief.

SHEPHERD. So 'tis said, sir, about his son, that should have married a shepherd's daughter.

AUTOLYCUS. If that shepherd be not now in handfast, let him fly. The curses he shall have, the torture he shall feel, will break the back of man, the heart of monster.

CLOWN. Think you so, sir?

AUTOLYCUS. Not he alone shall suffer what wit can make heavy and vengeance bitter; but those that are germane to him, though removed fifty times, shall all come under the hangman: which though it be great pity, yet it is necessary. An old sheep-whistling rogue, a ram-tender, to offer to have his daughter come into grace! Some say he shall be stoned; but that death is too soft for him, say I: draw our throne into a sheep-cote! All deaths are too few, the sharpest too easy.

CLOWN. Has the old man e'er a son, sir, do you hear, an 't like you, sir?

AUTOLYCUS. He has a son, who shall be flayed alive; then 'nointed over with honey, set on the head of a wasp's nest; then stand till he be three quarters and a dram dead; then recovered again with aqua-vitæ or some other hot infusion; then, raw as he is, and in the hottest day prognostication proclaims, shall he be set against a brick-wall, the sun looking with a southward eye upon him, where he is to behold him with flies blown to death. But what talk we of these traitorly rascals, whose miseries are to be smiled at, their offences being so capital? Tell me,—for you seem to be honest plain men,—what you have to the king. Being something gently considered, I 'll bring you where he is aboard, tender your persons to his presence, whisper him in your behalfs; and if it be in man besides the king to effect your suits, here is a man shall do it.

CLOWN. He seems to be of great authority. Close with him,

ACT IV : SCENE III

give him gold; and though authority be a stubborn bear, yet he is oft led by the nose with gold. Show the inside of your purse to the outside of his hand, and no more ado. Remember, 'stoned,' and 'flayed alive'!

SHEPHERD. An 't please you, sir, to undertake the business for us, here is that gold I have. I'll make it as much more and leave this young man in pawn till I bring it you.

AUTOLYCUS. After I have done what I promised?

SHEPHERD. Ay, sir.

AUTOLYCUS. Well, give me the moiety. Are you a party in this business?

CLOWN. In some sort, sir: but though my case be a pitiful one, I hope I shall not be flayed out of it.

AUTOLYCUS. O! that's the case of the shepherd's son. Hang him, he'll be made an example.

CLOWN. Comfort, good comfort! we must to the king and show our strange sights. He must know 'tis none of your daughter nor my sister; we are gone else. Sir, I will give you as much as this old man does when the business is performed; and remain, as he says, your pawn till it be brought you.

AUTOLYCUS. I will trust you. Walk before toward the seaside; go on the right hand; I will but look upon the hedge and follow you.

CLOWN. We are blessed in this man, as I may say, even blessed.

SHEPHERD. Let's before as he bids us. He was provided to do us good. *Exeunt Shepherd and Clown*

AUTOLYCUS. If I had a mind to be honest I see Fortune would not suffer me: she drops booties in my mouth. I am courted now with a double occasion, gold, and a means to do the prince my master good; which who knows how that may turn back to my advancement? I will bring these two moles, these blind ones, aboard him. If he think it fit to shore them again, and that the complaint they have to the king concerns him nothing, let him call me rogue for being so far officious; for I am proof against that title and what shame else belongs to 't. To him will I present them: there may be matter in it. *Exit*

ACT FIVE

SCENE ONE

Sicilia. A Room in the Palace of Leontes.

Enter Leontes, Cleomenes, Dion, Paulina, and Others

CLEOMENES. Sir, you have done enough, and have perform'd,
A saint-like sorrow. No fault could you make
Which you have not redeem'd; indeed, paid down
More penitence than done trespass. At the last,
Do as the heavens have done, forget your evil;
With them forgive yourself.

LEONTES. Whilst I remember
Her and her virtues, I cannot forget
My blemishes in them, and so still think of
The wrong I did myself; which was so much,
That heirless it hath made my kingdom, and
Destroy'd the sweet'st companion that e'er man
Bred his hopes out of.

PAULINA. True, too true, my lord;
If one by one you wedded all the world,
Or from the all that are took something good,
To make a perfect woman, she you kill'd
Would be unparallel'd.

LEONTES. I think so. Kill'd!
She I kill'd! I did so; but thou strik'st me
Sorely to say I did. It is as bitter
Upon thy tongue as in my thought. Now, good now,
Say so but seldom.

CLEOMENES. Not at all, good lady.
You might have spoken a thousand things that would
Have done the time more benefit, and grac'd
Your kindness better.

PAULINA. You are one of those

ACT V : SCENE I

Would have him wed again.

DION. If you would not so,
You pity not the state, nor the remembrance
Of his most sovereign name; consider little
What dangers, by his Highness' fail of issue,
May drop upon his kingdom and devour
Incertain lookers-on. What were more holy
Than to rejoice the former queen is well?
What holier than for royalty's repair,
For present comfort, and for future good,
To bless the bed of majesty again
With a sweet fellow to 't?

PAULINA. There is none worthy,
Respecting her that's gone. Besides, the gods
Will have fulfill'd their secret purposes;
For has not the divine Apollo said,
Is 't not the tenour of his oracle,
That King Leontes shall not have an heir
Till his lost child be found? Which that it shall,
Is all as monstrous to our human reason
As my Antigonus to break his grave
And come again to me; who, on my life,
Did perish with the infant. 'Tis your counsel
My lord should to the heavens be contrary,
Oppose against their wills.—(*To Leontes*) Care not for issue;
The crown will find an heir. Great Alexander
Left his to the worthiest, so his successor
Was like to be the best.

LEONTES. Good Paulina,
Who hast the memory of Hermione,
I know, in honour; O! that ever I
Had squar'd me to thy counsel! Then, even now,
I might have look'd upon my queen's full eyes,
Have taken treasure from her lips,—

PAULINA. And left them
More rich, for what they yielded.

LEONTES. Thou speak'st truth.
No more such wives; therefore, no wife: one worse,
And better us'd, would make her sainted spirit
Again possess her corpse and on this stage,—
Where we 're offenders now,—appear soul-vex'd,

And begin, 'Why to me?'
PAULINA.   Had she such power,
  She had just cause.
LEONTES.   She had; and would incense me
  To murder her I married.
PAULINA.   I should so.
  Were I the ghost that walk'd I'd bid you mark
  Her eye, and tell me for what dull part in't
  You chose her; then I'd shriek, that even your ears
  Should rift to hear me; and the words that follow'd
  Should be 'Remember mine.'
LEONTES.   Stars, stars!
  And all eyes else dead coals. Fear thou no wife;
  I'll have no wife, Paulina.
PAULINA.   Will you swear
  Never to marry but by my free leave?
LEONTES. Never, Paulina: so be bless'd my spirit!
PAULINA. Then, good my lords, bear witness to his oath.
CLEOMENES. You tempt him over much.
PAULINA.   Unless another,
  As like Hermione as is her picture,
  Affront his eye.
CLEOMENES.   Good madam,—
PAULINA.   I have done.
  Yet, if my lord will marry,—if you will, sir,
  No remedy, but you will,—give me the office
  To choose you a queen, she shall not be so young
  As was your former; but she shall be such
  As, walk'd your first queen's ghost, it should take joy
  To see her in your arms.
LEONTES.   My true Paulina,
  We shall not marry till thou bidd'st us.
PAULINA.   That
  Shall be when your first queen's again in breath;
  Never till then.

                    Enter a Gentleman

GENTLEMAN. One that gives out himself Prince Florizel,
  Son of Polixenes, with his princess,—she
  The fairest I have yet beheld,—desires access
  To your high presence.
LEONTES.   What with him? He comes not
  Like to his father's greatness; his approach,

ACT V : SCENE I

    So out of circumstance and sudden, tells us
    'Tis not a visitation fram'd, but forc'd
    By need and accident. What train?
GENTLEMAN.   But few,
    And those but mean.
LEONTES.   His princess, say you, with him?
GENTLEMAN. Ay, the most peerless piece of earth, I think,
    That e'er the sun shone bright on.
PAULINA.   O Hermione!
    As every present time doth boast itself
    Above a better gone, so must thy grave
    Give way to what's seen now. Sir, you yourself
    Have said and writ so,—but your writing now
    Is colder than that theme,—'She had not been,
    Nor was not to be equall'd'; thus your verse
    Flow'd with her beauty once: 'tis shrewdly ebb'd
    To say you have seen a better.
GENTLEMAN.   Pardon, madam:
    The one I have almost forgot—your pardon—
    The other, when she has obtain'd your eye,
    Will have your tongue too. This is a creature,
    Would she begin a sect, might quench the zeal
    Of all professors else, make proselytes
    Of who she but bid follow.
PAULINA.   How! not women?
GENTLEMAN. Women will love her, that she is a woman
    More worth than any man; men, that she is
    The rarest of all women.
LEONTES.   Go, Cleomenes;
    Yourself, assisted with your honour'd friends,
    Bring them to our embracement. Still 'tis strange,
            Exeunt Cleomenes, Lords, and Gentleman
    He thus should steal upon us.
PAULINA.   Had our prince—
    Jewel of children—seen this hour, he had pair'd
    Well with this lord. There was not full a month
    Between their births.
LEONTES. Prithee, no more: cease! Thou know'st
    He dies to me again when talk'd of. Sure,
    When I shall see this gentleman, thy speeches
    Will bring me to consider that which may
    Unfurnish me of reason. They are come.

Re-enter Cleomenes, with Florizel, Perdita, and Others
　　Your mother was most true to wedlock, prince;
For she did print your royal father off,
Conceiving you. Were I but twenty-one,
Your father's image is so hit in you,
His very air, that I should call you brother,
As I did him; and speak of something wildly
By us perform'd before. Most dearly welcome!
And you, fair princess,—goddess! O, alas!
I lost a couple, that 'twixt heaven and earth
Might thus have stood begetting wonder as
You, gracious couple, do: and then I lost—
All mine own folly—the society,
Amity too, of your brave father, whom,
Though bearing misery, I desire my life
Once more to look on him.
FLORIZEL.　　　　　　　By his command
Have I here touch'd Sicilia; and from him
Give you all greetings that a king, at friend,
Can send his brother: and, but infirmity,—
Which waits upon worn times,—hath something seiz'd
His wish'd ability, he had himself
The land and waters 'twixt your throne and his
Measur'd to look upon you, whom he loves—
He bade me say so—more than all the sceptres
And those that bear them living.
LEONTES.　　　　　　　O, my brother!—
Good gentleman,—the wrongs I have done thee stir
Afresh within me, and these thy offices
So rarely kind, are as interpreters
Of my behind-hand slackness! Welcome hither,
As is the spring to the earth. And hath he too
Expos'd this paragon to the fearful usage—
At least ungentle—of the dreadful Neptune,
To greet a man not worth her pains, much less
The adventure of her person?
FLORIZEL.　　　　　　　Good my lord,
She came from Libya.
LEONTES.　　　　　Where the war-like Smalus,
That noble honour'd lord, is fear'd and lov'd?
FLORIZEL. Most royal sir, from thence; from him, whose
　　daughter

ACT V : SCENE I

His tears proclaim'd his, parting with her: thence—
A prosperous south-wind friendly—we have cross'd,
To execute the charge my father gave me
For visiting your Highness. My best train
I have from your Sicilian shores dismiss'd;
Who for Bohemia bend, to signify
Not only my success in Libya, sir,
But my arrival and my wife's, in safety
Here where we are.

LEONTES. The blessed gods
Purge all infection from our air whilst you
Do climate here! You have a holy father,
A graceful gentleman; against whose person,
So sacred as it is, I have done sin:
For which the heavens, taking angry note,
Have left me issueless; and your father's bless'd—
As he from heaven merits it—with you,
Worthy his goodness. What might I have been,
Might I a son and daughter now have look'd on,
Such goodly things as you!

Enter a Lord

LORD. Most noble sir,
That which I shall report will bear no credit,
Were not the proof so nigh. Please you, great sir,
Bohemia greets you from himself by me;
Desires you to attach his son, who has—
His dignity and duty both cast off—
Fled from his father, from his hopes, and with
A shepherd's daughter.

LEONTES. Where's Bohemia? Speak.

LORD. Here in your city; I now came from him:
I speak amazedly, and it becomes
My marvel and my message. To your court
Whiles he was hastening,—in the chase it seems
Of this fair couple,—meets he on the way
The father of this seeming lady and
Her brother, having both their country quitted
With this young prince.

FLORIZEL. Camillo has betray'd me;
Whose honour and whose honesty till now
Endur'd all weathers.

LORD. Lay 't so to his charge.

He 's with the king your father.

LEONTES. Who? Camillo?

LORD. Camillo, sir. I spake with him, who now
Has these poor men in question. Never saw I
Wretches so quake. They kneel, they kiss the earth,
Forswear themselves as often as they speak.
Bohemia stops his ears, and threatens them
With divers deaths in death.

PERDITA. O my poor father!
The heaven sets spies upon us, will not have
Our contract celebrated.

LEONTES. You are married?

FLORIZEL. We are not, sir, nor are we like to be;
The stars, I see, will kiss the valleys first.
The odds for high and low 's alike.

LEONTES. My lord,
Is this the daughter of a king?

FLORIZEL. She is,
When once she is my wife.

LEONTES. That 'once,' I see, by your good father's speed,
Will come on very slowly. I am sorry,
Most sorry, you have broken from his liking
Where you were tied in duty; and as sorry
Your choice is not so rich in worth as beauty,
That you might well enjoy her.

FLORIZEL. Dear, look up:
Though Fortune, visible an enemy,
Should chase us with my father, power no jot
Hath she to change our loves. Beseech you, sir,
Remember since you ow'd no more to time
Than I do now; with thought of such affections,
Step forth mine advocate; at your request
My father will grant precious things as trifles.

LEONTES. Would he do so, I 'd beg your precious mistress,
Which he counts but a trifle.

PAULINA. Sir, my liege,
Your eye hath too much youth in 't. Not a month
'Fore your queen died, she was more worth such gazes
Than what you look on now.

LEONTES. I thought of her,
Even in these looks I made. (*To Florizel*) But your petition

Is yet unanswer'd. I will to your father.
Your honour not o'erthrown by your desires,
I am friend to them and you; upon which errand
I now go toward him. Therefore follow me,
And mark what way I make. Come, my lord. *Exeunt*

SCENE TWO

The Same. Before the Palace.

Enter Autolycus and a Gentleman

AUTOLYCUS. Beseech you, sir, were you present at this relation?

GENTLEMAN. I was by at the opening of the fardel, heard the old shepherd deliver the manner how he found it: whereupon, after a little amazedness, we were all commanded out of the chamber. Only this methought I heard the shepherd say; he found the child.

AUTOLYCUS. I would most gladly know the issue of it.

GENTLEMAN. I make a broken delivery of the business; but the changes I perceived in the king and Camillo were very notes of admiration. They seemed almost, with staring on one another, to tear the cases of their eyes; there was speech in their dumbness, language in their very gesture; they looked as they had heard of a world ransomed, or one destroyed. A notable passion of wonder appeared in them; but the wisest beholder, that knew no more but seeing, could not say if the importance were joy or sorrow; but in the extremity of the one it must needs be.

Enter another Gentleman

Here comes a gentleman that haply knows more. The news, Rogero?

SECOND GENTLEMAN. Nothing but bonfires. The oracle is fulfilled; the king's daughter is found. Such a deal of wonder is broken out within this hour that ballad-makers cannot be able to express it.

Enter a third Gentleman

Here comes the Lady Paulina's steward: he can deliver you more. How goes it now, sir? This news which is called true is so like an old tale that the verity of it is in strong suspicion. Has the king found his heir?

THIRD GENTLEMAN. Most true, if ever truth were pregnant by circumstance. That which you hear you'll swear you see, there is such unity in the proofs. The mantle of Queen Hermione, her jewel about the neck of it, the letters of Antigonus found with it, which they know to be his character; the majesty of the creature in resemblance of the mother, the affection of nobleness which nature shows above her breeding, and many other evidences proclaim her with all certainty to be the king's daughter. Did you see the meeting of the two kings?

SECOND GENTLEMAN. No.

THIRD GENTLEMAN. Then have you lost a sight, which was to be seen, cannot be spoken of. There might you have beheld one joy crown another, so, and in such manner that, it seemed, sorrow wept to take leave of them, for their joy waded in tears. There was casting up of eyes, holding up of hands, with countenances of such distraction that they were to be known by garment, not by favour. Our king, being ready to leap out of himself for joy of his found daughter, as if that joy were now become a loss, cries, 'O, thy mother, thy mother!' then asks Bohemia forgiveness; then embraces his son-in-law; then again worries he his daughter with clipping her; now he thanks the old shepherd, which stands by like a weather-bitten conduit of many kings' reigns. I never heard of such another encounter, which lames report to follow it and undoes description to do it.

SECOND GENTLEMAN. What, pray you, became of Antigonus that carried hence the child?

THIRD GENTLEMAN. Like an old tale still, which will have matter to rehearse, though credit be asleep and not an ear open. He was torn to pieces with a bear. This avouches the shepherd's son, who has not only his innocence—which seems much—to justify him, but a handkerchief and rings of his that Paulina knows.

FIRST GENTLEMAN. What became of his bark and his followers?

THIRD GENTLEMAN. Wracked, the same instant of their master's death, and in the view of the shepherd: so that all the instruments which aided to expose the child were even then lost when it was found. But, O! the noble combat that 'twixt joy and sorrow was fought in Paulina. She had one eye declined for the loss of her husband, another elevated that the oracle was fulfilled. She lifted the princess from the earth, and so locks her in embracing, as if she would pin her to her heart that she might no more be in danger of losing.

FIRST GENTLEMAN. The dignity of this act was worth the audience of kings and princes, for by such was it acted.

THIRD GENTLEMAN. One of the prettiest touches of all, and that which angled for mine eyes,—caught the water though not the fish,—was when at the relation of the queen's death, with the manner how she came to it,— bravely confessed and lamented by the king,—how attentiveness wounded his daughter; till, from one sign of dolour to another, she did, with an 'alas!' I would fain say, bleed tears, for I am sure my heart wept blood. Who was most marble there changed colour; some swounded, all sorrowed. If all the world could have seen 't, the woe had been universal.

FIRST GENTLEMAN. Are they returned to the court?

THIRD GENTLEMAN. No; the princess hearing of her mother's statue, which is in the keeping of Paulina—a piece many years in doing, and now newly performed by that rare Italian master, Julio Romano; who, had he himself eternity and could put breath into his work, would beguile Nature of her custom, so perfectly he is her ape: he so near to Hermione hath done Hermione that they say one would speak to her and stand in hope of answer. Thither with all greediness of affection are they gone, and there they intend to sup.

SECOND GENTLEMAN. I thought she had some great matter there in hand, for she hath privately, twice or thrice a day, ever since the death of Hermione, visited that removed house. Shall we thither and with our company piece the rejoicing?

FIRST GENTLEMAN. Who would be thence that has the benefit of access? Every wink of an eye some new grace will be born. Our absence makes us unthrifty to our knowledge. Let 's along. *Exeunt Gentlemen*

AUTOLYCUS. Now, had I not the dash of my former life in me, would preferment drop on my head. I brought the old man and his son aboard the prince; told him I heard them talk of a fardel and I know not what; but he at that time, over-fond of the shepherd's daughter,—so he then took her to be,—who began to be much sea-sick, and himself little better, extremity of weather continuing, this mystery remained undiscovered. But 'tis all one to me; for had I been the finder out of this secret, it would not have relished among my other discredits. Here come those I have done good to against my will, and already appearing in the blossoms of their fortune.

Enter Shepherd and Clown

SHEPHERD. Come, boy; I am past moe children, but thy sons and daughters will be all gentlemen born.

CLOWN. You are well met, sir. You denied to fight with me this other day, because I was no gentleman born. See you these clothes? Say you see them not and think me still no gentleman born. You were best say these robes are not gentlemen born. Give me the lie, do, and try whether I am not now gentleman born.

AUTOLYCUS. I know you are now, sir, a gentleman born.

CLOWN. Ay, and have been so any time these four hours.

SHEPHERD. And so have I, boy.

CLOWN. So you have. But I was a gentleman born before my father; for the king's son took me by the hand and called me brother; and then the two kings called my father brother; and then the prince my brother and the princess my sister called my father father; and so we wept: and there was the first gentleman-like tears that ever we shed.

SHEPHERD. We may live, son, to shed many more.

CLOWN. Ay; or else 'twere hard luck, being in so preposterous estate as we are.

AUTOLYCUS. I humbly beseech you, sir, to pardon me all the faults I have committed to your worship, and to give me your good report to the prince my master.

SHEPHERD. Prithee, son, do; for we must be gentle, now we are gentlemen.

CLOWN. Thou wilt amend thy life?

AUTOLYCUS. Ay, an it like your good worship.

CLOWN. Give me thy hand. I will swear to the prince thou art as honest a true fellow as any is in Bohemia.

SHEPHERD. You may say it, but not swear it.

CLOWN. Not swear it, now I am a gentleman? Let boors and franklins say it, I'll swear it.

SHEPHERD. How if it be false, son?

[152-163; 1-19] ACT V · SCENE II   1003

CLOWN. If it be ne'er so false, a true gentleman may swear it
in the behalf of his friend. And I'll swear to the prince
thou art a tall fellow of thy hands and that thou wilt not be
drunk; but I know thou art no tall fellow of thy hands and
that thou wilt be drunk. But I'll swear it, and I would thou
wouldst be a tall fellow of thy hands.
AUTOLYCUS. I will prove so, sir, to my power.
CLOWN. Ay, by any means prove a tall fellow. If I do not
wonder how thou darest venture to be drunk, not being a
tall fellow, trust me not. Hark! the kings and the princes,
our kindred, are going to see the queen's picture. Come,
follow us. We'll be thy good masters.   *Exeunt*

SCENE THREE

The Same. A Chapel in Paulina's House.

*Enter Leontes, Polixenes, Florizel, Perdita, Camillo,
Paulina, Lords, and Attendants*

LEONTES. O grave and good Paulina, the great comfort
That I have had of thee!
PAULINA.   What, sovereign sir,
I did not well, I meant well. All my services
You have paid home; but that you have vouchsaf'd,
With your crown'd brother and these your contracted
Heirs of your kingdoms, my poor house to visit,
It is a surplus of your grace, which never
My life may last to answer.
LEONTES.   O Paulina!
We honour you with trouble. But we came
To see the statue of our queen. Your gallery
Have we pass'd through, not without much content
In many singularities, but we saw not
That which my daughter came to look upon,
The statue of her mother.
PAULINA.   As she liv'd peerless,
So her dead likeness, I do well believe,
Excels whatever yet you look'd upon
Or hand of man hath done; therefore I keep it
Lonely, apart. But here it is. Prepare
To see the life as lively mock'd as ever

Still sleep mock'd death. Behold! and say 'tis well.

*Paulina draws back
a curtain, and discovers Hermione as a statue*

I like your silence: it the more shows off
Your wonder; but yet speak: first you, my liege.
Comes it not something near?

LEONTES. Her natural posture!
Chide me, dear stone, that I may say, indeed
Thou art Hermione; or rather, thou art she
In thy not chiding, for she was as tender
As infancy and grace. But yet, Paulina,
Hermione was not so much wrinkled; nothing
So aged as this seems.

POLIXENES. O! not by much.

PAULINA. So much the more our carver's excellence;
Which lets go by some sixteen years and makes her
As she liv'd now.

LEONTES. As now she might have done
So much to my good comfort, as it is
Now piercing to my soul. O! thus she stood,
Even with such life of majesty,—warm life,
As now it coldly stands,—when first I woo'd her.
I am asham'd. Does not the stone rebuke me
For being more stone than it? O royal piece!
There's magic in thy majesty, which has
My evils conjur'd to remembrance, and
From thy admiring daughter took the spirits,
Standing like stone with thee.

PERDITA. And give me leave,
And do not say 'tis superstition, that
I kneel and then implore her blessing. Lady,
Dear queen, that ended when I but began,
Give me that hand of yours to kiss.

PAULINA. O, patience!
The statue is but newly fix'd, the colour's
Not dry.

CAMILLO. My lord, your sorrow was too sore laid on,
Which sixteen winters cannot blow away,
So many summers dry. Scarce any joy
Did ever so long live; no sorrow
But kill'd itself much sooner.

POLIXENES. Dear my brother,

[54-85] ACT V : SCENE III

    Let him that was the cause of this have power
    To take off so much grief from you as he
    Will piece up in himself.
PAULINA.   Indeed, my lord,
    If I had thought the sight of my poor image
    Would thus have wrought you,—for the stone is mine,—
    I'd not have show'd it.
LEONTES.   Do not draw the curtain.
PAULINA. No longer shall you gaze on 't, lest your fancy
    May think anon it moves.
LEONTES.   Let be, let be!
    Would I were dead, but that, methinks, already—
    What was he that did make it? See, my lord,
    Would you not deem it breath'd, and that those veins
    Did verily bear blood?
POLIXENES.   Masterly done!
    The very life seems warm upon her lip.
LEONTES. The fixture of her eye has motion in 't,
    As we are mock'd with art.
PAULINA.   I'll draw the curtain;
    My lord's almost so far transported that
    He'll think anon it lives.
LEONTES.   O sweet Paulina!
    Make me to think so twenty years together!
    No settled senses of the world can match
    The pleasure of that madness. Let 't alone.
PAULINA. I am sorry, sir, I have thus far stirr'd you: but
    I could afflict you further.
LEONTES.   Do, Paulina;
    For this affliction has a taste as sweet
    As any cordial comfort. Still, methinks,
    There is an air comes from her. What fine chisel
    Could ever yet cut breath? Let no man mock me,
    For I will kiss her.
PAULINA.   Good my lord, forbear.
    The ruddiness upon her lip is wet.
    You'll mar it if you kiss it; stain your own
    With oily painting. Shall I draw the curtain?
LEONTES. No, not these twenty years.
PERDITA.   So long could I
    Stand by, a looker-on.
PAULINA.   Either forbear,

Quit presently the chapel, or resolve you
For more amazement. If you can behold it,
I 'll make the statue move indeed, descend,
And take you by the hand; but then you 'll think,—
Which I protest against,—I am assisted
By wicked powers.

LEONTES.   What you can make her do,
I am content to look on: what to speak,
I am content to hear; for 'tis as easy
To make her speak as move.

PAULINA.   It is requir'd
You do awake your faith. Then, all stand still;
Or those that think it is unlawful business
I am about, let them depart.

LEONTES.   Proceed:
No foot shall stir.

PAULINA.   Music, awake her! Strike!   *Music*
'Tis time; descend; be stone no more: approach;
Strike all that look upon with marvel. Come;
I 'll fill your grave up: stir; nay, come away;
Bequeath to death your numbness, for from him
Dear life redeems you. You perceive she stirs:
                          Hermione comes down
Start not; her actions shall be holy as
You hear my spell is lawful. Do not shun her
Until you see her die again, for then
You kill her double. Nay, present your hand.
When she was young you woo'd her; now in age
Is she become the suitor!

LEONTES. (*Embracing her*) O! she 's warm.
If this be magic, let it be an art
Lawful as eating.

POLIXENES.   She embraces him.

CAMILLO. She hangs about his neck.
If she pertain to life let her speak too.

POLIXENES. Ay; and make 't manifest where she has lived,
Or how stolen from the dead.

PAULINA.   That she is living,
Were it but told you, should be hooted at
Like an old tale; but it appears she lives,
Though yet she speak not. Mark a little while.
Please you to interpose, fair madam: kneel

And pray your mother's blessing. Turn, good lady;
Our Perdita is found.
> *Presenting Perdita, who kneels to Hermione*

HERMIONE. You gods, look down,
And from your sacred vials pour your graces
Upon my daughter's head! Tell me, mine own,
Where hast thou been preserved? where liv'd? how found
Thy father's court? For thou shalt hear that I,
Knowing by Paulina that the oracle
Gave hope thou wast in being, have preserv'd
Myself to see the issue.

PAULINA. There's time enough for that;
Lest they desire upon this push to trouble
Your joys with like relation. Go together,
You precious winners all: your exultation
Partake to every one. I, an old turtle,
Will wing me to some wither'd bough, and there
My mate, that's never to be found again,
Lament till I am lost.

LEONTES. O! peace, Paulina.
Thou shouldst a husband take by my consent,
As I by thine a wife. This is a match,
And made between's by vows. Thou hast found mine;
But how, is to be question'd; for I saw her,
As I thought, dead, and have in vain said many
A prayer upon her grave. I'll not seek far,—
For him, I partly know his mind,—to find thee
An honourable husband. Come, Camillo,
And take her by the hand; whose worth and honesty
Is richly noted, and here justified
By us, a pair of kings. Let's from this place.
What! look upon my brother. Both your pardons,
That e'er I put between your holy looks
My ill suspicion. This' your son-in-law,
And son unto the king,—whom heavens directing,
Is troth-plight to your daughter. Good Paulina,
Lead us from hence, where we may leisurely
Each one demand and answer to his part
Perform'd in this wide gap of time since first
We were dissever'd. Hastily lead away. *Exeunt*

NOTES

THE TEMPEST

I. i. 60. '*long heath, brown furze*'; so the Folios; Hammer's emendation has been generally accepted:—'*ling, heath, broom, furze.*'

I. ii. 100. '*Who having into truth*'; 'into,' used in the sense of 'unto,' and so emended in most editions; the sentence though very involved is intelligible without any alteration; '*into truth*' depends upon '*a sinner*'; and '*it*' refers vaguely to '*his own lie*'; '*to credit*' = 'as to credit.'

I. ii. 169. '*Now I arise*'; probably derived from astrology; 'now my star is in the ascendent;' it should be noted that the stage direction 'Resumes his mantle' is not in the Folios.

I. ii. 266. '*for one thing she did*'; Shakespeare does not tell us what he refers to here; perhaps he merely added the point in order to account for her preservation, or the incident may have been mentioned in his original.

I. ii. 379-380. '*Kiss'd the wild waves*'; so the Folios, *i.e.,* 'Kissed the wild waves into silence;' often printed with a comma after 'kissed.'

II. i. 5. '*The masters of some merchant*'; *i.e.,* 'the owners of some merchantman'; Steevens suggested '*mistress*' (old spelling '*maistres*'); the Cambridge editors '*master's*' (*i.e.,* 'master's wife').

II. i. 28. '*which, of he or Adrian*'; 'he' for 'him,' used somewhat substantively, probably owing to the use of the word in the previous sentence, '*he will be talking.*'

II. i. 36. The Folios read: 'Seb. *Ha, ha, ha!* Ant. *So you're paid.*' Theobald gives the whole line to Sebastian; and his reading is adopted by the Camb. ed. Possibly a better emendation is the transposition of the prefixes to the speeches; the point of the quibble is no doubt the old proverb 'let them laugh that win.' Capell ingeniously suggested that the Folio reading should stand with the slight change of '*you've paid*' for '*you're paid.*'

II. i. 123. '*who hath cause*'; the antecedent of 'who' is most probably '*she*'; some make the relative refer to '*eye,*' *i.e.* 'which hath cause to weep.'

II. i. 127. '*should bow*'; so Folios; seemingly unnecessary corrections have been made, *e.g.* '*she'd bow*'; '*which end the beam should bow*'; the omission of the pronoun 'it' or 'she' before 'should' can easily be paralleled in Shakespeare.

II. i. 238. '*But doubt discovery there*'; *i.e.* 'Cannot but doubt that anything can be discovered there.'

II. i. 245. '*She that from whom*'; the unnecessary 'that' is perhaps intentionally repeated, owing to the previous repetition of 'she that.'

II. i. 274. '*candied*'; generally explained as 'sugared over, and so insensible'; perhaps a better interpretation is 'made sweet as sugar,' as in the phrase 'the candied tongue.' Is Antonio possibly playing on 'candied' and 'candid' (a word not yet fully naturalised in the language, but probably familiar)?

II. ii. 74-75. '*I will not take too much for him*'; i.e. 'I will take as much as I can possibly get.'

II. ii. 167. '*Scamels*'; not found elsewhere in Shakespeare. Many emendations have been made; staniel (a species of hawk) has been adopted by some editors; the word occurs probably in *Twelfth Night* (II. v. 106), though the editions read 'stallion.' 'Scamel' is evidently the name of a rock-breeding bird; Mr. Wright has pointed out that, according to Stevenson's "Birds of Norfolk," "the female Bar-tailed God-wit is called a 'Scamell' by the gunners of Blakeney."

III. i. 15. '*Most busy lest, when I do it*'; so the first Folio. Various readings have been suggested; Pope, '*least busy when I do it*'; Theobald, '*most busie-less when I do it*'; Holt, '*most busiest, when I do it*'; Spedding, '*most busiest when idlest,*' &c., &c. It seems likely that the reading of the second, third, and fourth Folios throws light on the real meaning of the line—'*most busy least, when I do it*'; i.e., 'most busy when I indulge my thoughts, least busy when I am actually at work.' A comma after 'busy' instead of after 'least' would simplify this reading, but it is possible to understand it as punctuated in the Folios; Shakespeare probably wished to make the superlatives as antithetical as possible; perhaps we should read 'labour' for 'labours.'

III. iii. 39. '*Praise in departing*'; a proverbial expression; "stay your praises till you see how your entertainment will end."

IV. i. 64. '*pioned and twilled*'; various emendations have been suggested for these difficult words of the Folio:—'*peonied and lilied,*' '*tulip'd,*' '*tilled,*' &c. It is noted that 'piony' is an old spelling of 'peony,' and that the flower was formerly spoken of as 'the mayden piony' and 'virgin peonie.' In all probability the meaning of the words has not yet been discovered; they are evidently technical terms of horticulture. (*Cp.* Glossary.)

IV. i. 110. Mr. Wright suggests that '*earths*' should be read as a dissyllable, 'earthes'; the second, third, and fourth Folios read '*and*' before '*foison.*'

IV. i. 147. &c. In *The Tragedy of Darius*, by William Alexander, afterwards Earl of Sterling, published in the year 1603, occurs the following passage, which, according to Steevens, may have been the original of Shakespeare's Speech:

> *"Let greatnesse of her glascie sceptre vaunt:*
> *Not scepters, no, but reeds, soone brus'd, soone broken*
> *And let this worldlie pomp our wits inchant.*
> *All fades, and scarcelie leaues behind a token.*
> *Those golden pallaces, those gorgeous halles*
> *With fourniture superfluouslie faire:*
> *Those statelie courts, those sky-encountering walles*
> *Evanish all like vapours in the aire."*

IV. i. 195. The Folios read 'hang on them.'

IV. i. 224. 'O King Stephano! O Peer!' an allusion to the old song, often referred to in Elizabethan literature, "Take thy old cloak about thee":—

> "King Stephen was a worthy peere,
> His breeches cost him but a crowne,
> He held them sixpence all too deere;
> Therefore he called the taylor Lowne."

The ballad is printed in Percy's *Reliques*; Shakespeare quotes it also in Othello, II, iii. 84.

IV. i. 233. 'Let's alone'; some verb of motion must be understood, *i.e.*, 'let us go alone' (leaving Trinculo behind); 'alone' is possibly an error of the Folios for 'along,' as suggested by Theobald.

IV. i. 239. "An allusion to what often happens to people who pass the line. The violent fevers which they contract in that hot climate make them lose their hair."—Steevens.

V. i. 23-24. The first and second Folios place a comma after 'sharply,' making 'passion' a verb; the comma is omitted in the third and fourth Folios.

V. i. 310. The line is to be read, according to the Folios, 'to see our dear belov'd solémnizéd.'

THE TWO GENTLEMEN OF VERONA

DRAMATIS PERSONÆ. 'The names of all the actors' are given at the end of the play in the Folios; the form 'Protheus' is invariably used for 'Proteus,' 'Athonio' for 'Antonio,' and 'Panthion' for 'Panthino.'

I. i. 19. 'On a love-book pray for my success;' an allusion to the Roman Catholic custom of placing the beads on the prayer-book, and of counting the beads with the prayers. 'The love-book' is in this case to take the place of the prayer-book; some have supposed that Shakespeare is here referring to Marlowe's *Hero and Leander*, which however, though entered on the

Stationers' Registers in 1593, was not printed till 1598, after which date many references occur to it in contemporary literature; Shakespeare directly quotes from it in *As You Like It*, IV. i. 100.

I. ii. 51. '*What fool is she;*' the first three Folios read '*what fool is she,*' indicating the omission of the indefinite article, a not uncommon Elizabethan idiom.

I. ii. 134. '*I see you have a month's mind to them;*' Schmidt in his 'Shakespeare Lexicon' explains the phrase 'month's mind' as 'a woman's longing,' as though the expression had its origin in the longing for particular articles of food shown by women, but this interpretation seems to have no authority. Johnson rightly remarks on this passage:—'*A month's mind,* in the ritual sense, signifies not desire or inclination, but remembrance; yet I suppose this is the true original of expression.'

I. iii. 27. "Shakespeare has been guilty of no mistake in placing the emperor's court at Milan. Several of the first German Emperors held their courts there occasionally, it being at that time their immediate property, and the chief town of their Italian dominions." Steevens.

II. i. 34. '*none else would;*' *i.e.* 'no one else would perceive them.'

II. i. 71. '*to put on your hose;*' various suggestions have been made for the emendation of these words:—'*to beyond your nose,*' '*to put spectacles on your nose,*' '*to put on your shoes,*' '*to button your hose.*' It is not certain that a rhyming couplet was intended. Probably 'unable to see to put on one's hose' was a proverbial expression meaning 'unable to tell which leg to put into one's hose first,' *i.e.* 'not to have one's wits about one.'

II. i. 154. '*for in print I found it.*' Probably these lines are quoted from some old ballad or play, though their source has not yet been found. One cannot help thinking that Shakespeare is quoting from some play of the *Two Italian Gentlemen* type; the reprinted extracts contain passages strongly reminding one of these lines.

II. iii. 26. '*a wood woman*'; the Folios read '*a would woman*'; Theobald first changed '*would*' into '*wood*' (*i.e.* mad); others '*an ould* (*i.e.* old) *woman.*'

II. iv. 112. The Folios give this line to Thurio;' if the reading be right, he must have quitted the stage during the scene, probably immediately before the entrance of Proteus, after line 99.

II. iv. 126. *Whose high imperious thoughts have punished me;*' Johnson proposed to read '*those*' for '*whose,*' as if the imperious '*thoughts*' are Valentine's and not '*Love's*'; the word '*thoughts*' certainly presents a difficulty, being used here probably in the sense of 'dispositions of the mind.'

NOTES

II. iv. 193. '*Is it mine, or Valentine's praise;*' the first Folio reads, '*It is mine or Valentine's praise*'; the later Folios, '*Is it mine then, or Valentineans praise?*' Theobald's suggestion '*mine eye,*' has been generally adopted; 'if this were unsatisfactory,' the Camb. editors remark, 'another guess might be hazarded:—

'*Is it mine unstaid mind or Valentine's praise.*'

In the latter case 'Valentine's' must be read as a dissyllable; in the former as a quadrisyllable; it is not necessary to read, as has been proposed, 'Valentino's' or 'Valentinus'.' Two other ingenious emendations are noteworthy:—'*her mien,*' '*mine eyne,*' ('*thine eyne*' occurs as a rhyme in *A Midsummer-Night's Dream*, III. ii. 138).

II. v. 1; III. i. 81; V. iv. 129. The Cambridge editors have retained the reading of the Folios in these lines, 'Padua' in the first passage, and 'Verona' in the second and third, 'because it is impossible that the words can be a mere printer's, or transcriber's error. These inaccuracies are interesting as showing that Shakespeare had written the whole of the play before he had finally determined where the scene was to be laid'; the scene is in each case undoubtedly Milan (perhaps 'Milano,' *metri causa*).

III. i. 271. '*Condition;*' so the first three Folios; the fourth Folio reads '*conditions,*' adopted in many editions; '*condition*' is generally used by Shakespeare in the sense of 'temper,' 'quality.'

III. ii. 77. Malone suggests that some such line as the following has been lost after 'integrity':—'*as her obdurate heart may penetrate,*' but the meaning is perhaps rightly explained by Steevens:—"such ardour and sincerity as would be manifested by practising the directions given in the four preceding lines."

IV. i. 36. '*Robin Hood's fat friar,*' *i.e.* Friar Tuck. This allusion to 'Robin Hood's friar' by the Italian outlaw is somewhat unexpected; in the later play of *As You Like It* there is also an allusion to 'Robin Hood,' but Shakespeare is careful to add 'of England' ('*they live like the old Robin Hood of England,*' I. i. 115).

IV. i. 49. '*An heir, and near allied;*' the Folios read '*niece,*' for which Theobald suggested '*near,*' a reading generally accepted; possibly, but doubtfully, 'niece' may after all be correct, being used occasionally by Elizabethan writers to signify almost any relationship.

IV. iv. 53. '*Hangman boys;*' the Folios read '*hangman's boys;*' the reading in the text was given by Singer from a MS. note in a copy of the second Folio in his possession.

IV. iv. 71. The first Folio misprints, '*not leave her token.*'

V. iv. 2. Probably a better reading than the Folio is that generally adopted, due to Collier's MS.:—

1014 THE COMEDIES

'*these shadowy, desert, unfrequented woods.*'

V. iv. 47-50. '*Rend thy faith . . . perjury, to love me. Thou . . .*' The lines seem clear as they stand; a suggestion by Mr. Daniel is perhaps worthy of mention:—'*rain . . . perjury. To love me Thou,*' or '*hail . . . Discandied into perjury. To love me Thou . . .*'

V. iv. 71. A difficult line to scan; Johnson proposed '*O time most curst*'; others omit '*most*' or '*O*'; perhaps we have here an Alexandrine, 'O' counting as a monosyllabic foot; the second syllable of 'deepest' being an extra syllable before the pause:—

The pri'/vate wou'nd/ is de'epest;|| O'-/ time mo'st/ accur'st,/

THE MERRY WIVES OF WINDSOR

I. i. 19-20. '*The luce is the fresh fish; the salt fish is an old coat.*' No satisfactory explanation of this passage has as yet been offered; various suggestions have been made, *e.g.* 'salt-fish' = the hake borne by the stockfishmongers; 'same' for 'salt'; ''tis ott fish' (assigned to Evans), &c. May not, however, the whole point of the matter lie in Shallow's use of 'salt' in the sense of 'saltant,' the heraldic term, used especially for vermin? If so, 'salt fish' = 'the leaping louse,' with a quibble on 'salt' as opposed to 'fresh fish.' There is further allusion to the proverbial predilection of vermin for 'old coats,' used quibblingly in the sense of 'coat-of-arms.'

I. i. 81. '*Outrun on Cotsall,*' *i.e.* on the Cotswold hills (in Gloucestershire); probably an allusion to the famous Cotswold Games, which were revived at the beginning of the seventeenth century, though evidently instituted earlier; the allusion does not occur in the first and second Quartos.

I. i. 155. '*Scarlet and John*'; Robin Hood's boon companions; an allusion to Bardolph's red face.

I. iii. 25. '*A minute's rest*'; "*a minim's rest*" is the ingenious suggestion of Bennet Langton; *cp. Romeo and Juliet,* II, iv. 22, "*rests me his minim rest.*"

I. iii. 41. '*Carves*'; probably used here in the sense of 'to show favour by expressive gestures'; *cp.* "A carver: chironomus . . . one that useth apish motions with his hands."—Littleton's *Latin-English Dictionary* (1675).

I. iii. 61-62. '*Region of Guiana.*' Sir Walter Raleigh returned from his expedition to South America in 1596, and published his book on "The Discovery of the large, rich, and beautiful Empire of Guiana" in the same year.

NOTES   1015

I. iii. 85. '*By welkin and her star.*' This is no doubt the correct reading of the line, and there is no need to read *stars*, as has been suggested; 'star' is obviously used here for 'the sun'; the Quartos read 'fairies.'

II. i. 4, 5. '*Though Love use Reason for his physician.*' The Folios read '*precisian*'; the emendation adopted in the text was first suggested by Johnson, and has been generally accepted; *cp.* Sonnet CXLVII.: "*My reason the physician to my love.*"

II. i. 191, 193. In the Folios the name '*Broome*' is given instead of '*Brooke*'; but Falstaff's pun, "*Such Brooks are welcome to me, that overflow with liquor*," removes all doubt as to the correct reading, which is actually found in the Quartos.

II. i. 194. '*Will you go, An-hires?*' so the Folios and Quartos; Theobald's correction '*mynheers*' has been adopted by many modern editors. Other suggestions are "*on, here;*" "*on, hearts;*" "*on, heroes;*" "*cavaleires;*" &c.

II. iii. 75-76. '*Cried I aim?*' The Folios and Quartos read '*cried game*'; the ingenious emendation, due to Douce, was first adopted by Dyce.

III. i. 15, &c. Sir Hugh oddly confuses Marlowe's famous ditty, "*Come live with me and be my love,*" and the old version of the 137th Psalm, "*When we did sit in Babylon.*"

III. i. 86. '*Gallia and Gaul*'; so the Folios; the first and second Quartos read '*Gawle and Gawlia;*' Farmer's conjecture "*Gaullia and Gaul*" was adopted by Malone and other editors. *Gallia* = Wales.

III. ii. 66. '*He shall not knit a knot in his fortunes*' (which are now as it were unravelled).

III. iii. 36. '*Have I caught thee*'; probably the reading of the Quarto which omits 'thee' is the more correct; Falstaff quotes from the second song in Sydney's *Astrophel and Stella:*—

"*Have I caught my heav'nly jewell,
Teaching sleep most faire to be?
Now will I teach her that she
When she wakes is too-too cruell.*"

III. v. 4. The reading of the Quartos is seemingly preferable: —'*Have I lived to be carried in a basket, and thrown into the Thames like a barrow of butcher's offal.*'

III. v. 8. '*The rogues slighted me into the river,*' *i.e.* 'Threw me in contemptuously;' the Quartos read '*slided me in.*'

IV. i. 41. '*Hang-hog is Latin for bacon*'; probably suggested by the famous story told of Sir Nicholas Bacon. A prisoner named Hog, who had been condemned to death, prayed for mercy on the score of kindred. "Aye but," replied the judge, "you and I cannot be of kindred unless you are hanged; for Hog is not Bacon till it be well hanged" (Bacon's *Apophthegms*).

IV. ii. 17. 'Old lunes'; the Folios and third Quarto read 'lines;' the first and second Quartos 'vaine;' the correction is Theobald's; the same error occurs in *Troilus and Cressida*, II. iii. 128.

IV. ii. 84. '*The witch of Brentford*'; an actual personage of the sixteenth century. A tract is extant entitled "Jyl of Breyntford's Testament," whence it appears that the witch kept a tavern at Brentford; in Dekker & Webster's *Westward Ho* the following allusion is found:—"I doubt that old hag Gillian of Brainford has bewitched me."

IV. iv. 40. '*That Falstaff at that oak shall meet with us.*' After this line the following words from the Quartos have been added in many editions:—

"*We'll send him word to meet us in the field,
Disguised like Horne with huge horns on his head.*"

IV. iv. 56. '*To pinch*'; probably the correct reading should be 'to-pinch,' where 'to' is the intensitive prefix so common in old English, though it is possible to explain it as the ordinary infinitive prefix, omitted in the case of the former verb in the sentence.

IV. iv. 81. '*Send quickly to Sir John.*' Theobald ingeniously suggested '*Quickly*' for '*quickly.*'

IV. v. 68. '*Cozen-germans*'; the first Quarto reads:—
"*For there is three sorts of cosen garmombles,
Is cosen all the Host of Maidenhead and Readings,*"
where 'garmombles' is very possibly a perversion of Mömpelgard; Count Frederick of Mömpelgard visited Windsor in 1592; free post-horses were granted him by a passport of Lord Howard.

The Count became a "Duke of Jamany" (Wirtemberg) in 1593; considerable interest must have been taken in the Duke about 1598. A letter to the Queen, dated August 14, 1598, is extant, in which the following passage occurs:—"I have heard with extreme regret that some of my enemies endeavour to calumniate me and prejudice your majesty against me. I have given them no occasion for this. I hope that when your majesty has discovered this report to be false, you will have greater reason to continue your affection towards me, and give neither faith nor credit to such vipers." In the year 1602 appeared "An Account of the Duke's Bathing Excursion to the far-famed Kingdom of England" (*vide* Rye's *England as seen by Foreigners*).

V. v. 22. '*Bribe buck*'; the Folios read '*brib'd buck*,' which is probably the right reading: 'a bribed buck' was a buck cut up into portions (Old French *bribes* = 'portions of meat to be given away').

V. v. 37. '*Orphan heirs.*' Theobald suggested '*ouphen*' (elvish) for 'orphan,' and he has been followed by many editors, but the change is unnecessary. Cp. '*unfather'd heirs*' 2 *Henry IV.* iv. 122.

NOTES 1017

V. v. 40, 42. *'Toys,'* evidently to be read 'toyës,' rhyming with *'O-yes'* in the previous line; similarly *'unswept'* should probably be *'unswep'* rhyming with *'leap.'*

V. v. 105. *'These fair yokes';* the first Folio reads *'yoakes,'* the second *'okes.' 'Yokes'* must refer to the resemblance of the buck's horns to a yoke; a sort of sense can be got out of *'oaks,'* the antlers resembling the branches of oaks, but the first Folio reading seems preferable.

MEASURE FOR MEASURE

I. i. 8. There is no gap in the Folios, which is due to Theobald's plausible theory that the obscurity of the passage is due to some careless omission on the part of the printers. Various attempts have been made to explain the lines, *e.g.* "*But that to your sufficiencies your worth is abled*" (Johnson); "*But your sufficiency as worth is able*" (Farmer); Theobald supplied the missing words thus—
"*But that to your sufficiency you add
Due diligency as your worth is able.*"

I. i. 42. *'Hold therefore, Angelo;'* the Duke probably says these words on tendering commission to Angelo.

I. ii. 27-28. *'There went but a pair of shears between us;' i.e.* 'we are of one piece.'

I. ii. 116. *Cp. St. Paul to the Romans* ix. 15, 18: "For He saith to Moses, I will have mercy *on whom I will* have mercy," and again, "Therefore hath He mercy *on whom He will* have mercy, and *whom He will* He hardeneth."

I. ii. 127. *'Morality;'* the Folios misprint *'mortality.'*

I. ii. 143. *'Propagation;'* Folio 1 reads *propagation,* corrected in Folio 2; *prorogation, procuration, preservation,* have been suggested by various editors, but the text as it stands is probably correct, though not altogether clear; *'propagation'* = 'increase;' perhaps the word implies 'increase of interest,' and *'for propagation'* = 'that she might continue to receive the interest, which was to be hers while she remained unmarried.'

I. iii. 43. *'To do in slander;'* so the Folios; *'me'* and *'it'* have been suggested for *'in,'* but no change is necessary; *'do in'* = 'bring in, bring upon me.'

II. i. 39. *'Some run from brakes of ice, and answer none;'* the line as it stands in the Folios is obviously corrupt, and has occasioned much discussion. Shakespeare probably wrote *'brakes of vice;' brakes* = thickets, hence 'entanglements'; *'brakes of vice'* is antithetical to *'a fault alone,'* cp. *Henry VIII.* I. ii. 75—
"*the rough brake
That virtue must go through.*"

The line therefore means 'some escape from whole thickets of sin, and pay no penalty.' Judging by the passage in *Henry VIII*, *through* for *from* would perhaps be an improvement.

II. i. 124. '*An open room;*' Schmidt, "*public room;*" perhaps it means 'open to sun, light, cheerful.'

II. ii. 80. '*Like man new made;*' commentators are strongly tempted to refer the words to '*new made man,*' *i.e.* Adam; Holt White paraphrased thus:—"And you, Angelo, will breathe new life into Claudio, as the Creator animated Adam, by breathing into his nostrils the breath of life." Malone explains:—"You will then appear as tender-hearted and merciful as the first man was in his days of innocence, immediately after his creation." Schmidt and others, "like man redeemed and regenerated by divine grace." The lines are perhaps capable of this interpretation:— "And mercy will breathe within your lips, even as Mercy (*i.e.* God) breathed within the lips of new made man."

II. ii. 91. "*Dormiunt aliquando leges, moriuntur nunquam,*" is a well-known maxim in law (Holt White).

II. ii. 160. '*Where prayers cross,*' *i.e.* where his prayer to possess Isabella crosses with hers, "Heaven keep your *honour* safe!"

II. iii. 11. '*The flaws of her own youth;*' possibly Warburton's correction "*flames*" should be adopted; *cp.*
> '*To flaming youth let virtue be as wax,*
> *And melt in her own fire.*'
> —HAMLET, III. iv. 84, 85.

II. iii. 40. '*O injurious love*' (Folios 'loue'); Hanmer's suggestion, "*law*" for "*loue*," has been generally accepted; the law respited her 'a life whose very comfort' was 'a dying horror.'

II. iv. 9. '*Feared;*' probably an error of '*feared,*' *i.e.* '*seared,*' which, according to Collier, is the reading of Lord Ellesmere's copy of the first Folio.

II. iv. 104. '*That longing have been sick for,*' Rowe suggested "*I've been sick for.*"

II. iv. 173. '*O perilous mouths;*' the line is defective as it stands (?) "*O pernicious mouths*" (Walker), or "*these perilous*" (Seymour).

III. i. 92, 95. '*Prenzie!*' the source of this strange word has baffled students; it seems identical with the Scottish *primsie*, 'demure, precise,' which in its turn is connected with *prim* (in Old French *prin, pren*): under any circumstances there is no reason why the word should be changed, as has been proposed, to '*princely,*' the reading of the second Folio, or '*priestly,*' '*pensive,*' &c.

III. ii. 8. "The passage seems to us to imply, furred (that is, lined with lamb-skin fur inside, and trimmed with fox-skin fur outside) with both kinds of fur, to show that craft (fox-skin), being richer than innocency (lamb-skin), is used for decoration" (Clarke).

III. ii. 10, 11. *'Good father friar'* . . . *'good brother father;'* the joke, as Tyrwhitt pointed out, would be clearer in French. *'mon père frère'* . . . *'mon frère père.'*

III. ii. 37. *'From our faults, as faults from seeming, free!'* So Folio 1, Folio 2 and Folio 3, *'Free from our faults,'* &c.; Hanmer corrects the latter part of the line, *'As from faults seeming free.'* As it stands in the text, it would seem to mean "Would that we were as free from faults, as our faults are from seeming (hypocrisy)." One feels inclined to hazard—

'Free from our faults, as from false seeming, free!'

(*Cp.* II. iv. 15. *'thy false seeming.'*)

III. ii. 212, 213. *'Security enough to make fellowships accurst;'* cp. *Prov.* xi. 15.

III. ii. 241-262. These lines are in all probability not Shakespeare's, but by another hand.

III. ii. 244. *'Grace to stand, and virtue go;'* i.e. 'To have grace to stand firm, and virtue to go forward.'

III. ii. 253-256. *'How may likeness made in crimes,'* &c.; these lines do not readily admit of interpretation, and some corruption has probably crept into the text; Malone suggested *wade* for *made,* i.e. "How may hypocrisy wade in crimes;" Hanmer, "*the likeness shading crimes,*" &c. None of the suggestions seems very satisfactory. Perhaps *'to draw'* = *'to-draw,'* i.e. 'pull to pieces' (?).

IV. i. This song appears in Beaumont and Fletcher's *Bloody Brother,* with the addition of the following stanza, assuredly not Shakespeare's, though found in the spurious edition of his poems, (1640)—

"Hide, O hide those hills of snow
Which thy frozen bosom bears,
On whose tops the pinks that grow
Are of those that April wears;
But first set my poor heart free,
Bound by those icy chains by thee."

IV. i. 13. "Though the music soothed my sorrows, it had no tendency to produce light merriment" (Johnson).

IV. ii. 41, 42. *'If it be too little—thief;'* the Folios give this to *Clo.* (Pompey); Capell first transferred it to Abhorson, and he has been followed by most editors. Cowden Clarke defends the Folio arrangement; among other arguments he maintains that "the speech is much more in character with the clown's snip-snap style of chop-logic than with Abhorson's manner, which is remarkably curt and bluff."

IV. iv. 5. *'redeliver;'* Folio 1, *'re-liuer;'* Folio 2, *'deliuer*; Capell first suggested *'redeliver.'*

IV. iv. 25. *'bears of a credent bulk;'* so Folios 1, 2, 3; many emendations have been proposed; Dyce's seems the most plausible—'*bears so credent bulk;*' '*credent bulk*' = 'weight of credit.'

V. i. 64. '*Do not banish reason, For inequality;*' *i.e.* because of 'improbability,' 'incongruity,' or, according to some, 'partiality.'

V. i. 315. "These shops," according to Nares, "were places of great resort, for passing away time in an idle manner. By way of enforcing some kind of regularity, and perhaps at least as much to promote drinking, certain laws were usually hung up, the transgression of which was to be punished by specific *forfeitures*. It is not to be wondered, that laws of that nature were as often laughed at as obeyed."

V. i. 347. '*be hanged an hour*' seems to have been a cant phrase, meaning little more than 'be hanged!'

V. i. 494. '*Give me your hand;*' *i.e.* 'if you give me your hand.'

THE COMEDY OF ERRORS

I. i. 78. '*The latter-born;*' line 125 below seems to imply that this should be 'elder-born,' a change adopted by Rowe; but probably 'the children became exchanged in the confusion during the breaking-up of the ship.'

I. ii. 41. '*The almanac of my true date,*' because both were born in the same hour.

I. ii. 64. '*I shall be post indeed;*' a post stood in the middle of the shop, on which the scores of the customers were *scored*, or marked with chalk or notches.

I. ii. 66. '*Clock;*' Pope's emendation for '*cook,*' the reading of the Folios.

II. i. 109-113. These lines read as follows in the Folio:—

'*I see the Iewell best enameled*
Will loose his lustre; yet the gold bides still
That others touch, and often touching will,
Where gold and no man that hath a name,' &c.

The change of *where* to *wear* in the last line has been generally accepted, as also *and though* for *yet* in the second line; *yet* for *and* in the third; *and so a man* for *and no man* in the fourth; Warburton paraphrases this passage thus emended:—"Gold, indeed, will long bear the handling; however, often *touching* (*i.e.* assaying) will wear even gold: just so the greatest character, though as pure as gold itself, may in time be injured by the repeated attacks of falsehood and corruption." The Cambridge editors wisely abstain from these wholesale emendations, though so far no satisfactory explanation has been given of the lines. May not the meaning of the passage depend on some such interpretation as this:—The wife (the jewel) soon loses her beauty and

NOTES

ceases to attract, but man (the gold) still stands the test, assayed by other women, and although gold wears out if assayed too often, yet a man of good reputation is not shamed by his falsehood and corruption. 'Wherefore,' says Adriana, 'since I (the jewel) cannot please his eye, I'll weep what's left away,' &c.

II. ii. 90. *'Jollity;'* Staunton suggested that the reading is an error for *'policy,'* and the reading has been adopted by some modern editors.

II. ii. 119. As the line stands, it reads as an Alexandrine. Walker suggested *carv'd thee* for *carved to thee*; others propose the omission of *to thee*; neither change seems desirable.

II. ii. 147. *'I live distain'd, thou undishonoured;'* so read the Folios; *distain'd* has been changed to *unstain'd* in most modern editions; Heath proposed *'I live distained, thou dishonoured.'* The line as it stands in the text seems to mean, 'I live distained (*i.e.* stained), if untrue to my marriage vows; you, however, live undishonoured, however false you may be.'

II. ii. 186. *'this sure uncertainty,'* i.e. 'This to her surely a thing uncertain.'

II. ii. 191. The second Folio reads *'and Elves Sprites,'* which Rowe altered to *'Elvish sprites,'* a reading adopted by most editors. Theobald proposed to change *owls* to *ouphes*.

II. ii. 200. *' 'tis to an ass;'* the words remind one of Bottom's transformation in the *Midsummer-Night's Dream*.

III. i. 53. *'If thy name be called Luce': 'Luce'* = 'pike;' there is perhaps a play upon 'pike' in the sense of 'spear,' *cp.* 'Shall I set in my staff?' line 51.

III. ii. 66. *'I am thee;'* this reading of the Folio may surely, without risk, be emended:—*'I am thee,' i.e.* 'I aim at thee;' the transitive use of *aim* is found in Elizabethan writers.

III. ii. 125-126. *'armed and reverted, making war against her heir;'* Folio 2 substituted *hair* for *heir*, but the play upon words is the whole point of the passage, an allusion being intended to the War of the League against Henry of Navarre, the heir of Henry III. of France, whose cause was supported by Elizabeth; in 1591 she sent a body of 4000 men under Essex to help him. "Mistress Nell's brazen forehead seemed to push back her rough and rebellious hair, as France resisted the claim of the Protestant heir to the throne" (Clarke).

English enthusiasm for Henry of Navarre found expression, too, in Shakespeare's *Love's Labour's Lost*.

As regards the peculiar use of *reverted, i.e.* 'turned back,' Schmidt suggests that there may be a play upon the sense of 'fallen to another proprietor.'

IV. i. 21. *'I buy a thousand pound a year;'* some point in these words, familiar to Shakespeare's audience, is lost to us, and no satisfactory explanation has as yet been given, though Halliwell's comparison of the line with 3 *Henry VI.* II. ii. 144, is noteworthy:—

>   "A wisp of straw were worth a thousand crowns,
>   To make this shameless callet know herself."

IV. ii. 35. '*A fiend, a fury;*' the Folios read '*fairy,*' corrected by Theobald, who has been followed by most editors, including the Cambridge editors; a strong case can, however, be made for the original reading (*e.g. cp.* Hamlet I. i. 161-163).

IV. ii. 61. '*If Time be in debt;*' the Folios read '*If I,*' where *I* is probably an error for '*a* (*i.e. he*) or *he*; the reading in the text is Rowe's emendation.

IV. iii. 13. '*What, have you got the picture of old Adam new-apparelled?*' '*The picture of old Adam*' = the sergeant, who was clad '*in buff*'; in Elizabethan slang this latter phrase was used in the sense of 'bare skin,' *i.e.* 'naked'; hence the quibble. *New-apparelled* offers some difficulty, and depends on the general construction of the whole line. It has been ingeniously suggested that the idea is 'got him a new *suit,' i.e.* 'got rid of him.' On the other hand, there is a possibility that the phrase '*What have you got?*' is a vulgarism for '*What have you done with?*' Theobald proposed to read '*What, have you got rid of the picture,*' &c. In the latter cases *new-apparelled* must be regarded as merely a descriptive epithet, the whole phrase '*the picture of old Adam new-apparelled*' being an elaborate circumlocution for 'sergeant.'

IV. iii. 57. '*We'll mend our dinner,*' *i.e.* 'we'll buy something more for our dinner.'

IV. iv. 41-42. '*The prophecy like the parrot, beware the rope's-end;*' the Cambridge editors most ingeniously conjecture that we should read:—

>   "or, rather, '*prospice funem,*' beware the rope's end.
>   *Antipholus of E.* Wilt thou still talk like the parrot?"

Dyce proposed, '*or, rather, to prophecy, like,*' &c.

Parrots were taught uncomplimentary remarks in Elizabethan times, as they are at present; there are many allusions to the very phrase in the text: Ralpho, in Butler's *Hudibras,*

>   "Could tell what subtlest parrots mean,
>   That speak, but think contrary clean;
>   What member 't is of whom they talk,
>   When they cry rope, *and* walk, knave, walk."

V. i. 46. '*And much different,*' &c., the second Folio, for the sake of the metre, reads *much much*; a reading which does not commend itself; *too much* has been conjectured. The line as it stands is certainly doubtful: *différent* does not occur in Shakespeare.

V. i. 66. '*Glanced it;*' Pope's conjectural *at it* is unnecessary, though *glance* in the sense *to hint,* used transitively, does not otherwise occur; Folio 1 does not elide the *ed* of *glanced.*

V. i. 79. *'But moody and dull melancholy;'* something is obviously amiss with the line; *moody moping* has been suggested. *Kinsman* in the next line is used in its general sense of akin, which some editors have unnecessarily substituted; it has even been changed to *kinswoman*.

V. i. 170. *'Beaten the maids,'* &c. *i.e.* have beaten; but the previous verb has *are*,—a confusion of constructions which causes little difficulty, and fairly common in Elizabethan English.

V. i. 312. *'My feeble key of untuned cares;'* i.e. 'the feeble tone of my voice, which gives utterance to nothing but unharmonious grief.'

V. i. 390. *'These* ERRORS *are arose,'* so the Folios; *are* has been variously changed by scholars into *all, rare,* but no change is necessary; as far as rhythm is concerned the Folio reading is certainly preferable

V. i. 403. *'Thirty-three years;'* this reading of the Folios has been changed to *twenty-five* by most editors, following Theobald, who calculates the age of the twins by putting together what Ægeon says in Act I. i. 126 and in line 319 of Act V. Capell suggested *twenty-three,* from Act I. i. line 126 and line 133. On the other hand, the Duke states in line 325 of the present Act that he has been patron to Antipholus for *'twenty years'*; it looks as though Shakespeare changed his idea as to the age of the twins towards the end of the play, without troubling to make all his references fit in with one another.

V. i. 407. *'And you the calendars of their nativity;'* i.e., the two Dromios; *cp.* *'Here comes the almanac of my true date,'* I. ii. 41.

V. i. 409. *'After so long grief, such nativity;'* the labouring line harmonises well with the emotion of the speaker; the line is evidently intended to be read as follows:—

'After | so long | grief, súch | nativ | ity.'

There seems no reason for changing *nativity,* though Hanmer's conjecture *felicity* has been accepted by most editors; Johnson proposed *festivity*.

MUCH ADO ABOUT NOTHING

I. i. 192-193. The English story of "Mr. Fox" alluded to here was first written down by Blakeway, who contributed to Malone's Variorum Edition a version of the tale he had heard from an old aunt (*cp.* Jacobs' *English Fairy Tales*).

II. i. 193-194. *'As melancholy as a lodge in a warren'*: the phrase suggests "The daughter of Zion is left as a cottage in a vineyard, as a lodge in a garden of cucumbers." Isaiah i. 8.

II. ii. 39. Some editors substitute *'Borachio'* for *'Claudio'* in order to relieve the difficulty here, but, as the Cambridge editors point out, "Hero's supposed offence would not be enhanced by calling one lover by the name of the other. . . . Perhaps the author meant that Borachio should persuade her to play, as children say, at being Hero and Claudio."

II. iii. 33. The Folio reads:—'*Enter Prince, Leonato, Claudio and Jack Wilson*'; the latter was probably the singer who took the part of Balthasar.

III. ii. 24. '*Where is but a humour or a worm*': toothache was popularly supposed to be caused by a worm at the root of the tooth.

III. iii. It is an interesting fact that 'Dogberry,' the vulgar name of the *dogwood*, was used as a surname as far back as the time of Richard II., and that 'Verges,' a provincial corruption of *verjuice*, occurs in an ancient MS. (MS. Ashmol. 38) as the name of a usurer whose epitaph is given:—

"Here lies father Varges
Who died to save charges."

III. iii. 79-80. '*Keep your fellows' counsels and your own.*' It has been pointed out by students of Shakespeare's legal acquirements that these words still form part of the oath administered by judges' marshal to the grand jurymen at the present day.

III. v. 15. '*Comparisons are odorous.*' An elaborate extension of this joke occurs in the old play of *Sir Gyles Goosecappe* (c. 1603).

III. v. 33. '*When the age is in, the wit is out*'; a blunder for the old proverbial expression, "when the ale is in, wit is out"—

"When ale is in, wit is out,
When ale is out, wit is in,
The first thou showest out of doubt,
The last in thee hath not been."

HEYWOOD's *Epigrams and Proverbs*.

IV. ii. Nearly all the speeches of Dogberry throughout the scene are given to the famous comedian 'Kemp,' those of Verges to 'Cowley.' Willam Kempe and Richard Cowley are among the 'principall actors' enumerated in the first Folio. The retention of the names of the actors "supplies a measure of the editorial care to which the several Folios were submitted." Dogberry's speech is assigned to 'Andrew,' probably a familiar appellation of Kempe, who, according to the Cambridge Edition, often played the part of 'Merry Andrew.'

IV. ii. 5, 6. '*We have the exhibition to examine.*' Verges' blunder is not quite clear: possibly '*exhibition*' is used in the sense of 'allowance' or permission; otherwise he perhaps means 'examination to exhibit.'

V. i. 16. '*Bid sorrow wag, cry "hem!"*' The Quarto and the first and second Folios read, '*And sorrow wagge, crie hem*': Folio 3,

NOTES

'*And hallow, wag, cry hem*': Folio 4, '*And hollow wag, cry hem.*' Many emendations have been suggested. Capell's '*bid sorrow wag,*' is now generally adopted. Johnson proposed '*Cry, sorrow wag! and hem.*' ('Sorrow wag,' like 'care away,' was probably a proverbial phrase.) One other suggestion is perhaps noteworthy: —'*And, sorry wag, cry "hem."*'

V. iii. 18, 21. '*Heavily, heavily*'; so reads the Quarto; the Folios '*Heavenly, heavenly,*' adopted by many editors. The same error, however, of '*heavenly*' for '*heavily*' occurs in the Folio reading of *Hamlet* II. ii. 296.

"The slayers of the virgin knight are performing a solemn requiem on the body of Hero, and they invoke Midnight and the shades of the dead to assist, until *her* death be *uttered*, that is, proclaimed, published, sorrowfully, sorrowfully" (Halliwell).

V. iv. 120-121. '*There is no staff more reverend than one tipped with horn*'; *i.e.* having a ferrule of horn; there is, of course, a quibbling allusion in the words of the favourite Elizabethan joke.

LOVE'S LABOUR'S LOST

There is no list of 'Dramatis Personæ' in the Quartos and Folios: it should be remembered that 'Biron' is spelt 'Berowne,' rhyming with 'moon' in Act IV. iii. 227; 'Moth' was probably pronounced 'Mote' (*cp.* the quibble on 'nothing' in *Much Ado*, II. iii. 57, and on 'Goths' in *As You Like It*, III. iii. 6); 'Mercade' is generally 'Marcade'; 'Armado' is sometimes given as 'Armatho'; 'Boyet' rhymes with 'debt' in V. ii. 334; 'Longaville' with 'ill' in IV. iii. 120, and with 'mile' in V. ii. 53.

I. i. 62. '*feast*'; Quartos and Folios '*fast*,' corrected by Theobald.

I. i. 82. '*Who dazzling so*'; "that when he *dazzles,* that is, has his eye made weak, by fixing his eye upon a *fairer* eye, that *fairer* eye shall be his *heed*, his direction or *lodestar*, and give him light that was blinded by it" (Johnson).

I. i. 104. '*Any abortive,*' the reading of the Quartos and Folios; probably an error for '*an*' as corrected by Pope.

I. i. 106. '*shows*'; Theobald substituted '*earth*' for the sake of the rhyme; Walker proposed '*mirth.*' Malone supposes a line to be lost after line 104.

I. i. 108-109. '*So you to study . . . little gate*'; this is one of the instances where the reading of the first Quarto is better than that of the Folio:—

'*So you to studie now it is too late,*
That were to clymbe ore the house to unlocke the gate.'

Various emendations have been proposed; the only real difficulty is in the loose use of the word '*so.*' Biron says that he likes of each thing that in season grows; '*so*' presupposes, however, some statement to this effect; 'to wish for, or to do, a thing out of season is huge folly'; (*so* you, now that it is too late to study, climb o'er the house, &c.).

I. i. 181. '*Tharborough*'; the reading of the Quarto '*farborough*' probably gives us Dull's actual pronunciation of his office.

I. i. 190. '*heaven,*' so Quartos and Folios. Theobald proposed '*having*'; whatever may be the exact force of the phrase, it seems most probable that '*heaven*' is the right word, and no emendation is necessary.

I. ii. 87. '*A green wit*'; a probable allusion, according to the Cambridge editors, to the 'green withes' with which Samson was bound (*cp.* note *supra* on pronunciation of 'Moth').

I. ii. 101-102. The ballad of *King Cophetua and the Beggar-Maid* may be found in Percy's *Reliques.*

II. i. 45. '*Well fitted in arts*'; the second Folio inserts '*the,*' omitted in the earlier editions.

II. i. 113-127. The speakers in Quarto 1 are 'Berowne' and 'Katharine.'

II. i. 128. Shakespeare may have got a hint for this passage from Monstrelet's *Chronicles,* according to which Charles, King of Navarre, surrendered to the King of France the castle of Cherbourg, the country of Evreux, and other lordships for the Duchy of Nemours and a promise of 200,000 gold crowns (*vide Shakespeare's Library,* ed. Hazlitt, Part I. Vol. i.).

II. i. 235. '*Impatient to speak and not see,*' *i.e.,* 'not able to endure merely the faculty of speech without that of sight.'

III. i. 15-16. "It was a common trick among some of the most indolent of the ancient masters, to place the hands in the bosom or the pockets, or conceal them in some part of the drapery, to avoid the labour of representing them, or to disguise their own want of skill to employ them with grace and propriety" (Steevens).

IV. i. 1-4. These lines, as Spedding pointed out, were most probably introduced in the corrected copy. "It was thus that Shakespeare learnt to shade off his scenes, to carry the action beyond the stage."

IV. i. 142. '*Armado o' th' one side*'; the reading is due to Rowe; the first Quarto has '*Armatho ath toothen side,*' and the Folio '*Armathor ath to the side.*' Possibly the whole passage from '*O my troth . . . nit*' should have been printed in the previous scene, after line 136, and some editors make the transposition.

IV. ii. 40. '*The allusion holds in the exchange,*' *i.e.,* 'the riddle is as good when I use the name of Adam as when I use the name of Cain.'

IV. ii. 58. '*one sorel*'; the first Quarto has '*o sorell,*' and the

NOTES

Folios '*O sorell*'; Capell proposed '*O sore L,*' which is generally adopted.

IV. ii. 93, 94. The first Quarto and Folio give the following reading:—

'*Vermiche, vencha, que non te vnde, que non te perreche*';
the reading adopted by the Cambridge editors is from Florio's *Second Frutes* (1591), whence Shakespeare probably took it.

IV. ii. 117. '*apostrophas*'; this is taken by some editors to refer to the apostrophes in *vow'd* and *bow'd* (ll. 104, 106), and the words are accordingly printed '*vowed*' and '*bowed*'; this interpretation seems unsatisfactory, but so far nothing better has been advanced. Does not Holofernes' criticism bear directly on the last line of the canzonet? Nathaniel should have read:—

'*That singës heaven's praise with such an earthly tongue.*'

It was usual to mark *es* with two dots when sounded: Holofernes may mean by '*apostrophas*,' '*diæreses*.' The poem is printed with a few variant readings (*e.g.* '*to sing*') in the *Passionate Pilgrim*, where also are found ll. 57-70 and ll. 98-117 of the next scene, also with some interesting points of difference.

IV. iii. 103. '*Wish*,' so the Quartos and first Folio; in the *Passionate Pilgrim* '*wish'd*'; similarly in the line 109 '*thorn*' is due to the version printed in *England's Helicon*; the other editions read '*throne*.' Rowe first proposed the change.

IV. iii. 137. The second Folio omits '*one*.' Walker's suggestion '*One's*' makes the line rhythmic.

IV. iii. 141. '*Faith infringed*,' the reading of the Quartos and the Folio; '*faith so infringed*' seems the most satisfactory emendation proposed.

IV. iii. 161. '*a gnat*,' perhaps alluding to the fact that it sings, as it flies. Biron refers probably to the King's sonnets.

IV. iii. 243. '*wood*'; Quartos and Folios read '*word*.'

IV. iii. 251. '*School of night*'; so the early editions; '*scowl*,' '*stole*,' '*soul*,' '*scroll*,' '*seal*,' '*shade*,' have been proposed by various scholars; possibly, as the Cambridge editors suggest, '*school*' is an error for '*shoote*,' *i.e.* '*suit*.'

V. i. 27-28. In Quarto and Folio the line reads:—

'*Bome boon for boon priscian, a little scratcht 'twill serve.*'

V. i. 123. Capell proposed '*or*' for '*and*'; the passage is evidently corrupt.

V. ii. 67. '*perttaunt-like*'; this word is the *crux* of the play, the early editions read '*perttaunt-like*' and '*pertaunt-like*.' Theobald reads '*pedant-like*,' and other editors suggest '*portent-like*,' '*pageant-like*,' '*potently*,' '*persuant-like*.' It is perhaps worth while suggesting that the phrase (*tant*) *pour tant* (*quasi* 'tit for tat') perhaps underlies the word: it may well have been used in some game: Mr. Marshall quotes *pur Tant* from a poetical description of an old game, but no explanation has as yet been advanced.

1028 THE COMEDIES

V. ii. 332. 'To show his teeth as white as whale's bone'; this should certainly be printed *whalës bone,* the regular name for walrus tusk in old English.

V. ii. 338. '*Madman,*' obviously an error for '*man*'; '*mad*' probably due to '*madam*' in the next line.

V. ii. 560, 561. According to Plutarch, Alexander's head had a twist towards the left; he states also that Alexander's skin had "a marvellous good savour."

V. ii. 582. '*Canis*'; '*canus*' in the old editions, required for the sake of the rhyme.

V. ii. 730-731. The meaning of these somewhat obscure lines seems to be that 'the latest minute of the hour often fashions or moulds all causes or questions to the purposes of his speed, that is, to his own intents'; "the extreme parts are the end parts, '*extremities*'—as, of our body, fingers; of chains, the final links; of given portions of time, the last of those units into which we choose to divide them." Observe '*forms*' for '*form*' by attraction of '*time.*' In the next lines the metaphor is derived from archery.

V. ii. 742. '*Double*'; so Quartos and Folios; many modern editors adopt '*dull*' from the Collier MS.

V. ii. 753. '*Strange*'; the Quartos and Folios read '*straying,*' probably merely a variant spelling of '*strange.*'

V. ii. 865. '*Jack hath not Jill,*' cp. *Midsummer-Night's Dream,* III. ii. 462:—

"*Jack shall have Jill:
Nought shall go ill:
The man shall have his mare again, and all shall be well.*"

A MIDSUMMER-NIGHT'S DREAM

I. i. 10. '*new-bent*'; Rowe's correction of '*now bent,*' the reading of the Quartos and Folios.

I. i. 11. '*Philostrate*' is the name assumed by Arcite in Chaucer's *Knight's Tale*; it occurs too in Plutarch's *Lives*, where are to be found also the names, Lysander, and Demetrius.

I. i. 27. The second Folio reads '*this hath bewitched*'; the earlier edition '*this man*'; perhaps we should read '*this man hath 'witched.*'

I. i. 44. '*our law*'; Solon's laws gave a father the power of life and death over his child.

I. i. 159, 160. These lines should perhaps be transposed.

I. i. 167. '*to do observance to a morn of May,*' cp. *Knight's Tale,* 1500; '*And for to doon his observance to May.*'

I. i. 219. '*stranger companies*'; Theobald's emendation of '*strange companions,*' which is the reading of the Quartos and Folios.

NOTES

I. ii. 11. *'The most lamentable comedy,'* &c. *Cp.* the title of Preston's *Cambyses*, *'a lamentable tragedy mixed full of pleasant mirth'*; &c.

I. ii. 46. *'Thisne, Thisne,'* so the Quartos and Folios: perhaps this spelling was intentional to represent Bottom's attempt to speak the name 'in a monstrous little voice.' The words may, however, be an error for *'thisne, thisne,' i.e.* 'in this manner, in this manner,' *'thissen'* being used in this sense in various dialects.

II. i. 54, 55. The Quartos and Folios read *'coffe . . . loffe,'* for the sake of the rhyme.

II. i. 58. *'room'*; probably pronounced as a dissyllable.

II. i. 78. *'Perigenia,'* called *'Perigouna'* in North's *Plutarch;* she was the daughter of the famous robber Sinnis, by whom Theseus had a son, Menaloppus.

II. i. 79. *'Ægle'*; Rowe's correction for *'Eagles'* of the Quartos and Folios; probably *'Eagles'* was for *'Ægles,'* a form due to North's *Plutarch*, where it is stated that some think Theseus left Ariadne "because he was in love with another, as by these verses should appear,

'Ægles the nymph was lov'd of Theseus,
Who was the daughter of Panopeus.'"

II. i. 80. *'Antiopa,'* said to be the name of the Amazon queen, and the mother of Hippolytus.

II. i. 231. *'Daphne holds the chase'*; the story tells how Apollo pursued Daphne, who was changed into a laurel-tree as he reached her.

III. i. 33-41. This was probably suggested by an actual incident which occurred during the Kenilworth festivities, when one Harry Goldingham, who was to represent Arion upon the Dolphin's back, tore off his disguise and swore he was none of Arion (*cp.* Scott's use of this story in *Kenilworth*).

III. i. 171. *'Squash,' i.e.* an unripe peascod.

III. ii. 36. *'latch'd'*; the word *'latch'* in this passage, as Prof. Skeat has pointed out, is not connected with the ordinary *'latch,'* 'to catch,' but is etymologically the casual form of *'leak,'* and means 'to cause to drop, to drip.'

III. ii. 119. *'sport alone,' i.e.* 'by itself, without anything else'; others render *'alone'* by 'above all things, without a parallel.'

III. ii. 188. *'oes'*; *o* was used for anything round, among other things for circular discs of metal used for ornaments, *cp.* Bacon, Essay xxxvii.: "And Oes, and Spangs, as they are of no great cost, so they are of most glory."

III. ii. 204. *'needles,'* a monosyllable; *'needle'* was often spelt *'neeld'* in Old English.

III. ii. 212-214. "Helena says, 'we had two seeming bodies but one heart.' She then exemplifies her position by a simile—'we had two of the first, *i.e.* bodies, like the double coats in heraldry that belong to man and wife as one person, but which, like our single heart, have but one crest.'"

III. ii. 257. 'No no; he'll . . . seem'; the first Quarto 'heele seem'; the second 'hee'l seem'; the first Folio 'No, no, Sir, seem.' The passage is clearly corrupt in the old editions. I am inclined to accept Mr. Orson's ingenious suggestion:—

> "No no, sir; still
> Seeme to breake loose,"

'heele' being an easy misreading of 'stille.'

IV. i. 27. 'a reasonable good ear in music'; weavers were supposed to be fond of music, more especially of psalm-singing; cp. 1 Henry IV., II. iv. 130, 131. 'I would I were a weaver, I could sing psalms.'

IV. i. 40. 'So doth the woodbine the sweet honeysuckle'; commonly 'woodbine' is identical with 'honeysuckle,' but it is also used by Elizabethans for 'convolvulus' and 'ivy.' Shakespeare, however, uses the word in two other passages (II. i. 251 and Much Ado, III. i. 30) in the sense of 'honeysuckle'; hence Warburton suggested:—

> "So doth the woodbine, the sweet honeysuckle,
> Gently entwist the maple, ivy so," &c.

Johnson thought that 'woodbine' was the plant, and 'honeysuckle' the flower. These suggestions are not satisfactory: the simplest way out of the difficulty is to take 'woodbine' as equivalent to 'convolvulus' or 'bindweed'; cp. Ben Jonson's Vision of Delight:—

> "behold!
> How the blue bindweed doth itself unfold
> With honeysuckle."

IV. i. 71. 'Dian's bud'; it has been thought that perhaps 'Dian's bud' = 'Diana's rose,' 'the rose of England's Virgin Queen'; 'Diana's Rose' is actually used in this complimentary sense in Greene's Friar Bacon.

IV. i. 80. 'Than common sleep,' &c.; the Quartos and first two Folio read 'sleepe: of all these, fine the sense'; the correction is Theobald's.

IV. i. 88. 'prosperity'; so the first Quarto; the second and Folios 'posterity.'

IV. i. 114. 'fountains'; perhaps an error for 'mountains.'

V. i. 47. 'my kinsman Hercules'; cp. North's Plutarch, Life of Theseus: "they (Theseus and Hercules) were near kinsmen, being cousins removed by the mother's side."

V. i. 54. 'critical,' i.e. 'censorious' as in the well-known utterance of Iago, 'I am nothing, if not critical' (Othello, II. i. 119).

V. i. 59. 'wondrous strange snow'; 'strange' is hardly the epithet one would expect, and various emendations have been suggested: —'strange black,' 'strong snow,' 'swarthy snow,' 'sable-snow,' 'and, wondrous strange! yet snow.' Perhaps the most plausible

NOTES 1031

conjecture is Mr. S. W. Orson's *'wondrous flaming snow,'* cp. "What strange fits be these, Philautus, that burne thee with such a heat, that thou shakest for cold, and all thy body in a shivering sweat, in *a flaming ice*, melteth like wax and hardeneth like the adamant" (Lyly's *Euphues*, ed. Arber, p. 311).

V. i. 91. *'And what poor duty,'* &c.; Coleridge proposed:—
"*And what poor duty cannot do, yet would,*
    Noble respect takes it," &c.

The metre is defective as the lines stand. Theobald read *'poor willing duty . . . Noble respect.'* The meaning is sufficiently clear, and recalls *Love's Labour's Lost*, V. ii. 517, *'That sport best pleases that doth least know how,'* &c. *'Takes it in might'* = regards the ability or effort of the performance.

V. i. 118. *'stand upon points'*; Quince's punctuation reminds one of the reading of Roister Doister's letter to Mistress Constance in the old comedy (*cp. Roister Doister*, iii. 3).

V. i. 138. *'name'*; as there is no rhyme to *name*, the loss of a line is to be inferred, or perhaps we should read *'which by name Lion hight.'*

V. i. 205. *'mural down'*; the Quartos read *'Moon used'*; the Folios *'morall downe'*; the emendation *'mural'* was due to Pope.

V. i. 221. *'a lion-fell'*; the Quartos and Folios read *'a lion fell,'* i.e. a fierce lion, but Snug wishes to say 'he is not a lion,' wherefore the words have been hyphened by most modern editors, *'lion-fell,'* i.e. 'a lion's skin.' Johnson understood *'neither'* before *'a lion fell'*; Rowe read *'No lion fell.'* There is, I think, a more obvious emendation, and I propose:—

"*Then know that I, one Snug the joiner, n'am*
    A lion fell, nor else no lions dam,"

'n'am' being an archaic form, like *nill* (*i.e.* ne will). In Gascoigne's *Steele Glas* the following couplet occurs, remarkably suggestive of our text:—

"*I n'am a man, as some do think I am;*
    (*Laugh not good lord*), *I am indede a dame.*"

V. i. 261, 262. Spedding proposed to invert these lines.

V. 1. 265. *'gleams'*; the Quartos and Folio 1 read *'beams'*; Folio 2 *'streams.'*

V. i. 311-312. *'he for a man—God bless us,'* omitted in the Folios, probably in consequence of the statute of James I. forbidding profane speaking, or use of 'the holy name of God.'

V. i. 315. *'means,'* changed by Theobald to *'moans.'* *'Mean'* in the sense of 'to lament,' an archaic form, is really more correct than *'moan,'* and probably intentionally used by Shakespeare to harmonise with the archaisms of the interlude.

V. ii. 2. *'behowls'*; Theobald's emendation of *'beholds,'* the reading of the Quartos and Folios.

V. ii. 25. *'this ditty'*; Johnson supposes that two songs are lost, one led by Titania, and one by Oberon.

THE MERCHANT OF VENICE

The name 'Shylock' may have been derived by Shakespeare from a pamphlet called 'Caleb Shillocke his prophecies, or the Jewes Prediction'; the Pepysian ballad on this subject belongs to the year 1607; to the same year belongs a prose piece printed at the end of a rare tract called 'A Jewes prophecie, or Newes from Rome of two mighty armies,' &c. Its ultimate origin is unknown; it may have been an Italian name *Sciolocca*. According to Hunter, *Scialac* was the name of a Maronite of Mount Libanus, who was living in 1614.

I. i. 27. '*dock'd*'; Rowe's emendation for '*docks*,' the reading of the Quartos and Folios.

I. i. 113. '*Is that any thing new?*' The old editions read '*Is that any thing now*,' changed to '*new*' by Johnson. Rowe first suggested the interrogation.

I. ii. 70. '*the Scottish lord*'; in the first Folio '*Scottish*' is changed to '*other*.'

I. ii. 72-74. "Alluding to the constant assistance, or rather, constant promises of assistance, that the French gave the Scots in their quarrels with the English" (Warburton).

I. ii. 111. '*The four strangers*'; allusion has been made to six strangers. An interesting oversight on the poet's part.

I. iii. 60, 61. '*Is he yet possess'd How much ye would,*' so read the second and third Quartos; the Folios read '*he would*'; the first Quarto '*are you resolv'd how much he would have*': this is one of the important points in which the second Quarto is superior to the first.

I. iii. 67. *Cp.* Genesis xxx.

I. iii. 70. '*the third*,' *i.e.* 'reckoning Abraham himself as the first.'

I. iii. 130. '*A breed for barren metal*'; the reading of the Folio '*a breed of*'; '*for*' must be equivalent to 'in exchange for'; '*breed*' = 'interest money bred from the principal' (*cp.* Gr. τόκος).

II. i. The old stage direction ran as follows:—'*Enter Morochus a tawnie Moore all in white, and three or four followers accordingly, with Portia, Nerissa and their traine.*'

II. i. 25. '*the Sophy*,' *cp.* "Sofi, and Sofito, an ancient word signifying a wise man, learned and skillful in Magike Naturale. It has grown to be the common name of the Emperour of Persia" (Abraham Hartwell's translation of Minadoi's *History of the Wars between the Turks and the Persians*).

The '*Sefii of Persia*' is mentioned in the German play *Der Jude von Venedig*.

NOTES 1033

II. i. 35. *'page'*; Theobald's emendation for *'rage,'* the reading of all the old editions.

II. ii. 84. Gobbo's *'you,'* as a mark of respect, changes to *'thou,'* after the recognition.

II. ii. 148. "Long and deep lines from the Mount of Venus (the ball of the thumb) towards the line of life, signifieth so many wives.
. . . These lines visible and deep, so many wives the party shall have" (Saunder's *Chiromancie*, quoted by Halliwell).

II. iii. 11. *'did'*; the Quartos and first Folio read *'doe'*; the reading *'did'* was first given in the second Folio; if this is adopted, *'get'* = 'beget.'

II. v. 24. *'Black-Monday,'* i.e. Easter Monday, so called, because of a storm which occurred on April 14, 1360, being Easter Monday, when Edward III was lying with his army before Paris, and when many of his men-at-arms died of cold (Stowe).

II. v. 35. *'Jacob's staff'*; *cp.* Gen. xxxii. and Heb. xi. 21. 'A Jacob's staff' was generally used in the sense of 'a pilgrim's staff,' because St. James (or Jacob) was the patron saint of pilgrims.

II. v. 42. *'A Jewess' eye'*; the Quartos and Folios read *'a Jewes eye,'* probably pronounced *'Jewës'*; 'worth a Jew's eye' was a proverbial phrase: 'that worth was the price which the Jews paid for immunity from mutilation and death.' The reading *'Jewess'* seems very doubtful.

II. vi. 51. *'by my hood'*; this phrase is found nowhere else in Shakespeare; according to Malone, Gratiano is in a masqued habit, to which it is probable that formerly, as at present, a large cape or hood was affixed.

II. vii. 41. *'the Hyrcanian deserts'*; Shakespeare three times mentions the tigers of Hyrcania, 'the name given to a district of indefinite extent south of the Caspian,' where, according to Pliny, tigers were bred.

II. vii. 53. *'undervalued'*; "in the beginning of Elizabeth's reign, gold was to silver in the proportion of 11 to 1; in the forty-third year of her reign it was in the proportion of 10 to 1" (Clarendon).

II. vii. 69. *'tombs do'*; Johnson's emendation for the old reading *'timber do.'*

II. vii. 75. Halliwell notes that this line is a paraphrastical inversion of the common old proverb: 'Farewell, frost,' which was used in the absence or departure of anything that was unwelcome or displeasing.

III. i. 9. *'Knapped ginger'*; perhaps *'to knap ginger'* is to 'nibble ginger'; old women were fond of this condiment: Cotgrave invariably gives *'knap'* as a synonym of *'gnaw'* or *'nibble.'*

III. i. 60. *'humility,'* rightly explained by Schmidt as 'kindness, benevolence, humanity.'

III. i. 105. The special value of the 'turquoise' was its supposed virtue in indicating the health of the wearer: it was said to brighten or fade as its wearer was well or ill, and to give warning of approaching danger.

III. ii. 54. *'more love'*; because Hercules rescued Hesione not for love of the lady, but for the sake of the horses promised him by Laomedon.

III. ii. 99. *'veiling an Indian beauty'*; it has been pointed out that Montaigne in his Essay on 'Beauty' says: "The Indians describe it black and swarthy, with blabbered thick lips, with a broad and flat nose." If Shakespeare gives us a reminiscence of this, he must have read Montaigne in French, as Florio's translation was not published until 1603.

III. ii. 102. *'Hard food for Midas,'* who prayed that everything he touched might turn to gold, and soon regretted his prayer.

III. ii. 106. *'paleness'*; as Bassanio uses 'pale' of silver a few lines before, Theobald, on Warburton's suggestion, proposed to read *'plainness'*; but *'pale'* is a regular epithet of lead, and there seems no reason for changing the reading here.

III. ii. 112. *'rain'*; the reading of the second Quarto, *'rein,'* is generally preferred.

III. v. 69-70. *'And if on earth he do not mean it, then In reason'*; the second Quarto *'it, it'*; the Folios *'it, it is.'*

Various emendations have been suggested for *'mean,'* but no change is necessary: *'mean'* = 'aim at.' A kind correspondent, Mr. S. W. Orson, calls attention to Herbert's use of the word in *'The Church Porch'* (E. Stock's reprint of the first edition) "Shoots higher much than he that *means* a tree" (p. 12), and "Scorns his first bed of dirt, and *means* the sky" (p. 163).

IV. i. 36. *'Our holy Sabbath'*; so the first Quarto; the second reads *'Sabaoth'*; it is just possible that Shakespeare might have been misled by the expression, 'Lord God of Sabaoth,' which occurs in the New Testament. 'Sabbath' and 'Sabaoth' (*i.e.* 'hosts,' in the phrase 'Lord of hosts') were confused even by Sir Walter Scott, when in *Ivanhoe*, ch. x. he refers to "the gains of a week, aye the space between two Sabaoths." Similarly Spenser (F. Q. viii. 2):—

'But henceforth all shall rest eternally
With him that is the God of Sabaoth hight.'

Dr. Johnson treated the two words as identical in the first edition of his Dictionary.

IV. i. 50, 51. *'affection, Mistress of passion'*; the Quartos and Folios read *'affection. Master of passion.'* The reading now generally adopted was first suggested by Thirlby; *'Maistres'* or *'mastres,'* the old spelling of *'mistress'* evidently produced the error. *'Affection,'* when contrasted with *'passion,'* seems to denote 'emotions produced through the senses by external objects.'

NOTES

IV. i. 56. '*a wollen bag-pipe*'; the reading of all the old editions; '*wawling,*' '*swollen,*' '*bollen,*' have been variously suggested; '*woollen*' probably refers to the covering of the windbag.

IV. i. 181, 182. *Cp.* "Mercy is seasonable in the time of affliction, as clouds of rain in the time of drought," Ecclesiasticus, xxxv. 20.

IV. i. 252. '*Are there balance*'; '*balance*' was frequently treated as a plural by Elizabethan writers, though this is the only instance in Shakespeare.

V. i. 4. '*Troilus*'; the image is from Chaucer's *Troilus and Cresseide:* "Upon the wallis fast eke would he walke" (Bk. v. 666).

V. i. 7-14. '*Thisbe,*' &c. Hunter (*New Illustrations,* i. 309) ingeniously suggests that the old Folio of Chaucer was lying open before Shakespeare when he wrote this dialogue, and that there he found Thisbe, Dido, and Medea, as well as Troilus. It is certainly striking that Thisbe, Dido, and Medea follow each other in the '*Legend of Good Women.*' Shakespeare has seemingly transferred to Dido what he found in Chaucer's *Legend* concerning Ariadne ('*And to the stronde bare-fote faste she went*' —'*And turne agayne, and on the stronde hire fyinde.*'). Chaucer's *Medea* directed Shakespeare's mind to Ovid, *Metam.* VII.

V. i. 15. '*Jessica*'; Medea, who stole away from her father Æetes, with the golden fleece, suggests Jessica's own story to Lorenzo.

V. i. 60, &c. "The corresponding passage in Plato is in his tenth book *De Republica* where he speaks of the harmony of the Spheres, and represents a syren sitting on each of the eight orbs, and singing to each in its proper tone, while they are thus guided through the heavens, and consent in a diapason of perfect harmony, the Fates themselves chanting to this celestial music" (Du Bois, *The Wreath,* p. 60, quoted by Furness). The Platonic doctrine is, however, blended with reminiscences of Job xxxviii. 7, "The morning stars sang together."

V. i. 65. '*close it in*'; Quarto 1 and Folios read '*in it,*' which some editors have taken as equivalent to '*close-in-it.*'

V. i. 193. A similar repetition of the word '*love*' at the end of ten consecutive lines is found in '*The Fayre Mayde of the Exchange*' (1607); *cp. Edward III.* Act II. sc. i., where '*the sun*' ends eight consecutive lines.

AS YOU LIKE IT

DRAMATIS PERSONÆ. The pronunciation of '*Jaques*' is still somewhat doubtful, though the metrical test makes it certain

that it is always a dissyllable in Shakespeare: there is evidence
that the name was well known in England, and ordinarily
pronounced as a monosyllable; hence Harrington's *Metamorphosis of A-jax* (1596). The name of the character was probably
rendered '*Jakēs*'; the modern stage practice is in favour of
'*Jaqowes*.'

I. i. 1. '*it was upon this fashion: bequeathed*,' &c. The Folio
does not place a stop at '*fashion*,' but makes '*bequeathed*' a past
participle; the words '*charged*' ... '*on his blessing*' presuppose
'*he*' or '*my father*'; the nominative may, however, be easily
supplied from the context, or possibly, but doubtfully, '*a*'
(= '*he*') has been omitted before '*charged*.' There is very much
to be said in favour of the Folio reading; a slight confusion of
two constructions seems to have produced the difficulty. Warburton, Hanmer, and Capell proposed to insert '*my father*'
before '*bequeathed*.' Others punctuate in the same way as in the
present text, but read '*he bequeathed*' or '*my father bequeathed*';
the Cambridge editors hold that the subject of the sentence is
intentionally omitted.

I. ii. 75. The Folio prefixes '*Rosalind*' to the speech: Theobald first proposed the change to '*Celia*,' and he has been followed by most editors. Capell suggested '*Fernandine*' for
'*Frederick*' in the previous speech. Shakespeare does not give
us the name of Rosalind's father: he is generally referred to
as '*Duke Senior*'; Celia's father is mentioned as '*Frederick*' in
two other places (l. 219 of this scene, and V. iv. 151). One
has, however, a shrewd suspicion that Touchstone is referring
to the exiled king as '*old Frederick*,' and that Rosalind speaks
the words '*my father's love is enough to honour him*'; the expression is so much in harmony with her subsequent utterance, ll.
220:

'*My father loved Sir Rowland as his soul.*'

And again, in the next scene, l. 28:—

'*The Duke my father loved his father dearly.*'

I. ii. 189. '*You mean*'; Theobald proposed '*An' you mean*,'
and the Cambridge editors suggest that '*and*' for '*an*' (= if)
may be the right reading, omitted by the printer, who mistook
it for part of the stage-direction '*Orl. and*' for '*Orland*.'

I. ii. 254. '*the taller*'; but Rosalind is later on described as
'*more than common tall*,' and Celia as '*the woman low, and
browner than her brother*'; probably '*taller*' is a slip of Shakespeare's pen: '*shorter*,' '*smaller*,' '*lesser*,' '*lower*,' have been variously proposed; of these '*lesser*' strikes one perhaps as most
Shakespearian.

I. iii. 97. '*change*,' &c., Folio 1; the other Folios read '*charge*,'
i.e. 'burden,' probably the true reading.

I. iii. 123. There has been much discussion of the scansion

of this line; several critics, in their anxiety to save Shakespeare from the serious charge of using a false quantity, propose to accent 'Aliena' on the penultimate, but for all that it seems most likely that the line is to be read:—

'No lóng|er Cél|ya bút|Ali|ena.'

II. i. 5. *'here feel we but'*; Theobald first conjectured *'but'* for *'not'* of the Folios, and his emendation has been accepted by many scholars, though violently opposed by others. Most of the discussions turn on *'the penalty of Adam,'* which ordinarily suggests toil—'in the sweat of thy brow shalt thou eat bread'— but in this passage Shakespeare makes the penalty to be "the season's difference," cp. *Paradise Lost*, x. 678, 9:—
'Else had the spring Perpetual smiled on earth with vernant flowers.'

II. i. 13-14. *'like the toad, ugly and venomous,'* &c. A favourite Euphuistic conceit, e.g. 'The foul toade hath a faire stone in his head,' *Euphues*, p. 53 (ed. Arber), based on an actual belief in toadstones. The origin of the belief is traced back to Pliny's description of a stone as 'of the colour of a frog.'

II. iii. 12. *'no more do yours,'* a somewhat loose construction, but one easily understood, the force of the previous sentence being 'to some kind of men their graces serve them not as friends.'

II. iii. 71. *'seventeen'*; Rowe's emendation for *'seaventie'* of the Folios.

II. iv. 1. *'weary'*; Theobald's emendation for *'merry'* of the Folios, and generally adopted; some scholars are in favour of the Folio reading, and put it down to Rosalind's assumed merriment; her subsequent confession as to her weariness must then be taken as an aside.

II. iv. 46. *'from whom,'* i.e. from the peascod; similarly *'her'* in the next line: he was wooing the peascod instead of his mistress.

II. v. 3. *'turn,'* so the Folios: Pope substituted *'tune'*; but the change is unnecessary; according to Steevens *'to turn a tune* or *note'* is still a current phrase among vulgar musicians.

II. v. 56-57. *'I'll rail against all the first-born of Egypt.'* According to Johnson *'the first-born of Egypt'* was a proverbial expression for high-born persons, but it has not been found elsewhere. Nares suggests that perhaps Jaques is only intended to say that, if he cannot sleep, he will, like other discontented persons, rail against his betters. There is no doubt some subtler meaning in the words, and the following is possibly worthy of consideration:—Jaques says if he cannot sleep he'll rail against all first-borns, for it is the question of birthright which has caused him *'leave his wealth and ease,'* merely as he had previously put it *'to please a stubborn will'*; this idea has perhaps suggested

Pharaoh's stubbornness, and by some such association 'all first-borns' became *'all the first-born of Egypt'*; or, by mere association, the meaningless tag *'of Egypt'* is added by Jaques to round off the phrase, and to give it some sort of colour.

II. vii. 19. Touchstone of course alludes to the common saying 'Fortune favours fools,' *cp.* '*Every man out of his humour,*' I. i.

Sogliardo. Why, who am I, sir?
Macilente. One of those that fortune favours.
Carlo. [*Aside*] The periphrasis of a fool.

II. vii. 34, 36. '*A worthy fool*' . . . '*O, worthy fool*': the '*A*' and '*O*' should probably change places, according to an anonymous conjecture noted in the Cambridge Edition.

II. vii. 55. '*Not to seem*'; the words '*not to*' were first added by Theobald: the Folios read '*seem*'; Collier, following his MS. corrections, proposed '*but to seem*'; the meaning is the same in both cases. Mr. Furness follows Ingleby in maintaining the correctness of the text, and paraphrases thus:—"He who is hit the hardest by me must laugh the hardest, and that he must do so is plain; because if he is a wise man he must seem foolishly senseless of the bob by laughing it off. Unless he does this, viz., shows his insensibility by laughing it off, any chance hit of the fool will expose every nerve and fibre of his folly."

II. vii. 73. '*the weary very means*,' the reading of the Folios (Folios 1 and 2 '*wearie*'; Folios 3, 4, '*weary*'). Pope proposed '*very very*'; Collier (MS.) '*the very means of wear*'; Staunton '*weary-very,*' or '*very-weary.*' Others maintain the correctness of the original reading, and explained 'until that its very means, being weary or exhausted, do ebb.' A very plausible emendation was suggested by Singer, viz., '*wearer's*' for '*weary,*' and it has rightly been adopted by several editors: *cp. Henry VIII.* I. i. 83-85:—

'*O, many
Have broke their backs with laying manors on 'em
For this great journey.*'

II. vii. 178. '*because thou art not seen,*' *i.e.* "as thou art an enemy that dost not brave us with thy presence" (Johnson): several unnecessary emendations have been proposed, *e.g.* '*Thou causest not that teen*' (Hanmer); '*Because thou art foreseen*' (Staunton), &c.

II. vii. 189. '*As friend remember'd not,*' *i.e.* 'as forgotten friendship,' or 'as want an unremembered friend feels': *cp.* '*benefits forgot,*' *supra.*

III. ii. 104. '*the very false gallop,*' *cp.* Nashe's *Four Letters Confuted*, "I would trot a false gallop through the rest of his ragged verses but that if I should retort his rime dogrell aright, I must make my verses (as he doth his) run hobling like a

NOTES

Brewer's Cart upon the stones, and observe no length in their feet."

III. ii. 146. '*pulpiter*': Spedding's suggestion for '*Jupiter*' of the Folios.

III. ii. 384. '*living*,' *i.e.* lasting, permanent; the antithesis seems to require '*loving*,' which has been substituted by some editors: it is noteworthy that in some half-dozen instances in Shakespeare '*live*' has been printed for '*love*,' but it is questionable whether any change is justifiable here.

III. iii. 4. '*your features! . . . what features?*' Farmer's conjecture '*feature! . . . what's feature*' seems singularly plausible; cp. l. 17, '*I do not know what "poetical" is.*'

III. iii. 69. '*her*,' so Folios 1, 2: '*his*,' Folios 3, 4: the female bird was the falcon; the male was called 'tercel' or 'tassel.'

III. iv. 39. '*noble goose*'; Hanmer substituted '*nose-quilled*' for '*noble*,' which is, of course, used ironically.

III. v. 7. '*dies and lives*,' *i.e.* 'lives and dies,' *i.e.* 'subsists from the cradle to the grave'; the inversion of the words seems to have been an old idiom; cp. '*Romaunt of the Rose*,' v. 5790:—

"With sorwe they both die and live,
That unto Richesse her hertis yive."

Other passages in later literature might be adduced where the exigencies of metre do not exist.

IV. i. 136. '*like Diana in the fountain.*' Stowe mentions in his *Survey of London* (1603) that there was set up in 1596 on the east side of the cross in Cheapside "a curiously wrought tabernacle of grey marble, and in the same an alabaster image of Diana, and water conveyed from the Thames prilling from her naked breast." It is very doubtful whether Shakespeare is referring to this particular 'Diana,' as some have supposed.

IV. ii. 12. The words '*Then sing him home, the rest shall bear this burden,*' are printed as one line in the Folios. Theobald was the first to re-arrange, as in the text. Knight, Collier, Dyce, and others take the whole to be a stage-direction. Knight first called attention to the fact that possibly the original music for this song is to be found in John Hilton's '*Catch that Catch Can; or, a Choice Collection of Catches, Rounds,*' &c., 1652 (printed Furness, p. 230, 231).

IV. iii. 74. '*fair ones*'; Mr. Wright suggests that perhaps we should read 'fair *one*,' and Mr. Furness assents to the view that 'Shakespeare seems to have forgotten that Celia was apparently the only woman present.' But surely it is noteworthy that Oliver a few lines lower down gives the description:—'*The boy is fair,*' &c.

IV. iii. 86. '*like a ripe sister: the woman low*'; the pause at the woman low cæsura takes the place of a syllable.

IV. iii. 100. '*chewing the food,*' usually quoted as 'chewing the cud,' a correction of the line first suggested by Scott (cp. Introduction to *Quentin Durward*).

V. ii. 17. '*fair sister*'; Oliver addresses 'Ganymede' thus for he is Orlando's counterfeit Rosalind (cp. IV. iii. 92). Some interpreters of Shakespeare are of opinion that Oliver knows the whole secret of the situation.

V. ii. 65. '*which I tender dearly*'; probably an allusion to the Act "against Conjuracons, Inchantments, and Witchcraftes," passed under Elizabeth, which enacted that all persons using witchcraft, &c., whereby death ensued, should be put to death without benefit of clergy, &c.

V. iii. 15. Chappell printed the music of the song from a MS., now in the Advocates' Library, Edinburgh, belonging to the early part of the seventeenth century (cp. Furness, pp. 262, 263). In the Folios the last stanza is made the second. Mr. Roffe is of opinion that Shakespeare contemplated a trio between the Pages and Touchstone.

V. iv. 4. '*As those that fear they hope, and know they fear.*' A large number of unnecessary emendations have been proposed for this plausible reading of the Folios; e.g. '*fear, they hope, and know they fear*'; '*fear their hope and hope their fear*'; '*fear their hope and know their fear,*' &c. The last of these gives the meaning of the line as it stands in the text.

V. iv. 84. '*we quarrel in print, by the book*'; Shakespeare probably refers to "*Vincentio Saviolo his Practise. In two Bookes. The first intreating the use of the Rapier and Dagger. The second of Honor and honorable Quarrels*"; printed in 1594.

V. iv. 85. '*books for good manners,*' e.g. "*A lytle Booke of Good Manners for Chyldren with interpritation into the vulgare Englysshe tongue by R. Whittinton, Poet Laureat*"; printed at London in 1554; (cp. Dr. Furnivall's *Book of Norture of John Russell*, &c., published by the Early English Text Society, 1868). Cp. *Hamlet*, V. ii. 149, '*he* (i.e. *Laertes*) *is the card of calendar of gentry,*' a probable allusion to the title of some such 'book of manners.'

V. iv. 107. '*her hand with his*'; the first and second Folios '*his hand*'; corrected to '*her*' in the second and third Folios.

V. iv. 141. '*even daughter, welcome*'; Theobald proposed '*daughter-welcome,*' i.e. 'welcome as a daughter.' Folios 1, 2, 3, read '*daughter welcome*'; Folio 4, '*daughter, welcome.*' The sense is clear whichever reading is adopted, though the rhythm seems in favour of the reading in the text: 'O my dear niece,' says the Duke, 'nay, daughter, welcome to me in no less degree than daughter.'

Epilogue. 15. '*If I were a woman*'; the part of Rosalind was of course originally taken by a boy-actor: women's parts were not taken by women till after the Restoration.

THE TAMING OF THE SHREW

INDUCT. i. 7. *'go by, Jeronimy'*; a popular phrase from Kyd's *Spanish Tragedy*—"the common butt of raillery to all the poets in Shakespeare's time."

Induct. i. 13. *'Brach Merriman'*; *'brach'* usually means a female hound, as in the next line; the sequence of thought requires *'brach'* to be a verb: perhaps it is used in the sense of 'couple,' 'mate.' Hanmer proposed *'leech'*; Keightley, *'bathe'*; Singer (ed. 2), *'trash,'* &c.

Induct. i. 60. *'And when he says he is,'* &c., so the old eds. The reading is probably correct; the line means 'when he says he is mad, say that he dreams.' Rowe proposed *'And when he says he's poor'*; Keightley *'And when he says what he is,'* &c.

Induct. i. 84. The Folios and Quarto prefix *'Sincklo,'* the name of an actor in Shakespeare's company, who is mentioned also in stage-directions of Quarto edition (1600) of 2 *Henry IV.*, V. iv., and in the Folio, 3 *Henry VI.*, III. i.

Induct. i. 84. *'Soto'* is a character in Beaumont and Fletcher's *Women Pleased*.

I. i. 32. Cp. *The Taming of a Shrew*:—
'Welcome to Athens, my beloved friend,
To Plato's school and Aristotle's walks.'

I. i. 42. *'If Biondello, thou wert'*; the Collier MS. reads *'now were'*; Dyce adopts this emendation.

I. i. 64. *'To comb your noddle with a three-legg'd stool'*; an old expression occurring in Skelton's *Merrie Tales*. "Hys wife would divers times in the weeke kimbe his head with a iii. footed stoole."

I. i. 231. *'I, sir! ne'er a whit.'* Rowe proposed *'Ay, sir, ne'er,'* &c.; Dyce, *'Ay, sir.—Ne'er.'* It is difficult to determine whether 'I' is the personal pronoun, or stands, as is often the case, for 'Ay.'

I. i. 243. *'The presenters,' i.e.* Sly and his attendants in the balcony above.

I. ii. 28. *'what he 'leges in Latin'*; the Folios and Quarto, *'leges,'* an authorised form for *'alleges'*; Grumio, strange to say, though an Italian, mistakes Italian for Latin.

I. ii. 146-147. *'paper' . . . 'them'*; changed by Pope to *'papers'*: Mr. Daniel considers *'paper'* to be the note of the *'books,'* and *'them'* the books.

II. i. 75-82, arranged as verse in the Folios and Quarto, first printed as prose by Pope.

II. i. 200. *'no such jade as you'*; probably an error for *'no jade for such as you,'* as conjectured by Hudson: many other less obvious emendations have been proposed, *e.g.* "*no such load as you, sir*" (Singer), &c.

II. i. 205-207. '*buzzard*' in this passage is a crux: its three senses are, I think, punned on by the speakers:—(i.) a simpleton (l. 206); (ii.) a mean hawk (ll. 207, 208); in the latter case Petruchio interprets it as (iii.) 'a buzzing insect,' hence 'you wasp' (l. 209). Katharine's reply seems to mean:—'that, in calling her a turtle, he has mistaken a hawk for a dove'; underlying this retort there may be a suggestion of the proverbial 'blind buzzard.'

II. i. 287. '*morn*'; *cp. Troilus*, I. iii. 229:—
    '*Modest as morning when she coldly eyes
        The youthful Phœbus.*'
The Collier MS. has '*moone.*'

II. i. 316. '*We will have rings and things,*' probably a fragment of an old ballad. Collier quotes some lines bearing a very strong resemblance to these "from the recitation of an old lady"— a vague authority.

II. i. 368. '*Marseilles*' *road*,' Folio 1 and Quarto, '*Marcellus*'; the other Folios '*Marsellis*'; the word is obviously trisyllabic; the apostrophe is not needed, *cp.* '*Venice gold,*' '*Pisa walls*' in the previous speech.

III. i. 4. Theobald proposed '*she is a shrew, but, wrangling pedant, this is*'; evidently some words are lost, but it is useless to attempt the restoration of the line, as there is no evidence.

III. ii. 16. '*make friends, invite, and proclaim the banns*'; so Folio 1 and Quarto; Folios 2 and 3 insert '*yes*' before '*and.*' The more noteworthy suggestions are:—"*Make friends invite, Yes*" (Singer); "*make friends invite guests*" (Dyce); "*make feasts, invite friends*" (Dyce, ed. 2).

IV. i. 125. '*Where is the life that late I led*'; a line of an old song, quoted also by Pistol; *cp.* 2 *Henry IV.,* V. iii. 137. Similarly '*It was the friar of orders grey,*' &c., is a bit of an old ballad, now lost.

IV. i. 192. '*to kill a wife with kindness,*' a proverbial expression. Heywood's play, *A Woman Killed with Kindness,* was first produced in 1602.

IV. ii. 45. '*longeth*'; the Folios and Quartos correct '*longeth,*' without apostrophe; '*to long*' in the sense of 'to belong' is common in older English writings. Similarly '*pointed*' in old eds., III. ii. 1.

IV. ii. 61. '*An ancient angel*'; so the Folios and Quartos; Theobald suggested '*engle*' (a gull); other proposals have been *ayeul, gentle, morsel, antick,* &c., but no change is necessary. Cotgrave renders *Angelot à la grosse escaille* by "an old angell; and by metaphor, a fellow of the old, sound, honest and worthie stamp."

IV. iii. 60. 'ruffling treasure'; Pope changed 'ruffling' to 'rustling'; perhaps we should read 'russling' (for 'rustling'). Cp. Lear, II. iv. 299, where the Quarto reading is 'russel,' while the Folios have 'ruffle.' Mrs. Quickly's 'rushling in silk and gold' (Merry Wives, II. ii. 63) seems to be an important piece of evidence in favour of 'rustling.'

IV. iv. 62. 'Cambio,' probably an error for 'Biondello,' as suggested by the Cambridge editors, and more satisfactory from a metrical point of view. Again, "the supposed Cambio was not acting as Baptista's servant, and moreover, had he been sent on such an errand, he would have 'flown on the wings of love' to perform it. We must suppose that Biondello apparently makes his exit, but really waits till the stage is clear for an interview with his disguised master."

V. i. 25. 'his father has come from Padua,' so the Folios and Quartos; various changes have been proposed, e.g. 'to Padua,' 'from Pisa,' &c., but the Pedant means that he has been staying at Padua.

ALL'S WELL THAT ENDS WELL

I. i. 75-76.
> 'These great tears grace his remembrance more
> Than those I shed for him;'

i.e. "the big and copious tears she then shed herself, which were caused in reality by Bertram's departure, though attributed by Lafeu and the Countess to the loss of her father; and from this misapprehension of theirs graced his remembrance more than those she actually shed for him."

I. i. 105-154. These lines are struck out by some editors; the Cambridge editors rightly call them 'a blot on the play'; they were probably "an interpolation, 'to tickle the ears of the groundlings.'" The opening words of the speech which follows are obscure, and the enumeration of 'the loves' looks like 'the nonsense of some foolish conceited player.' Hanmer proposed:—

> 'Not my virginity yet.—You're for the Court:
> There shall your master,' &c.

I. ii. 54. 'He scatter'd not in ears, but grafted them.'; cp. the Collect in the Liturgy: "Grant we beseech thee, Almighty God, that the words which we have heard this day with our outward ears may through thy grace be so grafted inwardly in our hearts, that they may bring forth the fruit of good living," &c.

I. ii. 56. 'this,' so the Folio; Pope read 'Thus,' possibly the right word here.

I. iii. 22. '*service is no heritage*'; the idea seems to be that, 'if service is no blessing, children are'; Psalm cxxvii. 3 has been appropriately cited in connection with this expression:—"Lo, children are an heritage of the Lord."

I. iii. 48-49. '*Young Charbon the puritan and old Poysam the papist*'; '*Charbon*' possibly for '*Chair-bonne*,' and '*Poysam*' for '*Poisson*,' alluding to the respective lenten fares of the Puritan and Papist (*cp.* the old French proverb, '*Jeune chair et viel poisson*' = *young* flesh and *old* fish are the best).

I. iii. 104. '. . . *queen of virgins*'; Theobald inserted '*Dian no*' before '*queen.*'

II. i. 1, 2. '*lords*' . . . '*lords*'; probably the young noblemen are divided into two sections according as they intend to take service with the 'Florentines' or the 'Senoys' (*cp.* Note vi. Cambridge edition).

II. i. 12, 13. '*let higher Italy,—Those bated*,' &c.; the passage is probably corrupt. '*Higher Italy*' has been variously interpreted to mean (1) Upper Italy; (2) the side of Italy next to the Adriatic (but both Florence and Siena are on the other side); (3) Italy higher in rank and dignity than France; (4) the noblest of Italy, the worthiest among Italians. Johnson paraphrased as follows:—'Let upper Italy, *where you are to exercise your valour*, see that you come to gain honour, to the *abatement*, that is, to the disgrace and depression of those *that have now lost their ancient military fame*, and inherit but the fall of the last monarchy.' Schmidt proposed '*high*' for '*higher*': Coleridge '*hired*': Hanmer '*bastards*' for '*bated.*' Knight took '*bated*' to mean 'excepted,' Schmidt 'beaten down.'

II. i. 32-3. '*No sword worn but one to dance with*'; alluding to the light swords worn for dancing.

II. i. 61. '*I'll fee*'; Theobald's emendation. Folios, '*Ile see.*'

II. i. 77. '*To give great Charlemain a pen in 's hand*'; Charlemagne late in life attempted to learn to write.

II. i. 173-174.
'*ne worse of worst extended,*
With vilest torture let my life be ended';
So Folio 1; the other Folios read '*no*' for '*ne.*' Malone's '*nay*' for '*ne*' commends itself, though his explanation of '*extended*' as 'my body being extended on the rack' seems weak: it is probably used here simply in the sense of 'meted out to me,' or merely used for the purpose of emphasising '*worse of worst.*' A mass of conjectural emendations are recorded in the Cambridge edition of the play.

II. ii. 21-22. '*Tib's rush for Tom's forefinger*'; 'Tib and Tom' were used like 'Jack and Jill'; Tib was a cant term for any low or vulgar woman. 'Rush rings' were sometimes used at mar riage ceremonies, especially where the marriages were somewhat doubtful (*cp. Douce's Illustrations,* p. 196).

II. iii. 1-39. Johnson changed the distribution of the speakers, so as to bring out 'the whole merriment of the scene,' which, according to him, "consists in the pretensions of Parolles to knowledge and sentiments which he has not." Johnson has been generally followed by modern editors. The Folio arrangement has been kept in the Cambridge text.

II. iii. 24. '*a showing of a heavenly effect in an earthly actor*'; the title of some pamphlet is evidently ridiculed in these words.

II. iii. 73. '*Imperial Love*'; Folio 1, '*imperiall loue*'; Folio 2, '*imperiall Iove*'; Folio 3, '*impartiall Jove.*'

II. iii. 76. '*ames-ace,*' *i.e.* two aces; the lowest throw at dice; one would expect it, from the context, to mean just the contrary, but Lafeu is probably making 'a comparison by contraries,'—'an ironical comparison,' used with humorous effect. "One lauding a sweet-songed prima donna," aptly observed Brinsley Nicholson, "says, I'd rather hear her than walk a hundred miles with peas in my boots."

II. v. 26. '*end*'; the Folios have '*And*'; the correction, from the Ellesmere copy of the first Folio, has been generally adopted.

II. v. 44-45. '*Have or will to deserve*'; Malone proposed '*have qualities or will,*' &c.; Singer, '*wit or will*'; the later Folios omit '*to,*' and read '*have, or will deserve*'; the reading in the text is that of Folio 1.

III. i. 12-13.
> '*That the great figure of a council frames*
> *By self-unable motion*';

probably Clarke's explanation of these difficult lines is the best:—"The reasons of our state I cannot give you, excepting as an ordinary and uninitiated man, whom the august body of a government-council creates with power unable of itself to act, or with power incapable of acting of its own accord or independently." Others make '*that*' the subject of '*frames,*' explaining '*motion*' as 'mental sight,' or 'intuition.'

III. ii. 8-9. '*sold*'; so Folios 3, 4; Folios 1, 2, '*hold*'; Harness proposed '*holds a godly manner for.*'

III. ii. 62. '*If thou engrossest all the griefs are thine*'; the omission of the relative is common in Shakespeare. Rowe unnecessarily altered the line to '*all the griefs as thine.*'

III. ii. 88. '*holds him much to have*'; so the Folios; Theobald conjectured '*soils him much to have*'; others suggested '*hoves him not much to have*'; '*fouls him much to have,*' &c. Rolfe's view of the passage seems by far the most satisfactory:—"He has a deal of that too-much, *i.e.* excess of vanity, which makes him fancy he has many good qualities."

III. ii. 108. '*still-peering air*'; so Folio 1; Folio 2, '*still-piercing*'; probably an error for '*still-piecing*,' *i.e.* 'still-closing.' A passage in *The Wisdom of Solomon* has been appropriately compared, and may be the source of the thought:—"*As when an arrow is shot at a mark, it pareth the air, which immediately cometh together again, so that a man cannot know where it went through.*"

III. v. 63. '*I write, good creature,*' so Folio 1; Folios 2, 3, 4, '*I right*'; Rowe, '*Ah! right good creature!*' The Globe edition, '*I warrant, good creature*'; Kinnear, '*I war'nt* (= warrant), *good creature*' (cp. *Hamlet,* I. ii. 242, Quarto 2, '*I war'nt*').

III. vi. 34. '*John Drum's Entertainment*'; 'to give a person John Drum's Entertainment' probably meant to give him such an entertainment as the drum gets; hence 'to give a person a drumming,' to turn him forcibly out of your company. Theobald quotes the following from Holinshed's *Description of Ireland:*—"His porter, or none other officer, durst not, for both his ears, give the simplest man that resorted to his house, *Tom Drum his entertainment,* which is to hale a man in by the head, and thrust him out by both the shoulders." In Marston's interlude, *Jack Drum's Entertainment* (1601), Jack Drum is a servant who is constantly baffled in his knavish tricks.

IV. i. 38. '*Bajazet's mule*'; the allusion has not yet been explained; perhaps '*Bajazet's*' is a blunder on the part of Parolles for '*Balaam's.*'

IV. ii. 25. '*Jove's,*' probably substituted for the original '*God's,*' in obedience to the statute against profanity. Johnson conjectured '*Love's.*'

IV. ii. 36. '*Who then recover*'; the Folios read, '*who then recovers,*' changed unnecessarily by Pope to '*which then recover,*' but '*who*' is often used for 'an irrational antecedent personified,' though in this passage the antecedent may be '*of me*' implied in '*my*'; '*my sick desires*' = 'the sick desires of me'; in this latter case 'recovers' is the more common third person singular, instead of the first person after '*who.*'

IV. ii. 38. '*I see that men make rope's in such a scarre,*' the reading of Folios 1, 2; Folio 3, '*make ropes*'; Folio 4, '*make ropes . . . scar.*' This is one of the standing cruxes in the text of Shakespeare; some thirty emendations have been proposed for '*ropes*' and '*scarre,*' e.g. '*hopes . . . affairs*'; '*hopes . . . scenes*'; '*hopes . . . scare*'; '*slopes scarre*': other suggestions are, '*may cope's . . . sorte*'; '*may rope's . . . snarle*'; '*may rope's . . . snare,*' &c. The apostrophe in the first and second Folios makes it almost certain that '*'s*' stands for 'us.' Possibly '*make*' is used as an auxiliary; '*make rope's,*' would then mean 'do constrain, or ensnare us.' Or is '*make rope*' a compound verb? '*Scarre*' may be '*scare*' (*i.e.* 'fright'). The general sense seems to be, 'I see that men may reduce us to such a fright, that we'll forsake ourselves.'

NOTES 1047

IV. iii. 233. '*He will steal, sir, an egg out of a cloister,*' *i.e.* 'anything, however trifling, from any place, however holy.'

IV. iii. 261. '*and a perpetual succession for it*'; some such verb as '*grant*' is to be supplied. Hanmer altered '*for it*' to '*in it*'; Kinnear conjectured '*free in perpetuity.*'

IV. iv. 34. '*revives*'; so the Folios; '*reviles,*' '*invites,*' '*requires*' have been variously proposed; it is doubtful whether any change is necessary: 'Time,' says Helena, 'gives us fresh courage.'

IV. v. 35. '*an English name*'; Folios 1, 2, '*maine*'; Folio 3, '*main*'; Folio 4, '*mean*'; Rowe first suggested '*name*'; the allusion is obviously to the Black Prince.

IV. v. 35-36. '*his fisnomy is more hotter*'; Hanmer's proposal '*honour'd*' for '*hotter*' seems to be a most plausible emendation.

V. i. 6. '*Enter a Gentleman*'; Folio 1 reads 'A *gentle Astringer*'; Folio 2, 'A *gentle Astranger*'; Folios 3, 4, 'A *Gentleman a stranger.*' '*Astringer*' = a keeper of goshawks; the word occurs nowhere else in Shakespeare. There seems, however, no very particular reason for its omission in modern editions, though it is true that in the Folio the speeches given to 'the Astringer' all have the prefix '*Gent.*'

V. ii. 1. '*Good Monsieur Lavache*'; Folio 1, '*Lauatch*'; Folio 2, '*Lavatch*'; Folios 3, 4, '*Levatch*'; Tollet's conjecture '*Lavache*' has been generally adopted. Clark suggests that it may have been intended for *Lavage,* which, in familiar French, is used to express 'slop,' 'puddle,' 'washiness.' Something is to be said in favour of Jervis' proposed reading, '*Lapatch,*' *i.e.* 'patch' = clown, with the prefix '*la*' in imitation of '*Lafeu.*'

V. ii. 22. '*Similes of comfort*'; Theobald's certain emendation for the reading of the Folios, '*smiles of comfort.*'

V. iii. 65, 66.
Our own love waking cries to see what's done,
While shameful hate sleeps out the afternoon.
Johnson conjectured '*slept*' for '*sleeps,*' *i.e.* 'love cries to see what was done while hatred slept, and suffered mischief to be done.' Mason proposed '*old*' for '*own.*' W. G. Clarke ingeniously emended '*shameful hate*' into '*shame full late,*' but the emendation destroys the antithesis between '*love*' and '*hate.*' It is best to leave the lines as they stand, though the words '*our own love*' are somewhat doubtful: the general meaning is simple enough.

V. iii. 121. '*my fore-past proofs,*' &c.; *i.e.* "the proofs which I have already had are sufficient to show that my *fears* were not *vain* and irrational. I have rather been hitherto more easy than sought, and have *unreasonably* had *too little fear*" (Johnson).

V. iii. 193. '*He blushes, and 'tis it*'; Folios '*'tis hit,*' which has been variously explained as an Archaic form of 'it': as an error for '*'tis his,*' or '*is hit.*' It seems unnecessary to alter the Folio;

"*'tis hit*' can very well mean 'the blow has been well aimed, it has struck home,' 'it' being used impersonally.

V. iii. 214. '*Her infinite cunning, with her modern grace*'; Walker's certain emendation of the Folio reading '*her insuite comming*'; other suggestions have been made:—'*Her instant comity*' (Bubier); '*Her Jesuit cunning*' (Bulloch); '*Her own suit, coming*' (Perring).

Epil. 1. '*The King's a beggar*'; an allusion to the old story of 'The King and the Beggar' (*cp.* Percy's *Reliques*), often referred to by Shakespeare; *cp.* '*Is there not a ballad, boy, of the King and the Beggar?*' (*Love's Labour's Lost*, I. ii. 102-103); similarly *Richard II.*, V. iii. 79, 80:—

'*Our scene is alter'd from a serious thing,
And now chang'd to "The Beggar and the King."*'

TWELFTH NIGHT; OR, WHAT YOU WILL

I. i. 5. '*sound*'; so the Folios; Pope changed it to '*south,*' and editors have generally accepted this emendation, but it seems unnecessary: Grant White appropriately asks, "Did Pope, or the editors who have followed him, ever lie musing on the sward at the edge of a wood, and hear the low sweet hum of the summer air, as it kissed the coyly-shrinking wild flowers upon the banks, and passed on loaded with fragrance from the sweet salute?"

I. i. 22. '*like fell and cruel hounds*'; referring to the story of Actæon.

I. i. 38. '*all supplied, and filled*'; the comma after '*supplied*' is not in the Folio: its insertion simplifies the lines. Others leave the Folio reading, but bracket '*her sweet perfections*' in the next line; making them appositional to '*thrones.*'

I. ii. 14. '*Arion on the dolphin's back*'; the Folios misprint '*Orion*' for '*Arion.*'

I. iii. 64, 65. '*bring your hand to the buttery-bar and let it drink*'; "a proverbial phrase among Abigails, to ask at once for a kiss and a present" (Kenrick).

I. iii. 88. '*Then hadst thou had an excellent head of hair*'; Sir Toby evidently plays upon '*tongues*' and '*tongs*' (*i.e.* curling-tongs).

I. iii. 107. '*an old man*'; Theobald proposed to read '*a noble man,*' taking the allusion to be to Orsino. Clarke explains '*an old man*' as 'a man of experience'; "the word *old*," he adds, "gives precisely that absurd effect of refraining from competing in dancing, fencing, &c., with exactly the antagonist incapacitated by age over whom Sir Andrew might hope to prove his superiority."

NOTES 1049

I. iii. 125. '*That's sides and heart*'; Sir Andrew and Sir Toby are wrong in the parts assigned to Taurus in the old astrological figures of the human body. Taurus was supposed to govern the neck and throat.

I. iv. 3. '*three days*'; Mr. Daniel points out in his 'Time-Analysis' that this statement is inconsistent with the Duke's words in V. i. 102, '*Three months this youth hath tended upon me.*'

II. i. 15. '*Messaline*'; possibly an error for Mitylene, as Capell conjectured.

II. iii. 16. '*the picture of "we three"*'; "a common sign, in which two wooden heads are exhibited with this inscription under it, 'We three loggerheads be,' the spectator being supposed to make the third" (Malone).

II. iii. 22-23. '*Pigrogromitus . . . of Queubus,*' &c. Mr. Swinburne sees in these 'freaks of nomenclature' the direct influence of Rabelais (*cp. A Study of Shakespeare*, pp. 155, 156).

II. iii. 37. '*O mistress mine,*' &c. "this tune is contained in both the editions of Morley's *Consort Lessons*, 1599 and 1611. It is also found in Queen Elizabeth's Virginal Book, arranged by Boyd. As it is to be found in print in 1599, it proves either that Shakespeare's *Twelfth Night* was written in or before that year, or that, in accordance with the then prevailing custom, '*O mistress mine,*' was an old song, introduced into the play" (Chappell's *Popular Music of the Olden Time*).

II. iii. 105. '*Out o' tune, sir: ye lie*'; Theobald proposed '*time, sir?*' which has been very generally adopted. The reading of the Folios may well stand without change. Sir Toby says to the Clown that he is out of tune and lies in declaring '*no, no, no, you dare not*' (*i.e.* dare not bid Malvolio go). Hence next words '*Art any more than a steward,*' addressed to Malvolio.

II. v. 35. '*the lady of the Strachy*'; this is one of the unsettled problems in Shakespeare. Hunter ingeniously suggested that Shakespeare ridicules, in the scene between the Clown, as Sir Topas, and Malvolio (IV. ii.), the exorcisms by Puritan ministers, in the case of a family named Starchy (1596-99), and that the difficult Strachy was a hint to the audience to expect subsequent allusion to the Starchy affair. Others suggest '*Strozzi,*' '*Stracci,*' '*Stratarch.*' Halliwell refers to a Russian word meaning lawyer or judge. The incident of a lady of high rank marrying her steward is the subject of Webster's *Duchess of Malfy*.

II. v. 59. '*with cars*'; so Folio 1; the later Folios, '*with cares*'; Johnson, '*with carts*'; many emendations have been proposed. Clarke defends the original reading, and compares '*A team of horse shall not pluck that from me*' (*Two Gentlemen*, III. i. 264, 265). Hanmer's suggestion '*by th' ears*' has been generally adopted.

II. v. 141-142. '*yellow stockings*'; these were much worn in

Shakespeare's time, and have still survived to our own day in the yellow stockings worn by the 'Blue Coat boys.'

III. i. 47. *'these,'* i.e. these coins which Viola has given him.

III. i. 54. *'Cressida was a beggar'*; 'according to the story Cressida finally became a leper and begged by the roadside.'

III. i. 62. *'And, like the haggard, check at every feather'*; so the Folios; Johnson proposed *'not'* for *'and,'* and this reading has reasonably been adopted by most editors; *'to check'* is "a term in falconry, applied to a hawk when she forsakes her proper game, and follows some other of inferior kind that crosses her in her flight"; the meaning therefore of the Folio reading would be 'that he must catch at every opportunity,' but this does not suit the context: the wise Clown must be discriminative; hence Johnson's *'not.'*

III. i. 66. *'wise men, folly-fall'n, quite taint their wit'*; Folio 1, *'wisemens folly falne'*; Hanmer and Warburton, *'wise men's folly shown'*; the text is Theobald's, and is generally adopted.

III. i. 120. *'a cypress, not a bosom, Hides my heart'*; the force of these words has, it would seem, been missed; the point of the *'cypress'* is not its blackness but its transparency. Cp. *'The Ballad of Robin Hood, Scarlet and John'*:

"Cypress over her face,
Through which her rose-like cheeks did blush
All in a comely grace."

'Bosom' must, I think, be used in this passage in the sense of 'the bosom of the dress' which conceals the body. Olivia says, 'you can see my heart; a thin gauze as it were hides it, not a stomacher.'

III. ii. 23. *'sailed into the north,'* &c.; perhaps this is a reference to the discovery of Northern Nova Zembla by the Dutchman Barenz in 1596. (*Cp.* C. H. Coote's paper on *'the new map,'* l. 85. *New Shakespeare Society Publications,* 1878.)

III. ii. 59. *'youngest wren of nine'*; Folio, *'mine,'* emended by Theobald. The wren is said to lay nine or ten eggs at a time, and the last hatched nestling is usually the smallest of the whole brood.

III. ii. 71. *'the new map with the augmentation of the Indies'*; no doubt a reference to the map which Hallam, in his *Literature of Europe,* calls 'the best map of the 16th century': it is found in the first edition of Hakluyt's *Voyages* (1589), but as it records discoveries made at least seven years later, it was in all probability a separate map, well known at the time, and made so as to be inserted in Hakluyt: the author was probably Mr. Emmerie Mollineux, who was also the first Englishman to make a terrestrial globe. It is noteworthy that the map shows a marked development of the geography of India proper, &c. (*Cp. Transactions of New Shakespeare Society,* 1877-79.)

NOTES

III. iii. 15. '*And thanks; and ever . . . oft good turns.*' The Cambridge editors hold that some word has dropped out between '*ever*' and '*oft*.' Many emendations have been proposed; perhaps the simplest reading is that of the Old spelling Shakespeare:—

'*And thanks, and, ever oft, good turns . . .*'

'*ever oft*' in the sense of 'with perpetual frequency.' Theobald proposed:—

'*And thanks, and ever thanks; and oft good turns.*'

IV. i. 12-14. '*I am afraid this great lubber, the world, will prove a cockney*'; so the Folios; the lines evidently mean "I am afraid affectation and foppery will overspread the world" (Johnson); it has been proposed to change '*world*' into '*word*' (*i.e.* with reference to '*vent*'): others read '*this great lubberly world*'; Knight explains that the words are spoken aside, and mean, 'I am afraid the world will prove this great lubber (Sebastian) a cockney.' This seems very strained, and probably the simplest reading of the passage is the best.

IV. ii. 12-13. '*the old hermit of Prague*'; Douce points out that the allusion is "not to the celebrated heresiarch, Jerome of Prague, but another of that name, born likewise at Prague, and called the *hermit* of Camaldoli in Tuscany."

IV. ii. 37. '*clearstories*'; Folio 1, '*cleere stores*'; Folio 2, '*cleare stones*'; the reading adopted is Blakeway's conjecture in Boswell: '*clerestory*' is the name given to the windows above the arches of the nave of a Gothic church.

IV. ii. 127. '*goodman devil*'; Folio 1, '*good man diuell*'; Rowe's '*goodman Drivel*,' seems the most plausible emendation, if any is necessary; Folio 2 reads '*good man Direll.*'

V. i. 108. '*My soul the faithfull'st offerings hath breathed out*'; the Folios '*have*,' corrected by Capell, but probably Shakespeare's own reading; the plural for the singular, owing to the plural object ('*faithfull'st offerings*') preceding the verb.

V. i. 192. '*a passy measures pavin*'; Folio 1, '*panyn*'; Folio 2, '*Pavin*'; various emendations have been suggested, but there is little doubt that the reading in the text is the correct one. '*Passy measures*' is a corruption of the Italian '*passamezzo*,' which word Florio explains as 'a *passa-measure* in dancing, a cinque pace'; it was a slow dance, differing little from the action of walking. '*Pavin*' was a grave Spanish dance. According to Halliwell, the *passy measures pavin* is described as follows in an early MS. list of dances:—"*The passinge measure Pavyon*—2 singles and a double forward, and 2 singles syde.—Reprince back." Sir Toby means, therefore, that 'the surgeon is a rogue and a grave solemn coxcomb.'

V. i. 351. '*against.*' Tyrwhitt's conjecture '*in*' has a good deal in its favour; '*against*' may have been caught from line 368.

THE WINTER'S TALE

I. ii. 44. '*What lady she her lord*'; '*she*' has been variously interpreted; Collier and Dyce proposed '*should*,' destroying the beauty of the line; Schmidt makes the phrase '*lady she*' = 'a woman that is a lady,' taking '*she*' ≃ 'woman'; others print '*lady-she*'; perhaps the word may be best explained as the pleonastic pronoun so common in popular poetry; the rhythm seems to favour this latter view.

I. ii. 70. '*The doctrine of ill-doing, nor dream'd*'; so Folio 1; the later Folios, '*no nor dream'd*'; Spedding, '*neither dream'd*'; perhaps '*doctrine*' should be read as a trisyllable; a harsh line would, however, result; and the reading of the later Folios has much to commend it.

I. ii. 133-134. '*false As o'er-dyed blacks*'; Folios 1, 2, 3, '*o're dy'd*'; the words have been variously interpreted to mean 'fabrics dyed over with some other colour,' or, 'dyed too much'; Steevens saw in the phrase an allusion to the fact that black will receive no other hue without discovering itself through it; the passage may simply contain the idea, 'the blacker the garb, the less sincere the mourning.'

I. ii. 156. '*methoughts*'; so the Folios in this and other places; this erroneous form was probably due to '*methinks*'; it is noteworthy that the correct '*methought*' occurs a few lines below.

I. ii. 285. '*that*,' *i.e.* 'that of which you accuse her.'

II. i. 11. '*Who taught you this?*' Rowe's emendation of the reading of Folio 1, '*taught 'this*' (with an apostrophe before '*this*,' indicating an elision); the later Folios, '*taught this*.'

II. i. 24. '*A sad tale's best for winter*,' hence the title of the play.

II. i. 38-39. '*There may be in the cup A spider*,' &c.; it was formerly believed that spiders were venomous.

II. i. 133-134. '*I'll keep my stables where I lodge my wife*'; *i.e.* 'I'll degrade my wife's chamber into a stable or dog kennel.'

II. i. 142. '*I would land-damn him*'; so the Folios; '*land-damm*,' '*laudanum*,' '*lamback*,' (*i.e.* 'ebat'), '*half-damn*,' '*live-damn*,' '*landan* (*lantan, rantan*),' '*land-dam*,' are among the various emendations proposed; Schmidt suggests '*I would—Lord, damn him!*' In all probability the reading of the Folios should not be departed from, and it seems likely that Antigonus, having in the previous phrase used the word '*damn'd*,' here uses 'land-damn,' as a sort of grim quibble for 'landan,'—a Gloucestershire word still in use "to express the punishment meted out to slanderers and adulterers by rustics traversing from house to house along

NOTES 1053

the country side, blowing trumpets and beating drums or pans and kettles; when an audience was assembled the delinquents' names were proclaimed, and they were said to be landanned" (*cp.* Halliwell's *Dictionary of Archaic Words,* and *Notes and Queries* iii. 464): *landan, lantan, rantan,* were variants of the same word, which was probably imitative in its origin.

II. i. 152. '*As you feel doing thus,*' probably = my doing thus to you (*i.e.* touching him, or perhaps pulling his beard); '*the instruments that feel*' = my fingers.

II. iii. 177. '*to it own protection,*' so Folios 1, 2; Folios 3, 4, '*its*'; the old possessive form '*it,*' still in use in Lancashire, occurs again in this play (III. ii. 101); there are some dozen instances elsewhere: '*it own,*' may be regarded as a sort of idiomatic compound, the combination helping to maintain the archaism; '*its*' (Folio, *it 's*) *own,*' to be found in Act I. ii. 266 is said to be the only instance of its use in Shakespeare.

III. iii. 112. '*You 're a made old man*'; Theobald's emendation of the Folio reading '*mad,*' confirmed by a passage in Shakespeare's original:—"The goodman desired her to be quiet . . . if she could hold her peace they were made for ever."

IV. i. 15. '*to it,*' *i.e.* 'the present.'

IV. i. 4. '*It is fifteen years since,*' &c.; changed by Hanmer to '*sixteen,*' the number intended by Shakespeare.

IV. ii. 23, 24. '*when the kite builds, look to lesser linen*'; alluding to this bird's habit of carrying off small linen garments hung out to dry; Autolycus preferred more substantial prey.

IV. ii. 49. '*I' the name of me—*'; probably, as has been suggested, the Clown's exclamation of '*Mercy*' is interrupted by Autolycus.

IV. iii. 243. '*clamour your tongues*'; Hanmer's emendation '*charm*' has been generally adopted, but '*clamour*' is almost certainly correct (Taylor, the Water-Poet, wrote '*Clamour the promulgation of your tongues*'); '*clamour*' or rather '*clammer,*' is probably radically identical with '*clamber,*' the Scandinavian original of which '*klambra*' = 'to pinch closely together, to clamp.'

IV. iii. 269. '*another ballad of a fish*'; *cp. e.g.* "A strange report of a monstrous fish that appeared in the form of a woman from her waist upward, seen in the sea"; entered in the Stationers' Registers in 1604.

IV. iii. 428. '*Far than Deucalion off*'; '*far*' = 'farther'; the Folios all correctly read '*farre,*' *i.e.* the old form of the comparative of '*far.*'

IV. iii. 578. '*i' the rear o' her birth*'; Folios 1, 2, 3, '*'our birth*'; Rowe first emended the line as in the text, though in his second edition he read '*o' our*' for '*o' her.*'

IV. iii. 586. '*appear,*' *i.e.* appear so (like Bohemia's son).

IV. iii. 706. '*at palace*'; Folio 1, '*at 'Pallace*'; probably the apostrophe indicates "the omission of the article or its absorption in rapid pronunciation."

V. ii. 51. '*weather-bitten conduit*'; changed to '*weather-beaten*' in Folio 3; but '*weather-bitten*' is undoubtedly the correct form (*cp.* Skeat's *Etymological Dictionary*): *conduits* were frequently in the form of human figures.

V. ii. 90-91. '*that rare Italian master*'; Giulio Pippi, known as 'Giulio Romano,' was born in 1492, and died in 1546; his fame as a painter was widespread; Shakespeare, taking him as 'a type of artistic excellence,' makes him a sculptor; it must, however, be remembered that the statue was a 'painted picture.' Much has been made of this reference by the advocates of Shakespeare's alleged Italian journeys (*cp.* Elze's *Essays on Shakespeare*).

GLOSSARY

As.—As You Like It
A.W.—All's Well that Ends Well
C. of E.—The Comedy of Errors
L.L.L.—Love's Labour's Lost
M.A.—Much Ado about Nothing
M. for M.—Measure for Measure
M.N.D.—A Midsummer-Night's Dream
M. of V.—The Merchant of Venice
M.W.—The Merry Wives of Windsor
T. of S.—The Taming of the Shrew
Tp.—The Tempest
Tw.N.—Twelfth Night
Two G.—The Two Gentlemen of Verona
W.T.—The Winter's Tale

---

a', he. L.L.L. v. 2

abate, omit. L.L.L. v. 2; diminish. M.N.D. iii. 2

abode, delay. M. of V. ii. 6

abridgment, pastime, entertainment. M.N.D. v. 1

abstract, inventory. M.W. iv. 2

abuse, deceive. Tp. v. 1; etc.; ill-usage. M.W. v. 3; imposture. M. for M. v. 1

aby, suffer for. M.N.D. iii. 2

accountant, liable to give account. M. for M. ii. 4

adamant, diamond, loadstone. M.N.D. ii. 1

addition, title. M. W. ii. 2 A.W. ii. 3

address, prepare. M. W. iii. 5, &c.

admittance, admissibility. M. W. ii. 2; acceptance, sanction. M.W. iii. 3

adoptious christendoms, &c., christenings of adopted children for whom Cupid stands godfather. A.W. i. 1

advance, raise. Tp. i. 2; iv. 1

affied, betrothed. T. of S. iv. 4

affront, confront. W.T. v. 1

aglet-baby, doll decked with tagged laces. T. of S. i. 2

a-hold, close to the wind. Tp. i. 1

aim, guess, conjecture. Two G. iii. 1; T. of S. ii. 1

aim, cry, encourage, a term from archery. M.W. iii. 2

a-life, on my life. W.T. iv. 3

all-building, being the ground and foundation of all; or ? all-binding. M. for M. ii. 4

all hid, game of hide and seek. L.L.L. iv. 3

allicholy, allycholly, melancholy. Two G. iv. 2; M. W. i. 4

alligant, elegant. M.W. ii. 2

allottery, portion. As. i. 1

allow the wind, stand aside. A. W. v. 2

amain, at full speed. Tp. iv. 1; C. of E. i. 1

ames-ace, both aces, the lowest possible throw in dice. A. W. ii. 3

amort, dejected. T. of S. iv. 3

ample, well. A.W. iii. 5

an, if. Tp. ii. 1; &c.

anatomize, expose. As. i. 1; A. W. iv. 3

anatomy, walking skeleton. C. of E. v. 1

ancientry, elders. W.T. iii. 3; old-fashioned style. M.A. ii. 1

angel, a gold coin. M.W. i. 3; C. of E. iv. 3; M.A. ii. 3

answer, thrust after a parry. Tw. N. iii. 4

anthropophaginian, cannibal. M.W. iv. 5

ape-bearer, one who leads an ape. W.T. iv. 2

apes in hell, to lead, fancied consequence of dying a spinster. M.A. ii. 1; T. of S. ii. 1

appeached, give accusatory evidence. A.W. i. 3

apple of her eye, upon the, in obedience to her glance. L.L. L. v. 2

appliances, subservience. M. for M. iii. 1

apprehensive, fantastic. A.W. i. 2

approof, approval. M. for M. ii. 4; proof. A.W. i. 2; ii. 5

apricocks, apricots. M.N.D. iii. 1

araise, raise from the dead. A. W. ii. 1

arbitrement, decision. Tw.N. iii. 4

argosy, merchant vessel. M. of V. i. 1; T. of S. ii. 1

argument, subject for satire. M. A. i. 1; M.N.D. iii. 2; proof, token. M.A. ii. 3; L.L.L. i. 2; Tw.N. iii. 2

armigero, esquire. M.W. i. 1

armipotent, mighty in arms. L. L.L. v. 2; A.W. iv. 3

arras, tapestry placed round the walls of apartments, often at such a distance from them as to allow of people being concealed between. M.W. iii. 3; M.A. i. 3; T. of S. ii. 1

artificial, skilful. M.N.D. iii. 2

artist, medical practitioner. A. W. ii. 3

arts-man, scholar. L.L.L. v. 1

aspersion, shower, or spray. Tp. iv. 1

aspicious, blunder for suspicious. M.A. iii. 5

assay, accost, assail. M.W. ii. 1; M. for M. i. 2; test. M. for M. iii. 1; attempt. As. i. 3; make trial of. A.W. iii. 7

assured, betrothed. C. of E. iii. 2

Ates, mischiefs. L.L.L. v. 2

atomy, atom, mote. As. iii. 2; iii. 5

atone, are at one. As. v. 4

attaint, dishonour. C. of E. iii.2

attorney, duly appointed substitute. As. iv. 1

attorneyed, engaged as an attorney. M. for M. v. 1; performed by proxy. W.T. i. 1

aunt, old woman, gossip. M.N. D. ii. 1; loose woman. W.T. iv. 2

avised, advised. M.W. i. 1

avoid, begone. Tp. iv. 1; W.T. i.2

awful, law-abiding. Two G. iv. 1; awe-inspiring. T. of S. v. 2

GLOSSARY

backare, stand back, give place. T. of S. ii. 1

back-trick, caper backwards. Tw.N. i. 3

baffle, disgrace a knight with infamy. Tw.N. ii. 5; hoodwink. Tw.N. v. 1

bald, destitute of meaning. C. of E. ii. 2

balk, let slip, not forthcoming. Tw.N. iii. 2

balk logic, bandy words. T. of S. i. 1

Banbury cheese, nothing but paring. M.W. i. 1

band, bond. C. of E. iv. 2; A.W. iv. 2

bane, death. M. for M. i. 2

bare, shave. M. for M. iv. 2; A.W. iv. 1

barful, full of hindrances. Tw. N. i. 4

barm, froth, yeast. M.N.D. ii. 1

barn, barne, bairn, child. M.A. iii. 4; A.W. i. 3; W.T. iii. 3

barnacle, species of wild goose. Tp. iv. 1

base, bid the, challenge to a chase in the game of prisoners' base. Two G. i. 2

basilisk, fabulous serpent supposed to kill by its glance. W. T. i. 2

basta, enough. T. of S. i. 1

bastard, a kind of sweet wine. M. for M. iii. 2

bate, blunt with use. L.L.L. i. 1; except. M.N.D. i. 1; reduce. M. of V. iii. 3; flap the wing. T. of S. iv. 1

bat-fowling, catching birds by night, when at roost. Tp. ii. 1

batler, probably a heavy wooden implement for beating clothes in the wash. As. ii. 4

bawbling, paltry. Tw.N. v. 1

bawcock, fine fellow. Tw.N. iii. 4; W.T. i. 2

beadsman, one who prays for another. Two G. i. 1

beard, prickles on the ears of corn. M.N.D. ii. i

bearing-cloth, cloth in which a child was carried to be christened. W.T. iii. 3

bear in hand, keep in expectation. M. for M. i. 4; M.A. iv. 1; T. of S. iv. 2

bear up, take your course. Tp. iii. 2

beating in, puzzling. Tp. i. 2

beating on, thinking persistently. Tp. v. 1

become, make becoming. C. of E. iii. 2

bed-swerver, adulteress. W.T. ii. 1

beg, apply for the custody of a minor or an idiot; hence, to set down as a fool. L.L.L. v. 2

being, since. M.A. iv. 1

be-mete, measure. T. of S. iv. 3

bemoiled, bemired. T. of S. iv. 1

benched, raised to authority. W.T. i. 2

bent, hold the, keep the passion fresh. Tw.N. ii. 4

ben venuto, welcome. L.L.L. iv. 2; T. of S. i. 2

Bergomask, rustic dance from Bergamo. M.N.D. v. 1

Bermoothes, Bermudas. Tp. i. 2

beshrew, curse, with weakened force, as 'plague on.' Two G. i. 1; &c.

bestow, acquit. Two G. iii. 1; As. iv. 3; settle or give in marriage. As. v. 4; T. of S. i. 1; iv. 4

bestraught, distracted. T. of S. Ind. 2

beteem, accord, grant. M.N.D. i. 1

betid, befallen. Tp. i. 2

bias, preponderant tendency. L.L.L. iv. 2; Tw.N. v. 1; weight on one side of a bowl which affects its direction. T. of S. iv. 5

Biddy, a fowl. Tw.N. iii. 4

bilbo, a sword noted for the temper and elasticity of its blade. M.W. i. 1; iii. 5

bill, placard. M.A. i. 1; halberd. M.A. iii. 3; bonds. M.A. iii. 3

billets, small logs. M. for M. iv. 3

birdbolt, blunt-headed arrow. M.A. i. 1; L.L.L. iv. 3; Tw.N. i. 5

birding, bird-catching, fowling. M.W. iii. 3; iv. 2

bis coctus, twice cooked. L.L.L. iv. 2

black, dark-complexioned. M.A. iii. 1; black fabric. W.T. i. 2

Black-Monday, a name for Easter Monday. M. of V. ii. 5

blank, white spot in the centre of the target. W.T. ii. 3

blazon, description (heraldry). M.A. ii. 1; Tw.N. i. 5

blench, swerve, start aside. M. for M. iv. 5; W.T. i. 2

bless the mark, phrase used as apology after mentioning something horrible or indecent. Two. G. iv. 4

blow, fill with eggs. Tp. iii. 1; blossom, bloom. Two G. i. 1; &c.; inflate with vanity. Tw. N. ii. 5

blown, fly-blown, filled with eggs. L.L.L. v. 2

blue eye, a dark circle round the eye. Tp. i. 2; As. iii. 2

board, accost, make advances to, woo. M.W. ii. 1; &c.

bob, a jest, scoff. As. ii. 7

bodykins, God's body, an oath. M.W. ii. 3

boggle, take alarm. A.W. v. 3

bold-beating, brow-beating. M.W. ii. 2

bolt or shaft of it, make, risk making something or other out of it; make the venture. M.W. iii. 4

bombard, leather bottle or jug for liquor. Tp. ii. 2

bombast, padding used to stuff out garments. L.L.L. v. 2

boot, profit, avail. Two G. i. 1; &c.

boot, grace to, God help us. W. T. i. 2

boot-hose, overstocking which covered the leg like a jack-boot. T. of S. iii. 2

boots, torture of the boots. Two G. i. 1

bosky, bushy. Tp. iv. 1

bossed, studded. T. of S. ii. 1

bottle, bundle. M.N.D. iv. 1

bottom, wind as a skein. Two G. iii. 2; extent. M. for M. i. 1; vessel. M. of V. i. 1; Tw.N. v. 1; dell. As. iv. 3; ball. T. of S. iv. 3

bouncing, imperious. M.N.D. ii. 1

bourn, boundary. Tp. ii. 1; W. T. i. 2

bowget, budget, wallet. W.T. iv. 2

bow-hand, left hand. L.L.L. iv. 1

brabble, brawl. Tw.N. v. 1

brach, bitch hound. T. of S. Ind. 1

braid, deceitful. A.W. iv. 2

brake, thicket. M.N.D. ii. 1

GLOSSARY

bravery, finery. M. for M. i. 3; As. ii. 7; T. of S. iv. 3

brawl, French dance. L.L.L. iii. 1

breach of the sea, surf. Tw.N. ii. 1

break up, carve. L.L.L. iv. 1; open. M. of V. ii. 4

breathe, exercise. A.W. ii. 3

breathed, in good wind. L.L.L. v. 2; T. of S. Ind. 2; in full display of strength. As. i. 2

breeching, subject to the birch; T. of S. iii. 1

breed-bate, mischief-maker. M.W. i. 4

bribed buck, stolen deer. M.W. v. 5

brief, list. M.N.D. v. 1; in brief. As. iv. 3; contract. A.W. ii. 3; summary. A.W. v. 3

bring out, put out, disconcert. L.L.L. v. 2; As. iii. 2

bring to try, lay a ship with her side close to the wind. Tp. i. 1

broach, stab. M.N.D. v. 1

brock, badger, a term of contempt. Tw.N. ii. 5

broke, negotiate. A.W. iii. 5

broken, fallen out. Two G. ii. 5; with teeth missing. A.W. ii. 3

broken music, arranged for different instruments; part or concerted music. As. i. 2

broker, go-between. Two G. i. 2

Brownist, Independent (sect founded by Robert Brown, *c.* 1581). Tw.N. iii. 2

buck, with reference to the horns. M.W. iii. 3

buck-basket, washing-basket. M.W. iii. 3; &c.

bucking, washing linen with lye. M.W. iii. 3

buckler, shield, defend. T. of S. iii. 2

bucklers, give the, own oneself beaten. M.A. v. 2

buck of the first head, buck of the fifth year. L.L.L. iv. 2

bug, bug-bear. T. of S. i. 2; W.T. iii. 2

bugle, black glass bead. As. iii. 5; W.T. iv. 3

bully, term of familiarity and endearment. M.W. i. 3; ii. 3; M.N.D. iii. 1

bully-rook, boon companion. M.W. i. 3; ii. 1

bum-baily, bailiff. Tw.N. iii. 4

bush, a bush of ivy, used as a vintner's sign. As. Epil. 3

buttery, place for storing liquor or provisions. T. of S. Ind. i

buttonhole lower, a, without ceremony. L.L.L. v. 2

buttons, 'tis in his, he is sure to succeed. M.W. iii. 2

butt-shaft, blunt arrow used for shooting at the butt. L.L.L. i. 2

by'r lakin, by our Lady. Tp. iii. 3; M.N.D. iii. 1

caddis, worsted tape used for garters. W.T. iv. 3

caitiff, despicable wretch. M. for M. v. 1; A.W. iii. 2

cake is dough, project has failed of success. T. of S. i. 1; v. 1

callat, scold. W.T. ii. 3

can, can make. Tp. iv. 1

canary, light sweet wine from the Canary Islands. M.W. iii. 2; Tw.N. i. 3; lively Spanish dance. A.W. ii. 1; dance the canary. L.L.L. iii. 1; blunder for quandary. M.W. ii. 2

candied, covered with hoarfrost. Tp. ii. 1

canker, dog-rose. M.A. i. 3; worm. M.N.D. ii. 2

can't no other, is there no way. A.W. i. 3

canton, song. Tw.N. i. 5

canzonet, short song. L.L.L. iv. 2

capable, susceptible. As. iii. 5; A.W. i. 1

caparison, clothing. W.T. iv. 2

capon, type of dullness. C. of E. iii. 1; love-letter. L.L.L. iv. 1

capriccio, whim. A.W. ii. 3

captious, capacious. A.W. i. 3

carack, large ship of burden. C. of E. iii. 2

carbonado, score across for broiling. A.W. iv. 5; W.T. iv. 3

cardecu, quart d'écu, old French coin, worth about 2s. 1½d. A.W. iv. 3; v. 2

cardinally, blunder for 'carnally.' M. for M. ii. 1

card-maker, one who makes cards for combing wool. T. of S. Ind. 2

card of ten, face it with a, put on a bold front. T. of S. ii. 1

Carduus Benedictus, holy thistle. M.A. iii. 4

career, careire, short gallop at full speed. M.W. i. 1; M.A. v. 1; L.L.L. v. 2

carkanet, a jewelled necklace. C. of E. iii. 1

carlot, churl, peasant. As. iii. 5

carpet, table-cloth. T. of S. iv. 1

carpet consideration, for services in the Court. Tw.N. iii. 4

carpet-monger, one who frequents ladies' boudoirs or carpeted chambers. M.A. v. 2

carriage, burden. Tp. v. 1; bearing. C. of E. iii. 2; M.A. i. 3; management. W.T. iii. 1

cart, punishment akin to the ducking-stool. T. of S. i. 1

carve, ? to use great courtesy and affability. M.W. i. 3; L.L.L. v. 2

case, condition. Tp. iii. 2; to strip off the case or skin. A.W. iii. 6; skin, hide. Tw.N. v.1

cassock, a military cloak. A.W. iv. 3

cast, thrown up; with a play upon the sense of assigning parts to actors. Tp. ii. 1; emptied. M. for M. iii. 1; cast-off. As. iii. 4

Castiliano vulgo, nonsense phrase. Tw.N. i. 3

Cataian, thief, scoundrel, blackguard. M.W. ii. 1; Tw. N. ii. 3

catch, part song. Tp. iii. 2; Tw. N. ii. 3

cater-cousins, good friends. M. of V. ii. 2

cates, dainties. C. of E. iii. 1

caudle, gruel. L.L.L. iv. 3

centre, the earth, as supposed centre of universe. W.T. ii. 1

cerecloth, winding-sheet. M. of V. ii. 7

cesse, cease. A.W. v. 3

chairs of order, seats of the knights of an order. M.W. v.5

Cham, Great, Emperor of China, or Khan of Tartary. M. A. ii. 1

champian, open country. Tw. N. ii. 5

change, interchange. A.W. iii. 2; W.T. i. 2

chape, mounting of a scabbard. T. of S. iii. 2; A.W. iv. 3

charact, mark, stamp. M. for M. v. 1

GLOSSARY

character, write. Two G. ii. 7;
As. iii. 2; writing. M. for M. i.
1; W.T. v. 2

charactery, expression of
thought by symbols. M.W. v.
5

charge, put to expense. M.W.
ii. 2; entrust. C. of E. iii. 1;
cost, expense. M. of V. iv. 1;
W.T. iv. 3

chargeful, expensive. C. of E.
iv. 1

charge-house, school. L.L.L. v.
1

chariness, scrupulous integrity.
M.W. ii. 1

cheapen, bargain for. M.A. ii. 3

'cheator, escheator, an officer
who collected fines due to the
Exchequer. M.W. i. 3

check, restraint. M.W. iii. 4;
austere rule. T. of S. i. 1; to
forsake the 'quarry' and fly at
any chance bird. Tw.N. ii. 5;
iii. 1

cherry-pit, game with cherry-
stones. Tw.N. iii. 4

cheveril, kid-leather, very flex-
ible. Tw.N. iii. 1

childing, fruitful. M.N.D. ii. 1

chirurgeonly, surgeon-like. Tp.
ii. 1

chough, chatterer. Tp. ii. 1;
bird of the crow family. M.N.
D. iii. 2

chuck, term of endearment. L.
L.L. v. 1; Tw.N. iii. 4

cicatrice, scar-like mark. As.iii.
5; A.W. ii. 1

cinque-pace, lively dance. M.
A. ii. 1

circum circa, round and round.
L.L.L. v. 1

circummured, walled round.
M. for M. iv. 1

cittern-head, term of contempt,
with ref. to the grotesquely
carved head of a cittern or
guitar. L.L.L. v. 2

civil, orderly. Two G. v. 4;
grave. As. iii. 2; Tw.N. iii. 4;
courteous. Tw.N. i. 4

civil doctor, doctor of civil
law. M. of V. v. 1

clack-dish, wooden alms-dish
with a lid, clacked by beggars to attract attention. M.
for M. iii. 2

clamour, silence. W.T. iv. 3

clap, strike hands on conclud-
ing a bargain. W.T. i. 2

clapped up, concluded hastily.
T. of S. ii. 1

clapper-claw, thrash. M.W. ii.3

claw, flatter. M.A. i. 3; L.L.L.
iv. 2

clepe, call. L.L.L. v. 1

clew, ball of thread. A.W. i. 3

climate, sojourn. W.T. v. 1

clipping, embracing. W.T. v. 2

clodpole, blockhead. Tw.N. iii.
4

cloistress, nun. Tw.N. i. 1

clout, mark for archers. L.L.L.
iv. 1

cock, perversion of 'God.' T. of
S. iv. 1; woodcock (i.e. fool).
W.T. iv. 2

'cock and pie, by', an assevera-
tion, meaning possibly 'cock,'
God, and 'pie,' the ordinal of
the R.C. Church. M.W. i. 1

cockatrice, serpent, said to kill
by its mere glance. Tw.N. iii.
4

cockled, furnished with a shell.
L.L.L. iv. 3

cockney, petted child. Tw.N.
iv. 1

cod, peascod. As. ii. 4

codling, half-grown apple. Tw.
N. i. 5

cog, deceive, wheedle. M.W. iii. 1; &c.

coil, disturbance, confusion, ado. Tp. i. 2; &c.

collied, murky. M.N.D. i. 1

collop, piece of flesh. W.T. i. 2

colour, ensign. M.W. iii. 4; pretext. L.L.L. iv. 2; W.T. iv. 3; kind. As. i. 2

colourable, specious, plausible. L.L.L. iv. 2

colt, young or inexperienced person. M. of V. i. 2

combinate, betrothed. M. for M. iii. 1

come off, pay, disburse. M.W. iv. 3

comfect, sugar-plum. M.A. iv. 1

comfortable, of good comfort. As. ii. 6; comforting. A.W. i. 1

coming-in, income. M. of V. ii. 2

coming-on, complaisant. As. iv. 1

commerce, conversation. Tw. N. iii. 4

commixture, complexion. L.L.L. v. 2

commodity, advantage, interest. M. of V. iii. 3; W.T. iii. 2; parcel, quantity of wares. Tw. N. iii. 1

commodity of brown paper, a parcel of goods sold on credit by a usurer to a needy person, who immediately raised some cash by reselling them at a lower price, generally to the usurer himself. M. for M. iv. 3

commoner, prostitute. A.W. v. 3

commonty, blunder for 'comedy.' T. of S. Ind. 2

compact, leagued. M. for M. v. 1

companion, used as term of contempt. M.W. iii. 1; &c.

compass, accomplish. Two G. iv. 2; gain possession of. W.T. iv. 2

compassed, rounded, curved. T. of S. iv. 3

competitor, associate. Two G. ii. 6; companion. L.L.L. ii. 1; confederate. Tw.N. iv. 2

complements, accomplishments. L.L.L. i. 1

compt, account. A.W. v. 3

compter, counter. W.T. iv. 2

comptible, sensitive. Tw.N. i. 5

conceit, estimation, opinion. Two G. iii. 2; &c.; understanding. C. of E. iii. 2; a fancy article. M.N.D. i. 1; idea. W.T. iii. 2

conceited, imagined. Tw.N. iii. 4; witty, clever. W.T. iv. 3

conceitless, thoughtless. Two G. iv. 2

concern, befit. M.N.D. i. 1; is of importance. W.T. iii. 2

conclusions passed the careires, ? the end came very swiftly. M.W. i. 1

concolinel, a nonsense word. L.L.L. iii. 1

concupiscible, vehemently desirous. M. for M. v. 1

condition, social position, rank. Tp. iii. 1; character, behaviour. M.A. iii. 2; M. of V. i. 2; A.W. iv. 3

confidence, confidential communication. M.W. i. 4; M.A. iii. 5

confixed, fixed firmly, fastened. M. for M. v. 1

confound, destroy, ruin. C. of E. i. 2; M. of V. iii. 2

GLOSSARY

congee, pay one's respects at leaving. A.W. iv. 3

consort, company of musicians. Two G. iii. 2; fellowship. Two G. iv. 1; keep company with. C. of E. i. 2; L.L.L. ii. 1; M.N.D. iii. 2

constant, steady. Tp. ii. 2; self-possessed, M. of V. iii. 2; uniform. As. iii. 5; consistent. Tw.N. iv. 2

constantly, confidently. M. for M. iv. 1

conster, construe, explain. Tw.N. iii. 1

contempts, blunder for 'contents.' L.L.L. i. 1

continent, that which contains. M.N.D. ii. 1; that which comprises. M. of V. iii. 2

continue, let live. M. for M. iv. 3

contrive, conspire. M. of V. iv. 1; pass the time. T. of S. i. 2

control, to call to account. Tp. i. 2

convenience, propriety. A.W. iii. 2

convents, is convenient. Tw.N. v. 1

convented, summoned. M. for M. v. 1

conversation, behaviour. M.W. ii. 1; intercourse. A.W. i. 3

convertite, convert. As. v. 4

conveyance, impossible, incredible dexterity. M.A. ii. 1

cony, rabbit. As. iii. 2

cony-catch, cheat, trick. M.W. i. 1; &c.

copatain hat, high-crowned hat. T. of S. v. 1

cope, requite. M. of V. iv. 1; come into contact with. As. ii. 1; W.T. iv. 3

copulatives, persons about to be coupled in marriage. As. v. 4

coragio, courage. Tp. v. 1; A.W. ii. 5

coram, blunder for 'quorum.' M.W. i. 1

coranto, kind of dance. A.W. ii. 3; Tw.N. i. 3

cormorant, ravenous. L.L.L. i. 1

cornuto, cuckold. M.W. iii. 5

corollary, surplus, supernumerary. Tp. iv. 1

correspondent, responsive. Tp. i. 2

costard, apple of large size, head. M.W. iii. 1

Cotsall, Cotswold. M.W. i. 1

countenance, feigned appearance. M. for M. v. 1; patronage. As. i. 1; honour. T. of S. iv. 1

counter, following the scent in the reverse direction. C. of E. iv. 2; worthless wager. As. ii. 7

Counter-gate, gate of prison attached to city court. M.W. iii. 3

counterpoint, quilt, counterpane. T. of S. ii. 1

county, count. M.A. iv. 1; &c.

couplement, couple, pair. L.L.L. v. 2

courses, points of the compass. Tp. i. 1

cousin, nephew. M.A. i. 2; niece. As. i. 3; Tw.N. i. 3; uncle. Tw.N. i. 5

covent, convent. M. for M. iv. 3

cowl-staff, staff thrust through the handles of a tub to carry it. M.W. iii. 3

Cox my passion, an oath, 'God's my passion.' A.W. v. 2

coy, caress. M.N.D. iv. 1

THE COMEDIES

coystril, knave, base fellow. Tw.N. i. 3

cozen, cozener, cheat. M.W. iv. 5

cozier, cobbler. Tw.N. ii. 3

crack, boast. L.L.L. iv. 3; flaw. W.T. i. 2

crack-hemp, gallows'-bird. T. of S. v. 1

crazed, impaired, unsound. M.N.D. i. 1

cream, form a scum on the surface. M. of V. i. 1

credent, creditable, reputable. M. for M. iv. 4; credible. W.T. i. 2

crews, bands. Two G. iv. 1

crisp, rippled, wrinkled. Tp. iv. 1

cross, coin. L.L.L. i. 2; As. ii. 4

crowner, coroner. Tw.N. i. 5

cry, pack of hounds. M.N.D. iv. 1

cubiculo, bedchamber. Tw.N. iii. 2

cuckoo-buds, buttercup, marsh marigold, cowslip. L.L.L. v. 2

cullion, base fellow. T. of S. iv. 2

curious, particular, cautious. T. of S. iv. 4; A.W. i. 2; W.T. iv. 3

curious-knotted, laid out in elaborate plots. L.L.L. i. 1

curst, perverse, cantankerous. Two G. iii. 1; &c.

curtal, having tail docked. M.W. ii. 1; C. of E. iii. 2. See A.W. ii. 3

curtle-axe, cutlass. As. i. 3

cust-alorum, blunder for 'custos rotulorum.' M.W. i. 1

custard-coffin, crust of 'custard,' or open pie. T. of S. iv. 3

customer, associate. C. of E. iv. 4; prostitute. A.W. v. 3

cut, 'cut-tail horse,' or gelding; term of abuse. Tw.N. ii. 3

cypress, ? coffin of cypress-wood. Tw.N. ii. 4; Cyprus crape. Tw.N. ? ii. 4; iii. 1; W.T. iv. 3

daff, to thrust aside. M.A. ii. 3; v. 1

danger, mischief. M. of V. iv. 1; power to injure. M. of V. iv. 1

darkling, in darkness. M.N.D. ii. 2

dash, infusion, tinge. W.T. v. 2; abash. L.L.L. v. 2

daubery, work of a dauber, coarse work. M.W. iv. 2

day-woman, dairy-woman. L.L.L. i. 2

debatement, deliberation. M. for M. v. 1

debile, weak. A.W. ii. 3

deboshed, debauched, seduced. Tp. iii. 2; A.W. ii. 3

decern, concern. M.A. iii. 5

deck, sprinkled. Tp. i. 2

deface, cancel. M. of V. iii. 2

default, in the, at a pinch. A.W. ii. 3

defeat, cheat. M.N.D. iv. 1

defeature, marring of features. C. of E. ii. 1; v. 1

defect, blunder for 'effect.' M.N.D. iii. 1

defend, forbid. M.A. ii. 1; iv. 2

defiance, rejection. M. for M. iii. 1

definitive, resolved. M. for M. v. 1

degree, step towards. Tw.N. iii. 1

deliver, relate. Tp. v. 1; &c.; liberate. Tw.N. v. 1

GLOSSARY

denay, refusal. Tw.N. ii. 4

denier, a French copper coin of very small value. T. of S. Ind. 1

denunciation, formal announcement. M. for M. i. 2

deprave, decry, disparage. M. A. v. 1

deputation, deputyship. M. for M. i. 1

derivative, transmission by descent. W.T. iii. 2

descant, accompaniment to a musical theme. Two G. i. 2

detected, accused. M. for M. iii. 2

determinate, intended. Tw.N. ii. 1

determine, assign. M. for M. i. 1; limit. M. for M. iii. 1

detest, blunder for 'protest.' M.W. i. 4; M. for M. ii. 1

device, conceptions, aims. As. i. 1

diaper, napkin. T. of S. Ind. 1

dibble, pointed instrument to make holes for planting seeds. W.T. iv. 3

diet, fix. A.W. iv. 3; limit. A.W. v. 3

difference, i. e. in our social status. W.T. iv. 3

diffused, confused. M.W. iv. 4

digression, moral deviation. L.L.L. i. 2

dig-you-den, give you good evening. L.L.L. iv. 1

dilate, relate. C. of E. i. 1

dilated, prolonged. A.W. ii. 1

dildo, a word used in the refrains of ballads. W.T. iv. 3

dimension, bodily shape. Tw. N. i. 5; v. i

disable, disparage, undervalue. M. of V. ii. 7; As. iv. 1; v. 4; cripple. M. of V. i. 1

discase, unrobe, undress. Tp. v. 1; W.T. iv. 3

discharge, performance. Tp. ii. 1; perform. M.N.D. i. 2; iv. 2; v. i

discipled, educated. A.W. i. 2

discontenting, discontented. W.T. iv. 3

disfurnish, deprive, divest. Two G. iv. 1

dishonest, dishonesty, immodest, unchastity. M.W. iv. 2; As. v. 3

disliken, disguise. W.T. iv. 3

dismount, unsheathe. Tw.N. iii. 4

dispose, control. Two G. ii. 7; C. of E. i. 1

disputable, disputatious. As. ii. 5

dissemble, disguise. Tw.N. iv. 2

dissembly, blunder for 'assembly.' M.A. iv. 2

dissolutely, dissolved, blunders for 'resolutely,' 'resolved.' M W. i. 1

distemper, disorder. Tw.N. ii. 1

distemperature, disorder. C. of E. v. 1; M.N.D. ii. 1

disvouch, disown. M. for M. iv. 4

divulge, proclaim. M.W. iii. 2; A.W. ii. 1; Tw.N. i. 5

do, describe. W.T. v. 2

dog-ape, baboon. As. ii. 5

doit, a small Dutch coin, worth about half a farthing. Tp. ii. 2; M. of V. i. 3

dole, sorrow. M.N.D. v. 1; As. i. 2; share. A.W. ii. 3; W.T. i. 2

dominical, red letter in calendar indicating Sunday. L.L. L. v. 2

dowle, one of the fibres of a

feather. Tp. iii. 3

doxy, rogue's mistress. W.T. iv. 2

draff, refuse, swill given to pigs. M.W. iv. 2

draw, take draught of liquor. Tp. ii. 2; draw liquor for customers. M.W. i. 3; draw instrument from case, or draw bow across fiddle. M.A. v. 1; draw back. M. of V. ii. 9; Tw. N. i. 5; receive. M. of V. iv. 1

draw dryfoot, track game by the mere scent of the foot. C. of E. iv. 2

drawer, a tapster. M.W. ii. 2

drawn, with drawn swords. Tp. ii. 1; M.N.D. iii. 2; drunk. Tp. ii. 2

dribbling, falling short or wide of mark. M. for M. i. 3

drive, commute. M. of V. iv. 1

drovier, dealer in cattle. M.A. ii. 1

drumble, dawdle. M.W. iii. 3

Drum's entertainment, John, rough reception, turning an unwelcome guest out of doors. A.W. iii. 6

dry-beat, beat soundly. L.L.L. v. 2

duello, laws of the duel. L.L.L. i. 2; Tw.N. iii. 4

dump, plaintive melody or song. Two G. iii. 2; M.A. ii. 3

durance, imprisonment. M. for M. iii. 1; Tw.N. v. 1

durance, suit of, suit made of stout durable cloth (play on same word meaning 'imprisonment'). C. of E. iv. 3

eaning time, time of bearing lambs. M. of V. i. 3

eanling, young lamb. M. of V. i. 3

ear, plough. A.W. i. 3

ecstasy, state of being 'beside oneself'; frenzy or stupor caused by fear or passion. Tp. iii. 3; &c.

effect, accomplishment. Two G. i. 1; expression. M. for M. iii. 1; sign, symptom. M.A. ii. 3; purport, significance. As. iv. 3

eggs for money, take, put up with an affront. W.T. i. 2

eke, also, moreover. M.W. i. 3; ii. 3; M.N.D. iii. 1

eld, people of the old time. M.W. iv. 4; age. M. for M. iii. 1

elder, heart of, weak, fainthearted. M.W. ii. 3

element, air. Tw.N. i. 1; sphere. Tw.N. iii. 1

emboss, drive to extremity. A.W. iii. 6

embossed, foaming at mouth with exhaustion. T. of S. Ind. 1; swollen. As. ii. 7

embowelled, exhausted. A.W. i. 3

enchantingly, as though enchanted. As. i. 1

encounter, adversary. L.L.L. v. 2; greeting. T. of S. iv. 5; go toward. Tw.N. iii. 1; befall. W.T. ii. 1; behaviour. W.T. iii. 2

end, still an, continually. Two G. iv. 4

enfolding, garment. W.T. iv. 3

enforced, violated. M.N.D. iii. 1

enfreedoming, bringing into a state of freedom. L.L.L. iii. 1

engage, pledge. M.A. iv. 1; As. v. 4

engine, instrument of war. Tp. ii. 1; instrument. Two G. iii. 1

enlarge, release. Tw.N. v. 1

GLOSSARY 1067

enlargement, release. L.L.L. iii. 1

enmew, mew up, keep under. M. for M. iii. 1

enow, enough. M. of V. iii. 5

ensconce, shelter. M.W. ii. 2; iii. 3

enshield, shielded, concealed. M. for M. ii. 4

entertain, hire, take into service. Two G. ii. 4; &c.; maintain. M. of V. i. 1; desire to keep. M. for M. iii. 1

entertainment, employment, service. A.W. iii. 6; iv. 1; treatment. Tw.N. i. 5

entrenched, cut. A.W. ii. 1

envy, malice, spite. Tp. i. 2; M. of V. iv. 1

Ephesian, boon companion. M.W. iv. 5

epitheton, epithet, appellation. L.L.L. i. 2

Ercles, Hercules. M.N.D. i. 2

erection, direction. M.W. iii. 5

eringoes, candied root of sea holly, used as sweetmeat. M.W. v. 5

erst, little while since. As. iii. 5

escapes, sallies. M. for M. iv. i

estate, bestow, settle. Tp. iv. 1; M.N.D. i. 1; As. v. 2; state. M. of V. iii. 2; rank. A.W. iii. 7; wealth. W.T. iv. 2; affairs. W.T. iv. 3

estimable wonder, admiring judgment. Tw.N. ii. 1

even, make, grant. A.W. ii. 1; full. A.W. v. 3

everlasting garment, ? the buff jerkin of a sergeant. C. of E. iv. 2

evitate, avoid. M.W. v. 5

examine, question. A.W. iii. 5

exceed, be pre-eminent. M.A. iii. 4

except before excepted, a legal phrase, 'make objection.' Tw. N. i. 3

excess, interest. M. of V. i. 3

excrement, hair, moustache, beard. C. of E. ii. 2; &c.

exempt, separated. C. of E. ii. 2; remote. As. ii. 1; exclude. A.W. ii. 1

exhibition, allowance, maintenance. Two G. i. 3

exorcist, raiser of spirits. A.W. v. 3

experimental seal, stamp of experience. M.A. iv. 1

exploit, action, combat. A.W. i. 2; iv. 1

exposition, blunder for 'disposition.' M.N.D. iv. 1

expostulate, discuss. Two G. iii. 1

expressive, open or emphatic in expression. A.W. ii. i

expressure, expression. Tw.N. ii. 3; image, picture. M.W. v. 5

extent, seizure. As. iii. 1; assault. Tw.N. iv. 1

extermined, exterminated. As. iii. 5

extirp, root out. M. for M. iii. 2

extracting, ? distracting. Tw. N. v. i

extravagancy, vagrancy. Tw. N. ii. 1

eyas-musket, young hawk; sprightly child. M.W. iii. 3

eye, slight shade, tinge. Tp. ii. 1; limits. M. of V. i. 1

eyne, eyes. L.L.L. v. 2; M.N. D. i. 1

face, brave. C. of E. iii. 1; T. of S. iv. 3; v. 1

face out of, bully out of,

shamelessly exclude from. Tw.N. iv. 2; v. 1

face with card of ten, bluff, carry through by effrontery. T. of S. ii. 1

facinorous, infamous. A.W. ii. 3

fact, crime, deed. M. for M. iv. 2; W.T. iii. 2

fadge, fit, be suitable. L.L.L. v. 1; succeed. Tw.N. ii. 2

fading, refrain of popular song of indecent character. W.T. iv. 3

fail, failure. W.T. ii. 3; v. i

fain, wish to. Tp. i. 1; As. i. 2

fair, fairness, beauty. C. of E. ii. 1; &c.; in state, finery. T. of S. ii. 1

fairest grant is the necessity, best gift is that which meets the needs of case. M.A. iii. i

fairing, present. L.L.L. v. 2

faithless, unbelieving. M. of V. ii. 4

fall, let fall. Tp. ii. 1; &c.; be allotted. M. of V. i. 3; give birth to. M. of V. i. 3; happen. M. of V. iii. 2; A.W. v. 1; sinking of the note, cadence. Tw.N. i. 1

fallow, of a reddish-yellow colour. M.W. i. 1

false, falsehood. M. for M. ii. 4

falsing, deceptive. C. of E. ii. 2

familiar, spirit supposed to attend at call. L.L.L. i. 2

fancy, love. M.A. iii. 2; &c.

fancy-monger, dealer in love. As. iii. 2

fantastic, fop. M. for M. *Dram. Per.*; foppish. Two G. ii. 7

fap, drunk. M.W. i. 1

fardel, little pack. W.T. iv. 3; &c.

farthingale, framework of hoops of whalebone, for extending skirts of dresses; hooped petticoat. Two G. ii. 7; &c.

fartuous, blunder for 'virtuous.' M.W. ii. 2

fashion-monging, foppish. M.A. v. 1

fashions, farcy, disease of horses. T. of S. iii. 2

fat, make fat. M.N.D. ii. 1; cloying. Tw.N. v. i

favour, appearance, aspect, face. M. for M. iv. 2; &c.; present, token of love. L.L.L. v. 2; M.N.D. ii. 1; iv. 1

fay, faith. T. of S. Ind. ii

fear, frighten. M. for M. ii. 1; M. of V. ii. 1; T. of S. i. 2; peril, cause for fear. M.N.D. v. 1; fear for. M. of V. iii. 5; T. of S. v. 2

feater, more becoming. Tp. ii. 1

featly, neatly, gracefully. Tp. i. 2; W.T. iv. 3

federary, accomplice. W.T. ii. 1

feeder, servant. As. ii. 4

feeding, pasturage. W.T. iv. 3

fee-simple, unconditional possession. A.W. iv. 3

fell, enraged, savage. M.N.D. ii. 1; Tw.N. i. 1; fleece. As. iii. 2

fellow, equal, consort. Tp. ii. 1; &c.; accompany, be a partner. W.T. i. 2

fellowly, sympathetic. Tp. v. 1

fence, swordsmanship. M.W. i. 1; M.A. v. 1; Tw.N. iii. 4

feodary, accomplice. M. for M. ii. 4

festinately, hastily, speedily. L.L.L. iii. 1

GLOSSARY

fetch in, draw confession from. M.A. i. 1

few, in, in short. Tp. i. 2; T. of S. i. 2

fico, fig, expression of contempt. M.W. i. 3

fife, wry-necked, fife with upper part resembling the beak of a bird, or musician as looking away from his instrument. M. of V. ii. 5

fights, screen used during naval engagement to protect crew of a vessel. M.W. ii. 2

figure, figure of speech. Two G. ii. 1; L.L.L. i. 2; T. of S. i. 2; horoscope. M.W. iv. 2; phantasm. M.W. iv. 2; typify. M.N.D. i. 1

file, multitude. M. for M. iii. 2

fine, punish, punishment. M. for M. ii. 2; iii. 1; aim, end. M.A. i. 1; A.W. iv. 4; smart, T. of S. iv. 1; artful. A.W. v. 3

fine and recovery, absolute possession. M.W. iv. 2; C. of E. ii. 2

fine's the crown, end crowns all. A.W. iv. 4

firago, virago. Tw.N. iii. 4

fire, will-o'-the-wisp. M.N.D. iii. i

fire-new, brand-new. L.L.L. i. 1; Tw.N. iii. 2

fives, a disease in horses. T. of S. iii. 2

fixture, direction. W.T. v. 3

flap-dragon, snap-dragon, raisin caught out of burning brandy and eaten. L.L.L. v. 1

flap-dragoned, swallowed. W.T. iii. 3

flat-long, with the flat side. Tp. ii. 1

flatness, completeness. W.T. iii. 2

flatter with, deal falsely. Tw. N. i. 5

flaunts, finery. W.T. iv. 3

flaw, passionate outburst. M. for M. ii. 3

fleer, laugh, mock. M.A. v. 1; L.L.L. v. 2

fleet, company. M.A. ii. 1; fade, die away. M. of V. iii. 2; pass. iv. 1; As. i. 1

flesh, satiate. A.W. iv. 3

flewed, having large chaps. M.N.D. iv. 1

flight, shooting with arrows the greatest possible distance. M.A. i. 1

flote, wave. Tp. i. 2

flourish, embellish, gloss over. M. for M. iv. 1; fanfare of trumpets. M. of V. iii. 2

foil, put to, defeat, repulse. Tp. iii. 1

foin, thrust. M.W. ii. 3; M.A. v. 1

foison, plenty. Tp. ii. 1; iv. 1; M. for M. i. 4

folly-fallen, fallen into folly. Tw.N. iii. 1

fond, fondly, fondness, foolish, foolishly, foolishness. Two G. i. 1; &c.; valued by fools, trivial. M. for M. ii. 2; doting. M. for M. ii. 2; &c.; dote. Tw.N. ii. 2

fool, used as a term of endearment and pity. As. ii. 1; W.T. ii. 1; jester. T. of S. i. 1

fool-begged, foolishly demanded. C. of E. ii. 1

foot, kick, spurn. M. of V. i. 3; path. M. of V. ii. 4

foppery, folly. M.W. v. 5; M. for M. i. 2; M. of V. ii. 5

force, enforce. M. for M. iii. 1; scruple. L.L.L. v. 2; necessity. M.N.D. iii. 2; M. of V. iv. 1; W.T. iv. 3

fordone, wearied out. M.N.D. v. 2

'forehand, done at some earlier time. M.A. iv. 1

forehorse to a smock, squire of dames. A.W. ii. 1

forfend, forbid. W.T. iv. 3

forgery, invention. M.N.D. ii. 1

forked, horned. W.T. i. 2

formal, normal, sane. C. of E. v. 1; Tw.N. ii. 5

forted, fortified. M. for M. v. 1

forth-right, straight course or path. Tp. iii. 3

fortune, happen, chance. Two G. v. 4

foundered, lame, disabled. Tp. iv. 1

frame, form. M. for M. v. 1; scheme, order. M.A. iv. 1; L.L.L. iii. 1; contrivance. M.A. iv. 1; devise, plan. M.A. v. 1; W.T. v. 1

frampold, sour-tempered, disagreeable. M.W. ii. 2

franklin, yeoman. W.T. v. 2

fraught, cargo. Tw.N. v. 1; laden. Two G. iii. 2; M. of V. ii. 8; W.T. iv. 3

fraughtage, cargo. C. of E. iv. 1

fraughting, that form a cargo. Tp. i. 2

free, liberal. M. for M. v. i; innocent. As. ii. 7; Tw.N. ii. 4; W.T. ii. 3; noble. Tw.N. i. 5; W.T. ii. 2; accessible. W.T. ii. 1; ready. W.T. iv. 3

French crown, the baldness produced by the 'French disease.' M. for M. i. 2; M.N.D. i. 2; A.W. ii. 2

fresh, spring of fresh water. Tp. iii. 2; youthful. W.T. iv. 3

fret, chafe. M. of V. iv. 1; ring of gut placed on finger-board of musical instrument to regulate fingering. T. of S. ii. 1; spoil. T. of S. ii. 1

frippery, place where cast-off clothes are sold. Tp. iv. 1

frize, coarse woollen cloth. M.W. v. 5

from, different to, apart from. M.A. iii. 1; Tw.N. i. 5; v. 1

froth and lime, make a tankard froth, and put lime into sack to make it sparkle. M.W. i. 3

froward, refractory. T. of S. i. 1

fruitful, fruitfully, abundant, fully. M. for M. iv. 3; A.W. ii. 2

frutify, a confusion of 'notify' with 'fructify.' M. of V. ii. 2

fullam, die loaded at corner. M.W. i. 3

full-fraught, fully laden. Two G. iii. 2

fulsome, lustful. M. of V. i. 3; cloying, wearisome from excess. Tw.N. v. 1

gaberdine, loose upper garment. Tp. ii. 2; M. of V. i. 3

gaged, bound. M. of V. i. 1

galimaufry, gallimaufry, hotchpotch, medley. M.W. ii. 1; W.T. iv. 3

gall, harass, oppress. W.T. i. 2

galliard, lively dance in triple time. Tw.N. i. 3

galliass, heavy low-built vessel, larger than a galley. T. of S. ii. 1

gallows, gallows-bird. L.L.L. v. 2

gambold, gambol. T. of S. Ind. 2

gamester, gambler. M.W. iii.

GLOSSARY

1; L.L.L. i. 2; athlete. As. i. 1;
term of contempt. T. of S. ii.
1; lewd person. A.W. v. 3
garden-house, summer-house.
M. for M. v. 1
garner, granary. Tp. iv. 1
garnish, outfit, dress. M. of V.
ii. 6
gaskins, breeches or hose. Tw.
N. i. 5
gaud, gawd, trifle, finery. M.N.
D. i. 1; iv. 1; T. of S. ii. 1
gear, matter, purpose. M. of V.
i. 1; ii. 2
geck, fool, dupe. Tw.N. v. 1
geminy, couple. M.W. ii. 2
general, populace. M. for M. ii.
4
generation, offspring. W.T. ii. 1
generative, having the power
of generating. M. for M. iii. 2
generous, noble, high-born. M.
for M. iv. 6; L.L.L. v. 1
genius, one of two opposed
spirits by whom each person
was supposed to be attended;
spirit. Tp. iv. 1; C. of E. v. 1;
Tw.N. iii. 4
gentility, gentle bearing,
gentle birth. L.L.L. i. 1; As. i.
1
gentle, noble, well-born. Tp. i.
2; W.T. i. 2; gentleman, one
of good birth. M.W. iii. 2;
&c.; term of endearment. W.
T. iv. 3
gentry, rank by birth. M.W. ii.
1; W.T. i. 2
germane, kin, related. W.T. iv.
3
gest, time allotted for a halt or
stay. W.T. i. 2
gesture, bearing. As. v. 2
giddily, lightly. Tw.N. ii. 4
gig, whipping-top. L.L.L. iv.
3; v. 1

giglot, lewd woman. M. for M.
v. 1
gild, impart flush to. Tp. v. 1
Gillian, Juliana. C. of E. iii. 1
gillyvors, gillyflowers (a variety of wall-flower). W.T. iv.
3
gin, snare. Tw.N. ii. 5
ging, gang. M.W. iv. 2
Ginn, Jenny. C. of E. iii. 3
gird, gibe, hit. T. of S. v. 2
girdle, turn one's, ? find harmless outlet for anger. M.A. v. 1
give, display as armorial bearing, bear. M.W. i. 1; grant to
be. W.T. iii. 2
give out, proclaim. W.T. iv. 3
glance, allude, hint. C. of E. v.
1; M.N.D. ii. 1
glances, satirical allusions,
side hits. As. ii. 7
glass, hour-glass. W.T. i. 2
glasses, runnings of hour-glass.
Tp. i. 2; v. 1
glassy essence, essential nature
of man. M. for M. ii. 2
gleek, jest or gibe. M.N.D. iii.
1
glib, castrate. W.T. ii. 1
glozes, pretences, disguises. L.
L.L. iv. 3
God bless the mark, phrase
used as apology after mentioning something horrible or
indecent. Two G. iv. 4; M. of
V. ii. 2
*God dig you den, God ye good
even*, God give you a good
evening. L.L.L. iv. 1; As.
v. 1
God 'ild, God shield. As. iii. 3;
v. 4
Gogs-wouns, God's wounds,
an oath. T. of S. iii. 2
good, financially sound. M. of
V. i. 3

good deed, in very deed. W.T. i. 2

good den, good even. M.A. iii. 2

good even and twenty, twenty good evenings. M.W. ii. 1

good-jer, good year, a meaningless expletive. M.W. i. 4; M.A. i. 3

good life, lifelike truth. Tp. iii. 3; good name. M.W. iii. 3

good life, song of, moral song. Tw.N. ii. 3

gorge, throat, stomach. W.T. ii. 1

goss, gorse. Tp. iv. 1

gossip, woman's female friend, invited to be present at a birth. Two G. iii. 1; C. of E. v. i; to act as sponsor. A.W. i. 1; make merry. C. of E. v. 1; sponsor. W.T. ii. 3

gossips' bowl, used at christening feasts. M.N.D. ii. 1

go through, deal in succession. M. for M. ii. 1

gourd, a kind of false dice. M.W. i. 3

government, in, under control. M.N.D. v. 1

grace, favour granted. M.N.D. ii. 2; T. of S. i. 2; gain honour. As. i. 1; favour. A.W. v. 2; W.T. iii. 2; virtue. Tw. N. v. 1

graceful, full of nobility. W.T. v. 1

graff, graft. As. iii. 2

grained, furrowed. C. of E. v. 1

grain, in, fast, genuine, in the very nature. C. of E. iii. 2; Tw.N. i. 5

gramercy, thanks. M. of V. ii. 2; T. of S. i. 1

grange, country house. M. for M. iii. 1; granary. W.T. iv. 3

grated upon, harassed with importunities. M.W. ii. 2

gratify, fee, reward. M. of V. iv. 1; T. of S. i. 2

gratillity, blunder for 'gratuity.' Tw.N. ii. 3

gratulate, pleasing. M. for M. v. 1

grave, engrave, cut. M. of V. ii. 7

gravelled, at a standstill. As. iv. 1

greasily, indecently. L.L.L. iv. 1

Greek, roysterer. Tw.N. iv. 1

green, ? fresh, or freshly greased. T. of S. iii. 2

grize, step, stair. Tw.N. iii. 1

grizzle, sprinkling of grey hairs. Tw.N. v. 1

groat, English coin worth about 4d. M.W. i. 1

gross, palpable. M. for M. i. 2; A.W. i. 3; total. As. iv. 1

grossly, awkwardly. M.W. ii. 2; obviously, palpably. C. of E. ii. 2; A.W. i. 3; materially. M. of V. v. 1

grossness, density. M.N.D. iii. 1; enormity, flagrancy. M. of V. iii. 2; Tw.N. iii. 2

growing, accruing. C. of E. iv. 1

grow to, have a tendency. M. of V. ii. 2

guard, ornamental trimming. M. for M. iii. 1; M.A. i. 1; L.L.L. iv. 3; ornament, trim. M.A. i. 1; M. of V. ii. 2

guerdon, reward, requital. M.A. v. 3; L.L.L. iii. 1

guilder, gold coin once current in Netherlands. C. of E. i. 1; iv. 1

guiled, treacherous. M. of V. iii. 2

GLOSSARY

gull, trick, deception. M.A. ii. 3; dupe, simpleton. Tw.N. iii. 2; v. 1

gull-catcher, trickster. Tw.N. ii. 5

gust, pleasure. Tw.N. i. 3; taste, relish. W.T. i. 2

H, i. e. ache (pron. aitch). M.A. iii. 4

hack, become vile and vulgar. M.W. ii. 1

haggard, haggerd, wild female hawk. M.A. iii. 1; &c.

hag-seed, offspring of witch. Tp. i. 2

hale, haul, draw, drag. M.A. ii. 3; &c.

half-cheek, side-face. L.L.L. v. 2

halidom, holy relic, anything regarded as sacred. Two G. iv. 2

Hallowmas, feast of All Saints. Two G. ii. 1; M. for M. ii. 1

hammered of, pondered on. W.T. ii. 2

hand, lay hands on. W.T. ii. 3

hand, at or **in any,** on any account, in any case. T. of S. i. 2; A.W. iii. 6

handfast, custody. W.T. iv. 3

hands, of all, in any case. L.L.L. iv. 3

hangman boys, young rascals. Two G. iv. 4

haply, perhaps. Tw. N. i. 2

happily, haply, perhaps. M. for M. iv. 2; T. of S. iv. 4; Tw.N. iv. 2

happiness, aptitude. M.A. ii. 3

harlot, lewd fellow. C. of E. v. 1; adulterous. W.T. ii. 3

hatch, half-door. C. of E. iii. 1

haud credo, hardly I believe. L.L.L. iv. 2

have at, I'll try. W.T. iv. 3

have to, we'll go to. T. of S. i. 1

have with, I'll go with. L.L.L. iv. 2; As. i. 2

hawking, hawk-like, keen. A.W. i. 1

hawthorn-buds, dandies. M.W. iii. 3

hay, country dance. L.L.L. v. 1

head, behead. M. for M. ii. 1; face. M.A. v. 1; M.N.D. i. 1; fountain-head. A.W. i. 3

head, of the first, said of a deer at the age when the antlers are first developed. L.L.L. iv. 2

head-stall, part of bridle that fits round head. T. of S. iii. 2

heart, affection. As. i. 1

heat, run swiftly over. W.T. i. 2; course. Tw.N. i. 1

heaviness, sadness. Tp. v. 1; M. of V. ii. 8

heavings, sighs. W.T. ii. 3

heavy, drowsy. Tp. ii. 1; sad, sorrowful. M. for M. iv. 1; M. of V. v. 1; W.T. iii. 3

hedge, shift, dodge. M.W. ii. 2; restrict. M. of V. ii. 1

hedge-priest, illiterate priest of inferior status. L.L.L. v. 2

heft, heaving. W.T. ii. 1

height, highest degree. M.A. iv. 1

Helen, blunder for 'Hero,' M.N.D. v. 1

helm, steer, guide. M. for M. iii. 2; helmet. A.W. iii. 3

helpless, unavailing. C. of E. ii. 1

hent, reached, occupied. M. for M. iv. 6; lay hold of. W.T. iv. 2

herb of grace, rue. A.W. iv. 5

hereby, as it may happen. L.L.L. i. 2

hest, behest, command. Tp. i. 2; iii. 1

hic jacet (here lies), die in the attempt. A.W. iii. 6

Hiems, winter. M.N.D. ii. 1

high and low, two kinds of false dice. M.W. i. 3

high bent, turned full. A.W. v. 3

high-cross, market-cross. T. of S. i. 1

high-proof, in the highest degree. M.A. v. 1

hight, is called. L.L.L. i. 1; M.N.D. v. 1

hilding, good-for-nothing. T. of S. ii. 1; A.W. iii. 6

hind, servant, agricultural labourer. M.W. iii. 5; L.L.L. i. 2; As. i. 1; female of the deer. As. iii. 2

hint, occasion, opportunity. Tp. i. 2; ii. 1

hip, on or *upon the*, at a disadvantage. M. of V. i. 3; iv. 1

hipped, having the hip injured or dislocated. T. of S. iii. 2

hobby-horse, frivolous or foolish fellow. M.A. iii. 2; prostitute. W.T. i. 2

hob, nob, have or have not, give or take. Tw.N. iii. 4

hodge-pudding, pudding made of a medley of ingredients. M.W. v. 5

hold, remain. M.A. i. 1; keep promise. M.N.D. i. 2; maintain. A.W. i. 1

holding, consistency. A.W. iv. 2

holidame, halidom, q.v. T. of S. v. 2

holp, helped. Tp. i. 2; C. of E. iv. 1

home, thoroughly. Tp. v. 1; &c.; a home-thrust. L.L.L. v. 1

home, and home, effectively, out and out. M. for M. iv. 3

hoodman, blindfolded player in blindman's buff. A.W. iv. 3

hoodwink, to cover up from sight. Tp. iv. 1

hornbook, primer. L.L.L. v. 1

horn-mad, mad with rage at having been made a cuckold. M.W. i. 4; C. of E. ii. 1; M.A. i. 1

host, lodge, put up. C. of E. i. 2; A.W. iii. 5

host, lay at, were left at. C. of E. v. i

hot-house, bathing-house, brothel. M. for M. ii. 1

hovel-post, support of the roof of an outhouse. M. of V. ii. 2

hox, hamstring, hough. W.T. i. 2

hoy, small vessel; a sloop. C. of E. iv. 3

hull, float, anchor. Tw.N. i. 5

Hungarian, thievish, beggarly. M.W. i. 3

hungerly, hungry-looking. T. of S. iii. 2

hurly, hurly-burly. T. of S. iv. 1

hurtling, conflict. As. iv. 3

husband, housekeeper, steward. M. for M. iii. 2; T. of S. v. 1

hyen, hyena. As. iv. 1

i'fecks, in faith. W.T. i. 2

ignomy, ignominy. M. for M. ii. 4

ignorant fumes, fumes producing unconsciousness. Tp. v. i

ill-ta'en, misconceived. W.T. i. 2

illustrate, illustrious. L.L.L. iv. i; v. 1

image, idea. M.W. iv. 6

imagined speed, all speed imaginable. M. of V. iii. 4

imbrue, stain with blood. M.N. D. v. i

immediately, purposely. M.N. D. i. 1

imp, child. L.L.L. i. 2; v. 2

impawned, in pledge. W.T. i. 2

impeticos, burlesque word for 'to pocket,' perhaps intended to suggest 'petticoat.' Tw.N. ii. 3

importance, importunity. Tw. N. v. 1; import, meaning. W.T. v. 2

important, importunate. C. of E. v. 1; M.A. ii. 1

importing, of much import. A.W. v. 3

impose, injunction. Two G. iv. 3; command. M.A. v. 1

imposition, imputation, accusation, charge. M. for M. i. 2; W.T. i. 2; injunction. M. of V. i. 2; imposed task. M. of V. iii. 4; A.W. iv. 4

incardinate, incarnal, blunders for 'incarnate.' M. of V. ii. 2; Tw.N. v. 1

incense, instigate. M.A. v. 1; W.T. v. 1

inch-meal, by, by inches, inch by inch. Tp. ii. 2

incidency, incident. W.T. i. 2

include, bring to a close. Two G. v. 4

incontinent, immediately. As. v. 2

incony, pretty, 'nice.' L.L.L. iii. 1; iv. 1

incorporate, made one body. M.N.D. iii. 2

increase, vegetable produce, crops. Tp. iv. 1

incredulous, incredible. Tw.N. iii. 4

Ind, Inde, India, or the Indies (E. or W.). Tp. ii. 2; L.L.L. iv. 3; As. iii. 2

indifferent, equally. T. of S. i. 2; of medium quality or character. T. of S. iv. 1; fairly. Tw.N. i. 3; i. 5

indubitate, undoubted. L.L.L. iv. 1

inequality, variableness. M. for M. v. 1

infection, blunder for 'affection.' M.W. ii. 2

infest, vex. Tp. v. 1

informal, ? disordered in mind. M. for M. v. 1

inherit, win. Two G. iii. 2

inkle, a kind of tape. L.L.L. iii. 1; W.T. iv. 3

inland, in or towards interior of country. As. ii. 7; having refinements characteristic of inlying parts of country. As. iii. 2

inly, inwardly. Tp. v. 1; heartfelt. Two G. ii. 7

innocent, idiot. A.W. iv. 3

insanie, madness. L.L.L. v. 1

insculped, engraved. M. of V. ii. 7

insinuate, convey notion by indirect suggestion. L.L.L. v. 1; ingratiate. As. Epil. 8; intermeddle. W.T. iv. 3

instalment, place wherein some one is installed. M.W. v. 5

intellect, purport. L.L.L. iv. 2

intelligencing, conveying information. W.T. ii. 3

intelligent, communicative. W.T. i. 2

intend, pretend. M.A. ii. 2; M.N.D. iii. 2; T. of S. iv. 1

intendment, intention. As. i. 1

intenible, incapable of holding or containing. A.W. i. 3

intermission, action to while

away time. M. of V. iii. 2
intestine, internal. C. of E. i. 1
invectively, with inveighing or denunciation. As. ii. 1
inward, secret, confidential. M.A. iv. 1; L.L.L. v. 1; familiar acquaintance. M. for M. iii. 2; inwardly. M. of V. iii. 2
inwardness, intimacy. M.A. iv. 1
issued, born, descended. Tp. i. 2
issues, purposes. M. for M. i. 1
it, them. L.L.L. i. 1
I wis, certainly, truly. M. of V. ii. 9; T. of S. i. 1

Jack, knave. Tp. iv. 1; &c.; a leather vessel for liquor. T. of S. iv. 1
Jack-a-Lent, figure set up to be pelted during Lent. M.W. iii. 3; v. 5
jade, worthless nag. T. of S. i. 2; befool. Tw.N. ii. 5
jar, discordant sound. As. ii. 7; tick. W.T. i. 2
jay, showy person. M.W. iii. 3
jerk, short sharp witty speech. L.L.L. iv. 2
jerkin, close-fitting jacket. Tp. iv. 1; Two G. ii. 4
jet, strut, swagger. Tw.N. ii. 5
jills, drinking vessels made of metal. T. of S. iv. 1
joinder, conjunction, union. Tw.N. v. 1
joint-stool, a kind of folding chair. T. of S. ii. 1
joul, knock, push. A.W. i. 3
journal, daily. M. for M. iv. 3
jump, agree. M. of V. ii. 9; T. of S. i. 1; Tw.N. v. 1
junket, sweetmeat. T. of S. iii. 2
just, justly, exactly, precisely. M. for M. iii. 1; &c.
justify, prove. Tp. v. 1; A.W. iv. 3; confirm. W.T. v. 2; v. 3
juvenal, juvenile. L.L.L. i. 2; iii. 1; M.N.D. iii. 1

keel, cool boiling liquid by stirring, skimming, or pouring in something cold. L.L.L. v. 2
keep, restrain. Two G. iv. 4; reside. M. for M. i. 3; M. of V. iii. 3; charge; an article which serves for containing something. T. of S. i. 2
keeping, maintenance. As. i. 1
Keisar, kaiser, emperor. M.W. i. 3
kennel, gutter. T. of S. iv. 3
kersey, coarse narrow cloth. M. for M. i. 2; T. of S. iii. 2; plain, homely. L.L.L. v. 2
kibe, chilblain, esp. on the heel. Tp. ii. 1; M.W. i. 3
kickshaws, toy, trifle, gewgaw. Tw.N. i. 3
kicky-wicky, ludicrous term for wife. A.W. ii. 3
kid-fox, fox-cub. M.A. ii. 3
kiln-hole, fire-hole of kiln. M.W. iv. 2; W.T. iv. 3
kind, kindred. Two G. ii. 3; natural. M.A. i. 1; respect. M.N.D. i. 1; nature. As. iv. 3; A.W. i. 3
kind, deed of, sexual function. M. of V. i. 3
kissing-comfits, perfumed comfits for sweetening the breath. M.W. v. 5
kitchen, entertain in the kitchen. C. of E. v. 1
knack, knick-knack. M.N.D. i. 1; T. of S. iv. 3; W.T. iv. 3
knap, nibble. M. of V. iii. 1
knit, texture. T. of S. iv. 1
knot (folded arms). Tp. i. 2

GLOSSARY

labras, blunder for 'labra,' plural of 'labrum,' a lip. M. W. i. 1

laced mutton, strumpet. Two G. i. 1

lakin, form of Lady; *by'r lakin* = by our Lady. Tp. iii. 3; M. N.D. iii. 1

lampass, disease of horses. T. of S. iii. 2

land-damn, make a hell on earth for. W.T. ii. 1

languishing, attack of faintness, such as proceeds from disease. A.W. i. 3

lapsed, surprised, apprehended. Tw.N. iii. 3

large, licentious, gross. M.A. ii. 3; iv. 1

latch, secure. M.N.D. iii. 2

latten, mixed metal of yellow colour. M.W. i. 1

laying on, wagering on. T. of S. v. 2

leaguer, camp, investing force. A.W. iii. 6

leasing, lying, falsehood. Tw. N. i. 5

leavened, tempered, modified. M. for M. i. 1

led, carried. A.W. iv. 3

leer, countenance. As. iv. 1

leet, court which lords of certain manors were empowered to hold. T. of S. Ind. 2

'lege, allege, say. T. of S. i. 2

leg, make a, bow, make obeisance. A.W. ii. 2

leiger, resident ambassador. M. for M. iii. 1

leisure, by my good, gradually. M. for M. iii. 2

leman, lover. M.W. iv. 2; Tw. N. ii. 3

lenten, poor, scanty. Tw. N. i. 5

l'envoy, epilogue. L.L.L. iii. 1

let, hinder, delay. Two G. iii. 1; &c.

Lethe, a river in Hades, the water of which produced forgetfulness. Tw.N. iv. 1

level, guess. M. of V. i. 2; equipoised, steady. Tw.N. ii. 4; range of missile. W.T. ii. 3; direction, aim. W.T. iii. 2

lewdster, lewd person. M.W. v. 3

libbard, leopard. L.L.L. v. 2

lie, lodge, dwell. Two G. iv. 2; &c.

light, wanton. C. of E. iv. 3

lighter, inferior. Tw.N. v. 1

liking, appearance, condition. M.W. ii. 1

Limander, Leander. M.N.D. v. 1

limbo, prison, confinement. C. of E. iv. 2; region on the border of hell. A.W. v. 3

lime, birdlime. Tp. iv. 1; Two G. iii. 2; put lime into wine. M.W. i. 3; catch as with birdlime. M.A. iii. 1; Tw.N. iii. 4

limit, appointed time. M. for M. iii. 1; appoint, fix. M. for M. iv. 2; prescribed time of repose after child-bearing. W.T. iii. 2

line, draw, trace. As. iii. 2

line-grove, grove of lime-trees. Tp. v. 1

ling, fish, meagre food. A.W. iii. 2

link, blacking, lamp-black. T. of S. iv. 1

linsey-woolsey, medley, nonsense. A.W. iv. 1

lion-fell, lion's skin. M.N.D. v. 1

liquor, dress boots with oil or grease. M.W. iv. 5

list, like, care to. Tp. iii. 2; W. T. iv. chor.; limit, boundary.

M. for M. i. 1; *A.W.* ii. 1; *Tw. N.* iii. 1

livelihood, activity, vigour. *A.W.* i. 1

lively, lifelike. *As.* v. 4; *W.T.* v. 3

liver, supposed to be the seat of love and of passion generally. *Tp.* iv. 1; &c.

liver-vein, style of men in love. *L.L.L.* iv. 3

lob, clown. *M.N.D.* ii. 1

lock, love-lock. *M.A.* iii. 3; v. 1

lode-star, pole-star. *M.N.D.* i. 1

long, belong. *M. for M.* ii. 2

'long of, on account of, through. *L.L.L.* ii. 1; *M.N.D.* iii. 2

longly, for a long time. *T. of S.* i. 1

look out, blush. *W.T.* iv. 3

loose, last moment. *L.L.L.* v. 2; shoot, let fly. *M.N.D.* ii. 1

lordings, lordlings. *W.T.* i. 2

'Lord's sake, for the,' supplication of imprisoned debtors to passers-by. *M. for M.* iv. 3

Lord's tokens, plague-spots. *L.L.L.* v. 2

lose, forget. *M.N.D.* i. 1; cause the loss of. *Tw.N.* ii. 2

loss of question, in the, for the sake of argument. *M. for M.* ii. 4

love-broker, go-between. *Tw. N.* iii. 2

loves, affects. *L.L.L.* iv. 3

loves, of all, phrase of strong entreaty. *M.W.* ii. 2; *M.N.D.* ii. 2

love-springs, tender shoots of love. *C. of E.* iii. 2

lower chair, easy chair. *M. for M.* ii. 1

lower messes, people dining at the lower end of the table; hence, inferiors. *W.T.* i. 2

lozel, worthless person. *W.T.* ii. 3

luce, pike, fish. *M.W.* i. 1

lumpish, low-spirited, dejected. *Two G.* iii. 2

lunes, fits of frenzy. *M.W.* iv. 2; *W.T.* ii. 2

lurch, remain about a place furtively. *M.W.* ii. 2

lure, apparatus used to recall hawks. *T. of S.* iv. 1

lustihood, vigour of body, robustness. *M.A.* v. 1

luxurious, unchaste. *M.A.* iv. 1

luxury, lust. *M.W.* v. 5; *M. for M.* v. 1

maculate, spotted, defiled. *L.L.L.* i. 2

Magnifico, magnate of Venice. *M. of V.* iii. 2

mail, bag. *L.L.L.* iii. 1

main-course, main-sail. *Tp.* i. 1

making, outward form. *C. of E.* iv. 2

malapert, presumptuous, impudent. *Tw.N.* iv. 1

Mall, Mary. *Tp.* ii. 2; *Tw.N.* i. 3

malmsey, strong sweet wine. *L.L.L.* v. 2

malt-horse, heavy horse used by maltsters, term of abuse. *C. of E.* iii. 1; *T. of S.* iv. 1

manage, manager, wield, wielder. *Two G.* iii. 1; *L.L.L.* i. 2

mankind, masculine, furious. *T.W.* ii. 3

manner, taken with the, caught in the act. *L.L.L.* i. 1; *W.T.* iv. 3

mantle, cloud, become covered over. *M. of V.* i. 1

margent, margin with marginal notes. *L.L.L.* ii. 1; bor-

GLOSSARY

der, edge. M.N.D. ii. 1
mark, thirteen shillings and fourpence. M. for M. iv. 3; pattern. W.T. iv. 3
marl, clay. M.A. ii. 1
marmozet, small monkey. Tp. ii. 2
marry, asseverative exclamation. Tw.N. iv. 2
mart, bargain. T. of S. ii. 1; W.T. iv. 3
match, bargain. M. of V. iii. 1
mated, confounded, stupefied. C. of E. iii. 2; v. 1
material, full of matter or sense. As. iii. 3
matter, important matter. Tp. ii. 1
maugre, in spite of. Tw.N. iii. 1
maze, figure marked on village greens for rustic sports. M.N.D. ii. 1; perplex. M.N.D. ii. 1
meacock, effeminate. T. of S. ii. 1
mealed, spotted, stained. M. for M. iv. 2
mean, tenor or alto. Two G. i. 2; L.L.L. v. 2; W.T. iv. 2; means, method. Two G. ii. 7; &c.; opportunity. C. of E. i. 2
meander, crooked and winding path. Tp. iii. 3
measure, grave and stately dance. M.A. ii. 1; &c.; judge. W.T. ii. 1
mechanical, vulgar, vile. M.W. ii. 2; artisan. M.N.D. iii. 2
medicinable, healing. M.A. ii. 2
medicine, physician. A.W. ii. 1; W.T. iv. 3
meet, even, quits. M.A. i. 1
mell, meddle. A.W. iv. 3
men of hair, dressed in goatskins. W.T. iv. 3
mercatante, a merchant. T. of S. iv. 2
mere, absolute, downright. L.L.L. i. 1; &c.; merely. A.W. iii. 5
merely, altogether. Tp. i. 1; M.A. ii. 3
mess, group of four. L.L.L. iv. 3; v. 2; course. T. of S. iv. 4; W.T. iv. 3
mete, aim. L.L.L. iv. 1
mete-yard, measuring rod. T. of S. iv. 3
metheglin, spiced variety of mead. M.W. v. 5; L.L.L. v. 2
mew, mew up, confine. M.N.D. i. 1; T. of S. i. 1
mewl, whimper, cry feebly. As. ii. 7
mickle, much. C. of E. iii. 1
middle-earth, earth as placed between heaven and hell. M.W. v. 5
milch-kine, cows giving milk. M.W. iv. 4; T. of S. ii. 1
mill-sixpences, sixpences struck by coining-mill instead of hammer. M.W. i. 1
mind, spirit, temper. M. for M. ii. 4; M. of V. ii. 8; mean, intend. M.N.D. v. 1; remind. W.T. iii. 2
mine, undermine. As. i. 1; my kinsmen. A.W. i. 3
minimus, small insignificant creature. M.N.D. iii. 2
minion, favourite. Tp. iv. 1; &c.; spoilt favourite. Two G. i. 2; saucy wench. T. of S. ii. 1
minstrelsy, for my, instead of music. L.L.L. i. 1
misgraffed, badly matched. M.N.D. i. 1
misprise, despise, scorn. M.A. iii. 1; As. i. 1; i. 2; mistake. M.N.D. iii. 2; A.W. iii. 2
misprision, mistake, misunder-

standing. M.A. iv. 1; &c.; contempt. A.W. ii. 3
miss, do without. Tp. i. 2
missingly, with sense of loss. W.T. iv. 1
misuse, deceive. M.A. ii. 2
mo, moe, more. M. for M. iii. 1; &c.
modern, ordinary, commonplace. As. ii. 7; iv. 1; A.W. ii. 3; modest, or modish. A.W. v. 3
moiety, part, share. A.W. iii. 2; W.T. ii. 3; half. W.T. iii. 2
monarcho, the title assumed by Italian who fancied himself emperor of the world; one who is an object of ridicule. L.L.L. iv. 1
montant, upright blow or thrust. M.W. ii. 3
month's mind, good mind, inclination. Two G. i. 2
monument, memory. M.A. v. 2
monumental, serving as memento also as a proof of identity. A.W. iv. 3
mood, anger. Two G. iv. 1; C. of E. ii. 2
moonish, variable, fickle. As. iii. 2
mop, grimace. Tp. iv. 1
moralize, moral on, point the moral of. As. ii. 1; ii. 7
morning's love, i.e. Cephalus. M.N.D. iii. 2
morris-pike, a pike supposed of Moorish origin. C. of E. iv. 3
mort, note sounded on a horn at the death of the deer. W.T. i. 2
mortifying, killing. M.A. i. 3
mose in the chine, suffer from glanders. T. of S. iii. 2
motion, puppet-show. Two G. ii. 1; M. for M. iii. 2; W.T. iv. 2; proposal. M.W. i. 1; C. of E. i. 1; incitement. M. for M. i. 4; emotion, impulse. Tw.N. ii. 4
motive, instrument. A.W. iv. 4
motley, parti-coloured, as fool's dress. As. ii. 7; Tw.N. i. 5; fool. As. iii. 3
motley-minded, variegated, changeable. As. v. 4
mountanto, an upright blow or thrust. M.A. i. 1
move, appeal to. C. of E. ii. 2
mow, grimace. Tp. ii. 2; iv. 1
murmur, rumour. Tw.N. i. 2
murrain, plague, used as an imprecation. Tp. iii. 2
murrion, having died of disease. M.N.D. ii. 1
mystery, art of a trade guild. M. for M. iv. 2; A.W. iii. 6

napkin, handkerchief. As. iv. 3; T. of S. Ind. 1
native, by nature. L.L.L. i. 2; closely related. A.W. i. 1
natural, half-witted person. Tp. iii. 2; As. i. 2
nature, natural affection. Tp. v. 1; C. of E. i. 1; special duty. As. iii. 1; life. M. for M. ii. 4; temperament. A.W. iii. 1; way. A.W. iv. 3
naught, efface oneself, withdraw. As. i. 1
naughty, morally bad, wayward. M. for M. ii. 1; M. of V. iii. 2; good for nothing. A.W. v. 3
nayward, denial, disbelief. W. T. ii. 1
nay-word, watch word, catchword. M.W. ii. 2; v. 2; byword. Tw.N. ii. 3
neaf, fist. M.N.D. iv. 1
near-legged, knock-kneed in forelegs. T. of S. iii. 2

GLOSSARY

neat, ox, oxen. Tp. ii. 2; &c.
neat-herds, cow-herds. W.T. iv. 3
neb, mouth. W.T. i. 2
necessitied, in need of. A.W. v. 3
neeze, sneeze. M.N.D. ii. 1
nerve, sinews. Tp. i. 2
nick, reckoning, account. Two G. iv. 2; indent. C. of E. v. 1
night-rule, night revelry or riot. M.N.D. iii. 2
nine men's morris, a game between two players, each with nine disks of wood, or pegs, often played in the open. M.N.D. ii. 1
nit, gnat, or small fly; term of contempt or fun. L.L.L. iv. 1; T. of S. iv. 3
noddy, noodle. Two G. i. 1
noise, low or melodious sound. Tp. iii. 2
non-come, blunder for 'non compos' (out of one's right mind). M.A. iii. 5
note, mark of distinction. A.W. i. 3; be known. Tw.N. iv. 3; notice. W.T. i. 1; sign. W.T. i. 2; list. W.T. iv. 2
notedly, particularly. M. for M. v. 1
novum, game at dice, principal throws being nine and five. L.L.L. v. 2
nowl, head. M.N.D. iii. 2
number, metre. Tw.N. ii. 5
nuncio, messenger. Tw.N. i. 4
nuthook, beadle, constable. M.W. i. 1

O, anything round; circle, round spot, orb. L.L.L. v. 2; M.N.D. iii. 2
obscenely, blunder for 'seemly.' M.N.D. i. 2
occasion, husband's, opportunity for getting the better of one's husband. As. iv. 1
Od, minced form of 'God.' M.W. i. 1; &c.
oeilliades, amorous glances. M.W. i. 3
o'erflourished, elaborately carved. Tw.N. iii. 4
o'erlooked, perused. Two. G. i. 2; bewitched. M.W. v. 5; M. of V. iii. 2
o'erparted, with too difficult a part, or too many parts to play. L.L.L. v. 2
o'er-raught, outwitted, cheated. C. of E. i. 2
o'erslip, slips by without notice. Two G. ii. 2
offer, essay, try, endeavour. As. iii. 2; contribute. As. v. 4; make an attempt. W.T. iv. 3
office, service. M. for M. v. 1; perform by way of service. A.W. iii. 2
officed, functioned. W.T. i. 2
old, great, plentiful, excessive. M.W. i. 4; &c.
omit, neglect. Tp. i. 2; ii. 1; Two G. ii. 4
open, (of hounds) to begin to cry when in pursuit of a scent. M.W. iv. 2; clear, easy to understand. M. for M. ii. 1; Tw.N. ii. 5; openly. Tw.N. iii. 3
opinion, self-conceit. L.L.L. v. 1; reputation, estimation. M. of V. i. 1
opinioned, blunder for 'pinioned.' M.A. iv. 2
or, before. Tp. i. 2; v. 1; &c.
orb, orbit. M.A. iv. 1; circles, rings. M.N.D. ii. 1; star. M. of V. v. 1; the earth, the world. Tw.N. iii. 1
ordinary, public meal at eating-house or tavern. A.W. ii. 3

ostent, ostentation, display, appearance, exhibition. M.A. iv. 1; &c.

othergates, otherwise, in another way. Tw.N. v. 1

otherwhere, elsewhere. C. of E. ii. 1

ounce, lynx. M.N.D. ii. 2

ouph, goblin child. M.W. iv. 4; v. 5

ousel, blackbird, merle. M.N.D. iii. 1

out, completely, quite. Tp. i. 2; iv. 1; M.A. iii. 2; exhausted. Tp. iii. 2; out of practice. L.L.L. iv. 1; at a loss from failure of memory or self-possession. L.L.L. v. 2; As. iv. 1; into confusion or perplexity. L.L.L. v. 2; As. iii. 2; at variance. M. of V. iii. 5; over. A.W. i. 2; in error, mistaken. Tw.N. ii. 3; W.T. ii. 1; dislocated. W.T. iv. 2

outvied, out-done. T. of S. ii. 1

outward, uninitiated. A.W. iii. 1

overture, opening of negotiations or proceedings. A.W. iv. 3; Tw.N. i. 5; disclosure. W.T. ii. 1

owe, own, possess. Tp. i. 2; &c.

oyes, call or exclamation of 'Oyez,' 'Hear ye!' M.W. v. 5

pace, train, exercise. M. for M. iv. 3; prescribed walk. A.W. iv. 5

pack, compact, plot. M.W. iv. 2; C. of E. iv. 4; T. of S. v. 1

packed, leagued. C. of E. v. 1; M.A. v. 1

pain, penalty. M. for M. ii. 4; trouble. M. for M. v. 1; toil. T. of S. iii. 1

painted cloth, hanging for room painted or worked with figures, mottoes, or texts; tapestry. L.L.L. v. 2; As. iii. 2

palabras, i.e. pocas palabras (Sp.), few words. M.A. iii. 5

pale, bounds, region. W.T. iv. 2

panderly, base. M.W. iv. 2

pantaloon, dotard, old fool. As. ii. 7; T. of S. iii. 1

pantler, officer in charge of pantry. W.T. i . 3

parcel, part. M.W. i. 1; C. of E. v. 1; in part, partly. M. for M. ii. 1; company, collection, assemblage. L.L.L. v. 2; M. of V. i. 2; A.W. ii. 3; detail. As. iii. 5

pard, leopard, or panther. Tp. iv. 1; M.N.D. ii. 2; As. ii. 7

parfect, blunder for 'present.' L.L.L. v. 2

parish-top, top kept for the use of villagers. Tw.N. i. 3

'paritor (apparitor), summoning officer of ecclesiastical court. L.L.L. iii. 1

parle, conversation. Two G. i. 2; speak. L.L.L. v. 2; parly. T. of S. i. 1

parlous, perilous. M.N.D. iii. 1; As. iii. 2

particular, part. A.W. ii. 5

partlet, hen. W.T. ii. 3

pash, head. W.T. i. 2

pass, indulge in as a jest. M.W. i. 1; pass description. M.W. i. 1; iv. 2; thrust in fencing. M.W. ii. 1; ii. 3; Tw.N. iii. 1; pronounce verdict. M. for M. ii. 1; course of action. M. for M. v. 1; pass for. L.L.L. v. 1; transfer to. T. of S. iv. 4; transact. T. of S. iv. 4; impose. Tw.N. v. 1; surpass. W.T. ii. 2

passado, thrust in fencing. L.L.L. i. 2

passage, passing of people. C.

GLOSSARY

of E. iii. 1; occurrence. A.W. i. 1; act, transaction, proceeding. Tw.N. iii. 2; course, process. W.T. iii. 2

passant (of a beast, in heraldry), walki g. M.W. i. 1

passion, passionate speech or outburst. M.N.D. v. 1; feel deeply. Tp. v. 1; L.L.L. i. 1; grieving. Two G. iv. 4

pass of pate, sally of wit. Tp. iv. 1

passy-measures pavin, slow dance. Tw.N. v. 1

patch, fool, clown. Tp. iii. 2; &c.

patched, motley. M.N.D. iv. 1

pathetical, moving, affecting. L.L.L. i. 2; iv. 1; As. iv. 1

patine, thin circular plate of metal. M. of V. v. 1

pattern, match. W.T. iii. 2

pauca, pauca verba, paucas pallabris, few words. M.W. i. 1; L.L.L. iv. 2; T. of S. Ind. 1

paunch, stab or wound in the stomach. Tp. iii. 2

pavin, stately dance. Tw.N. v. 1

peach, impeach, betray. M. for M. iv. 3

peaking, sneaking. M.W. iii. 5

peascod, pea-pod. M.N.D. iii. 1; As. ii. 4; Tw.N. i. 5

peat, pet, spoilt girl. T. of S. i. 1

peculiar, private. M. for M. i. 2

pedant, pedascule, schoolmaster. L.L.L. iii. 1; T. of S. iii. 1; &c.

peer, appear. W.T. iv. 2; iv. 3

peevish, foolish. M.W. i. 4; C. of E. iv. 1; Tw.N. i. 5; wayward, saucy. As. iii. 5

Peg-a-Ramsey, name of old ballad. Tw.N. ii. 3

peise, weigh down. M. of V. iii. 2

pelting, paltry. M. for M. ii. 2; M.N.D. ii. 1

pensioner, gentleman-at-arms, body-guard. M.W. ii. 2; M.N.D. ii. 1

Penthesilea, queen of the Amazons. Tw.N. ii. 3

pent-house, shelter, porch, shed, outhouse. M.A. iii. 3; L.L.L. iii. 1; M. of V. ii. 6

perdurably, everlastingly. M. for M. iii. 1

perdy, Par Dieu, an oath. C. of E. iv. 4; Tw.N. iv. 2

peregrinate, having air of a traveller. L.L.L. v. 1

perfect, instruct or inform completely. Tp. i. 2; M. for M. iv. 3; sure. W.T. iii. 3

perge, go on, proceed. L.L.L. iv. 2

perpend, ponder, consider. M. W. ii. 1; As. iii. 2; Tw.N. v. 1

persever, persevere. As. v. 2

personage, personal appearance. M.N.D. iii. 2; Tw.N. i. 5

perspective, magnifying glass, telescope. A.W. v. 3; picture or figure constructed so as to produce a fantastic effect. Tw.N. v. 1

persuaded, best, having the best opinion. Tw.N. ii. 3

pertly, promptly, quickly. Tp. iv. 1

perttaunt-like, a word not yet explained. L.L.L. v. 2

pettitoes, pigs' trotters; W.T. iv. 3

phantasime, fantastic being. L L.L. iv. 1; v. 1

pheezar, see 'pheeze' below. M.W. i. 3

pheeze, beat, pay you out. T. of S. Ind. 1

Phibbus, Phoebus. M.N.D. i. 2

Philip and Jacob, St. Philip's and St. James's Day. M. for M. iii. 2

physics, heals, cures. W.T. i. 1

pia mater, brain. L.L.L. iv. 2; Tw.N. i. 5

picked, finical, particular. L.L.L. v. 1

piece, exemplification. Tp. i. 2; work of art. W.T. v. 2; v. 3; complete. W.T. v. 2

piety, blunder for 'impiety.' M.A. iv. 2

piled, having a pile or long nap, as velvet. M. for M. i. 2

pilot's glass, hour-glass. A.W. ii. 1

pin, mere nothing. M.W. i. 1; stud fixed in centre of target. L.L.L. iv. 1

pin and web, disease of the eye; ?cataract. W.T. i. 2

pinched, made ridiculous. W.T. ii. 1

pinfold, place for confining stray cattle. Two G. i. 1

pioned, ? dug, excavated, trenched; ? covered with marsh-marigolds. Tp. iv. 1

pip, each of the spots on playing-cards. T. of S. i. 2 (allusion to card-game called 'one-and-thirty')

pipe-wine, wine drawn directly from cask or 'wood' (with play upon musical 'pipe' and 'canary' the dance). M.W. iii. 2

pitch, degree, elevation, status. Tw.N. i. 1

place, house, dwelling. As. ii. 3; precedence. A.W. i. 1; position, station. W.T. i. 2

placket, pocket, especially in woman's skirt. L.L.L. iii. 1; W.T. iv. 3

plain, mere, absolute. Tp. v. 1

plain-song, singing simple melody. M.N.D. iii. 1

plantain, plantain leaf used to stop bleeding. L.L.L. iii. 1

plash, pool, puddle. T. of S. i. 1

plausive, plausible, pleasing, specious. A.W. i. 2; iv. 1

pleached, formed by intertwisting of boughs and twigs. M.A. i. 2; iii. 1

please, pay. C. of E. iv. 4

please-man, man-pleaser, sycophant. L.L.L. v. 2

pluck up, rouse thyself. M.A. v. 1

plummet, 'Ignorance itself is a plummet o'er me' = 'I am a plummet's depth below ignorance itself.' M.W. v. 5

point, smallest detail. Tp. i. 2; suggest. L.L.L. ii. 1; tagged lace for attaching hose to doublet. T. of S. iii. 2; Tw.N. i. 5; W.T. iv. 3

point-device, -devise, extremely neat, precise, scrupulous. L.L.L. v. 1; As. iii. 2; exactly. Tw.N. ii. 5

poising us, adding our weight (of patronage). A.W. ii. 3

poke, pocket. As. ii. 7

poking-sticks, rods used for stiffening plaits of ruffs. W.T. iv. 3

pole, quarter-staff. L.L.L. v. 2

pole-clipt, hedged in by poles. Tp. iv. 1

pollusion, blunder for 'allusion.' L.L.L. iv. 2

pomander, ball of perfume. W.T. iv. 3

GLOSSARY

pomewater, large juicy apple. L.L.L. iv. 2

Poor-John, hake (or ? other fish) salted and dried for food. Tp. ii. 2

porpentine, porcupine. C. of E. iii. 1

porringer, small basin. T. of S. iv. 3

port, gate. A.W. iii. 5; deportment, style of living, importance. M. of V. i. 1; iii. 2; T. of S. i. 1

possess, inform. M. for M. iv. 1; &c.

possession, mental endowment. Two G. v. 2; i.e. by the devil. C. of E. v. 1

possitable, blunder for 'positively.' M.W. i. 1

post, letter-carrier. Tp. ii. 1; &c.; post-haste. C. of E. i. 2; iii. 2; W.T. ii. 1; tavern door-post on which reckonings were scored. C. of E. i. 2

posy (i.e. poesy), short motto, line of poetry, inscribed on a knife or in a ring. M. of V. v. 1

pottle, two quarts. M.W. ii. 1; iii. 5

powdered, salted and pickled. M. for M. iii. 2

practice, scheming, machination, trickery. M. for M. v. 1; &c.

practise, intrigue. Two G. iv. 1; As. i. 1; play a trick. T. of S. Ind. i

praise, appraise, value. Tw.N. i. 5

prank, dress. Tw.N. ii. 4; W.T. iv. 3

preceptial, instructive. M.A. v. 1

preeches, breeched for flogging. M.W. iv. 1

prefer, promote. Two G. ii. 4; recommend. M. of V. ii. 2; T. of S. i. 1; press forward. M. for M. i. 1; submitted for approval. M.N.D. iv. 2

pregnant, clear, obvious. M. for M. ii. 1; W.T. v. 2; inventive, resourceful. M. for M. i. 1; Tw.N. ii. 2; receptive, disposed, ready. Tw.N. iii. 1

prejudicates, prejudices. A.W. i. 2

premises, previous circumstances. Tp. i. 2

prenzie, doubtful word, prob. an error. M. for M. iii. 1

preposterous, blunder for 'prosperous.' W.T. v. 2

prest, constrained. M. of V. i. 1

Prester John, a legendary Christian king and priest ruling in the extreme East, or in Abyssinia. M.A. ii. 1

prevailment, influence, ascendancy. M.N.D. i. 1

pribbles and prabbles, petty wranglings. M.W. i. 1

prick, the spine. Tp. ii. 2; spot in centre of target. L.L.L. iv. 1; sting. As. iii. 2; stick. T. of S. iii. 2; incite. T. of S. iii. 2

pricket, buck in its second year. L.L.L. iv. 2

prig, thief. W.T. iv. 2

primero, gambling card-game. M.W. iv. 5

principality, one of the nine orders of angels. Two G. ii. 4

print, in, with exactness or preciseness. Two G. ii. 1; L.L.L. iii. 1; As. v. 4

priser, prize-fighter. As. ii. 3

probation, proof. M. for M. v. 1; trial. Tw.N. ii. 5

process, course, story. M. of V. iv. 1

prolixious, long in duration. M. for M. ii. 4

prolonged, postponed. M.A. iv. 1

prompture, instigation. M. for M. ii. 4

proper-false, handsome and deceitful. Tw.N. ii. 2

property, mere means to an end. M.W. iii. 4; fulfilment. A.W. ii. 1; make a tool of, exploit. Tw.N. iv. 2

proportions, fortune. M. for M. v. 1

propose, converse, conversation. M.A. iii. 1

propriety, individuality. Tw. N. v. 1

provincial, belonging to an ecclesiastical province. M. for M. v. 1

provoke, invoke. M. for M. iii. 1

pruning, adorning. L.L.L. iv. 3

puddings, bowels, entrails. M.W. ii. 1

pugging, ? 'p, igging,' thievish, or 'pug-tooth,' eye-tooth. W.T. iv. 2

puisny, puny, insignificant. As. iii. 4

pumpion, pumpkin. M.W. iii. 3

punk, prostitute. M.W. ii. 2; M. for M. v. 1

punto, stroke or thrust with sword-point. M.W. ii. 3

purgation, vindication, proof. As. i. 3; v. 4; W.T. iii. 2

push, pish! make a push at = treat with disdain. M.A. v. 1; impulse, impetus. W.T. v. 3

push-pin, child's game. L.L.L. iv. 3

put, compelled; called upon. M. for M. i. 1

put in, plead, intercede. M. for M. i. 2

put on, urge onward. M. for M. iv. 2; ? to lay on as a blow. L.L.L. iv. 1; communicate, impart. As. i. 2; Tw.N. v. 1

putter-on, instigator. W.T. ii. 1

putter-out, one who lends money at interest. Tp. iii. 3

quail, overpower. M.N.D. v. 1; fail. As. ii. 2

quarter, to add another's coat to one's hereditary coat-of-arms. M.W. ii. 1; conduct, relations. C. of E. ii. 1

quatch-buttock, squat buttock. A.W. ii. 2

quean, ill-behaved woman. M.W. iv. 2

queasy, nice, delicate. M.A. ii. 1

quell, kill. M.N.D. v. 1

quern, handmill. M.N.D. ii. 1

quest, inquiry, pursuit, search. M. for M. iv. 1; M. of V. i. 1

questant, seeker. A.W. ii. 1

question, consideration. M. for M. i. 1; that's the question. M.A. v. 2; talk, discourse. M.N.D. ii. 1; &c.

question, loss of, for the sake of argument. M. for M. ii. 4

quick, running. Tp. iii. 2; living. M.W. iii. 4; &c.; pregnant. L.L.L. v. 2

quillets, casuistries. L.L.L. iv. 3

quintain, stout post, used as mark in tilting. As. i. 2

quire, company. M.N.D. ii. 1; sing in concert. M. of V. v. 1

quirk, witty turn, conceit. M.A. ii. 3; fit, sudden stroke. A.W. iii. 2; trick of behaviour. Tw. N. iii. 4

quit, leave. Tp. i. 2; M. for M. ii. 4; remit. C. of E. i. 1; M. of V. iv. 1; acquit. As. iii. 1; A.

GLOSSARY

W. v. 3; renounce, dismiss. Tw.N. v. 1

quittance, receipt. M.W. i. 1

quoif, cap. W.T. iv. 3

quote, regard, mention. L.L.L. iv. 3; v. 2; A.W. v. 3

quotidian, intermittent fever. As. iii. 2

rabato, kind of stiff collar. M.A. iii. 4

race, natural or inherited disposition. Tp. i. 2; M. for M. ii. 4; a herd of horses. M. of V. v. 1; root. W.T. iv. 2

rack, driving mist. Tp. iv. 1; stretch or raise beyond the normal degree. M.A. iv. 1; M. of V. i. 1

ragged, harsh, discordant. As. ii. 5

rank, abundantly. M.W. iv. 6; lustful. M. of V. i. 3; position. As. i. 2; movement in line or file. As. iii. 2; row. As. iv. 3

rankness, pride, rebellion. As. i. 1

rascal, inferior deer of a herd. As. iii. 3

rate, estimation, consideration. Tp. i. 2; ii. 1; value. M. for M. ii. 2; M. of V. ii. 7; mode of living. M. of V. i. 1; scold. T. of S. i. 1; price. A.W. v. 3

rato-lorum, blunder for 'rotulorum.' M.W. i. 1

raught, reached. L.L.L. iv. 2

ravel, become entangled. Two G. iii. 2

ravin, ravenously devour. M. for M. i. 2; ravenous. A.W. iii. 2

rayed, befouled, soiled. T. of S. iii. 2; iv. 1

razure, effacement. M. for M. v. 1

reason, anything reasonable. Tp. iii. 2; possibility of action. Two G. ii. 4; T. of S. ii. 1; discourse. L.L.L. v. 1; As. i. 2; argue. M. of V. ii. 8; 'it is just.' W.T. iv. 3

reave, deprive. A.W. v. 3

rebate, make blunt. M. for M. i. 4

rebused, blunder for 'abused.' T. of S. i. 2

recheat, notes sounded on a horn to call together the hounds in a hunt. M.A. i. 1

reclusive, secluded. M.A. iv. 1

record, render in song. Two G. v. 4; memory. Tw.N. v. 1

recorder, wind instrument. M.N.D. v. 1

recountment, relation, recital. As. iv. 3

red-lattice, lattice painted red as the mark of an inn, hence an alehouse or inn. M.W. ii. 2

reechy, smoky, dirty. M.A. iii. 3

reed, reedy or squeaking. M. of V. iii. 4

reeling-ripe, drunk to the point of reeling. Tp. v. i

refell, refuse, reject. M. for M. v. 1

refer, have recourse. M. for M. iii. 1

reformed, blunder for 'informed.' M.A. v. 1

regreet, greeting. M. of V. ii. 9

rehearse, sing over. M.N.D. v. 2

rein, submit to the rein. Tw.N. iii. 4

religious, faithful. A.W. ii. 3

relish, realize. W.T. ii. 1

remember thy curtsy, put on thy hat. L.L.L. v. 1

remorse, compassion. Tp. v. 1. &c.

remorseful, compassionate. Two G. iv. 3

remove, absence. M. for M. i. 1; post-stage. A.W. v. 3

removed, removedness, secluded, seclusion. M. for M. i. 3; &c.; distant in relationship. As. v. 4; separated by time. Tw.N. v. 1

render, describe as. As. iv. 3; pay, exhibit. M.A. v. 3; to make. M. of V. iii. 2

renegado, apostate. Tw.N. iii. 2

rent, rend. M.N.D. iii. 2

repair, come back. L.L.L. v. 2; restores, revives. A.W. i. 2; restoration. W.T. v. 1

repasture, repast. L.L.L. iv. 1

repetition, remembrance. A.W. v. 3

report, reputation. M. for M. ii. 3; M.A. iii. 1; testimony. L.L.L. ii. 1

reportingly, by report or hearsay. M.A. iii. 1

reprehend, misused for 'represent.' L.L.L. i. 1

reproach, blunder for 'approach.' M. of V. ii. 5

reprove, disprove. M.A. ii. 3

require, deserve. W.T. ii. 3; iii. 2

requit, repay, requite. Tp. iii. 3

rere-mice, bats. M.N.D. ii. 2

resolve, bring to a clear understanding. Tp. v. 1; M. for M. iv. 2; inform. M. for M. iii. 1; answer. L.L.L. ii. 1; T. of S. iv. 2; solve. As. iii. 2

resolvedly, definitely. A.W. v. 3

resolve you, prepare yourselves. W.T. v. 3

respect, value. Two G. i. 2; regard, care for. Two G. iii. 1; &c.; consideration, estimation. L.L.L. v. 2; M.N.D. ii. 1; regard to circumstances. M. of V. v. 1; reason. A.W. ii. 5

respected, blunder for 'suspected.' M. for M. ii. 1

respecting, in comparison with. W.T. v. 1

respective, worthy of regard. Two G. iv. 4; careful. M. of V. v. 1

'rest, arrest. C. of E. iv. 2; &c.

restrained, forbidden. M. for M. ii. 4; drawn tightly. T. of S. iii. 2

rest, set up one's, resolve, determine. C. of E. iv. 3; M. of V. ii. 2; A.W. ii. 1

retention, power to retain. Tw.N. ii. 4

retort, refer back. M. for M. v. 1

reverse, back-handed stroke. M.W. ii. 3

rheum, cold or catarrh. M. for M. iii. 1; C. of E. iii. 2; W.T. iv. 3; saliva. M. of V. i. 3; tears. M.A. v. 2

rheumatic, inducing catarrhal affections. M.W. iii. 1; characterized by rheum. M.N.D. ii. 1

Rialto, quarter of Venice in which the Exchange was situated. M. of V. i. 3

rib, enclose as with ribs. M. of V. ii. 7

rid, destroy. Tp. i. 2

right, exactly. M.N.D. iv. 2

ring-carrier, go-between. A.W. iii. 5

Ringwood, name of a dog. M.W. ii. 1

riping, point of becoming ripe. M. of V. ii. 8

ronyon, abusive term applied to a woman. M.W. iv. 2

rope-tricks, ? blunder or pun for 'rhetoric.' T. of S. i. 2

round, bring to completeness.

GLOSSARY 1089

Tp. iv. 1; plain spoken. C. of E. ii. 1; Tw.N. ii. 3; circle. M.N.D. ii. 1; encircle. M.N.D. iv. 1; whisper. W.T. i. 2; develop to a full round form. W.T. ii. 1

roundel, round dance. M.N.D. ii. 2

roundly, promptly. As. v. 3; T. of S. v. 2; bluntly. T. of S. iii. 2; without needless ceremony. T. of S. iv. 4

rout, rabble. C. of E. iii. 1

roynish, coarse, base. As. ii. 2

rub, encounter (in playing bowls) some impediment which diverts the bowl from its proper course. L.L.L. iv. 1

rubious, ruby-coloured. Tw.N. i. 4

rudesby, insolent fellow. T. of S. iii. 2; Tw.N. iv. 1; ruffling, rising in ruffles. T. of S. iv. 3

rule, procedure. M. of V. iv. 1; Tw.N. ii. 3

rushling, blunder for 'rustling.' M.W. ii. 2

russet, homespun. L.L.L. v. 2

russet-pated, grey-headed. M.N.D. iii. 2

ruttish, lustful. A.W. iv. 3

sack, white wine. Tp. ii. 2; T. of S. Ind. 2; Tw.N. ii. 3

Sackerson, name of a famous bear. M.W. i. 1

sad, sadness, serious, seriousness. Two G. i. 3; &c.

sain, said. L.L.L. iii. 1

sale-work, ready-made goods. As. iii. 5

salt, salt-cellar. Two G. iii. 1; lustful. M. for M. v. 1

saltiers, blunder for 'satyrs.' W.T. iv. 3

sanctimonious, holy, consecrated. Tp. iv. 1

sanctimony, sanctity. A.W. iv. 3

sand-blind, half-blind, dim-sighted, purblind. M. of V. ii. 2

sanded, of a sandy colour. M.N.D. iv. 1

sans, without. Tp. i. 2; L.L.L. v. 2; As. ii. 7

saucy, wanton, lascivious. M. for M. ii. 4; A.W. iv. 4

scale, weigh as in scales, estimate. M. for M. iii. 1

scall, scabby. M.W. iii. 1

scambling, scrambling. M.A. v. 1

scamel, meaning uncertain. Tp. ii. 2

scandaled, scandalous. Tp. iv. 1

scape, transgression. W.T. iii. 3

scarfed, beflagged. M. of V. ii. 6

scarfs and bannerets, silken ornaments worn on various parts of the attire. A.W. ii. 3

scathful, hurtful, harmful. Tw.N. v. 1

sconce, head. C. of E. i. 2; ii. 2; defence. C. of E. ii. 2

scour, to depart in haste, run away, decamp. W.T. ii. 1

scrip, written list. M.N.D. i. 2; small bag. As. iii. 2

scrippage, contents of a scrip. As. iii. 2

scrubbed, stunted. M. of V. v. 1

scruple, quantity. M. for M. i. 1

scut, tail. M.W. v. 5

search, probe. As. ii. 4

season, influence. M. for M. ii. 2; opportunity. C. of E. iv. 2; that which preserves. M.A. iv. 1; preserve. A.W. i. 1; Tw.N. i. 1

second, helpful. W.T. ii. 3

secure, careless. M.W. ii. 1

seedness sowing of the seed. M. for M. i. 1

seeming, appearance, hypocrisy. M. for M. ii. 4; M.A. iv. 1; seemingly, becomingly. As. v. 4; freshness. W.T. iv. 3

seen, well, well-skilled. T. of S. i. 2

seldom when, rarely. M. for M. iv. 2

semblative, resembling, like. Tw.N. i. 4

se'nnight, a week. As. iii. 2

Senoys, Sienese. A.W. i. 2

sense, feelings. Tp. ii. 1; sensual passions. M. for M. ii. 2; reason. M. of V. v. 1; A.W. i. 1

sensible, sensitive. Tp. ii. 1; C. of E. iv. 4; M. of V. ii. 8; capable of feeling. M.N.D. v. 1; substantial. M of V. ii. 9

sentences, sententious sayings. M.A. ii. 3

sequent, following. M. for M. v. 1; follower. L.L.L. iv. 2

serpigo, skin eruption. M. for M. iii. 1

sessa, exclamation urging to speed. T. of S. Ind. 1

set, set to music, value. Two G. i. 2; seated. Two G ii. 1; a set at tennis. L.L.L. v. 2

several, belonging to private owner. L.L.L. ii. 1; individual. W.T. ii. 2

Shafalus, i.e. Cephalus. M.N.D. v. 1

sheep-biter, sheep-biting, thief, thieving. Tw.N. ii. 5; M. for M. v. 1

sheep-whistling, sheep-tending. W.T. iv. 3

sheer, mere, nothing but. T. of S. Ind. 2

shent, rated, reviled. M.W. i. 4; Tw.N. iv. 2

sheriff's post, post to which proclamations were affixed. Tw.N. i. 5

shield, defend, grant. M. for M. iii. 1

ship-tire, headdress. M.W. iii. 3

shot, reckoning. Two G. iii. 5

shoulder-shotten, with dislocated shoulder. T. of S. iii. 2

shovel-board, shilling used in game of that name. M.W. i. 1

'shrew, beshrew, plague. W.T. i. 2

shrewd, mischievous, bad. M.W. ii. 2; &c.; shrewish. M.A. ii. 1

shrieve, sheriff. A.W. iv. 3

shrift, absolution. M. for M. iv. 2

shrow, shrew. L.L.L. v. 2

sicles, shekels. M. for M. ii. 2

side sleeves, long hanging sleeves. M.A. iii. 4

siege, stool, excrement. Tp. ii. 2; seat. M. for M. iv. 2

significant, something to express meaning. L.L.L. iii. 1

signory, lordship, domain, territory. Tp. i. 2

silly, defenceless. Two G. iv. 1; homely. Tw.N. ii. 4

simple, herb used in medicine. M.W. i. 4; iii. 3; As. iv. 1; foolish. T. of S. v. 2

since once, that once upon a time. M.N.D. ii. 1; T. of S. Ind. 1; when. W.T. v. 1

singled, separated. L.L.L. v. 1

sinister, left. M.N.D. v. 1; A.W. ii. 1

sink, make fall. Tp. ii. 1

sinking-ripe, ready to sink. C. of E. i. 1

sirrah, familiar style of address. Tp. v. 1

sir-reverence, corruption of

GLOSSARY

'save-reverence,' an apologetic expression. C. of E. iii. 2

Sisters Three, the Fates. M.N.D. v. 1

sith, since. M. for M. i. 3; &c.

sithence, since. A.W. i. 3

skill, matter. T. of S. iii. 2; Tw. N. v. 1; cunning. W.T. ii. 1; reason. W.T. iv. 3

skill-less, skilless, ignorant. Tp. iii. 1; Tw.N. iii. 3

skipper, thoughtless fellow. T. of S. ii. 1

slack, neglect. M.W. iii. 4

sleeve-hand, a wristband. W. T. iv. 3

'slid, God's lid, an oath. M.W. iii. 4; Tw.N. iii. 4

'slight, God's light, an oath. Tw.N. ii. 5; iii. 2

slighted, chucked, threw contemptuously. M.W. iii. 5

slop, slops, loose breeches. M. A. iii. 2; L.L.L. iv. 3

slubber, slur over. M. of V. ii. 8

sluggardized, made indolent. Two G. i. 1

smack, savour. M. for M. ii. 2; M. of V. ii. 2; the small of the leg. L.L.L. v. 2; smattering. A.W. iv. 1

small, boy's or woman's treble voice; shrill-voiced. M.N.D. i. 2; Tw.N. i. 4

smother, suffocating smoke. As. i. 2

smug, trim, spruce. M. of V. iii. 1

snatches, repartees. M. for M. iv. 2

sneap, check, nip. L.L.L. i. 1; W.T. i. 2

sneck up, expression of contempt. Tw.N. ii. 3

snipt-taffeta, dressed in silks and ribbons. A.W. iv. 5

snuff, object of loathing. A.W. i. 2

sod, sodden. L.L.L. iv. 2

solely, absolutely. A.W. i. 1; alone. W.T. ii. 3

solemn, ceremonious. A.W. iv. 3

something, somewhat. M. of V. i. 1

sonties, ? corruption of 'sante,' 'sanctity,' or 'saints.' M. of V. ii. 2

sooth, truth. M.N.D. ii. 2; &c.

Sophy, Shah of Persia. Tw.N. ii. 5; iii. 4

sore, buck of the fourth year. L.L.L. iv. 2

sorel, buck of the third year. L.L.L. iv. 2

sot, fool. Tp. iii. 2; C. of E. ii. 2; Tw.N. i. 5

soud, a sigh of fatigue. T. of S. iv. 1

sovereignty, efficacy. A.W. i. 3

spare, forbear to offend. M. for M. ii. 3

specialties, articles of a contract. L.L.L. ii. 1; T. of S. ii. 1

speciously, blunder for 'specially.' M.W. iii. 4; iv. 5

sped, done for, prospered. M. of V. ii. 9; W.T. i. 2

speed, succeed. Two G. iv. 4; T. of S. i. 2; help. As. i. 2; fortune, progress. T. of S. ii. 1; W.T. iii. 2

sphery, starry. M.N.D. ii. 2

spinner, spider. M.N.D. ii. 2

splay, castrate. M. for M. ii. 1

spleen, supposed seat of emotion of laughter. M. for M. ii. 2; quick movement. M.N.D. i. 1; passion. As. iv. 1; ill-temper. T. of S. iii. 2; laughter. Tw.N. iii. 2; &c.

sprag, quick, sharp. M.W. iv. 1

sprat, worthless fellow. A.W. iii. 6

spring, beginning. M.N.D. ii. 1

springe, trap. W.T. iv. 2

spurs, roots. Tp. v. 1

squandered, scattered. M. of V. i. 3

squandering, random. As. ii. 7

square, quarrel. M.N.D. ii. 1; embroidery about the bosom of garment. W.T. iv. 3; shape. W.T. v. 1

squarer, brawler, braggart. M.A. i. 1

squash, unripe peascod. M.N.D. iii. 1; Tw.N. i. 5; W.T. i. 2

squire, squier, square, rule, measure. L.L.L. v. 2; W.T. iv. 3

stage, exhibit. M. for M. i. 1

stagger, staggering, hesitate, hesitation. M.W. iii. 3; M. for M. i. 2; As. iii. 3

staggers, apoplexy in horses. T. of S. iii. 2; bewilderment. A.W. ii. 3

stain, tinge, characteristic. A.W. i. 1

stale, decoy. Tp. iv. 1; T. of S. iii. 1; dupe, laughing-stock. M.W. ii. 3; T. of S. i. 1; prostitute. C. of E. ii. 1; M.A. ii. 2; iv. 1

stall, keep close, as in a stall. A.W. i. 3

stamps, impressed coins. M.W. iii. 4

stand, withstand. T. of S. i. 2; fight. W.T. iii. 2

standing, duration. W.T. i. 2

standing-bed, bed standing on posts. M.W. iv. 5

standing water, between ebb and flood of tide. Tw.N. i. 5

stand upon, be of importance to. C. of E. iv. 1

staniel, kestrel-hawk. Tw.N. ii. 5

stanze, stanzo, stanza. L.L.L. iv. 2; As. ii. 5

staple, thread. L.L.L. v. 1

star, pole star. M.A. iii. 4; fortune. Tw.N. ii. 5

start-up, upstart. M.A. i. 3

starve, nip with cold. Two G. iv. 4

state, attitude. L.L.L. iv. 3; estate, fortune. M. of V. iii. 2; &c.; chair of state. Tw.N. ii. 5; authority. Tw.N. ii. 5; condition. Tw.N. v. 1

statute-caps, woollen caps, worn by citizens in accordance with an Act of Parliament of 1571. L.L.L. v. 2

stead, be of service. Tp. i. 2; &c.

stead up, supply, take the place of. M. for M. iii. 1

steely, unyielding. A.W. i. 1

stew, cauldron. M. for M. v. 1

stigmatical, marked with deformity. C. of E. iv. 2

still an end, perpetually. Two G. iv. 4

still-piecing, doubtful word. A.W. iii. 2

still-vexed, always disturbed. Tp. i. 2

stoccado, thrust in fencing. M.W. ii. 1

stock, thrust in fencing. M.W. ii. 3; stocking. T. of S. iii. 2; Tw.N. i. 3

stock-fish, dried cod. Tp. iii. 2; M. for M. iii. 2

stockish, insensible. M. of V. v. 1

stomach, courage. Tp. i. 2; temper. Two G. i. 2; appetite. C. of E. i. 2; M.A. i. 3; T. of S. iv. 1; pride. T. of S. v. 2; inclination. A.W. iii. 6

GLOSSARY

stone-bow, cross-bow for shooting stones. Tw.N. ii. 5

story, subject of mirth. M. for M. i. 4

stoup, drinking-cup. Tw.N. ii. 3

stout, haughty, proud. Tw.N. ii. 5

stover, fodder for cattle. Tp. iv. 1

strain, pervert oneself. W.T. iii. 2

strained, constrained. M. of V. iv. 1; turned from right course. W.T. iii. 2

strait, strict. M. for M. ii. 1

straited, at a loss. W.T. iv. 3

straitness, strictness. M. for M. iii. 2

strange, original. L.L.L. v. 1; reserved, distant. Tw.N. ii. 5; estranged. Tw.N. v. 1

strangely, extraordinarily well. Tp. iv. 1

strangeness, reserve, distant manner. Tw.N. iv. 1

strayed, led astray. C. of E. v. 1

stricture, strictness. M. for M. i. 3

strond, strand. M. of V. i. 1

struck, advanced. T. of S. ii. 1

stuck-in, thrust in fencing. Tw. N. iii. 4

studied, practised, instructed. M. of V. ii. 2

stuffed, complete. M.A. i. 1; W.T. ii. 1

subscribe, be surety. A.W. iii. 6; iv. 5; admit, acknowledge. M. for M. ii. 4; declare. M.A. v. 2

subscribe to, admit, acknowledge. Two G. v. 4; A.W. v. 3

substractors, detractors. Tw.N. i. 3

subtilties, illusions, false appearances. Tp. v. 1

succeed, inherit. M. for M. ii. 4; descend by order of succession; A.W. iii. 7

succeeding, consequence. A. W. ii. 3

success, the issue. M.A. iv. 1; succession. W.T. i. 2

succession, others from doing the same. A.W. iii. 5

sufferance, suffering. M.W. iv. 2; &c.

sufficiency, ability. W.T. ii. 1

suffigance, blunder for 'sufficient.' M.A. iii. 5

suggest, tempt. Two G. iii. i; L.L.L. v. 2; A.W. iv. 5

suggestion, prompting, temptation. Tp. ii. 1; iv. 1; L.L.L. i. 1

suit, service due to a feudal superior. M. for M. iv. 4; fit. M.A. v. 1; Tw.N. i. 2; furnish. As. i. 3; petition, dress. As. ii. 7

suits, respects. T. of S. Ind. 1

suits with fortune, out of, dismissed from Fortune's service. As. i. 2

superfluous, luxurious. A.W. i. 1

superscript, address. L.L.L. iv. 2

supportance, keeping. Tw.N. iii. 4

supposed, blunder for 'deposed,' M. for M. ii. 1; spurious. M. of V. iii. 2

supposition, beguile the, deceive the opinion. A.W. iv. 3

suspect, suspicion. C. of E. iii. 1; blunder for 'respect.' M.A. ii. 2

swabber, one who scrubs the deck of a ship. Tp. ii. 2; Tw. N. i. 5

swarth, grass cut by one sweep of scythe. Tw.N. ii. 3

swashing, swaggering. As. i. 3

swayed, strained. T. of S. iii. 2

sweat, plague. M. for M. i. 2; sweated. M. of V. iii. 2; As. ii. 3

sweetness, self-indulgence. M. for M. ii. 4

sweet-suggesting, sweetly tempting. Two G. ii. 6

swinge, beat. Two G. ii. 1; &c.

sworn out, forsworn. L.L.L. ii. 1

sympathized, mutually suffered. C. of E. v. 1; suitably matched. L.L.L. iii. 1

table, writing tablet. Two G. ii. 7; palm of the hand. M. of V. ii. 2; tablet. A.W. i. 1

table-book, memorandum-book. W.T. iv. 3

tables, backgammon. L.L.L. v. 2

tabor, small drum. Tp. iii. 2; &c.

ta'en, given. T. of S. i. 2

ta'en up, arranged amicably. As. v. 4

taffeta, plain wove glossy silk. L.L.L. v. 2; Tw.N. ii. 4; florid, bombastic. L.L.L. v. 2

take, strike. M. for M. ii. 1; T. of S. iii. 2; Tw.N. ii. 5; strike with disease. M.W. iv. 4; captivate. Tp. v. 1; W.T. iii. 2; iv. 3; take to. C. of E. i. 2

take air, get abroad. Tw.N. iii. 4

take in, conquer. W.T. iv. 3

take order, take measures. M. for M. ii. 1

taken up, arrested; and obtained on credit. M.A. iii. 3

take up, take to task. Two G. i. 2; make up, arrange amicably. As. v. 4; Tw.N. iii. 4; assume. Tw.N. v. 1

tall, fine, doughty. M.W. i. 4; &c.

tang, ? pungent or stinging effect; or an unpleasant tone, twang. Tp. ii. 2; utter with a ringing tone. Tw.N. ii. 5; iii. 4

tardy, retard. W.T. iii. 2

targe, light shield or buckler. L.L.L. v. 2

tarriance, tarrying, delay, procrastination. Two G. ii. 7

Tartar, Tartarus, hell. C. of E. iv. 2; Tw.N. ii. 5

taste, experience. Tp. v. 1; to try, to test. Tw.N. iii. 1; iii. 4

tawdry-lace, woman's silk necktie. W.T. iv. 3

tax, taxing, charge, accusation, censure. M.A. i. 1; As. ii. 7; A.W. ii. 1

taxation, censure, satire. As. i. 2

tear a cat, rant. M.N.D. i. 2

teen, grief. Tp. i. 2; L.L.L. iv. 2

tell, count. Tp. ii. 1; W.T. iv. 3

temper, mix. M.A. ii. 2

temperance, temperature. Tp. ii. 1

temperate, chaste. Tp. iv. 1

tempered, disposed. As. i. 2

temporary meddler, cleric who meddles with temporal affairs. M. for M. v. 1

tender, regard, especially with care or tenderness. Tp. ii. 1; &c.; dear. Two G. v. 4; tend. T. of S. Ind. 1; introduce. W.T. iv. 3

tents, bed hangings. T. of S. ii. 1

terminations, terms. M.A. ii. 1

tester, sixpence, money in general. M.W. i. 3

GLOSSARY

testern, present with a tester. Two G. i. 1

testimonied, attested. M. for M. iii. 2

testril, sixpence. Tw.N. ii. 3

tharborough, constable. L.L.L. i. 1

theorick, theory. A.W. iv. 3

thereabouts, of that import. W.T. i. 2

thereto, in addition, besides. W.T. i. 2

thick-pleached, thickly intertwined. M.A. i. 2

thick-skin, blockhead. M.W. iv. 5; M.N.D. iii. 2

thill-horse, shaft-horse. M. of V. ii. 2

third-borough, constable. T. of S. Ind. 1

thought, care, anxiety, melancholy. As. iv. 1; Tw.N. ii. 4; the swiftness of thought. Tp. iv. 1

Thracian singer, Orpheus. M.N.D. v. i

thrasonical, boastful. L.L.L. v. 1; As. v. 2

thread and thrum, everything in general. M.N.D. v. 1

three-pile, richest kind of velvet. W.T. iv. 2

three-piled, having a thick pile, richest. M. for M. i. 2; superfine. L.L.L. v. 2

thrift, success. M. of V. i. 1; profits. M. of V. i. 3

throughly, thoroughly. Tp. iii. 3; Two G. i. 2; T. of S. iv. 4

throw, venture (as in dice). Tw.N. v. 1

thrum, tufted end of a thread in weaving. M.N.D. v. 1

thrummed hat, hat made of very coarse woollen stuff. M.W. iv. 2

tickle, tottering. M. for M. i. 2

tick-tack, sort of backgammon. M. for M. i. 2

'tide, betide. M.N.D. v. 1

tightly, briskly, smartly. M.W. i. 3; ii. 3

tillyvally, an expression of contempt. Tw.N. ii. 3

tilth, tillage. Tp. ii. 1; M. for M. i. 4

time, youth. M. of V. i. 1

timeless, untimely. Two G. iii. 1

tinct, grand elixir sought by alchemists. A.W. v. 3

tire, headdress. Two G. iv. 4; M.W. iii. 3; M.A. iii. 4

tire-valiant, fanciful headdress. M.W. iii. 3

tiring-house, dressing-room of a theatre. M.N.D. iii. 1

tithe, ? tilth. M. for M. iv. 1

tittles, trifles. L.L.L. iv. 1

to, compared to. Tp. i. 2; ii. 1; L.L.L. ii. 1; A.W. ii. 3; for, as. Tp. ii. 1; Two G. ii. 4; at. Two G. i. 1; with. M.A. ii. 1

toaze, drag out. W.T. iv. 3

tod, 28 lbs. of wool, yield a tod. W.T. iv. 2

tofore, before. L.L.L. iii. 1

tongue, to denounce. M. for M. iv. 4

tongues, foreign languages. Two G. iv. 1; M.A. v. 1

took, gave. T. of S. iii. 2

top, forelock. M.A. i. 2; head. A.W. i. 2

torcher, torch-bearer. A.W. ii. 1

touch, action. M.N.D. iii. 2; trait. As. iii. 2; v. 4

touse, pull, tear. M. for M. v. 1

toward, in preparation. M.N.D. iii. 1; As. v. 4; T. of S. i. 1; tractable. T. of S. v. 2

trace, traverse. M.A. iii. 1; M.N.D. ii. 1

train, entice, allure. C. of E. iii. 2

traject, ferry. M. of V. iii. 4

translate, change, transform. M.N.D. i. 1; iii. 1

transport, remove to another world. M. for M. iv. 3; M.N.D. iv. 2; carried away by feeling. W.T. iii. 2; v. 3

trash, lop, cut off high branches. Tp. i. 2

travel of regard, grave survey. Tw.N. ii. 5

traverse, make a thrust. M.W. ii. 3; crosswise. As. iii. 4

tray-trip, a game of dice in which success depended on throwing the three. Tw.N. ii. 5

tremor cordis, trembling of the heart. W.T. i. 2

trench, cut. Two G. iii. 2

trencher-knight, servant who waits at table. L.L.L. v. 2

trencher-man, good feeder. M.A. i. 1

trick, custom, habit. M. for M. v. 1; toy. T. of S. iv. 3; W.T. ii. 1; special peculiarity of look, voice, &c. A.W. i. 1; W.T. ii. 3

tricking, ornaments, costumes. M.W. iv. 4

tricksy, sportive. Tp. v. 1; M. of V. iii. 5

trifle, appearance. Tp. v. 1; toy. M.N.D. i. 1

triple, third. A.W. ii. 1

triplex, triple-time in music. Tw.N. v. 1

triumph, festival. Two G. v. 4; M.N.D. i. 1

troll, sing in rotation. Tp. iii. 2

trol-my-dames, French game of 'trou madame.' W.T. iv. 2

trot, troth. M.W. iv. 5; term of contempt. M. for M. iii. 2; hag. T. of S. i. 2

troth, truth. M.W. i. 4; M.N.D. ii. 2

trow, wonder. M.W. i. 4; ii. 1; think ye. M.A. iii. 4; know. As. iii. 2

Troyan, used as term of contempt. L.L.L. v. 2

truant, play truant. C. of E. iii. 2

truckle-bed, low bed, which can be pushed under another. M.W. v. 5

trumpet, herald. W.T. ii. 2

trunk sleeve, full sleeve. T. of S. iv. 3

try, bring a ship as close to wind as possible. Tp. i. 1

tub, process of curing venereal disease by sweating. M. for M. iii. 2

tuck, rapier. Tw.N. iii. 4

tucket, flourish on a trumpet. M. of V. v. 1; A.W. iii. 5, stage direction

tug, contend. W.T. iv. 3

tuition, guardianship. M.A. i. 1

tundish, funnel. M. for M. iii. 2

Turk, turn, become wicked. M.A. iii. 4

turn, change. Two G. ii. 2; modulate, tune. As. ii. 5

turtle, turtle-dove. T. of S. ii. 1

twelve score, twelve score yards. M.W. iii. 2

twilled, covered with reeds. Tp. iv. 1

twink, twinkling, instant. Tp. iv. 1; T. of S. ii. 1

tyrant, pitiless critic. M.A. i. 1

umber, red ochre. As. i. 3

unadvised, unintentionally. Two G. iv. 4

unbreathed, unexercised. M.N.D. v. 1

GLOSSARY

uncape, uncouple, throw off the hounds. M.W. iii. 3

uncase, undress. L.L.L. v. 2; T. of S. i. 1

unchary, carelessly. Tw.N. iii. 4

unchecked, not contradicted. M. of V. iii. 1

unconfirmed, inexperienced. M.A. iii. 3; L.L.L. iv. 2

uncurrent, extraordinary. W.T. iii. 2

underbear, face, trim. M.A. iii. 4

undertaker, surety, or agent for others. Tw.N. iii. 4

undervalued, inferior in value. M. of V. i. 1; ii. 7

unfolding star, the star that bids shepherd let sheep out of fold. M. for M. iv. 2

unfool, take away reproach of folly. M.W. iv. 2

unfurnish, deprive. W.T. v. 1

unfurnished, without companion. M. of V. iii. 2

ungalled, unblemished. C. of E. iii. 1

ungenitured, without power of procreation. M. for M. iii. 2

ungot, unbegotten. M. for M. v. 1

unhandsome, unsuitable. As. Epil.

unhappiness, mischief. M.A. ii. 1

unhappy, mischievous. C. of E. iv. 4; L.L.L. v. 2; A.W. iv. 5

unhatched, undrawn, undisclosed. Tw.N. iii. 4

unintelligent, unconscious. W.T. i. 1

unjust, dishonest. W.T. iv. 3

unkind, unnatural. As. ii. 7

unlike, unlikely. M. for M. v. 1

unmuzzled, as of dogs worrying bear. Tw.N. iii. 1

unpeeled, stripped, desolate. L.L.L. ii. 1

unpinked, not pierced with eyelet holes. T. of S. iv. 1

unpitied, unmerciful. M. for M. iv. 2

unpregnant, dull, without sense. M. for M. iv. 4

unprizable, invaluable. Tw.N. v. 1

unprofited, with nothing gained. Tw.N. i. 4

unquestionable, unwilling to be conversed with. As. iii. 2

unraked, not made up for night. M.W. v. 5

unreverend, unreverent, irreverent. Two G. ii. 6; T. of S. iii. 2

unrolled, struck off the roll. W.T. iv. 2

unroosted, henpecked. W.T. ii. 3

unseasoned, inexperienced. A.W. i. 1

unshape, throw into disorder. M. for M. iv. 4

unshunned, unavoidable. M. for M. iii. 2

unsisting, ? unresting. M. for M. iv. 2

unstanched, incontinent. Tp. i. 1

unthrift, unthrifty, good-for-nothing. M. of V. i. 3; v. 1

unthrifty to, not to increase. W.T. v. 2

untoward, unmannerly. T. of S. iv. 5

untowardly, unluckily. M.A. iii. 2

untread, retrace. M. of V. ii. 6

untried, unexamined. W.T. iv. Chorus

untrussing, unloosing 'points' of hose. M. for M. iii. 2

up and down, exactly. Two G. ii. 3; M.A. ii. 1

upshoot, deciding shot. L.L.L. iv. 1

up-staring, standing on end. Tp. i. 2

urchin, hedgehog, goblin. Tp. i. 2; M.W. iv. 4

urchin-shows, apparitions of goblins. Tp. ii. 2

usance, interest of money. M. of V. i. 3

use, interest. M. for M. i. 1; M. A. ii. 1; Tw.N. iii. 1; custom. M. for M. i. 4; A.W. v. 1; trust. M. of V. iv. 1

usurping, counterfeit, false. L. L.L. iv. 3

utter, pass from one to another. L.L.L. ii. 1; cause so to pass. W.T. iv. 3

vagrom, mistake for 'vagrant.' M.A. iii. 3

vail, lower, let fall. M. for M. v. 1; L.L.L. v. 2; M. of V. i. 1; T. of S. v. 2

vain, 'for vain' = uselessly. M. for M. ii. 4; light of tongue. C. of E. iii. 2

vanity, illusion. Tp. iv. 1

vantage, opportunity. M.W. iv. 6; M. for M. v. 1; M. of V. iii. 2; superiority. M.N.D. i. 1

vara, very. L.L.L. v. 2

varlet, knave. Tp. iv. 1; M.A. iv. 2

vast, dreary stretch of sea. W. T. i. 1

vastidity, extent, immensity. M. for M. iii. 1

vaward, vanguard. M.N.D. iv. 1

velure, velvet. T. of S. iii. 2

venew, veney, a bout at fencing. M.W. i. 1; L.L.L. v. 1

vengeance, mischief. As. iv. 3

ventricle, cavity. L.L.L. iv. 2

verse love, make love in verse. M.N.D. ii. 1

via, go forward; away with you. M.W. ii. 2; M. of V. ii. 2; come on. L.L.L. v. 1

vice, the buffoon. Tw.N. iv. 2; screw. W.T. i. 2

vie, stake, as at cards. T. of S. ii. 1

viewless, invisible. M. for M. iii. 1

vigitant, blunder for 'vigilant.' M.A. iii. 3

villagery, village people. M.N. D. ii. 1

villain, used good-humouredly. C. of E. i. 2; Tw.N. ii. 5; W.T. i. 2; serf. As. i. 1

viol-de-gamboys (blunder for 'da gamba'), violoncello. Tw. N. i. 3

virginalling, playing with fingers, as upon virginal. W.T. i. 2

virtue, essence, very being. Tp. i. 2; M.N.D. iv. 1; efficacy. M. of V. v. 1

visited, infected. L.L.L. v. 2

visor, mask. M.A. ii. 1; L.L.L. v. 2

vizaments, advisements, counsel. M.W. i. 1

vizarded, masked. M.W. iv. 6

vlouting-stog, laughing-stock. M.W. iii. 1

voice, name, behalf. M. for M. i. 2; vote. M.N.D. i. 1; As. ii. 4

void, emit. M. of V. i. 3

volable, quick-witted. L.L.L. iii. 1

vow-fellow, companions in oath. L.L.L. ii. 1

vulgar, vulgar tongue. As. v. 1; common. Tw.N. iii. 1; common person. W.T. ii. 1

GLOSSARY

vulgarly, publicly. M. for M. v. 1

waft, beckon. C. of E. ii. 2; M. of V. v. 1; turn. W.T. i. 2

waftage, passage by water. C. of E. iv. 1

wag, to go one's way. M.W. i. 3; ii. 1; M.A. v. 1; shake. M. of V. iv. 1

wailful, doleful. Two G. iii. 2

wainropes, waggon-ropes. Tw. N. iii. 2

waist, part of ship between quarterdeck and forecastle. Tp. i. 2

wake, late revels. L.L.L. v. 2; W.T. iv. 2

wanton, luxuriant. M.N.D. ii. 1; play, dally. W.T. ii. 1

wantonness, lasciviousness. M.W. iv. 2

ward, guard in fencing. Tp. i. 2; M.W. ii. 2; W.T. i. 2; defence. L.L.L. iii. 1

warden, large baking pear. W.T. iv. 2

warp, deviate. M. for M. i. 1; twist, pervert. As. ii. 7; A.W. v. 3

warrant, secure, protect. M. for M. iv. 2; C. of E. iv. 4; As. iii. 3; attest. M.A. iv. 1

warranted need, upon a, if the question required a guarantee. M. for M. iii. 2

warrener, gamekeeper. M.W. i. 4

watch, tame by keeping awake. M.W. v. 5; T. of S. iv. 1

waters, for all, fit for anything. Tw.N. iv. 2

watery star, the moon. W.T. i. 2

waxen, grow, increase. M.N.D. ii. 1

wear, fashion. M. for M. iii. 2; &c.; wear out, tire. As. ii. 4; A.W. v. 1; are in fashion. A.W. i. 1; grow fitted by use. Tw.N. ii. 4

weather-fend, shelter. Tp. v. 1

web, disease of the eye, ? cataract. W.T. i. 2

weed, garment. Two G. ii. 7; &c.

weeding, weeds. L.L.L. i. 1

welkin, sky. Tp. i. 2; Tw.N. ii. 3; iii. 1; blue. W.T. i. 2

well, at rest. W.T. v. 1

well-advised, deliberate, in right mind. L.L.L. v. 2

well entered, being initiated. A.W. ii. 1

well found, found to be well skilled. A.W. ii. 1

well-liking, in good condition. L.L.L. v. 2

wezand, windpipe. Tp. iii. 2

whelm, overwhelm. M.W. ii. 2

when, exclamation of impatience. Tp. i. 2; T. of S. iv. 1

whe'r, whether. Tp. v. 1; C. of E. iv. 1

where, whereas. Two G. iii. 1; L.L.L. ii. 1; M. of V. iv. 1; to where. M.N.D. iv. 1

wherein, in what dress. As. iii. 2

where you are, what you mean. As. v. 2

whey-face, covered with youthful down. M.W. i. 4

while-ere, not long ago. Tp. iii. 2

whist, hushed, silent. Tp. i. 2

white, bull's-eye in target. T. of S. v. 2

whiting-time, bleaching-time. M.W. iii. 3

whitster, bleacher. M.W. iii. 3

whoo-bub, hubbub. W.T. iv. 3

whooping, out of all, beyond expression. As. iii. 2

whoreson, bastard. Tp. i. 1; &c.

wide, far from, indifferent to. M.W. iii. 1; distractedly. M.A. iv. 1

wide-chapped, open-mouthed. Tp. i. 1

widow, dower. M. for M. v. 1

widowhood, rights of a widow. T. of S. ii. 1

wightly, nimble. L.L.L. iii. 1

wild, rash, heedless. W.T. ii. 1; iv. 3

wilderness, wildness. M. for M. iii. 1

wimpled, blindfolded. L.L.L. iii. 1

wind, blow. M.A. i. 1; to fold. M.N.D. iv. 1

windgalls, swelling in horse's legs. T. of S. iii. 2

windring, winding. Tp. iv. 1

windy, windward, safe. M.A. ii. 1; Tw.N. iii. 4

wish, commend. T. of S. i. 1; i. 2; desire. M. for M. v. 1

wit, wisdom. Two G. i. 1; &c.; sense. M.A. i. 1

witcracker, jester. M.A. v. 4

withal, not do, not help it. M. of V. iii. 4

withering out, delaying enjoyment of. M.N.D. i. 1

without-door, external. W.T. ii. 1

witness, evidence. M.W. iv. 2

wit-snapper, man ready at repartee. M. of V. iii. 5

'*wit, whither wilt?*' expression used to check anyone talking too much. As. iv. 1

wittol, contented cuckold. M.W. ii. 2

woe, sorry. Tp. v. 1

woman me to it, make me show my woman's weakness. A.W. iii. 2

woman-tired, henpecked. W.T. ii. 3

womb, enclose. W.T. iv. 3

wonder, wondering, admiration. W.T. iv. chor.; v. 1

wondered, wonder-working. Tp. iv. 1

wood, mad. Two G. ii. 3; M.N.D. ii. 1

woodbine, bindweed, honeysuckle, or convolvulus. M.N.D. ii. 1; iv. 1

woodcock, fool. M.A. v. 1; &c.

woollen, blankets. M.A. ii. 1

woolward, go, wear wool instead of linen next skin. L.L.L. v. 2

word, promise. A.W. ii. 1

word, at a, in short. M.W. i. 1; as good as my word. M.W. i. 3

working, scope. As. i. 2

working-day, common, ordinary. As. i. 3

world, wonder. M.A. iii. 5; T. of S. ii. 1

world, go to the, be married. M.A. ii. 1; A.W. i. 3

worm, creature. Tp. iii. 1; M.W. v. 5; serpent. M. for M. iii. 1; M.N.D. iii. 2

worn times, old age. W.T. v. 1

worship, honour, dignity. W.T. i. 2

wort, root. M.W. i. 1; sweet unfermented beer. L.L.L. v. 2

wot, wotting, know, knowing. L.L.L. i. 1; W.T. iii. 2

wrack of sea, shipwreck. C. of E. v. 1

wrath, wrathful. M.N.D. ii. 1; ardour. As. v. 2

wring, writhe. M.A. v. 1

writ, scripture. A.W. ii. 1; written, claimed. A.W. ii. 3

write, claim to be. A.W. ii. 3
wroth (so spelt for rhyme), wrath. M. of V. ii. 9
wry-necked, see *fife.*

yare, yarely, ready, readily; nimble, active, briskly. Tp. i. 1; &c.
Yead, diminutive for 'Edward.' M.W. i. 1
yearn, grieve, vex. M.W. iii. 5
years, in, into wrinkles. L.L.L. v. 2

yellow, emblem of jealousy. W.T. ii. 3
yellowness, jealousy. M.W. i. 3
yellows, jaundice in horses. T. of S. iii. 2
yest, foam, froth. W.T. iii. 3
yield you forth, expose you. M. for M. v. 1
younker, youth. M. of V. ii. 6

zany, buffoon. L.L.L. v. 2; Tw.N. i. 5
zodiacs, years. M. for M. i. 2

The Best of the World's Best Books
COMPLETE LIST OF TITLES IN
THE MODERN LIBRARY

For convenience in ordering use number at right of title

ADAMS, HENRY	The Education of Henry Adams 76
AIKEN, CONRAD (Editor)	A Comprehensive Anthology of American Poetry 101
AIKEN, CONRAD (Editor)	20th-Century American Poetry 127
ALCOTT, LOUISA M.	Little Women 258
ANDERSON, SHERWOOD	Winesburg, Ohio 104
AQUINAS, ST. THOMAS	Introduction to St. Thomas Aquinas 259
ARISTOTLE	Introduction to Aristotle 248
ARISTOTLE	Politics 228
ARISTOTLE	Rhetoric and Poetics 246
AUGUSTINE, ST.	The Confessions of 263
AUSTEN, JANE	Pride and Prejudice and Sense and Sensibility 264
BALZAC	Droll Stories 193
BALZAC	Père Goriot and Eugénie Grandet 245
BEERBOHM, MAX	Zuleika Dobson 116
BELLAMY, EDWARD	Looking Backward 22
BENNETT, ARNOLD	The Old Wives' Tale 184
BERGSON, HENRI	Creative Evolution 231
BIERCE, AMBROSE	In the Midst of Life 133
BLAKE, WILLIAM	Selected Poetry & Prose of 285
BOCCACCIO	The Decameron 71
BOSWELL, JAMES	The Life of Samuel Johnson 282
BRONTË, CHARLOTTE	Jane Eyre 64
BRONTË, EMILY	Wuthering Heights 106
BROWNING, ROBERT	Selected Poetry of 198
BUCK, PEARL	The Good Earth 15
BURCKHARDT, JACOB	The Civilization of The Renaissance In Italy 32
BURK, JOHN N.	The Life and Works of Beethoven 241
BUTLER, SAMUEL	Erewhon and Erewhon Revisited 136
BUTLER, SAMUEL	The Way of All Flesh 13
BYRNE, DONN	Messer Marco Polo 43
BYRON, LORD	The Selected Poetry of 195
BYRON, LORD	Don Juan 24
CALDWELL, ERSKINE	God's Little Acre 51
CALDWELL, ERSKINE	Tobacco Road 249
CANFIELD, DOROTHY	The Deepening Stream 200
CARROLL, LEWIS	Alice in Wonderland, etc. 79
CASANOVA, JACQUES	Memoirs of Casanova 165
CELLINI, BENVENUTO	Autobiography of Cellini 150
CERVANTES	Don Quixote 174
CHAUCER	The Canterbury Tales 161
CICERO	The Basic Works of 272
COLERIDGE	Selected Poetry and Prose of 279
COMMAGER, HENRY STEELE & NEVINS, ALLAN	A Short History of the United States 235

CONFUCIUS	The Wisdom of Confucius 7
CONRAD, JOSEPH	Lord Jim 186
CONRAD, JOSEPH	Nostromo 275
CONRAD, JOSEPH	Victory 34
COOPER, JAMES FENIMORE	The Pathfinder 105
CORNEILLE & RACINE	Six Plays of Corneille and Racine 194
CORVO, FREDERICK BARON	A History of the Borgias 192
CRANE, STEPHEN	The Red Badge of Courage 130
CUMMINGS, E. E.	The Enormous Room 214
DANA, RICHARD HENRY	Two Years Before the Mast 236
DANTE	The Divine Comedy 208
DAY, CLARENCE	Life with Father 230
DEFOE, DANIEL	Moll Flanders 122
DEFOE, DANIEL	Robinson Crusoe and A Journal of the Plague Year 92
DEWEY, JOHN	Human Nature and Conduct 173
DICKENS, CHARLES	David Copperfield 110
DICKENS, CHARLES	Pickwick Papers 204
DICKENS, CHARLES	A Tale of Two Cities 189
DICKINSON, EMILY	Selected Poems of 25
DINESEN, ISAK	Out of Africa 23
DINESEN, ISAK	Seven Gothic Tales 54
DONNE, JOHN	Complete Poetry and Selected Prose of 12
DOS PASSOS, JOHN	Three Soldiers 205
DOSTOYEVSKY, FYODOR	The Brothers Karamazov 151
DOSTOYEVSKY, FYODOR	Crime and Punishment 199
DOSTOYEVSKY, FYODOR	The Possessed 55
DOUGLAS, NORMAN	South Wind 5
DOYLE, SIR ARTHUR CONAN	The Adventures and Memoirs of Sherlock Holmes 206
DREISER, THEODORE	Sister Carrie 8
DUMAS, ALEXANDRE	Camille 69
DUMAS, ALEXANDRE	The Three Musketeers 143
DU MAURIER, DAPHNE	Rebecca 227
DU MAURIER, GEORGE	Peter Ibbetson 207
ELLIS, HAVELOCK	The Dance of Life 160
EMERSON, RALPH WALDO	Essays and Other Writings 91
FAULKNER, WILLIAM	Absalom, Absalom! 271
FAULKNER, WILLIAM	Light in August 88
FAULKNER, WILLIAM	Sanctuary 61
FAULKNER, WILLIAM	The Sound and the Fury and As I Lay Dying 187
FIELDING, HENRY	Joseph Andrews 117
FIELDING, HENRY	Tom Jones 185
FLAUBERT, GUSTAVE	Madame Bovary 28
FORESTER, C. S.	The African Queen 102
FRANCE, ANATOLE	Penguin Island 210
FRANKLIN, BENJAMIN	Autobiography, etc. 39
FREUD, SIGMUND	The Interpretation of Dreams 96
FROST, ROBERT	The Poems of 242
GALSWORTHY, JOHN	The Apple Tree (in Great Modern Short Stories 168)
GAUTIER, THEOPHILE	Mlle. De Maupin and One of Cleopatra's Nights 53
GEORGE, HENRY	Progress and Poverty 36
GODDEN, RUMER	Black Narcissus 256

GOETHE	Faust 177
GOGOL, NIKOLAI	Dead Souls 40
GRAVES, ROBERT	I, Claudius 20
GUNTHER, JOHN	Death Be Not Proud 286
HACKETT FRANCIS	The Personal History of Henry the Eighth 265
HARDY, THOMAS	Jude the Obscure 135
HARDY, THOMAS	The Mayor of Casterbridge 17
HARDY, THOMAS	The Return of the Native 121
HARDY, THOMAS	Tess of the D'Urbervilles 72
HART & KAUFMAN	Six Plays by 233
HARTE, BRET	The Best Stories of 250
HAWTHORNE, NATHANIEL	The Scarlet Letter 93
HEGEL	The Philosophy of 239
HELLMAN, LILLIAN	Four Plays by 223
HENRY, O.	Best Short Stories of 4
HERODOTUS	The Persian Wars 255
HERSEY, JOHN	A Bell for Adano 16
HOFFENSTEIN, SAMUEL	The Complete Poetry of 225
HOMER	The Iliad 166
HOMER	The Odyssey 167
HORACE	The Complete Works of 141
HOWELLS, WILLIAM DEAN	The Rise of Silas Lapham 277
HUDSON, W. H.	Green Mansions 89
HUGHES, RICHARD	A High Wind in Jamaica 112
HUGO, VICTOR	The Hunchback of Notre Dame 35
HUXLEY, ALDOUS	Antic Hay 209
HUXLEY, ALDOUS	Point Counter Point 180
IBSEN, HENRIK	A Doll's House, Ghosts, etc. 6
IRVING, WASHINGTON	Selected Writings of 240
JAMES, HENRY	The Portrait of a Lady 107
JAMES, HENRY	The Turn of the Screw 169
JAMES, HENRY	Washington Square 269
JAMES, HENRY	The Wings of the Dove 244
JAMES, WILLIAM	The Philosophy of William James 114
JAMES, WILLIAM	The Varieties of Religious Experience 70
JEFFERS, ROBINSON	Roan Stallion; Tamar and Other Poems 118
JEFFERSON, THOMAS	The Life and Selected Writings of 234
JOYCE, JAMES	Dubliners 124
JOYCE, JAMES	A Portrait of the Artist as a Young Man 145
KAFKA, FRANZ	Selected Stories of 283
KANT	The Philosophy of 266
KAUFMAN & HART	Six Plays by 233
KEATS	The Complete Poetry and Selected Prose of 273
KIPLING, RUDYARD	Kim 99
KOESTLER, ARTHUR	Darkness at Noon 74
LAOTSE	The Wisdom of 262
LARDNER, RING	The Collected Short Stories of 211
LAWRENCE, D. H.	The Rainbow 128
LAWRENCE, D. H.	Sons and Lovers 109
LAWRENCE, D. H.	Women in Love 68
LEWIS, SINCLAIR	Dodsworth 252
LONGFELLOW, HENRY W.	Poems 56
LOUYS, PIERRE	Aphrodite 77

LUDWIG, EMIL	Napoleon 95
MACHIAVELLI	The Prince and The Discourses 65
MALRAUX, ANDRÉ	Man's Fate 33
MANN, THOMAS	Death in Venice (in Great German Short Novels and Stories 108)
MANSFIELD, KATHERINE	The Garden Party 129
MARQUAND, JOHN P.	The Late George Apley 182
MARX, KARL	Capital and Other Writings 202
MAUGHAM, W. SOMERSET	Cakes and Ale 270
MAUGHAM, W. SOMERSET	The Moon and Sixpence 27
MAUGHAM, W. SOMERSET	Of Human Bondage 176
MAUPASSANT, GUY DE	Best Short Stories 98
MAUROIS, ANDRÉ	Disraeli 46
MEAD, MARGARET	Coming of Age in Samoa 126
MELVILLE, HERMAN	Moby Dick 119
MEREDITH, GEORGE	Diana of the Crossways 14
MEREDITH, GEORGE	The Egoist 253
MEREDITH, GEORGE	The Ordeal of Richard Feverel 134
MEREJKOWSKI, DMITRI	The Romance of Leonardo da Vinci 138
MILTON, JOHN	The Complete Poetry and Selected Prose of John Milton 132
MOLIÈRE	Plays 78
MONTAIGNE	Selected Essays of 218
MORIER, JAMES	The Adventures of Hajji Baba of Ispahan 289
MORLEY, CHRISTOPHER	Parnassus on Wheels 190
NASH, OGDEN	The Selected Verse of Ogden Nash 191
NEVINS, ALLAN & COMMAGER, HENRY STEELE	A Short History of the United States 235
NEWMAN, CARDINAL JOHN H.	Apologia Pro Vita Sua 113
NIETZSCHE, FRIEDRICH	Thus Spake Zarathustra 9
NOSTRADAMUS	Oracles of 81
ODETS, CLIFFORD	Six Plays of 67
O'HARA, JOHN	Appointment in Samarra 42
O'NEILL, EUGENE	The Emperor Jones, Anna Christie and The Hairy Ape 146
O'NEILL, EUGENE	The Long Voyage Home: Seven Plays of the Sea 111
PALGRAVE, FRANCIS (Editor)	The Golden Treasury 232
PARKER, DOROTHY	The Collected Short Stories of 123
PARKER, DOROTHY	The Collected Poetry of 237
PARKMAN, FRANCIS	The Oregon Trail 267
PASCAL, BLAISE	Pensées and The Provincial Letters 164
PATER, WALTER	Marius the Epicurean 90
PATER, WALTER	The Renaissance 86
PEPYS, SAMUEL	Passages from the Diary of 103
PERELMAN, S. J.	The Best of 247
PETRONIUS ARBITER	The Satyricon 156
PLATO	The Republic 153
PLATO	The Works of Plato 181
POE, EDGAR ALLAN	Best Tales 82
POLO, MARCO	The Travels of Marco Polo 196
POPE, ALEXANDER	Selected Works of 257
PORTER, KATHERINE ANNE	Flowering Judas 284
PORTER, KATHERINE ANNE	Pale Horse, Pale Rider 45
PROUST, MARCEL	The Captive 120
PROUST, MARCEL	Cities of the Plain 220

PROUST, MARCEL	The Guermantes Way 213
PROUST, MARCEL	The Past Recaptured 278
PROUST, MARCEL	Swann's Way 59
PROUST, MARCEL	The Sweet Cheat Gone 260
PROUST, MARCEL	Within a Budding Grove 172
RACINE & CORNEILLE	Six Plays by 194
READE, CHARLES	The Cloister and the Hearth 62
REED, JOHN	Ten Days that Shook the World 215
RENAN, ERNEST	The Life of Jesus 140
RICHARDSON, SAMUEL	Clarissa 10
ROSTAND, EDMOND	Cyrano de Bergerac 154
ROUSSEAU, JEAN JACQUES	The Confessions of 243
RUSSELL, BERTRAND	Selected Papers of Bertrand Russell 137
SAKI	The Short Stories of 280
SCHOPENHAUER	The Philosophy of Schopenhauer 52
SCHULBERG, BUDD	What Makes Sammy Run? 281
SHAKESPEARE, WILLIAM	Tragedies, 1, 1A—complete, 2 vols.
SHAKESPEARE, WILLIAM	Comedies, 2, 2A—complete, 2 vols.
SHAKESPEARE, WILLIAM	Histories, 3 Histories, Poems, 3A } complete, 2 vols.
SHAW, BERNARD	Four Plays by 19
SHELLEY	The Selected Poetry & Prose of 274
SMOLLETT, TOBIAS	Humphry Clinker 159
SPINOZA	The Philosophy of Spinoza 60
STEINBECK, JOHN	In Dubious Battle 115
STEINBECK, JOHN	The Grapes of Wrath 148
STEINBECK, JOHN	Of Mice and Men 29
STEINBECK, JOHN	Tortilla Flat 216
STENDHAL	The Red and the Black 157
STERNE, LAURENCE	Tristram Shandy 147
STEWART, GEORGE R.	Storm 254
STOKER, BRAM	Dracula 31
STONE, IRVING	Lust for Life 11
STOWE, HARRIET BEECHER	Uncle Tom's Cabin 261
STRACHEY, LYTTON	Eminent Victorians 212
SUETONIUS	Lives of the Twelve Caesars 188
SWIFT, JONATHAN	Gulliver's Travels, A Tale of a Tub, The Battle of the Books 100
SYMONDS, JOHN A.	The Life of Michelangelo 49
TACITUS	The Complete Works of 222
TCHEKOV, ANTON	The Stories of
TCHEKOV, ANTON	The Plays of
THACKERAY, WILLIAM	Henry Esmond 80
THACKERAY, WILLIAM	Vanity Fair 131
THOMPSON, FRANCIS	Complete Poems 38
THOREAU, HENRY DAVID	Walden and Other Writings 155
THUCYDIDES	The Complete Writings of 58
TOLSTOY, LEO	Anna Karenina 37
TROLLOPE, ANTHONY	Barchester Towers and The Warden 41
TROLLOPE, ANTHONY	The Eustace Diamonds 251
TURGENEV, IVAN	Fathers and Sons 21
TWAIN, MARK	A Connecticut Yankee in King Arthur's Court 162
VEBLEN, THORSTEIN	The Theory of the Leisure Class 63
VIRGIL'S WORKS	The Aeneid, Eclogues & Georgics 75
VOLTAIRE	Candide **47**

WALPOLE, HUGH	Fortitude 178
WALTON, IZAAK	The Compleat Angler 26
WARREN, ROBERT PENN	All The King's Men 170
WEBB, MARY	Precious Bane 219
WELLS, H. G.	Tono Bungay 197
WELTY, EUDORA	Selected Stories of 290
WHARTON, EDITH	The Age of Innocence 229
WHITMAN, WALT	Leaves of Grass 97
WILDE, OSCAR	Dorian Gray, De Profundis 125
WILDE, OSCAR	The Plays of Oscar Wilde 83
WILDE, OSCAR	Poems and Fairy Tales 84
WORDSWORTH	Selected Poetry of 268
WRIGHT, RICHARD	Native Son 221
YEATS, W. B. (Editor)	Irish Fairy and Folk Tales 44
YOUNG, G. F.	The Medici 179
ZOLA, EMILE	Nana 142
MISCELLANEOUS	An Anthology of American Negro Literature 163
	An Anthology of Irish Literature 288
	An Anthology of Light Verse 48
	The Arabian Nights' Entertainments 201
	Best Amer. Humorous Short Stories 87
	Best Russian Short Stories 18
	A Comprehensive Anthology of American Poetry 101
	The Consolation of Philosophy 226
	Eight Famous Elizabethan Plays 94
	Eighteenth-Century Plays 224
	Famous Ghost Stories 73
	The Federalist 139
	Five Great Modern Irish Plays 30
	Fourteen Great Detective Stories 144
	Great German Short Novels and Stories 108
	Great Modern Short Stories 168
	Great Tales of the American West 238
	The Greek Poets 203
	The Latin Poets 217
	The Making of Man: An Outline of Anthropology 149
	The Making of Society: An Outline of Sociology 183
	Outline of Abnormal Psychology 152
	Outline of Psychoanalysis 66
	The Poetry of Freedom 175
	Restoration Plays 287
	Seven Famous Greek Plays 158
	The Short Bible 57
	Six Modern American Plays 276

	Three Famous French Romances 85
	   Sapho, by Alphonse Daudet
	   Manon Lescaut, by Antoine Prevost
	   Carmen, by Prosper Merimee

	Twentieth-Century American Poetry 127